D0890976

LASTOVO (PHOTO: TZ DUBOVNIK)

Acknowledgements

This book has truly been an international effort and is the result of terrific support from every Mediterranean island country and several beyond. I would first like to thank those without whose special contributions the book could never have been completed – Penelope Matsouka for her tireless research into Greek islets and Arlen Abramic, who has been contributing information on Croatian islets since the book was first conceived in 1994.

Extremely valuable information has also been received from Dr Vesna Mikacic of the Institute for Tourism in Zagreb, Manos Hatzimalonas of the Greek National Tourism Organisation in London and Dr Tea Duplancic Leder of the Hydrographic Institute of Croatia in Split.

We have had help from the tourism organisations of all countries and I would particularly like to thank the Italian State Tourist Board in London for assembling a wonderful collection of photographs, Tulin Sermin Ozduran of the Turkish Tourism Office for her continuing enthusiasm, as well as the Croatian National Tourist Board, the Tunisian National Tourist Office and the London offices of the Spanish, Malta and Cyprus tourist organisations.

Institutions which have helped with valuable information are the Istituto Idrografico della Marina in Genova, the Hellenic Navy Hydrographic Service, the State Geodetic Administration in Zagreb, the Office de la Topographie et de la Cartographie in Tunis, the Govern de les Illes Balears, and ISTAT with population figures for Italian islands.

A large number of individuals have given very willing help and I would single out Talin Etyemez of Adalar Kultur Dernegi for her research on Turkish islands, Fabio Pittella for repeated help on Italian island matters, Agenc in Bastia and Gilles Cheylan for detailed information about the islets of Corsica and Provence respectively, Dr Pier Giovanni d'Ayala of Insula in Paris, and Tassos Labropoulos and Despina Psychi of National Technical University of Athens for their information about small islands in Greece. Among all the immense help that we have received from the islands themselves I would like to give special thanks to Stjepan Felber for his great efforts on the islands of Zadar county and to Josip Sladic for detailed information about the islands of Murter-Kornati.

Among the 'home team', we have had terrific support and illustrative material from our guest authors, beautiful drawings of marine creatures from Lucy Wilson and a marvellous range of photographs assembled by Kate Buckle and Hassina Christian. I have relied from the outset on the unerring advice of Bryn Thomas, and Stephen Mesquita and Kevin Fitzgerald have made valuable contributions from their huge experience.

Our editorial team has carried off the difficult task of keeping me on the right track, with Peter Read giving unfailing support and guidance, Tricia Hayne helping on many matters in addition to editing, John King doing a most efficient job with proof-reading and Gerard Gorman and Paul Sterry contributing additional essays on Mediterranean plant life and wildlife.

Carol Farley has conducted the marketing of the book with her usual good judgment, Andrew Duncan has contributed his wide experience on international syndication, Graham Vickers has made key contributions on the presentation of the book, Steve Plackett has dealt with all printing matters with great courtesy and Di Tolland has always been there to find the solution to problems that nobody else can resolve.

What started off as a simple idea has been transformed into a book more beautiful than I ever imagined by the inspired work of Pearce Marchbank and he in turn has had terrific support from Ben May of his studio staff in putting the whole book together, from Alan Grimwade and his team at Cosmographics who have drawn all the large maps with great style and Nick Hill who has done a most efficient job in producing all the islet and island maps.

The result is a unique and lovely thing which I hope people will enjoy looking at and using and which I hope also we will be able to develop further as more information comes to hand.
Charles Arnold

Compiled and edited by
Charles Arnold

Design and production by
Pearce Marchbank RDI

Feature maps and atlas by
Cosmographics

Island and Islet maps by
Nick Hill Design

First published 2008

British Library Cataloguing in Publication Data.
A CIP record for this book is available from the British Library.

ISBN: 978-0-9556489-1-5

Printed and bound in India by Ajanta Offset

Mediterranean Islands
c/o Survival Books
26 York Street
London W1U 6PZ
United Kingdom
Telephone: +44 (0)20-7788 7644
Fax: +44 (0)870-762 3212
email: info@mediterraneanislands.org
www.mediterraneanislands.org

Mediterranean Islands

www.mediterraneanislands.org

The Mediterranean is the world's most important holiday region and its islands are visited by millions of people every year – some 40 million people in 2006.

Yet, surprisingly, no attempt has previously been made to produce a comprehensive book about the islands of the Mediterranean. Until now.

Mediterranean Islands is a unique guide, providing detailed information about every one of the 218 islands which offer accommodation, in addition to cataloguing and mapping over 1,000 islands and islets for the first time. It includes essays on many key aspects of the Mediterranean, including its geology, history, plantlife, environment, tourism, wildlife, sailing and privately-owned islands – each written by a leading expert in the field.

Mediterranean Islands is essential reading for those who love the Mediterranean, island devotees, sailors and anyone planning (or dreaming about) a Mediterranean holiday, and is a unique reference and a mine of information. Not only is it the only place where the vital statistics of all the islands are at your fingertips (such as size, highest point and population), it also provides a unique assessment of each island. This includes a concise synopsis of the main characteristics of each island, its tourism rating, vegetation ('greenness'), the quality of beaches, historical interest, and a precise ranking of its size, population and 'Crowdfactor' – essential information for those who do not want to share their holiday with a million others!

There are also summaries of air and sea communications for each island, the best maps to buy and - for sailors - the ports where fuel can be found. Every island page also features a photograph depicting the character of the island, an outline map showing the main town or port and a location map showing the island's precise position.

In addition to the millions travelling for pleasure, those employed in the travel industry will find *Mediterranean Islands* a unique and valuable reference book. It is, for example, the only place where the accommodation capacity of each island can be found.

For those engaged in planning and development for the tourism industry, unique statistics are published for the first time, including the bed capacity of each island and the annual turnover of beds – an important measure of the industry's efficiency. There are also literally thousands of organisations working in the Mediterranean region who will find the information provided in *Mediterranean Islands* an invaluable resource. Last but not least, the islanders themselves will be fascinated to see how their island compares with their neighbours.

We have tried, where possible, to use national languages throughout the book, using English only for narrative. Place names have been written in national languages as a general rule, but inevitably there are a few inconsistencies. Although national spellings may look odd in those cases where a more familiar version is commonplace, we concluded that an international balance could only be achieved by using national place names, which would also give the book wider international accessibility. For Greek place names we have used ELOT 743, the international standard for the romanisation of Greek geographical names.

While we have made every effort to ensure that all the facts and figures contained in *Mediterranean Islands* are as accurate and complete as possible (much of the information was provided by official sources in the countries concerned) there will inevitably be some errors. Please let us know if you find any inaccuracies or omissions, along with any suggestions you may have for improvements, and we will send you a free copy of the next edition of *Mediterranean Islands* as a token of our appreciation.

Charles Arnold, January 2008

MOLAT: THE ISLANDS OF NORTH DALMATIA ARE A HAVEN FOR SAILORS (PHOTO: ZADAR COUNTY TOURIST BOARD)

The Mediterranean

A series of essays written by leading international specialists give some background about the Mediterranean Sea

Satellite Atlas Page 380

All the islands that offer accommodation are shown in these state-of-the-art maps
A large poster version is also available...see inside back cover for details

The Islands Page 84

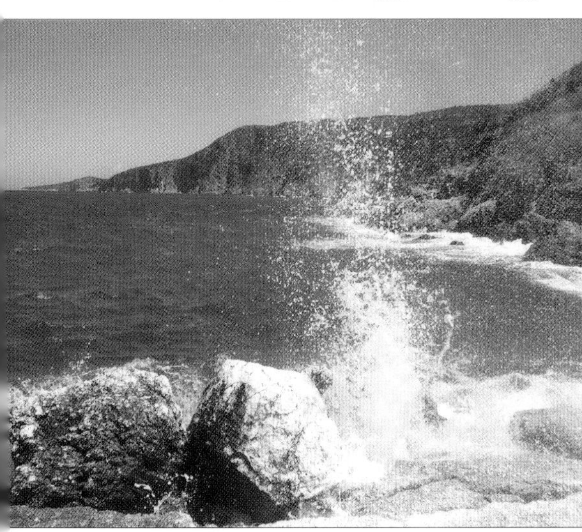

A page each on 218 islands that offer accommodation with key information, photographs and mini-maps

Page 316 The Islets

All islets larger than one-tenth of a square kilometre listed and mapped

Island Locator Page 396

Alphabetical index of all islands, islets and private islands listed in the book, with regions and groups

Page 360 Statistics

Islands listed and compared by size, population, accommodation, visitors and Crowdfactor, with country statistics, coastline lengths and other listings

THE SOUTH COAST CLIFFS OF GOZO (PHOTO: MALTA TOURISM AUTHORITY)

In this book the Mediterranean is divided into seven coloured zones, as shown on this map. Each island and islet has a four-figure identification number.

3000-3999
Italy

2000-2999
France, Monaco

4000-4999
Croatia, Slovenia, Bosnia, Montenegro, Albania

1000-1999
Spain, Morocco, Gibraltar

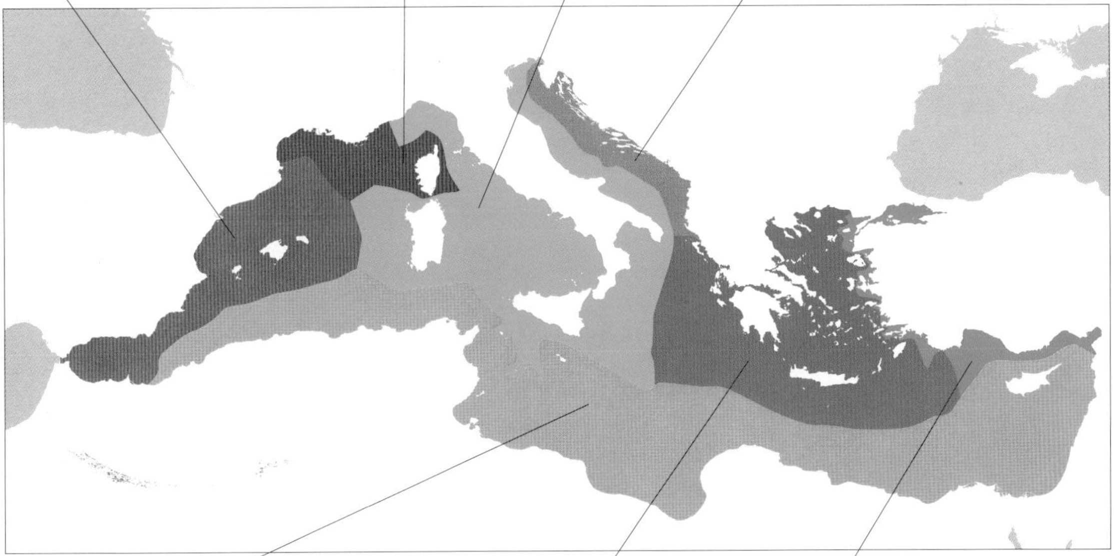

9000-9999
Cyprus, Malta, Tunisia, Algeria, Libya, Egypt, Gaza, Israel, Lebanon, Syria

8000-8999
Turkey

5000-5999
Greece, west of Cape Sounion

6000-6999
Greece, Crete,Cyclades, Evvoia, Sporades

7000-7999
Greece, Dodecanese, North Aegean

Professor Eleftheria Papadimitriou discusses how today's Mediterranean basin was formed by continental shifts

Perpetual evolution and shifting continents

The name given to the Mediterranean by the ancient Greeks, Mesogeios (meaning in the middle of the Earth), is self-explicit of its position. It is a closed sea, formed completely differently from the oceans, lying between the land areas of Africa and Europe. It is divided into marine sub-areas, namely the Balearic Sea, the Tyrrhenian Sea, the Adriatic Sea, the Ionian Sea, the Aegean Sea and the Levantine Sea, separated by the biggest Mediterranean islands and land areas. Thus, the Tyrrhenian Sea is separated from the Balearic Sea to the west by Corsica and Sardinia, while the Italian peninsula and Sicily separate it to the east from the Adriatic and the Ionian Sea.

As happens all over the world, island areas are associated with high seismic and volcanic activity, which are symptoms that have the same cause as the formation of the islands by themselves, deriving from the geodynamic properties of the places where they are located. However, people started to wonder about these physical phenomena and tried to give explanations for them long before observations and experiments were put on a scientific basis. Earthquakes and volcanoes are among the most frightening and at the same time most impressive phenomena for which descriptions and explanations were sought.

Legend

In Greek mythology, in the very old days, the Giants fought with the Gods of Olympus for the government of the world, and the Giants tried to expel the Gods from Mt Olympus. The leader of the Giants was Engelados, son of Tartaros and of Earth. The Gods finally won and the goddess Athena chased and defeated the giant Engelados, threw a huge piece of earth (which was Sicily) over him and completely covered him. Since then, because the Giants are immortal, occasionally Engelados moves and sighs in his grave, tries to free himself from the burden that squashed him and causes earthquakes and volcanic eruptions.

Not only was the formation of the Mediterranean Sea explored by our ancient ancestors, but the Sea itself. The Sea was personified by the primordial goddess Thalassa (Thalassa in Greek means sea), who was daughter of Aether (personification of the 'upper sky', space and heaven, and the elemental god of the 'Bright, Glowing, Upper Air') and Hemera (personification of the day).

A counterpart of Thalassa was Tethys, daughter of Uranus (sky) and Gaia (Earth). She was a Titaness and sea goddess who was both sister and wife of Oceanus. She was mother of the chief rivers of the world known to the Greeks, including the Nile, the Alpheus, the Maeander and about three thousand daughters called the Oceanides. She was considered the embodiment of the waters of the world.

We must admit that scientists nowadays have given us a more plausible explanation about the origin and evolution of the structure of the countries around the Mediterranean and of the Mediterranean islands in particular, which we shall now explore.

History

Some 225 million years ago, all the world's land masses were joined together into one supercontinent. This is based on the theory of continental drift, which states that parts of the Earth's crust slowly drift atop a liquid core, first proposed in 1912 by Alfred Wegener, a German geologist and meteorologist. Wegener hypothesised that the original, gigantic supercontinent, which he named Pangaea (meaning 'all the earth' in Greek), consisted of all of Earth's land masses. Pangaea was surrounded by a single universal sea, Panthalassa (meaning 'all the sea' in Greek), and existed from the Permian to the Jurassic period. It started to break up, during the Jurassic period, into two smaller supercontinents, called Laurasia and Gondwana, separated by the Tethys Sea. By the end of the Cretaceous period, the continents were separating into land masses that look like our continents today.

Facing page:
A NASA space photo showing a plume of smoke from Mount Etna passing over Malta 200 kilometres away and continuing to the coast of north Africa

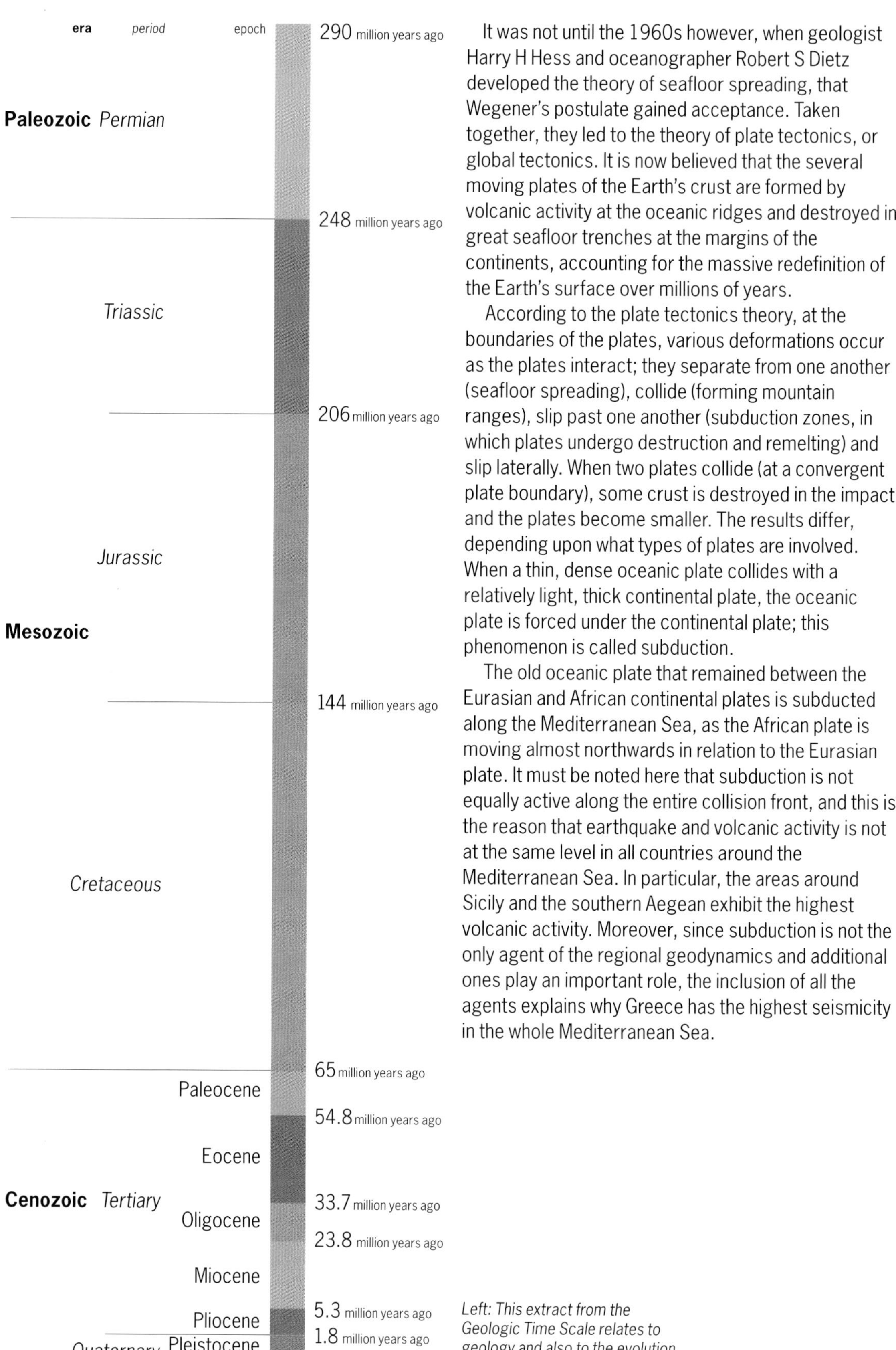
era
period
epoch
290 million years ago
Paleozoic
Permian
248 million years ago
Triassic
206 million years ago
Jurassic
Mesozoic
144 million years ago
Cretaceous
65 million years ago
Paleocene
54.8 million years ago
Eocene
Cenozoic
Tertiary
33.7 million years ago
Oligocene
23.8 million years ago
Miocene
5.3 million years ago
Pliocene
1.8 million years ago
Quaternary
Pleistocene
Holocene
Last 10,000 years

It was not until the 1960s however, when geologist Harry H Hess and oceanographer Robert S Dietz developed the theory of seafloor spreading, that Wegener's postulate gained acceptance. Taken together, they led to the theory of plate tectonics, or global tectonics. It is now believed that the several moving plates of the Earth's crust are formed by volcanic activity at the oceanic ridges and destroyed in great seafloor trenches at the margins of the continents, accounting for the massive redefinition of the Earth's surface over millions of years.

According to the plate tectonics theory, at the boundaries of the plates, various deformations occur as the plates interact; they separate from one another (seafloor spreading), collide (forming mountain ranges), slip past one another (subduction zones, in which plates undergo destruction and remelting) and slip laterally. When two plates collide (at a convergent plate boundary), some crust is destroyed in the impact and the plates become smaller. The results differ, depending upon what types of plates are involved. When a thin, dense oceanic plate collides with a relatively light, thick continental plate, the oceanic plate is forced under the continental plate; this phenomenon is called subduction.

The old oceanic plate that remained between the Eurasian and African continental plates is subducted along the Mediterranean Sea, as the African plate is moving almost northwards in relation to the Eurasian plate. It must be noted here that subduction is not equally active along the entire collision front, and this is the reason that earthquake and volcanic activity is not at the same level in all countries around the Mediterranean Sea. In particular, the areas around Sicily and the southern Aegean exhibit the highest volcanic activity. Moreover, since subduction is not the only agent of the regional geodynamics and additional ones play an important role, the inclusion of all the agents explains why Greece has the highest seismicity in the whole Mediterranean Sea.

Left: This extract from the Geologic Time Scale relates to geology and also to the evolution of plants and wildlife

(PHOTO: THOMAS REICHART)

Evolution of the Mediterranean Sea

The development of the Mediterranean through the Mesozoic and Cenozoic eras was a consequence of relative movements between North America, Eurasia and Africa, and those movements have been recorded by the 'magnetic tape' on the sea floor, namely the magnetic stripes of the Atlantic. Following the separation of the Triassic Pangaea, during the 'geosynclinal' (or Tethyan) phase, Africa moved sinistrally away from North America and Eurasia, which continued to be bound together. The seafloor spreading during the Jurassic and early Cretaceous periods created the Atlantic between Africa and North America, and the Tethys, or the ancestral Mediterranean, between Africa and Eurasia.

When Eurasia started to move away from North America in the late Cretaceous, the movement between Europe and Africa became dextral and compressional. By that time, volcanic activity was common, and some oceanic volcanoes grew tall enough for their peaks to emerge above the surface of the sea, creating new islands.

The coming together of the two plates gave rise to the Alps and the gradual elimination of the Tethys Ocean, of which the eastern Mediterranean is its last remnant. Tethys closed during the Cenozoic era about 50 million years ago when continental fragments of Gondwana – India, Arabia and Apulia (consisting of parts of Italy, the Balkan states, Greece and Turkey) – finally collided with the rest of Eurasia. The result was the creation of the modern Alpine-Himalayan ranges, which extend from Spain (the Pyrenees) and northwest Africa (the Atlas) along the northern margin of the Mediterranean Sea (the Alps and Carpathians) into southern Asia (the Himalayas) and then to Indonesia. Remnants of the Tethys Sea remain today as the Mediterranean, Black, Caspian and Aral seas.

Between the Eurasian and African lithospheric plates, two main motions take place: namely, a dextral motion of the Eurasian plate with respect to the African plate along the Azores-Gibraltar fault and a north-south convergence of the two plates, particularly revealed by the compressional tectonics along the Hellenic Arc in the eastern Mediterranean region. However, these main motions are not adequate to explain the peculiarities in seismic and volcanic activities in different parts of the Mediterranean Sea. For this reason, it is widely accepted among scientists that smaller rigid microplates exist between Eurasia and Africa, which contribute to the current geodynamic regime.

Microplates are smaller plates defined by active boundaries, which are manifested by seismic and volcanic activity. When this activity ceases, the microplate becomes part of the adjacent plate. There is a dispute among scientists on the number of active microplates around the Mediterranean. Nevertheless, there is a consensus that the highest activity, which is observed nowadays around the Aegean in comparison with other Mediterranean areas, is due to the existence and relative motion of three microplates, namely the Anatolian, Aegean and Apulian (Papazachos and Papazachou, 2003).

Above: Stromboli, said to be the most active volcano in the world with signs of activity every few minutes

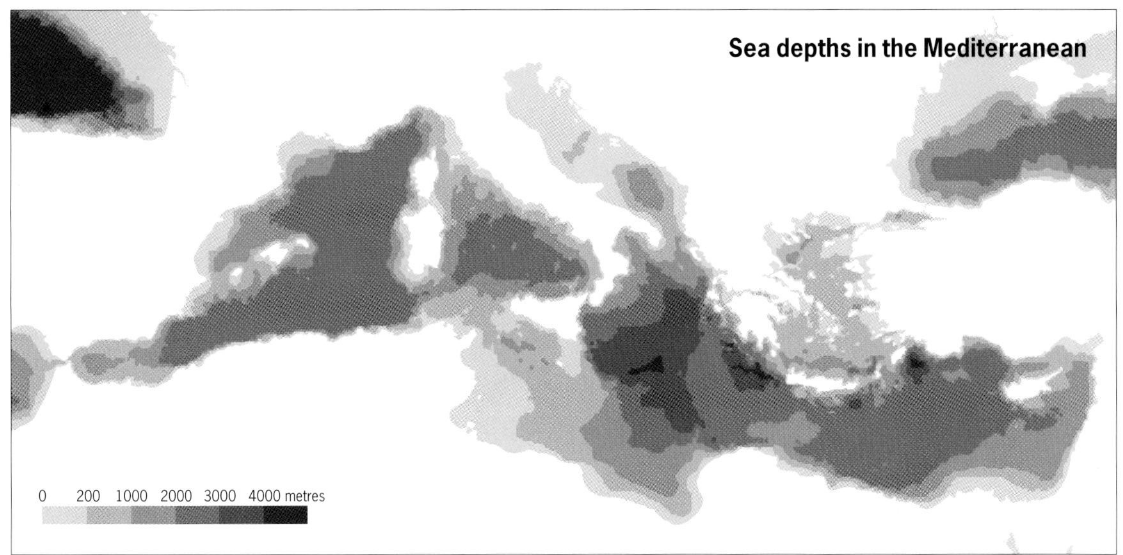
Sea depths in the Mediterranean
0 200 1000 2000 3000 4000 metres

Origin of the Mediterranean basins and islands
Islands, territorial units isolated by a barrier of waters, but with close ties to the nearby mainland shores, constitute geographical units. Although the largest Mediterranean islands (Sicily, Sardinia, Cyprus, Corsica) are connected with active boundaries between lithospheric plates or microplates and are not in Greek territory, the majority, more than 3000, are located in the Aegean Sea. The explanation of this spatial distribution lies in the geodynamics that cause the present relief in the Mediterranean and surrounding coastal areas.

Thus, going from west to east, one sees first the Balearic Islands in the Sea of the same name, which was created around the upper Oligocene by the oblique continental collision between Africa and western Europe. The opening of the Balearic basin ceased around the upper Miocene when the Corsica-Sardinia microplate reached its present position.

The Tyrrhenian Sea is one of the young basins of the Mediterranean and started to open in the Late Miocene along a north-south trending rift corresponding to the eastern Sardo -Corsican continental margin. At present, the Tyrrhenian Sea has a triangular shape and in the southern sector it is characterised by an abyssal plain (Central Abyssal Plain), more than 3500 metres deep, from which many basement highs rise.

Geodynamic processes in the region led firstly to the opening of the Ligurian Sea and the separation of the Corsica-Sardinia microplate from the European plate during the lower Miocene, and secondly to the opening of the Northern Tyrrhenian Sea, which began in the Upper Miocene. The Tyrrhenian Sea is bounded to the south by Sicily, the biggest island in the Mediterranean with the active volcano Etna in its eastern part, 3300 metres high, which is the highest in Europe.

The Adriatic Sea is the marine portion of a foreland basin that is deformed between the Apennines, the Alps and the Dinarides-Hellenides chains (Moretti and Royden, 1988). It is one of the major regional sub-basins of the Mediterranean Sea. It is an elongated NW-SE basin, almost entirely surrounded by mountain ridges and communicating with the Ionian Sea through the Otranto Strait (Zavatarelli and Pinardi, 2003). The northern part of the basin is characterized by very shallow depths (35 metres on average). In the central part, depths increase gently to 100 m, and the distinctive morphological features are two small bottom depressions (the so-called 'Pomo' and 'Jabuka' Pits) with a maximum depth of 250 m. The southern part of the basin contrasts markedly with the northern one, as depths rapidly increase to a maximum of about 1200 metres. The connection with the Ionian Strait is characterised by a sill with a depth of 875 m.

The Aegean Sea is a back arc basin located on the Aegean microplate, which overrides the eastern Mediterranean oceanic old lithospheric plate, being part of the frontal African lithospheric plate, which is nowadays moving almost northwards. This convergence results in an active subduction zone, along the Hellenic arc that extends from the Ionian

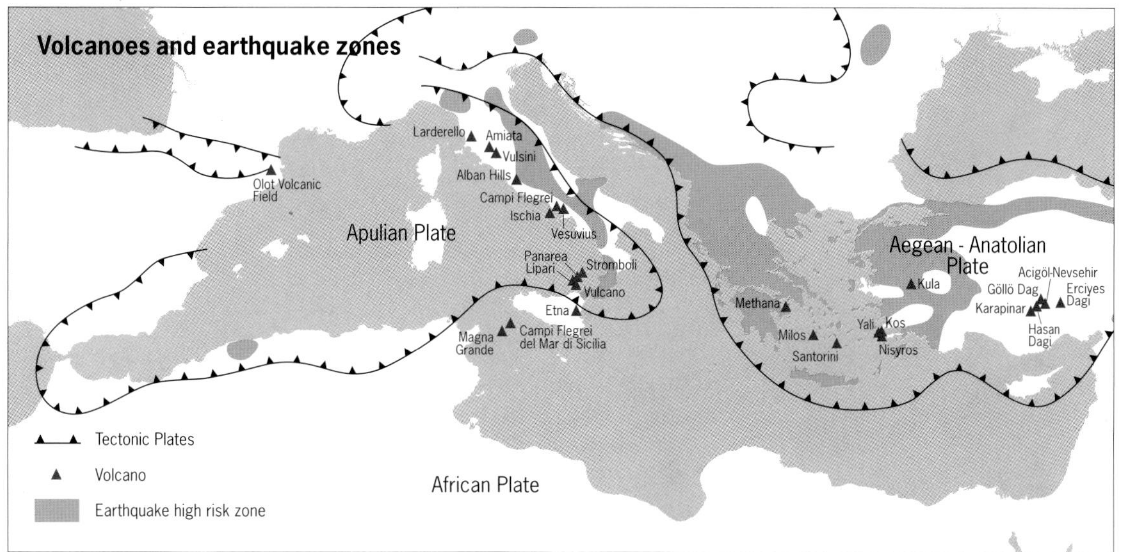
Volcanoes and earthquake zones
Larderello
Amiata
Vulsini
Alban Hills
Campi Flegrei
Ischia
Vesuvius
Olot Volcanic Field
Apulian Plate
Panarea
Lipari
Stromboli
Vulcano
Etna
Magna Grande
Campi Flegrei del Mar di Sicilia
Methana
Milos
Santorini
Yali
Kos
Nisyros
Aegean - Anatolian Plate
Kula
Acigöl-Nevsehir
Göllö Dag
Erciyes Dagi
Karapinar
Hasan Dagi
Tectonic Plates
Volcano
Earthquake high risk zone
African Plate

Islands in the northwest to Rhodes in the east. Crete is the biggest island located on this active boundary, while there are many islands in the Aegean, several of them being of volcanic origin (the most famous one being Santorini with a spectacular caldera). The existence of numerous Aegean islands, along with the high seismicity of the area, is the manifestation of the active tectonics of the region, which result in the rapid southwestwards motion of the Aegean microplate, with the influence of the Anatolian microplate from the east and Adriatic microplate from the west.

The Levantine basin, once considered to be a remnant of the Palaeozoic Tethys, is now thought to be either a remnant of a Mesozoic ocean basin created south of Palaeotethys or a subsided portion of thin continental crust. The Island of Cyprus, formed there by a series of unique and complicated geological events, was part of the bottom of 'Tethys'. Tectonic movements at that time resulted in the collision of the African with the Eurasian plate ultimately giving birth to Cyprus. Troodos and the Pentadactylos range first rose above the surface of the sea about 20 million years ago.

Summary

The Mediterranean Sea comprises a number of geodynamic units, which have interacted in the course of their formation, as briefly described above. The characteristics of the Mediterranean geodynamic setting can be summarised as a combination of...

1. The presence of old oceanic crust currently being destroyed in subduction zones
2. Continental collision
3. The volcanic arcs
4. The active crustal deformation in many areas, which is manifested by strong and frequent earthquakes.

These geodynamic properties account for the formation of the various sea basins, both larger and smaller, as well as the formation of the numerous islands and the variety of their size, shape and geographical distribution. The geodynamic state of the Mediterranean region has evolved over a very long period and it is still evolving.

Professor Eleftheria Papadimitriou is Professor of Seismology at Aristotle University of Thessaloniki.

Further reading

Hsu K J. *Alpine Mediterranean geodynamics: past, present and future.* AGU Geodynamics Series, Vol 7, 1982.
Mantovani E, Albarello D, Babucci D, Tamburelli C & Viti M. *Trench arc-back arc systems in the Mediterranean area: examples of extrusion tectonics.* Journal of the Virtual Explorer 3, 17-44, 2002.
Moretti I & Royden L. *Deflection, gravity anomalies and tectonics of doubly subducted seismic continental lithosphere: Adriatic and Ionian Seas.* Tectonics 7, pp 875-893, 1988.
Papazachos B C & Papazachou C. *The earthquakes of Greece,* Ziti Publications, Thessaloniki, pp 317 ff, 2003.
Zavatarelli M & Pinardi N. *The Adriatic Sea modeling system: a nested approach.* Annales Geophysicae 21, pp 345-364, 2003.

An introduction to the flora of the Mediterranean islands

Paul Sterry of our editorial team takes a walk through the rich plant life of a typical Mediterranean island

A walk across a Mediterranean island

Visit any Mediterranean island in spring and you will find stunning floral displays that stand comparison with the best wildlife wonders on earth. But, like many natural events, the spectacle is a brief one and the peak flowering season in the Mediterranean is short. To see it at its best, visit the region between late March and early May.

Climate and plantlife

The Mediterranean climate is what draws most visitors to the region, especially its hot, dry summers, almost guaranteed blue skies and warm seas. Temperature and rainfall are also the most significant factors influencing the region's plants and to survive native species have evolved to cope with the Mediterranean's climatic extremes. In many areas there is almost no rain from June to August and midday summer temperatures can soar to 35C or more. Most rain falls from November to February and, although temperatures drop considerably in winter, frosts are rare; the thermometer does not dip below 5C in some years.

Water loss and retention are clearly problems for Mediterranean plants. Most native shrubs and trees are evergreen and reduce evaporation from their leaves in a variety of ways: some have narrow leaves with small surface areas; others having waxy or aromatic oily coatings to reduce transpiration. For smaller, herbaceous plants the problem is more profound and the solution often more drastic. Many species are annual and simply die after producing seeds in spring. Even many perennial plants wither entirely above ground in summer and persist as dormant underground bulbs, tubers or corms until the first autumn rains revive their fortunes. Consequently, from July to September much of the vegetation looks parched and lifeless and for almost all native Mediterranean plants winter is the main growing season.

Facing page:
Lavender
(Lavandula stoechas)

Origins of Mediterranean plants

Man has lived in the Mediterranean region for millennia and his impact on the environment has been profound. Indeed, while the landscape may retain a natural look, in many regions its character and the plants that thrive result directly from the actions of people. Much of the Mediterranean's primary woodland cover has long since been cleared, replaced most obviously by villages and cultivated land. But even the scrub-covered hillsides, such a feature of today's Mediterranean, would also have been wooded in the distant past. With their natural tree cover removed, stunningly colourful shrubs and herbaceous plants have filled the gap and flourished. And man's grazing animals – goats in particular – have also had a profound influence: many of the plants that do best are ones with some form of grazing deterrent such as spines, thorns or aromatic scents or taste.

Many of the plants that we associate most closely with the Mediterranean nowadays are not native to the region, or at least their natural range has been greatly extended by planting. Understandably, most of them are sources of food and the best-known example is the olive *Olea europaea.* Often used as a botanical indicator of a Mediterranean climate (it is intolerant of frost), its true origins are hard to discern although its ties are certainly with the east and Asia minor. The same is true of orange *Citrus sinensis* and lemon *Citrus limon,* which perfume the outskirts of many villages. Other species with edible parts, and whose natural ranges are blurred by centuries of planting (and subsequent naturalisation), include fig *Ficus carica*, grape *Vitis vinifera*, caper *Capparis ovata* and pistachio *Pistachia vera*; a close relative of the latter, lentisc *Pistacia lentiscus,* also grows wild, particularly in the east of the region and is sometimes cultivated for its resin, mastic. Planted nowadays as much for ornament as

Left to right: Bougainvillea (*Bougainvillea spectabilis*), Wild basil (*Clinopodium vulgare*) and Tamarisk (*Tamarix parviflora*)

(PHOTO: PIA HELENA FALK)

for food the date palm *Phoenix dactylifera* comes originally from N Africa and the Arabian peninsula.

Most of the Mediterranean's more traditional edible plants have been cultivated for thousands of years and their origins lie either within the region as a whole, or on its fringes. But more recently, introductions have come from farther afield. From the 15th century onwards plants have been brought from the New World. Most striking of these is the century plant *Agave mexicana*, grown today often for its appearance rather than as a source of fibre. But perhaps the most valued introduction, in culinary terms at least, is the ubiquitous tomato *Lycopersicon esculentum* – there can hardly be a Mediterranean menu on which it does not feature. Some introductions are purely decorative and bougainvillea *Bougainvillea glabra*, which looks so at home festooning walls and houses, hails from Brazil. With others their role is more functional and shade trees such as blackwood acacia *Acacia melanoxylon* come from Australia.

A sensory experience

Although studying Mediterranean plantlife is primarily a visual experience, it can involve all the senses. The air is heavily perfumed by many species of flowers, and brushing through hillside vegetation yields the pungent and aromatic scents of herbs. Although not strictly speaking botanical, colourful meadows and hillside scrub can be deafening with the sound of bees buzzing, and grasshoppers and crickets chirping; these insects would not be there but for the plantlife.

Moving on to the sense of touch, unless you watch your step, wandering through Mediterranean scrub can be a painful experience with many of the plants being spiny or prickly. And to complete the sensory complement, you can feast on a wild-grown fig, caper bud or some other Mediterranean delicacy as a reward for your efforts.

With several thousand native species growing wild in the Mediterranean, anyone with an interest in botany could happily spend a lifetime studying them. And with most of the larger islands boasting numerous endemic plant species and subspecies variations some keen botanists do just that, visiting a different island each spring. With so much variety, an introduction to the region's plantlife must, of necessity, paint a broad picture. To do this I will take you on an imaginary journey through the Mediterranean landscape that starts with our arrival by boat at a small harbour. From here we will stroll through the nearby village, wander among peaceful olive groves, and eventually emerge onto scrub-covered hills that look back to the sea. A steep climb then takes us to woodland whose shade provides a welcome relief from the heat of the day.

The coast

After time spent at sea, it is nice to stroll on dry land for a change. Paddling in the shallows as you walk along the beach, you may notice fibrous, spherical objects – known as sea balls – some the size of a tennis ball, washed up on the seashore. These are tangible reminders of plantlife beneath the waves and are the matted and rolled remains of Neptune Grass *Posidonia oceanica*, a grass-like flowering plant that, in life,

(PHOTO: PAUL STERRY/NATURE PHOTOGRAPHERS)

(PHOTO: PAUL STERRY/NATURE PHOTOGRAPHERS)

grows on shallow seabeds. Further up the beach, colonising plants such as sea stock *Matthiola sinuata* flourish if human disturbance is not great and keen-eyed observers may spot the strap-like leaves of sea daffodil *Pancratium maritimum* emerging from the sand; breaking all the botanical rules for the Mediterranean, this species' lily-like flowers appear in autumn. Broken, sandy slopes above the beach in Crete, Cyprus and other islands in the eastern Mediterranean often support thriving colonies of Jersualem sage *Phlomis fruticosa* while throughout the region tamarisk *Tamarix* sp. is a familiar coastal feature and is often planted as a windbreak or for shade; *T. gallica* is common in the west, although not on the Balearic islands or Sardinia while *T. parviflora* is native in the east but widely planted in the west. Stone pines *Pinus pinaster* are often planted to stabilise coastal sands.

Village life

To combat midday heat, Mediterranean gardens are often planned and planted with shade in mind, which is where grape vines come in extremely useful. But with an eye to colour, the highly poisonous oleander *Nerium oleander* is widely grown and often naturalised and stately Italian cypress trees *Cupressus sempervirens* add an architectural tone to the landscape.

Wandering out of the village, roadside verges are often amazingly colourful and plants that thrive in arable fields also find roadside soil disturbance to their liking. Species of poppy *Papaver* sp. are a common sight but most impressive of all is giant fennel *Ferula communis*, with its bright yellow umbels of flowers; it can reach a height of three metres.

Olive groves and agricultural land

There is something rather magical about a good olive grove in spring. The ground below the trees is often tilled, sometimes annually, to discourage scrub encroachment, but the result is that plants that thrive on disturbance (and are also found in arable fields) do well. And the shade provided by the trees prolongs the flowering season. The precise mix of species varies considerably and a good site may have several hundred species. But common components include crown daisy *Chrysanthemum coronarium*, corn marigold *Chrysanthemum segetum*, gladiolus species, notably *Gladiolus illyricus*, poppies *Papaver* sp., corncockle *Agrostemma githago* and pheasant's-eye *Adonis annua*. Tassel hyacinth *Muscari comosum* is distinctive and especially common in the east while rosy garlic *Allium roseum* is more widespread. Members of Pea family are well represented in olive groves and grassy fields: bladder vetch *Anthyllis tetraphylla* is found on most islands except the Balearics; several clover species *Trifolium* sp. are abundant with starry clover *T. stellatum* being obvious in the west and eastern starry clover *T. dasyurum* largely replacing it in the east; trefoils *Lotus* sp., many of which have yellow flowers, are an attractive sight and vetches *Vicia* sp. clamber through the vegetation. Many islands boast specialities within each genus.

(PHOTO: PAUL STERRY/NATURE PHOTOGRAPHERS)

(PHOTO: PAUL STERRY/NATURE PHOTOGRAPHERS)

Scrub habitats

Mediterranean scrub habitats have evolved, and flourish, in the wake of tree clearance by man. Depending on the degree of erosion and degradation (by grazing animals) they vary in appearance from dense and impenetrable (referred to as *maquis*) to areas dominated by sparse vegetation, typically under 1 metre in height (referred to as *garrigue*, or *phrygana* in Greece). Compared with the original vegetation (woodland), maquis and garrigue are degraded habitats in ecological terms. But tree clearance has had a positive effect upon the diversity of herbaceous plants and it is in these scrubby habitats that, arguably, the region's greatest botanical interest lies.

The dominant group of plants in many scrub areas are members of the rockrose family, with clump- or shrub-forming *Cistus* species being most obvious. Regional specialities abound (many of which look very similar to one another) but widespread representatives include the white-flowered sage-leaved cistus C. *monspeliensis* and the pink-flowered *C. creticus*. Smaller rockrose family members, such as spotted rockrose *Tuberaria guttata* grow between the clumps of larger species and this is also the place to look for aromatic plants such as lavenders *Lavandula* sp., basil *Clinopodium vulgare*, sage species *Salvia* sp., rosemaries *Rosmarinus* sp., marjoram *Origanum vulgare* and thymes Thymus sp.; *Thymus capitatus* is a particularly showy, pungent and widespread example.

Larger, striking scrub species include spurges (*Euphorbia characias* is a feature of the Balearics), colourful brooms, *Cytisus* sp., Spanish broom *Spartium junceum* (a mainly western species), thorny brooms such as *Calycotome infesta* (widespread in the west and on Sicily), and Mt Etna broom *Genista aetnensis*, native to Sardinia and Sicily but widely planted elsewhere. Asphodels, although impressive to look at, are a sign of chronic overgrazing – they are unpalatable to animals. Common asphodel *Asphodelus aestivus* and yellow asphodel *Asphodeline lutea* are both widespread, the latter particularly in the east.

Further botanical interest is provided by species of cyclamens, many of which have only limited ranges; *Cyclamen graecum* is one of the most widespread in the east and *C. balearicum* is restricted to the Balearics. But it is for the orchids that maquis and garrigue habitats are most renowned. Of course, orchids are not restricted to these habitats by any means but it is here that you find the greatest diversity and abundance, especially where soils are calcareous. Showy and intriguing examples include the Italian man orchid *Orchis italica*, tongue orchid *Serapias lingua* and giant orchid *Barlia robertiana*. But pride of place goes to members of the bee orchid family *Ophrys*: if the experts are to be believed, almost every island in the Mediterranean has its own *Ophrys* species or unique subspecies and the variation in floral appearance, although subtle, is bewildering for the beginner. Common and reasonably widespread examples with brown furry lips include the sawfly orchid *O.*

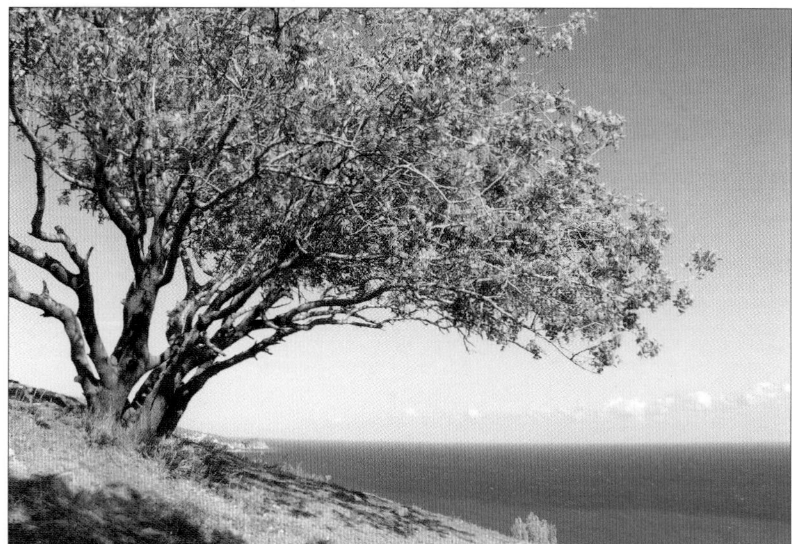

Left to right:
Eastern yellow bee orchid (Ophrys sicula),
Mirror orchid (Ophrys speculum) and Pistachio (Pistachia vera)

tenthredinifera, the woodcock orchid *O. scolopax*, the mirror orchid *O. speculum*, and the bumblebee orchid *O. bombylifera*; for enthusiasts, the Majorcan speciality Berteloni's bee orchid *O. bertelonii* is considered one of the finest examples. Yellow-lipped species also occur with *O. lutea* being widespread in the west.

Maquis represents the shrubby end of the scrub habitat spectrum and stature is lent to the vegetation by towering tree heathers (*Erica arborea* is found mainly in the west while *E. terminalis* is dominant on Corsica and Sardinia). Junipers such as the pricky juniper *Juniperus oxycedrus* and Phoenician juniper *J. phoenicea* can provide dense cover and strawberry trees are also common with *Arbutus unedo* in the west and *A. andrachne* in the east.

Woodland and forest

In most parts of the Mediterranean, native remnant or planted woodland and forests are dominated by evergreen trees; deciduous species only flourish at cooler, humid high altitudes. Aleppo pine *Pinus halepensis* is widespread and Black pine *Pinus nigra* is also a familiar sight, the latter represented in different parts of the region by a range of subspecies. Stone pine *Pinus pinea*, the source of edible pine nuts, is native and widely planted and various cedars such as Cedar of Lebanon *Cedrus libani* are also popular, partly for ornament. Cyprus cedar *C. brevifolia* is endemic to that island.

At ground level most Mediterranean woodlands are rather lacking in botanical interest. However, particularly under mature pines, showy masses of violet limodore orchids *Limodorum abortivum* can sometimes be found and closer scrutiny may reveal several other, less striking orchid species such as dense-flowered orchid *Neotinea maculata*.

Pause for thought

Having retraced your steps back to the coast it is worth reflecting on the wealth of plantlife you have just seen, preferably over a glass of locally produced wine and a plate of regional olives.

In botanical terms, the Mediterranean really is special and whichever island you visit it pays to follow the flowers even if your floral interests are superficial. Because doing so will take you off the beaten track and reveal what for many is the real Mediterranean, a place where a slow pace of life allows for a greater degree of harmony between people and their environment that exists in few other places in the world.

An in-depth look at Mediterranean island plant life
Professor Frédéric Médail explores the rich diversity of Mediterranean island plant life

A natural history of the islands' unique flora

The unique nature of Mediterranean island floras
The unusual geographical, climatic and topographical diversity and the complex historical biogeography explain the exceptionally high plant diversity and endemism of the Mediterranean Basin. The numerous islands constitute a significant component of Mediterranean plant biodiversity, notably with the presence of range-restricted plants (endemic plants) and isolated plant populations from a genetic point of view. This highly diversified insular flora is the result of the different geographical situations, of the varied paleogeography linked to important tectonic movements, and of the wide ranges of size, altitude, morphology and geology. The considerable diversity of insular landscapes is also explained by the heritage of human activities which have had profound consequences on the distribution and dynamics of plant species and ecosystems.

Main patterns of vegetation and plant biodiversity of the major islands and archipelagos
In the larger Mediterranean islands plant endemism is generally 10-12% (see map on page 32) but the overall range of flora is greater than expected, with between 1600 and 2800 taxa (species and subspecies). On insular mountain ranges, the endemism level is clearly higher since at altitudes above 1700 metres endemic plants represent about 35-40% of the vascular flora in Corsica and in Crete. Even small islands play an important role in plant biodiversity: for example, on 71 satellite islands of Sardinia, which represent only 1.1% of the total surface of the main island, 1200 plants have been identified, i.e. almost half of the total Sardinian flora.

Balearic islands The Balearic archipelago has a relatively high plant richness with about 1730 native plant taxa (including varieties) and 173 endemic and subendemic plants of which about 121 are restricted endemics. The distribution of the flora reflects deeply the complex palaeogeography of the western Mediterranean, and these islands form two distinct units. The flora of the western islands (Formentera and Ibiza) possess strong Iberian or Ibero-Maghrebian affinities whereas those of the eastern islands (Majorca, Minorca, Cabrera) have clear Tyrrhenian affinities with the unique presence of monospecific genera (*Femeniasia, Naufraga, Soleirolia*) and other palaeoendemics (*Daphne rodriguezii, Pimpinella bicknellii, Lotus tetraphyllus*…). Therefore, according to this clear biogeographical segmentation, it is not really surprising that only few endemics are common to all the Balearic islands (*Hypericum balearicum, Bupleurum barceloi*…). If tourism and land-use changes have profoundly altered and modified the habitats in Majorca and Ibiza, the islands of Menorca and Formentera are less impacted and rural landscapes are still prevalent.

The vegetation is mainly composed of typical trees and shrubs (*Quercus ilex, Ceratonia siliqua, Olea europaea, Pistacia lentiscus, Myrtus communis*…), but there are some singularities in the plant communities with the presence of the shrubs *Cneorum tricoccon* and *Buxus balearica*. Along windy and rocky coasts of the eastern islands, there is a remarkable plant community made up of spiny and cushion endemics locally named *socarrell* (*Launaea cervicornis, Anthyllis hystrix, Astragalus balearicus, Dorycnium pentaphyllum* subsp. *fulgurans*). Another *socarrell* community defined notably by *Teucrium subspinosum* is also present on the ridges of the upper part of the Serra de Tramuntana de Mallorca, above 1100 metres.

Corsica This mountainous island comprises 2325 indigenous plant taxa (including varieties), of which 316 are endemics or subendemics, i.e. a 13.6% rate of endemism. 146 plant taxa are strictly localised to Corsica, and the mountain alpine flora above 2100 metres is highly specific as it includes ca. 43% endemics of the 131 alpine taxa, with 34 strict Corsican endemics. Nevertheless, the most numerous group of the endemics is centered at medium altitudes, and several endemics are very common at this level

Facing page:
Bug orchid
(Orchis coriophora)

Left to right:
Cyprus cedar (Cedrus brevifolia), Oleander (Nerium oleander) and Stone pine (Pinus pinea)

(PHOTO: ANDREW CLEAVE/NATURE PHOTOGRAPHERS)

(*Thymus herba-barona, Stachys corsica, Genista corsica...*). Corsica is the most wooded Mediterranean island with almost 30% of its surface covered by forests and mature maquis. In the mountains, the dominant tree is the Corsican pine or Laricio (*Pinus nigra* subsp. *laricio*) which often forms pure and impressive stands. The upper limits of forests are roughly at 1600 metres on northern slopes and 1800 metres on southern ones, but *Abies alba* can reach 1900 metres locally. In the alpine zone, north-facing slopes are covered by *Alnus viridis* subsp. *suaveolens* scrub and grasslands, but south-facing slopes with xerophytic dwarf-shrubs (*Astragalus genargenteus, Berberis aetnensis, Genista salzmannii*) dominate the landscape. Between 1600 and 2400 metres particular vegetation (named locally pozzines) have a high conservation value with several endemics (*Bellis bernardii, Bellium nivale, Pinguicula corsica...*). Other very rich and generally still well preserved habitats, despite their location at low altitude, include temporary pools with a huge contingent of rare and restricted plants (*Isoetes, Pilularia*), and rocky or sandy coasts with several particular plants (*Armeria soleirolii, Erodium corsicum, Silene velutina...*).

Sardinia As in the other large Mediterranean islands, sclerophyllous species dominate the landscape notably with *Quercus suber* forests that were favoured by man. The dwarf-palm (*Chamaerops humilis*) is commonly found along the warm slopes of the coasts whereas this south-Mediterranean species is absent in neighbouring Corsica. There are some deciduous trees (*Quercus pubescens, Fraxinus ornus*) and more sparsely maples, together with populations of *Taxus baccata* and *Ilex aquifolium* that make up the treeline at an exceptionally low altitude of 1400-1500 metres. The absence of trees above this limit is certainly due to ancient human deforestation and pasture and the upper part of the Gennargentu massif is characterised by the the same shrubs as in the mountains of Corsica.

Sardinia is rather rich in flora with about 2300 species and subspecies and a well-documented plant endemism (254 endemics and subendemics), with clear affinities to Corsica since 80 endemics are solely shared between these two islands. Furthermore, the existence of several closely related plants (vicarious plants: eg. *Ruta corsica* and *R. lamarmorae*) attest the strong biogeographical link between Sardinia and Corsica. Some exclusive Sardinian endemics also deserve attention, notably in two genera whose distribution is Alpine-centered, *Aquilegia* with three local endemics (*A. barbaricina, A. nuragica, A. nugorensis*) and *Ribes* (*R. sandalioticum, R. sardoum*).

Sicily Sicily, the largest Mediterranean island, is an area of major botanical interest, with around 2800 plant species and 321 endemics and subendemics notably located in the north-eastern part of the island.The flora of the hills of Madonie alone includes 50% of Sicily's species and 40 endemics in less than 2% of the island's area. Etna contains 21 endemic plants and shows a remarkable vertical distribution of the vegetation, from the foothills with an evergreen vegetation belt, to the presence above 1000 metres of deciduous broadleaved trees with *Quercus pubescens* and then *Fagus sylvatica* enriched by Laricio pine

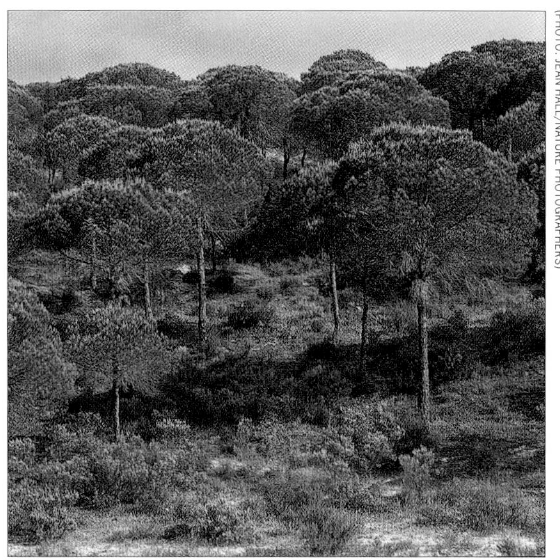

(PHOTO: JEAN HALL/NATURE PHOTOGRAPHERS)

woodlands, and finally a shrubby vegetation dominated by *Astragalus siculus,* an endemic thorny-cushion plant present up to 2450 metres. Sicily includes also several endemic trees, which is uncommon in the Mediterranean Basin. Two of these species are very rare and endangered: *Abies nebrodensis* with only about thirty individuals located on the Madonie mountain, and the relict *Zelkova sicula* with only one population of 250 individuals discovered ten years ago in the south-east of the island (Iblei mountains). Some endemic trees are found only on Etna: *Betula aetnensis* and *Celtis aetnensis* are strict endemics whereas *Pinus nigra* subsp. *laricio* and *Genista aetnensis* are also located on other Tyrrhenian islands. Some less disturbed areas show a trend toward a gradual replacement of evergreen forests with *Quercus ilex* by broad-leaved trees (*Quercus pubescens, Fraxinus ornus, Ostrya carpinifolia*) and *Quercus suber.*

Malta The vegetation of the Maltese archipelago has been seriously modified by man for millennia and only very reduced and isolated patches of woods with *Quercus ilex* and *Pinus halepensis* still exist. Maquis with *Ceratonia siliqua, Pistacia lentiscus* and *Euphorbia dendroides,* and garigues dominated by *Corydothymus capitatus, Erica multiflora, Anthyllis hermanniae, Teucrium fruticans* are mostly derived formations. Of the 16 strict endemic species and sub-species, two monotypic genera (*Cremnophyton lanfrancoi* and *Palaeocyanus crassifolius*) deserve attention because they represent relict and rare species restricted to some sheer cliffs in SW Malta and Gozo. From a biogeographical point of view, the Maltese islands are linked to other islands of the strait of Sicily (Lampedusa, Linosa, Pantelleria), but some relationships with North Africa are noticeable, such as the presence of the coniferous tree *Tetraclinis articulata.*

Nevertheless, the deep and ancient human impact is responsible for the local extinction of at least fifty indigenous plants and a severe impoverishment of the plant diversity and vegetation types.

Crete Isolated for around 5.2 million years and almost entirely spared by Quaternary glaciations, this island has a unique flora with 209 endemics out of a total of 1735 native species. The high biogeographical interest of this Cretan flora is also related to the presence of diverse elements from the Balkans, Anatolia and to a lesser extent North Africa. Calcareous cliffs and treeless mountain areas with cushion-shaped and spiny dwarf shrubs (*Berberis cretica, Acantholimon ulicinum, Astracantha cretica…*) harbour a high number of endemic plants. Indeed, if the high-mountain flora of the three main massifs (Levka Ori, Psiloritis and Dhikti) is very poor, 35% of the 217 plants censused above 1500 metres are endemic. The level, clay-based mountain habitat is very particular with a distinct vegetation and the presence of several very rare plants and endemics such as the recently described herb *Horstrissea dolinicola,* a monospecific genus.

Scrub communities dominate the Cretan landscape, with maquis or garigues including *Ceratonia siliqua, Cistus spp., Olea europaea, Pistacia terebinthus,*

(PHOTO: ANDREW CLEAVE/NATURE PHOTOGRAPHERS)

(PHOTO: ANDREW CLEAVE/NATURE PHOTOGRAPHERS)

Arbutus unedo, Erica arborea and *Quercus coccifera*, and phrygana composed of spiny, hemispherical dwarf shrubs (*Anthyllis hermanniae, Coridothymus capitatus, Euphorbia acanthothamnos*…). Woodlands are mainly composed of sclerophyllous trees at low to mid altitudes (*Ceratonia siliqua, Phillyrea latifolia, Quercus ilex, Quercus coccifera*) with *Pinus brutia*, whereas deciduous oaks (*Quercus brachyphylla, Q. ithaburensis* subsp. *macrolepis*) occur nowadays only as scattered trees. In mountain areas, *Acer sempervirens* and *Cupressus sempervirens* are the dominant trees with *Quercus coccifera*; one of the most interesting trees is Ambelitsiá (*Zelkova cretica*), a relict elm-like tree present sparsely in the western mountains between 850 and 1800 metres.

Cyprus Natural habitats in Cyprus are mainly composed of pine forests, with Brutia pine forests from sea level to 1200 m, and the Black pine (*Pinus nigra* subsp. *pallasiana*) forests which occupy a restricted area of 6000 hectares in the Troodos massif between 1200 and 1900 metres. Mainly resulting from the destruction of forests by human activities, garigues and maquis cover a large part of the island, with evergreen shrubs but also with several dwarf shrubs (*Genista sphacelata, Nonea mucronata, Sarcopoterium spinosum, Asperula cypria*…) in dry and eroded soils.

Cyprus comprises about 1620 plant species with 170 endemics and subendemics. The flora has clear biogeographical affinities with Anatolia, but several plants with an African-Arabian distribution (*Prosopis farcta, Pteranthus dichotomus, Zygophyllum album*) are the testimony of arid conditions which occur in the lowlands. Some of the most remarkable endemics are *Onobrychis venosa* and *Bosea cypria*, whereas three endemic species of *Crocus* are recorded. Of about 25 endemic plants located in rocky areas, six species are included in the Stonecrop family (*Sedum, Rosularia*).

The most interesting sector from a botanical point of view is the Troodos massif with unique forests of the endemic trees *Cedrus brevifola* and *Quercus alnifolia* and the existence of about 65 endemic plants mainly on serpentine soils.

Natural history and biogeography of Mediterranean island floras

Mediterranean islands constitute major refugia areas, since they represent conservatories of old (often mid-Tertiary) and relict plants with a restricted distribution, termed palaeoendemics. This pattern is well supported by the presence of several monotypic endemic plant genera, restricted to one or few of these islands (see table on page 33), and by the existence of some relict plants of the subtropical tertiary environments, eg. the genus *Zelkova*. An outstanding example of the importance of ancient palaeogeography to explain current patterns of plant distribution and biogeographical links is provided by the Tyrrhenian islands. The eastern Balearic Islands (Menorca and Majorca), Corsica, Sardinia and part of Sicily are some of the remnant areas that once belonged to the Protoligurian massif, a west Mediterranean Hercynian formation that was fragmented in the mid-Tertiary period (Oligocene-Miocene), causing notably the rotation and migration of the Corsica-Sardinia block between 23 and 16

(PHOTO: IBATUR GOVERN ILLES BALEARS MANFRED)

Left to right:
European fan palm (Chamaerops humilis),
Yellow asphodel (asphodeline lutea) and Fig (Ficus carica)

million years ago. The distribution of numerous Tyrrhenian endemic plants shared between these islands (e.g. *Arenaria balearica, Delphinium pictum, Dracunculus muscivorus, Teucrium marum, Thymus herba-barona*) reflects this crucial event (see map on page 33).

Another fascinating pattern is that offshore islands determine quite often the limits of geographical ranges of some range-restricted plants. Indeed, despite its closeness (about 10 km) from Cape Bon in Tunisia, the island of Zembra harbours the southernmost populations of plants located mainly in Italy, Sicily (*Erodium maritimum, Iberis semperflorens*) or in the eastern Mediterranean (*Sarcopoterium spinosum*). The Hyères archipelago, a remnant of the ancient Protoligurian massif, comprises several Tyrrhenian endemics (*Delphinium pictum, Ptilostemon casabonae, Teucrium marum*) which are totally absent along the nearby mainland of Provence, even if environmental conditions are similar.

For explaining in part these current patterns of plant distribution and endemism on the Mediterranean islands, two determinant geological periods must be invoked. First, the Messinian salinity crisis of the Late Miocene, provoked by the interruption of marine relationships between the Atlantic Ocean and the Mediterranean Sea, induced an almost complete desiccation of the Mediterranean Sea between 5.96 and 5.33 million years ago. Five million years ago, the beginning of the Pliocene was marked by the return of the sea and this resulted in the final separation of some major islands (Crete and Karpathos, Corsica, Sardinia, the Balearic islands) from the mainland. Second, the severe cooling episodes beginning at the late Pliocene (ca. 1.75 million years ago) caused severe regressions of the sea level (between 100 and 150 metres below the actual), inducing numerous terrestrial migration of more competitive cool-temperate flora on offshore islands. But if Mediterranean islands have served as refugia, their role in local and more recent differentiation of plants is also important. Therefore, islands frequently harbour polymorphic species and younger endemic plants (neoendemics such as *Limonium* and *Centaurea*).

One of the most fascinating and intriguing patterns is related to the ecological uniqueness of islands. Some close islands show very different plant species composition. This is the case of the distribution of about 60 plant species (notably *Campanula, Dianthus, Erysimum, Helichrysum*) restricted to mostly maritime cliffs of the Aegean, with marked differences between islands even less than 10-20 km apart. Furthermore, on very small islands, it is possible to find some "islet specialists", i.e. plants that grow exclusively or are very abundant locally, but not on the mainland or on the closest larger island. Their distribution and abundance can be explained by their optimal specialisation in highly harsh and unusual environmental conditions. Islet specialists often possess a good ability for dispersal by sea drift over distances of hundreds of

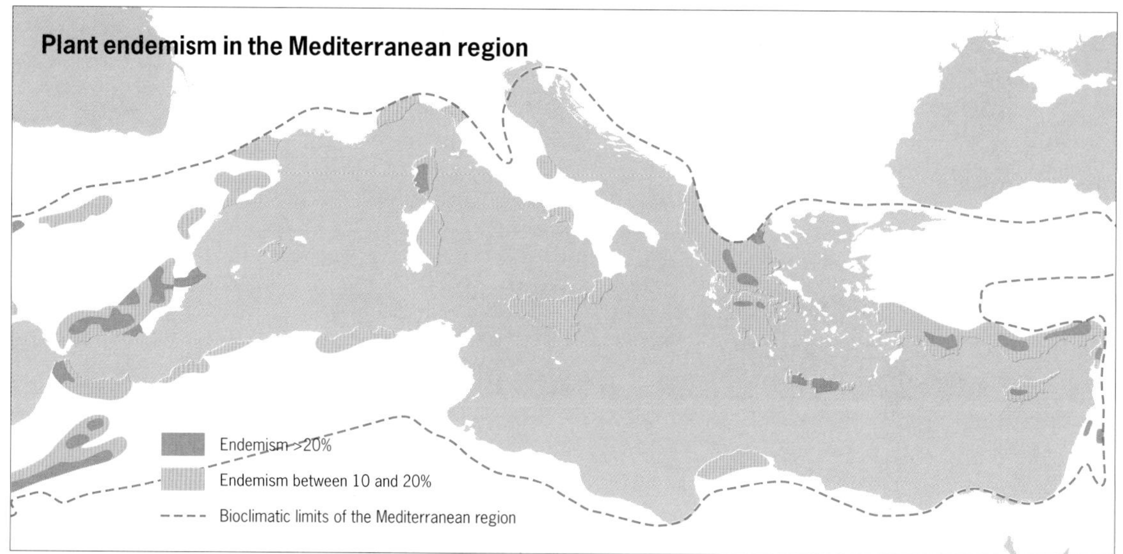
Plant endemism in the Mediterranean region
Endemism >20%
Endemism between 10 and 20%
Bioclimatic limits of the Mediterranean region

kilometres since floating diaspores can stand up to a month in the sea water. Some possess a large peri-Mediterranean distribution (*Allium commutatum, Hymenolobus procumbens, Lavatera arborea*), while others constitute narrow endemics: *Atriplex recurva* and *Silene holzmannii* in the Aegean islands, or *Nananthea perpusilla* in several satellite islets around Corsica and Sardinia. Some remote islands exhibit a pattern of flora similar to those of remote oceanic islands: this is the case for Alborán island (7.1 hectares, 15 metres above sea level) isolated between Spain (85 km) and Morocco (55 km) which includes a very reduced plant richness (20 species) but with the presence of three endemic plants (*Anacyclus alboranensis, Diplotaxis siettiana, Senecio alboranicus*) restricted only to this flat island.

Threats to Mediterranean island plants

As for other Mediterranean areas, the main threats faced by island plants are mostly due to direct and indirect human impacts. These threats are manifold and they can be ranked by decreasing order of importance: urbanisation, tourism and recreation, environmental changes (land-use and global warming), biological invasions, fires, collecting pressures.

From a demographic point of view, two different situations exist. The major islands are usually characterised by an increase of human population, whereas the smaller islands (with the exception of hotspots of tourism such as Capri, Corfu and Djerba) are subject to a clear demographic decline. Since the 1960s, tourism on islands has increased extensively, with a paroxysm on some Balearic islands (Majorca and Ibiza) where a peak was reached in 2000-2001 with 11 million tourists. This huge human pressure induces a strong urban development which is concentrated along the coasts, destroying or threatening several fragile ecosystems such as sand-dunes, wetlands and to a lesser extent coastal rocky habitats. For example, on the Greek island of Skiathos tourism development since the 1970s has produced an 80% reduction of these coastal ecosystems.

Changes in agricultural and livestock farming extending inland have induced a recent collapse of the traditional Mediterranean tryptique of land-use (agriculture, pastoral, forestry) which has moulded insular landscapes during several centuries. Diverse trends in landscape dynamics cause major modifications to the structure and composition of insular ecosystems. Mediterranean islands and islets are also in places seriously threatened by aggressive alien plants, notably along coasts, in lowlands and along rivers. Exotic plant species represent 17% (473 taxa) of Corsican flora, even if only 6% are well established (171 naturalized taxa), 9.2% (184 taxa) of Sardinian flora, and 8.4% (124 taxa) of Balearic Islands flora.

Despite these diverse threats and the fact that a large number of endemic plant species are narrowly distributed in a single island with low populations, only a small number of plants seems to have become extinct in the Mediterranean islands. But each disappearance constitutes an irreparable loss of evolutionary history. Of about forty Mediterranean plants presumed extinct, ten species are strict insular endemics. Two of these species are only extinct in the wild, *Lysimachia minoricensis* from Minorca and *Diplotaxis siettiana* from the Alborán islet but in this

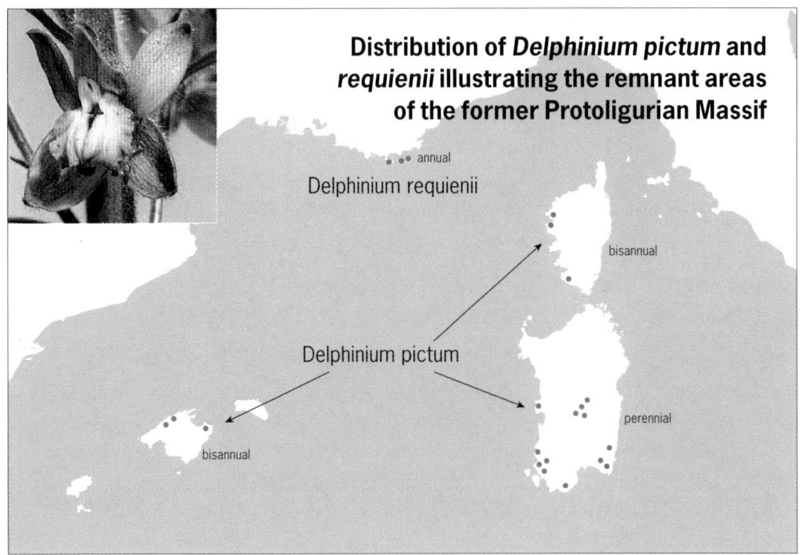
Distribution of Delphinium pictum and requienii illustrating the remnant areas of the former Protoligurian Massif
annual
Delphinium requienii
bisannual
Delphinium pictum
perennial
bisannual

latter case the plant reintroduction was successful. Sicily seems to be the most impacted island with the extinction of four endemics (*Allium permixtum, Anthemis abrotanifolia, Carduus rugulosus, Limonium catanense*) and one from Lampedusa (*Limonium intermedium*). In the eastern Mediterranean, two endemics from Thasos (*Geocaryum bornmuelleri* and *Paronychia bornmuelleri*) are presumed extinct, and one pink (*Dianthus multinervis*) from the remote islet of Jabuka in Croatia. Therefore, the unique flora of Mediterranean islands is on the whole deeply threatened, especially the endemic species which grow in coastal and low altitude habitats. On large islands, the percentage of taxa that are threatened ranges from 2% (Corsica) to 11% (Crete). In Corsica, as much as 90% of local extinct plants (74 taxa) occurred at low altitude, between sea level and 800 m, and they were mainly located in arable fields, wetlands, coastal areas and rocky grasslands.

Owing to their uniqueness and fragility, Mediterranean islands, even the smallest ones, urgently need some integrated and ambitious conservation planning for the long-term preservation of this outstanding biotic heritage.

Professor Frédéric Médail is Professor of plant ecology at University Paul Cezanne, Aix-Marseille and has written (with P.Quezel) *Ecologie et Biogeographie des forets du bassin mediterraneen* (Elsevier 2003) and (with B.Fady) *Peut-on preserver la biodiversite?* (Editions Le Pommier 2006).

Further reading

Alomar G, Mus M & Rossello J A. *Flora endemica de les Balears.* Consell Insular de Mallorca, Palma, 1997.
Delanoe O, Montmollin B de & Olivier L. *Conservation of Mediterranean island plants, 1 Strategy for action*, p 106, IUCN, Gland & Cambridge, 1996.
Fielding J & Turland N. *Flowers of Crete*, xix & p 650, Royal Botanic Garden, Kew, 2005.
Gamisans J. *La vegetation de la Corse*, p 408, Edisud, Aix-en-Provence, 1999.
Gamisans J & Marzocchi J-F. *La flore endemique de la Corse*, p 208, Edisud, Aix-en-Provence, 1996.
Jeanmonod D & Gamisans J. *Flora Corsica*, p 921 & cxxxiv, Edisud, Aix-en-Provence, 2007.
Marras N. *Flora Sarda, piante endemiche*, p 143, Zonza Editori, Sestu, 2000.
Meikle R D. *Flora of Cyprus*, The Bentham-Moxon Trust, Royal Botanic Gardens, Kew, 1977-1985.
Montmollin B de & Strahm W (eds). *The Top 50 Mediterranean island plants : wild plants at the brink of extinction, and what is needed to save them*, x & p 110, IUCN/SSC Mediterranean Islands Plant Specialist Group, IUCN, Gland & Cambridge, 2005.
Olivier L & Muracciole M (eds). *Connaissance et conservation de la flore des iles de la Mediterranee*, Ecologia Mediterranea 21, 1995.
Raimondo F, Gianguzzi L & Ilardi V. *Inventaria delle specie « a rischio » nella flora vascolare native della Sicilia*, pp 65-132, Quad. Bot. Ambientale Appl. 3, 1994.
Romo A M. *Flores silvestres de Baleares*, p 412, Editorial Rueda, Alcorcon, 1994.
Tsintides T C. *The endemic plants of Cyprus*, p 123, Bank of Cyprus Group, Cyprus Association of Professional Foresters, Nicosia, 1998.

Indigenous plant richness and endemism, and threatened vascular plants of seven important Mediterranean island groups

islands	areas (km2)	plant species	endemic plant species	endemism level %	endemic genera	extinct and endangered plants
Sicily	25 708	2793	321	11	Petagnaea	87
Sardinia	24 090	2295	254	11	Castroviejoa Morisia Nananthea Soleirolia	63
Cyprus	9 250	1620	170	10		51
Corsica	8 748	2325	316	11	Castroviejoa Morisia Nananthea Naufraga? Soleirolia	47
Crete	8 729	1735	209	12	Horstrissea Petromarula	193
Balearic islands	4987	1729	173	10	(only on Menorca, Mallorca, Cabrera) Femeniasia Naufraga Soleirolia	69
Malta	316	700	16	2	Cremnophyton Palaeocyanus	16

Our editorial team's *Gerard Gorman* introduces some of the more interesting wildlife species to be encountered in the Mediterranean islands

Dolphins and tortoises, geckos and cicadas

A varied and fascinating blend of wildlife, including mammals, amphibians, reptiles, birds and insects, inhabits the islands of the Mediterranean Sea. Many species found on mainland Europe also occur on these islands but, living as they have in splendid isolation, some animals have evolved into distinct island races, whilst others have gone a step further and become endemic (unique to a particularly area) species found nowhere else on the planet.

Reptiles

Reptiles are not only abundant on most Mediterranean islands, but they are usually easy to observe: well worth remembering when holidaying with the children or, for that matter, a serious herpetologist.

The Mediterranean chameleon *Chamaeleo chamaeleon* is a popular and often photogenic reptile found on Malta, Sicily, Crete and some Aegean islands. Starred agama *Laudakia stellio* can be seen on islands in the Aegean and, like the chameleon, it is able to change colour. Geckos are endearing little lizards, often seen on, and even inside, buildings where they prey on insects attracted to lights. Moorish gecko *Tarentola mauritanica* and Turkish gecko *Hemidactylus turcicus* are widespread, Kotschy's gecko *Cyrtopodion kotschyi* is found in the very east and European leaf-toed gecko *Euleptes europaea*, the smallest of the three at about 8 cm, is restricted to Corsica, Sardinia and some smaller Tyrrhenian islands. Several islands are home to lizards that do not occur anywhere else. The Balearics host two: Lilford's wall lizard *Podarcis lilfordi* on islets off Majorca and Minorca and Ibiza wall lizard *Podarcis pityusensis* on Ibiza, Formentera and adjacent islets.

Not to be outdone, Corsica and Sardinia host Bedriaga's rock lizard *Lacerta bedriagae* and Tyrrhenian rock lizard *Podarcis tiliguerta*. Sicilian wall lizard *Podarcis wagleriana* lives on the Egadi Islands and, as its name suggests, Sicily. Aeolian wall lizard *Podarcis raffonei* has an even more restricted range, being confined to the Aeolian islands off the north-east of Sicily, while the Maltese wall lizard *Podarcis filfolensis* is found on Malta, Gozo, Linosa, Lampione and islets nearby. The strikingly marked Milos wall lizard *Podarcis milensis* scurries around small islands in the Cyclades and Skyros wall lizard *Podarcis gaigeae* is on Skyros, Piperi and other islands in the Aegean. Pygmy algyroides *Algyroides fitzingeri* is restricted to Corsica and Sardinia and to see Columbretes wall lizard *Podarcis atrata* one has no choice but to visit these islands off the east coast of Spain, as it occurs nowhere else in the world.

The Gyaros whip snake *Coluber gyarosensis* is endemic to that Aegean island and Malta is probably the only place in Europe with Algerian whip snake *Coluber algirus*. The boldly marked leopard snake *Elaphe situla* is arguably the most attractive snake in the region and can be seen on Sicily, Malta and throughout the Adriatic and Aegean. Four viper species occur, though they are absent from most of the larger islands such as Sardinia, Corsica, Malta and Crete. All are venomous and should never be harassed or handled. The stern looking nose-horned viper *Vipera ammodytes* lives in the Adriatic and Aegean, asp viper *Vipera aspis* (of Cleopatra fame) on Sicily and smaller islands off Italy, Ottoman viper *Vipera xanthina* in the eastern Aegean and Milos viper *Vipera schweizeri* in the Cyclades.

Tortoises are more approachable. Three species occur with Hermann's tortoise *Testudo hermanni* being the most widespread, trundling around most of the larger islands. Spur-thighed *Testudo graeca* and marginated tortoises *Testudo marginata* are only likely to be encountered in the Aegean, though they have been introduced elsewhere. Being essentially aquatic, European pond terrapin *Emys orbicularis* is only found on islands that have freshwater wetlands where they can be spotted basking on logs and rocks during the day. The closely related Balkan terrapin *Mauremys rivulata* is mainly confined to the Aegean. Sadly, sea turtles have disappeared from much of the

Facing page:
Hoopoe (Upupa epops)

Left to right:
Mediterranean horseshoe bat (Rhinolophus euryale), Cicada (cicadetta argentata) and the Short-toed eagle (Circaetus gallicus)

(PHOTO: S.C. BISSEROT/NATURE PHOTOGRAPHERS)

Mediterranean. The species most likely to be encountered is loggerhead turtle *Caretta caretta* an impressive creature that can reach over a metre in length. Females come ashore to lay eggs on Sicily, the Isole Pelagie, north-west Crete and some smaller Greek islands. Green turtle is even bigger, sometimes 1.5 metres long, but much rarer, today breeding only on Cyprus and some Aegean islands.

Amphibians

Amphibians have permeable skins and thus cannot live in salt water nor in very arid places, hence there is a paucity of these sensitive creatures on Mediterranean islands. Yet, where they do occur, they are invariably unique. For example, Corsican fire salamander *Salamandra corsica,* Corsican brook newt *Euproctus montanus* and Corsican painted frog *Discoglossus montalentii* are found on Corsica and nowhere else. Not to be outdone, Sardinia has Sardinian brook newt *Euproctus platycephalus* and four species of endemic cave salamander: Gene's, Scented, Supramontane and Monte Albo, all troglodyte *Speleomantes* species. Further east, Luschan's salamander *Mertensiella luschani* is easy to identify as it is the only tailed amphibian in the south-east Aegean. Tyrrhenian tree frog *Hyla sarda* and Tyrrhenian painted frog *Discoglossus sardus* are almost entirely restricted to Corsica, Sardinia and a few islands off the Tuscan coast, while Majorcan midwife toad *Alytes muletensis* lives in uplands in north-west Majorca. Further east,Karpathos water frog *Rana cerigensis* only hops around this Aegean island and Cretan water frog *Rana cretensis* is confined to Crete.

Birds

Many Mediterranean islands are used as stop-over sites by birds migrating between Europe and Africa. In peak periods in autumn the number of storks, herons, egrets, birds of prey, wildfowl, waders, terns and songbirds, dropping into islands to rest and refuel, runs into the millions. Many others spend their winters on these islands or the surrounding seas. Breeding birds include some of Europe's most colourful: bee-eater *Merops apiaster,* roller *Coracias garrulus,* hoopoe *Upupa epops,* rock thrush *Monticola saxatilis* and golden oriole *Oriolus oriolus* are all fairly widespread. Also brightly coloured, but somewhat larger, are purple gallinule *Porphyrio porphyrio,* which is resident on the Balearics, Sardinia and Sicily, and greater flamingo *Phoenicopterus ruber* which in most years attempts to establish colonies on Sardinia. Some islands are internationally important as nesting havens for seabirds such as Cory's shearwater *Calonectris diomedea,* Balearic shearwater *Puffinus mauretanicus,* Yelkouan shearwater *Puffinus yelkouan* and Audouin's gull *Larus audouinii,* one of the world's most attractive and rarest larids.

Breeding raptors include a few pairs of lammergeier *Gypaetus barbatus* on Corsica and Crete, griffon vulture *Gyps fulvus* on Sardinia, Crete and the Croatian island of Cres, and the huge black vulture *Aegypius monachus* on Majorca. The graceful Eleonora's falcon *Falco eleonorae* nests on island sea-cliffs throughout the Mediterranean, raising its brood late in the year in order to take advantage of the many songbirds that fly

(PHOTO: PAUL STERRY/NATURE PHOTOGRAPHERS)

(PHOTO: PAUL STERRY/NATURE PHOTOGRAPHERS)

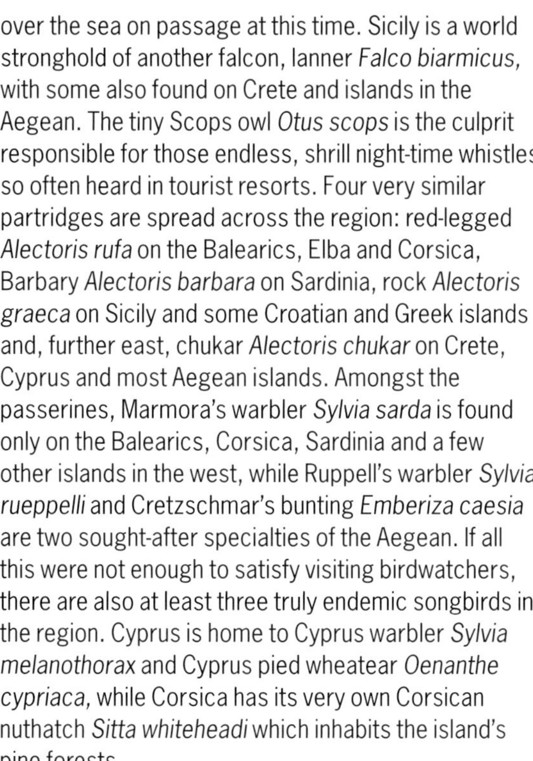

over the sea on passage at this time. Sicily is a world stronghold of another falcon, lanner *Falco biarmicus,* with some also found on Crete and islands in the Aegean. The tiny Scops owl *Otus scops* is the culprit responsible for those endless, shrill night-time whistles so often heard in tourist resorts. Four very similar partridges are spread across the region: red-legged *Alectoris rufa* on the Balearics, Elba and Corsica, Barbary *Alectoris barbara* on Sardinia, rock *Alectoris graeca* on Sicily and some Croatian and Greek islands and, further east, chukar *Alectoris chukar* on Crete, Cyprus and most Aegean islands. Amongst the passerines, Marmora's warbler *Sylvia sarda* is found only on the Balearics, Corsica, Sardinia and a few other islands in the west, while Ruppell's warbler *Sylvia rueppelli* and Cretzschmar's bunting *Emberiza caesia* are two sought-after specialties of the Aegean. If all this were not enough to satisfy visiting birdwatchers, there are also at least three truly endemic songbirds in the region. Cyprus is home to Cyprus warbler *Sylvia melanothorax* and Cyprus pied wheatear *Oenanthe cypriaca,* while Corsica has its very own Corsican nuthatch *Sitta whiteheadi* which inhabits the island's pine forests.

Mammals

Most islands lack large mammals and large predators, such as wolf, have long since vanished. Exceptions are mouflon *Ovis orientalis,* a stocky, wild sheep found in mountain woodlands on Sardinia, Corsica and Cyprus, and Cretan wild goat *Capra aegagrus,* which roams rocky uplands on Crete and some Aegean islands. These two ungulates are not entirely native, having being introduced in Neolithic times. Both males have impressive horns: the mouflon's are curved in a spiral and the wild goat's are long, ridged and pointed.

Bats

The cave systems that riddle many Mediterranean islands are ideal roosting and nursery sites for bats. Over half of all the species found in Europe occur here, including some of the most endangered. Many species, including long-fingered bat *Myotis capaccinii,* Schreiber's Bat *Miniopterus schreibersii* and Savi's pipistrelle *Pipistrellus savii,* are best sought in areas with limestone caves. Being fairly large and with a protruding tail, European free-tailed bat *Tadarida teniotis* is one of the easiest bats to identify when it emerges to hunt flying insects at dusk.

Marine mammals

The Mediterranean monk seal *Monachus monachus* is the only seal species in the Mediterranean. Once widespread, today this endangered mammal probably numbers less than 500 in the wild. Just 20 or so breeding sites are known worldwide, a few tucked away in coves and marine caves on the more remote

(PHOTO: PAUL STERRY/NATURE PHOTOGRAPHERS)

(PHOTO: JAMES SUTHERLAND/NATURE PHOTOGRAPHERS)

Mediterranean islands. Dolphins are most likely to be seen from ferries and boats rather than from land. The common dolphin *Delphinus delphis* is the most widespread cetacean in the region, though it has declined in number. Most are some 2m long, mainly black with pale underparts and yellow flanks. The striped dolphin *Stenella coeruleoalba* and the highly intelligent bottle-nosed dolphin *Tursiops truncatus,* the species that most performs in dolphinariums, are less common. The more bulky Risso's dolphin *Grampus griseus* can grow over 3m in length, lacks a beak and is often marked with weird scratch marks. The harbour porpoise *Phocoena phocoena* is more nondescript, being mostly plain grey and with a small triangular dorsal fin and short flippers - true dolphins have sharp, curved dorsal fins and long flippers. Up to 10 species of whale are, from time to time, sighted in the western Mediterranean. Though nowhere common, and never easy to see, Cuvier's beaked whale *Ziphius cavirostris* and killer whale *Orcinus orca* do rove over the whole Mediterranean.

Invertebrates

In summer the islands of the Mediterranean positively buzz with the sound of insects. In particular, it is impossible to miss the high pitched buzzing calls of cicadas, though they can be frustratingly difficult to see, usually going silent as one gets close. There are innumerable moths, dragonflies, grasshoppers, crickets, flies, bees, wasps, bugs and beetles, as well as many other non-insect invertebrates such as scorpions, spiders and snails. Together, invertebrates (animals without backbones) comprise the overwhelming majority of all animal species on the islands. The sun douses the region for most of the year and this results in a rich and colourful range of day-flying butterflies. Many spectacular species occur, such as the swallowtails and two-tailed pasha *Charaxes jasius*, but it is the localised island species that attract most visiting lepidopterists. These include Corsican swallowtail *Papilio hospiton,* Corsican dappled white *Euchloe insularis,* Corsican Fritillary *Argynnis elisa,* Corsican grayling *Hipparchia neomiris* and Corsican heath *Coenonympha corinna*, which occur solely on Corsica and Sardinia. The tiny Sardinian blue *Pseudophilotes barbagiae* and Sardinian meadow brown *Maniola nurag* have even more precise ranges, being endemic to Sardinia, whilst Cretan grayling *Hipparchia cretica* and Cretan small heath *Coenonympha thyrsis* are only found on Crete. From spring through summer, islands with freshwater wetlands are home to a superb variety of dragonflies. Larger islands can host over 30 species and, amongst the hawkers, club-tails, emeralds, chasers, skimmers, darters, demoiselles and damselflies, are some that are found nowhere else. Island bluetail *Ischnura genei* is a Tyrrhenian endemic

(PHOTO: GRAEME CRESSWELL/NATURE PHOTOGRAPHERS)

common on Corsica, Sardinia, Sicily and adjacent islands. Crete has two endemics, Cretan bluet *Coenagrion intermedium* and the rare Cretan spectre *Boyeria cretensis*. Volcanic wetlands on Pantelleria host the only oasis bluetails *Ischnura fountaineae* in all Europe. Other, easy to see, insects include Egyptian grasshopper *Anacridium aegyptium,* the females of which can measure 7cm long, and slant-headed grasshopper *Acrida ungarica* which can reach 7.5 cm and resembles a stick insect. At up to 8 cm in length the praying mantis *Mantis religiosa* is a formidable predator of grassy places on most islands. When disturbed mantises splay their limbs, spread their wings, gape their jaws, and if provoked will bite and pinch threatening fingers. Scorpions, like spiders, are arachnids and thus have eight legs. Several islands, including the Balearics, Montecristo and Cyprus, have endemic species. Most are dark in colour though some, such as the yellow scorpion *Mesobuthus gibbosus,* are often rather translucent. Scorpions are mainly nocturnal, hiding during the day under stones and in crevices in rocks, walls, ruins and inhabited buildings. Though seldom deadly, a sting from that famous scorpion tail can be extremely painful, and thus these largely placid creatures should never be knowingly disturbed.

Above, left to right: Scops owl (Otus scops), Loggerhead turtle (Caretta caretta) and Short-beaked common dolphin (delphinus delphis)

Professor Jacques Blondel and *Dr Marc Cheylan* look at the evolution of endemic wildlife species in the islands

Lost species and animal survivors

Biologists have always been fascinated by the biology of island life, particularly in relation to factors determining species diversity, adaptive radiation and evolutionary changes. The Mediterranean possesses one of the largest archipelagos in the world and the total coastal length of Mediterranean islands is over 20000 km. Each island, especially the larger ones, shows a unique array of bioclimatic and biological features, mostly because the larger islands have been entirely disconnected from any continent since at least the Messinian crisis, some 5 million years ago, when the Mediterranean Sea almost completely dried out. This means that plant and animal species had to colonise islands from nearby mainland areas. Several islands are ancient submarine volcanoes and Mt. Troödos in Cyprus emerged as an oceanic island at the end of the Cretaceous period, 60 million years ago.

The extant biodiversity

A classic feature of islands is that, compared with mainland areas of similar size, they are heavily impoverished but species impoverishment is compensated by high levels of endemism. Almost every island in the Mediterranean has its own set of native plant and animal species. Indeed, local differentiation giving rise to endemic species and subspecies was especially likely in the Mediterranean Basin because of the exceedingly complex history of this region which is divided into thousands of biological isolates - islands, peninsulas and mountain ranges. Endemism levels in the Mediterranean by far exceed those that can be found in any other part of Europe.

Levels of endemism are high in most groups of animals. In some isolated mountain ranges and larger islands, endemic species of insects may account for 15-20% of the insect fauna, a figure which may rise to 90% in some caves. Amphibians include twelve endemic species in the Mediterranean archipelago, equivalent to 41% endemism (see the table on page 45). Examples of highly endemic amphibian species in the western Mediterranean islands are two species of salamanders (*Euproctus montanus* in Corsica and *E. platycephalus* in Sardinia). These are very particular archaic species which, unlike closely related newts, do not have lungs. In the Balearic Islands (Mallorca), the recently discovered toad *Alytes muletensis* is the last survivor of an endemic fauna which has been enriched by several species of reptiles and three species of amphibians, all introduced by man.

In reptiles the average endemism rate is 10% (see the table on page 45). Some lineages are Mediterranean-specific, for example, the genus *Archeolacerta* in Corsica and Sardinia and the genus *Euleptes* (ex *Phyllodactylus*) on several Tyrrhenian islands.

There are few endemic species of birds in Mediterranean islands because they are too close to the mainland for differentiation having a chance to occur. There are two species in Cyprus: the Cyprus wheatear (*Oenanthe cypriaca*) and the Cyprus warbler (*Sylvia melanothorax*); and one in Corsica, the Corsican nuthatch (*Sitta whiteheadi*). Another warbler, the Marmora's warbler (*Sylvia sarda*) occurs in several islands in the western part of the Mediterranean basin. However, at the subspecific level, morphological changes on islands led taxonomists to recognise many subspecies. For instance, on Corsica more than half the species of birds are recognised as subspecies.

Historical determinants of biodiversity

Climatic events of the Quaternary period, with the alternation of glacial and interglacial episodes are crucial for understanding when and how species and ecosystems established in Mediterranean islands. All the larger islands have been colonised by humans and deeply transformed for millennia. Recent evidence from archaeological sites in Cyprus shows that human colonisation of that island began very soon after the end of the last glacial episode and Cyprus, Malta, and Crete in particular were home to some of the most brilliant civilisations in the Ancient World.

Facing page: Praying mantis (Mantis religiosa)

Left to right:
Mouflon (Ovis musimon),
Bee-eater (Merops apiaster)
and Agama (Agama stellio)

(PHOTO: JAN-GERD TENBERGE)

Patterns of distribution of animals have been deeply disturbed by introductions and extinctions of endemic species caused by humans since the beginning of the Holocene, some 10,000 years ago. During the Quaternary period, most of the larger Mediterranean islands were populated with odd assemblages of animals including tortoises, giant rodents, flightless owls, dwarf deer, hippos and elephants. Many of these endemic animals evolved striking adaptations such as gigantism or dwarfism. For example, no less than twelve species of dwarf descendants of the ancestor elephant *Palaeoloxodon antiquus* inhabited Mediterranean islands during the Upper Pleistocene. These species varied greatly in size and are an interesting example of evolutionary convergence, because the different species evolved independently from the ancestor mainland species. Even the small island of Tilos in the Aegean Sea had its own species of dwarf elephant. The smallest species *Palaeoloxodon falconeri*, less than one metre high, from Sicily possibly gave rise to the myth of the cyclops Polyphemus in the Odyssey, because the large frontal hollow between the nostrils looks like an enormous single eye.

In Mediterranean islands, after the mass extinction of this archaic endemic mammal fauna that started in the late Pleistocene, only a few endemic mammal species were left. They include three species of shrews, one in Sicily, *Crocidura sicula*, one in Crete, *Crocidura zimmermanni*, and we presume one in Cyprus, *Crocidura cypria*, as well as some endemic rodents such as *Mus cypriacus* in Cyprus, recently discovered by François Bonhomme. These small mammals presumably differentiated recently and have been discovered through genetic studies. In any case these are not "old endemics" like most reptiles and amphibians.

Life on islands

When some individuals of a species succeed in immigrating and then colonising an island, they are confronted with new sets of environmental factors. Moreover its genetic background is different from that of the mother mainland population because of a bottleneck effect that reduces genetic diversity. These new ecological and genetic conditions result in new selection pressures that inevitably lead the founding population to diverge from its mainland mother population. However, evolution and genetic differentiation of endemic forms is only one aspect of the story of island life. Several ecological and evolutionary processes occur as a result of isolation. The most obvious character of island communities is that they are impoverished in comparison with communities occupying areas of similar size on the nearby mainland. For example, 108 species of birds regularly breed on Corsica, an island of 8680 km^2, as compared with 170 to 173 species found breeding in three areas of similar size in continental France. Moreover, the smaller the island, the lower the number of species. As a general rule, rates of species impoverishment are a function of dispersal abilities of organisms. Compared with species richness on the mainland, impoverishment in Corsica is 38% in birds which are good dispersers but rises to up to 43% in reptiles and 68% in non-flying mammals. Similarly, in

(PHOTO: KAREN NICHOLS)

butterflies, most of the variation in species richness on Mediterranean islands can be explained by differences in the islands' surface area. For example there are only 24 species of butterflies in Formentera, one of the smaller islands, but as many as 89 species in Sicily, the largest of all Mediterranean islands.

Species impoverishment on islands results in a cascade of changes in ecological and evolutionary processes at the levels of communities, species and populations, which may be briefly summarised in four points. i) There is selection among candidates for island colonisation. In birds the most successful colonists are species that are small, widespread and flexible in habitat selection and foraging habits; in plants small generalist dioecious flowers are favoured. ii) Population sizes of the species that occur on islands are often much larger than those of their mainland counterparts. iii) Many species on islands often occupy more habitats and forage over a larger spectrum of microhabitats than on mainland areas. This process of 'niche enlargement' has been observed in many species of both animals and plants. iv) The social behaviour of many territorial animals, e.g. reptiles, mammals, and birds, reveals remarkable shifts such as reduced territory size, increased territory overlap, acceptance of subordinates, reduced situation-specific aggressiveness and abandonment of territorial defence, as compared with mainland populations. Many lizard species on small islands are darker than their mainland counterparts or closely related species and have shorter legs and tail, which contributes to making them less dispersive. Insular forms of the lizard *Podarcis lilfordi* of the Balearic Islands are completely black although they live on a white limestone substrate ! Another adaptation is a trend towards herbivory in many insular species.

Threats to biodiversity

The biodiversity of Mediterranean islands was under threat as soon as humans started to colonise them, as is sadly illustrated by the extermination of all the large "mega-nano-mammals" of Mediterranean islands, for example the dwarf hippos and elephants of Cyprus, Malta, Sicily and other islands, following their colonisation by humans at the beginning of the Holocene. All these islands are still threatened by many factors including human pressure, over-harvesting and poaching, habitat degradation and invasive species. This makes the unique flora of Mediterranean islands locally threatened, especially the endemic species which grow on coastal and low altitude habitats. On large islands, the percentage of species that are threatened on a global scale ranges from 2% (Corsica) to 11% (Crete). In contrast with what happened to mammals, amphibians and reptiles did not suffer from

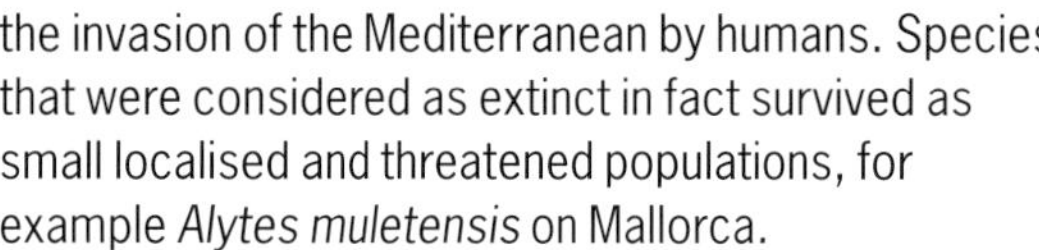

the invasion of the Mediterranean by humans. Species that were considered as extinct in fact survived as small localised and threatened populations, for example *Alytes muletensis* on Mallorca.

The Mediterranean is the leading tourist destination in the world and well over 8800 km of Mediterranean seacoasts (19%) are now occupied by tourist installations, concrete structures and diverse roadways. On the island of Mallorca, for example, 48% of the coastline has been irreversibly 'artificialised', threatening many coastal habitats of great interest.

Another serious threat is hunting and poaching. Direct persecution results in the death of millions of birds annually and particularly sad examples are the large-scale destructions of migrant birds that take place in Malta, Cyprus and other islands. In these islands migrating birds, including the smallest birds such as warblers and kinglets, provide twice a year a providential amount of food for local people. It is estimated that up to 1000 million birds are illegally killed annually in the basin when they stop over during migration. Recent studies based on the analysis of recoveries of ringed birds strongly suggest that a decline in survival rates of many migratory birds throughout Europe may be directly related to excessive hunting and trapping pressures which occur in many Mediterranean islands.

It would be beyond the scope of this chapter to discuss the pros and cons of human action in Mediterranean islands, which is a difficult and controversial issue. During their long-lasting common history with humans, landscapes have been designed and re-designed for almost 10,000 years in the eastern part of the basin and 8000 years in its western part. Landscape changes have not necessarily resulted in degradation and many studies show that humans have often contributed to preserving Mediterranean landscapes as they progressively established since the last glacial episode. Sometimes human impact has resulted in an increase in biodiversity through the shaping of a large variety of cultural landscapes.

Professor Jacques Blondel and **Dr Marc Cheylan** are both members of Centre d'Ecologie Fonctionelle et Evolutive, CNRS, Montpellier and Professor Blondel is the author (with J.Aronson) of *Biology and Wildlife of the Mediterrranean Region* (O U P 1999) and of *Man as Designer of Mediterranean Landscapes* (2006).

Further reading

Blondel J & Aronson J. *Biology and wildlife of the Mediterranean Region*, Oxford University Press, 1999.

Delaguerre M & Cheylan M. *Atlas de repartition des Batraciens et Reptiles de Corse*, Parc Naturel Regional de la Corse, Ajaccio, 1992.

Lister A M. *Dwarfing in island elephants and deer: processes in relation to time and isolation*, pp 277-292, Symp. Zool. Soc. Lond. 69, 1996.

Shay C T, Shay J M & Zwiazek J. *Paleobotanical investigations at Kommos, Crete. Plant Animal Interactions in Mediterranean-type ecosystems*, Maleme, Crete, University of Athens, 1991.

Simmons A H. *Extinct pygmy hippopotamus and early man in Cyprus*, pp 554-7, Nature 333, 1988.

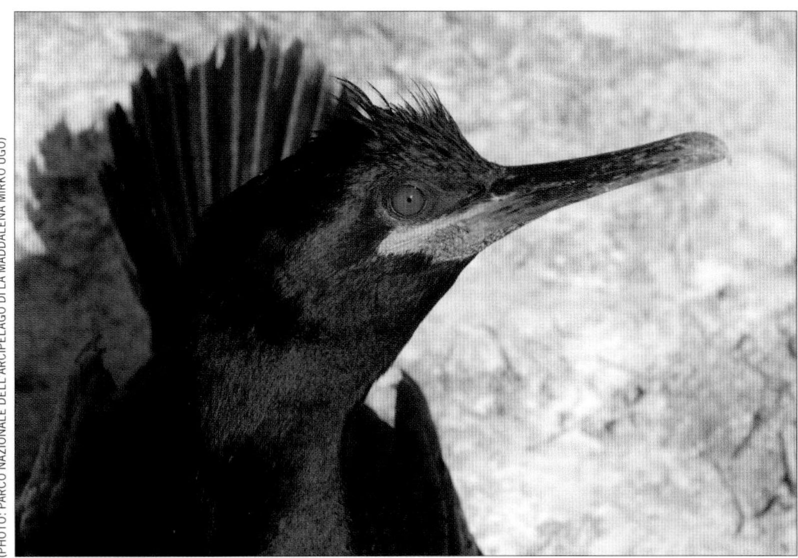

(PHOTO: PARCO NAZIONALE DELL'ARCIPELAGO DI LA MADDALENA MIRKO UGO)

Left to right:
Turkish gecko (Hemidactylus turcicus), Griffon vulture (Gyps fulvus) and Shag (Phalacrocorax aristotelis)

Endemic species of reptiles and amphibians in the larger Mediterranean Islands (various sources)

species	family	distribution
Amphibia (Urodela)		
Salamandra corsica	Salamandridae	Corsica
Euproctus montanus	Salamandridae	Corsica
Euproctus platycephalus	Salamandridae	Sardinia
Speleomantes genei	Plethodontidae	Sardinia
Speleomantes flavus	Plethodontidae	Sardinia
Speleomantes supramontis	Plethodontidae	Sardinia
Speleomantes imperialis	Plethodontidae	Sardinia
Amphibia (Anura)		
Discoglossus sardus	Discoglossidae	Tyrrhenian islands
Discoglossus montalentii	Discoglossidae	Corsica
Alytes muletensis	Discoglossidae	Mallorca
Rana cerigensis	Ranidae	Aegean islands (Karpathos)
Rana cretensis	Ranidae	Crete
Sauria		
Anatololacerta troodica ?	Lacertidae	Cyprus
Archaeolacerta bedriagae	Lacertidae	Corsica and Sardinia
Podarcis wagleriana	Lacertidae	Sicily
Podarcis raffonei	Lacertidae	Eolie Islands
Podarcis filfolensis	Lacertidae	Malta archipelago and Pelagian archipelago (Linosa & Lampione)
Podarcis gaigeae	Lacertidae	Skyros archipelago (Sporades)
Podarcis milensis	Lacertidae	Milos archipelago
Podarcis tiliguerta	Lacertidae	Corsica and Sardinia
Podarcis pityusensis	Lacertidae	Ibiza and Formentera
Podarcis lilfordi	Lacertidae	Minorca and Mallorca
Algyroides fitzingeri	Lacertidae	Corsica and Sardinia
Ophidia		
Hierophis cypriensis	Colubridae	Cyprus
Macrovipera schweizeri	Viperidae	Cyclades islands

Some common fish of the Mediterranean

Dr Rio Sammut illustrates a wide range of common species shown with their names in all the languages

Barbouni and John Dory, vongole and langoustines

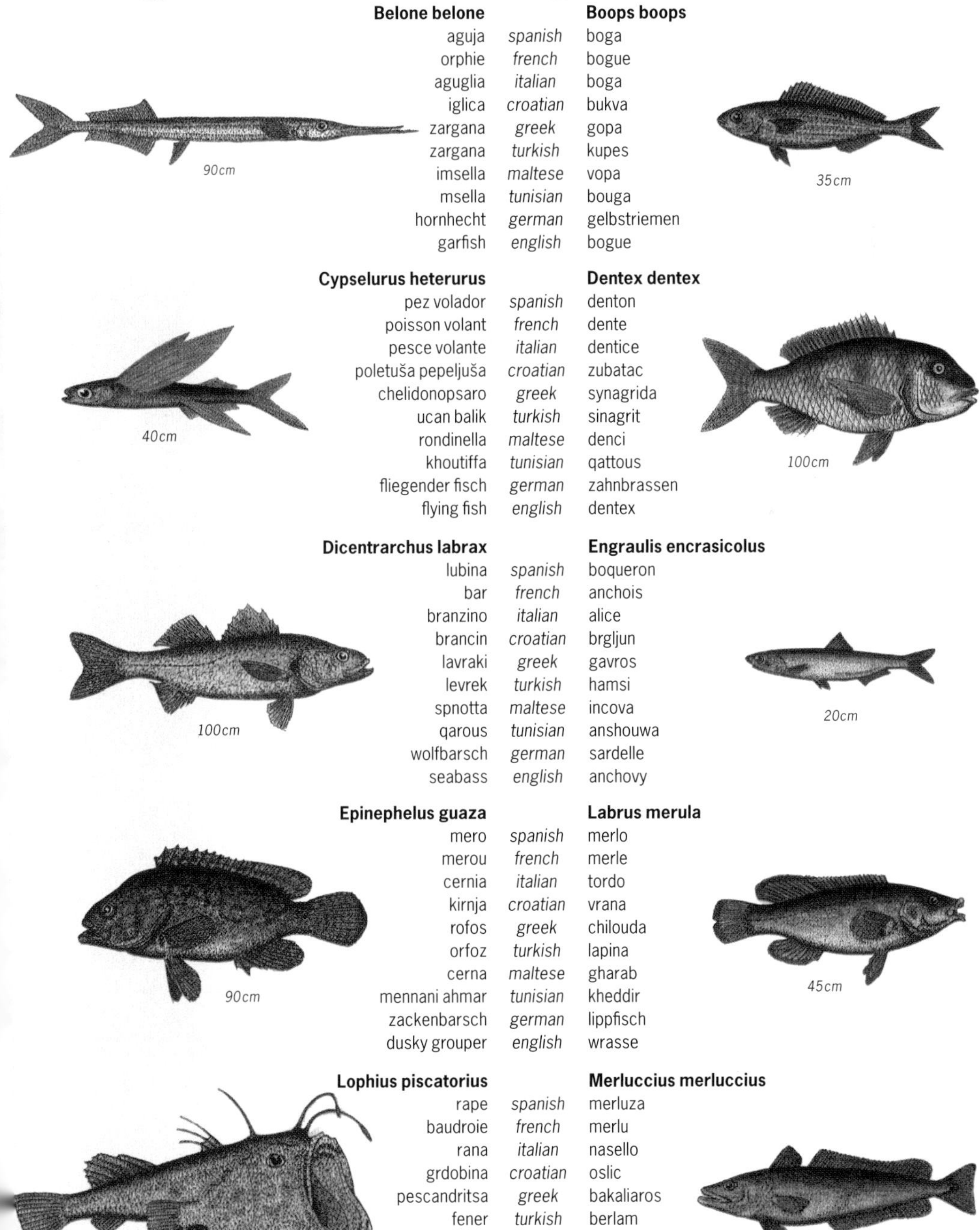

90cm
35cm
40cm
100cm
100cm
20cm
90cm
45cm
200cm
80cm

Belone belone		**Boops boops**
aguja	*spanish*	boga
orphie	*french*	bogue
aguglia	*italian*	boga
iglica	*croatian*	bukva
zargana	*greek*	gopa
zargana	*turkish*	kupes
imsella	*maltese*	vopa
msella	*tunisian*	bouga
hornhecht	*german*	gelbstriemen
garfish	*english*	bogue

Cypselurus heterurus		**Dentex dentex**
pez volador	*spanish*	denton
poisson volant	*french*	dente
pesce volante	*italian*	dentice
poletuša pepeljuša	*croatian*	zubatac
chelidonopsaro	*greek*	synagrida
ucan balik	*turkish*	sinagrit
rondinella	*maltese*	denci
khoutiffa	*tunisian*	qattous
fliegender fisch	*german*	zahnbrassen
flying fish	*english*	dentex

Dicentrarchus labrax		**Engraulis encrasicolus**
lubina	*spanish*	boqueron
bar	*french*	anchois
branzino	*italian*	alice
brancin	*croatian*	brgljun
lavraki	*greek*	gavros
levrek	*turkish*	hamsi
spnotta	*maltese*	incova
qarous	*tunisian*	anshouwa
wolfbarsch	*german*	sardelle
seabass	*english*	anchovy

Epinephelus guaza		**Labrus merula**
mero	*spanish*	merlo
merou	*french*	merle
cernia	*italian*	tordo
kirnja	*croatian*	vrana
rofos	*greek*	chilouda
orfoz	*turkish*	lapina
cerna	*maltese*	gharab
mennani ahmar	*tunisian*	kheddir
zackenbarsch	*german*	lippfisch
dusky grouper	*english*	wrasse

Lophius piscatorius		**Merluccius merluccius**
rape	*spanish*	merluza
baudroie	*french*	merlu
rana	*italian*	nasello
grdobina	*croatian*	oslic
pescandritsa	*greek*	bakaliaros
fener	*turkish*	berlam
petrica	*maltese*	marlozz
raasha	*tunisian*	nazalli
seeteufel	*german*	seehecht
anglerfish	*english*	hake

All lengths are average

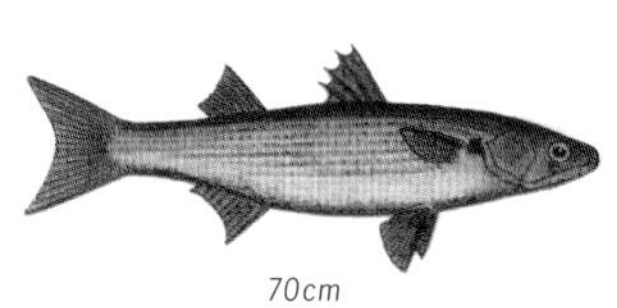

70cm

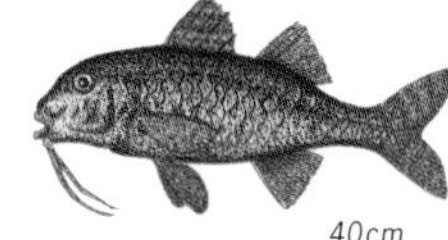

40cm

Mugil cephalus		Mullus barbatus
pardete	*spanish*	salmonete
mulet	*french*	rouget
cefalo	*italian*	triglia
cipal	*croatian*	trlja
kefalos	*greek*	barbouni
has kefal	*turkish*	tekir
mulett	*maltese*	trilja
bouri	*tunisian*	mellou
meeraesche	*german*	meerbarbe
grey mullet	*english*	red mullet

150cm

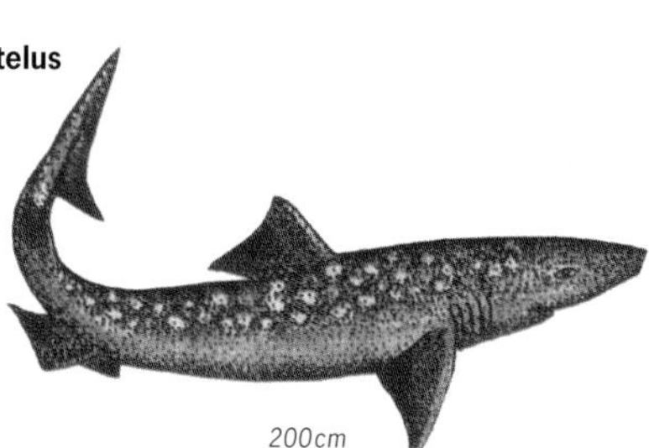

200cm

Muraena helena		Mustelus mustelus
morena	*spanish*	musola
murene	*french*	emissole
murena	*italian*	palombo
murina	*croatian*	pas glusac
smerna	*greek*	galeos
merina	*turkish*	kopek baligi
morina	*maltese*	mazzola
mrina	*tunisian*	ktat
murane	*german*	glatthai
moray eel	*english*	smoothhound

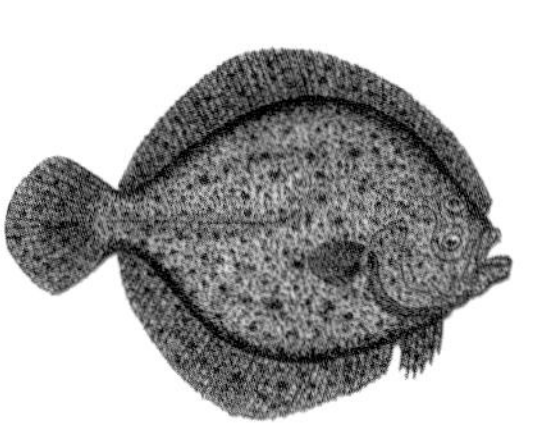

80cm

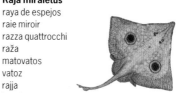

50cm

Psetta maxima		Raja miraletus
rodaballo	*spanish*	raya de espejos
turbot	*french*	raie miroir
rombo chiodato	*italian*	razza quattrocchi
iverak	*croatian*	raža
kalkani	*greek*	matovatos
kalkan	*turkish*	vatoz
barbun imperjali	*maltese*	rajja
mdess moussa	*tunisian*	hassira
steinbutt	*german*	roche
turbot	*english*	brown ray

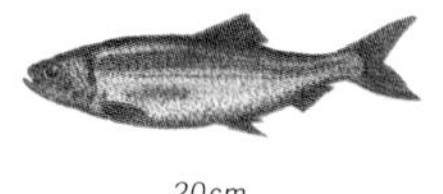

20cm

50cm

Sardina pilchardus		Scomber scombrus
sardina	*spanish*	caballa
sardine	*french*	maquereau
sardina	*italian*	sgombro
srdela	*croatian*	skuša
sardella	*greek*	skoumbri
sardalya	*turkish*	uskumru
sardina	*maltese*	pizzintun
sardina	*tunisian*	sqoumri
sardine	*german*	makrele
sardine	*english*	mackerel

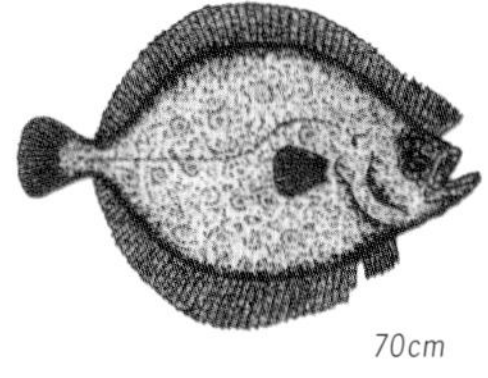

70cm

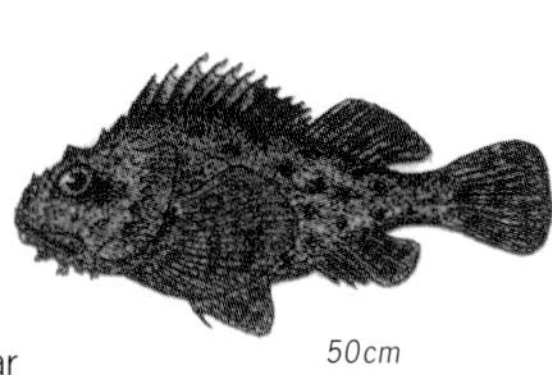

50cm

Scophthalmus rhombus		Scorpaena scrofa
remol	*spanish*	cabracho
barbue	*french*	rascasse
rombo liscio	*italian*	scorfano
oblić	*croatian*	škrpina
romvos	*greek*	skorpios
civisiz kalkan	*turkish*	lipsoz
barbun lixx	*maltese*	cippullazza
mdess moussa	*tunisian*	bou keshesh ahmar
glattbutt	*german*	drachenkoepfe
brill	*english*	scorpionfish

45cm

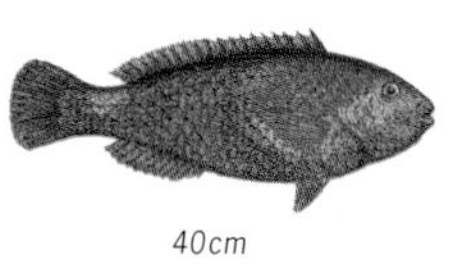

40cm

Solea solea		Sparisoma cretense
lenguado	*spanish*	viela
sole	*french*	poisson perroquet
sogliola	*italian*	scaro
list	*croatian*	papigica
glossa	*greek*	skaros
dil	*turkish*	iskaroz baligi
lingwata	*maltese*	marzpan
mdass	*tunisian*	
seezunge	*german*	seepapagei
sole	*english*	parrotfish

All lengths are average

60cm

100cm

Sparus aurata		**Sphyraena sphyraena**
dorada	*spanish*	espeton
dorade	*french*	brochet
orata	*italian*	luccio
orada	*croatian*	barakuda
tsipoura	*greek*	loutsos
cipura	*turkish*	iskarmoz
awrata	*maltese*	lizz
ourata	*tunisian*	moghzel
goldbrasse	*german*	pfeilhecht
gilthead sea bream	*english*	barracuda

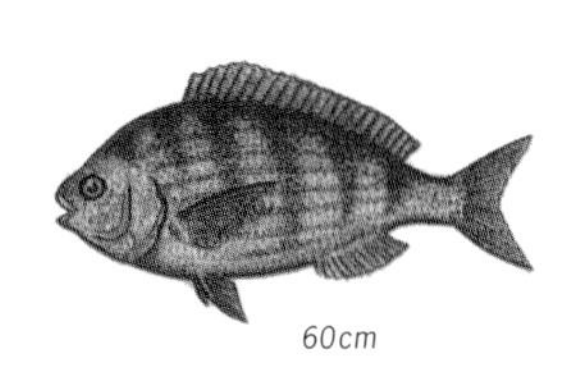

60cm

15cm

Spondyliosoma cantharus		**Sprattus sprattus**
chopa	*spanish*	espadin
griset	*french*	sprat
tanuta	*italian*	papalina
kantar	*croatian*	papalina
skathari	*greek*	papalina
saragoz	*turkish*	caca
tannuta	*maltese*	lacca kahla
kannouta	*tunisian*	
streifenbrassen	*german*	sprotte
black sea bream	*english*	sprat

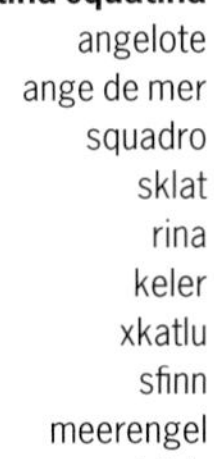

200cm

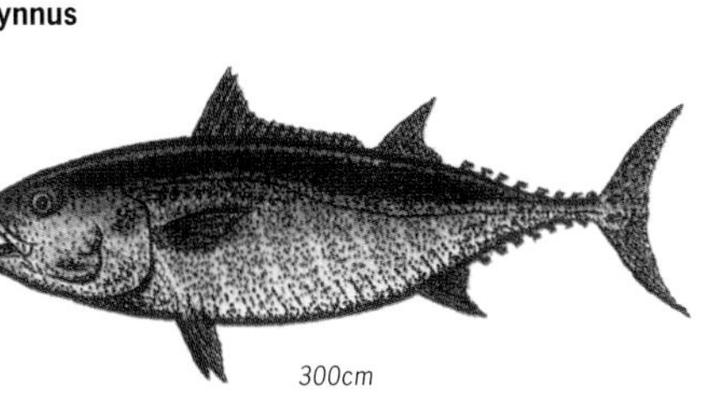

300cm

Squatina squatina		**Thunnus thynnus**
angelote	*spanish*	atun
ange de mer	*french*	thon
squadro	*italian*	tonno
sklat	*croatian*	tunj
rina	*greek*	tonos
keler	*turkish*	orkinos
xkatlu	*maltese*	tonna
sfinn	*tunisian*	toun ahmar
meerengel	*german*	roter thun
monkfish	*english*	tunny

40cm

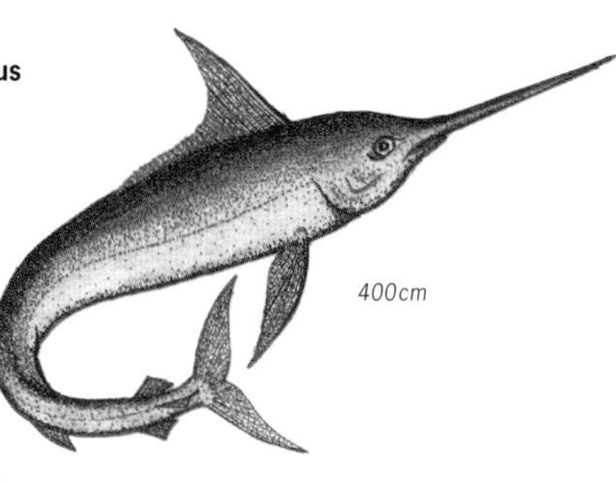

400cm

Trachinus draco		**Xiphias gladius**
escorpion	*spanish*	pez espada
grande vive	*french*	espadon
dragone	*italian*	pesce spada
pauk bijeli	*croatian*	sabljarka
drakena	*greek*	xifias
trakonya	*turkish*	kilic baligi
sawt	*maltese*	pixxispad
billem kbir	*tunisian*	bou sif
petermannchen	*german*	schwertfisch
weever	*english*	swordfish

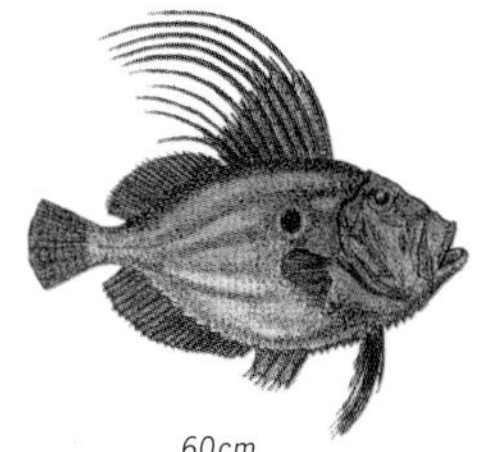

60cm

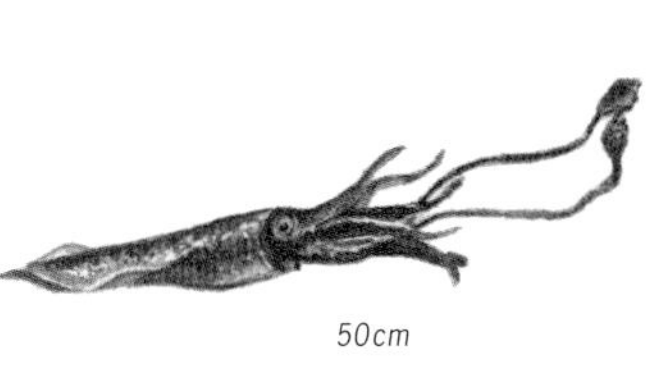

50cm

Zeus faber		**Loligo vulgaris**
san pedro	*spanish*	calamar
saint-pierre	*french*	encornet
san pietro	*italian*	calamaro
kovač	*croatian*	lignja
christopsaro	*greek*	kalamari
dulger	*turkish*	kalamar
huta san pietru	*maltese*	klamar
hout sidi sliman	*tunisian*	mettig
petersfisch	*german*	kalmar
john dory	*english*	squid

300cm

40cm

Octopus vulgaris		**Sepia officinalis**
pulpo	*spanish*	jibia
poulpe	*french*	seiche
polpo	*italian*	seppia
hobotnica	*croatian*	sipa
chtapodi	*greek*	soupia
ahtapot	*turkish*	supya
qarnita	*maltese*	sicca
qarnit kbir	*tunisian*	shoubia
tintenfisch	*german*	sepia
octopus	*english*	cuttlefish

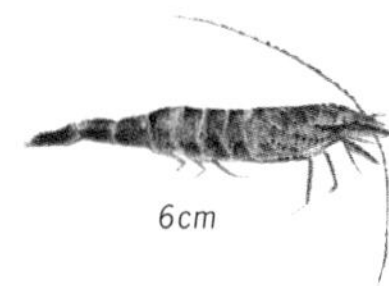

6cm

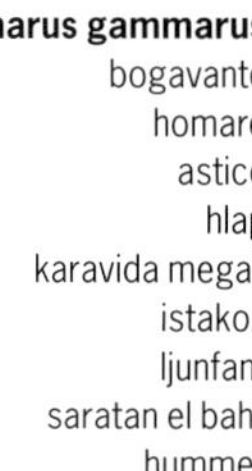

6cm

Carcinus mediterraneus		**Crangon crangon**
cangrejo	*spanish*	quisquilla
crabe vert	*french*	crevette
granchio	*italian*	gamberetto
grancigula	*croatian*	kozica
kavouras	*greek*	garida
cingene	*turkish*	tekke
granc tal-marsa	*maltese*	gamblu
aghreb bahr	*tunisian*	brgouth bahr
taschenkrebs	*german*	garnele
shore crab	*english*	shrimp

15cm

50cm

Homarus gammarus		**Maja squinado**
bogavante	*spanish*	centolla
homard	*french*	araignee de mer
astice	*italian*	grancevola
hlap	*croatian*	rakovica
karavida megali	*greek*	kavouromana
istakoz	*turkish*	ayna
ljunfant	*maltese*	ghaguza
saratan el bahr	*tunisian*	rtila bahr
hummer	*german*	seespinne
lobster	*english*	spider crab

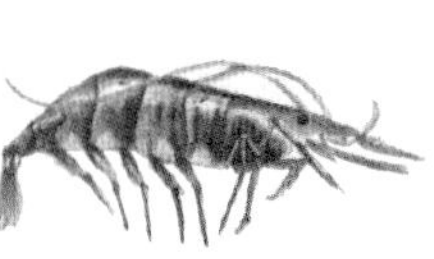

7cm

20cm

Nephrops norvegicus		**Palaemon serratus**
cigala	*spanish*	camaron
langoustine	*french*	bouquet
scampo	*italian*	gamberello
škamp	*croatian*	kozica
karavida	*greek*	garida
deniz kereviti	*turkish*	teke karidesi
ragustelli	*maltese*	gamblu tax-xatt
jarradh el bahr	*tunisian*	gembri
kaisergranat	*german*	saegegarnele
langoustine	*english*	prawn

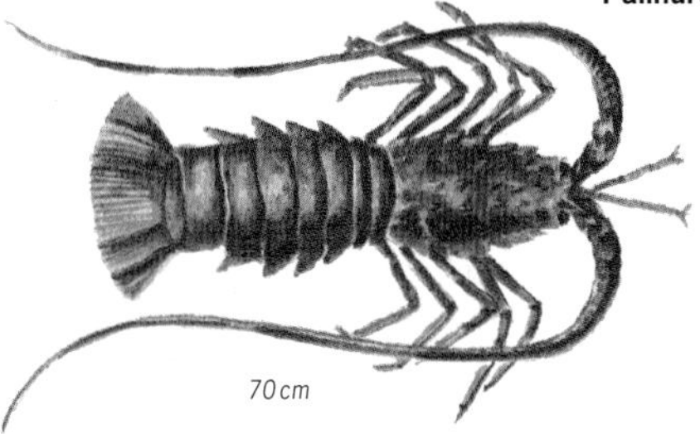

70cm

5cm

Palinurus elephas		**Cerastoderma edule**
langosta	*spanish*	berberecho
langouste	*french*	coque
aragosta	*italian*	cuore
jastog	*croatian*	čančica
astakos	*greek*	kydoni
bocek	*turkish*	acivades
awwista	*maltese*	arzella tal-marsa
langouste	*tunisian*	babouche
languste	*german*	herzmuschel
crayfish	*english*	cockle

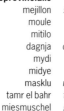

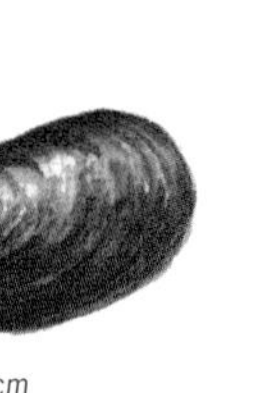

8cm

10cm

Mytilus galloprovincialis		**Ostrea edulis**
mejillon	*spanish*	ostra
moule	*french*	huitre
mitilo	*italian*	ostrica
dagnja	*croatian*	kamenica
mydi	*greek*	stridi
midye	*turkish*	istiridye
masklu	*maltese*	koccla
tamr el bahr	*tunisian*	istridia
miesmuschel	*german*	auster
mussel	*english*	oyster

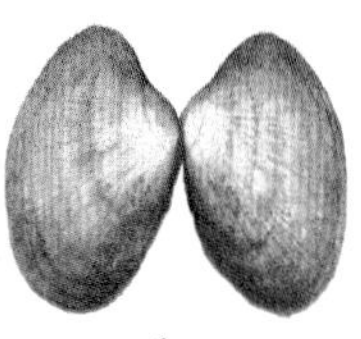

6cm

Ruditapes decussatus	
almeja	*spanish*
palourde	*french*
vongola	*italian*
vongola	*croatian*
chavaro	*greek*
kum midyesi	*turkish*
arzella	*maltese*
clovisse	*tunisian*
teppichmuschel	*german*
carpetshell	*english*

All lengths are average

Dr Rio Sammut is Commissioner for Kummissjoni Ambjent, Malta and has published *Mediterranean Sea Fishes* (2001). His illustrations of fishes from this book appear on these pages. Drawings of the other marine creatures have been made by **Lucy Wilson** and some of her illustrations are used here with the kind permission of Imray Laurie Norie & Wilson, publishers of the *Mediterranean Cruising Handbook* by Rod Heikell, author of our feature on sailing in the Mediterranean.

How the Mediterranean was defined by its islands
Charles Freeman summarises the key events that have shaped the history of the Mediterranean over the millennia

Many layers of history upon every island

In one of the great epic journeys of history, Homer's Odyssey, the hero Odysseus makes his way across the Mediterranean towards his island home on Ithaca where his wife Penelope awaits patiently in the hope he has survived. The journey takes ten years and is a marvellous account of the hazards and opportunities of travel in 'the Great Sea'. For seven years the nymph Calypso holds Odysseus as a captive lover on her legendary island Ogygie. Freed, he washes up on another island, Scheria, the home of the ordered and civilized Phaeacians who are skilled at seafaring and who help him further on his way. In contrast there are the unruly Cyclops, one of whom, Polyphemus, eats men raw. Later legend placed their caves in Sicily. So even in the 8th century BC the islands of the Mediterranean have become inseparable from its history.

The Setting

The Mediterranean is not tidal but there are local currents and variable prevailing winds. From early times there have been favoured routes which have exploited both of these, sometimes using a current to counteract a contrary wind. Some islands such as Ibiza benefited from being on routes from both east and west, others from the resources they have to offer in fertile land or minerals. Obsidian was being taken from Melos to the Greek mainland as early as 10,000 BC while Sicily, Corsica, Sardinia and the Balearic Islands were colonised by 9000 BC. By 6000 a community in Sicily was involved in intensive fish farming and the Temple Period in Malta (3600-2500 BC) saw the earliest free-standing buildings known.

This is a testament not only to the benign nature of the Mediterranean (at least from March to October), but to the skills of her early seafarers. One of the most fascinating aspects of Mediterranean history is the adaptation of shipping, through hull, oar or sail, to exploit its particular characteristics.

Facing page:
The Knights Hospitaller have left an unforgettable imprint on two Mediterranean islands: they held Rhodes for 213 years before moving to Malta, where they spent a further 267 years

The First Civilizations

It was Crete which established the first sustained island civilization, at the beginning of the second millennium BC. The legendary Cretan king Minos was reputed to rule over the southern Aegean and his trading network extended from the still more ancient civilization of Egypt, across the islands of the Aegean and as far west as Lipari and Sicily. The Minoan frescos show the vitality and sophistication of their way of life although it was to end in the fifteenth century when a mammoth volcanic explosion on Santorini disrupted the entire region. The beneficiaries were an aggressive chieftain culture from mainland Greece, the Mycenaeans. They took over the devastated sites of Crete and expanded their own tentacles of trade from Sardinia, Ischia and Sicily in the west to the eastern coastlines of the Aegean. Legends of the siege of Troy, which guarded the routes to the Black Sea, are rooted in Mycenaean civilization.

The Mycenaeans collapsed about 1200 BC, probably as a result of the fragmentation of their over-extended trade routes. The sources tell of refugee groups, including the shadowy 'sea peoples', rampaging across the sea. There are only a few sites, such as Lefkandi in Euboea, where a trading settlement survived. In Lefkandi's case, the burial of a chieftain with his horses suggests the 'heroic' culture of the Mycenaeans persisted.

The revival of the Mediterranean economy begins in the ninth to eighth centuries BC and the pioneers were the Phoenicians from the Levant. They probed westwards to find metals in Spain and its adjacent islands. Phoenician settlements were to be found in Malta, Sicily, Sardinia and the Balearic islands. Their enterprise encouraged the Greeks to revive their own seafaring and by the end of the eighth century the fertile coastline of Sicily was dotted with Greek colonies. Pithecoussai, an important Greek-Phoenician trading post on Ischia, acted as an entrepot for trade with the Etruscans on the Italian mainland. Corinth was another major trading state: her colonies included Corcyra in Corfu and Syracuse in Sicily. For the next five hundred years Carthaginians (the descendants of those Phoenicians who had settled in the west), Greeks and Etruscans battled with each other over influence in the western Mediterranean.

In the east the Greek city states extended their culture over the entire Aegean and along the coastline of modern Turkey. Two invasions by the Persians, in 490 and 480 BC, were fought off. This was the age of the trireme, a fighting machine manned by hundreds of oarsmen and devastating in battle. The Athenians used their well trained fleet to see off the Persian invading fleet at Salamis in 480. By 440 the Aegean and its islands had become part of an Athenian empire although this fragmented when Athens was defeated by the Spartans at the end of the century. A dramatic moment came when the Macedonian Alexander the Great led his army into Asia Minor to defeat the Persians and establish a Greek cultural hegemony which extended throughout the eastern Mediterranean and beyond into Egypt and central Asia. After his death in 323 BC, his successors fought over the spoils.

There was a famous siege of Rhodes by Demetrius Poliorcetes (the Besieger) in 305, whose failure the Rhodians celebrated by building the Colossus of Rhodes by their harbour entrance. For a hundred years Rhodes flourished as one of the most important trading posts of the Mediterranean.

The complex history of these centuries can be seen in the changing fortunes of Cyprus, an important source of copper and a stepping stone for travellers heading west from Syria and the Levant. Independent in the seventh century, it then became part of the Persian empire in the sixth. It rebelled against the Persians in 499 with Athenian support but the Persians restored control until Alexander the Great renewed its independence. After his death it eventually became part of the Ptolemaic kingdom of Egypt. The Romans took it in 58 BC but it was then offered back to Cleopatra by her lover Mark Antony before being brought back under Roman rule on their defeat by Octavian, later the emperor Augustus, in 31 BC.

The Pax Romana

The fragmentation of the Mediterranean in both east and west was brought to an end by the rise of Rome. First came the Roman absorption of the Etruscans, then the conquest of Sicily and a confrontation with the Carthaginians which nearly brought Rome to her knees but whose success left Rome with a navy and control of the western Mediterranean. The subjection of Greece followed in the second century BC and then in the first Syria, Palestine, Cyprus and finally Egypt when Cleopatra was defeated. Up to this time the Mediterranean had been seen as a series of local seas but now it was *mare nostrum*, 'our sea'. (The name Mediterranean, 'the inland sea' is only recorded for the first time in the sixth century AD.) The Romans had to clean up piracy but once they had trade could flourish. Large galleys (examples as large as 300 to 400 tons have been found in wrecks) brought grain, wine and oil from north Africa to Rome, the hub of the empire. The islands of Malta, Sicily, Rhodes and Cyprus were all vital stopping points while Delos, in the central Aegean, became a slave market with 12,000 transactions a day. With trade came the circulation of peoples and cults. Christianity would never have been able to spread without this secure network of routes.

When the Roman empire collapsed in the fifth century AD, trade in the western Mediterranean slumped and shipping was not to reach similar levels until the sixteenth century. The Byzantine empire survived in the east as the successor of the Romans and attempted in the sixth century to regain the west. Many islands including Corsica, Sardinia, the Balearics and Sicily came, somewhat bizarrely perhaps, under Greek-speaking rulers but it was the expansion of the Arabs which was to prove lasting. They swept across north Africa in the eighth century and by the ninth had occupied Malta and Sicily as well as the Balearics. The Normans were to displace them in Sicily and Malta in the twelfth century adding another level of complexity to Mediterranean history.

Venice and the rebirth of Mediterranean trade

A new phase began with the slow rise of the Italian city states from the tenth century. The Venetians, who were technically subordinate members of the Byzantine empire, ruthlessly exploited the enormous potential of the emerging Arab economies, even though they had to fight off competition from rival cities, notably Pisa and Genoa, to do so. The Adriatic became a Venetian lake, its islands jealously guarded from Italian rivals. Luxury goods and spices from the east were traded for metals, wood and slaves. These enterprises went hand in hand with the Crusades, a desperate attempt to regain the Holy Land from Muslim domination. The Fourth Crusade of 1204, a shameful enterprise when the Venetians led a Crusade which was destined for the Holy Land to sack the city of Constantinople, saw the seizure from the Byzantines of a string of trading posts, including Corfu and the Ionian Islands, Crete and later Cyprus.

The major Venetian routes were now secure. For those heading east there were three. One went around the Peloponnese stopping at Negroponte (the island of Euboea) and then northwards across the Aegean to Constantinople and the Black Sea. The other two headed first southwards to Crete where the routes would diverge to Alexandria or eastwards via Rhodes and Cyprus to Beirut. The western routes would converge on Sicily which would be the staging post for the north African coast, Palma (on Majorca) or western Italy and the French coast.

A wide range of ships evolved in these centuries. The galley with its mixture of sails for the open sea and oarsmen for manoeuvring into harbour took a smaller cargo but it was ideal for precious goods which needed fast transport and it could be diverted to duty as a warship. The larger, rounded *nefs* were the slower workhorse cargo ships, with ten times as much capacity as the galley, but much more cost effective. The mass of Mediterranean trade always remained in staple goods, grain, oil, textiles or timber. All depended on frequent halts, so a network of ports was scattered along the coastlines of the Mediterranean.

The Ottoman Challenge

A fresh turning point came with the capture of Constantinople by the Ottoman Turks in 1453. The Italians were now on the defensive in the east as the Ottomans expanded right along the coast of north Africa as well as through the Balkans and Greece. One casualty was Rhodes. Held by the Knights Hospitaller, an order which protected Christian pilgrims to the Holy Land, after they had been expelled from Jerusalem and then Acre in 1291, it had been transformed by the Knights into a military stronghold whose fortifications still survive intact today. It finally fell in 1522 and the Knights moved westwards to Malta.

By now Italy itself was consumed by internal struggles and its trade began to suffer. Spain emerged as the new western power as, in the joint reign of Ferdinand and Isabella, the Moorish kingdom of Grenada was crushed (1492) and the Jews expelled to make a resolutely Catholic state. It was a Spanish led fleet which held off the Ottomans at the battle of Lepanto in 1571. The Knights, now based on Malta under Spanish protection, also defended its vital position in the central Mediterranean, fortifying its harbour Valletta with an impressive array of walls which remain largely intact. There was thus a stalemate between Ottoman east and Spanish west although the loss of Cyprus by Venice in 1571 was a further symbol of her own decline as the great trading power of the east. Crete, another acquisition from the Fourth Crusade, was to be lost to the Ottomans in 1669.

The Mediterranean and the European Powers 1600 -1900

By the sixteenth century Mediterranean trade was beginning to falter as that of the Atlantic flourished and routes were opened by the Portuguese and Dutch to the Far East. In the next century the Ottoman empire and Spain both began a slow decline. In the ensuing vacuum, the Mediterranean became the playground of pirates and corsairs, both Christian and Muslim. It was France who was to become the new dominant power in the eighteenth century and she was prepared to work with the Ottomans as she feared that their weakness would lead to the expansion of France's main rivals, the Austrians and Russians.

However, with the vitality lost from Mediterranean trade, the main islands became bargaining chips in the wars between the European powers. Gibraltar went to Britain in 1704, Sardinia became part of the Kingdom of Piedmont in 1718. Corsica was purchased by France from Genoa in 1768 just in time for the son of a minor aristocratic family,the Bonapartes, to be born French the following year.

Napoleon was to throw Europe including the Mediterranean into turmoil, extinguishing the Venetian Republic in 1797 and seizing Malta from the Knights. He launched an invasion of Egypt but it was his defeat there by Nelson in the Battle of the Nile (1798) which inaugurated a new era. After the final collapse of his empire in 1815, the British were left as the dominant naval power in the Mediterranean. The Ionian islands, which had remained Venetian, ended up as a British protectorate (1815-64), which is why cricket is still played there. Malta was also ceded to Britain.

In an age of romantic fervour for the lost civilization of Greece, the British backed Greek independence and it was a British fleet, with Russian and French support, which won the last battle between sailing ships in the Mediterranean, against the Turks at the Bay of Navarino in 1827. Greece emerged free, but it was a slow process to regain the islands around her.

Later, pragmatism took over and the British turned to backing the Ottomans out of fear of Russian expansion into the eastern Mediterranean from the Black Sea. They even fought the Russians on their behalf in the inconclusive Crimean War (1854-6). The British determination to maintain their influence in the Mediterranean intensified with the opening of the Suez Canal in 1869. Britain leased Cyprus from the Ottomans (1878) and established a protectorate over Egypt so that through Gibraltar, Malta and Cyprus she had strategic command over the sea.

Into the 20th century

No single power was able to sustain the Ottoman Empire. Its grip on the peoples of North Africa was lost and the European colonisers moved in with France taking Algeria (1831) and Tunisia (1882) and the Italians (now a single state incorporating Sardinia and Sicily) Libya and the islands of the Dodecanese in 1912. The First World War saw the final collapse of the Ottoman empire although there remained a tragic and disorderly disentangling of Greek and Turk, with Greek communities expelled from Turkey and Muslims from Crete. The Turkish invasion of Cyprus in 1974 showed how the fallout of Ottoman rule still lingers.

The Second World War saw the Mediterranean as a major theatre of war as both Germany and Italy attempted to dominate the sea. German occupation of Greece and her islands was especially harsh. Malta held out heroically against intense German bombardment while Sicily was to provide a staging post for theAllied invasion of Italy.

The post-war Mediterranean festered with the political tensions of the Cold War, civil war in Greece, the dictatorship of Tito in Yugoslavia and the subsequent breakdown of order on his death.

Yet the underlying strengths of the region have reasserted themselves. Mass tourism has its hedonistic side but there is a growing awareness of just how rich the ancient cultures of the Mediterranean have been. Layer upon layer of history remains on every island, whether it is traces of Arabic cooking or Greek temples in Sicily, memories of Italian occupation in the Dodecanese, Minoan palaces in mainland Crete, Venetian castles in the Aegean or a wealth of different civilizations in Cyprus, Malta or the Balearics. It is impossible to do justice to the interplay of so many different sophisticated and complex civilizations over so many millennia but it is hoped that this introduction has provided an incentive to explore further.

Charles Freeman sits on the Blue Guides Editorial Board as Historical Consultant and among the books that he has published are *Egypt Greece and Rome* (second edition Oxford University Press 2004), *The closing of the Western Mind: The Rise of Faith and the Fall of Reason* (Klopf 2005), *The Greek Achievement: The Foundation of the Western World* (Penguin Press 1999) and *The horses of St Marks* (Little Brown 2004).

Further reading

Abulafia, David (ed). *The Mediterranean in History*, London, 2003. Essays covering the entire history of the Mediterranean. Well illustrated.
Braudel, Fernand. *The Mediterranean and the Mediteranean World at the time of Philip II*, London, 1972. Famous meditation on the ebb and flow of Mediterranean life which finally comes to roost in the events of the sixteenth century.
Braudel, Fernand. *The Mediterranean in Ancient History*, London, 2002. Sweeping and perceptive appraisal of the ancient Mediterranean.
Casson, Lionel. *Ships and Seafaring in Ancient Times*, Austin,Texas, 1994. Excellent introduction to the shipping of the ancient Mediterranean.
Freeman, Charles. *Egypt, Greece and Rome, Civilizations of the Ancient Mediterranean*, second edition, Oxford, 2004. Comprehensive survey of Mediterranean history up to 600 AD.
Norwich, John Julius. *The Middle Sea: A History of the Mediterranean*, London, 2006. Rollicking account of Mediterranean history concentrating more on personalities and events than the underlying economic and social issues.

Venetian names for selected islands

Croatia

Bisevo	Busi
Brac	Labrasa
Ciovo	Bua
Cres	Cherso
Dugi Otok	Lunga
Hvar	Lesina
Korcula	Curzola
Kornat	Corona
Krk	Veglia
Lastovo	Lagosta
Lokrum	Lacroma
Lopud	Mezzo
Losinj	Lussino
Mljet	Meleda
Murter	Morter
Olib	Ulbo
Pag	Pago
Rab	Arbe
Silba	Selve
Ugljan	Ugliano
Vir	Puntadura
Vis	Lissa

Greece

Aigina	Engia
Alonnisos	Dromo
Amorgos	Amurgo
Anafi	Namphio
Andros	Andro
Astypalaia	Stampalia
Chalki	Carchi
Chios	Scio
Evvoia	Negroponte
Folegandros	Policandro
Ikaria	Nicaria
Ios	Nio
Kalymnos	Colmine
Karpathos	Scarpanto
Kasos	Caso
Kea	Zia
Kefalonia	Cefalonia
Kerkyra	Corfu
Kimolos	Argenteria
Kythira	Cerigo
Kos	Stancio
Kriti	Candia
Kythnos	Termia
Lefkada	Santa Maura
Leros	Leria
Lesvos	Metellino
Limnos	Stalimene
Megisti	Castelrosso
Milos	Millo
Mykonos	Micoli
Naxos	Nicsia
Nisyros	Nissaro
Oinousses	Spalmatori
Paros	Pario
Patmos	Palmosa
Paxoi	Paxo
Poros	Sanari
Rodos	Rodi
Salamina	Culuri
Samos	Sciamo
Samothraki	Samandrachi
Serifos	Serphino
Sifnos	Siphano
Sikinos	Sicandro
Skiathos	Sciati
Skopelos	Scopulo
Skyros	Sciro
Spetses	Spezzia
Symi	Simie
Syros	Sira
Thasos	Tasso
Thira	Sant'Erini
Tilos	Piscopia
Tinos	Tine
Ydra	Idria
Zakynthos	Zante

Turkey

Bozcaada	Tenedo
Gokceada	Lembro

Facing page: The gateway to a Venetian manor house on the island of Paxoi

FREE

Mediterranean islands at the start of the 21st century

Professor Emile Kolodny describes the forces that have shaped today's varied island populations

Where many different cultures meet

The islands of the Mediterranean consist of a multitude of minor islands, and a few ones of medium size on a European scale. Around two hundred permanently populated islands covering a total of 103,100 square kilometres together have 10,900,000 inhabitants, equivalent to the population of Greece in 2001. In the western Mediterranean, in Sicily, Sardinia, Corsica and the Balearics there is a common Latin heritage and Catholic faith. In the eastern there is more diversity: Greek language and Orthodoxy from Corfu to Cyprus are accompanied by Catholic Slavs in the Dalmatian islands (Croatia); Turks in the islands of Marmara and the Dardanelles and in Kos, Rhodes and Cyprus and Berbers and Arabs (in Djerba, Kerkennah, and Arwad in Syria) are all Muslims; while the Maltese combine a semitic language with a fervent Catholicism.

Within this exceptional framework of a sea between mountains, this *succession de plaines liquides* (Braudel) there are many *pays de montagnes dans la mer* (Ratzel about Corsica). Etna reaches a height of 3323 metres, the Lefka Ori in Crete rise to 2453 metres less than eight km from the shore. Steep gradients are frequent in the Aegean: Samothrace (178 sq km) has a highest point of 1600 metres.

On these islands the climate matches the terrain. They dictate an agriculture founded on cultivation of olives, vines, almonds, chestnuts, the lentisk of Chios, citrus. These islands, where rock limits pasture of goats and sheep, maintain until recently traditional societies of herdsmen and peasants. There are many *landsmen* islands, which have long turned their back on the sea: Corsica, Sardinia, Crete, Cyprus, Rhodes, Lesbos. These contrast with the islands of seamen and merchants, which are numerous in Greece - Chios, Cephalonia, Ithaca, Andros, Hydra, Syros, Kalymnos - but rare in the western Mediterranean : Carloforte on San Pietro, Malta, the Cap Corse and Venice are among the few examples.

The *seamen's islands* contrast with those where the agricultural economy goes hand in hand with a long ignorance of city life: Corsica before the Genoese occupation, Samos under the Ottomans. Today almost all the islands have a share in the tourism business.

Facing page:
Malta was not occupied by the Turks, but has had a taste of many other cultures

A history of dominating powers

In this inland sea, where the proximity of the mainland leads to the intervention of coastal powers, island towns bear the imprint of their colonisers. These are the port cities founded or reshaped by the merchant republics of Pisa (Bonifacio), Genoa (Corsica, Sardinia, Chios, Lesbos, Cyprus) and Venice. Genoa secured her Gulf with a line of towns grafted on to the Corsican coast; Venice established from Dalmatia to Cyprus a string of fortified ports. They constituted *la flotte immobile de Venise* (Braudel). They fell, with the exception of the Adriatic and Heptanese, into the hands of the Ottomans, giving these Italian-made towns an Islamic stamp. We should mark the imprint of the Knights Hospitaller of the Order of St John on Rhodes (1308-1522) and then on Malta. We owe to them the foundation of Valletta (1566) and the fortification of the Grand Harbour.

We should note also the lasting intervention of a power from outside the Mediterranean. The English were present in Minorca in the 18th century; they disputed with France first Corsica, ceded by Genoa in 1768, then drove her from Malta in 1800 and from the Ionian islands in1815, and supplanted the authority of the Sultan in Cyprus in 1878.

The only islands which are independent today are the two ancient colonies of the Crown: Cyprus and Malta, held under British rule until the 1960s. Both joined the European Union in 2004.

We should insist on calling the Mediterranean islands *continental*, as opposed to *oceanic* islands which are often mini-states. These islands cannot be studied without reference to the countries that surround them and serve for the most part as political, economic and cultural points of reference. The only exceptions are Malta and Cyprus, for whom the decision-making centre was for a long time in London. Twenty states share the Mediterranean coast, of which ten have practically no islands. The two sovereign states gather

9% of the total island area and 12% of their population. Most of it belongs to nine continental countries, of which six have island populations of over 100,000: Italy, Greece, Spain, France, Croatia and Tunisia. Two countries have an *'island ratio'* of over 10%: Italy and Greece. The shares are unequal, since Italy has double the island area of Greece (50160 against 25150 sq km), with an island population four times bigger (6,576,000 inhabitants or 11.7% of the Italian total).

The importance of the Greek islands is not negligible: with 1,622,000 islanders in 2001, covering 19% of the country's area, Greece is in first place: 14.8% of the total population (24.4% in 1920). The *'island ratio'* is 2.6% in Croatia and only 1.5% in Tunisia. These percentages appear quite small. In Greece the situation was affected up to 1970 by the islands contributing to the growth of Athens. In fact the ratios in Greece and Italy are exceptional for, with the exception of island states, countries combining significant island and mainland areas are rare.

Spain, with the Balearics (2.1% of national population) in the Mediterranean and the Canaries in the Atlantic, has a combined *'island ratio'* of 6.5%. Outside the Mediterranean, Denmark is the best example of a combined island-mainland country, with Copenhagen being on the island of Zealand.

The fact that most islands belong to coastal countries is the consequence of geographic proximity, history and culture. This has preserved, or rather renewed, the Latin and Greek character of the populations, in spite of Islam having invaded most of the islands. The Arab occupation of Sicily and Malta came to an end in 1090-91; the Muslims, having been in a 75% majority in 1240, were driven from Malta five years later. In the Balearics, the *Reconquista* and Catalan colonisations (1229-35) came after five centuries of Saracen presence. The second phase of the reconquest is still with us today.

The wars between Greeks and Turks from 1821 to 1923 emptied the Archipelago of Muslims, of which the remnants were the subject of forced exchange with the Greek refugees of Asia Minor. The Cypriot conflict is linked to the maintenance of the last Turkish bastion in the eastern Mediterranean. The intervention of the Turkish army in 1974 and the proclamation of a *'Turkish Republic of North Cyprus'* in 1983 may be considered as the start of a new phase of reconquest.

Continental dependence is the consequence of processes of appropriation and integration by the coastal states. In Corsica, the decline of Genoa led from 1737 to French interventions. The cession of Sardinia to the Dukes of Savoy in 1718 put an end to four centuries of dominance by Aragon and Spain. In 1847 the Sardinians 'merged' with Piedmont and thenceforth the *Sardinian States* were governed from Turin. Sicily ceased to be an independent state from 1409, undergoing various vicissitudes under the Aragonese, the Bourbons of Naples and the Kingdom of the *Two Sicilies*, before the landing of the *Mille* in 1860 and integration into the Italian state.

The rebirth of Greece was fed by successive island and mainland annexations. Euboea and the Cyclades made up the initial core in 1830 and the Heptanese (Ionian islands) was attached in 1864.With the First Balkan War of 1912 were added the eastern islands of the Aegean and Crete. The annexation put an end to the Principality of Samos and the short-lived *Cretan State* (1898-1912). Finally Greece took over the Dodecanese, which had been a possession of colonial Italy from 1912 to 1944.

In Cyprus, independence in 1960 resulted in a compromise between the two communities, the Greek majority (77%) renouncing *Enosis*, the union with Greece, and the Turks (18%) *Taksim*, partition. This cohabitation was put in question by the events of 1963-64, then irremediably overthrown by the invasion of 1974. This led to a de facto partition, accompanied by a massive exodus, with the *Attila line* dividing in two the island and its capital Nicosia.

Today the authority of the Republic extends only to the Greek sector, while the northern part (36% of the land area) houses a Turkish state recognised only by Ankara. Adding the two 'sovereign bases' of the British army one realises that Cyprus comprises two or rather three mini-states. The reunification of the island, in a confederate form proposed by the UN in 2002, will realistically only come to pass if Turkey joins the EU.

The only island to exercise full authority is Malta, which has been an independent republic since 1964, the last bases having been evacuated in 1979. This miniscule archipelago of 316 sq km has the highest density in Europe: 1240 inhabitants per sq km. Two thirds are concentrated in the area surrounding

Valletta. The special ethno-cultural nature of Malta has been protected from outside interference by the presence of the Knights and more than one and a half centuries of British rule.

The period between the 18th and the beginning of the 20th century saw the incorporation of islands into emerging coastal states and the reinforcement of the British presence in the Mediterranean. The end of the second world war led to the culmination of this process in Greece (Dodecanese).British disengagement in Cyprus thwarted annexation plans of neighbouring powers. The aftermath of war brought in a new phase in the political condition of the principal islands. The inauguration of the Italian republic led to special laws giving a wide autonomy to border regions as well as Sicily and Sardinia (1948). They have an elected council, a *Giunta regionale* and presidency with extensive powers. The Balearics became a *Comunidad Autonoma* in 1983, with a government and parliament within the framework of a Kingdom of Spain divided into 19 entities. In Corsica, a regional *Assemblée de Corse* has been elected since 1982.

If there are still autonomous or separatist impulses present in the western Mediterranean, there is no such feeling in the Greek islands, where the aspiration has always been integration with Greece: one does not find any nostalgia for the *Cretan State*. A country where everything is decided in Athens, Greece has engaged in an administrative decentralisation, manifested by the demarcation of 13 regions. The five *nomes* of the Archipelago, comprising the regions of North and South Aegean are covered by a Ministry of the Aegean. In Crete, the four prefectures answer to a regional governor based in Heraklion. He is not assisted by an elected council.

The islands are reasserting their independence

With Cyprus and Malta having reached independence and the proliferation of laws of autonomy and regionalisation, it is necessary to moderate the view of islands totally subjugated to the mainland. Even when this dependence remains obvious - notably at an economic level - one cannot any more *consider* the islands as simple appendages of the mainland.

They have gained in population stability, increased their revenues by expanding tourism and added - as with Malta and Cyprus - new resources: light industries, civil conversion of the Malta drydocks, creation of free zones, of financial centres for offshore companies and the proliferation of *convenience flag* merchant fleets. We note also the opening of universities in Corte (1981), Corfu, in the Aegean and Crete and in Nicosia (1992). In the Greek islands the faculties are spread: arts subjects are in Mytilene, economics in Chios, mathematics in Samos, the education institute in Rhodes. In Crete the university is shared between Heraklion, Chania and Rethymnon.

One of the phenomena marking the recent evolution of the islands is the recovery of their populations. In spite of lower fertility and a less and less important natural balance, the islands have gained one and a half million inhabitants in 40 years. This is shown by an almost uninterrupted growth (Balearics, Cyprus, Crete, Malta, Sardinia) or by a recovery following a prolonged recession (Corsica, Ionian islands, Cyclades, Dodecanese). The recovery is a consequence of the reversal of migratory flows. The labour pool for the civil service and the army (Corsica and the southern Italian islands), crews for the Greek merchant fleet, builders and workers for the industries of Piedmont, Lombardy, Lorraine and Germany, migrants to western Europe and overseas, has been transformed into an area of inflow. There enters into the process the interruption of outflow overseas, with the crisis of the 1970s accelerating returns.

The development of tourism activities, building and public works, attracts a new kind of labour: *Murcianos* (Andalucians) and Catalans to the Balearics; Maghrebins, principally Moroccans, who are taking the place of Sardinians and *Lucchesi* (Tuscans) in Corsica; workers from the third world and eastern Europe - some illegal - employed in the Italian and Greek islands: Albanians, Bulgarians, Poles, Moroccans and Tunisians, Asians and other Africans.

We should emphasise the transfer of former emigrants, affected by the dissolution of colonial empires: *Pieds Noirs* repatriated from north Africa; Italians from Tunisia, Libya and Egypt; Greeks from Alexandria, the Black Sea and the former Soviet Union. To the category of refugees should be added Greek and Turkish Cypriots driven from one side or other of the *Attila Line*, the Lebanese transferred to Cyprus during the civil war, the Croats and Bosnians quartered or interned in the Dalmatian islands (1992-1995), the Turkish and Kurdish colonists implanted in north Cyprus. Let us add also the permanent transfer of Europeans who have acquired residences in the tourist islands: the Balearics, the Aegean and Crete. In the future, a new wave of migrants may be the desperate *boat people* who, in trying to reach the European countries, run aground at Malta, Lampedusa, Sardinia and Eastern Aegean islands.

Three islands of similar size: Corsica, Crete and Cyprus

The reversal of population flows is illustrated by the revival of Corsica. The island, which had reached its peak around 1881 (273,000), underwent a depopulation until the middle of the twentieth century, the population being estimated at 170,000 in 1955. Emigration to the continent and the colonies, aggravated by the bloodbath of the first world war, accelerated the loss of population. The arrival of repatriates, whether or not of Corsican stock, followed by workers from the North Africa and the reduction of traditional outlets elsewhere, fed the revival: 227,000 inhabitants in 1975, 240,000 in 1982 and 260,000 in 1999. At that date 10% of the population was composed of foreigners (of which 70% were Maghrebins). After *Ile de France,* Corsica has the highest proportion of foreigners in France.

The Corsican experience calls for comparison with Cyprus and Crete, all three islands having been modestly populated at the beginning of the nineteenth century. Around 1820 Corsica and Crete had between 180,000 and 220,000 inhabitants, more than Cyprus.

While Corsica started a slow but regular growth, Crete suffered murderous revolutions. The insurrection of 1821-29 cost the island half its population. Those of 1858, 1866 and 1896 reduced the number of Greek-speaking Muslim Cretans (who had been converted after the taking of Candia in 1669) and drove them to the towns: 27% of the population in 1881 was Muslim and 7% in 1920. In spite of this instability, Crete caught Corsica up again in about 1880. But while Corsica was rocked by massive emigration, the last *Turcocretans* left the island in 1923 and it received 34,000 Greek refugees. These made a decisive contribution to the development of the island. The German occupation and famine did not have a lasting effect on Cretan vitality, nor did the wave of migrations of 1960-70. In 2001 Crete's population was more than double that of Corsica at 601,000 (72 inhabitants per sq km).

Cyprus, the least populated of the three, was to eclipse its rivals. It avoided the carnage of the Cretan uprisings. The British presence protected it from the direct blows of the two world wars. It took no part in the Greek-Turkish exchanges of 1923 and suffered neither occupation nor famine. The result was a continuous growth in population, which tripled between 1881 (186,000) and 1960 (574,000). Cyprus overtook Corsica in 1910, then caught up Crete at the end of the second world war.

The aftermath of independence rocked Cyprus in ways similar to those experienced by Crete in the 19th century, turning 40% of the two communities into refugees, of which a part left the country. The restructuring of the Greek sector, with the rehabilitation of 198,000 refugees mainly in the towns, compensated for the civil and military losses and the doubling of emigration. It was not until the 1980s that a revival was registered, with the return of emigrants and new inflows: workers from the Balkan countries, from the Middle and Far East. In the Turkish sector, the transfer of Anatolians compensated for the departure of many Turkish Cypriots.

This divergence of fortunes needs thinking about. How could Corsica, which is not the worst endowed island in the Mediterranean and which - apart from its great contribution of military casualties in World War I - has not undergone a continued civil war like Crete, have registered such a downturn? It was the result of a steady migratory outflow lasting over a century.

But Corsica did not have an exclusivity on massive emigration: Malta, Sicily, the Dalmatian islands, the Heptanese and the Aegean all have a long tradition in this regard. Some islands have undergone even more spectacular losses: Kythira (280 sq km) has gone from 14,000 inhabitants in 1860 to 8,000 in 1940 and 3354 in 2001. Between 1890 and 1940 this island of poor peasants contributed one fifth of all Greek emigrants to Australia, where it monopolised the oyster and fish market, as well as restaurant business.

The worst losses have affected above all small islands or island groups, whose balance between resources and population is precarious. Kastellorizo (10 sq km) to the east of Rhodes had 10,000 inhabitants at the start of the twentieth century, when it was a sponge fishing and active trading port; it dropped to 2,700 in 1922 and to 430 today.

The vulnerability of small islands does not inhibit growth in the long term. With a population estimated at 20,000 after the Great Siege of 1565, Malta did not take off until the following century (48,000 in 1632). Malta then underwent a plague epidemic, which claimed 12,000 victims in 1675-76, but at the time of the French conquest its population had reached 114,000 in 1798, with a density even then of 361 inhabitants per sq km. Two centuries later the population has tripled, despite a strong flow of emigrants which has been reversed in the last three decades.

Opportunities and challenges in the future

Certainly being an island has not always been a handicap and it is not necessarily the first factor in marginalisation or backwardness. This is true not only for the Balearics, but also for Sardinia and Sicily in comparison with southern Italy, as well as for Crete, which is more prosperous than Epirus or Thrace. It is true for the Greek community in Cyprus, whose per capita GNP is comparable to that of Greece, and this is a country whose territory has been divided, populations displaced and economy profoundly reshaped. The case of the Balearics shows that Mediterranean islands can be leaders of a continental nation.

The examples of Malta and Cyprus confirm the vitality and entrepreneurial capacity of small island states. Though less striking, the revival of population in Corsica is something that deserves consideration. Who would have thought 40 years ago that an island which continued to waste away could recover some stability? It is true that the revival is confined to areas close to the towns, while the mountains continue to empty. Moreover, a growth in population does not in any way mean rectification of economic imbalance. Furthermore, the putting in place of new regional structure has not put an end to demands for autonomy or even independence.

Today almost all the Mediterranean islands make up the southern and eastern sea frontiers of the European Union. The planned adherence of Croatia, and perhaps later Turkey, would complete the process. The islands have acquired, thanks to new activities and in particular tourism, a diversity in their populations and a firm degree of prosperity. Their populations, revived by a now positive migratory balance, show more mobility, helped in part by the development of means of transport. Nevertheless, an unbroken continuity between mainland and island will never be totally assured, even if one can hope that the bridge between Calabria and Sicily will be built in the medium term. At the end of June 2006, all maritime traffic in the Aegean was brought to a standstill for three consecutive days by raging winds and seas.

With tourist and urban development, environmental problems have taken on an increased importance. The 'balearisation' of the coastline by numerous residential and hotel buildings, the degradation of the natural heritage – notably by forest fires such as those in Corsica and Euboea in the summer of 2007 – require new thought about the future of the island sector. The islands of the Mediterranean, changing ever more rapidly, are starting to encounter an overloading of people, permanent or seasonal, which needs to be taken seriously into account.

Professor Emile Kolodny is Directeur de recherche honoraire au CNRS and among his many publications are *La Population des Iles de la Grece* (3 volumes, Edisud 1974) and *La geographie urbaine de la Corse* (SEDES 1962).

Further reading

For those interested in exploring this subject in more depth, Professor Kolodny has kindly supplied the following bibliography of the major works on the subject written since 1960...

Barceló Pons, B. : *"Evolución reciente y estructura actual de la población en las Islas Baleares"*. Madrid-Ibiza (1970), 399 p. (thesis).

Barceló Pons, B. et alia : *"Atlas de les illes Balears"*. Barcelone (1979), 88 p.

Biagini, E. : *"Le isole Maltesi"*. Gênes (1974), 223 p.

Bisson, J. : *"La terre et l'homme aux îles Baléares"*. Aix en Provence (1977), 415 p.(thesis)

Bowen-Jones, H., Dewdney, J.C. et Fisher, W.B. : *"Malta - Background for Development"*. Durham, s. d. (1960-61), 356 p.

Brigand, L. : *"Les îles en Méditerranée - Enjeux et perspectives"*. Paris (1991), 98 p.

Cori, B. : *"La penisola di Capo Corso"*. Pisa (1966), 246 p. (thesis).

Faugères, L. and Kolodny, E., : *"Samothrace : Etude géographique d'un milieu insulaire"* in *"Recherches sur la Grèce rurale"*. Paris, *Mémoires et Documents du CNRS* (1972) vol.13, pp.63-124.

Gentileschi, M.L. et Simoncelli, R. : *"Rientro degli emigrati e territorio..."*. Cagliari - Naples (1983), 399 p. Sardinia, pp. 265-349.

King, R. : *"Sicily"*. Newton Abbot - Harrisburg (1973), 208 p.

King, R. : *"Sardinia"*. Newton Abbot - Harrisburg (1975), 216 p.

King, R.(ed.) : *"Geography, Environment and Development in the Mediterranean"*. Sussex Academic press, Brighton-Portland (2001), 292 p.

Kolodny, E. : *"La géographie urbaine de la Corse"*. Paris (1962), 334 p. (thesis).

Kolodny, E. : *"La population des îles en Méditerranée"*. *Méditerranée*, n°1 (1966), pp. 3-31.

Kolodny, E. : *"La Crète : Mutations et évolution d'une population insulaire grecque"*. *Revue de Géographie de Lyon*, n° 3 (1968), pp.227-290.

Kolodny, E. : *"Hermoupolis-Syra : Naissance et évolution d'une ville insulaire grecque"*. *Méditerranée*, n° 2 (1969), pp.189-219.

Kolodny, E. : *"Chios : Evolution récente et structures du peuplement d'une île de navigateurs"*. *Recherches Méditerranéennes - Etudes et Travaux de Méditerranée* n° 8 (1969), pp.313-351.

Kolodny, E. : *"Une communauté insulaire en Méditerranée orientale : les Turcs de Chypre"*. *Revue de Géographie de Lyon* n°1 (1971), pp. 5 - 56.

Kolodny, E. : "La population des îles de la Grèce - Essai de géographie insulaire en Méditerranée orientale". Aix en Provence, (1974), 829 p. and atlas (thesis).

Kolodny, E. : *"Un village cycladien : Chora d'Amorgos"*. Aix en Provence (1992), 269 p.

Kolodny, E. : *"Des Musulmans dans une île grecque : les "Turcocrétois"*. Mediterranean World, XIV, Tokyo (1995), pp. 1-16.

Kolodny, E. : *"Insularité méditerranéenne et spécificité de la Corse"* in *"Méditerranée, Mer Ouverte"*. *Actes du colloque de Marseille, 21-23 septembre 1995*. International Foundation - Malta . (1997), tome II, pp. 767-787.

Kolodny, E. : *"La population des îles dalmates"*. *Rivista Geografica Italiana*, n°107 (2000), pp. 161-174.

Kolodny, E. : *"Iles et populations en Méditerranée orientale" Analecta Isisiana LXXIX*, Istanbul, *Les Editions Isis* (2004), 342 p. Collection of 15 published papers (1966-2003).

Kolodny, E. and Darques, R. : *"Turcs, Grecs et réfugiés dans l'île de Lesbos au XXe siècle"*. *Méditerranée*, n°3-4 (2004), pp.65-74.

Martinetti, J. : *"Insularité et marginalité en Méditerranée occidentale"*. Ajaccio (1989), 215 p. (thesis).

Miossec, J.M. : *"L'archipel maltais"*. *Bulletin de la Société Languedocienne de Géographie*, tome 14 vol. n° 1(1980), pp. 43-95.

Mori, A. : *"Sardegna"*. Turin (1966), 676 p.

Papadopoullos, T.: *"Social and Historical Data on Population (1570-1881). Texts and Studies of the History of Cyprus - I"*. Nicosia (1965), 248 p.

Péchoux, P.Y. : *"Les dimensions géographiques d'une guerre localisée : Chypre, 1974 - 1976"*. *Hérodote*, n° 3 (1976) pp. 11 - 44.

Péchoux, P.Y. : *"Chypre : géopolitique d'une île fracturée"*. *Hérodote*, n° 48 (1988), pp.127 - 142.

Péchoux, P.Y. : *"Chypre et les Chypriotes : vers une double insularité"* in *"Territoires et sociétés insulaires"*. Paris - Brest (1991), pp. 189-195.

Pecora, A. : *"Sicilia"*. Turin (1968), 644 p.

Pracchi, R., Terrosu Asole, A. et Riccardi, M. : *"Atlante della Sardegna"*. Cagliari - Rome (1971-1980), 2 vol.

Ravis-Giordani, G. : *"Bergers corses - Les communautés villageoises du Niolu"*. Aix en Provence (1983), 505 p.(thesis).

Ravis-Giordani, G. (ed.) : *"Atlas ethnohistorique de la Corse"*. Ed. du Comité des travaux historiques et scientifiques (2004) 253 p.

Renucci, J. : *"Corse traditionnelle et Corse nouvelle"*. Lyon (1974), 454 p. (thesis).

Rochefort, R. : *"Le travail en Sicile"*. Paris (1961), 363 p. (thesis).

Rombai, L. : *"Le isole minori italiane - Studi comparati di geografia della popolazione*. Florence, (1977 - 6), 107 p. et tableaux.

Simi, P. : *"L'adaptation humaine dans la dépression centrale de la Corse"*. Aix en Provence (1966), 260 p. (thesis).

Simi, P. : *"Précis de géographie physique, humaine... de la Corse"*. Bastia (1982), 608 p.

Tlatli, S.-E. : *"Djerba l'île des Lotophages"*. Tunis (1967), 193 p.

"Iles de Méditerranée". Paris (1981), 148 p.; 9 papers.

"Territoires et sociétés insulaires". Paris - Brest (1991), 456 p. Include15 papers on Mediterranean Islands.

Professor Maria Sala assesses the natural and social factors that impact upon the Mediterranean's environment

Fires and floods, trees and tourism

The Mediterranean environment is characterised by its climate, with rainfall occurring only during the winter, and dry summers – this last a decidedly unusual phenomenon. While this is good news for tourists, it is less so for vegetation, because it is in summer that plants need water to grow and survive. In addition, rainfall when it occurs is often torrential, prone to producing floods and with them increased erosion.

Despite the importance of floods and droughts in determining the region's climate, several climatic varieties can be distinguished, ranging from sub-humid in the north and in the mountains, to semi-arid in the most southerly locations, which lie adjacent to desert environments.

If climate plays a key role in defining the Mediterranean environment, so too does the region's topography. The mountainous terrain that extends around the Mediterranean Sea is the result of tectonic activity related to the collision of the African and European plates. Not only do these mountains define the location; they also impact on the type of drainage and consequent erosion when subject to torrential rain. Predominant among the rock types are granites, slates, limestones and loose sediments. Limestones, when subjected to rain, undergo solution processes that produce karst landscapes, in which water drains away easily, thus producing a very dry environment.

Granites, on the other hand, undergo weathering processes that produce a mantle of silt and sandy material that retains water, which can be used for vegetation during a certain period after rainfall, resulting in a more humid landscape. Sedimentary rocks are often silty clays, which are rather impermeable and favour bare landscapes where gullying and erosion are common. Typically, soils across the region are thin and poorly developed, with the main differences related to the underlying rock and the type and density of vegetation.

Facing page:
A view of southern Greece from the NASA Space Shuttle showing the smoke plumes from the massive fires during the summer of 2007

Land degradation

Mediterranean islands, in common with mainland regions, are suffering from considerable land degradation, brought about by a number of factors. Although some of the causes of this, such as flooding and erosion, are related to the fragile nature of the environment, others, such as vegetation clearing, intensive agricultural practices, and construction, are the result of human intervention.

Vegetation has suffered from the clearance of trees and shrubs for shipbuilding, fuel and agricultural purposes. Forest fires have also played a significant role for thousands of years, each causing an adjustment of the ecosystem to the new conditions.

In addition to natural fires arising from a combination of drought, tinder-dry vegetation and lightning during storms, fire has long been the means of clearing forested areas in order to obtain land for grazing and agriculture. In recent years, the extent and frequency of the fires has increased notably, mostly related to human causes, such as tourist developments in coastal mountains and forests, the increasing use of forest roads by motorbikes and cars, and human negligence and arson. Even today, shepherds and cow-hands light illegal fires in order to put the land to pasture.

Most vegetation, especially the *macchia* and *garriga* shrubs, is capable of self-regeneration within just a year after a light fire, although this can take three or four years in the case of heavy fires.The recovery time of trees, however, is much longer, and in the case of the few deciduous species the loss may be irreversible. The tree most resistant to burning is the cork oak, with its protective bark, yet the main reforestation species, pines and eucalyptus, are highly combustible.

Loss of vegetation and fauna due to forest fires is enormous, but the illegal trade of species, such as

(ALL PHOTOS: PROFESSOR MARIA SALA)

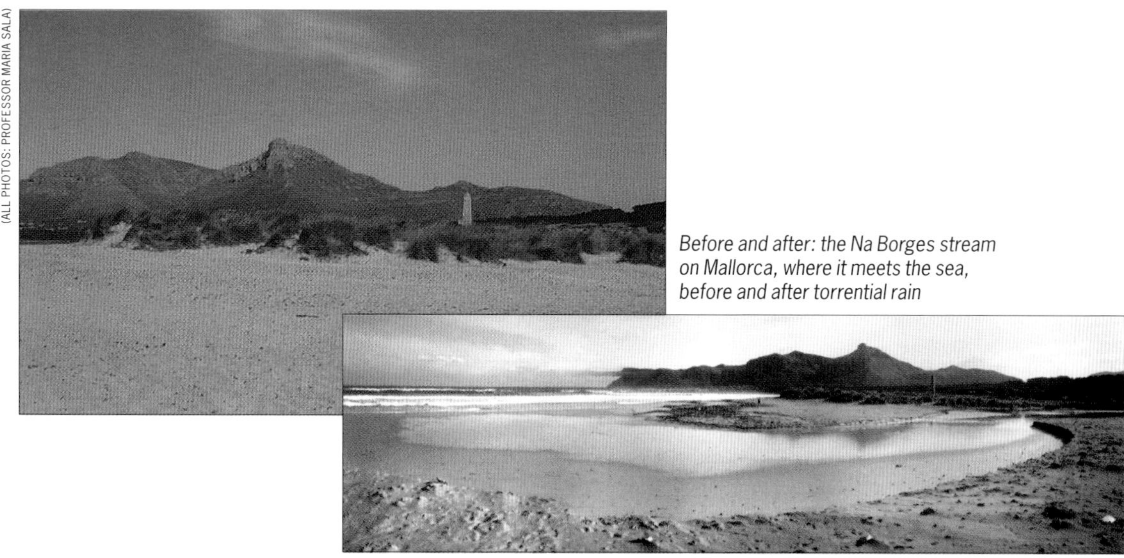

Before and after: the Na Borges stream on Mallorca, where it meets the sea, before and after torrential rain

chameleons, spiny tailed lizards and tortoises, is a further factor contributing to the decline of the region's indigenous wildlife.

A far more recent environmental issue is the level of coastal erosion. A large part of Mediterranean coasts are only a narrow strip, unable to accommodate strong urban pressures. The natural equilibrium that prevailed until the early 1900s has given way to a rate of erosion that was in the 1960s and 1970s put down to excavation of gravel from river beds and beaches. But while this activity nearly ceased from the early 1980s, beach erosion has continued at almost the same rate. This has been accelerated because of inappropriate coastal works, such as T groynes and parallel reefs, constructed without any preliminary study of the dynamics of the coastal system. Often, the beach replenishment has been undertaken using earth-rich material, whereas the natural materials were pebbles, leading to pollution of the sea floor with mud.

Despite this, urbanisation often goes uncontrolled. Holiday houses are built where once there were dunes, or directly on the beach. In some places, the strong coastal retreat of recent decades is resulting in the complete destruction of the rear-beach environment.

Land uses and their impact

For centuries, land use in the Mediterranean environment centred on agriculture, pasture and forestry. Although these sometimes produced extensive erosion, this was a far cry from the impact of today's increasing demands on the land. At the root of the problem lies the combination of progressive industrialisation and increasing tourism. Undoubtedly the main causes of economic progress in Mediterranean countries, they are also the major factors in environmental degradation.

During the summer season tourists may increase the total population by more than three times, causing enormous pressure on the environment – and with tourist numbers expected to grow further by the year 2025, there is no sign of immediate improvement.

The combined impact of building and road construction represents one of the major forces in land degradation in the region, with the islands suffering at least as badly as the mainland. In addition to restricting the area available for other uses, such as agriculture, such wholesale construction has an altogether more serious consequence: that of increased flooding. Building leads to a huge extension of impervious surfaces where rainfall, instead of filtering into the soil, remains on the surface. The result is a dramatic increase of catastrophic floods, especially because many of the new buildings are located either on the coast or along river floodplains. Added to this, the steep slopes behind many buildings and roads along the coasts increase the risk of flash floods in urban areas, while roadbuilding in mountain areas tends to act as a trigger for landslides.

A further consequence of development is an increase in pollution. Water that flows from urbanised areas contains a high level of dissolved and suspended sediments, which in turn have the potential to pollute both rivers and underground water. Less obvious, perhaps, are the environmental effects – both positive and negative – of modern agricultural practice. On the one hand, intensive cultivation practices still contribute significantly to the erosion of soils; on the other, EU

Before and after: the Torrent de Pareis, also on Mallorca, was so full after a storm that it could only be photographed from the air

policies have favoured a reduction in overgrazing. This in turn has led to the recolonisation of shrub vegetation in many areas, which favours soil regeneration but increases the risk of fires. In Sardinia and part of Sicily, however, the land is widely grazed by sheep, with minimal negative effects on soil erosion.

The marine environment

Many parts of the world, including the Mediterranean regions, are experiencing depletion of fish stocks. Overfishing is diminishing the number and diversity of species, as is the extraction, often illegal, of corals. There are also increasing threats to fish stocks from onshore pollutants such as agricultural nutrients and industrial effluents, as well as urban sewage.

Any waste material dumped by cities and ships will be carried by the currents, eventually reaching the shoreline. In the case of oil pollution, this leads to the formation of tar, which particularly affects bathing beaches. Such marine pollutants are severely prohibited in the Mediterranean Sea, being an almost closed inner sea, and strict regulations have been imposed on oil tankers, prohibiting the disposal of ballast water into the open sea. As a result, tar pollution of the beaches has been reduced, although it remains an issue on the beaches of the eastern Mediterranean. One means of measuring the efficacy of such measures is the Blue Flag scheme, whereby beaches are monitored annually according to strict criteria which include water quality and environmental management, as well as safety and provision of services. There have been some notable successes on Mediterranean islands, including – in 2007 – 52 beaches on Cyprus alone, as well as several on Crete and other Greek islands, and others in the Balearics.

Preserving the environment

There is a need to balance short-term economic and production needs against long-term environmental goals. Increasingly, governments are attempting to reconcile these imperatives through the development of sustainable development policies.

In European countries, the Common Agricultural Policy (CAP) will have a strong impact on both land degradation and its protection. The main points of the reforms are price cuts for key products such as cereals; the withdrawal of land from production; and accompanying measures for agri-environmental protection, afforestation of agricultural land and early retirement of farmers.

In agricultural practices, reducing land degradation by adapting cultivation practices to the susceptibility of land to erosion is an ancient practice in Mediterranean areas. It is possible to reduce erosion by ploughing along the contour lines, by leaving herbs to grow between the crops, or by rebuilding the cultivation terraces.

Measures to reduce the fire hazard include diversification of land use, management of recreation and illegal dumping, and environmental education. The number and intensity of forest fires can be reduced by co-ordinating action between the various authorities. Other recommended measures are to decrease the time required to develop and apply new techniques for extinguishing fires.

Reforestation – both spontaneous and through replanting – is considered effective in stabilising

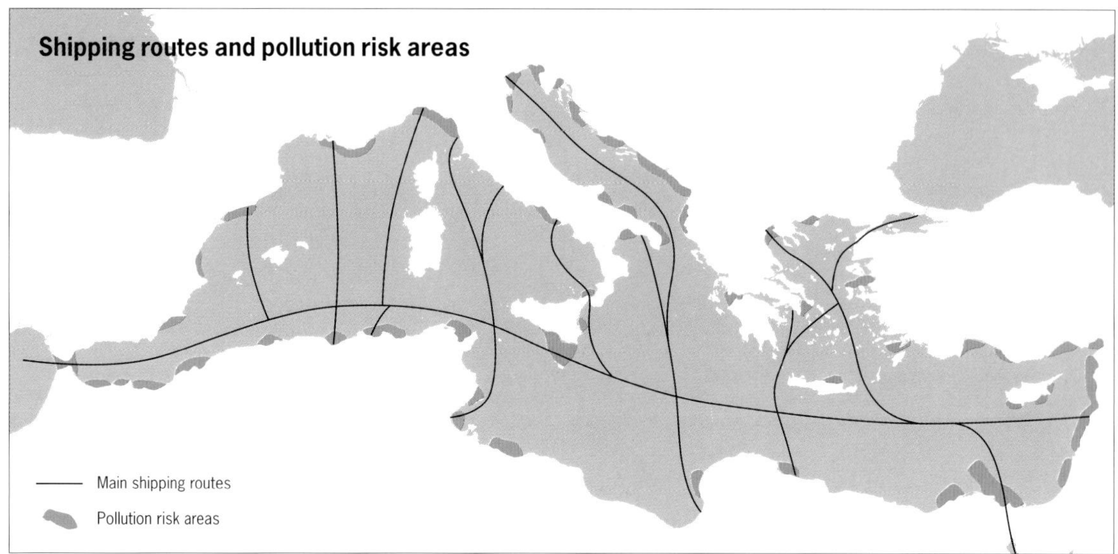
Shipping routes and pollution risk areas
Main shipping routes
Pollution risk areas

slopes, but it does not constitute an efficient means of combating floods, as runoff tends to concentrate on the forest floor. Thus a favoured practice is 'down-cutting', creating channels that allow a more rapid evacuation of flood water. Forests must also be defended against pest attacks, such as that of the procession caterpillar, which attacks pine trees, but the costs can be high.

Flood control also requires a better knowledge of the impact of river flows, both upstream and down-stream. Check dams, used since Roman times, but widespread since the 1950s, are effective in reducing the movement of sediment, but not in the reduction of erosion. In fact, due to siltation, erosion is reduced upstream but is increased downstream as the clear waters have a higher erosive capability. Thus, industrial and urban construction should be banned from the coastal margins and within floodplains. On the contrary, re-naturalisation of channels should be encouraged. Improved flood warning systems are being implemented, and floodwater can be diverted from coastal streams to recharge the aquifer.

In addition to such practical measures, economic and social solutions to the problem of land degradation need to be considered. Working on the carrot-and-stick approach, economic solutions balance the provision of tax incentives and direct subsidies to encourage good management practices, with the imposition of financial penalties to punish harmful practices. Social measures may include the relocation of people from badly degraded areas, and education and improved com-munication to change attitudes or to improve land-holders' skills.

Tourists can also play a part

If such measures seem detached from the holiday plans of most tourists, there is still plenty that the individual visitor can do to minimise or even redress the situation. It is perhaps obvious to state that re-cycling bottles or ensuring that cigarette butts are properly extinguished can help, but it is all too easy to forget that these are imperatives on holiday even more than at home.

Saving water is particularly important in the Medi-terranean: it is not necessary to shower with fresh water after each swim and, as a matter of fact, keep-ing your body salty is healthy and good for your skin. Visitors are also in a unique position to influence attitudes. Ask questions about the environmental impact of a property before investing in it. Find out if a boat captain is disposing of waste safely. Give the car a miss and explore on foot – or by bus. Put on a mask and fins, and see for yourself the state of the under-water world. If so many of the Mediterranean's environmental problems are being laid at the foot of tourists, then it is also up to those tourists to form part of the solution.

Professor Maria Sala is Professor Emeritus at University of Barcelona and Founder of IGU Commission on Land Degradation and is the author (with A.Conacher) of *Land Degradation in Mediterranean Environments of the World* (John Wiley 1998).

Facing page:
75% of beach litter is plastic, but attitudes towards littering beaches are becoming much more responsible

The prospects for tourism in the Mediterranean
Dr Mara Manente looks at the development of island tourism and its future challenges

The changing face of island tourism

The Mediterranean and its islands represent an important cultural, natural, tourist and economic resource, both for individual Mediterranean countries and for Europe in general, which is reflected in their international influence and the number of visitors they attract. The islands are a huge tourist attraction and offer a significant opportunity for economic development, particularly of marginal undeveloped areas linked to conservation and 'exploitation' (making the most of natural advantages) projects, which would benefit not only individual countries but Mediterranean tourism as a whole.

The Mediterranean as a tourist destination

In terms of tourist movements, the Mediterranean is the world's most important region, with more than 265 million visitors in 2005, or a third of all international tourism, which, according to the World Tourism Organisation, totalled 806 million arrivals in 2005. While the region's rapid development and economic progress of the last 30 years is linked primarily to the boom in 3S (sun, sand and sea) tourism, its capacity to maintain its appeal is derived mainly from the four principal assets that characterise the area (PNUE/PAM 2005): its favourable climate and coastal fringe; the rich variety of natural, cultural, historic and artistic attractions; its physical proximity and cultural similarity to the European market; and its image as a traditional tourist destination.

The Mediterranean has maintained its leadership by emphasising its historical, artistic and cultural heritage, which has enabled it to distinguish itself from other regions offering solely (or mainly) beach holidays. Thanks to these factors, the Mediterranean has shown steady tourism growth, although this has been overshadowed by global trends. Between 1999 and 2005, the average annual growth of international tourism in the region was 3.2%, compared with world growth estimated at 4%. The performance of individual countries varies, which reflects their different levels of tourist development and what they offer. In contrast to the modest growth that has characterised mature destinations such as Italy (0.9% average growth between 1999 and 2005) and France (0.6%), strong growth has been seen in a number of countries. These include Turkey (19.7%), Croatia (14.3%) and Egypt (10.2%), all of which have made considerable investments in their tourist industries in recent years, resulting in a significant increase in their market share between 1999 and 2005: from 3.2% to 7.7% for Turkey, from 1.7% to 3.2% for Croatia, and from 2.2% to 3.2% for Egypt. Among the other leading destinations, Spain and Greece have maintained more or less constant market shares of 21 and 5.5% respectively, while the greatest losses have been recorded by France (from 33.5 to 28.5%) and Italy (from 16.7 to 14. 4%).

Facing page: Kefalonia's world famous Myrtos beach was almost unknown before the 1990s

Tourism in the Mediterranean islands

The islands of the Mediterranean attract over 37 million visitors annually, including both international and domestic (i.e. tourists from the mainland) arrivals. Taking the international component separately, it is estimated that these constitute around 5% of total tourist numbers in the Mediterranean region.

Visitor capacity, measured in terms of the number of beds, totals around 1.9 million; there are some 50 islands with at least 3,000 beds, which together represent 95% of the total capacity. The top ten islands by capacity are, in size order (largest first), Mallorca with 286,000 beds, followed by Crete, Sardinia, Sicily, Cyprus, Ibiza, Rhodes, Djerba, Corsica and finally Menorca, with 49,000 beds. These ten islands comprise 85% of the total Mediterranean island population, with 66% of visitor beds and 76% of visitors. The same ten islands, together with Malta, are the only islands to register over a million annual visitors, with a maximum of 9.6 million for Mallorca down to 1.06 million for Rhodes. Cyprus and Malta, the only independent islands, receive 3.1 million and 1.1 million visitors respectively, which together comprise 11% of total island visitors.

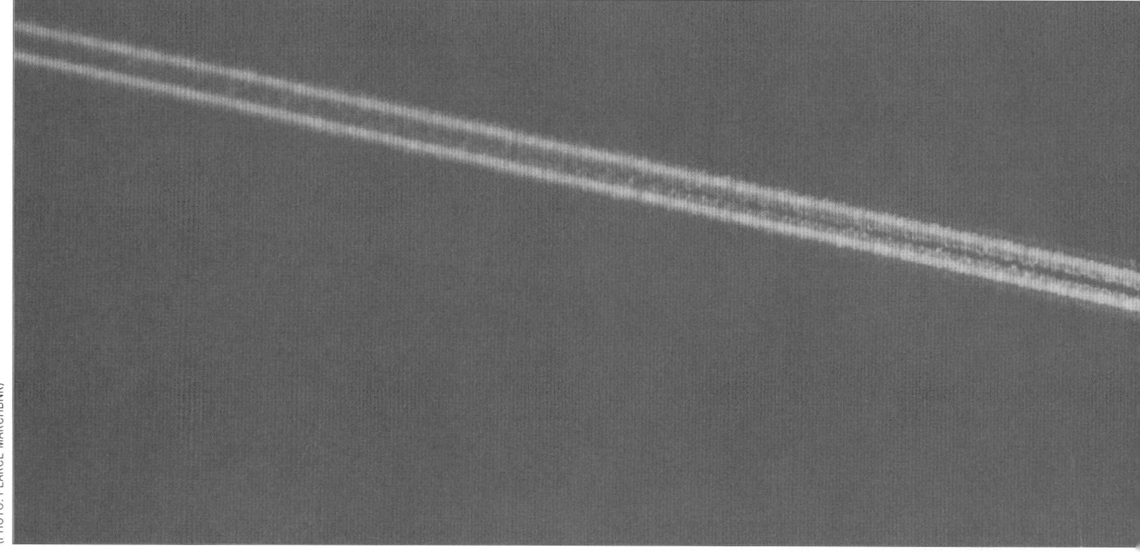
(PHOTO: PEARCE MARCHBNK)

The impact of tourism can be assessed by comparing the ratio of arrivals (or more correctly, the number of overnight stays) with the population and the area of an island. When the number of visitors in relation to the population is too high, social and other problems can result, while, with regard to the ratio to area, a disproportionate number of visitors in a relatively small island will have an impact on land use and the environment, which in turn effectively defines the capacity limits.

Compared with an average visitor/population ratio of 3.3, and 2.9 for the top ten islands (among which Ibiza has the highest ratio of 17), five smaller islands attract over 25 visitors per inhabitant, four of which are in Croatia: Cres 82, Avsa (in Turkey) 57, Murter 33, Krk 30 and Losinj 29. Among these, only Krk has a population of over 10,000. Assuming a minimum average stay of three nights, Ibiza is already showing signs of reaching a critical ratio between tourist numbers and resident population, particularly when we consider that a destination with the highest tourist congestion, such as Venice, has a visitor/population ratio of 53. As is well known, such a critical ratio results in an overload of services (e.g. transport, healthcare, water supply, refuse collection etc.) and increases the cost of such services – costs which weigh heavily on the resident population. The problem is more acute when one considers that tourism is usually concentrated within a few months of the year, resulting in a significantly higher seasonal ratio than the average annual figure reported here.

It is, however, with regard to the second indicator of visitor/area ratio, that it is possible to quantify the stress that tourism can place on an island's environment. Again, assuming a minimum stay of three nights, around 40 Mediterranean islands would register over 500 people per square kilometre. The most critical situations (over 3,000 visitors per sq km, or 9,000 people on the three-night assumption) are Capri (over 16,000 visitors per sq km), Ischia (11,000), Murter (9,000) and Avsa (7,000), followed by Malta, Ibiza and Losinj. It is significant that only Murter, Avsa and Losinj appear in the above visitor/population group, while among the top ten islands, only Ibiza appears. It is also important to stress that in most cases the location of an island makes it difficult or virtually impossible for excess flows to be directed elsewhere.

Tourism as a development factor

In an economic context, tourism represents the mainstay of the economy in almost all the Mediterranean islands, a fact which is illustrated by the proportion of GDP produced by the tourist industry and the ratio of employment within the sector. International tourism makes a vital contribution to the balance of payments, as international tourism receipts are similar to exports (i.e. foreign currency earnings), differing only in the fact that it is people rather than goods which travel. Tourist receipts add to demand and stimulate the local economy by increasing production, employment and added value. As for domestic tourism, however important it may be, its impact is less, as it needs to be offset against the amount that would have been spent, in any case, by resident 'tourists'.

The tourist industry generates over 50% of GDP in the Balearics and Corsica, and constitutes over 10% of national wealth in Cyprus and Malta. In Cyprus, which is

Direct flights are a key factor in determining the development of tourism on an island

the third-largest Mediterranean island, tourism represents some 50% of the service sector, employs 12% of the working population and produces 40% of export earnings. In Malta, tourism is also the island's principal industry, generating 30% of GDP and 25% of exports.

The future outlook

Tourism has proved a liberating force for the islands of the Mediterranean. In the past they have always been at an economic disadvantage due to their size, their dependence on the mainland and the restricted mobility (and supply) of labour, goods and services. Tourism outweighs these disadvantages at a stroke, and, being more profitable than traditional activities such as fishing and agriculture, it provides an immediate and direct stimulus for an island's economy.

There are, of course, some drawbacks. Tourism results in a greatly increased consumption of water, a scarce resource in most Mediterranean islands, and leads to an increase in pollution and waste. Agricultural land is lost, the natural environment is destroyed and coastal degradation increases; in the Balearics and Malta, 30% of the coast is built up (compared with 80% on the Cote d'Azur). Property prices rise to uncomfortable levels (almost 40% of the Balearics are in foreign ownership), making it difficult or impossible for locals to buy a home. Perhaps the biggest danger of all is that tourism could ultimately destroy the character of an island which attracted the visitors in the first place.

A recent independent analysis (Easterley & Kraay 2000) has, however, concluded that the positive benefits of tourist development are two and a half times greater than the negative effects.

It should also be borne in mind that tourism is no longer a fast growing industry in most parts of the Mediterranean. As illustrated above, growth in the more mature markets has been modest in recent years and current expectations are that growth up to 2025 will average just 2 to 2.5% a year in Spain, France, Italy, Greece, Cyprus and Malta. Only a few Mediterranean countries are expecting to see tourism grow faster than the world average: for example, by 7% a year in Croatia (where tourism currently accounts for 29% of GDP) and Egypt, and by 5% in Morocco and Turkey (which is expected to rise from eleventh to fourth place in the Mediterranean tourism standings).

What will undoubtedly be seen, especially in the more developed markets, are changes in the forms that tourism takes. One of the most encouraging trends is the awareness of the harmful effects of tourism and the efforts that are increasingly being made to reduce them. New, less harmful forms of tourism, such as agricultural tourism, sailing, cruising (Cyprus and the Balearics are the two top cruise passenger destinations in the Mediterranean) and cultural tourism are being encouraged and are growing. With these changes comes a gradual shift in attitudes on the part of tourists, and recent years have seen an increasing respect for the environment and culture of the countries of the Mediterranean, which are – lest we forget – the birthplace of western civilisation.

Dr Mara Manente is Director of CISET (International Centre of Studies on Tourism Economics) at University Ca'Foscari, Venice.

427

Sailing in the Mediterranean

A summary by *Rod Heikell* of the rapid expansion of sailing in the Mediterranean

From flotilla to superyacht: a thirty-year boom in sailing

It may or may not have been in the Mediterranean where man first hopped on a log and stretched some animal skin on a couple of sticks to sail downwind, but we can be sure that sailing developed from these crude beginnings to the construction of boats and the squaresail in the southeast of the Mediterranean.

Ancient beginnings

For two millennia BC the Mediterranean was quartered by ships under sail trading right around this sea. Homer in *The Odyssey* gives us a few clues on the knowledge of winds and the use of stars for navigation and, in the 5th or 6th century BC, Skylax of Karyanda wrote the first *Periplus* (sailing directions) for the Mediterranean. Off Ulu Burun, a cape on the Turkish coast, a shipwreck from the 14th century BC has been excavated, a modest 50 foot long coaster loaded with items from all around Europe and Asia Minor. Off the island of Antikythira, sponge divers recovered what is in effect the first analogue computer, dated to the 1st century BC, with complex gear wheels to determine the position of the sun, moon and stars: a sort of clock of the heavens.

The constant summer winds, the Etesians (the modern Meltemi), of the Aegean provided a predictable timetable for boats trading under sail to make their voyages. In the summer the etesians blow from the north curving around to the west in the south and ships would sail from around Athens to the islands in the Cyclades and the coast of Asia Minor.

Navigation was simplified by the fact that navigators were rarely out of sight of land and could sail from island to island using the naked eye. Later passages out of sight of land utilised the stars and the moon and an instinctive reckoning of course and speed. Homer tells Odysseus to keep the Great Bear or the Plough on his left to reach Greece from Calypso's Island in Malta and this is exactly the direction to steer to get east to the Ionian islands.

The first concrete reference we have to sailing for pleasure is from the Roman poet Catullus who calls his yacht a 'bean-pod boat' and describes how he had her built in the Black Sea and sailed her around the Aegean. Like most boat owners he asserts 'that she's been the fastest piece of timber under sail or oar afloat'. There must surely have been others around sailing for pleasure in the Mediterranean, but the records reveal little until the 19th century when yachts ventured down from northern Europe and even across from the USA as the archaeological and historical sites dotted around the inland sea were 'rediscovered'.

The 20th century

After World War II increasing numbers of yachts began to cruise down to the Mediterranean and, inspired by the exploits of Humphrey Barton and Adlard Coles who showed that extended voyages could be made in small yachts, many of them were humbler craft than the large yachts that visited in the 19th and early 20th century. Although more yachts were visiting the Mediterranean, right up until the 1960s it remained an adventure akin to sailing to the Caribbean or the Pacific, though with much shorter distances involved.

In the latter part of the 20th century marinas were built and yacht facilities improved in the western Mediterranean, though the eastern Mediterranean remained a little visited place. This all began to change in the 1980s when yacht numbers began to increase and by the beginning of the 21st century there was an explosion in the number of yachts. Yacht charter blossomed and in countries like Croatia, Greece and Turkey, where the norm had been to berth in local fishing harbours or anchor off, an increasing number of marinas have been built, with more in the pipeline. By this time Spain, France and Italy had marinas dotted all around the coast.

Today there is still a definite split between the western and eastern ends of the Mediterranean in

Facing page:
Anchoring at Sa Calobra, Mallorca

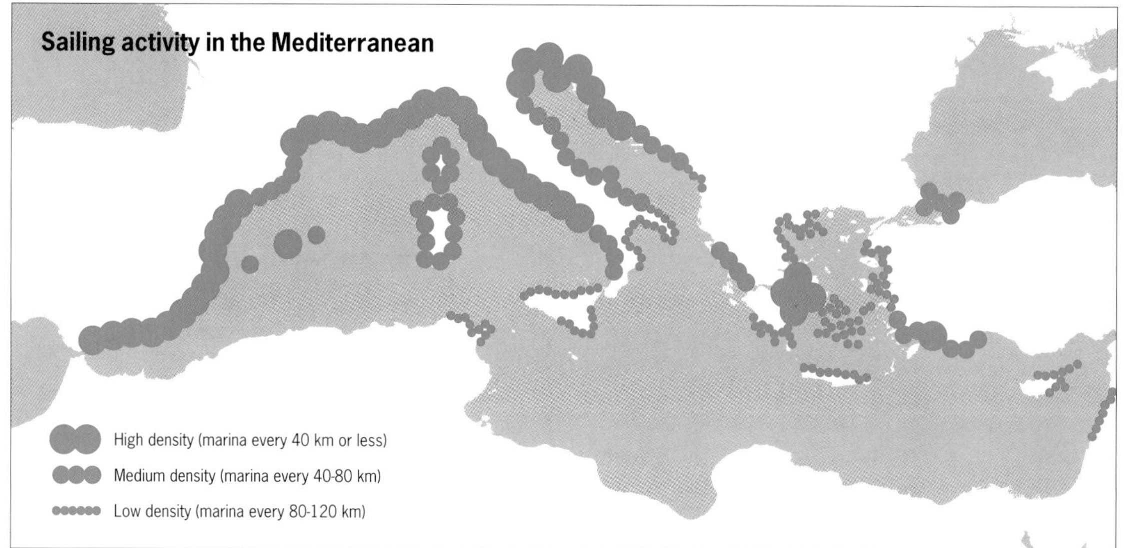
Sailing activity in the Mediterranean
High density (marina every 40 km or less)
Medium density (marina every 40-80 km)
Low density (marina every 80-120 km)

terms of cruising styles and possibilities. Around the coasts of Spain and France there are hundreds of marinas, many of them luxurious affairs with a berthing cost to match the facilities. Palma Mallorca in the Balearics is the superyacht base in the Mediterranean, though older favourites around the French and Italian Riviera and in other parts of the western Mediterranean figure in the superyacht itinerary as well.

The eastern Mediterranean is a little more homespun with a lot of good anchorages and fishing harbours offering less in the way of facilities with the bonus of down-to-earth ambience. Yachts still sail the ancient routes from island to island utilising the naked eye in the way the ancients did.

In recent years some up-market marinas have been built around the coasts and islands of Croatia, Greece and Turkey in an attempt to attract larger yachts from the western Mediterranean circuit.

A much more crowded sea

As in other parts of the world, the numbers of yachts in the Mediterranean have increased dramatically in the last decade. This is partly because of increased prosperity in the EU countries bordering the Mediterranean where locals have bought boats for their leisure activities and also because a lot of yachts from central and northern Europe now visit the Mediterranean or base their boats there on a permanent basis.

In France there is an estimated shortfall of some 80,000 yacht berths, in Spain the marinas are full to overflowing with yachts and berths in new marinas are paid for and reserved before construction of the marina is finished. In Italy many of the old fishing harbours and parts of commercial harbours have been modified for yacht berths.

In Croatia it is difficult to find a permanent berth as large numbers of Germans and Austrians keep their boats there, just a few hours drive away from the top of the Adriatic, from where they can cruise down through the archipelago of islands off the Dalmatian coast. In Greece and Turkey marina berths are filling up quickly and in the Ionian there are boatyard clusters storing thousands of yachts over the winter.

This dramatic increase in the number of boats kept in the Mediterranean has significantly altered the local economies of many places and contributes significantly by providing work for the local population, both skilled and unskilled, and in the amount of money spent ashore in local shops. Some islands in Croatia and Greece rely on the revenue from visiting yachts for a significant part of their livelihood, probably more than 50% of the total. Yacht tourism is also more evenly distributed throughout the year compared with the annual pilgrimage of package tourists in the summer months, with some hotels on the islands busy for just a few months of the year.

Yachts require hauling out in the winter or gardiennage afloat, with winter work repairing and refitting yachts in the off season and yacht owners returning in April and sailing throughout the year until September or October.

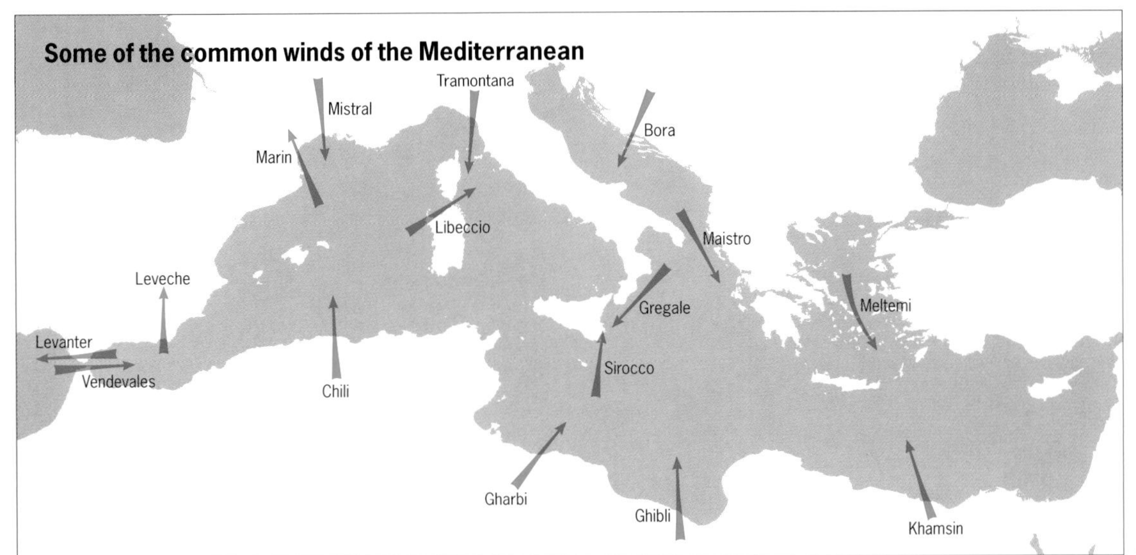
Some of the common winds of the Mediterranean
Tramontana
Mistral
Bora
Marin
Libeccio
Maistro
Leveche
Gregale
Meltemi
Levanter
Vendevales
Sirocco
Chili
Gharbi
Ghibli
Khamsin

Cruising areas around the islands

Spain The Balearics are the jewel of Mediterranean Spain and have become increasingly popular in recent years, so much so that it can be difficult to find a berth in a marina or somewhere to anchor in the calas and bays. The three main islands, Ibiza, Mallorca and Minorca, have marinas all around the coast and a number of natural harbours and anchorages. Alboran, closer to Gibraltar, has no useful anchorages.

France The offshore island of Corsica has often been described as a lump of granite deposited in the sea and the view from seawards is just so. The coast has a number of marinas and many spectacular protected bays. It is a perennial favourite for yachts to visit in the summer. Around the coast of mainland France there are smaller islands like Porquerolles and Iles Lerins.

Italy The two islands of Sardinia and Sicily are quite different. Sardinia has a long history of yachting infrastructure in the north, and the south is now being developed as well. Sicily has long been relatively underdeveloped and although it has a few marinas around its long coastline, most yachts will use fishing harbours or a few natural anchorages. Sicily also has the popular Lipari Islands and the Egadi Islands lying close by. Off the coast of Italy the Tuscan Islands are popular and a bit further south the Pontine Islands are a useful cruising ground. Off the Bay of Naples lie Ischia, Capri and Procida.

Malta The two main islands that make up Malta are known as a popular base for yachts to winter over rather than as an extensive cruising area.

Croatia The archipelago of islands scattered down the eastern side of the Adriatic make up a vast cruising area that has been extensively developed in recent years and there are now a large number of marinas and many of the bays have laid moorings.

Greece Our idea of Greece is moulded more by the idea of islands than it is of the mainland. It is the quintessential island cruising ground and like the ancients you can navigate from island to island all the way across the Ionian and the Aegean. There are a few marinas scattered around the islands, but for the most part yachts use fishing harbours and anchorages in bays and coves.

Turkey Turkey has a few islands dotted along its coast, but is better known for the indented gulfs running into the mainland coast.

Cyprus The island has a modest infrastructure and like Malta is known as a popular spot for yachts to spend the winter rather than a cruising area.

Tunisia There are a few islands off the coast, though the main cruising area is around the mainland coast. There are several marinas and fishing harbours and anchorages. Shallow waters and a significant tide, at least for the Mediterranean, pose some interesting pilotage problems.

Winds

Weather in the Mediterranean can come as a bit of a shock to sailors from northern Europe. A common image and prevailing stereotype is of turquoise seas ruffled by the occasional zephyr blowing out of a cloudless azure sky. The reality is that there is on average more wind in the Mediterranean than in places like the English Channel and other areas in northern Europe. Add to that the fact that the weather changes relatively quickly compared with many other areas and in half an hour it can go from 5 knots to a screaming 30-40 knots. This can catch sailors out who are used to the plodding progress of Atlantic lows changing the weather around northern Europe. Even with more wind, at least the sea and spray are warm and the skies blue.

Chartering a yacht

Fifty years ago you could find a few luxury skippered yachts to charter, but for most people the idea of chartering a yacht in the Mediterranean was beyond their wildest dreams.

Today there are charter companies of all types scattered all around the Mediterranean, though the eastern Mediterranean accounts for some 70% of charter bases with Greece and Turkey the most popular destinations. Cheap charter flights and improved facilities have meant that chartering a yacht can be around the same price as a land-based hotel if you take the cheaper options available.

Yacht charter can be roughly divided into three categories. Flotilla sailing suits the less experienced and you sail in company with a group of yachts (typically 10-12) on a loosely defined itinerary with a lead boat on which there is a skipper and hostess and sometimes an engineer. Bareboat charter is where you hire the boat and equipment and skipper it yourself. Skippered charter is typically on larger yachts and you will have a skipper and crew to sail the yacht and cook and keep you entertained.

Environment

Compared with tourist infrastructure ashore and all the hotels, apartment blocks and self-catering villas built around the coast and islands, yachting in the Mediterranean has had little impact on the environment. Nevertheless in the last few decades the increasing numbers of yachts have started to impact on the environment in a number of ways. The increase in motor boats, large and small, has resulted in a significant amount of hydrocarbon pollution, as well as noise pollution and coastline damage from the wash of motorboats (sailing boats produce little wash).

The habitats of various species including some seabirds and the Mediterranean monk seal have suffered from the intrusion of more boats (particularly rigid inflatable boats and small hire boats) into what were relatively isolated coastlines. In enclosed bays yachts pumping out toilets have caused some problems and a number of countries including Spain and Turkey require that yachts have holding tanks and only pump out black water (toilet effluent) at least three miles off the coast. It is likely other countries will introduce similar regulations conforming to MARPOL (Marine Pollution Convention 1973-8) regulations.

The yachtsman can expect more stringent regulations in the future to protect the marine environment. Several countries, in particular Italy, have established marine reserves which are often around the comparatively unspoilt coasts of small islands. There are restrictions on yacht navigation within these areas, and these are likely to be expanded throughout other countries. Any thinking yachtsman can only applaud measures which keep the waters we sail upon unsullied by our activities.

Rod Heikell has written many books on sailing in the Mediterranean, all published by Imray Laurie Norie & Wilson, including the *Mediterranean Almanac 2007-8, Mediterranean Cruising Handbook, Pilots to: Mediterranean France and Corsica, Turkish Waters and Cyprus, Italian Waters, Greek Waters* and *Cruising companions to the Ionian, West Aegean and East Aegean.*

Facing page. Sailing in the Mediterranean is usually a relaxed, low-key, family affair

GARMIN

Argyronisos, between north Evvoia and the mainland, 40 minutes from Athens by helicopter, can be rented and is also for sale, at a price to be disclosed on request

Private ownership of islands in the Mediterranean
Dr Farhad Vladi looks at today's private island market in the Mediterranean and its future prospects

Buying a private piece of paradise

Few people can resist the idea of owning a private island, far from the stresses of the modern world. An island feels infinite and the surrounding water creates a natural boundary that gives an impression of freedom and security that isn't found anywhere on the mainland.

During three decades in the island business, I have had the opportunity of meeting island owners with the most varying personalities. But, irrespective of their backgrounds or achievements, they are all individuals who love nature and are determined to find it. For them, an island is the one place that catches the spirit of solitude, tranquillity and privacy that they seek. The Greek shipping magnate, Aristotle Onassis, was not the first person to own an island hideaway (Skorpios, a gem in the Ionian Sea), but he was the first to instil into public consciousness the concept of the private island as the ultimate retreat. Other well-known island owners have included Marlon Brando, Malcolm Forbes, Charles Heidsieck, Rudolf Nureyev, Baron Rothschild, the Shah of Iran and John Wayne. Today's high profile island owners include Bjorn Borg, Richard Branson, Nicolas Cage, Tony Curtis, Diana Ross, Brooke Shields and Ted Turner.

The practicalities

While an island is just a piece of real estate surrounded by water, there are huge differences in terms of practicalities and use. Some infrastructure difficulties have been overcome in recent years, with the development of electricity generating systems, water purification, comfortable prefabricated houses, new road building techniques and satellite communications. While people have different views on such things as good access and climate, one factor which is of vital importance to everyone is the availability of emergency medical services, which must be no more than 90 minutes from an island by boat, plane or helicopter.

Islands are usually private resorts for holidays. Normally people buy a holiday home where they are familiar with the social and natural environment, but these parameters can be very different on an island. I would strongly recommend that anyone seeking to buy a private island first rents one, either the one he is looking to purchase or one nearby.

Buying an island is about making compromises, as the perfect island for everyone doesn't exist.

Buying an island

The following checklist of twelve vital criteria is designed to help buyers evaluate a private island and decide which points they are willing to compromise on. All criteria are usually negotiable, with the exception of the availability of medical services nearby, which is essential!

When rating islands, we assign each of the following twelve checkpoints a score of two points, making a maximum of 24 points. If an island scores 16 points, then we consider it to be habitable.

1. Access Is the island accessible? For example, harbour, anchorage and/or landing.
2. Building Permit What is the availability of building permits, the size of house and type of development that is permitted?
3. Climate Thoroughly investigate the weather and climatic conditions, and whether they appeal to you.
4. Fauna Can you live with (or eradicate) the indigenous wildlife on the island, e.g. mosquitoes, etc?
5. Flora Make a note of the island's trees, shrubs and plants, and their pros and cons.
6. Host Country What is the social environment and acceptance of foreign ownership of the island?
7. Infrastructure Does the island have water, sewage, electricity, telephone and internet services (or can they be provided)?
8. Medical Emergency medical services **must** be available by boat or air within 90 minutes of an island.
9. Seller Will you be dealing with the owner directly, a licensed agent or a third party?

Skorpios, near Lefkada in the Ionian Islands, is the best known private island in the Mediterranean, having once belonged to the shipowner Aristotle Onassis

Santo Stefano, near Ventotene in the Pontine Islands, is for sale at €20 million which includes 16 houses and a church, but not including the large 18th century prison

(ALL PHOTOS: WWW.VLADI-PRIVATE-ISLANDS.DE)

10. *Surroundings* What is the immediate neighbourhood like – amenities, services and crime level?
11. The Title Must be freehold and unencumbered.
12. Value (Investment) Is the market locally-driven and/or driven by foreign investors?

The island market

As with all commodities, supply and demand determine the price for private islands, but there is one aspect which is different from other property purchases, which is the intangible value. An island can have a beauty or an emotional 'value' which often reminds me of the art market, where paintings can also be emotional assets: it is not the quantity of paint or size of canvas that determines the price of a painting.

Apart from the intangible value, the market for islands is also driven by the availability of surplus cash. When the stock market is strong, the island market also flourishes. When people have surplus cash, the decision making process speeds up: instant decisions can be made with instantly available cash, and vendors are persuaded to sell by rising prices. However, when there is a stock market crash or a recession, prices in the island market can fall sharply, as it is easier to sell a holiday home than a house in which your family is living (few people live permanently on an island).

Until recently, islands have been cheaper than mainland properties, due to the infrastructure disadvantage. That disadvantage has been eroded by innovations such as satellite communications, water makers and desalination plants; solar and renewable energies; and wind generators – and island prices have balanced out with those for mainland properties. More recently we have seen island prices outstrip those of mainland properties, especially in places such as the Mediterranean, where islands are unique, there are no infrastructure disadvantages and a high emotional value is placed on an island's beauty. On the other hand, in countries where islands are plentiful, such as Sweden, Norway, Finland and Canada, the market is more stable - and it is said 'if you can afford a car, you can afford an island'.

Islands in the Mediterranean

The hot spots in the Mediterranean are Spain, France and Italy. Few if any islands are available and they go for almost any price. There are always more buyers than sellers and when owners decide to sell they can, in many cases, simply ask any price they want. There is a ceiling, however, which is the price of a comparable nearby island or islands in other areas. In the final analysis, a Japanese investor, for example, is not too concerned whether an island is in Spain or France, or on the other side of the Atlantic in the Bahamas or Florida. Therefore if a Spanish island is too expensive, the Japanese investor will go for an island in Florida. It must be borne in mind that the European continent has many wealthy people and their demands determine the market.

The only counter force in Europe is the nature conservancy laws. In France, even if you have an island with no building, you are not allowed to build one.

Sa Ferradura, near San Miguel in north Ibiza, with luxury facilities including home entertainment theatre and pool with waterfall, has just been sold for €33 million

Kistak, near Bodrum, is one of very few private islands in Turkey and is on offer for €5 million to include one house and building permission granted to build two more

If there is a building on a Spanish island, the owner might get a permit to renovate it, but not to enlarge it. Therefore there are limits. The island market in Greece is completely different and, since Onassis and Stavros Niarchos bought their islands, island owners have believed that any island is worth millions of Euros, irrespective of its size. For decades, unrealistic prices have been asked, but there has been very little movement, what with the difficulty of obtaining building permits, drought and infrastructure disadvantages. I have seldom seen or heard of realistic prices in Greece, but I hope this will change in the future.

Other areas in the Mediterranean, such as Croatia and the African coast, are emerging markets. The African coast does not have too many islands, while Croatia has many beautiful ones, but it may be a little premature to talk about them. Currently, the title system is in need of a complete overhaul and professionals are biding their time, despite the fact that some islands have been sold for substantial prices. The Adriatic will, in my opinion, be the focal point of island buyers in the future.

Dr Farhad Vladi is President of Vladi Private Islands in Hamburg, which he founded in 1975 and is the author of *Luxury Private Islands* (teNeues 2006).

Some private islands in the Mediterranean

Spain
Aire
Aucanada
Bleda Gorra
Bleda Plana
Bosque
Colom
Conejera (Eivissa)
Conills
Escull Esparlar
Escull Vermell
Espalmador
Espardell
Espartar
Formentor
Frares
Gran d'Addaia
Llarga
Malgrats
Na Bosc
Petita d'Addaia
Porros
Ravells
Redona
Sa Porrassa
Sargantana
Ses Mones
Ses Rates
Soller
Tagomago
Vedra
Vedranell

France
Bendor
Camaro Canto
Cavallo
Cornuta
Elbu
Embiez
Farina
Fautea
Finocchiarola
Forana
Grain de sable
Maestro Maria
Mezzana
Palazzu
Piana (Ajaccio)
Piana (Cerbicale)
Piana (Lavezzi)
Pietricaggiosa
Port
Saint Honorat
San Bainsu
San Ciprianu
Sulana
Terra

Italy
Capo Passero
Galli
Gallinara
Gavi
Santa Maria
S Stefano (Ponziane)

Croatia
Daksa
Gustac (Zut)
Obonjan
Oruda
Palacol

Greece
Agios Athanasios
Agios Georgios
Agios Thomas
Alatas
Ano Antikeri
Anydros
Apaso
Argyronisi
Arkoudi
Aspronisi
Atokos
Dokos
Drakonera
Glaronisi
Gravari
Kalogiros
Kardiotissa
Karlonisi
Kato Antikeri/Drima
Koronida/Koilada
Kythros
Lambrinos
Lygia/Pera Pigadi
Madouri
Makri
Makropoula
Modi
Oxia
Patroklou
Petalas
Pistros
Pontikos
Praso
Provatio
Revmatonisi
Rinia
Skorpidi
Skorpios
Skyropoula
Sofia
Soros
Spalathro
Sparti
Spetsopoula
Tsakalonisi
Velopoula/Parapola

Turkey
Domuz
Garip
Kasikada
Kistak

Tunisia
Gattaya el Baharia

The Islands

This section has a page for each of the 218 islands in the Mediterranean which offer some form of accommodation. The variety is enormous and we have attempted to assemble, as briefly as possible, a wide range of data to enable readers to form a judgement about each island.

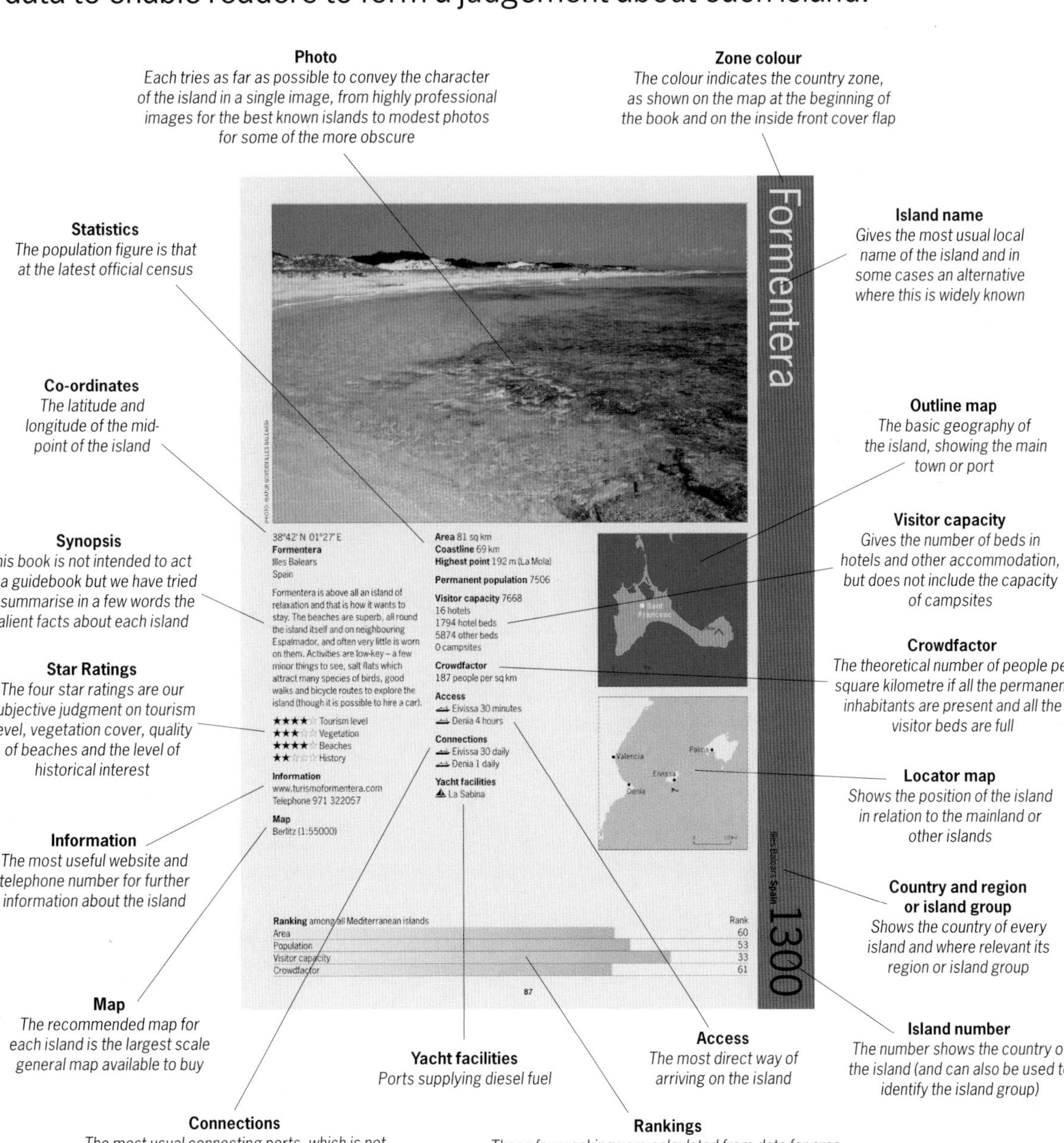

Photo
Each tries as far as possible to convey the character of the island in a single image, from highly professional images for the best known islands to modest photos for some of the more obscure
Zone colour
The colour indicates the country zone, as shown on the map at the beginning of the book and on the inside front cover flap
Statistics
The population figure is that at the latest official census
Island name
Gives the most usual local name of the island and in some cases an alternative where this is widely known
Co-ordinates
The latitude and longitude of the mid-point of the island
Outline map
The basic geography of the island, showing the main town or port
Synopsis
This book is not intended to act
s a guidebook but we have tried
 summarise in a few words the
salient facts about each island
Visitor capacity
Gives the number of beds in hotels and other accommodation, but does not include the capacity of campsites
Star Ratings
The four star ratings are our
ubjective judgment on tourism
evel, vegetation cover, quality
of beaches and the level of historical interest
Crowdfactor
The theoretical number of people per square kilometre if all the permanent inhabitants are present and all the visitor beds are full
Locator map
Shows the position of the island in relation to the mainland or other islands
Information
The most useful website and telephone number for further information about the island
Country and region or island group
Shows the country of every island and where relevant its region or island group
Map
The recommended map for each island is the largest scale general map available to buy
Island number
The number shows the country of the island (and can also be used to identify the island group)
Yacht facilities
Ports supplying diesel fuel
Access
The most direct way of arriving on the island
Connections
The most usual connecting ports, which is not intended to be a definitive list. One of the joys of the Mediterranean islands is that it is often possible to get almost anywhere if you have the ingenuity and patience
Rankings
These four rankings are calculated from data for area, population, visitor capacity and Crowdfactor. The resulting rank (number) is where an island ranks in relation to all other Mediterranean islands
Formentera
38°42' N 01°27' E
Formentera
Illes Balears
Spain
Formentera is above all an island of relaxation and that is how it wants to stay. The beaches are superb, all round the island itself and on neighbouring Espalmador, and often very little is worn on them. Activities are low-key – a few minor things to see, salt flats which attract many species of birds, good walks and bicycle routes to explore the island (though it is possible to hire a car).
Tourism level
Vegetation
Beaches
History
Information
www.turismoformentera.com
Telephone 971 322057
Map
Berlitz (1:55000)
Area 81 sq km
Coastline 69 km
Highest point 192 m (La Mola)
Permanent population 7506
Visitor capacity 7668
16 hotels
1794 hotel beds
5874 other beds
0 campsites
Crowdfactor
187 people per sq km
Access
Eivissa 30 minutes
Denia 4 hours
Connections
Eivissa 30 daily
Denia 1 daily
Yacht facilities
La Sabina
Valencia
Palma
Eivissa
Denia
Ranking among all Mediterranean islands
Rank
Area 60
Population 53
Visitor capacity 33
Crowdfactor 61
87
Illes Balears Spain
1300

Eivissa (Ibiza)

BENIRRAS (PHOTO: GOVERN DE LES ILLES BALEARS IBATUR ANTONIO GARRIDO)

San Antoni
Eivissa
0
10km

Valencia
Palma
Denia
Alicante
0
100km

39°03′ N 01°32′ E
Eivissa (Ibiza)
Illes Balears
Spain

Eivissa has a lovely town, dominated by the fortress that encloses the old town with its cathedral, bishop's palace and castle, and flanked by the quarter of Sa Penya with its picturesque narrow streets. The interior of the island is rewarding, with some fine old villages and lovely walks along mountain ridges giving views over the whole island and over to Formentera, Mallorca and the mainland. Eivissa is widely thought to be the best island for nightlife in the Mediterranean.

★★★★★ Tourism level
★★★★☆ Vegetation
★★★★☆ Beaches
★★★☆☆ History

Information
www.eivissa.es
Telephone 971 301900

Map
Berlitz (1:55000)

Area 568 sq km
Coastline 210 km
Highest point 476 m (Sa Talaia)

Permanent population 111107

Visitor capacity 79864
120 hotels
37152 hotel beds
42712 other beds
1 campsite

Crowdfactor
335 people per sq km

Access
✈ Eivissa
⛴ Denia, Palma 2 hours
⛴ Valencia, Alicante 3 hours

Connections
⛴ Denia 7 daily
⛴ Palma 3 daily
⛴ Barcelona 2 daily
⛴ Valencia, Alicante 1 daily

Yacht facilities
⛵ Eivissa, S Antonio, S Eulalia

1200 **Spain** Illes Balears

Ranking among all Mediterranean islands	Rank
Area	14
Population	11
Visitor capacity	6
Crowdfactor	35

38°42′ N 01°27′ E
Formentera
Illes Balears
Spain

Formentera is above all an island of relaxation and that is how it wants to stay. The beaches are superb, all round the island itself and on neighbouring Espalmador, and often very little is worn on them. Activities are low-key – a few minor things to see, salt flats which attract many species of birds, good walks and bicycle routes to explore the island (though it is possible to hire a car).

★★★★☆ Tourism level
★★★☆☆ Vegetation
★★★★☆ Beaches
★★☆☆☆ History

Information
www.turismoformentera.com
Telephone 971 322057

Map
Berlitz (1:55000)

Area 81 sq km
Coastline 69 km
Highest point 192 m (La Mola)

Permanent population 7506

Visitor capacity 7668
16 hotels
1794 hotel beds
5874 other beds
0 campsites

Crowdfactor
187 people per sq km

Access
Eivissa 30 minutes
Denia 4 hours

Connections
Eivissa 30 daily
Denia 1 daily

Yacht facilities
La Sabina

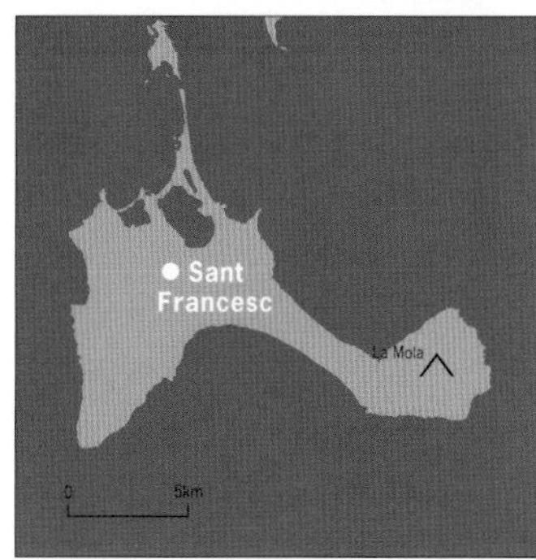
Sant Francesc
La Mola
0
5km

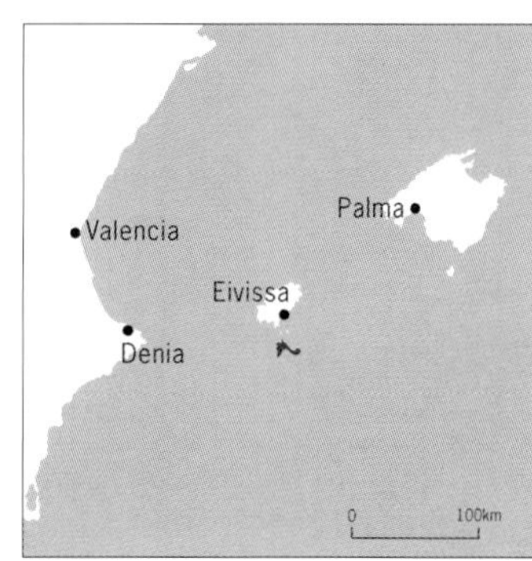
Valencia
Palma
Eivissa
Denia
0
100km

Ranking among all Mediterranean islands

	Rank
Area	60
Population	53
Visitor capacity	33
Crowdfactor	61

Puig Mayor
Palma
0
25km

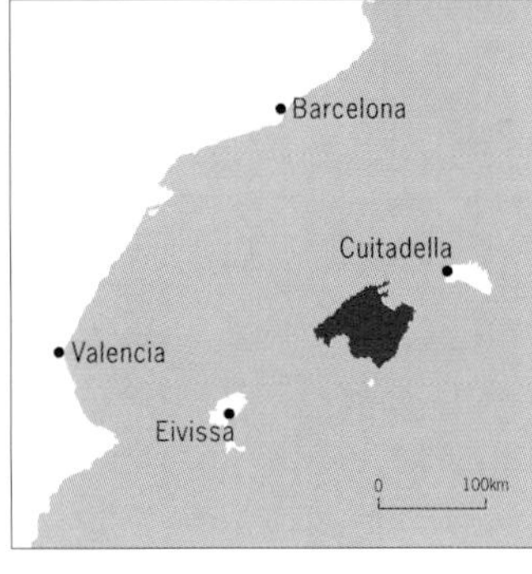
Barcelona
Cuitadella
Valencia
Eivissa
0
100km

39°34' N 02°39' E
Mallorca
Illes Balears
Spain

Mallorca is an island of magnificent scenery, particularly in the Sierra del Norte and the drive from Andratx through Valldemosa, Deya, Soller (including the branch down to Sa Calobra) and then through Pollensa to Formentor is not to be missed. The other principal sights are the gothic cathedral and fine old residences of Palma, the east coast caves of Drach, Hams and Arta and the talayots (prehistoric stone towers) of Capicorp Vey.

★★★★★ Tourism level
★★★★☆ Vegetation
★★★★☆ Beaches
★★★☆☆ History

Information
www.infomallorca.net
Telephone 971 939393

Map
Reise-Know-How (1:80000)

Area 3620 sq km
Coastline 554 km
Highest point 1445 m (Puig Mayor)

Permanent population 777821

Visitor capacity 286408
740 hotels
190042 hotel beds
96366 other beds
0 campsites

Crowdfactor
293 people per sq km

Access
Palma
Cuidadella 1 hour
Eivissa 2 hours
Valencia, Barcelona 4 hours

Connections
Ciutadella, Eivissa, Valencia 3 daily
Barcelona 4 daily

Yacht facilities
19 ports

Ranking among all Mediterranean islands	Rank
Area	7
Population	4
Visitor capacity	1
Crowdfactor	38

Menorca

39°53' N 04°14' E
Menorca
Illes Balears
Spain

An island of many beautiful beaches and two fine towns. The capital Mao has a magnificent natural harbour and the former capital Ciutadella has a picturesque port. There is a splendid view of the whole island from Monte Toro and the island has an abundance of prehistoric remains. The Naveta Es Tudons with its burial chambers is the oldest building anywhere in Spain dating back some 3500 years.

★★★★☆ Tourism level
★★★☆☆ Vegetation
★★★★☆ Beaches
★★★☆☆ History

Information
www.e-menorca.org
Telephone 971 363790

Map
Kompass (1:50000)

Area 693 sq km
Coastline 285 km
Highest point 357 m (Monte Toro)

Permanent population 86697

Visitor capacity 49172
100 hotels
23014 hotel beds
26158 other beds
2 campsites

Crowdfactor
195 people per sq km

Access
Mahon (air)
Alcudia 1 hour (fast ferry)
Barcelona 4 hours (fast ferry)
Barcelona 7 hours (ferry)

Connections
Alcudia 3 daily (fast ferry)
Barcelona 1 daily (fast ferry)
Barcelona 2 daily (ferry)

Yacht facilities
Mahon, Cuidadella, Tamarinda

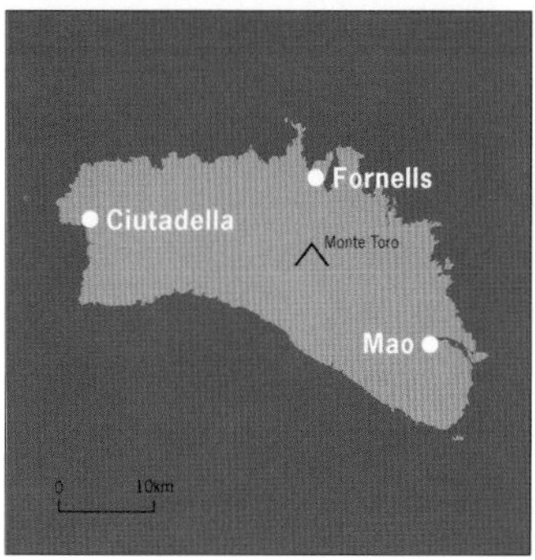
Fornells
Ciutadella
Monte Toro
Mao
0 10km

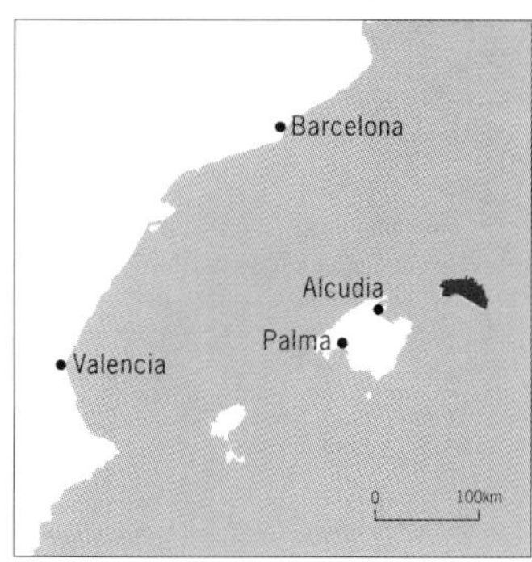
Barcelona
Alcudia
Palma
Valencia
0 100km

Illes Balears **Spain** 1100

Ranking among all Mediterranean islands

	Rank
Area	12
Population	14
Visitor capacity	10
Crowdfactor	59

Nueva Tabarca

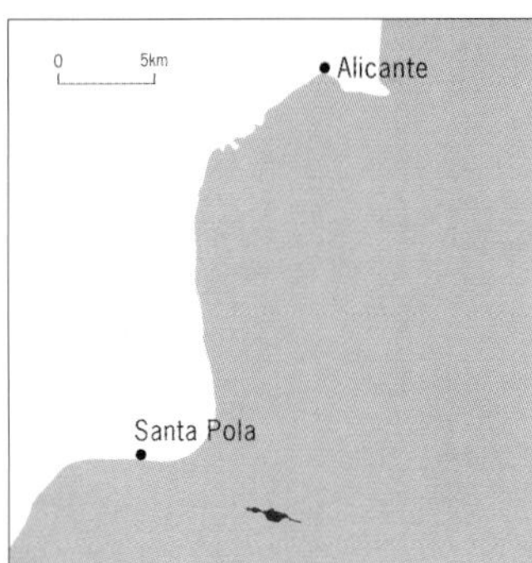
0
5km
Alicante
Santa Pola

38°09' N 00°28' W
Nueva Tabarca
Spain

The island has been a Protected Marine Reserve for the last 20 years, which prohibits the collection of any flora or fauna, scuba diving or any motorised sport. San Pedro y San Pablo at the western end of the island is a fortified 18th century walled village with three gates in its walls. The only sandy beach is at the isthmus which links the village to the larger eastern part of the island. The island gets crowded with day trippers in summer.

★★★☆☆ Tourism level
★★☆☆☆ Vegetation
★★☆☆☆ Beaches
★★★☆☆ History

Information
Telephone 965 230160
676 486427

Map
None

Area 0.43 sq km
Coastline 4 km
Highest point 14 m (Tabarca)

Permanent population 66

Visitor capacity 63
2 hotels
40 hotel beds
23 other beds
0 campsites

Crowdfactor
300 people per sq km

Access
Santa Pola 30 minutes
Alicante 60 minutes

Connections
Santa Pola 10 daily
Alicante 2 daily

Yacht facilities
no fuel

Ranking among all Mediterranean islands	Rank
Area	49
Population	17
Visitor capacity	16
Crowdfactor	3

1400 Spain

Bendor

(PHOTO: JOHN HENRY WALZL)

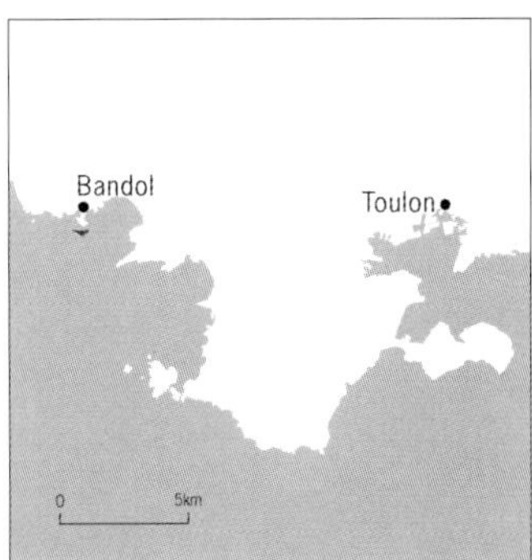
Bandol
Toulon
0
5km

43°07' N 05°44' E
Bendor
France

This small island still has room for a reasonably large wooded area. The hotel is in two main buildings and also has converted cottages with their own private gardens. Other attractions include a wine and spirits museum, art gallery, diving club, tennis courts and a port said to be the smallest in the Mediterranean.

★★★★☆ Tourism level
★★★☆☆ Vegetation
★★★☆☆ Beaches
★★☆☆☆ History

Information
www.bendor.com
Telephone 494 055494

Map
IGN (1:25000)

Area 0.08 sq km
Coastline 1.5 km
Highest point 17 m

Permanent population 0

Visitor capacity 140
1 hotel
140 hotel beds
0 other beds
0 campsites

Crowdfactor
1750 people per sq km

Access
Bandol 10 minutes

Connections
Bandol 30 daily

Yacht facilities
no fuel

2800 France

Ranking among all Mediterranean islands	Rank
Area	C
Population	C
Visitor capacity	148
Crowdfactor	11

(PHOTO: B A OVERY)

41°55′ N 08°44′ E
Corse (Corsica)
France

By far the least crowded of the large Mediterranean islands, Corsica is a strong contender for the most beautiful island in the Mediterranean, with the Gulf of Porto particularly breathtaking. The Regional Nature Park of Corsica covers 40% of the island and there are nature reserves at Biguglia and the islands of Scandola, Finocchiarola, Cerbicale and Lavezzi. Napoleon looms large in Ajaccio, his birthplace, and the setting of italianate Bonifacio is unforgettable.

★★★☆☆ Tourism level
★★★★☆ Vegetation
★★★★☆ Beaches
★★★☆☆ History

Information
www.visit-corsica.com
Telephone 495 517777

Map
Reise-Know-How (1:135000)
IGN covers the island in 19 sheets at 1:25000

Area 8679 sq km
Coastline 920 km
Highest point 2706 m (Monte Cinto)

Permanent population 260196

Visitor capacity 54000
400 hotels
21000 hotel beds
33000 other beds
189 campsites

Crowdfactor
36 people per sq km

Access
✈ Ajaccio, Bastia, Calvi, Figari
Hydrofoil: Nice 3 hours
Ferry: Santa Teresa Gallura 1 hour
Ferry: Livorno, Piombino 4 hours
Ferry: Nice, Genova 5 hours

Connections
Hydrofoil: Nice 4 daily
Ferry: Nice, Santa Teresa 5 daily
Ferry: Livorno 4 daily
Ferry: Piombino 2 daily
Ferry: Genova 1 daily

Yacht facilities
⛵ 18 ports

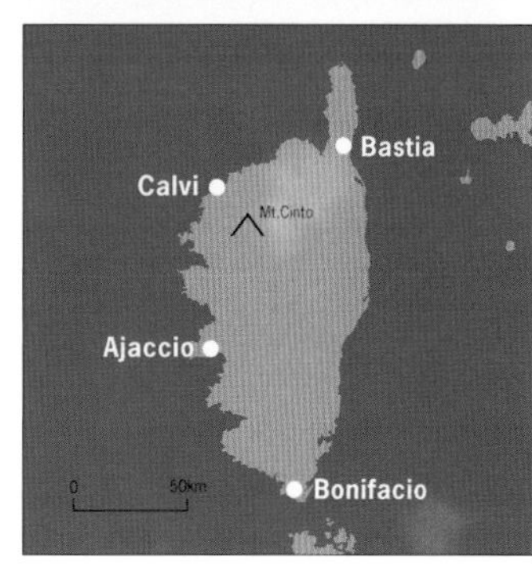
Bastia
Calvi
Mt.Cinto
Ajaccio
Bonifacio
0
50km

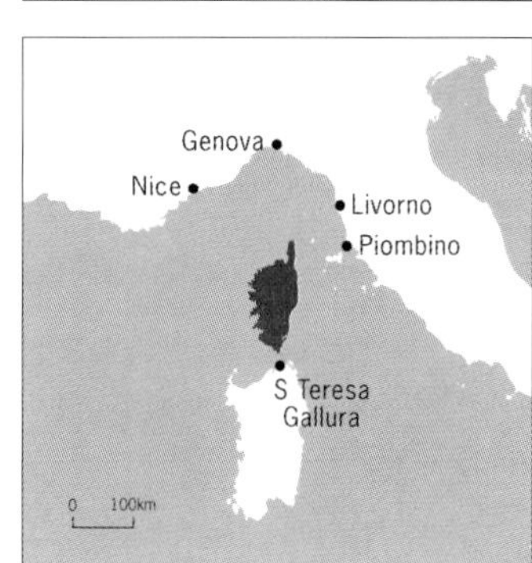
Genova
Nice
Livorno
Piombino
S Teresa Gallura
0
100km

Ranking among all Mediterranean islands

	Rank
Area	4
Population	7
Visitor capacity	9
Crowdfactor	151

Corse (Corsica)

France 2000

Embiez

France

(PHOTO: JOHN HENRY WALZL)

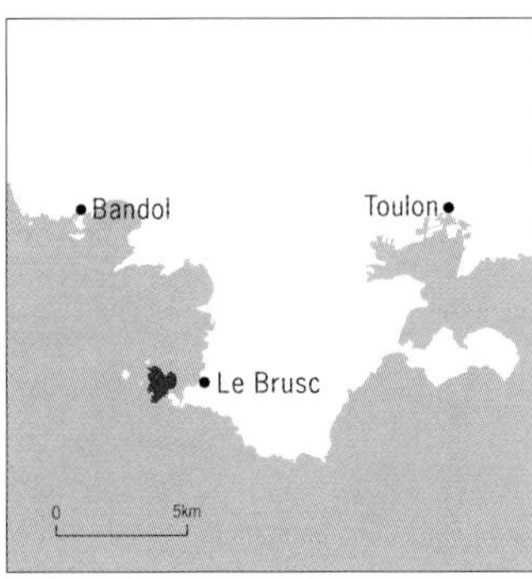
Bandol
Toulon
Le Brusc
0
5km

43°04′ N 05°46′ E
Embiez
France

There are two sides to Embiez, largest of a small archipelago of four islands. The north side of the island has a marina with 750 berths and an oceanographic institute with interesting aquariums and a museum. The southern part of the island has pine woods, a number of small beaches and vineyards producing over 20000 bottles of wine a year. There are 3 different places to stay and 9 places to eat.

★★★★☆ Tourism level
★★★☆☆ Vegetation
★★★☆☆ Beaches
★★☆☆☆ History

Information
www.les-embiez.com
Telephone 494 106610

Map
IGN (1:25000)

Area 0.9 sq km
Coastline 6 km
Highest point 57 m

Permanent population 50

Visitor capacity 580
2 hotels
160 hotel beds
420 other beds
0 campsites

Crowdfactor
700 people per sq km

Access
Le Brusc 10 minutes

Connections
Le Brusc 25 daily

Yacht facilities
St Pierre

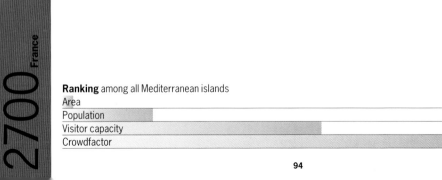

Ranking among all Mediterranean islands	Rank
Area	378
Population	185
Visitor capacity	109
Crowdfactor	18

FRIOUL WITH CHATEAUX D'IF IN THE FOREGROUND (PHOTO: MARSEILLE TOURISME)

43°17' N 05°18' E
Frioul
France

The islands of Ratonneau and Pomegues, which lie just beyond the chateau d'If, are joined by a causeway to form Frioul. The island has over 300 apartments, some of which can sometimes be rented, and the port has a capacity of 600 berths. There is also a holiday centre, which is used by diving clubs and school groups.

★★★★☆ Tourism level
★☆☆☆☆ Vegetation
★★☆☆☆ Beaches
★★☆☆☆ History

Information
www.frioul.net
Telephone 491 590173

Map
IGN (1:25000)

Area 1.84 sq km
Coastline 31 km
Highest point 86 m (Pomegues)

Permanent population 150

Visitor capacity 154
0 hotels
Leisure centre

Crowdfactor
165 people per sq km

Access
Marseille 25 minutes

Connections
Marseille 25 daily

Yacht facilities
Port du Frioul

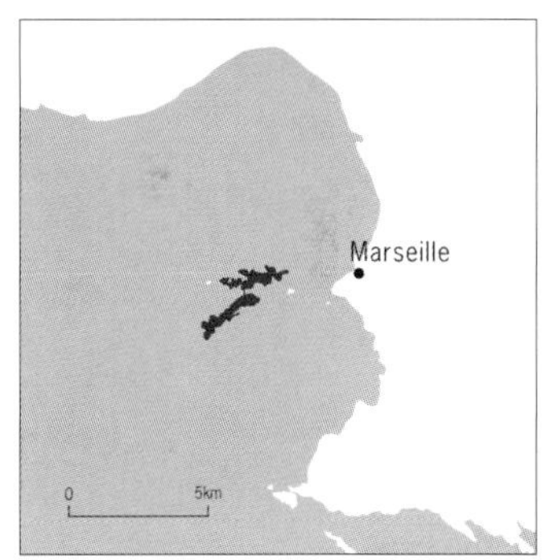
Marseille
0
5km

Ranking among all Mediterranean islands

	Rank
Area	291
Population	162
Visitor capacity	146
Crowdfactor	65

Le Levant

(PHOTO: SYNDICAT D'HELIOPOLIS)

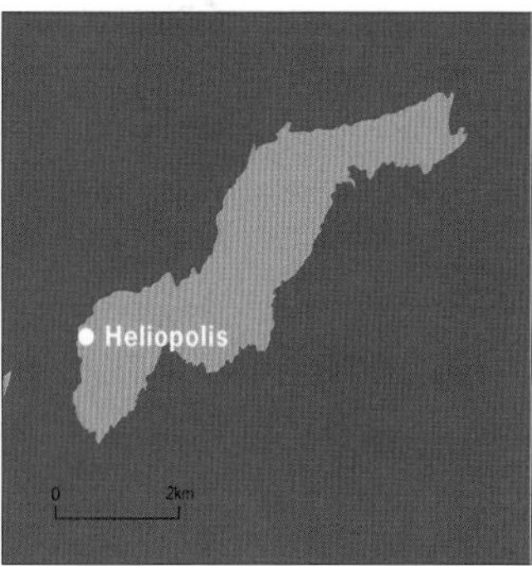
Heliopolis
0
2km

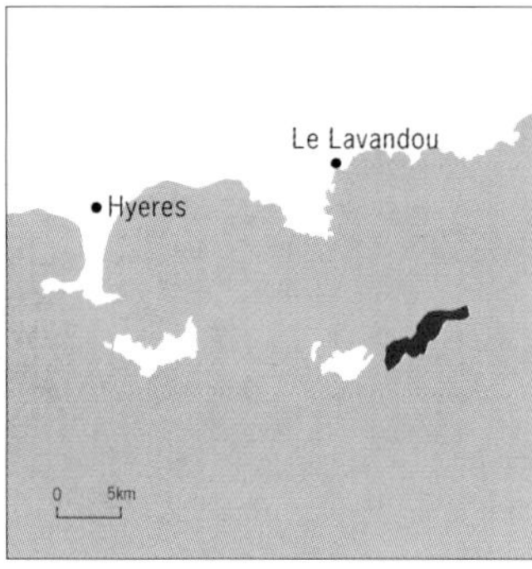
Le Lavandou
Hyeres
0
5km

43°01' N 06°25' E
Le Levant
Iles d'Hyères
France

94% of this lovely island is occupied by the French navy and is not accessible to the public. This leaves only 61 hectares for the naturist area of Heliopolis, which is therefore rather cramped (crowdfactor 1075). The village is relaxed and charming with exotic flora, but the walks around are disappointingly short and the area for bathing is very restricted.

★★★★☆ Tourism level
★★★☆☆ Vegetation
★★☆☆☆ Beaches
★☆☆☆☆ History

Information
www.iledulevant.com
Telephone 494 059352

Map
IGN (1:25000)

Area 9 sq km
Coastline 26 km
Highest point 138 m (Mont des Salins)

Permanent population 186

Visitor capacity 470
6 hotels
205 hotel beds
265 other beds
2 campsites

Crowdfactor
65 people per sq km

Access
Le Lavandou 1 hour

Connections
Le Lavandou 6 daily

Yacht facilities
no fuel

2200 **France** Iles d'Hyeres

Ranking among all Mediterranean islands	Rank
Area	159
Population	155
Visitor capacity	114
Crowdfactor	111

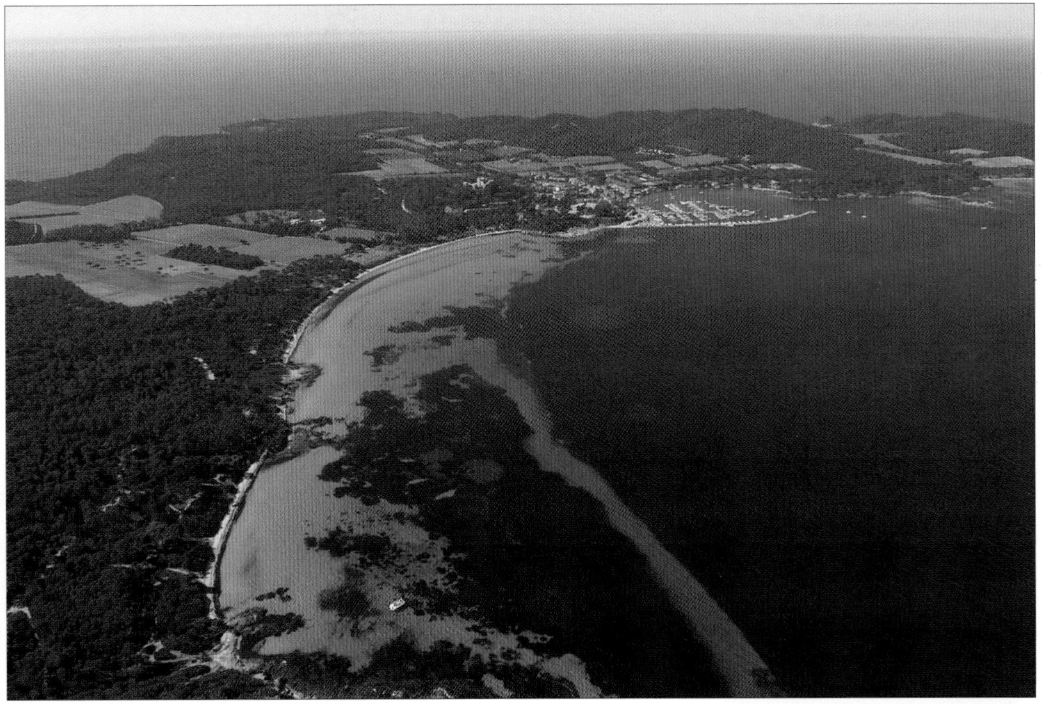

43°00' N 06°11' E
Porquerolles
Iles d'Hyères
France

The largest and liveliest of the Iles d'Hyeres, Porquerolles has a relaxed small town and fertile countryside. With no cars allowed, the island is best explored by bicycle or by a series of lovely walks over to the steep southern side of the island. There are fine views and plenty of secluded bathing places.

★★★★☆ Tourism level
★★★☆☆ Vegetation
★★★☆☆ Beaches
★★☆☆☆ History

Information
www.porquerolles.com
Telephone 494 583376

Map
IGN (1:25000)

Area 12 sq km
Coastline 45 km
Highest point 140 m (Semaphore)

Permanent population 342

Visitor capacity 949
7 hotels
368 hotel beds
581 other beds
0 campsites

Crowdfactor
102 people per sq km

Access
La Tour Fondue 20 minutes

Connections
La Tour Fondue 20 daily

Yacht facilities
Porquerolles

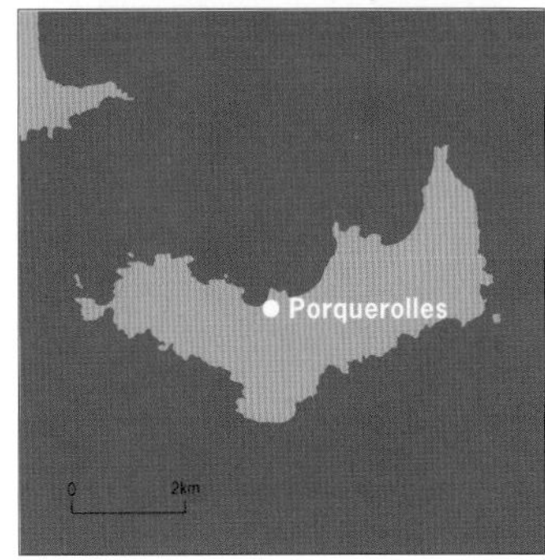
Porquerolles
0
2km

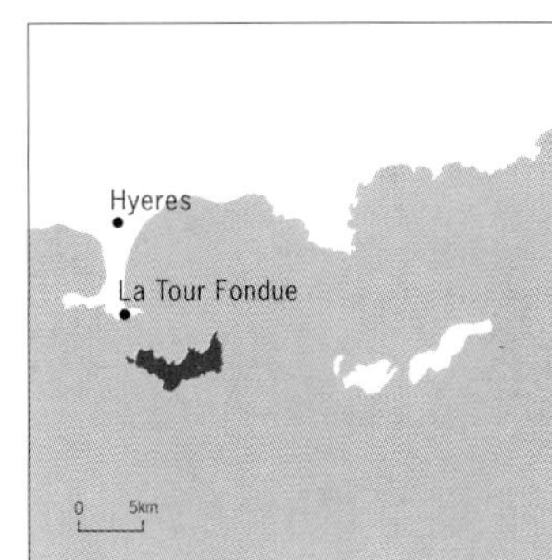
Hyeres
La Tour Fondue
0
5km

Ranking among all Mediterranean islands

	Rank
Area	144
Population	130
Visitor capacity	89
Crowdfactor	86

Port-Cros

(PHOTO: OFFICE DE TOURISME DE HYERES)

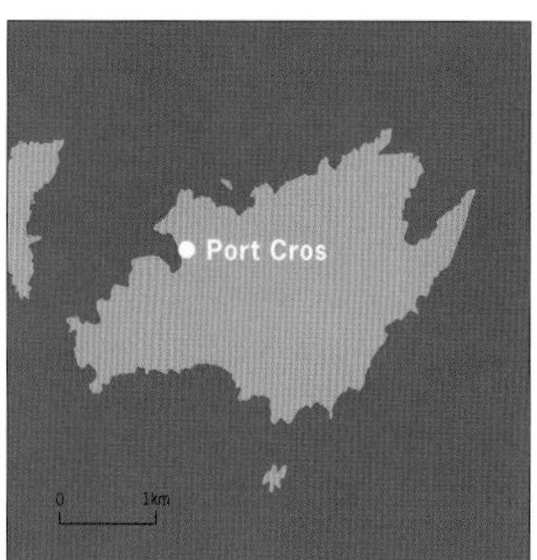
Port Cros
0
1km

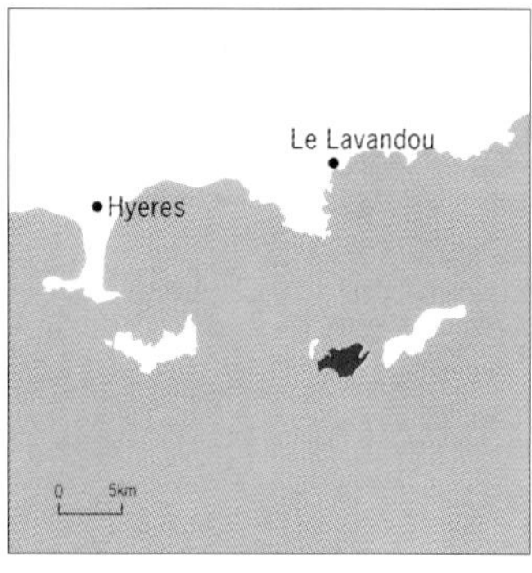
Le Lavandou
Hyeres
0
5km

43°00' N 06°22' E
Port-Cros
Iles d'Hyères
France

The island has been a nature reserve for over 40 years and has more of a tropical feel than perhaps anywhere else in Europe. The island can only be explored on foot, with lovely walks through the luxuriant vegetation teeming with all manner of interesting species.

★★★☆☆ Tourism level
★★★★★ Vegetation
★★☆☆☆ Beaches
★★☆☆☆ History

Information
www.hyeres-tourisme.com
Telephone 494 018450

Map
IGN (1:25000)

Area 6 sq km
Coastline 23 km
Highest point 199 m (La Vigie)

Permanent population 48

Visitor capacity 135
2 hotels
75 hotel beds
60 other beds
0 campsites

Crowdfactor
27 people per sq km

Access
Le Lavandou 1 hour

Connections
Le Lavandou 3 daily

Yacht facilities
no fuel

Ranking among all Mediterranean islands	Ran
Area	18
Population	18
Visitor capacity	15
Crowdfactor	16

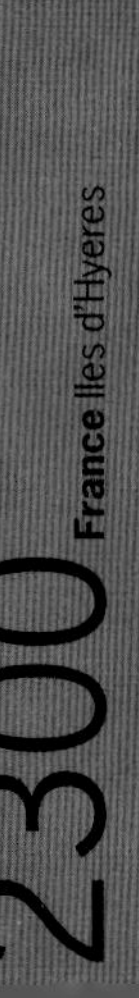
2300 France Iles d'Hyeres

43°30′ N 07°02′ E
Saint Honorat
Iles Lérins
France

This lovely island is owned by the Cistercian abbaye de Lerins. Visitor numbers have been more than halved in recent years to help preserve the tranquillity of the island. Accommodation in the 11th century abbey is confined to people (of either sex) seeking a peaceful retreat for up to a week, during which they will share the life of the monks, rising early, eating in silence and helping with the domestic work of the abbey including the production of its renowned liqueur and wines.

★★☆☆☆ Tourism level
★★★★☆ Vegetation
★★☆☆☆ Beaches
★★★☆☆ History

Information
www.iles-de-lerins.net
Telephone 492 995400

Map
IGN (1:25000)

Area 0.36 sq km
Coastline 3.3 km
Highest point 6 m

Permanent population 57

Visitor capacity 40
0 hotels
monastery

Crowdfactor
269 people per sq km

Access
Cannes 30 minutes

Connections
Cannes 10 daily

Yacht facilities
no fuel

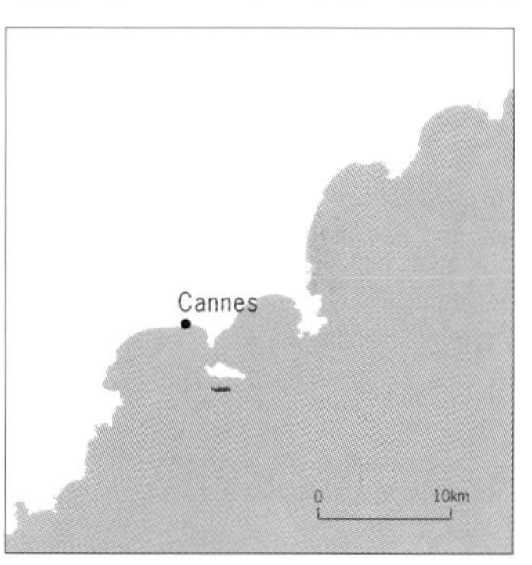
Cannes
0
10km

Ranking among all Mediterranean islands	Rank
Area	534
Population	182
Visitor capacity	179
Crowdfactor	45

Saint Honorat

Iles Lerins **France** 2500

Sainte Marguerite

(PHOTO: PALAIS DES FESTIVALS CANNES)

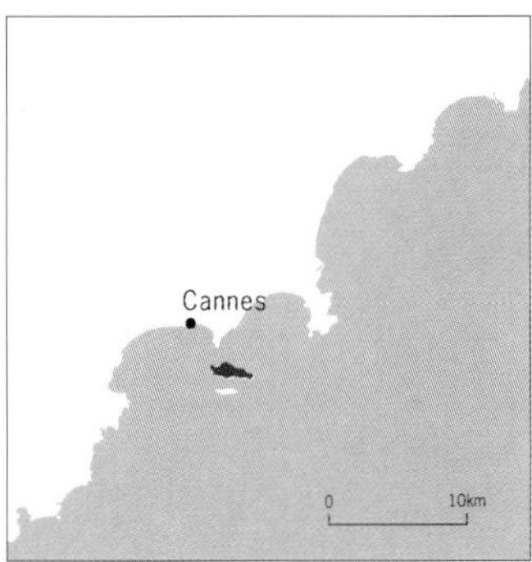
Cannes
0
10km

43°31′ N 07°02′ E
Sainte Marguerite
Iles Lérins
France

This heavily wooded island has lovely walks through allées of wonderfully scented pines and fine eucalyptus. There are many picnic places and two restaurants. The main sights are the Fort Royal, where the Man in the Iron Mask was imprisoned, which now houses a maritime museum, and the Etang du Bateguier with its many migrant bird species.

★★★★☆ Tourism level
★★★★★ Vegetation
★★☆☆☆ Beaches
★★★☆☆ History

Information
www.iles-de-lerins.net
Telephone 493 434924

Map
IGN (1:25000)

Area 2.1 sq km
Coastline 7 km
Highest point 28 m

Permanent population 28

Visitor capacity 200
0 hotels
Leisure centre

Crowdfactor
108 people per sq km

Access
Cannes 15 minutes

Connections
Cannes 12 daily

Yacht facilities
no fuel

Ranking among all Mediterranean islands	Ran
Area	28
Population	19
Visitor capacity	13
Crowdfactor	8

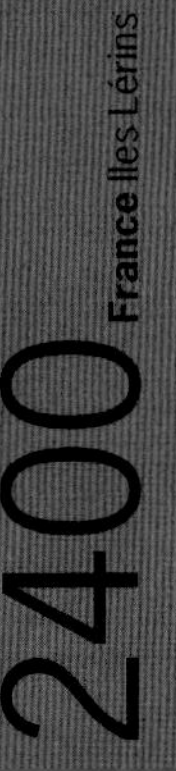
2400
France Iles Lérins

Alicudi

(PHOTO: INGO AURIN)

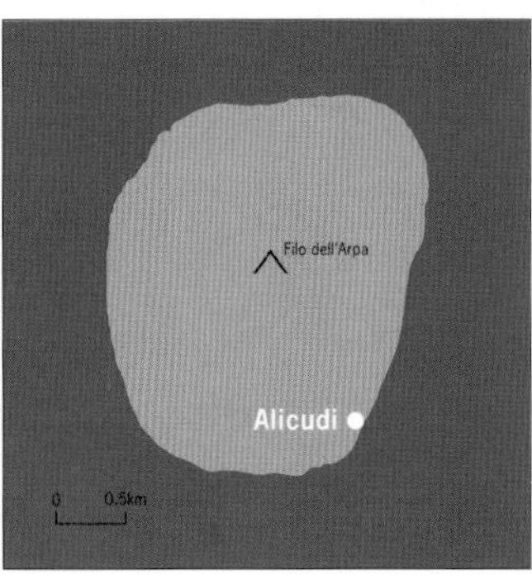
Filo dell'Arpa
Alicudi
0 0.5km

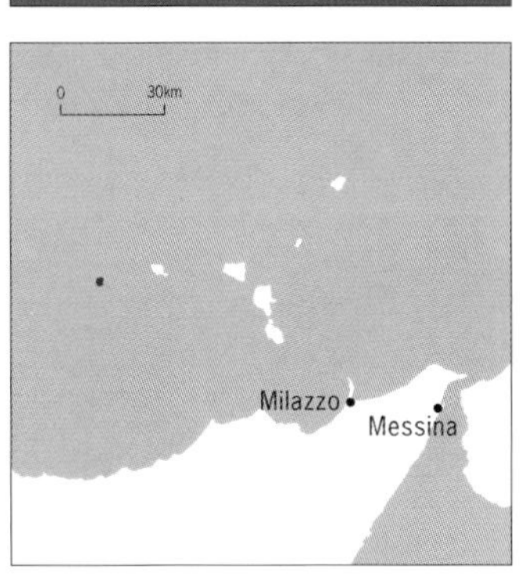
0 30km
Milazzo
Messina

38°32' N 14°21' E
Alicudi
Isole Eolie
Italy

A remote peaceful island of fishermen, with green terraces, heather, sheep and clear waters.

★★☆☆☆ Tourism level
★★☆☆☆ Vegetation
★☆☆☆☆ Beaches
★★☆☆☆ History

Information
www.isolelipari.it
Telephone 090 988 0095

Map
Kompass (1:25000)

Area 5 sq km
Coastline 8 km
Highest point 675 m (Filo dell'Arpa)

Permanent population 105

Visitor capacity 40
1 hotel
24 hotel beds
16 other beds
0 campsites

Crowdfactor
28 people per sq km

Access
Milazzo 3 hours

Connections
Milazzo 2 daily

Yacht facilities
no fuel

3350 **Italy** Isole Eolie

Ranking among all Mediterranean islands	Ran
Area	20
Population	16
Visitor capacity	17
Crowdfactor	15

(PHOTO: ALESSANDRO GALLIONE)

43°02′ N 09°49′ E
Capraia
Arcipelago Toscano
Italy

A quiet pretty hilly island, with good diving and interesting caves such as the Grotta della Foca and the Grotta di Parino. The port is dominated by the impressive fortress of San Giorgio.

★★★☆☆ Tourism level
★★☆☆☆ Vegetation
★☆☆☆☆ Beaches
★★★☆☆ History

Information
www.aptelba.it
Telephone 0565 939737

Map
Multigraphic (1:25000)

Area 19 sq km
Coastline 27 km
Highest point 447 m (Monte Castello)

Permanent population 333

Visitor capacity 343
3 hotels
316 hotel beds
27 other beds
1 campsite

Crowdfactor
35 people per sq km

Access
Livorno 2½ hours

Connections
Livorno daily

Yacht facilities
Porto Capraia

Capraia
0
2km

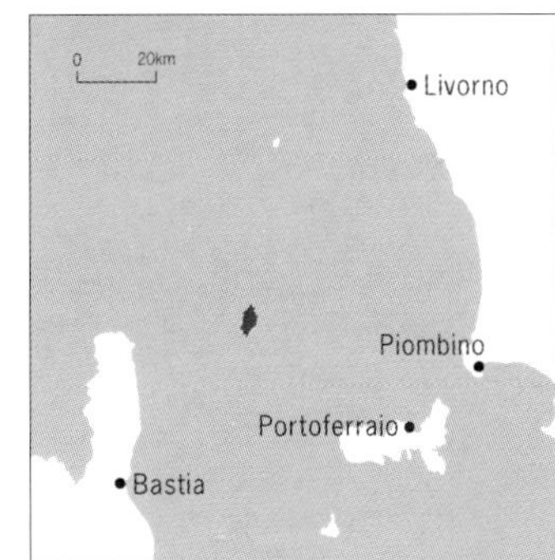
0
20km
Livorno
Piombino
Portoferraio
Bastia

Ranking among all Mediterranean islands

	Rank
Area	118
Population	132
Visitor capacity	125
Crowdfactor	152

CALA ADREANI (PHOTO: PARCO NAZIONALE DELL'ARCIPELAGO DI LA MADDALENA)

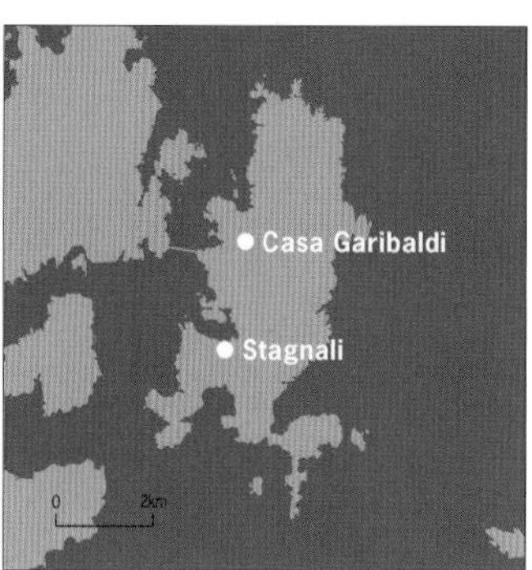
Casa Garibaldi
Stagnali
0
2km

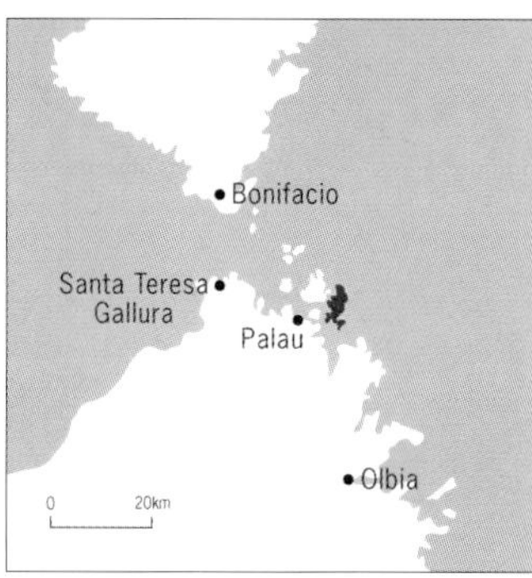
Bonifacio
Santa Teresa
Gallura
Palau
Olbia
0
20km

41°12' N 09°28' E
Caprera
Arcipelago Maddalenino
Italy

A peaceful island mostly covered in pine trees, Caprera is much visited for Garibaldi's house which is now a museum. The island is a nature reserve and has lovely white sand beaches, while much of the terrain is rugged and there are magnificent views from the tops of Teialone and Poggio Stefano.

★★★☆☆ Tourism level
★★★★☆ Vegetation
★★★☆☆ Beaches
★★★☆☆ History

Information
www.lamaddalena.it
Telephone 0789 892080

Map
FMB (1:25000)

Area 15 sq km
Coastline 45 km
Highest point 212 m (Teialone)

Permanent population 77

Visitor capacity 1384
0 hotels
0 hotel beds
1384 other beds (holiday centre)
0 campsites

Crowdfactor
92 people per sq km

Access
Bridge to Maddalena

Yacht facilities
⛵ no fuel

Ranking among all Mediterranean islands	Rank
Area	130
Population	177
Visitor capacity	73
Crowdfactor	96

(PHOTO: AZIENDA TURISMO CAPRI)

40°33′ N 14°14′ E
Capri
Italy

Steep-sided Capri, though crowded mainly by day-trippers, could never lose its beauty. The walks that radiate from the small town, filled with boutiques and restaurants, pass beautifully kept gardens and afford some of the most memorable views in the Mediterranean. Famous sights include the imperial Villa Jovis, the Gardens of Augustus, the blue grotto, the natural arch and the Villa San Michele.

★★★★★ Tourism level
★★★★☆ Vegetation
★☆☆☆☆ Beaches
★★★★☆ History

Information
www.capritourism.com
Telephone 081 837 0686

Map
DeAgostini (1:18000)

Area 10 sq km
Coastline 16 km
Highest point 589 m (M Solaro)

Permanent population 12919

Visitor capacity 3824
64 hotels
3489 hotel beds
335 other beds
0 campsites

Crowdfactor
1622 people per sq km

Access
Sorrento 20 minutes
Napoli 40 minutes
Sorrento 50 minutes
Napoli 1½ hours
Napoli 20 minutes

Connections
Napoli 8 daily
Sorrento 4 daily
Napoli 6 daily
Sorrento 5 daily

Yacht facilities
Marina Grande

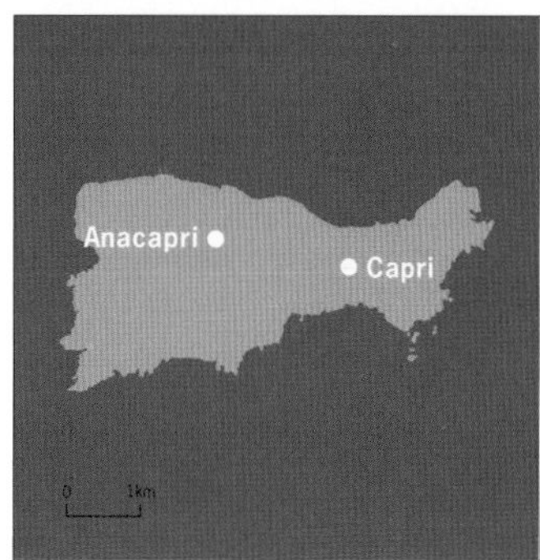
Anacapri
Capri
0
1km

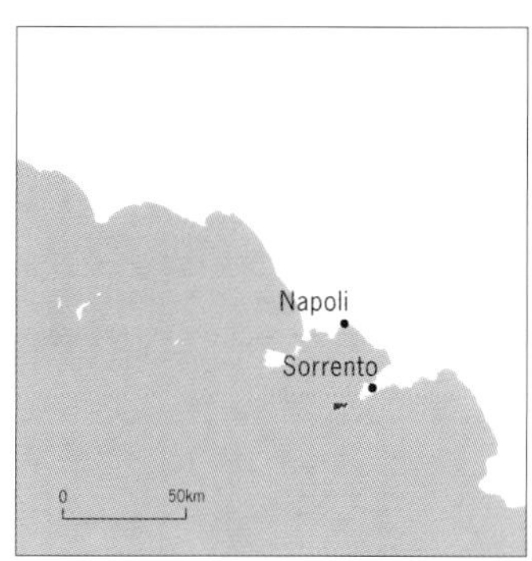
Napoli
Sorrento
0
50km

Ranking among all Mediterranean islands

	Rank
Area	156
Population	35
Visitor capacity	46
Crowdfactor	14

(PHOTO: FOTOTECA ENIT DEAGOSTINI)

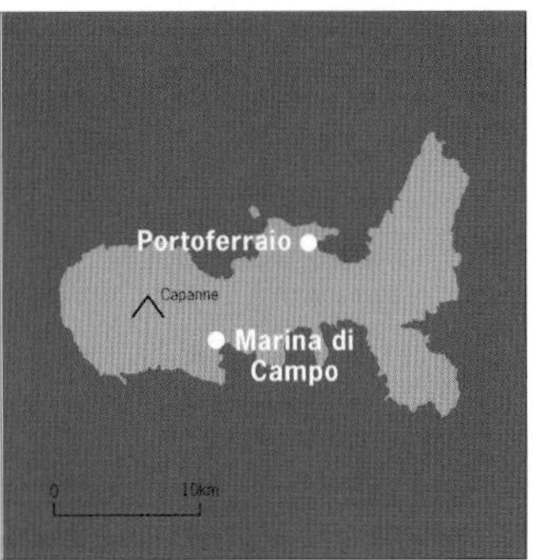
Portoferraio
Capanne
Marina di
Campo
0
10km

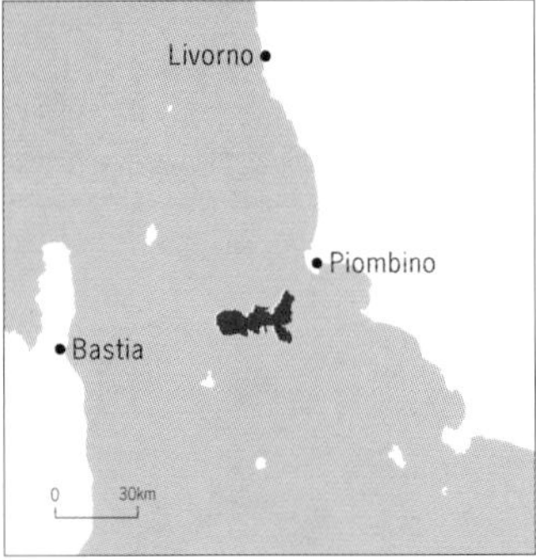
Livorno
Piombino
Bastia
0
30km

42°49′ N 10°19′ E
Elba
Arcipelago Toscano
Italy

Italy's third largest island attracts a lot of visitors, probably more than 2 million a year including day-trippers. The result is that it is difficult to get away from the crowds in summer, even though the island has many beaches. The most rewarding excursion is to take the cable-car to the top of Monte Capanne and enjoy a terrific view of the Tuscan archipelago, Corsica and the mainland. The west coast is the loveliest and the east has eerie iron ore deposits. The small airport serves Pisa, Milan, Switzerland and Germany.

★★★★★ Tourism level
★★★☆☆ Vegetation
★★★☆☆ Beaches
★★★☆☆ History

Information
www.aptelba.it
Telephone 0565 939727

Map
Multigraphic (1:25000)

Area 223 sq km
Coastline 147 km
Highest point 1018 m (Capanne)

Permanent population 24988

Visitor capacity 22181
201 hotels
15744 hotel beds
6437 other beds
27 campsites

Crowdfactor
211 people per sq km

Access
⛴ Piombino 50 minutes

Connections
⛴ Piombino 14 daily

Yacht facilities
⛵ 7 ports

Ranking among all Mediterranean islands	Rank
Area	35
Population	23
Visitor capacity	19
Crowdfactor	55

Favignana

CALA ROSSA (PHOTO: APT TRAPANI ANTONIO NOTO)

37°56′ N 12°20′ E
Favignana
Egadi
Italy

Favignana is probably best known for the mattanza, the annual slaughter of migrating tunny fish in May and June. Easily the most visited of the Egadi islands, this wild island appears rather unkempt and the many old tufa quarries add to this impression. The best natural features are the Grotta del Uccerie and the Faraglione and the medieval fortresses of Santa Caterina and San Giacomo are impressive too but are not open to the public.

★★★★☆ Tourism level
★★☆☆☆ Vegetation
★★☆☆☆ Beaches
★★☆☆☆ History

Information
www.egadiweb.it
Telephone 0923 545511

Map
Proloco (1:12000)

Area 19 sq km
Coastline 33 km
Highest point 314 m (Santa Caterina)

Permanent population 3176

Visitor capacity 1484
7 hotels
1085 hotel beds
399 other beds
3 campsites

Crowdfactor
233 people per sq km

Access
Trapani 20 minutes
Marsala 40 minutes

Connections
Trapani, Marsala 5 daily

Yacht facilities
Favignana

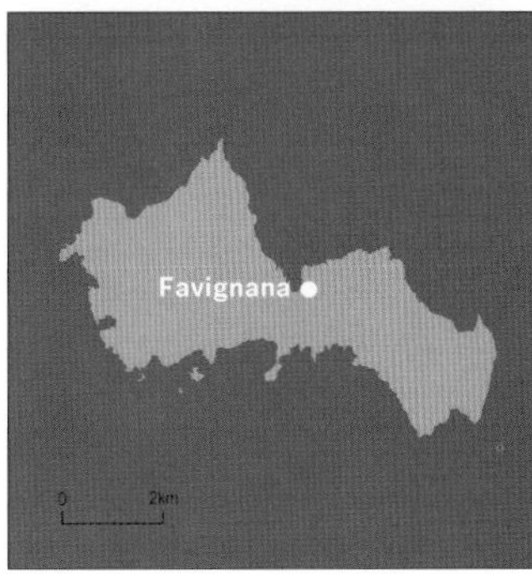
Favignana
0
2km

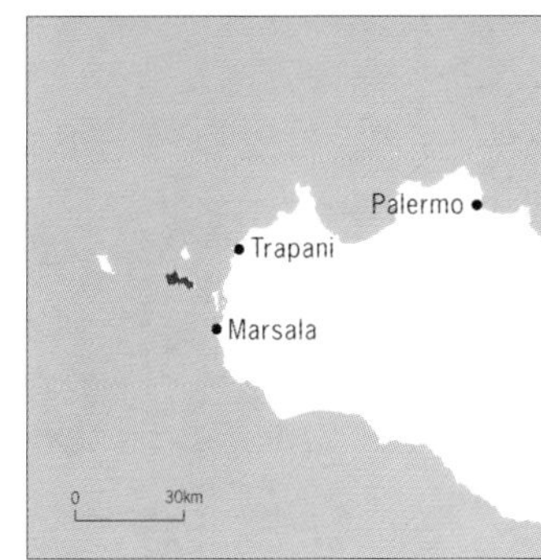
Palermo
Trapani
Marsala
0
30km

Ranking among all Mediterranean islands	Rank
Area	116
Population	73
Visitor capacity	70
Crowdfactor	50

Egadi **Italy** 3100

Filicudi

(PHOTO: CLAUDIO MOSSINO)

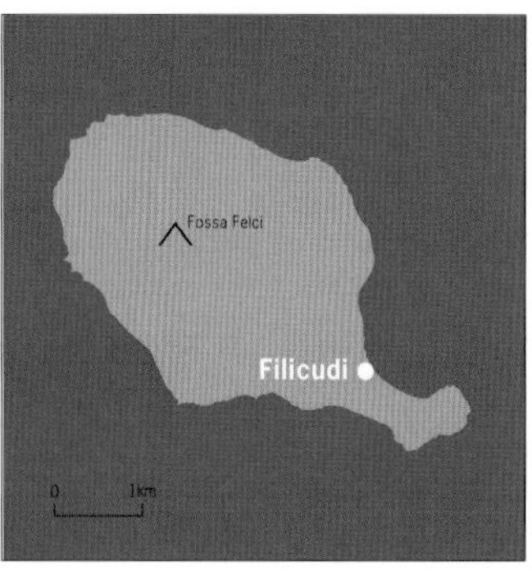
Fossa Felci
Filicudi
0
1km

0
30km
Milazzo
Messina

38°34' N 14°34' E
Filicudi
Eolie
Italy

A quiet terraced island, with a coastline of precipices, unusual rock formations, caves and basalt columns, popular with divers.

★★☆☆☆ Tourism level
★★☆☆☆ Vegetation
★★☆☆☆ Beaches
★★★☆☆ History

Information
www.isolelipari.it
Telephone 090 988 0095

Map
Kompass (1:25000)

Area 9 sq km
Coastline 9 km
Highest point 773 m (Fossa Felci)

Permanent population 225

Visitor capacity 123
2 hotels
85 hotel beds
38 other beds
0 campsites

Crowdfactor
37 people per sq km

Access
⛴ Milazzo 2½ hours

Connections
⛴ Milazzo 2 daily

Yacht facilities
⛵ no fuel

Ranking among all Mediterranean islands	Rank
Area	161
Population	149
Visitor capacity	152
Crowdfactor	146

3340 Italy Eolie

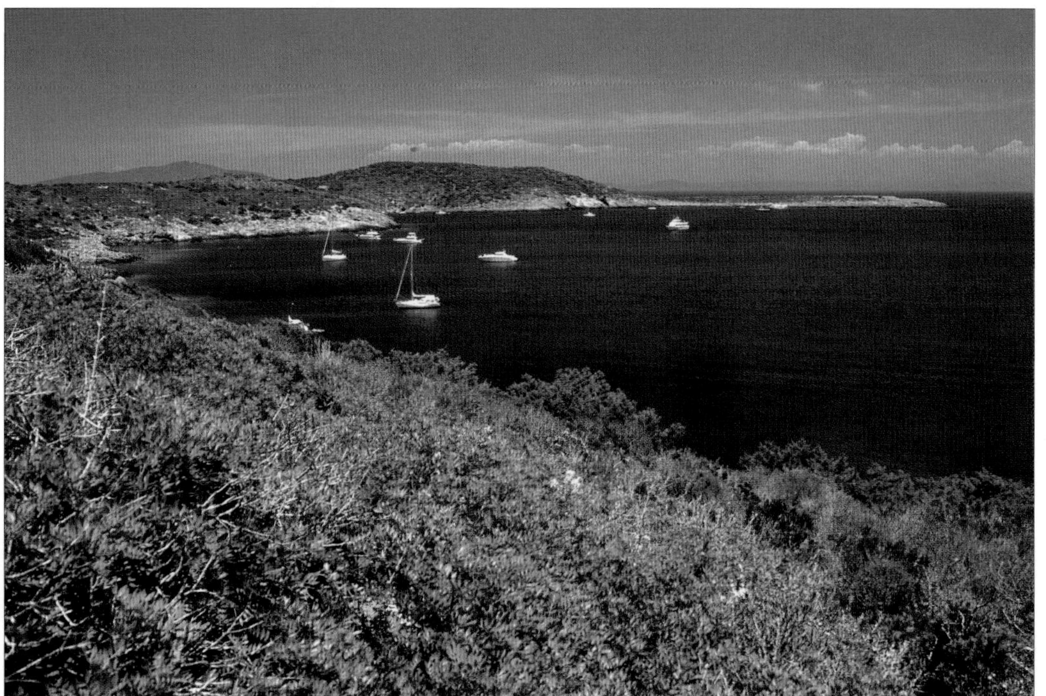

42°15' N 11°06' E
Giannutri
Arcipelago Toscano
Italy

A very pretty little island, ideal for walking, with many coves and lovely swimming, good tree cover, hilly terrain and interesting caves. There are two small ports and the remains of a Roman villa.

★★☆☆☆ Tourism level
★★★☆☆ Vegetation
★☆☆☆☆ Beaches
★★☆☆☆ History

Information
www.giannutri.org
Telephone 0564 898859

Map
Multigraphic (1:25000)

Area 2.39 sq km
Coastline 11 km
Highest point 88 m (Capel Rosso)

Permanent population 23

Visitor capacity 100
0 hotels
0 hotel beds
100 other beds
0 campsites

Crowdfactor
51 people per sq km

Access
Giglio 1 hour
Porto Santo Stefano 1½ hours

Connections
Porto Santo Stefano daily
Giglio 3 weekly

Yacht facilities
no fuel

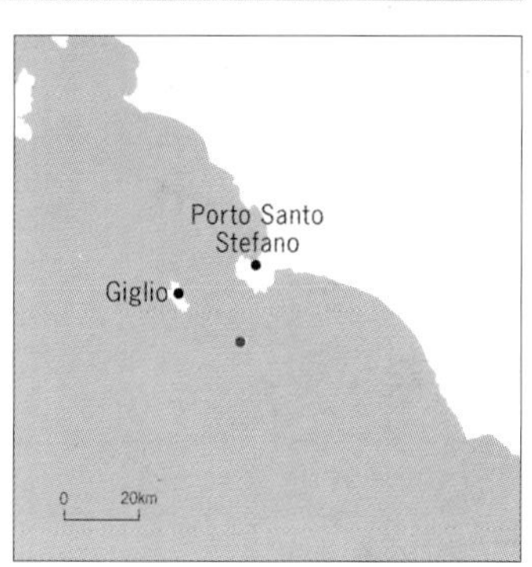
Porto Santo
Stefano
Giglio
0
20km

Ranking among all Mediterranean islands

	Rank
Area	270
Population	194
Visitor capacity	155
Crowdfactor	132

(PHOTO: APT LA MAREMMA)

Giglio Castello
Giglio Campese
Giglio Porto
0 2km

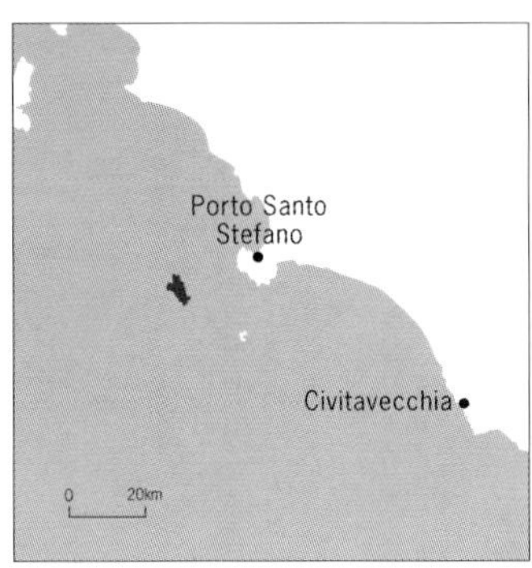
Porto Santo Stefano
Civitavecchia
0 20km

42°21' N 10°54' E
Giglio
Arcipelago Toscano
Italy

Giglio looks attractive from the Argentario peninsula, but a large number of visitors make it rather crowded in summer. The medieval town of Giglio Castello is very attractive.

★★★★☆ Tourism level
★★★☆☆ Vegetation
★★☆☆☆ Beaches
★★★☆☆ History

Information
www.isoladelgiglio.biz
Telephone 0564 809400

Map
Multigraphic (1:25000)

Area 21 sq km
Coastline 28 km
Highest point 498 m (Pagana)

Permanent population 1390

Visitor capacity 768
13 hotels
548 hotel beds
220 other beds
1 campsite

Crowdfactor
101 people per sq km

Access
Porto Santo Stefano 1 hour

Connections
Porto Santo Stefano 10 daily

Yacht facilities
Giglio Porto

Ranking among all Mediterranean islands	Ran
Area	10
Population	9
Visitor capacity	9
Crowdfactor	8

40°45' N 13°57' E
Ischia
Italy

A handsome island, with the imposing Monte Epomeo clad in luxuriant green of pine woods, olives and vineyards which produce renowned red and white wines. The colourful cubic architecture of the coastal towns has been the background for over 20 films and Ischia's hot springs make the island one of the world's most important thermal spas.

★★★★★ Tourism level
★★★★☆ Vegetation
★★★★☆ Beaches
★★★☆☆ History

Information
www.infoischiaprocida.it
Telephone 081 507 4231

Map
DeAgostini (1:28000)

Area 46 sq km
Coastline 34 km
Highest point 788 m (Epomeo)

Permanent population 56105

Visitor capacity 22936
312 hotels
21133 hotel beds
1803 other beds
3 campsites

Crowdfactor
1702 people per sq km

Access
Napoli 40 minutes
Pozzuoli I hour
Napoli 20 minutes

Connections
Napoli 18 daily
Pozzuoli 12 daily
Procida 7 daily

Yacht facilities
4 ports

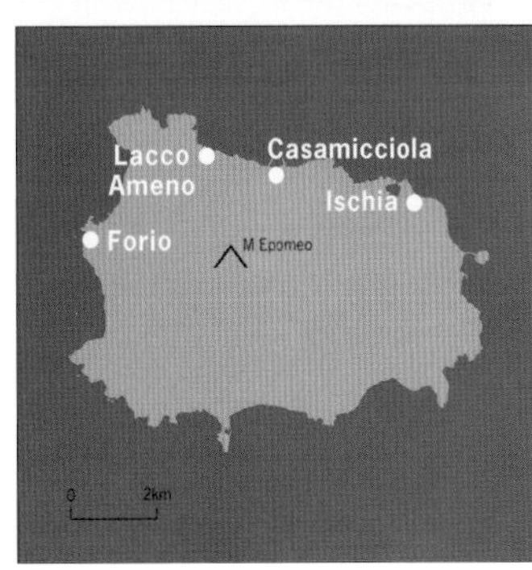
Lacco Ameno
Casamicciola
Ischia
Forio
M Epomeo
0
2km

Napoli
Pozzuoli
0
50km

Italy 3810

Ranking among all Mediterranean islands	Rank
Area	80
Population	15
Visitor capacity	17
Crowdfactor	12

Lampedusa

Lampedusa
0 2km

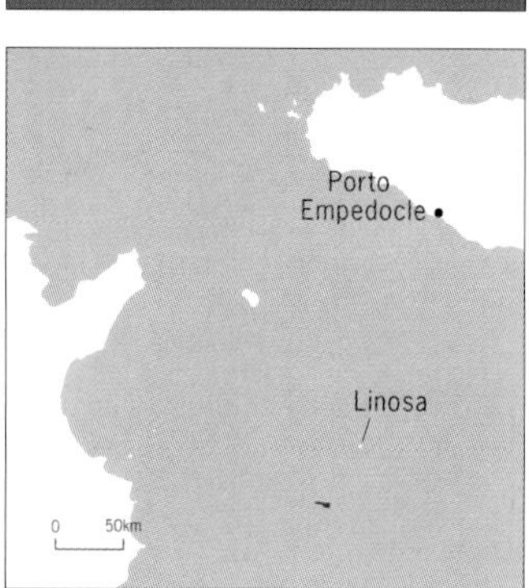
Porto Empedocle
Linosa
0 50km

35°30′ N 12°36′ E
Lampedusa
Pelagie
Italy

A barren windswept island with very little vegetation, Lampedusa is renowned for its clean sea and attracts visitors for its diving. The island has pretty coves on the south coast and impressive cliffs and rock formations which are best explored by taking a boat round it.

★★★☆☆ Tourism level
★☆☆☆☆ Vegetation
★★★☆☆ Beaches
★★☆☆☆ History

Information
www.lampedusa.to
Telephone 0922 973573

Map
None

Area 20 sq km
Coastline 26 km
Highest point 133 m (Albero Sole)

Permanent population 5703

Visitor capacity 1616
25 hotels
1028 hotel beds
588 other beds
1 campsite

Crowdfactor
357 people per sq km

Access
Lampedusa
Porto Empedocle 4 hours
Porto Empedocle 8 hours

Connections
Porto Empedocle daily
Porto Empedocle daily

Yacht facilities
Lampedusa

3200 **Italy** Pelagie

Ranking among all Mediterranean islands	Rank
Area	11
Population	61
Visitor capacity	67
Crowdfactor	30

38°00' N 12°20' E
Levanzo
Egadi
Italy

Levanzo is a rocky island with an inaccessible coast, whose inhabitants are mainly engaged in fishing. The most impressive things to see are the Grotta del Genovese with its prehistoric paintings, the impressive Faraglione rock and the pleasant inland pasture where cattle graze, all of which can be taken in on the same walk.

★★☆☆☆ Tourism level
★★☆☆☆ Vegetation
★★☆☆☆ Beaches
★★☆☆☆ History

Information
www.egadiweb.it
Telephone 0923 545511

Map
None

Area 5 sq km
Coastline 15 km
Highest point 278 m (Monaco)

Permanent population 235

Visitor capacity 69
2 hotels
48 hotel beds
21 other beds
0 campsites

Crowdfactor
51 people per sq km

Access
Trapani 30 minutes

Connections
Trapani 6 daily

Yacht facilities
no fuel

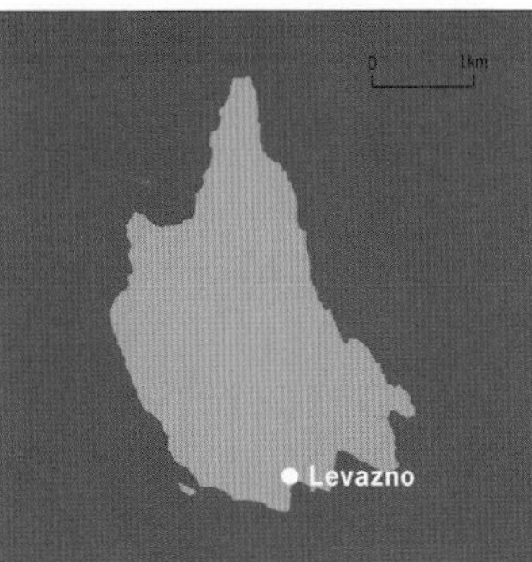
0 1km
Levazno

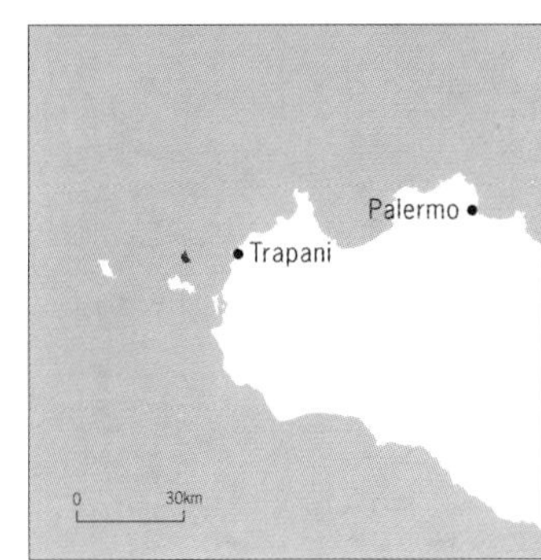
Palermo
Trapani
0 30km

Ranking among all Mediterranean islands

	Rank
Area	189
Population	147
Visitor capacity	164
Crowdfactor	132

Linosa

3210 **Italy** Pelagie

(PHOTO: FABIO TUCCIO)

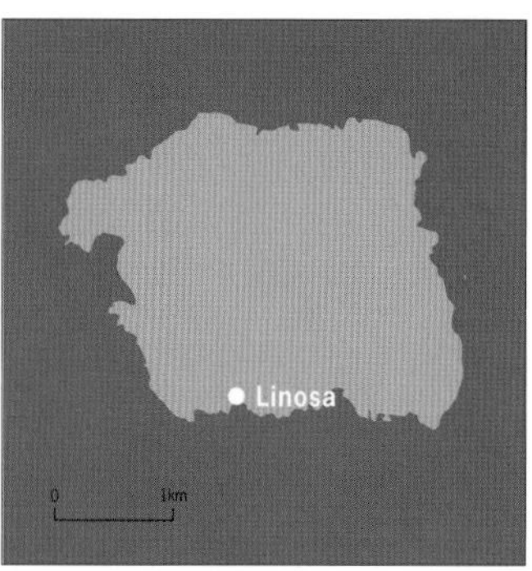

Linosa
0
1km

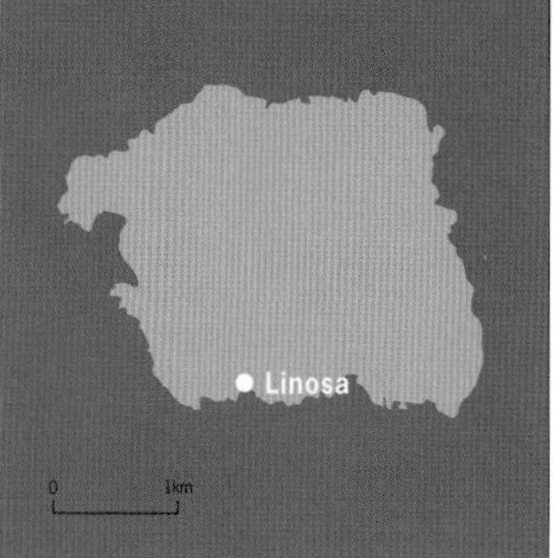

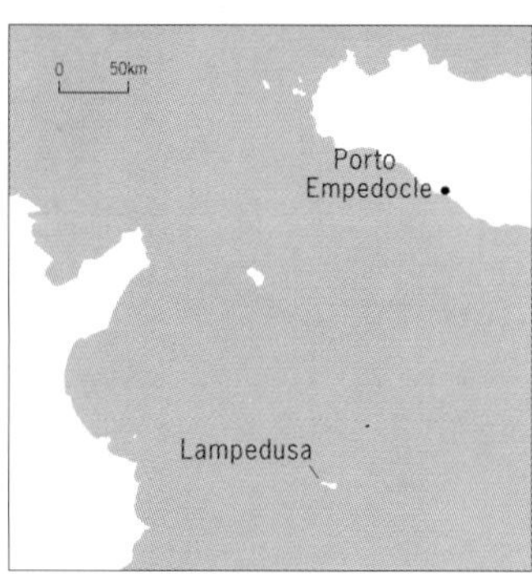

0
50km
Porto
Empedocle
Lampedusa

35°51' N 12°51' E
Linosa
Pelagie
Italy

A volcanic island comprised of three extinct craters, remote Linosa retains a quiet charm while attracting many more visitors in recent years .The coast has both cliffs and lava beaches and inland there is a certain amount of agriculture. Much less windy than Lampedusa, Linosa is renowned for being very hot.

★★★☆☆ Tourism level
★★☆☆☆ Vegetation
★★☆☆☆ Beaches
★☆☆☆☆ History

Information
www.linosa.biz
Telephone 333 684 6636

Map
None

Area 5 sq km
Coastline 11 km
Highest point 195 m (M Vulcano)

Permanent population 438

Visitor capacity 485
2 hotels
39 hotel beds
446 other beds
1 campsite

Crowdfactor
169 people per sq km

Access
Porto Empedocle 3 hours
Porto Empedocle 6 hours

Connections
Porto Empedocle daily
Porto Empedocle daily

Yacht facilities
no fuel

Ranking among all Mediterranean islands	Rank
Area	197
Population	126
Visitor capacity	113
Crowdfactor	63

38°28′ N 14°58′ E
Lipari
Eolie
Italy

The most populous and fashionable of the Eolian islands, Lipari has many points of interest. The often almost vertical coast has fascinating rock formations and a significant part of the island is covered by white pumice quarries and fields of obsidian. Agriculture is also important with capers, figs and currants all plentiful. The fine town has a walled medieval quarter, a 16th century castello enclosing the cathedral and three churches and a very interesting archaeological museum. There are marvellous views from the Quattrocchi belvedere.

★★★★☆ Tourism level
★★★☆☆ Vegetation
★★☆☆☆ Beaches
★★★☆☆ History

Information
www.isolelipari.it
telephone 090 988 0095

Map
Kompass (1:25000)

Area 37 sq km
Coastline 30 km
Highest point 602 m (Monte Chirica)

Permanent population 8677

Visitor capacity 2100
32 hotels
1486 hotel beds
614 other beds
1 campsite

Crowdfactor
288 people per sq km

Access
Milazzo 1 hour
Milazzo 2½ hours

Connections
Milazzo 15 daily
Milazzo 4 daily

Yacht facilities
Marina Lunga, Pignataro, Marina Corta

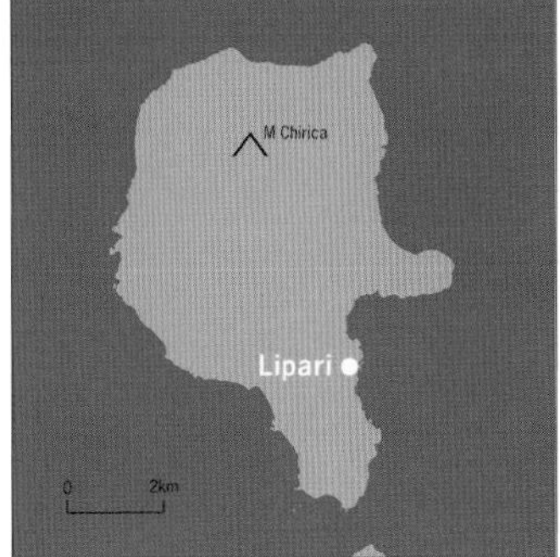
M Chirica
Lipari
0
2km

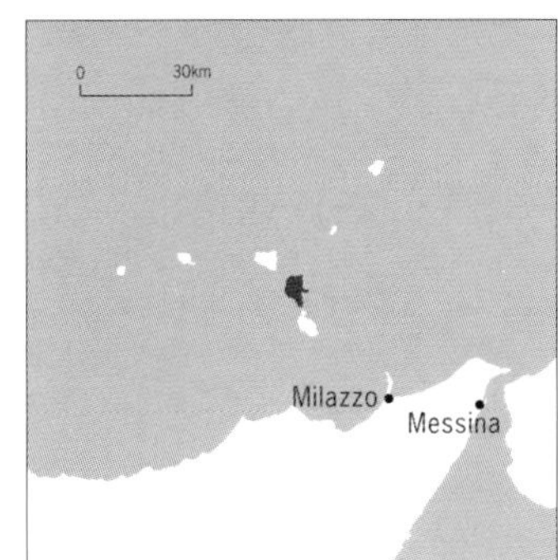
0
30km
Milazzo
Messina

Ranking among all Mediterranean islands

	Rank
Area	87
Population	47
Visitor capacity	63
Crowdfactor	40

BAIA TRINITA (PHOTO: PARCO NAZIONALE ARCIPELAGO MADDALENA

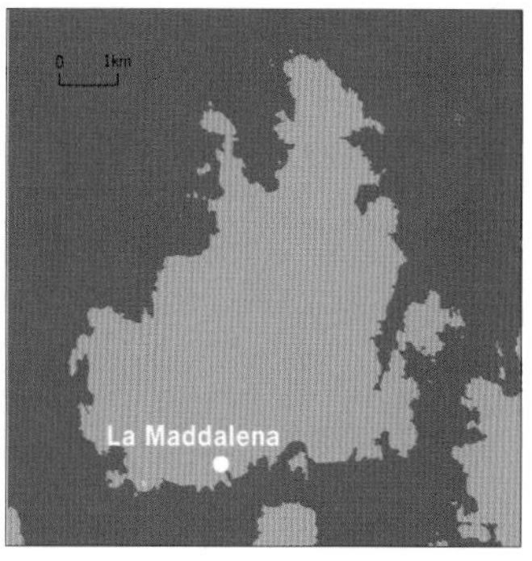
0 1km
La Maddalena

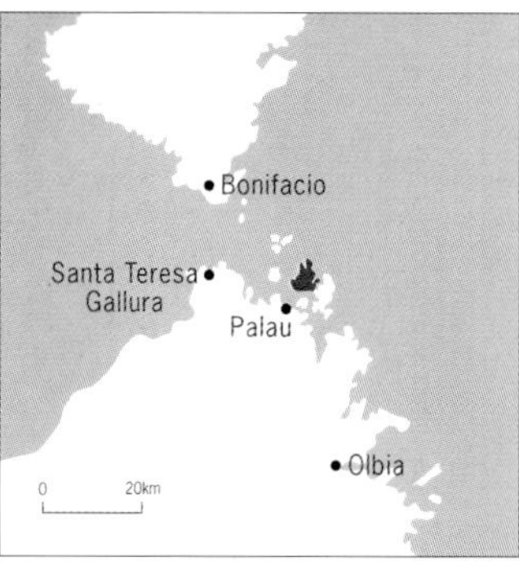
Bonifacio
Santa Teresa
Gallura
Palau
Olbia
0 20km

41°12' N 09°25' E
Maddalena
Arcipelago Maddalenino
Italy

The relatively large town of La Maddalena has a prosperous feel and is home to a NATO base. The island has a beautiful coastline and it is well worth driving the length of the coast road.

★★★☆☆ Tourism level
★★★☆☆ Vegetation
★★★☆☆ Beaches
★★☆☆☆ History

Information
www.lamaddalena.it
Telephone 0789 892080

Map
FMB (1:25000)

Area 20 sq km
Coastline 43 km
Highest point 152 m (Guardia Vecchia)

Permanent population 11275

Visitor capacity 1059
14 hotels
712 hotel beds
347 other beds
3 campsites

Crowdfactor
611 people per sq km

Access
Palau 15 minutes

Connections
Palau 84 daily

Yacht facilities
La Maddalena

Ranking among all Mediterranean islands	Rar
Area	11
Population	3
Visitor capacity	8
Crowdfactor	2

Marettimo

37°57′ N 12°02′ E
Marettimo
Egadi
Italy

Remote and quite independent of the other Egadi islands, Marettimo is very much a fishing community. The port is attractive and the rugged interior can be accessed on foot. The coast is magnificent, with fascinating rock formations and caves, dramatic cliffs on the western side and wonderful views from the Castello di Punta Troia.

★★☆☆☆ Tourism level
★★★☆☆ Vegetation
★★★☆☆ Beaches
★★☆☆☆ History

Information
www.egadiweb.it
Telephone 0923 545511

Map
None

Area 12 sq km
Coastline 16 km
Highest point 686 m (Monte Falcone)

Permanent population 725

Visitor capacity 181
0 hotels
0 hotel beds
181 other beds
0 campsites

Crowdfactor
74 people per sq km

Access
Trapani 1 hour

Connections
Trapani 4 daily

Yacht facilities
no fuel

Marettimo
0
1km

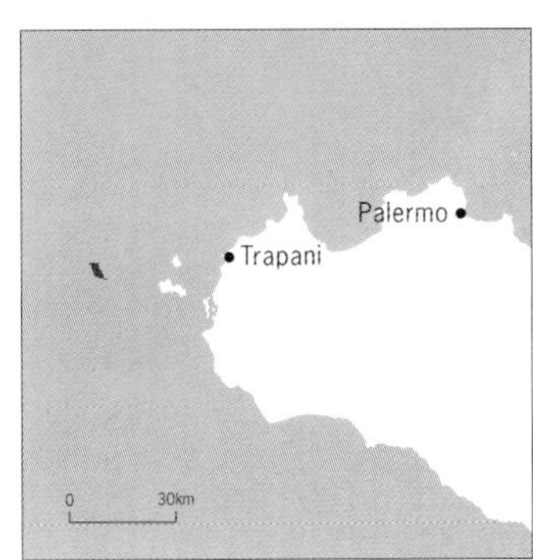
Palermo
Trapani
0
30km

Ranking among all Mediterranean islands

	Rank
Area	146
Population	114
Visitor capacity	142
Crowdfactor	103

Egadi **Italy** 3120

Palmarola

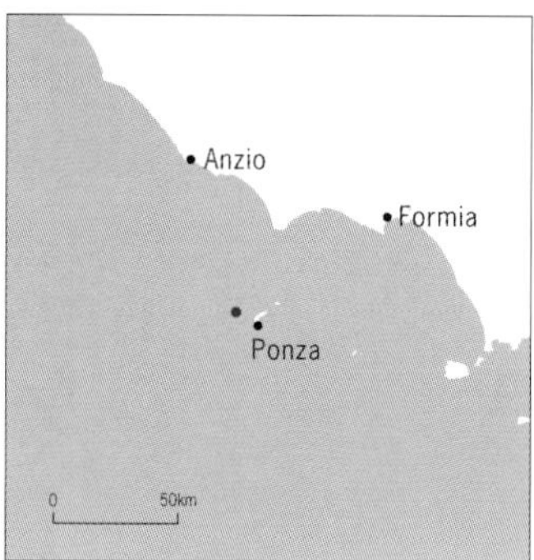
Anzio
Formia
Ponza
0
50km

40°56' N 12°51' E
Palmarola
Isole Ponziane
Italy

A beautiful and majestic island surrounded with rocks of many shapes and colours, with terraced vineyards on the higher ground. Palmarola is now inhabited only in the summer, when a couple of small eating places open on the island's attractive beach.

★☆☆☆☆ Tourism level
★★★★☆ Vegetation
★★☆☆☆ Beaches
★★☆☆☆ History

Information
www.palmarola.it
Telephone 0771 808417

Map
Brigantino (1:15400)

Area 1.24 sq km
Coastline 15 km
Highest point 249 m (Monte Guarniere)

Permanent population 0

Visitor capacity 10
0 hotels
0 hotel beds
10 other beds
0 campsites

Crowdfactor
8 people per sq km

Access
Private boat from Ponza

Connections
None scheduled

Yacht facilities
⛵ no fuel

3710 **Italy** Isle Ponziane

Ranking among all Mediterranean islands	Ran
Area	33
Population	
Visitor capacity	20
Crowdfactor	20

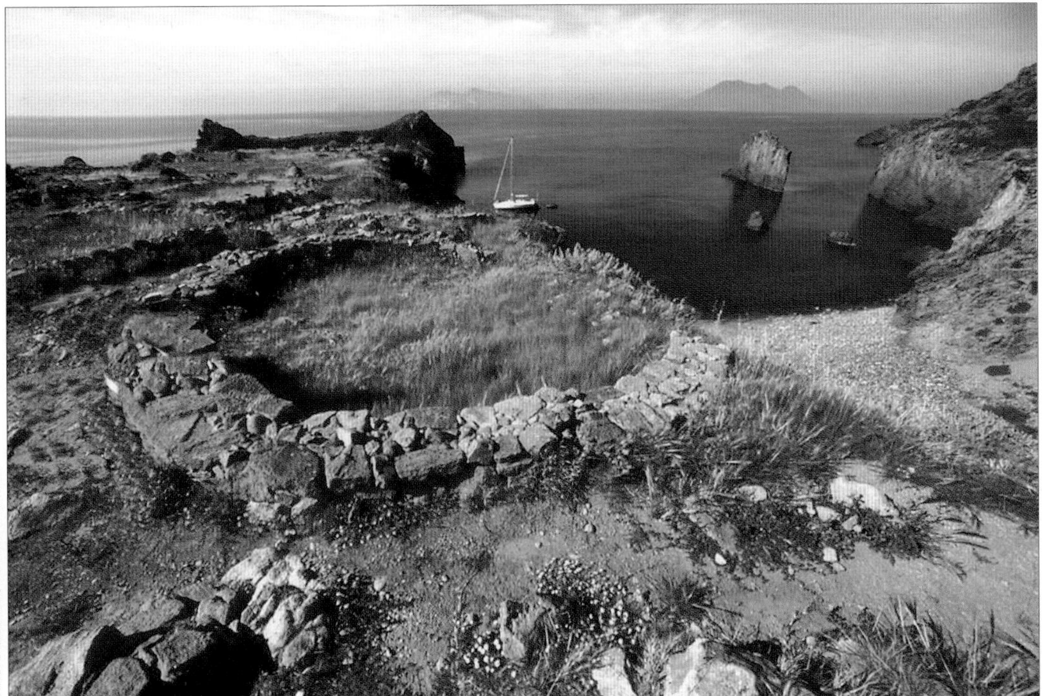
BAIA DI CALAJUNCO (PHOTO: APT MESSINA)

38°38' N 15°03' E
Panarea
Eolie
Italy

A chic relaxed volcanic island, with terraces, hot springs, underwater fumaroles and a bronze age village. The archipelago of smaller islands to the east is a delight to explore, particularly Basiluzzo with its giant columns, many Roman remains now surrounded with capers and rosemary and exotic marine species.

★★★☆☆ Tourism level
★★★☆☆ Vegetation
★★☆☆☆ Beaches
★★☆☆☆ History

Information
www.isolelipari.it
Telephone 090 988 0095

Map
Kompass (1:25000)

Area 3.38 sq km
Coastline 7 km
Highest point 420 m (Punta del Corvo)

Permanent population 230

Visitor capacity 534
12 hotels
389 hotel beds
145 other beds
0 campsites

Crowdfactor
226 people per sq km

Access
Milazzo 2½ hours
Reggio 30 minutes

Connections
Milazzo 5 daily

Yacht facilities
no fuel

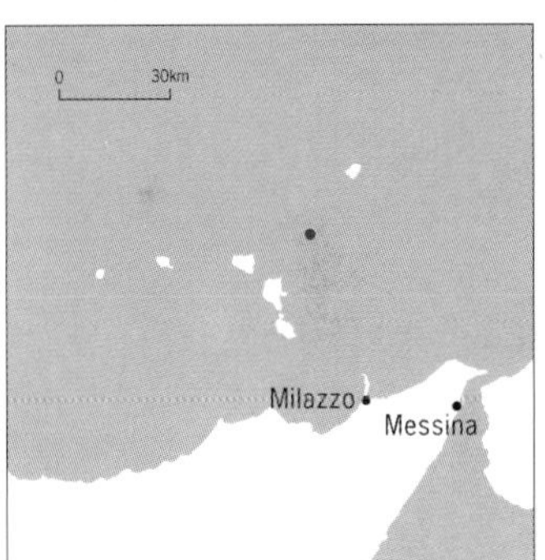
0
30km
Milazzo
Messina

Ranking among all Mediterranean islands

	Rank
Area	239
Population	148
Visitor capacity	111
Crowdfactor	51

LIPARI (PHOTO: EOLIENELMONDO)

Pantelleria

3050 Italy

LAGO SPECCHIO DI VENERE (PHOTO: WALTER LEONARDI)

Pantelleria
Montagna Grande
0 3km

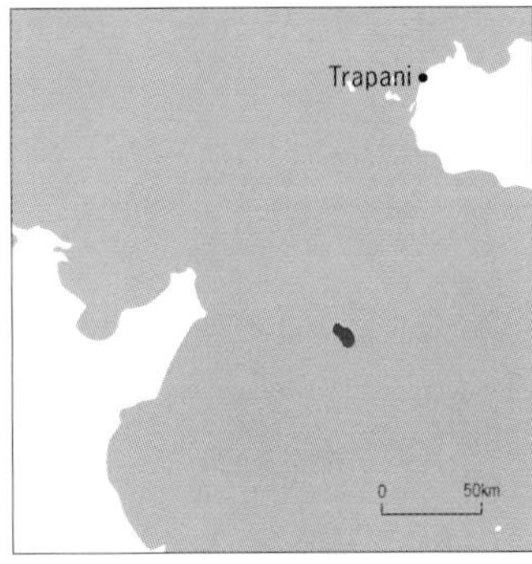
Trapani
0 50km

36°48' N 12°00' E
Pantelleria
Italy

There are about a dozen volcanic peaks on this unusual island, famous for its radioactive waters and many varied wines. Interesting too are the sesi, megalithic circular chamber tombs and particularly the dammusi, domed cubic Moorish houses. A drive round the picturesque rocky coast of the island is rewarding, with many features including the lovely Cala Cinque Denti, the pretty village of Gadir, the Arco Elefante, the cliffs of Dietro Isola and the fine port of Scauri. The interior is lovely too with its vines, capers and wooded areas and is full of Arabic placenames like Bugeber above Lago Specchio di Venere.

★★★☆☆ Tourism level
★★★☆☆ Vegetation
★★☆☆☆ Beaches
★★☆☆☆ History

Information
www.pantelleria.com
Telephone 0923 695037

Map
Valenza (1:40000)

Area 84 sq km
Coastline 51 km
Highest point 836 m (Montagna Grande)

Permanent population 7224

Visitor capacity 1481
12 hotels
1228 hotel beds
253 other beds
0 campsites

Crowdfactor
103 people per sq km

Access
Pantelleria
Trapani 2½ hours
Trapani 6 hours

Connections
Trapani daily
Trapani 2 daily

Yacht facilities
Pantelleria

Ranking among all Mediterranean islands	Rar
Area	5
Population	5
Visitor capacity	7
Crowdfactor	8

(PHOTO: CONDOMINIO VILLAMARINA)

39°11′ N 08°19′ E
Isola Piana
Arcipelago Sulcitano
Italy

Isola Piana is a privately run island with a condominium of holiday apartments and a marina with 77 berths

★★★☆☆ Tourism level
★★☆☆☆ Vegetation
★★☆☆☆ Beaches
★☆☆☆☆ History

Information
www.isolapiana.com
Telephone 0781 854460

Map
None

Area 0.21 sq km
Coastline 1.8 km
Highest point 19 m

Permanent population 0

Visitor capacity 400
0 hotels
0 hotel beds
400 other beds (condominium)
0 campsites

Crowdfactor
1904 people per sq km

Access
Private boat from San Pietro

Connections
None scheduled

Yacht facilities
⛵ no fuel

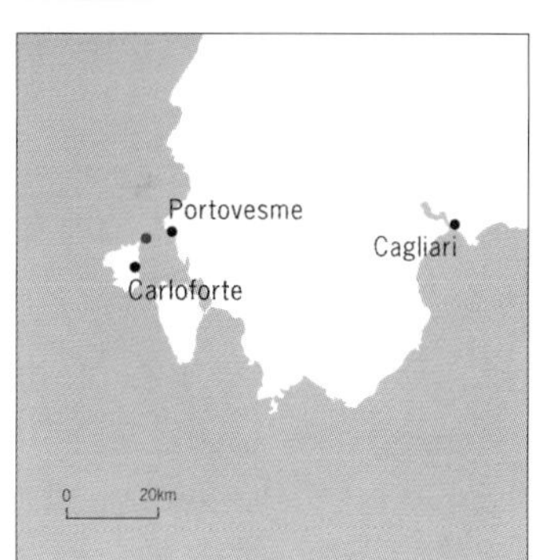
Portovesme
Cagliari
Carloforte
0
20km

Ranking among all Mediterranean islands	Rank
Area	683
Population	0
Visitor capacity	119
Crowdfactor	9

Ponza

VEDUTA DEL PORTO (PHOTO: APT LATINA TURISMO)

Ponza
0
2km

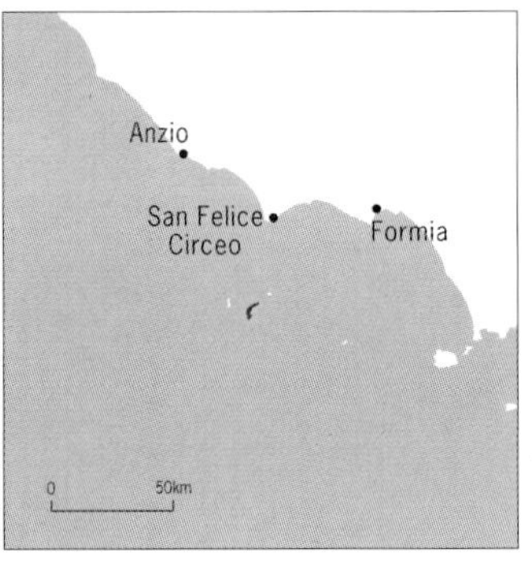
Anzio
San Felice Circeo
Formia
0
50km

40°54' N 12°58' E
Ponza
Isole Ponziane
Italy

A unique and picturesque island situated along the rim of an old volcanic crater, Ponza is best seen by going round the island in a boat, which will reveal all the amazing shapes of the rocks, islets and coves. The crescent beach of Chiaia di Luna under its cliff is famously striking. The town is pretty too with its brightly painted cubic houses and attractive shops and restaurants. There are plenty of Roman traces around the island and surprisingly large areas of terraced vineyards.

★★★★☆ Tourism level
★★☆☆☆ Vegetation
★★★★☆ Beaches
★★★☆☆ History

Information
www.ponza.it
Telephone 0771 80031

Map
Brigantino (1:15400)

Area 7 sq km
Coastline 41 km
Highest point 283 m (Monte Guardia)

Permanent population 3107

Visitor capacity 958
17 hotels
689 hotel beds
269 other beds
0 campsites

Crowdfactor
542 people per sq km

Access
Formia, Anzio 1½ hours
S Felice Circeo 1½ hours
Formia, Anzio 2½ hours

Connections
Formia, Anzio daily
S Felice Circeo, Formia, Anzio daily
Ventotene 2 daily

Yacht facilities
Ponza

Ranking among all Mediterranean islands

	Ran
Area	17
Population	7
Visitor capacity	8
Crowdfactor	2

ABBAZIA S MICHELE ARC (PHOTO: APT ISCHIA PROCIDA)

40°46' N 14°02' E
Procida
Italy

Procida is enchanting, like an imaginary Italian island come true. The architecture, with houses apparently blending into each other or separated by intertwining passages in a riot of pastel colours, is like something from a film set. Beyond Marina Grande and Corricella the island is very green with many campsites near the beaches on either side of the island. An island of sailors and fishermen, Procida's simplicity is well summed up by the combination of its excellent fish, outstanding lemons and pleasant white wine.

★★★☆☆ Tourism level
★★★☆☆ Vegetation
★★★☆☆ Beaches
★★★☆☆ History

Information
www.ischiaprocida.it
Telephone 081 507 4231

Map
DeAgostini (1:28000)

Area 3.89 sq km
Coastline 16 km
Highest point 91 m (Terra Murata)

Permanent population 10575

Visitor capacity 810
8 hotels
202 hotel beds
608 other beds
6 campsites

Crowdfactor
2926 people per sq km

Access
Pozzuoli, Ischia 15 minutes
Napoli 30 minutes

Connections
Pozzuoli 16 daily
Napoli 10 daily
Ischia 7 daily

Yacht facilities
Procida Marina, Chiaiolella

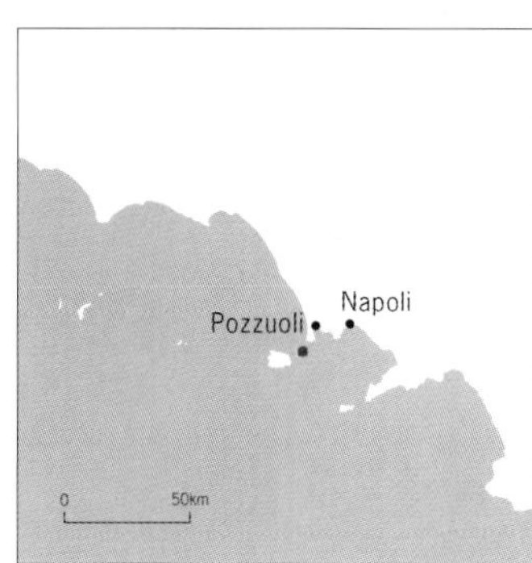
Napoli
Pozzuoli
0
50km

Ranking among all Mediterranean islands	Rank
Area	224
Population	41
Visitor capacity	92
Crowdfactor	5

Italy
3820

Salina

POLLARA (PHOTO: APT MESSINA)

Santa Marina Salina
Fossa delle Felci
0
2km

0
30km
Milazzo
Messina

38°32' N 14°52' E
Salina
Eolie
Italy

This green very fertile island is the highest in the Eolian archipelago and is formed of two extinct volcanoes. The atmosphere is quiet and pleasant and the road round the island is magnificent, passing through fields of vines and capers, with terrific views in every direction. The coast is spectacular with beautiful sheer rocks and grottoes.

★★★☆☆ Tourism level
★★★☆☆ Vegetation
★★☆☆☆ Beaches
★★☆☆☆ History

Information
www.isolelipari.it
Telephone 090 988 0095

Map
Kompass (1:25000)

Area 26 sq km
Coastline 24 km
Highest point 962 m (Fossa delle Felci)

Permanent population 2300

Visitor capacity 577
14 hotels
422 hotel beds
155 other beds
1 campsite

Crowdfactor
110 people per sq km

Access
Milazzo 2 hours
Milazzo 3½ hours

Connections
Milazzo 8 daily
Milazzo 2 daily

Yacht facilities
Santa Maria

3310 **Italy** Eolie

Ranking among all Mediterranean islands	Rank
Area	97
Population	87
Visitor capacity	110
Crowdfactor	80

San Domino

Tremiti **Italy** 3900

42°06' N 15°29' E
San Domino
Tremiti
Italy

A lovely forest-covered island but rather swamped by the hordes of visitors who come for the day to the only islands off the Adriatic coast of Italy. Apart from the crowded bathing places the main attraction is to explore the caves of Bue Marino, Viole and Rondinelle and the impressive crag of the Ripa dei Falconei.

★★★★★ Tourism level
★★★★★ Vegetation
★☆☆☆☆ Beaches
★★☆☆☆ History

Information
www.comune.isoletremiti.fg.it
Telephone 0882 463063

Map
None

Area 2.07 sq km
Coastline 9 km
Highest point 116 m (Colle dell'Eremita)

Permanent population 236

Visitor capacity 1366
20 hotels
670 hotel beds
696 other beds
0 campsites

Crowdfactor
773 people per sq km

Access
San Nicola 5 minutes
Foggia 30 minutes

Connections
San Nicola 36 daily

Yacht facilities
no fuel

Ortona
Vasto
Termoli
Rodi
Garganico
Vieste
Peschici
Foggia
0
30km

Ranking among all Mediterranean islands	Rank
Area	282
Population	146
Visitor capacity	74
Crowdfactor	17

San Nicola

(PHOTO: APT FOGGIA)

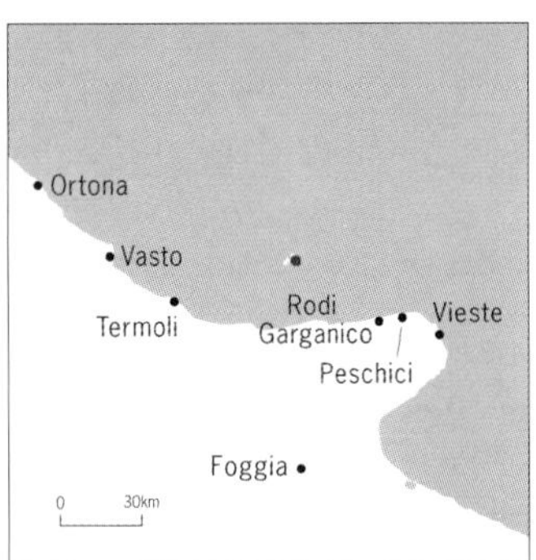
Ortona
Vasto
Termoli
Rodi Garganico
Vieste
Peschici
Foggia
0 30km

42°07' N 15°30' E
San Nicola
Tremiti
Italy

The administrative centre of the Tremiti islands, San Nicola has a lovely little walled town with the impressive looking abbey fortress of Santa Maria a Mare, of which little but the church remains. The rest of the island is bleak and of little interest.

★★★☆☆ Tourism level
★★☆☆☆ Vegetation
★☆☆☆☆ Beaches
★★★☆☆ History

Information
www.comune.isoletremiti.fg.it
Telephone 0882 463063

Map
None

Area 0.44 sq km
Coastline 3.7 km
Highest point 75 m (Pianoro)

Permanent population 131

Visitor capacity 50
0 hotels
0 hotel beds
50 other beds
0 campsites

Crowdfactor
411 people per sq km

Access
San Domino 36 daily
Termoli, Vasto, Rodi Garganico 1 hour

Connections
Termoli 4 daily
Vasto, Rodi, Peschici, Vieste, Ortona daily

Yacht facilities
no fuel

Ranking among all Mediterranean islands

	Ran
Area	48
Population	16
Visitor capacity	17
Crowdfactor	2

39°09' N 08°13' E
San Pietro
Arcipelago Sulcitano
Italy

A peaceful island that is starting to attract more visitors, San Pietro has a coastline with interesting caves and pine woods inland. In May/June there is a mattanza of tunny fish.

★★★☆☆ Tourism level
★★★☆☆ Vegetation
★★★☆☆ Beaches
★★☆☆☆ History

Information
www.carloforte.net
Telephone 0781 854009

Map
Coedisar (1:50000)

Area 50 sq km
Coastline 33 km
Highest point 211 m (Guardia d Mori)

Permanent population 6444

Visitor capacity 973
8 hotels
434 hotel beds
539 other beds
0 campsites

Crowdfactor
145 people per sq km

Access
Calasetta 30 minutes
Portovesme 45 minutes

Connections
Calasetta 20 daily
Portovesme 16 daily

Yacht facilities
Carloforte

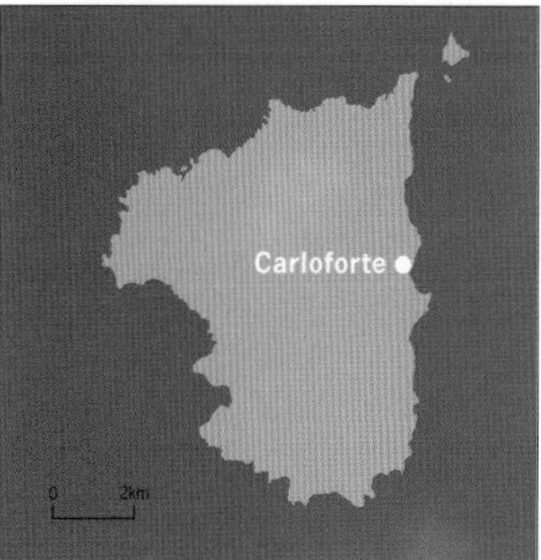
Carloforte
0
2km

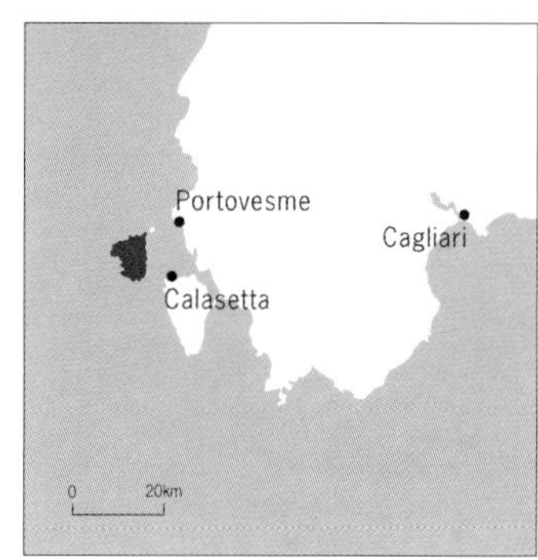
Portovesme
Cagliari
Calasetta
0
20km

Ranking among all Mediterranean islands

	Rank
Area	75
Population	58
Visitor capacity	87
Crowdfactor	70

Santa Maria

3640 **Italy** Arcipelago Maddalenino

FARO SANTA MARIA (PHOTO: PARCO NAZIONALE DELL'ARCIPELAGO DI LA MADDALENA)

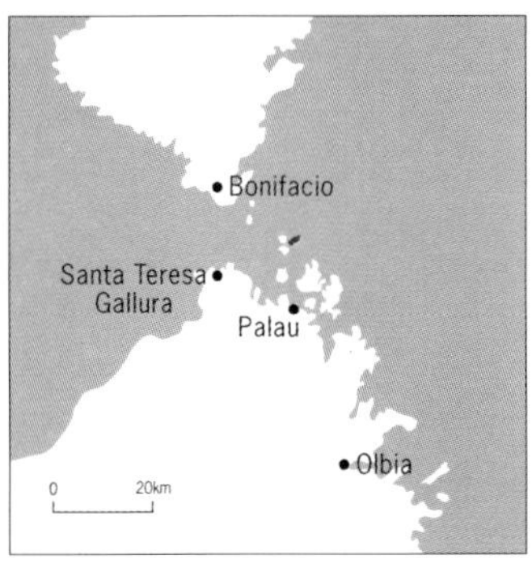

Bonifacio
Santa Teresa Gallura
Palau
Olbia
0
20km

41°18' N 09°23' E
Santa Maria
Arcipelago Maddalenino
Italy

This granite island has lovely coves and a few summer houses. There are other islands in every direction, the nearest being Budelli with its spiaggia rosa, but Santa Maria still retains a very remote feel.

★☆☆☆☆ Tourism level
★★☆☆☆ Vegetation
★★☆☆☆ Beaches
★★☆☆☆ History

Information
www.lamaddalena.it
Telephone 0789 892080

Map
FMB (1:25000)

Area 1.86 sq km
Coastline 10 km
Highest point 49 m (Guardia del Turco)

Permanent population 4

Visitor capacity 10
0 hotels
0 hotel beds
10 other beds
0 campsites

Crowdfactor
7 people per sq km

Access
Private boat from La Maddalena

Connections
None scheduled

Yacht facilities
⛵ no fuel

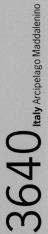

Ranking among all Mediterranean islands	Ran
Area	28
Population	21
Visitor capacity	20
Crowdfactor	20

Sant'Antioco

39°04' N 08°27' E
Sant'Antioco
Arcipelago Sulcitano
Italy

Volcanic in origin, Sant'Antioco is a hilly island with fine cliffs on the west coast. The island is known for its strong wine and increasingly for attracting tourism. The town of Calasetta is attractive with a levantine feel.

★★★☆☆ Tourism level
★★★☆☆ Vegetation
★★★☆☆ Beaches
★★☆☆☆ History

Information
www.comune.santantioco.ca.it
Telephone 0781 82031

Map
Coedisar (1:50000)

Area 109 sq km
Coastline 42 km
Highest point 271 m (Perdas de Fogu)

Permanent population 11670

Visitor capacity 2139
13 hotels
639 hotel beds
1500 other beds
2 campsites

Crowdfactor
126 people per sq km

Access
Bridge to Sardegna

Connections
Carloforte 20 daily

Yacht facilities
Calasetta

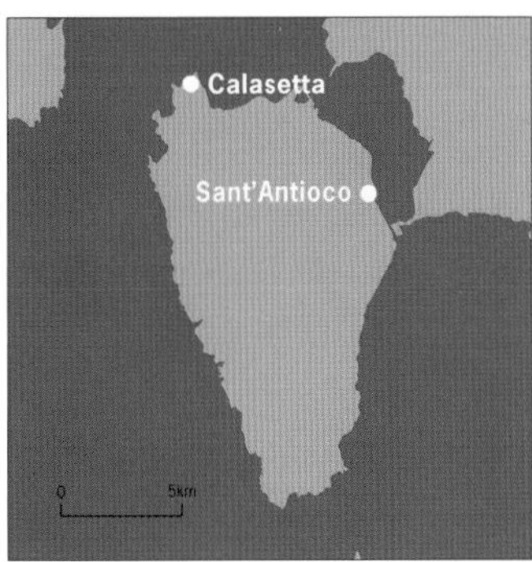
Calasetta
Sant'Antioco
0
5km

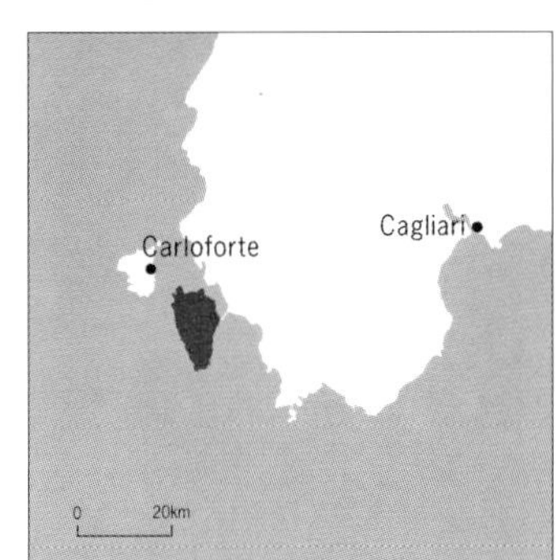
Cagliari
Carloforte
0
20km

Ranking among all Mediterranean islands

	Rank
Area	47
Population	38
Visitor capacity	62
Crowdfactor	77

Arcipelago Sulcitano **Italy** 3510

Santo Stefano

(PHOTO: VALTUR SPA)

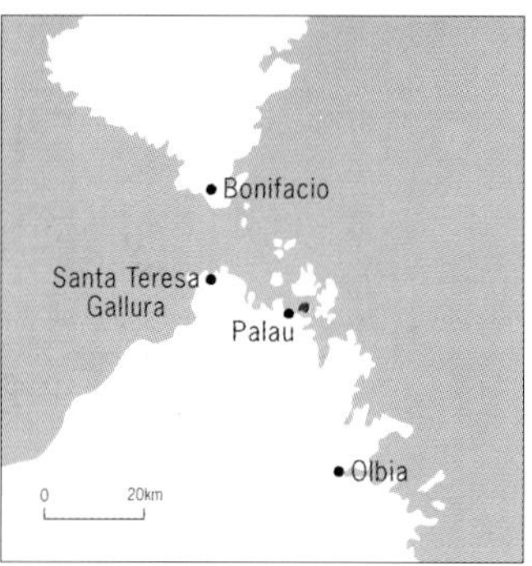
Bonifacio
Santa Teresa Gallura
Palau
Olbia
0
20km

41°12' N 09°25' E
Santo Stefano
Arcipelago Maddalenino
Italy

Santo Stefano has a holiday village at Spiaggia del Pesce, a fine beach at La Fumata and a NATO base, which is out of bounds to the public.

★★★☆☆ Tourism level
★★★☆☆ Vegetation
★★☆☆☆ Beaches
★★★☆☆ History

Information
www.lamaddalena.it
Telephone 0789 709812

Map
FMB (1:25000)

Area 3 sq km
Coastline 11 km
Highest point 101 m (Monte Zucchero)

Permanent population 1

Visitor capacity 639
1 hotel
639 hotel beds
0 other beds
0 campsites

Crowdfactor
212 people per sq km

Access
⛴ La Maddalena 10 minutes
⛴ Palau 15 minutes

Connections
⛴ La Maddalena 10 daily
⛴ Palau 4 daily

Yacht facilities
⛵ no fuel

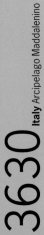

Ranking among all Mediterranean islands

	Rank
Area	248
Population	238
Visitor capacity	102
Crowdfactor	54

3630 **Italy** Arcipelago Maddalenino

39°12' N 09°06' E
Sardegna
Italy

A large island, similar in size to Sicily and more than 2½ times larger than any other Mediterranean island. Sardinia has by far the best beaches of anywhere in Italy and is ideal for exploring. The massif of the Gennargentu is wild and the loveliest parts of the coast are between Cagliari and Nuoro in the east and between Alghero and Oristano in the west. There are over 7000 nuraghe, fortified tower houses around 3000 years old, Sassari has a lovely medieval centre and the Grotta di Nettuno is a wonderful cave.

★★★☆☆ Tourism level
★★★☆☆ Vegetation
★★★★☆ Beaches
★★★☆☆ History

Information
www.sardegnaturismo.it
Telephone 070 991350

Map
TCI (1:200000)

Area 23812 sq km
Coastline 1232 km
Highest point 1834 m (Marmora)

Permanent population 1602406

Visitor capacity 175869
822 hotels
95843 hotel beds
80026 other beds
83 campsites

Crowdfactor
74 people per sq km

Access
Cagliari, Olbia, Alghero
Civitavecchia, Piombino 4 hours
Livorno 5 hours
Bonifacio 1 hour

Connections
Civitavecchia, Piombino, Livorno daily
Bonifacio 5 daily

Yacht facilities
34 ports

Sassari
Olbia
Alghero
Marmora
Oristano
Cagliari
0 50km

Livorno
Piombino
Civitavecchia
Bonifacio
0 100km

Ranking among all Mediterranean islands

	Rank
Area	2
Population	2
Visitor capacity	3
Crowdfactor	103

Italy 3500

SEGESTA DORIC TEMPLE (PHOTO: APT TRAPANI ARTURO SA

Messina
Palermo
Etna
Catania
Agrigento
Siracusa
0 50km

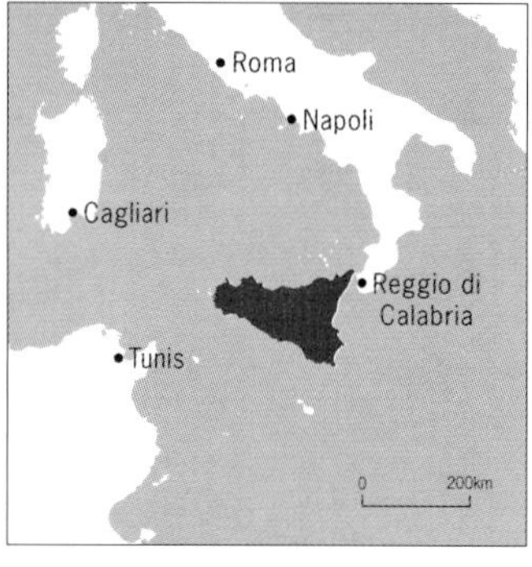
Roma
Napoli
Cagliari
Reggio di Calabria
Tunis
0 200km

38°07' N 13°22' E
Sicilia
Italy

The largest island in the Mediterranean, Sicily has a population almost equal to all the other Mediterranean islands put together. Dominated for nearly 3000 years by foreign cultures (Greek, Carthaginian, Roman, Saracen, Norman, Spanish) Sicily regards herself today as a country of her own. Outstanding examples of this diversity are the temples of Agrigento and Segesta, the theatres of Siracusa and Taormina and the 12th century cathedrals of Monreale, Cefalu and Palermo.

★★★☆☆ Tourism level
★★★☆☆ Vegetation
★★★☆☆ Beaches
★★★★★ History

Information
www.regione.sicilia.it
Telephone 091 707 8015

Map
TCI (1:200000)

Area 25426 sq km
Coastline 1152 km
Highest point 3323 m (Etna)

Permanent population 4937301

Visitor capacity 128750
1080 hotels
102832 hotel beds
25918 other beds
102 campsites

Crowdfactor
199 people per sq km

Access
✈ Palermo, Catania, Trapani

Connections
Reggio Calabria 20 daily

Yacht facilities
43 ports

Ranking among all Mediterranean islands

	Ran
Area	
Population	
Visitor capacity	
Crowdfactor	5

38°47' N 15°12' E
Stromboli
Eolie
Italy

Said to be the most active volcano in the world, Stromboli gives some signs of activity every few minutes. The climb to the top of the island is fascinating and unforgettable. Impressive too is the view from the basalt cliff of Strombolicchio, as is watching the island's activity from out at sea by night. A visit should also be made to the charming village of Ginostra, cut off from the rest of the island by the Sciara del Fuoco lava channel.

★★★☆☆ Tourism level
★★★☆☆ Vegetation
★☆☆☆☆ Beaches
★★☆☆☆ History

Information
www.isolelipari.it
Telephone 090 988 0085

Map
Kompass (1:25000)

Area 12 sq km
Coastline 15 km
Highest point 924 m (Vancori)

Permanent population 568

Visitor capacity 596
9 hotels
420 hotel beds
176 other beds
0 campsites

Crowdfactor
93 people per sq km

Access
Milazzo 3 hours

Connections
Milazzo 5 daily

Yacht facilities
no fuel

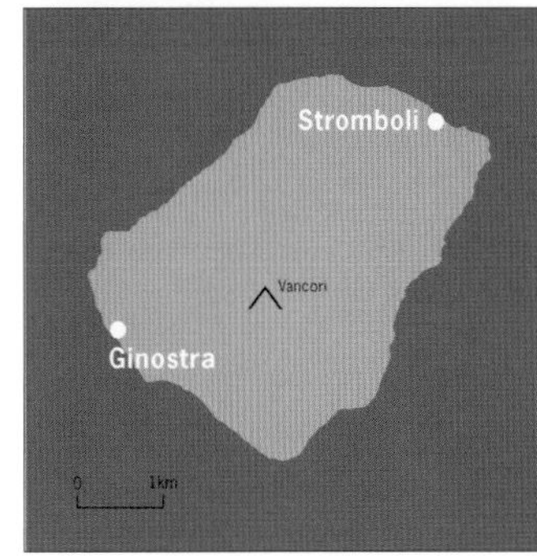
Stromboli
Vancori
Ginostra
0
1km

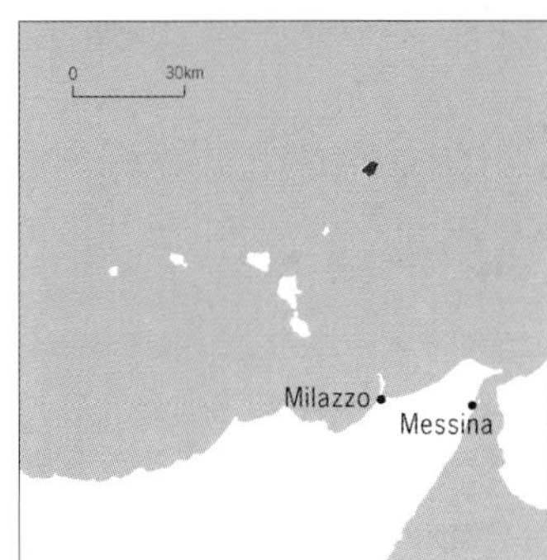
0
30km
Milazzo
Messina

Ranking among all Mediterranean islands	Rank
Area	145
Population	119
Visitor capacity	106
Crowdfactor	94

Ustica

(PHOTO: ASSESSORATO AL TURISMO DELLA REGIONE SICILIANA)

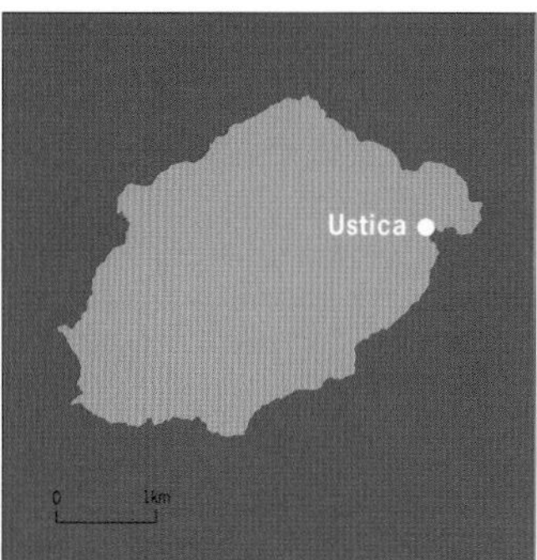

Ustica
0
1km

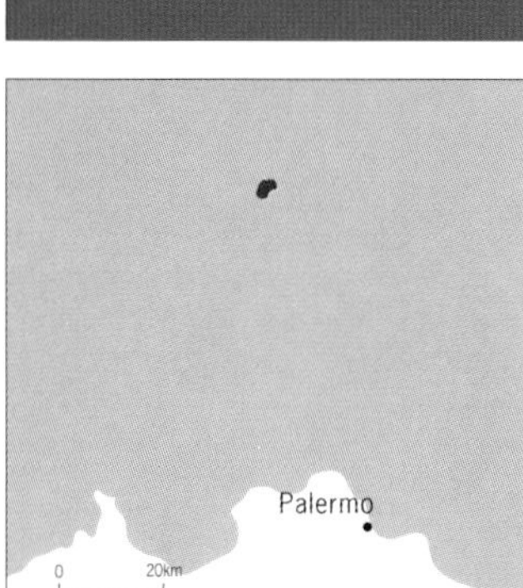

Palermo
0
20km

38°43' N 13°11' E
Ustica
Italy

The volcanic island of Ustica is now a marine reserve. Diving is one of the main activities and is well regulated, while inland there are peaceful walks through country rich in vines, capers, lentils, figs and other fruit. The most spectacular way to see the island is by boat, around a coast with a fine array of caves, rocks, cliffs and coves.

★★★☆☆ Tourism level
★★★☆☆ Vegetation
★★☆☆☆ Beaches
★★☆☆☆ History

Information
www.ustica.net
Telephone 091 844 9045

Map
Kaleghe (1:8500)

Area 8 sq km
Coastline 12 km
Highest point 248 m (M Guardia dei Turchi)

Permanent population 1335

Visitor capacity 1067
7 hotels
561 hotel beds
506 other beds
0 campsites

Crowdfactor
291 people per sq km

Access
Palermo 1½ hours
Palermo 3 hours

Connections
Palermo 3 daily
Palermo daily

Yacht facilities
Cala Santa Maria

3020 Italy

Ranking among all Mediterranean islands

	Rank
Area	17[illegible]
Population	9[illegible]
Visitor capacity	8[illegible]
Crowdfactor	3[illegible]

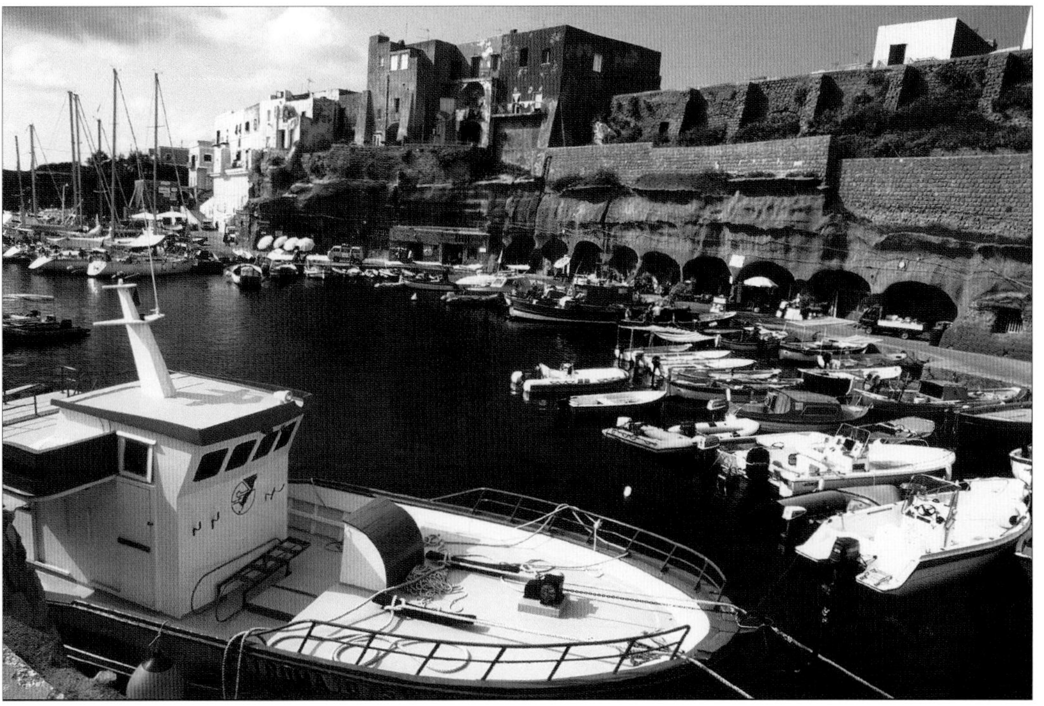

40°47' N 13°25' E
Ventotene
Isole Ponziane
Italy

Ventotene is a flat green island occupying part of an old volcanic crater. The village lies between the new port and the striking Roman port and the interior of the island has a rather rural feel with fields of lentils and other crops. It is worth taking a boat round the island to see its rock formations and over to the neighbouring island of Santo Stefano with its imposing 18th century prison.

★★★★☆ Tourism level
★★★☆☆ Vegetation
★★☆☆☆ Beaches
★★★☆☆ History

Information
www.ventotene.it
Telephone 0771 85257

Map
Brigantino (1:13600)

Area 1.4 sq km
Coastline 7 km
Highest point 139 m (Monte dell'Arco)

Permanent population 633

Visitor capacity 239
9 hotels
178 hotel beds
61 other beds
0 campsites

Crowdfactor
622 people per sq km

Access
Ponza 50 minutes
Casamicciola 1 hour
Formia, Napoli 2 hours

Connections
Formia 3 daily
Casamicciola, Napoli, Ponza 2 daily

Yacht facilities
Cala Rossano

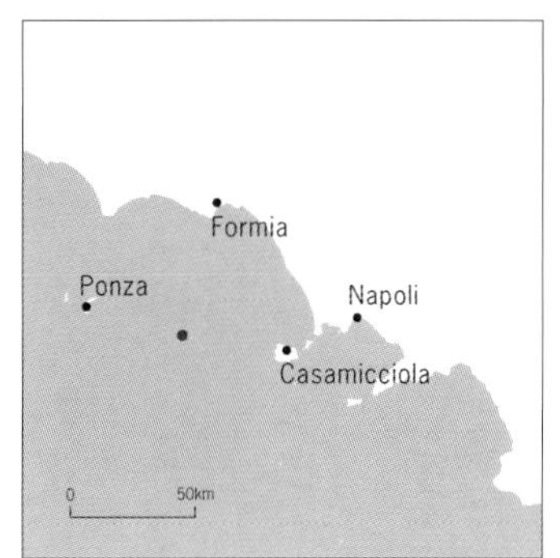
Formia
Ponza
Napoli
Casamicciola
0
50km

Ranking among all Mediterranean islands	Rank
Area	322
Population	117
Visitor capacity	133
Crowdfactor	20

Vulcano

PORTO DI PONENTE (PHOTO: ART MESSINA)

Porto di Levante
0
2km

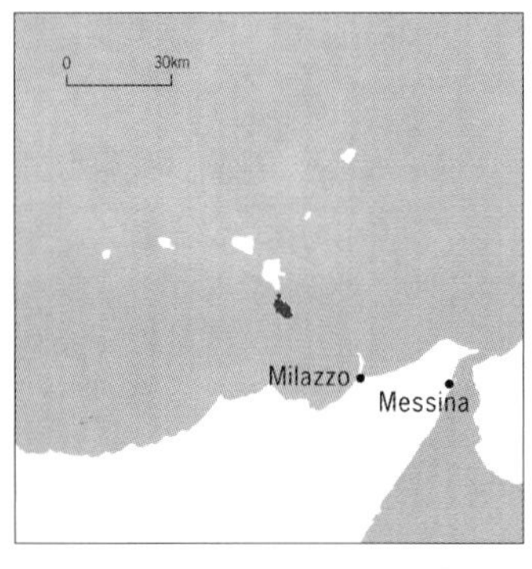
0
30km
Milazzo
Messina

38°22′ N 15°00′ E
Vulcano
Eolie
Italy

Composed of four volcanoes, Vulcano is a living study of the science that bears its name. An island of sometimes desolate beauty, it has soils coloured yellow, orange and red, fumaroles, underwater jets of steam sometimes heating the seawater almost to boiling point and sulphurous hot and evil-smelling mud. Incongruously, there are also woods and even sheep grazing inland and the views over the great crater should not be missed; nor should a boat trip round the amazing coastline.

★★★☆☆ Tourism level
★★☆☆☆ Vegetation
★★★☆☆ Beaches
★★☆☆☆ History

Information
www.isolelipari.it
Telephone 090 988 0095

Map
Kompass (1:25000)

Area 21 sq km
Coastline 28 km
Highest point 500 m (Monte Aria)

Permanent population 749

Visitor capacity 1187
14 hotels
923 hotel beds
264 other beds
0 campsites

Crowdfactor
92 people per sq km

Access
Milazzo 2 hours

Connections
Milazzo 4 daily

Yacht facilities
no fuel

Ranking among all Mediterranean islands

	Rar
Area	10
Population	11
Visitor capacity	7
Crowdfactor	9

3320 **Italy** Eolie

Brač

(PHOTO: CROATIAN NATIONAL TOURIST BOARD D FABIJANIC)

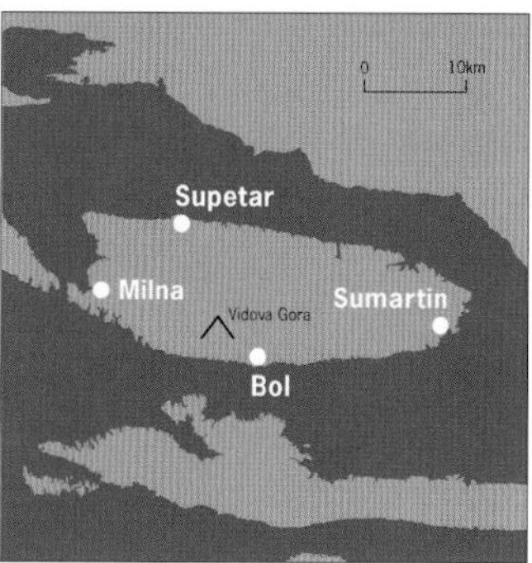

0
10km
Supetar
Milna
Vidova Gora
Sumartin
Bol

Split
Makarska
Jelsa
Dubrovnik
0
30km

43°19' N 16°26' E
Brač
Central Dalmatia
Croatia

Brač has a beautiful interior and the highest peak in all the Croatian islands, from which there are very fine views. Brač is famous for its white marble, used for Diocletian's Palace in Split and the White House in Washington. The Blaca monastery is interesting and Milna is a pretty port now with a marina offering 200 berths. The famous Zlatni Rat beach is usually very crowded but there are many other beaches and coves round the island. The small airport handles charter flights and a scheduled service to Zagreb.

★★★☆☆ Tourism level
★★★☆☆ Vegetation
★★★☆☆ Beaches
★★☆☆☆ History

Information
www.supetar.hr
www.bol.hr
Telephone 021 630551

Map
Freytag & Berndt (1:100000)

Area 394 sq km
Coastline 175 km
Highest point 780 m (Vidova Gora)

Permanent population 14031

Visitor capacity 19009
10 hotels
4831 hotel beds
14178 other beds
9 campsites

Crowdfactor
83 people per sq km

Access
✈ Brač
⛴ Split, Makarska 1 hour

Connections
Jelsa daily
⛴ Split 12 daily
⛴ Makarska 5 daily

Yacht facilities
⛵ Supetar, Bol, Milna

Ranking among all Mediterranean islands	Rank
Area	21
Population	32
Visitor capacity	20
Crowdfactor	99

4700 **Croatia** Central Dalmatia

43°30' N 16°20' E
Čiovo
Central Dalmatia
Croatia

Joined to Trogir by a bridge, Čiovo is a pleasant green island growing vines, oranges, lemons, figs and olives. There are good sandy beaches and coves and excellent food at Slatin. The Dominican monastery of Sv Kriz has a fine cloister and there are lovely views from the top of the island.

★★★☆☆ Tourism level
★★★☆☆ Vegetation
★★★☆☆ Beaches
★★★☆☆ History

Information
Telephone 021 881412

Map
Freytag & Berndt (1:100000)

Area 28 sq km
Coastline 43 km
Highest point 217 m (Rudine)

Permanent population 4455

Visitor capacity 4182
182 hotel beds
4000 other beds
0 campsites

Crowdfactor
299 people per sq km

Access
Bridge from Trogir

Connections
None scheduled

Yacht facilities
⛵ Marina Trogir

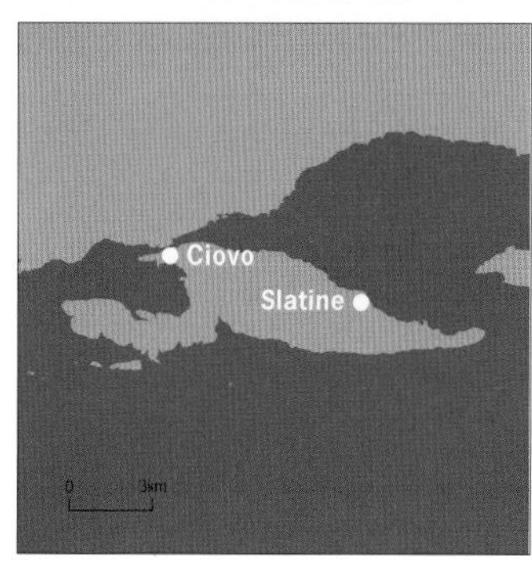
Čiovo
Slatine
0
3km

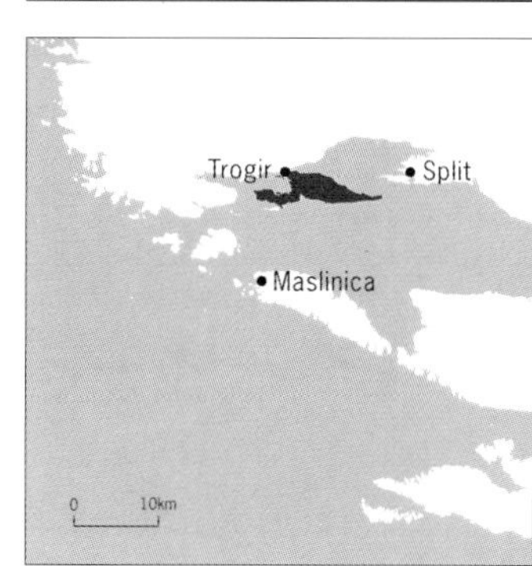
Trogir
Split
Maslinica
0
10km

Ranking among all Mediterranean islands	Rank
Area	95
Population	65
Visitor capacity	45
Crowdfactor	37

(PHOTO: MALI LOSINJ TOURIST BOARD)

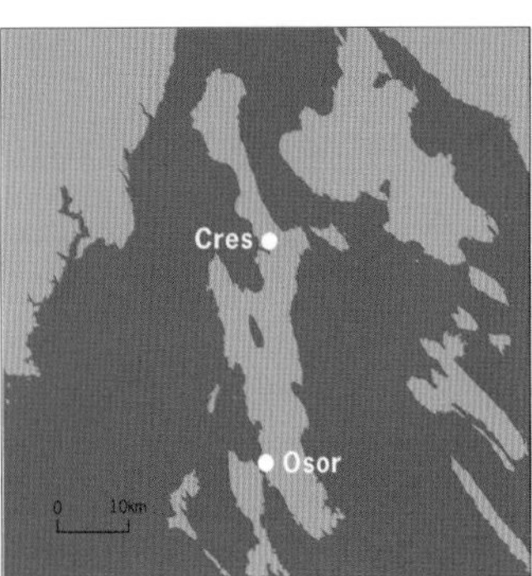
Cres
Osor
0 10km

Rijeka
Brestova
Valbiska
Pula
Zadar
Split
0 50km

45°07′ N 14°16′ E
Cres
Kvarner
Croatia

Large and uncrowded, Cres is an attractive island with extensive forests and pretty villages. The north east of the island is still home to the griffon vulture and in the centre of the island is Lake Vrana, the largest lake in the Croatian islands. The port of Cres is extremely picturesque and Osor is a fine old town, while Beli on the east coast has a lovely setting.

★★★☆☆ Tourism level
★★★☆☆ Vegetation
★★★★☆ Beaches
★★★☆☆ History

Information
www.island-cres.net
Telephone 051 571535

Map
Freytag & Berndt (1:100000)

Area 405 sq km
Coastline 247 km
Highest point 648 m (Gorica)

Permanent population 3184

Visitor capacity 4365
2 hotels
1137 hotel beds
3228 other beds
3 campsites

Crowdfactor
18 people per sq km

Access
Brestova 30 minutes
Valbiska 45 minutes

Connections
Brestova 20 daily
Valbiska 12 daily

Yacht facilities
Cres

Ranking among all Mediterranean islands	Ran
Area	1
Population	7
Visitor capacity	4
Crowdfactor	17

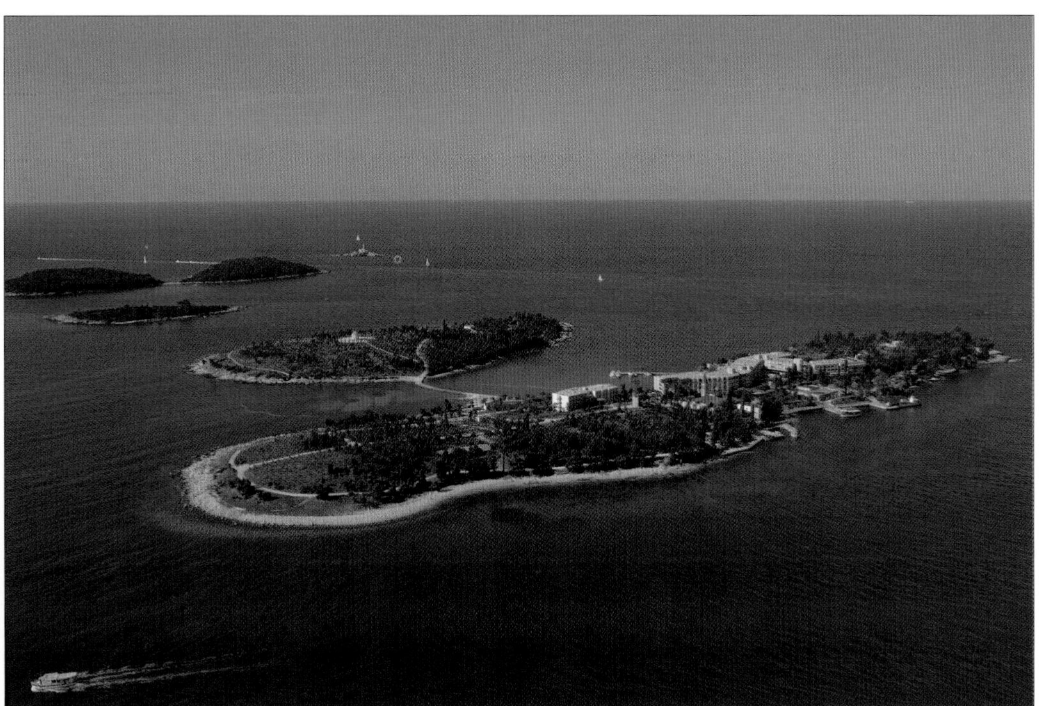

45°03′ N 13°37′ E
Crveni Otok
Istria
Croatia

Crveni Otok is a double island – Sv Andrija has a hotel and is joined by an isthmus to Maskin which has a nudist campsite.

★★★★☆ Tourism level
★★★★☆ Vegetation
★★★☆☆ Beaches
★★☆☆☆ History

Information
www.maistra.com
Telephone 052 802500

Map
None

Area 0.23 sq km
Coastline 3.1 km
Highest point 16 m

Permanent population 0

Visitor capacity 721
1 hotel
721 hotel beds
0 other beds
1 campsite

Crowdfactor
3134 people per sq km

Access
Rovinj 15 minutes

Connections
Rovinj 18 daily

Yacht facilities
no fuel

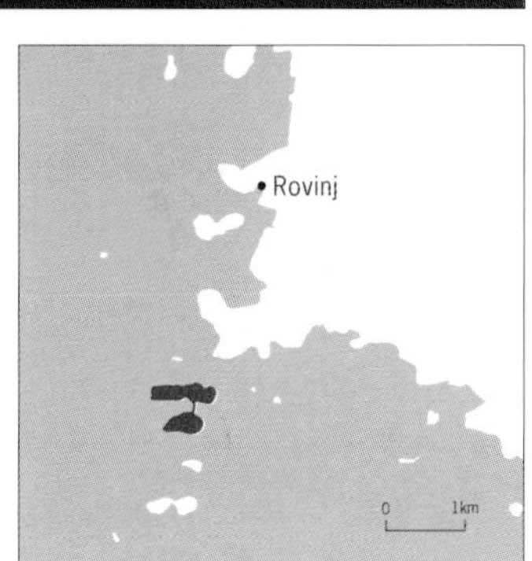
Rovinj
0
1km

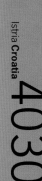

Ranking among all Mediterranean islands	Rank
Area	660
Population	0
Visitor capacity	98
Crowdfactor	3

(PHOTO: TZ ZADAR)

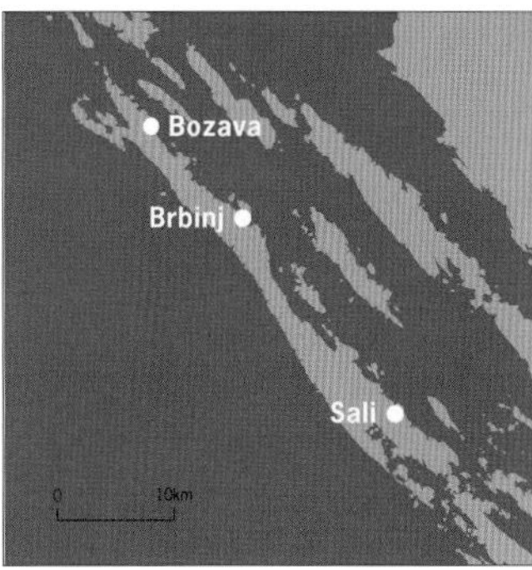
Bozava
Brbinj
Sali
0
10km

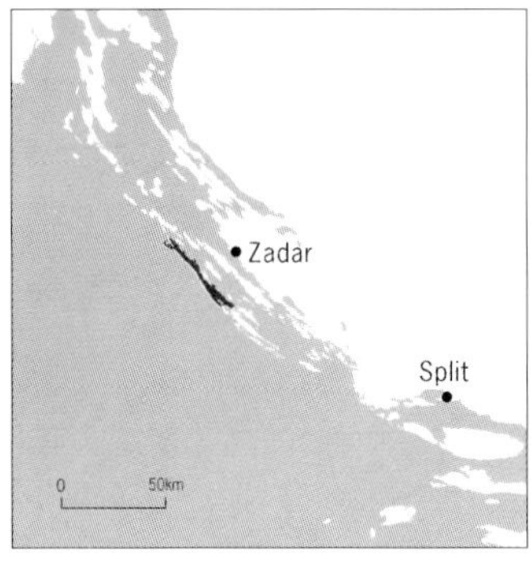
Zadar
Split
0
50km

44°00′ N 15°03′ E
Dugi Otok
North Dalmatia
Croatia

The long island has only one road and is best explored by boat. It has some stunning scenery, with cliffs, woods and picturesque villages. There is a terrific view over the many surrounding islands from the top of Brucastac and the cave of Strasna Pecina is worth visiting. Bozava is an attractive resort and there is a Franciscan monastery at Zaglav. The beautiful Telascica Bay in the south is now a nature park. The island is quiet, with friendly people and very good fishing and is regularly visited by sailors.

★★★☆☆ Tourism level
★★★☆☆ Vegetation
★★☆☆☆ Beaches
★☆☆☆☆ History

Information
www.dugiotok.hr
Telephone 023 377094

Map
Freytag & Berndt (1:100000)

Area 114 sq km
Coastline 170 km
Highest point 338 m (Vela Straza)

Permanent population 1772

Visitor capacity 2563
3 hotels
852 hotel beds
1711 other beds
0 campsites

Crowdfactor
37 people per sq km

Access
Zadar 1 hour
Zadar 1½ hours

Connections
Zadar 3 daily
Zadar 4 daily

Yacht facilities
Zaglav

Ranking among all Mediterranean islands	Rar
Area	4
Population	9
Visitor capacity	5
Crowdfactor	14

43°51′ N 15°26′ E
Gangaro
North Dalmatia
Croatia

Private accommodation on this little island, which lies to the south of Pašman, can be arranged in Murter together with boat transfer.

★☆☆☆☆ Tourism level
★★★☆☆ Vegetation
★★☆☆☆ Beaches
★☆☆☆☆ History

Information
Telephone 022 436544

Map
None

Area 0.79 sq km
Coastline 4.6 km
Highest point 27 m

Permanent population 0

Visitor capacity 30
0 hotels
0 hotel beds
30 other beds
0 campsites

Crowdfactor
37 people per sq km

Access
Private boat from Murter

Connections
None scheduled

Yacht facilities
⛵ no fuel

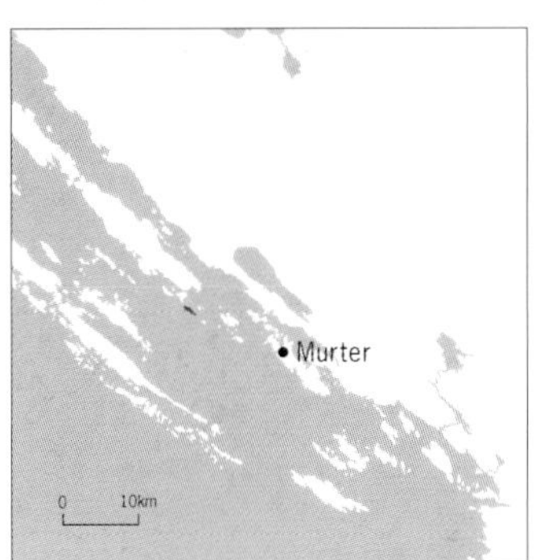
Murter
0 10km

Ranking among all Mediterranean islands

	Rank
Area	393
Population	0
Visitor capacity	191
Crowdfactor	146

(PHOTO: CROATIAN NATIONAL TOURIST BOARD J KOPAC)

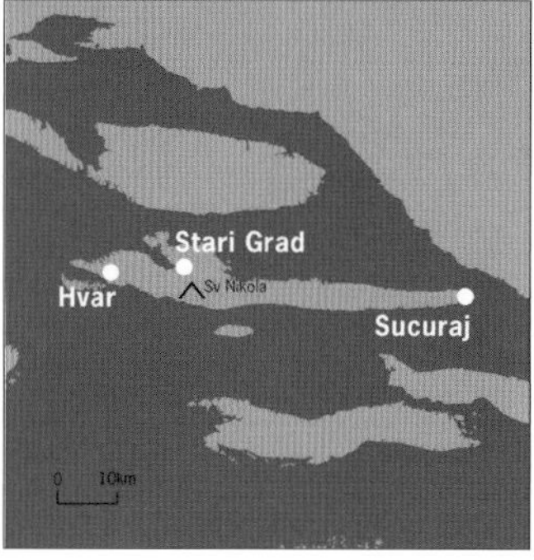
Stari Grad
Hvar
Sv Nikola
Sucuraj
0 10km

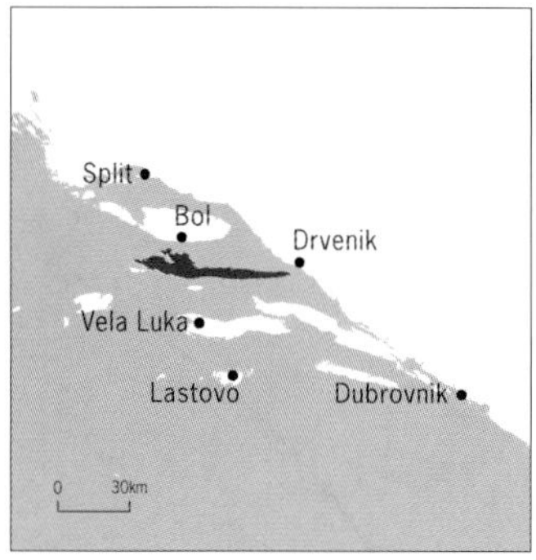
Split
Bol
Drvenik
Vela Luka
Lastovo
Dubrovnik
0 30km

43°09′ N 16°38′ E
Hvar
Central Dalmatia
Croatia

A beautiful green island best explored by car, Hvar is famous for its lavender, good food and beaches. The town of Hvar is extremely attractive, with its cathedral, bishop's palace, Franciscan monastery and lovely old houses and churches, and the view from the Spanjol fortress is lovely too. Stari Grad is well worth visiting for its Dominican monastery and the fortified Trvdalj summer residence of the poet Hektorovic. Vrboska is a charming and picturesque little town.

★★★★☆ Tourism level
★★★★☆ Vegetation
★★★★☆ Beaches
★★★☆☆ History

Information
www.hvar.hr
Telephone 021 741059

Map
Freytag & Berndt (1:100000)

Area 299 sq km
Coastline 254 km
Highest point 628 m (Sv Nikola)

Permanent population 11103

Visitor capacity 17714
19 hotels
5476 hotel beds
12238 other beds
7 campsites

Crowdfactor
96 people per sq km

Access
✈ Split 1 hour
⛴ Drvenik 30 minutes
⛴ Split 2 hours

Connections
✈ Split 2 daily
✈ Lastovo, Bol, Vela Luka daily
⛴ Drvenik 12 daily
⛴ Split 7 daily

Yacht facilities
⛵ Hvar, Vrboska, Jelsa

Ranking among all Mediterranean islands

	Rank[illegible]
Area	2[illegible]
Population	4[illegible]
Visitor capacity	2[illegible]
Crowdfactor	9[illegible]

44°27′ N 14°33′ E
Ilovik
Kvarner
Croatia

Ilovik is a fertile island with abundant water and is well known for its lovely flowers, oranges, lemons, vegetables and eucalyptus.

★★☆☆☆ Tourism level
★★★★☆ Vegetation
★★★☆☆ Beaches
★★☆☆☆ History

Information
www.tz-malilosinj.hr
Telephone 051 231547

Map
Drzavna Geodetska Uprava (1:25000)

Area 5 sq km
Coastline 14 km
Highest point 88 m (Did)

Permanent population 104

Visitor capacity 25
0 hotels
0 hotel beds
25 other beds
0 campsites

Crowdfactor
23 people per sq km

Access
Mali Losinj 1 hour

Connections
Mali Losinj 3 daily

Yacht facilities
no fuel

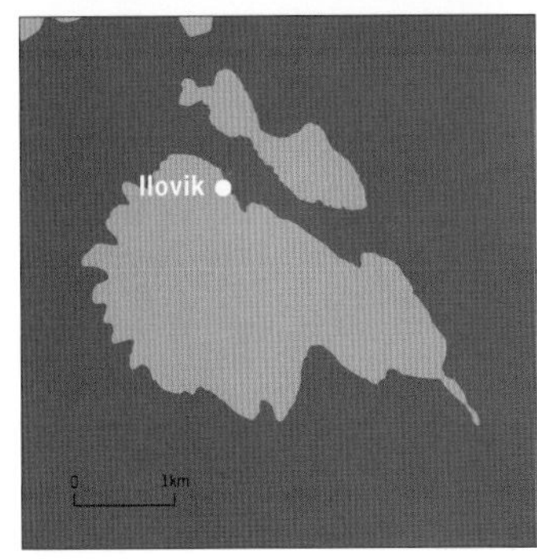
Ilovik
0 1km

Mali Lošinj
0 10km

Ranking among all Mediterranean islands

	Rank
Area	195
Population	170
Visitor capacity	195
Crowdfactor	167

Ist

(PHOTO: TZ ZADAR)

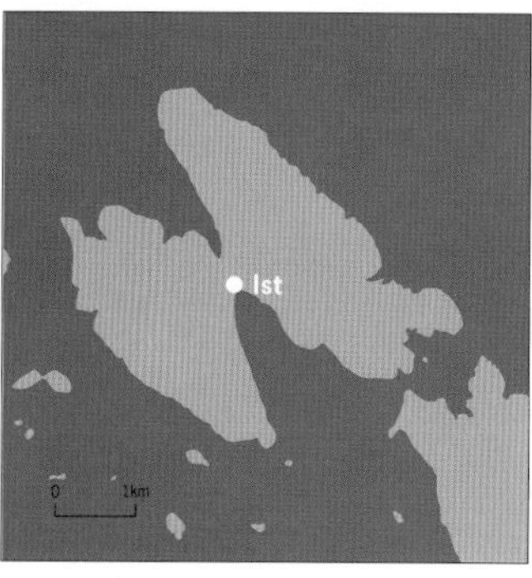
Ist
0 1km

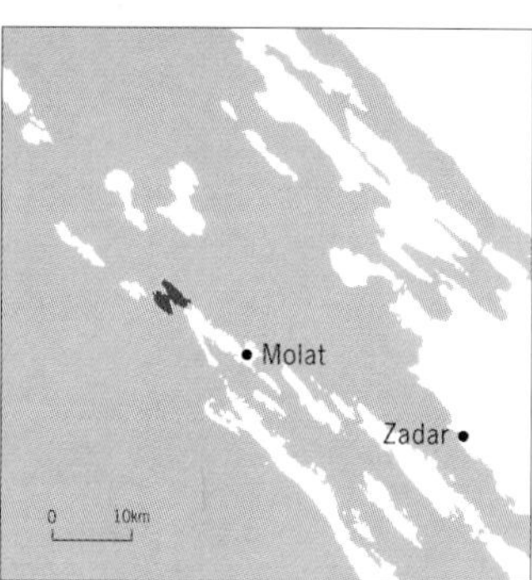
Molat
Zadar
0 10km

44°16' N 14°46' E
Ist
North Dalmatia
Croatia

A hilly wooded quiet island with pleasant coves, Ist has a fertile centre growing mainly vines and olives.

★★☆☆☆ Tourism level
★★★☆☆ Vegetation
★★★☆☆ Beaches
★☆☆☆☆ History

Information
Telephone 023 316166

Map
Drzavna Geodetska Uprava (1:25000)

Area 9 sq km
Coastline 23 km
Highest point 174 m (Straza)

Permanent population 202

Visitor capacity 192
0 hotels
0 hotel beds
192 other beds
0 campsites

Crowdfactor
40 people per sq km

Access
Zadar 2 hours
Zadar 2½ hours

Connections
Zadar daily
Zadar 4 weekly

Yacht facilities
no fuel

Ranking among all Mediterranean islands	Ran
Area	16(
Population	15
Visitor capacity	14
Crowdfactor	14

44°02′ N 15°06′ E
Iž
North Dalmatia
Croatia

Iž has a dense forest of pine trees, with two quiet villages of fishermen and farmers growing olives fruit and vines.

★★☆☆☆ Tourism level
★★★★☆ Vegetation
★★★☆☆ Beaches
★★☆☆☆ History

Information
Telephone 023 316166

Map
Freytag & Berndt (1:100000)

Area 17 sq km
Coastline 35 km
Highest point 168 m (Korinjak)

Permanent population 557

Visitor capacity 640
1 hotel
204 hotel beds
436 other beds
0 campsites

Crowdfactor
68 people per sq km

Access
Zadar 1½ hours

Connections
Zadar 3 daily

Yacht facilities
no fuel

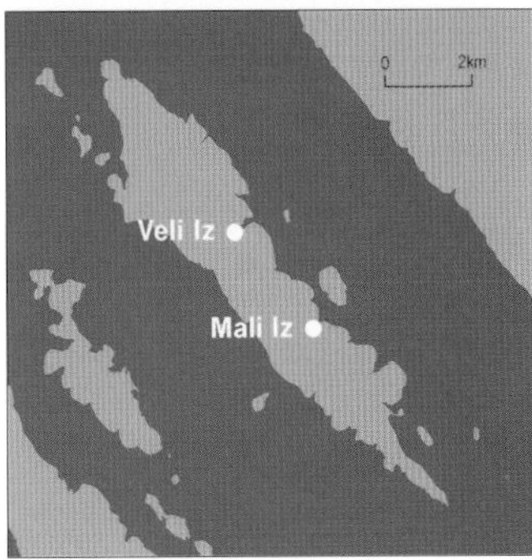
0
2km
Veli Iz
Mali Iz

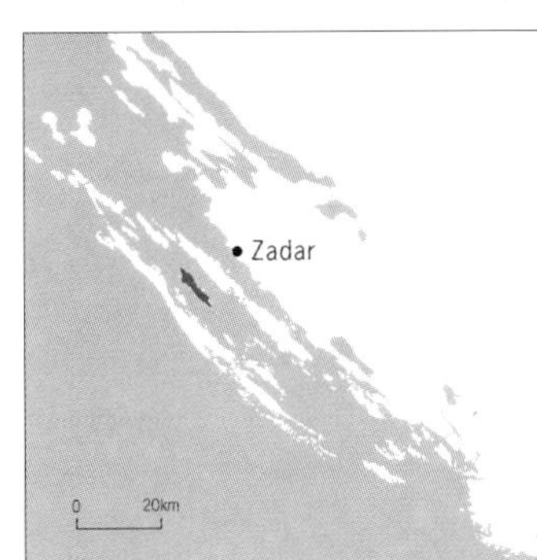
Zadar
0
20km

Ranking among all Mediterranean islands

	Rank
Area	125
Population	120
Visitor capacity	101
Crowdfactor	109

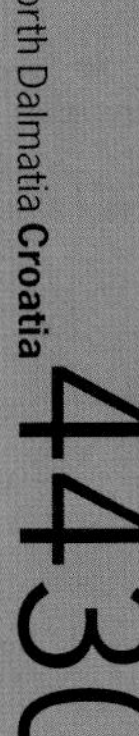
North Dalmatia **Croatia**
4430

Kaprije

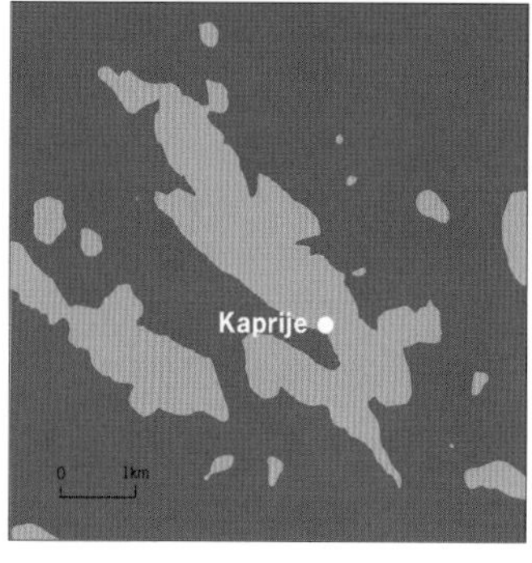
Kaprije
0 1km

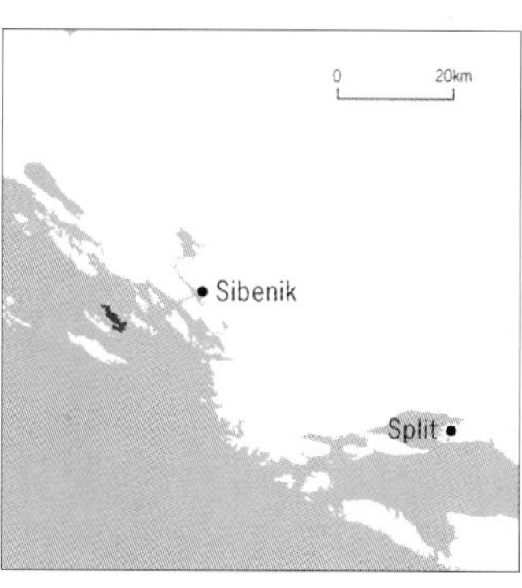
0 20km
Sibenik
Split

43°40′ N 15°43′ E
Kaprije
North Dalmatia
Croatia

Kaprije is a quiet hilly island with no cars. It has pretty coves, olives and pine trees and makes good wine.

★★☆☆☆ Tourism level
★★★☆☆ Vegetation
★★☆☆☆ Beaches
★☆☆☆☆ History

Information
Telephone 022 212075

Map
Drzavna Geodetska Uprava (1:25000)

Area 6 sq km
Coastline 24 km
Highest point 129 m (Vela Glavica)

Permanent population 143

Visitor capacity 125
0 hotels
0 hotel beds
125 other beds
0 campsites

Crowdfactor
38 people per sq km

Access
Sibenik 30 minutes
Sibenik 1½ hours

Connections
Sibenik daily
Sibenik daily

Yacht facilities
no fuel

4650 Croatia North Dalmatia

Ranking among all Mediterranean islands

	Ran
Area	18
Population	16
Visitor capacity	15
Crowdfactor	14

42°39' N 18°01' E
Koločep
South Dalmatia
Croatia

The smallest of the three main Elafiti islands, Koločep is a luxuriant island with beautifully scented pine forest, no cars, good beaches and a number of ruined churches.

★★★☆☆ Tourism level
★★★★☆ Vegetation
★★☆☆☆ Beaches
★★☆☆☆ History

Information
www.dubrovnikandislands.com
Telephone 020 323907

Map
None

Area 2.4 sq km
Coastline 12 km
Highest point 125 m (Kriz)

Permanent population 294

Visitor capacity 407
1 hotel
369 hotel beds
38 other beds
0 campsites

Crowdfactor
288 people per sq km

Access
Dubrovnik 30 minutes

Connections
Dubrovnik 4 daily

Yacht facilities
no fuel

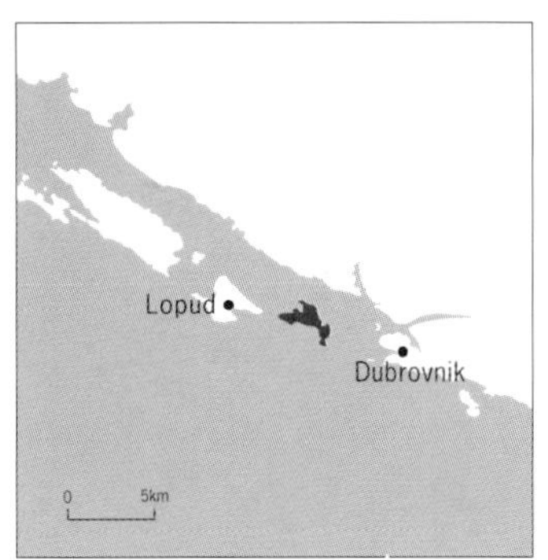
Lopud
Dubrovnik
0
5km

Ranking among all Mediterranean islands

	Rank
Area	267
Population	137
Visitor capacity	118
Crowdfactor	40

Korčula

(PHOTO: CROATIAN NATIONAL TOURIST BOARD / J. KOPAC)

Vela Luka
Blato
Korcula
0 10km

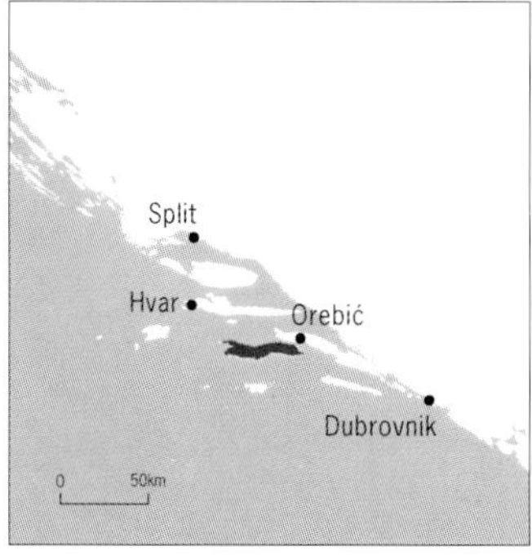

Split
Hvar
Orebić
Dubrovnik
0 50km

42°56′ N 16°53′ E
Korčula
South Dalmatia
Croatia

A beautiful island with fine pine forests, Korčula is best explored by car. The walled town of Korčula is magnificent with its cathedral, Bishop's Palace, Prince's Palace and Dominican monastery. It is also worth visiting the Franciscan monastery with its fine cloister on the island of Badija. Korčula is well known for its cakes and produces very good white wines. There are good beaches on the islets of Osjak and Proizd reached from Vela Luka.

★★★☆☆ Tourism level
★★★★☆ Vegetation
★★★☆☆ Beaches
★★★★☆ History

Information
www.korculainfo.com
Telephone 020 715867

Map
Freytag & Berndt (1:100000)

Area 276 sq km
Coastline 181 km
Highest point 569 m (Klupca)

Permanent population 16182

Visitor capacity 9616
15 hotels
3378 hotel beds
6238 other beds
9 campsites

Crowdfactor
93 people per sq km

Access
✈ Split 2 hours
⛴ Orebic 15 minutes
⛴ Split 3 hours

Connections
✈ Split daily
⛴ Orebic 18 daily
⛴ Split 2 daily

Yacht facilities
⛵ 4 ports

Ranking among all Mediterranean islands	Ran
Area	3
Population	3
Visitor capacity	2
Crowdfactor	9

4800 **Croatia** South Dalmatia

43°50′ N 15°15′ E
Kornat
North Dalmatia
Croatia

Kornat is the main island in an archipelago of over 100 islands which is a national park and very popular with sailors (there is a marina on Piskera with120 berths). The west side of the island has fine cliffs and the middle of the island, although for the most part sparsely vegetated, supports isolated fields of oranges, lemons, figs, vines and olives. It is possible to rent a cottage on Kornat through agencies in Murter to enjoy a remote holiday with good walking and snorkelling. Day trips can also be arranged.

★★☆☆☆ Tourism level
★★☆☆☆ Vegetation
★★☆☆☆ Beaches
★★★☆☆ History

Information
www.kornati.hr
Telephone 022 436544

Map
Freytag & Berndt (1:100000)

Area 32 sq km
Coastline 66 km
Highest point 237 m (Metlina)

Permanent population 7

Visitor capacity 200
0 hotels
0 hotel beds
200 other beds
0 campsites

Crowdfactor
6 people per sq km

Access
Private boat from Murter

Connections
None scheduled

Yacht facilities
⛵ no fuel

Lucice
Vrulje
0
5km

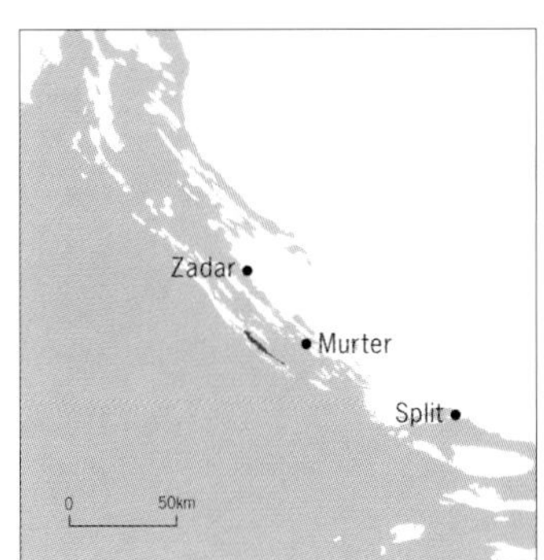
Zadar
Murter
Split
0
50km

Ranking among all Mediterranean islands	Rank
Area	93
Population	212
Visitor capacity	136
Crowdfactor	209

Kornat

North Dalmatia **Croatia** 4500

Krapanj

(PHOTO: CROATIAN NATIONAL TOURIST BOARD D FABIJANIĆ)

Sibenik
Brodarica
0
10km

43°40′ N 15°54′ E
Krapanj
North Dalmatia
Croatia

This very small wooded island has a Franciscan monastery with a beautiful cloister and is famous for its good food especially shellfish.

★★★☆☆ Tourism level
★★★☆☆ Vegetation
★☆☆☆☆ Beaches
★★★☆☆ History

Information
www.krapanj.com
Telephone 022 350612

Map
None

Area 0.35 sq km
Coastline 3.6 km
Highest point 7 m

Permanent population 237

Visitor capacity 2268
1 hotels
65 hotel beds
2203 other beds
0 campsites

Crowdfactor
7157 people per sq km

Access
Brodarica 10 minutes

Connections
Brodarica 10 daily

Yacht facilities
no fuel

Ranking among all Mediterranean islands

	Rank
Area	542
Population	145
Visitor capacity	58
Crowdfactor	2

4690 **Croatia** North Dalmatia

45°13' N 14°36' E
Krk
Kvarner
Croatia

With an airport in the north of the island and some crowded resorts, Krk has more than twice the number of visitors of any other Croatian island. The south is less crowded, with some forest and widespread vineyards and olive groves. Krk is a fine town with a castle and cathedral and Vrbnik has a charming medieval centre. A much visited tourist attraction is the Franciscan monastery on the wooded islet of Kosljun.

★★★★☆ Tourism level
★★★☆☆ Vegetation
★★★☆☆ Beaches
★★★☆☆ History

nformation
www.krk.hr
Telephone 051 221359

Map
Freytag & Berndt (1:100000)

Area 405 sq km
Coastline 189 km
Highest point 568 m (Obzovo)

Permanent population 17860

Visitor capacity 36860
12 hotels
8540 hotel beds
28320 other beds
7 campsites

Crowdfactor
134 people per sq km

Access
✈ Krk
Bridge to mainland

Connections
⛴ Merag 12 daily
⛴ Lopar 3 daily

Yacht facilities
⛵ Krk, Malinska

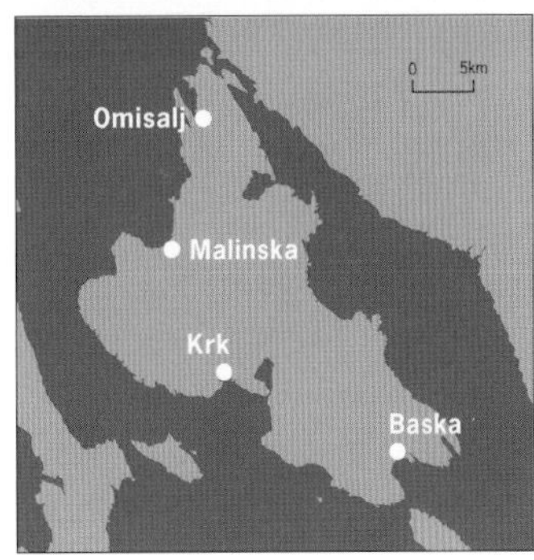
0 5km
Omisalj
Malinska
Krk
Baska

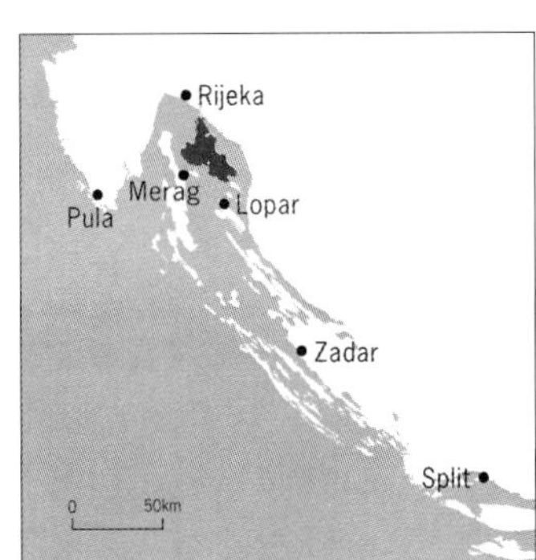
Rijeka
Merag
Lopar
Pula
Zadar
Split
0 50km

Ranking among all Mediterranean islands	Rank
Area	19
Population	26
Visitor capacity	14
Crowdfactor	74

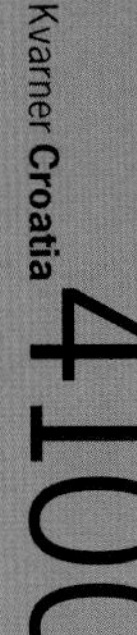
4100

Lastovo

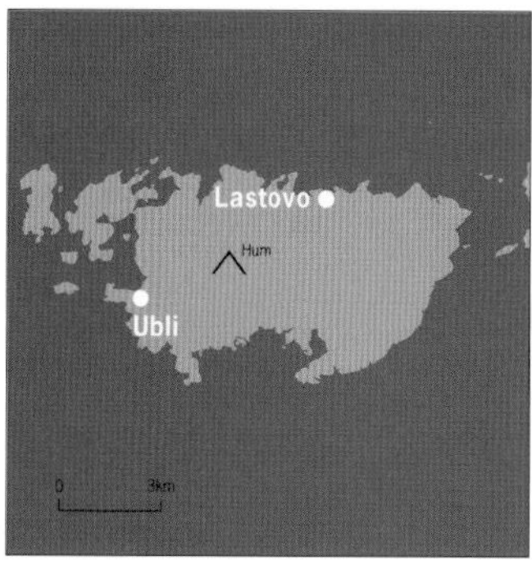
Lastovo
Hum
Ubli
0
3km

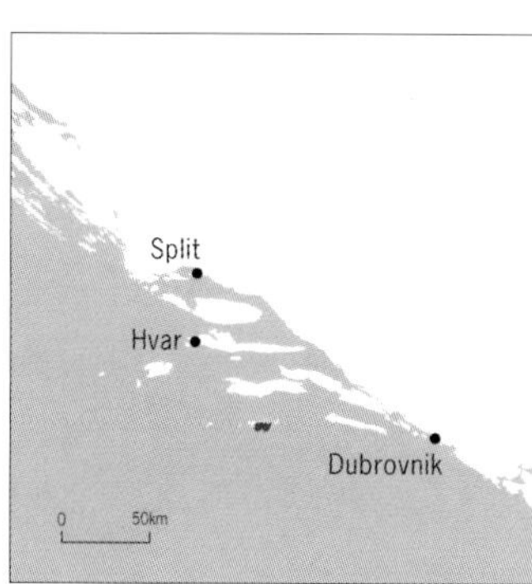
Split
Hvar
Dubrovnik
0
50km

42°43' N 16°53' E
Lastovo
South Dalmatia
Croatia

A lovely quiet island with an isolated feel, Lastovo has beautiful pine forests and good fish and wine. The town has fine old churches and a number of pretty islands lie offshore, reached by boats from the harbour.

★★☆☆☆ Tourism level
★★★☆☆ Vegetation
★★★☆☆ Beaches
★★☆☆☆ History

Information
www.lastovo-tz.net
Telephone 020 801018

Map
Freytag & Berndt (1:100000)

Area 46 sq km
Coastline 46 km
Highest point 415 m (Hum)

Permanent population 835

Visitor capacity 633
1 hotel
176 hotel beds
457 other beds
1 campsite

Crowdfactor
31 people per sq km

Access
Split 3 hours
Split 5 hours

Connections
Split daily
Split daily

Yacht facilities
Ubli

Ranking among all Mediterranean islands	Ran
Area	7
Population	11
Visitor capacity	10
Crowdfactor	15

4900 **Croatia** South Dalmatia

43°56′ N 15°12′ E
Lavdara
North Dalmatia
Croatia

A lovely little pine-clad island where you can escape from the world to enjoy nothing but the simple pleasures of walking, fishing, diving and eating delicious local produce.

★☆☆☆☆ Tourism level
★★★★☆ Vegetation
★★☆☆☆ Beaches
★☆☆☆☆ History

Information
www.lavdaraturist.com
Telephone 023 321884

Map
None

Area 2.27 sq km
Coastline 9 km
Highest point 88 m (V Vrh)

Permanent population 0

Visitor capacity 18
0 hotels
0 hotel beds
18 other beds
0 campsites

Crowdfactor
7 people per sq km

Access
Sali 15 minutes

Connections
None scheduled

Yacht facilities
no fuel

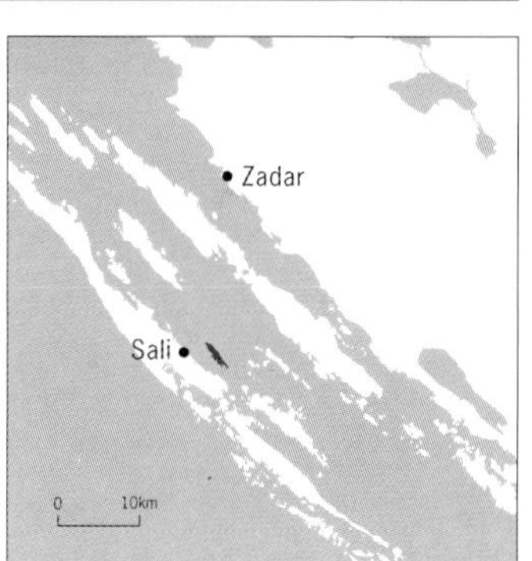
Zadar
Sali
0
10km

Ranking among all Mediterranean islands

	Rank
Area	276
Population	0
Visitor capacity	199
Crowdfactor	205

Lavsa

(PHOTO: DIGITAL FILM SIBENIK)

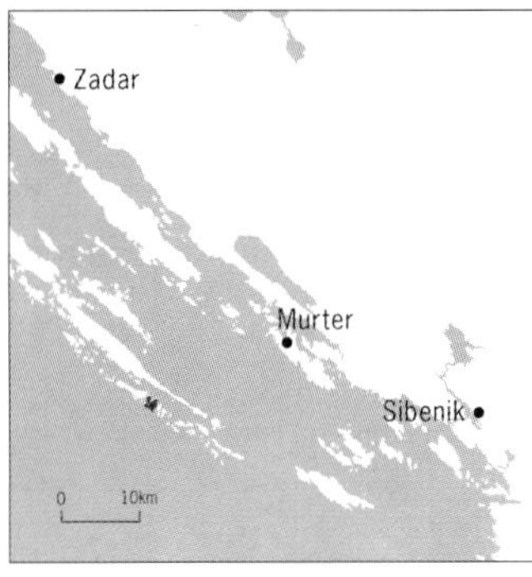
Zadar
Murter
Sibenik
0 10km

43°45' N 15°22' E
Lavsa
North Dalmatia
Croatia

Private accommodation on this little island, which lies on the seaward side of Kornat, can be arranged in Murter together with boat transfer. Lavsa has an attractive bay, much visited by sailors, and there are three restaurants on the island.

★☆☆☆☆ Tourism level
★☆☆☆☆ Vegetation
★☆☆☆☆ Beaches
★☆☆☆☆ History

Information
Telephone 022 436544

Map
None

Area 1.78 sq km
Coastline 9 km
Highest point 111 m (V Vrh)

Permanent population 0

Visitor capacity 20
0 hotels
0 hotel beds
20 other beds
0 campsites

Crowdfactor
11 people per sq km

Access
Private boat from Murter

Connections
None scheduled

Yacht facilities
⛵ no fuel

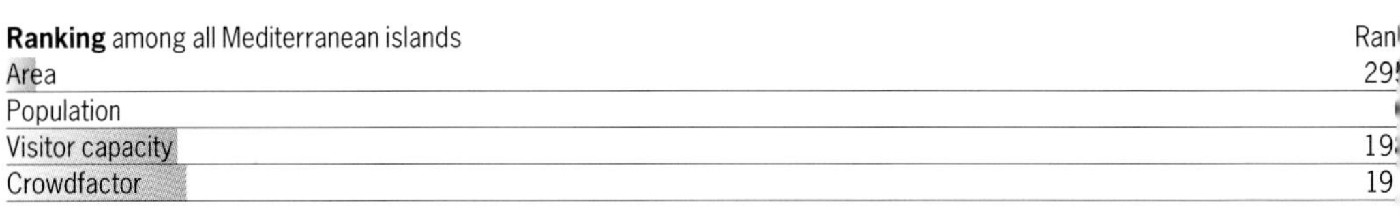
Ranking among all Mediterranean islands
Area
Population
Visitor capacity
Crowdfactor

4514 **Croatia** North Dalmatia

Lopud

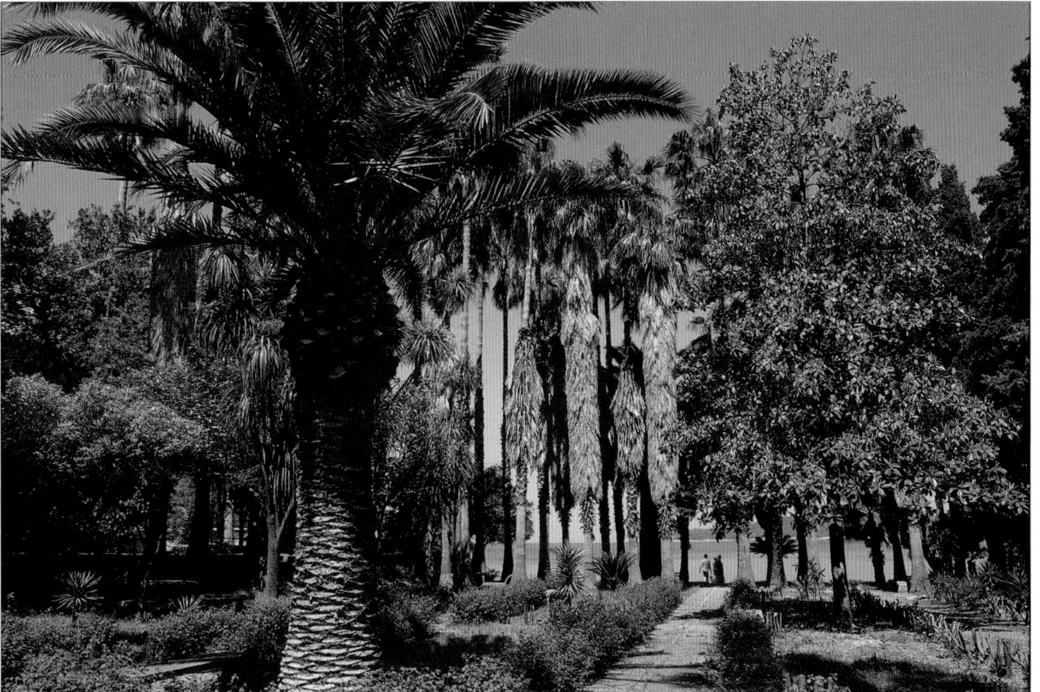

42°41' N 17°57' E
Lopud
South Dalmatia
Croatia

Lopud is the liveliest of the Elafiti islands and the beach at Sunj can get crowded. The vegetation is luxuriant, with palms and cypresses in the gardens of the fine stone houses. There are two monasteries on the island, now both deserted, and the interesting old church of Sv Ilija with its museum.

★★★☆☆ Tourism level
★★★★☆ Vegetation
★★☆☆☆ Beaches
★★★☆☆ History

nformation
www.dubrovnikandislands.com
elephone 020 759086

lap
lone

Area 4.3 sq km
Coastline 14 km
Highest point 216 m (Polacica)

Permanent population 269

Visitor capacity 779
3 hotels
487 hotel beds
292 other beds
0 campsites

Crowdfactor
239 people per sq km

Access
⛴ Dubrovnik 45 minutes
Connections
⛴ Dubrovnik 4 daily

Yacht facilities
⛵ no fuel

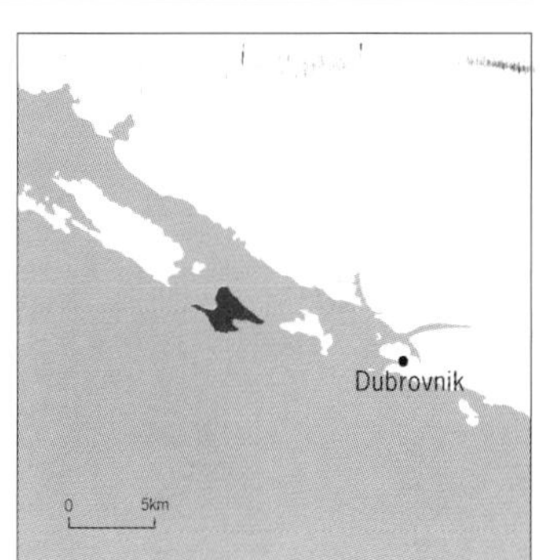
Dubrovnik
0
5km

anking among all Mediterranean islands	Rank
rea	211
pulation	141
sitor capacity	93
rowdfactor	49

South Dalmatia **Croatia** 4970

Lošinj

(PHOTO: CROATIAN NATIONAL TOURIST BOARD

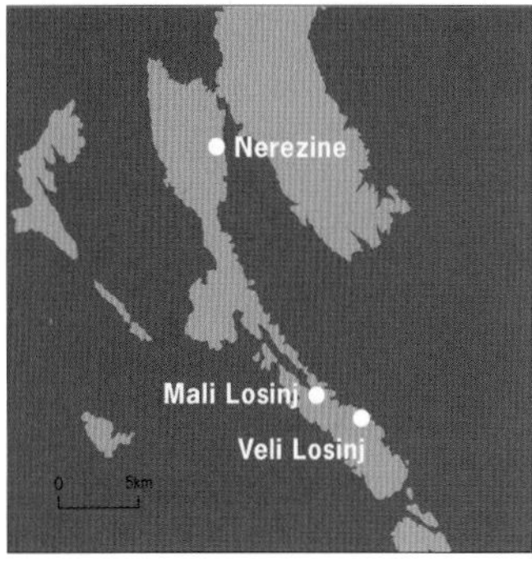
Nerezine
Mali Losinj
Veli Losinj
0
5km

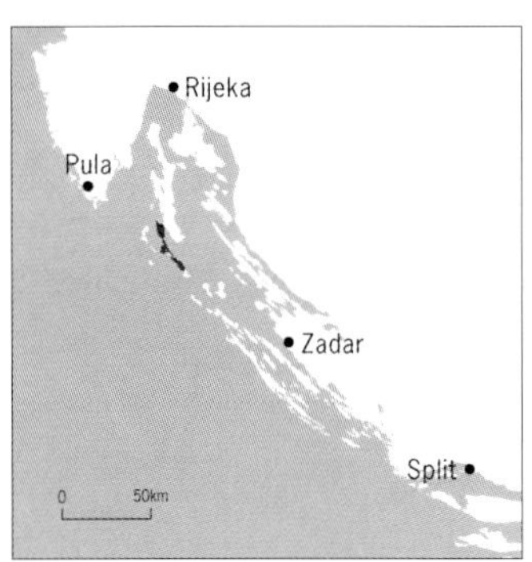
Rijeka
Pula
Zadar
Split
0
50km

44°33' N 14°22' E
Lošinj
Kvarner
Croatia

Of the two attractive old towns, Mali Lošinj is now a package tour centre while Veli Lošinj is much quieter. The island is the most crowded of the Croatian islands after Murter, but the interior is still attractive for walking and there is a superb view from the top of Televrina over the surrounding islands. It is also easy to take day trips to a number of different outlying islands. There is a small airport for private planes with a flight to the island of Unije three times a week.

★★★★☆ Tourism level
★★★☆☆ Vegetation
★★★☆☆ Beaches
★★★☆☆ History

Information
www.tz-malilosinj.hr
Telephone 051 231547

Map
Freytag & Berndt (1:100000)

Area 74 sq km
Coastline 112 km
Highest point 589 m (Televrina)

Permanent population 7771

Visitor capacity 13465
9 hotels
5895 hotel beds
7570 other beds
3 campsites

Crowdfactor
284 people per sq km

Access
Bridge to Cres
Rijeka 4 hours

Connections
Rijeka 2 daily

Yacht facilities
Mali Losinj

Ranking among all Mediterranean islands	Ran
Area	6
Population	5
Visitor capacity	2
Crowdfactor	4

4120 **Croatia** Kvarner

43°27′ N 16°05′ E
Mali Drvenik
Central Dalmatia
Croatia

Mali Drvenik is a very quiet fishing island that also grows olives. It has good sandy and rocky beaches and coves, the best being at Vela Rina bay.

★★☆☆☆ Tourism level
★★★☆☆ Vegetation
★★★☆☆ Beaches
★☆☆☆☆ History

Information
Telephone 021 881412

Map
Drzavna Geodetska Uprava (1:25000)

Area 3.42 sq km
Coastline 12 km
Highest point 79 m (Glavica)

Permanent population 54

Visitor capacity 15
0 hotels
0 hotel beds
15 other beds
0 campsites

Crowdfactor
20 people per sq km

Access
Trogir 1½ hours

Connections
Trogir 2 daily

Yacht facilities
no fuel

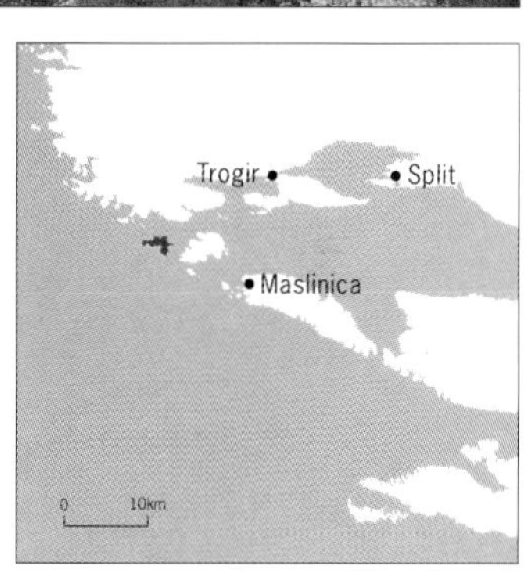
Trogir
Split
Maslinica
0
10km

Ranking among all Mediterranean islands

	Rank
Area	236
Population	183
Visitor capacity	202
Crowdfactor	174

Mljet

(PHOTO: CROATIAN NATIONAL TOURIST BOARD)

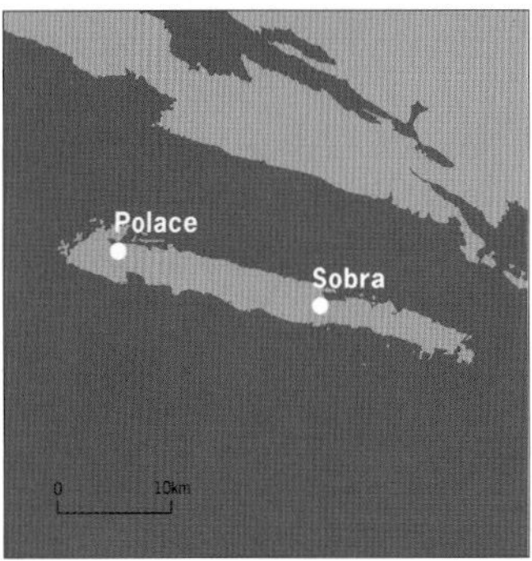

Polace
Sobra
0
10km

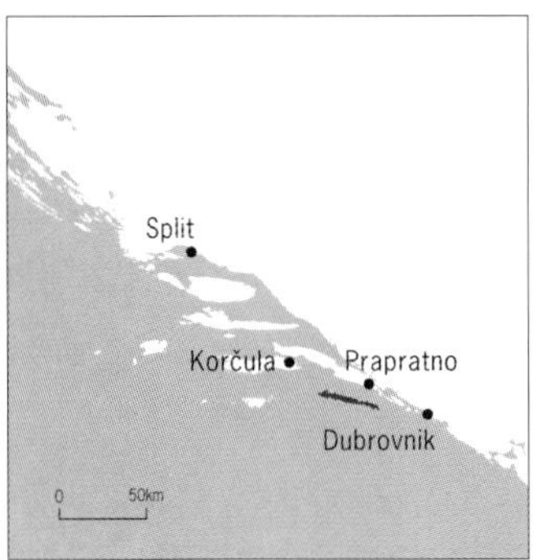

Split
Korčula
Prapratno
Dubrovnik
0
50km

42°44' N 17°31' E
Mljet
South Dalmatia
Croatia

A beautiful island mostly covered by forest, the west end of which is a national park, where there are two saltwater lakes and a pretty islet with the monastery of Sv Marija. Mljet is a good place for cycling and walking and is also known for its good food, especially its fish, cheese and wine. Mongooses, originally introduced to reduce the large number of snakes, have now become wild. The caves of Movrica, Otasevica and Rikavica near Babino Polje are worth visiting.

★★☆☆☆ Tourism level
★★★★☆ Vegetation
★★★☆☆ Beaches
★★☆☆☆ History

Information
www.mljet.hr
Telephone 020 746025

Map
Freytag & Berndt (1:100000)

Area 100 sq km
Coastline 131 km
Highest point 513 m (Veliki Grad)

Permanent population 1111

Visitor capacity 1349
1 hotel
345 hotel beds
1004 other beds
0 campsites

Crowdfactor
24 people per sq km

Access
Korčula 1 hour
Dubrovnik 1½ hours
Prapratno 1 hour
Dubrovnik 2½ hours

Connections
Dubrovnik, Korčula daily
Prapratno 5 daily
Korčula daily

Yacht facilities
Luka Sobra

Ranking among all Mediterranean islands	Ra
Area	4
Population	10
Visitor capacity	
Crowdfactor	16

44°12′ N 14°50′ E
Molat
North Dalmatia
Croatia

An island visited mainly by people in boats, Molat is green and fertile and produces good sheep's cheese. It has good beaches and coves and an active fishing community.

★★☆☆☆ Tourism level
★★★★☆ Vegetation
★★★☆☆ Beaches
★☆☆☆☆ History

Information
Telephone 023 316166

Map
Freytag & Berndt (1:100000)

Area 22 sq km
Coastline 48 km
Highest point 148 m (Lokardenik)

Permanent population 207

Visitor capacity 210
0 hotels
0 hotel beds
210 other beds
0 campsites

Crowdfactor
18 people per sq km

Access
Zadar 1 hour
Zadar 3 hours

Connections
Zadar daily
Zadar daily

Yacht facilities
no fuel

Zapuntel
Molat
0
2km

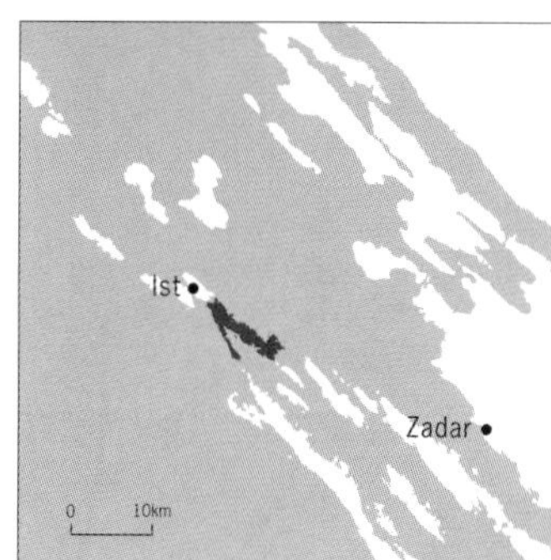
Ist
Zadar
0
10km

Ranking among all Mediterranean islands	Rank
Area	105
Population	150
Visitor capacity	135
Crowdfactor	176

Mrcara

PHOTO: VISIT-TROGIR DENIS PAVELIN

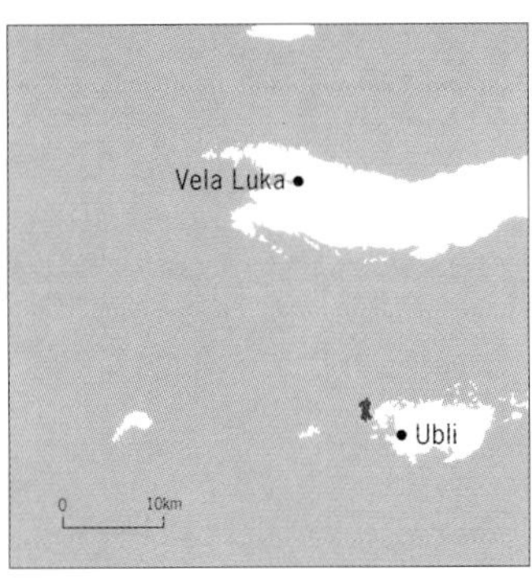

Vela Luka
Ubli
0
10km

42°46′ N 16°47′ E
Mrcara
South Dalmatia
Croatia

Mrcara is a most attractive small island, with pine forests and olive trees, goats and mouflon sheep. Accommodation consists of a hunter's lodge and three cottages and the island offers simple pleasures such as fishing (very good crayfish), boating and swimming.

★☆☆☆☆ Tourism level
★★★★☆ Vegetation
★★☆☆☆ Beaches
★☆☆☆☆ History

Information
www.lastovo-tz.net
Telephone 020 801018

Map
None

Area 1.45 sq km
Coastline 7 km
Highest point 123 m

Permanent population 0

Visitor capacity 26
0 hotels
0 hotel beds
26 other beds
0 campsites

Crowdfactor
17 people per sq km

Access
Ubli 30 minutes

Connections
None scheduled

Yacht facilities
no fuel

Ranking among all Mediterranean islands	Ra
Area	31
Population	
Visitor capacity	19
Crowdfactor	18

43°46′ N 15°37′ E
Murter
North Dalmatia
Croatia

Murter is joined to the mainland by a swing bridge and is the most crowded of the Croatian islands. Nevertheless it has good beaches and is fertile in the north with olives, fruit, vegetables and vines producing a good wine. The island has marina space for over 400 berths and is the gateway for visits to the Kornati archipelago.

★★★☆☆ Tourism level
★★★☆☆ Vegetation
★★★☆☆ Beaches
★★☆☆☆ History

nformation
vww.tzo-murter.hr
'elephone 022 434995

1ap
reytag & Berndt (1:100000)

Area 18 sq km
Coastline 38 km
Highest point 125 m (Raduc)

Permanent population 5060

Visitor capacity 7449
2 hotels
1198 hotel beds
6251 other beds
1 campsite

Crowdfactor
672 people per sq km

Access
Bridge to mainland

Connections
None scheduled

Yacht facilities
⛵ Jezera, Hramina

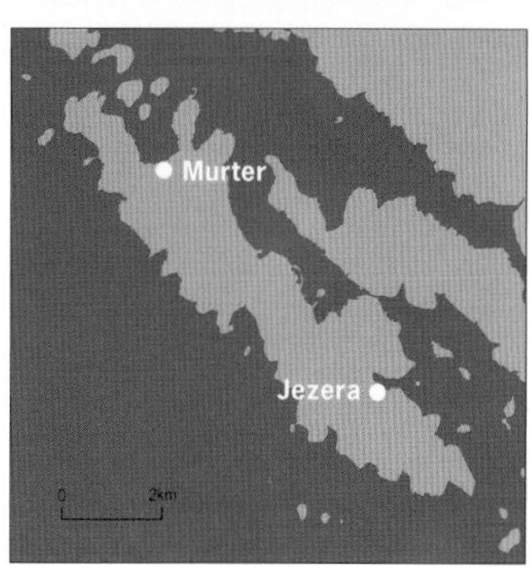
Murter
Jezera
0
2km

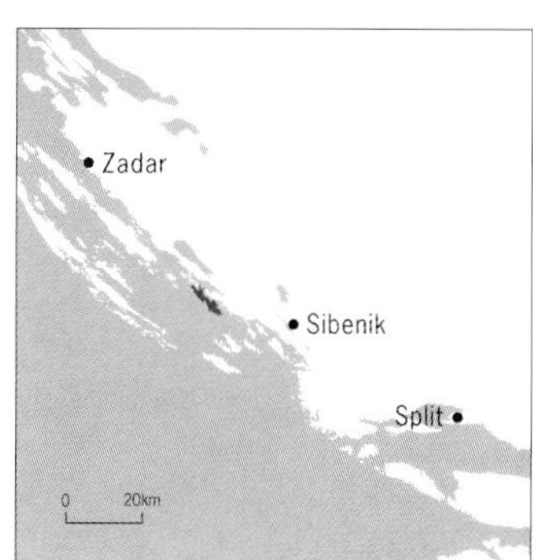
Zadar
Sibenik
Split
0
20km

anking among all Mediterranean islands

	Rank
rea	119
opulation	62
sitor capacity	34
rowdfactor	19

Obonjan

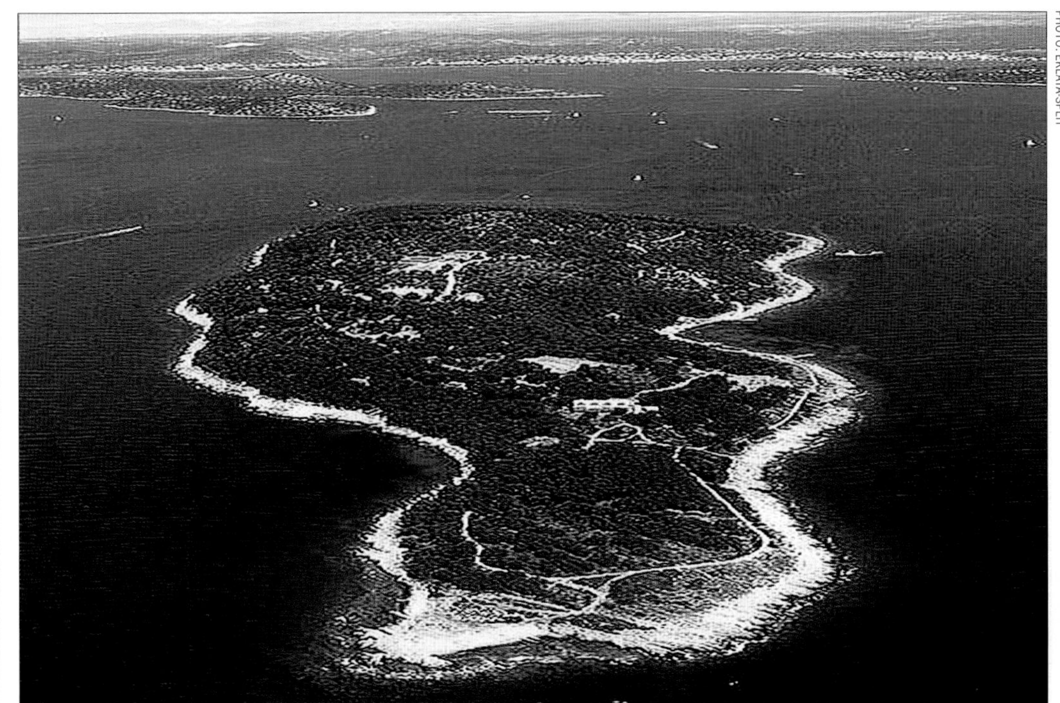

PHOTO: EKLATA-SPLIT

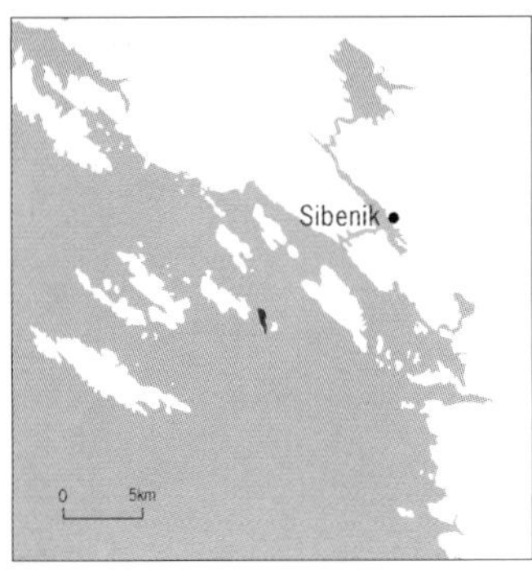
Sibenik
0
5km

43°41' N 15°47' E
Obonjan
North Dalmatia
Croatia

Obonjan is a youth holiday camp, with accommodation split evenly between rooms and tents. It has various sports facilities, a theatre, a self-service restaurant and cafes. It also has a heliport.

★★★☆☆ Tourism level
★★★★☆ Vegetation
★★☆☆☆ Beaches
★☆☆☆☆ History

Information
www.eklata.com
www.otok-mladosti.hr

Map
None

Area 0.55 sq km
Coastline 3.7 km
Highest point 55 m

Permanent population 0

Visitor capacity 1000
0 hotels
0 hotel beds
1000 youthcamp

Crowdfactor
1818 people per sq km

Access
Sibenik 45 minutes

Connections
Sibenik daily

Yacht facilities
no fuel

Ranking among all Mediterranean islands	Ran
Area	44
Population	
Visitor capacity	8
Crowdfactor	1

4671

Croatia North Dalmatia

44°22' N 14°47' E
Olib
North Dalmatia
Croatia

Olib is a green fertile island with many kinds of produce including good wine, fish and a very good sheep's cheese. There are no cars and the island has a relaxing friendly atmosphere and many pleasant coves.

★★☆☆☆ Tourism level
★★★☆☆ Vegetation
★★★☆☆ Beaches
★★☆☆☆ History

Information
Telephone 023 316166

Map
Freytag & Berndt (1:100000)

Area 26 sq km
Coastline 31 km
Highest point 72 m (Kalac)

Permanent population 147

Visitor capacity 50
0 hotels
0 hotel beds
50 other beds
0 campsites

Crowdfactor
7 people per sq km

Access
Zadar 2½ hours
Zadar, Mali Losinj 3½ hours

Connections
Zadar daily
Zadar, Mali Losinj daily

Yacht facilities
no fuel

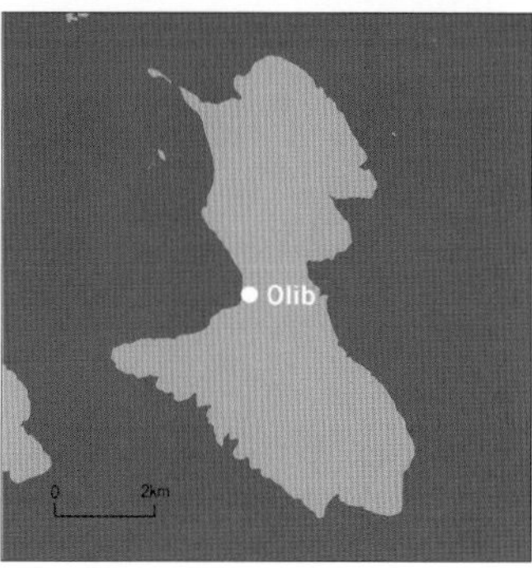
Olib
0
2km

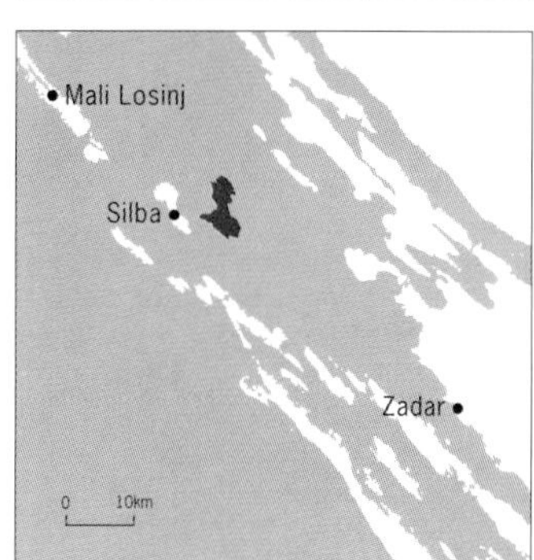
Mali Losinj
Silba
Zadar
0
10km

Ranking among all Mediterranean islands	Rank
Area	98
Population	163
Visitor capacity	173
Crowdfactor	205

Ošljak

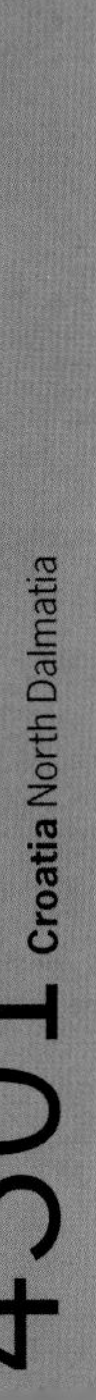

4301
Croatia North Dalmatia

(PHOTO: TZ PREKO)

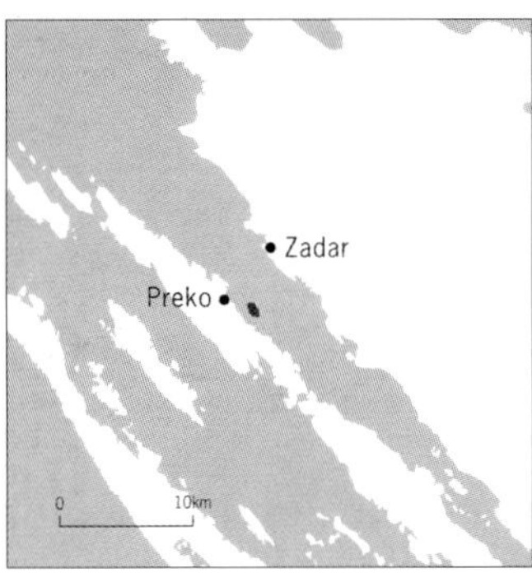

Zadar
Preko
0
10km

44°04′ N 15°12′ E
Ošljak
North Dalmatia
Croatia

A quiet wooded island with no cars, lovely cypresses, an attractive fishing harbour and the remains of old windmills.

★★☆☆☆ Tourism level
★★★☆☆ Vegetation
★★☆☆☆ Beaches
★★☆☆☆ History

Information
www.osljak.com
Telephone 023 288011

Map
None

Area 0.33 sq km
Coastline 2.4 km
Highest point 89 m

Permanent population 0

Visitor capacity 57
0 hotels
0 hotel beds
57 other beds
0 campsites

Crowdfactor
172 people per sq km

Access
⛴ Preko 10 minutes
⛴ Zadar 20 minutes

Connections
⛴ Preko, Zadar 2 daily

Yacht facilities
⛵ no fuel

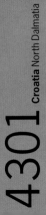

Ranking among all Mediterranean islands	Rar
Area	56
Population	
Visitor capacity	17
Crowdfactor	6

44°34′ N 14°59′ E
Pag
North Dalmatia
Croatia

Pag is one of the least attractive of Croatia's larger islands. Though mostly barren and hot, it does have some cultivation of vegetables, fruit and olives and, with the longest coastline of all the islands, it has a number of sandy beaches. Pag town is attractive and relatively quiet, while Novalja in the north has become a centre for Croatia's clubbers. The island is famous for its salt production, white wine and delicious hard sheep's cheese.

★★★☆☆ Tourism level
★★☆☆☆ Vegetation
★★★★☆ Beaches
★★☆☆☆ History

Information
www.otokpag.com
Telephone 023 611286

Map
Freytag & Berndt (1:100000)

Area 284 sq km
Coastline 269 km
Highest point 349 m (Sv Vid)

Permanent population 8398

Visitor capacity 24788
6 hotels
1545 hotel beds
23243 other beds
4 campsites

Crowdfactor
116 people per sq km

Access
Bridge to mainland
Ferry: Prizna 30 minutes
Ferry: Rab 45 minutes

Connections
Ferry: Prizna 20 daily
Ferry: Rab daily

Yacht facilities
5 ports

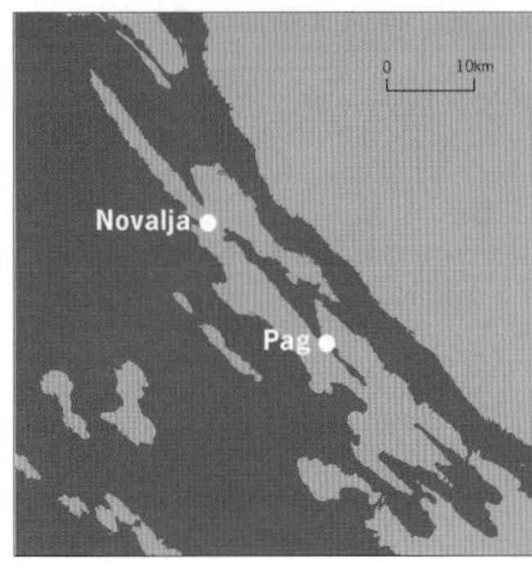
0 10km
Novalja
Pag

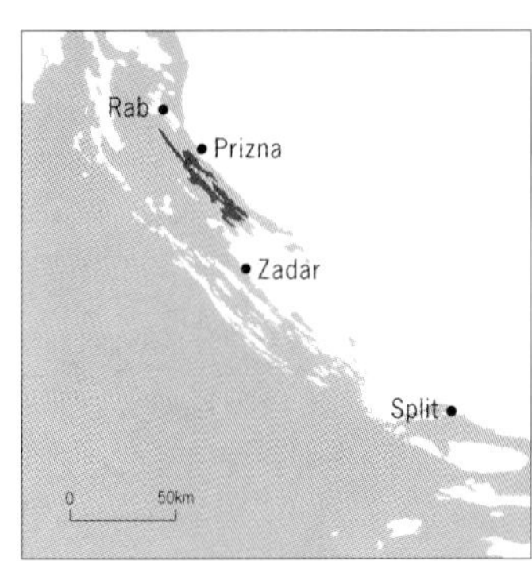
Rab
Prizna
Zadar
Split
0 50km

Ranking among all Mediterranean islands

	Rank
Area	29
Population	48
Visitor capacity	16
Crowdfactor	78

North Dalmatia Croatia 4200

Palagruža

(PHOTO: PLOVPUT-SPLIT)

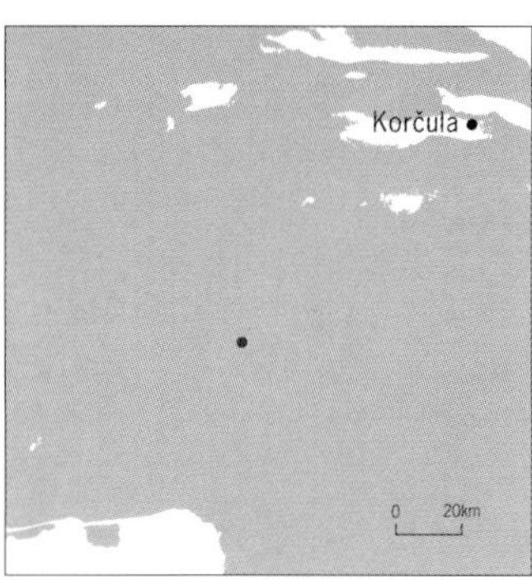
Korčula
0 20km

42°23' N 16°15' E
Palagruža
South Dalmatia
Croatia

The largest of a small group of four islands, Palagruža is the remotest place in Croatia, about 50 kilometres from Lastovo and 40 from the Tremiti islands. It is a steep island, with very interesting vegetation and two beaches suitable for children. Apart from the lighthouse which can be rented, there is the small medieval church of St Michael.

★☆☆☆☆ Tourism level
★★☆☆☆ Vegetation
★★★☆☆ Beaches
★★☆☆☆ History

Information
www.lighthouses-croatia.com
Telephone 021 390609

Map
None

Area 0.28 sq km
Coastline 3.6 km
Highest point 23 m

Permanent population 0

Visitor capacity 8
0 hotels
0 hotel beds
8 other beds
0 campsites

Crowdfactor

Access
Korčula 3 hours

Connections
None scheduled

Yacht facilities
no fuel

Ranking among all Mediterranean islands	Ran
Area	60
Population	
Visitor capacity	21
Crowdfactor	

43°57' N 15°21' E
Pašman
North Dalmatia
Croatia

A very pleasant tranquil island with woods, fishing villages and beautiful beaches and coves. The island grows fruit, vegetables, vines and olives and is known for its good food. There is a Benedictine abbey near Tkon and a Franciscan monastery at Kraj.

★★★☆☆ Tourism level
★★★☆☆ Vegetation
★★★☆☆ Beaches
★★☆☆☆ History

Information
www.pasman.hr
Telephone 023 260155

Map
Freytag & Berndt (1:100000)

Area 63 sq km
Coastline 65 km
Highest point 259 m (Ostro)

Permanent population 2711

Visitor capacity 2146
0 hotels
0 hotel beds
2146 other beds
4 campsites

Crowdfactor
76 people per sq km

Access
Bridge to Ugljan
Biograd 30 minutes

Connections
Biograd 10 daily

Yacht facilities
no fuel

0
5km
Pasman
Tkon

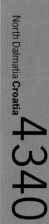

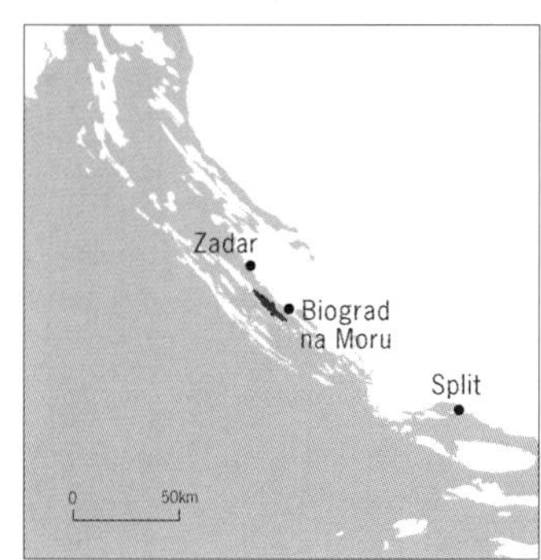
Zadar
Biograd na Moru
Split
0
50km

Ranking among all Mediterranean islands	Rank
Area	69
Population	78
Visitor capacity	61
Crowdfactor	102

PALMIZANA RESORT ON SV KLEMENT (PHOTO: MENEGHELLO PALMIZANA)

Pločica

(PHOTO: PLOVPUT-SPLIT)

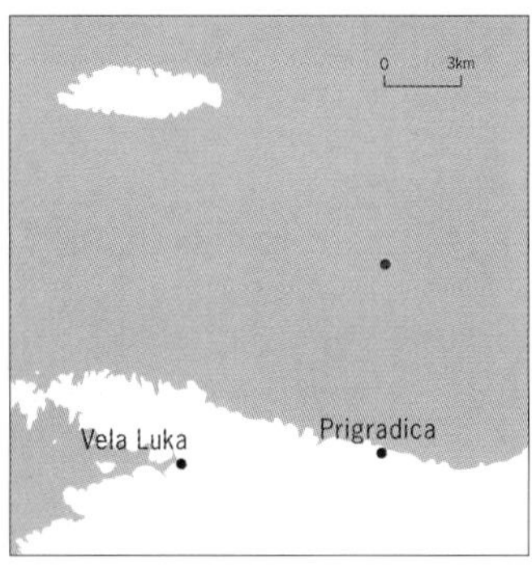
0 3km
Vela Luka
Prigradica

44°02′ N 16°49′ E
Pločica
South Dalmatia
Croatia

A most attractive lighthouse island, with shade from tamarisks and fig trees, good diving and a shallow sandy beach suitable for children.

★☆☆☆☆ Tourism level
★★☆☆☆ Vegetation
★★☆☆☆ Beaches
★☆☆☆☆ History

Information
www.lighthouses-croatia.com
Telephone 021 390609

Map
None

Area 0.07 sq km
Coastline 1.9 km
Highest point 12 m

Permanent population 0

Visitor capacity 14
0 hotels
0 hotel beds
14 other beds
0 campsites

Crowdfactor

Access
Prigradica 30 minutes

Connections
None scheduled

Yacht facilities
no fuel

4801 **Croatia** South Dalmatia

Ranking among all Mediterranean islands	Rar
Area	
Population	
Visitor capacity	2C
Crowdfactor	

44°45' N 13°53' E
Porer
Istria
Croatia

The smallest island in the book, some 21 million times smaller than Sicily. The lighthouse stands on a rock just 40 metres across and is surrounded by strong currents. While some might consider this a little restrictive, others might relish the challenge.

★☆☆☆☆ Tourism level
★☆☆☆☆ Vegetation
★☆☆☆☆ Beaches
★☆☆☆☆ History

Information
www.lighthouses-croatia.com
Telephone 021 390609

Map
None

Area 0.0012 sq km
Coastline 0.1 km
Highest point 7 m

Permanent population 0

Visitor capacity 8
0 hotels
0 hotel beds
8 other beds
0 campsites

Crowdfactor

Access
Premantura 30 minutes

Connections
None scheduled

Yacht facilities
no fuel

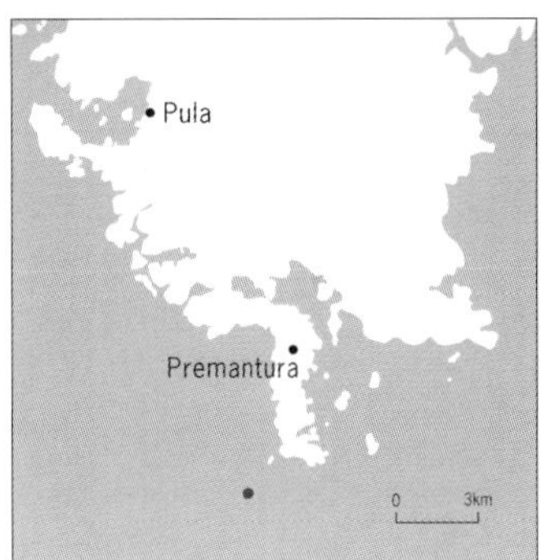
Pula
Premantura
0
3km

Ranking among all Mediterranean islands

	Rank
Area	0
Population	0
Visitor capacity	212
Crowdfactor	0

Premuda

(PHOTO: TZ ZADAR)

Premuda
0
2km

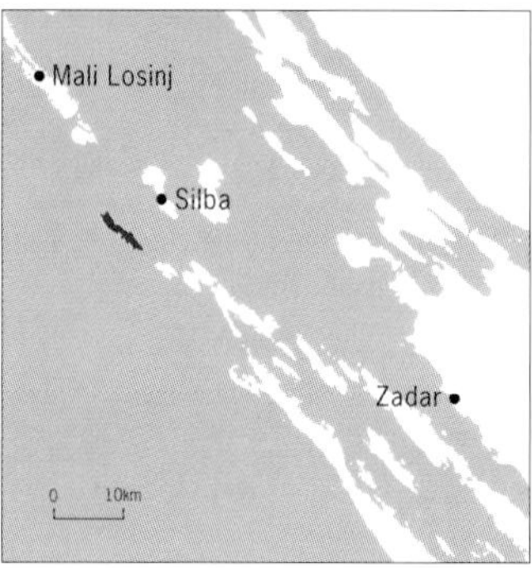
Mali Losinj
Silba
Zadar
0
10km

44°19' N 14°37' E
Premuda
North Dalmatia
Croatia

A mainly green island growing fruit, vines and olives, Premuda is a quiet place with no cars and several nice bays, visited mostly by people in boats. It has an active fishing community.

★★☆☆☆ Tourism level
★★★☆☆ Vegetation
★★★☆☆ Beaches
★☆☆☆☆ History

Information
Telephone 098 299232

Map
Freytag & Berndt (1:100000)

Area 9 sq km
Coastline 23 km
Highest point 90 m (Vrh)

Permanent population 58

Visitor capacity 45
0 hotels
0 hotel beds
45 other beds
0 campsites

Crowdfactor
11 people per sq km

Access
Zadar 1½ hours
Mali Losinj 2 hours
Zadar 5 hours

Connections
Zadar daily
Mali Losinj, Zadar daily

Yacht facilities
no fuel

4250 **Croatia** North Dalmatia

Ranking among all Mediterranean islands	Ran
Area	16
Population	18
Visitor capacity	17
Crowdfactor	19

43°49' N 15°33' E
Prisnjak
North Dalmatia
Croatia

An attractive little island with a lighthouse, a pine wood, stone walls and shallow water suitable for children.

★☆☆☆☆ Tourism level
★★☆☆☆ Vegetation
★★☆☆☆ Beaches
★☆☆☆☆ History

Information
www.lighthouses-croatia.com
Telephone 021 390609

Map
None

Area 0.064 sq km
Coastline 1 km
Highest point 21 m

Permanent population 0

Visitor capacity 4
0 hotels
0 hotel beds
4 other beds
0 campsites

Crowdfactor

Access
Murter 45 minutes

Connections
None scheduled

Yacht facilities
no fuel

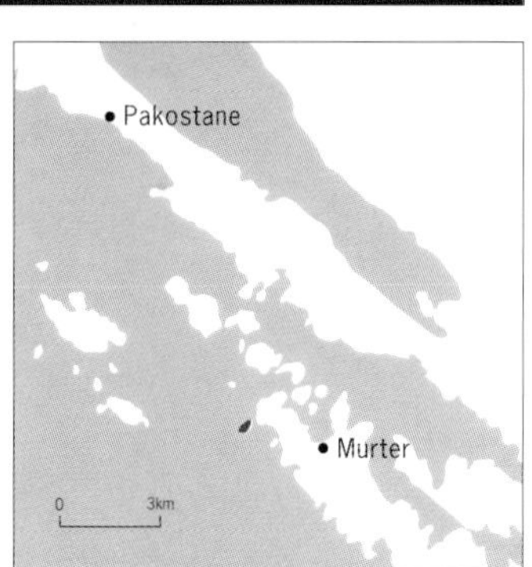
Pakostane
Murter
0
3km

Ranking among all Mediterranean islands	Rank
Area	0
Population	0
Visitor capacity	218
Crowdfactor	0

Prvić

(PHOTO: DIGITAL FILM SIBENIK)

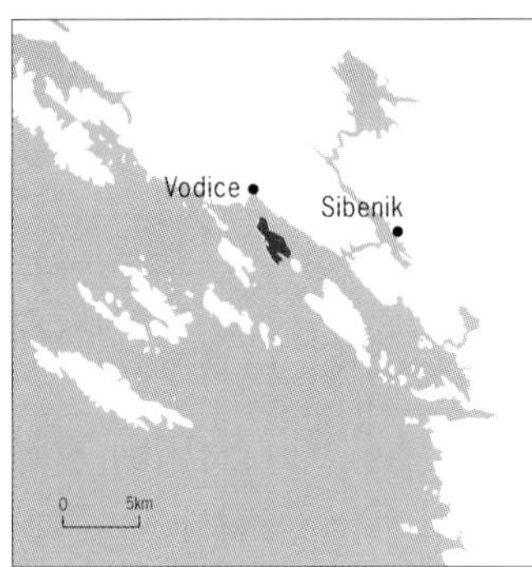

Vodice
Sibenik
0
5km

43°43' N 15°47' E
Prvić
North Dalmatia
Croatia

Prvićis a quiet island with two unspoilt towns, good beaches, pine forests, a 15th century monastery and no cars.

★★★☆☆ Tourism level
★★★☆☆ Vegetation
★★★☆☆ Beaches
★★☆☆☆ History

Information
www.prvic.netfirms.com
Telephone 022 448083

Map
None

Area 2.4 sq km
Coastline 10 km
Highest point 75 m (Vitkovic)

Permanent population 453

Visitor capacity 618
1 hotel
23 hotel beds
595 other beds
0 campsites

Crowdfactor
446 people per sq km

Access
Vodice 15 minutes
Sibenik 1 hour

Connections
Vodice, Sibenik 5 daily

Yacht facilities
no fuel

4660 **Croatia** North Dalmatia

Ranking among all Mediterranean islands	Rar
Area	26
Population	12
Visitor capacity	10
Crowdfactor	2

Rab

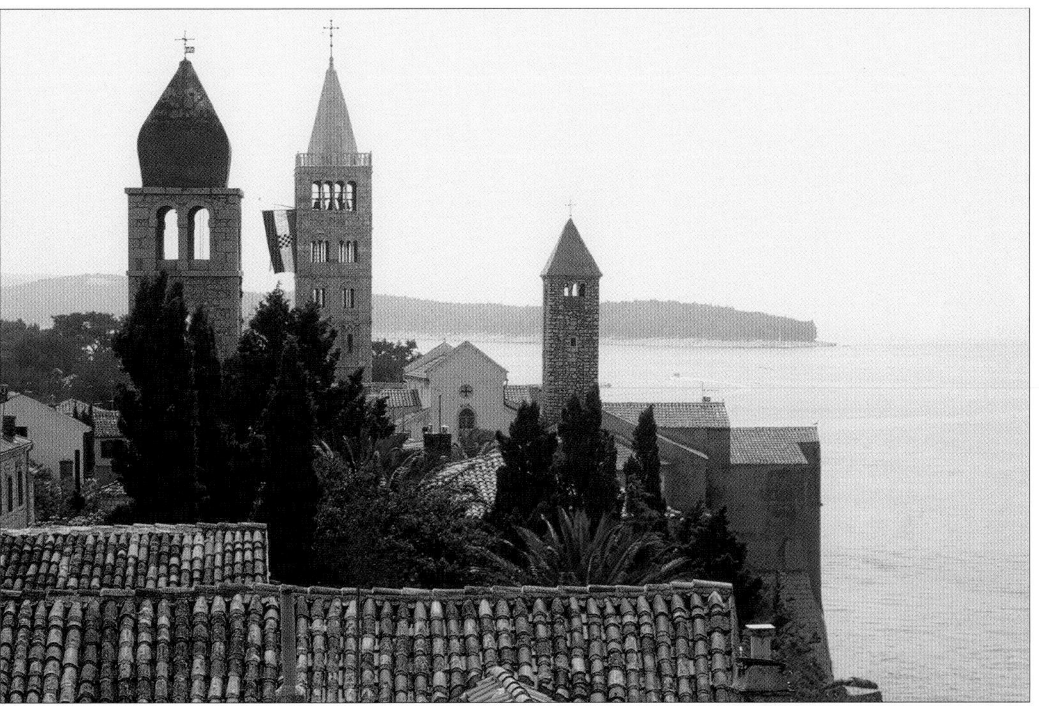

44°44' N 14°46' E
Rab
Kvarner
Croatia

Although its landward side is barren and dull, Rab is heavily wooded on its western side and has fine beaches. The capital is a lovely medieval town known for its four campaniles and the fine gardens of Komrcar Park. Kampor is a pleasant fishing village with a Franciscan monastery.

★★★★☆ Tourism level
★★★★☆ Vegetation
★★★★☆ Beaches
★★★☆☆ History

nformation
www.rab-croatia.com
elephone 051 724064

Map
reytag & Berndt (1:100000)

Area 90 sq km
Coastline 103 km
Highest point 410 m (Straza)

Permanent population 9480

Visitor capacity 22847
8 hotels
3716 hotel beds
19131 other beds
6 campsites

Crowdfactor
355 people per sq km

Access
Jablanac 15 minutes
Baska 1½ hours
Novalja 45 minutes

Connections
Jablanac 20 daily
Baska 4 daily
Novalja daily

Yacht facilities
Rab

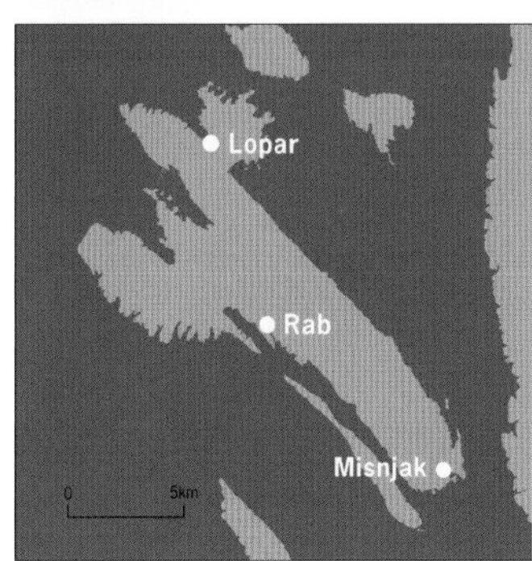
Lopar
Rab
Misnjak
0
5km

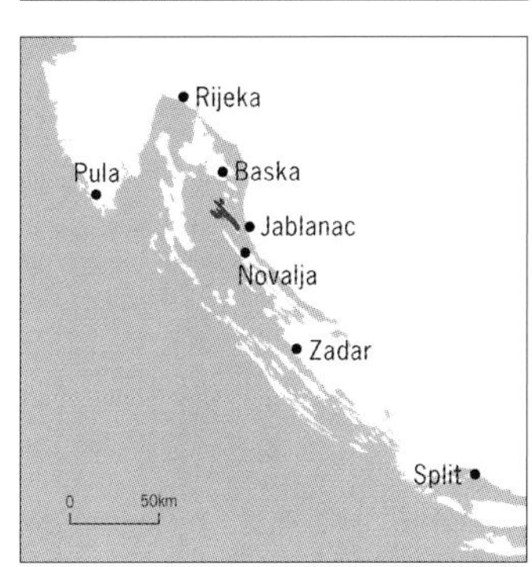
Rijeka
Pula
Baska
Jablanac
Novalja
Zadar
Split
0
50km

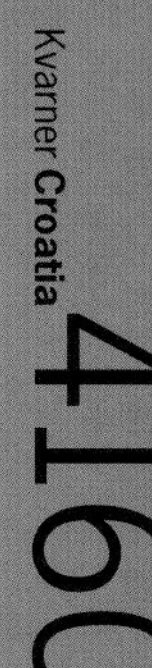
Kvarner Croatia
4160

anking among all Mediterranean islands	Rank
rea	55
opulation	42
isitor capacity	18
rowdfactor	32

Rava

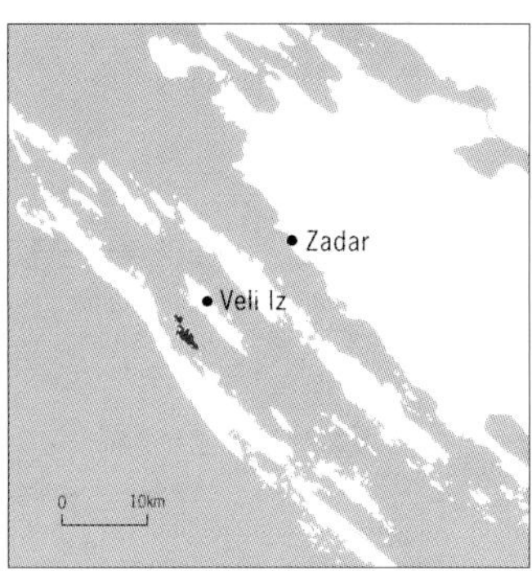

Zadar
Veli Iz
0
10km

44°01' N 15°03' E
Rava
North Dalmatia
Croatia

A mostly green island growing vines and olives, Rava has two villages and an active fishing community. It has very nice coves and is visited mostly by sailors.

★★☆☆☆ Tourism level
★★★☆☆ Vegetation
★★☆☆☆ Beaches
★☆☆☆☆ History

Information
Telephone 023 316166

Map
Drzavna Geodetska Uprava (1:25000)

Area 3.63 sq km
Coastline 15 km
Highest point 98 m (Babikovac)

Permanent population 98

Visitor capacity 17
0 hotels
0 hotel beds
17 other beds
0 campsites

Crowdfactor
31 people per sq km

Access
⛴ Zadar 2½ hours

Connections
⛴ Zadar daily

Yacht facilities
⛵ no fuel

Ranking among all Mediterranean islands	Rar
Area	23
Population	17
Visitor capacity	20
Crowdfactor	15

4420 **Croatia** North Dalmatia

44°10' N 15°01' E
Rivanj
North Dalmatia
Croatia

Rivanj is a green island visited by sailors, with a number of houses which let rooms.

★★☆☆☆ Tourism level
★★☆☆☆ Vegetation
★★☆☆☆ Beaches
★☆☆☆☆ History

Information
Telephone 023 286108

Map
None

Area 3.61 sq km
Coastline 10 km
Highest point 112 m (Lukocina)

Permanent population 22

Visitor capacity 8
0 hotels
0 hotel beds
8 other beds
0 campsites

Crowdfactor
8 people per sq km

Access
Zadar 1 hour

Connections
Zadar daily

Yacht facilities
no fuel

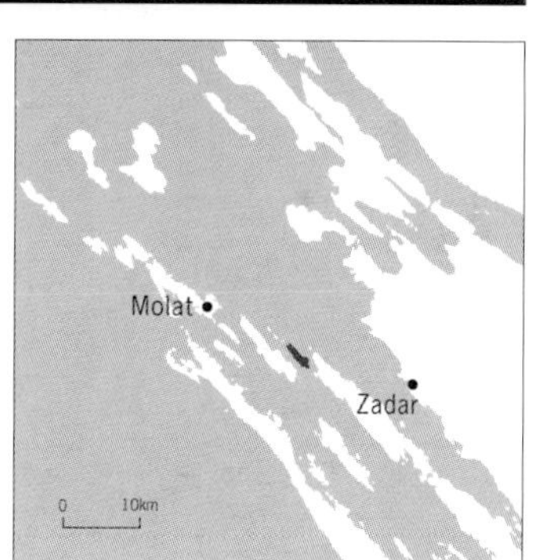
Molat
Zadar
0
10km

Ranking among all Mediterranean islands

	Rank
Area	233
Population	195
Visitor capacity	212
Crowdfactor	203

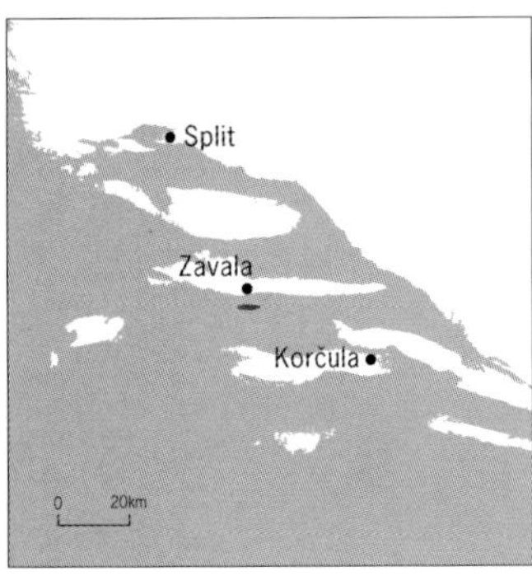
Split
Zavala
Korčula
0 20km

43°05' N 16°42' E
Šćedro
Central Dalmatia
Croatia

A wooded island with a tiny settlement in a sheltered bay and the remains of a Dominican monastery. It is possible to stay in a family house and enjoy simple recreations such as fishing with local fishermen and walking through maquis, vineyards and olive groves.

★☆☆☆☆ Tourism level
★★★★☆ Vegetation
★★★☆☆ Beaches
★★☆☆☆ History

Information
www,adventure-island.net
Telephone 09892 36040

Map
None

Area 8 sq km
Coastline 26 km
Highest point 112 m (V Glava)

Permanent population 0

Visitor capacity 10
0 hotels
0 hotel beds
10 other beds
0 campsites

Crowdfactor
1 person per sq km

Access
Zavala 30 minutes

Connections
Zavala daily

Yacht facilities
no fuel

Ranking among all Mediterranean islands	Ran
Area	17
Population	
Visitor capacity	20
Crowdfactor	21

44°08' N 15°01' E
Sestrunj
North Dalmatia
Croatia

Sestrunj is a green island engaged in fishing and the growing of vines and olives, much visited by sailors.

★★☆☆☆ Tourism level
★★★☆☆ Vegetation
★★★☆☆ Beaches
★★☆☆☆ History

Information
Telephone 023 288011

Map
Freytag & Berndt (1:100000)

Area 15 sq km
Coastline 27 km
Highest point 159 m (Drakovac)

Permanent population 48

Visitor capacity 30
0 hotels
0 hotel beds
30 other beds
0 campsites

Crowdfactor
5 people per sq km

Access
Zadar 1½ hours

Connections
Zadar daily

Yacht facilities
no fuel

Sestrunj
0
2km

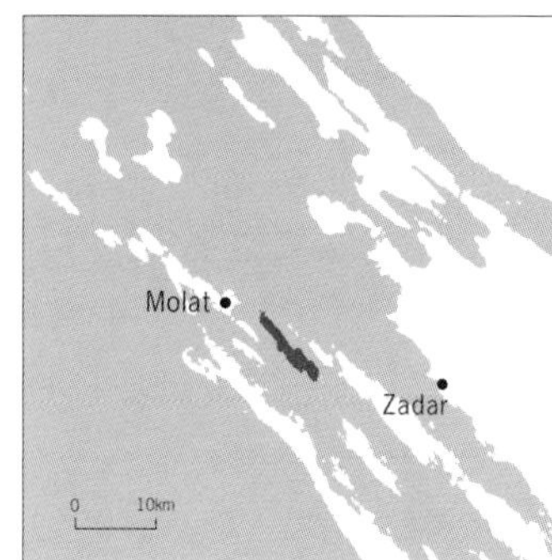
Molat
Zadar
0
10km

Ranking among all Mediterranean islands	Rank
Area	132
Population	187
Visitor capacity	191
Crowdfactor	211

PHOTO: IVAN JURAS

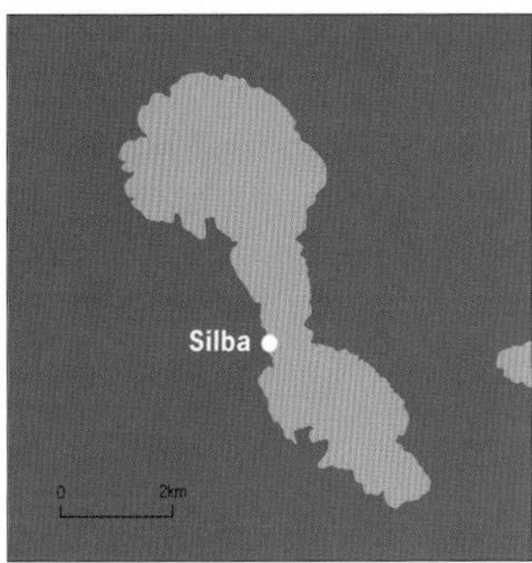
Silba
0 2km

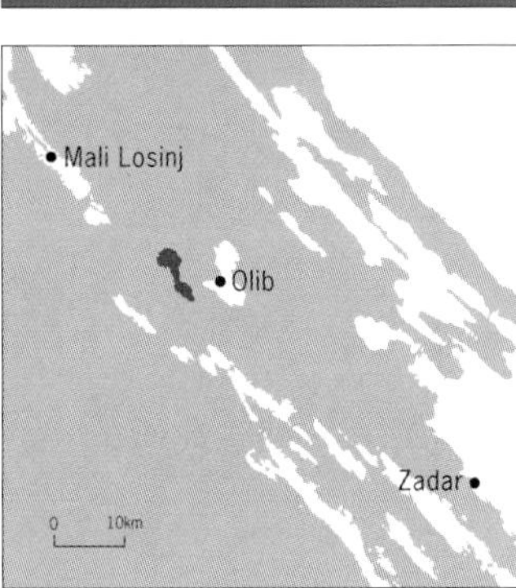
Mali Losinj
Olib
Zadar
0 10km

44°22' N 14°42' E
Silba
North Dalmatia
Croatia

Silba is a green island based on fishing and wine-growing, with nice coves and beaches. It has no cars and produces good cheese and other food.

★★★☆☆ Tourism level
★★★☆☆ Vegetation
★★★☆☆ Beaches
★★☆☆☆ History

Information
www.silba.org
Telephone 023 316166

Map
Freytag & Berndt (1:100000)

Area 14 sq km
Coastline 25 km
Highest point 83 m (Vrh)

Permanent population 265

Visitor capacity 700
0 hotels
0 hotel beds
700 other beds
0 campsites

Crowdfactor
64 people per sq km

Access
Zadar 2 hours
Mali Losinj 2½ hours
Zadar 4 hours

Connections
Zadar daily
Mali Losinj, Zadar daily

Yacht facilities
no fuel

Ranking among all Mediterranean islands	Ran
Area	13
Population	14
Visitor capacity	9
Crowdfactor	11

42°45' N 17°51' E
Šipan
South Dalmatia
Croatia

By far the quietest of the Elafiti islands, Šipan is a lovely island with walks through pine and cypress-clad hills and plains growing oranges and lemons, figs, vines and olives. Sights are the fortified castle at Sudjurad and the ducal palace above Sipanska Luka. The island has a number of quiet small beaches and coves.

★★☆☆☆ Tourism level
★★★★☆ Vegetation
★★★☆☆ Beaches
★★☆☆☆ History

Information
www.dubrovnikandislands.com
Telephone 020 323887

Map
Freytag & Berndt (1:100000)

Area 15 sq km
Coastline 28 km
Highest point 234 m (Velji Vrh)

Permanent population 436

Visitor capacity 301
1 hotel
168 hotel beds
133 other beds
0 campsites

Crowdfactor
46 people per sq km

Access
Ferry: Dubrovnik 1 hour

Connections
Ferry: Dubrovnik 5 daily

Yacht facilities
no fuel

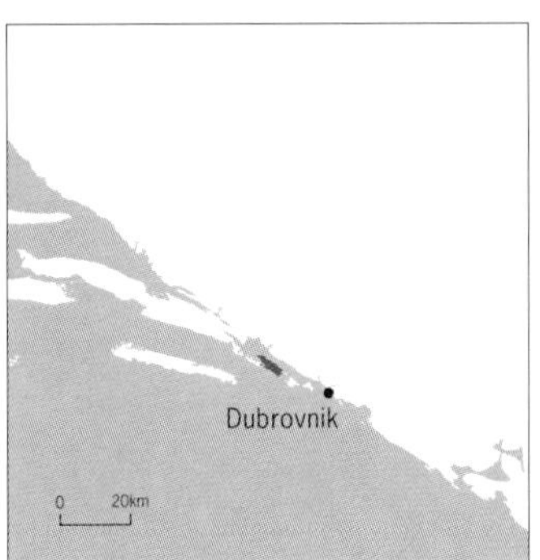
Dubrovnik
0 20km

Ranking among all Mediterranean islands

	Rank
Area	129
Population	127
Visitor capacity	126
Crowdfactor	135

(PHOTO: PHOTOSERVIS/

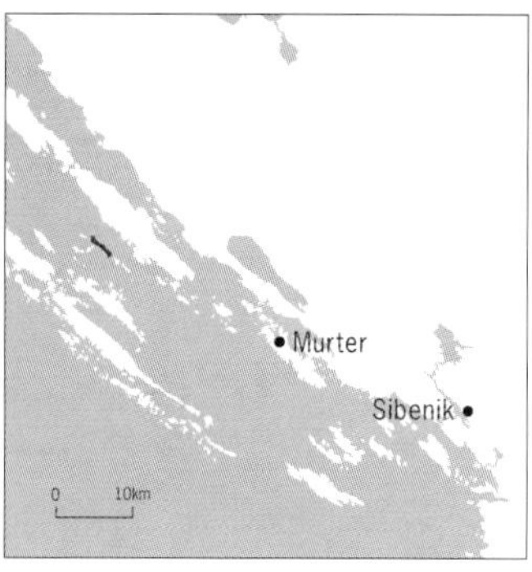

Murter
Sibenik
0
10km

43°55' N 15°18' E
Sit
North Dalmatia
Croatia

Private accommodation on this small island, which lies between Pašman and Žut, can be arranged in Murter together with boat transfer. Sit is rather a bare island with two small ports.

★☆☆☆☆ Tourism level
★★★☆☆ Vegetation
★★☆☆☆ Beaches
★☆☆☆☆ History

Information
Telephone 022 436544

Map
None

Area 1.77 sq km
Coastline 9 km
Highest point 84 m (Runjevac)

Permanent population 0

Visitor capacity 40
0 hotels
0 hotel beds
40 other beds
0 campsites

Crowdfactor
22 people per sq km

Access
Private boat from Murter

Connections
None scheduled

Yacht facilities
⛵ no fuel

Ranking among all Mediterranean islands

	Ran
Area	29
Population	
Visitor capacity	17
Crowdfactor	16

43°43′ N 15°28′ E
Smokvica
North Dalmatia
Croatia

Private accommodation on this little island, which lies off the southern tip of Kornat, can be arranged in Murter together with boat transfer. Smokvica is quite a green island with a little port.

★☆☆☆☆ Tourism level
★★☆☆☆ Vegetation
★★☆☆☆ Beaches
★☆☆☆☆ History

Information
Telephone 022 436544

Map
None

Area 1.04 sq km
Coastline 6 km
Highest point 94 m (V Vrh)

Permanent population 0

Visitor capacity 25
0 hotels
0 hotel beds
25 other beds
0 campsites

Crowdfactor
24 people per sq km

Access
Private boat from Murter

Connections
None scheduled

Yacht facilities
⛵ no fuel

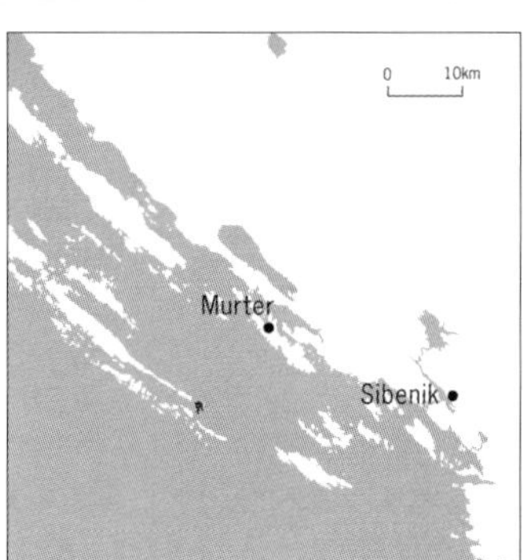
0 10km
Murter
Sibenik

Ranking among all Mediterranean islands	Rank
Area	357
Population	0
Visitor capacity	195
Crowdfactor	164

Smokvica

North Dalmatia **Croatia** 4523

Šolta

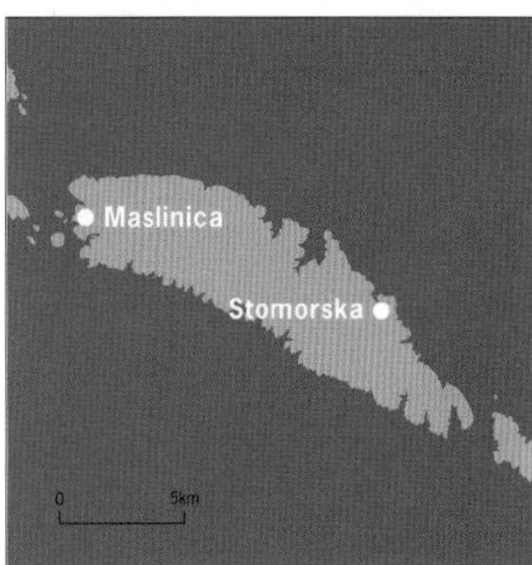
Maslinica
Stomorska
0
5km

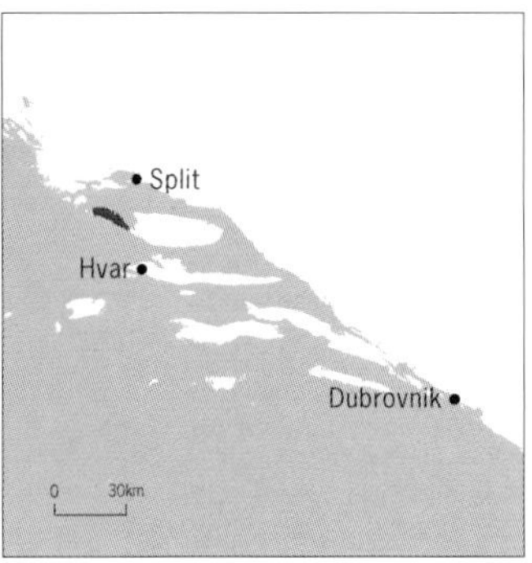
Split
Hvar
Dubrovnik
0
30km

43°22′ N 16°17′ E
Šolta
Central Dalmatia
Croatia

A lovely wooded island with many fine beaches, coves and bays, Šolta has good food and is famous for its honey, mulberries, olives and rosemary. There are castles at Grohote and Rogac, the fishing village of Maslinica has a beautiful setting and there is an apartment complex at Necujam set against a background of rich vegetation.

★★★☆☆ Tourism level
★★★★☆ Vegetation
★★★★☆ Beaches
★★★☆☆ History

Information
www.solta.hr
Telephone 021 654151

Map
Freytag & Berndt (1:100000)

Area 58 sq km
Coastline 73 km
Highest point 211 m (V Straza)

Permanent population 1479

Visitor capacity 1766
2 hotels
716 hotel beds
1050 other beds
1 campsite

Crowdfactor
55 people per sq km

Access
Split 30 minutes
Split 1½ hours

Connections
Split daily
Split 6 daily

Yacht facilities
Rogac

Ranking among all Mediterranean islands	Rar
Area	7
Population	9
Visitor capacity	6
Crowdfactor	12

4710 **Croatia** Central Dalmatia

42°45′ N 16°29′ E
Sušac
South Dalmatia
Croatia

By far the largest of the 6 lighthouse islands in the book, Sušac has pine trees and maquis, a good beach and several coves.

★☆☆☆☆ Tourism level
★☆☆☆☆ Vegetation
★★☆☆☆ Beaches
★☆☆☆☆ History

Information
www.lighthouses-croatia.com
Telephone 021 390609

Map
None

Area 4.02 sq km
Coastline 16 km
Highest point 239 m (Sušac)

Permanent population 0

Visitor capacity 8
0 hotels
0 hotel beds
8 other beds
0 campsites

Crowdfactor

Access
Vela Luka 3 hours

Connections
None scheduled

Yacht facilities
no fuel

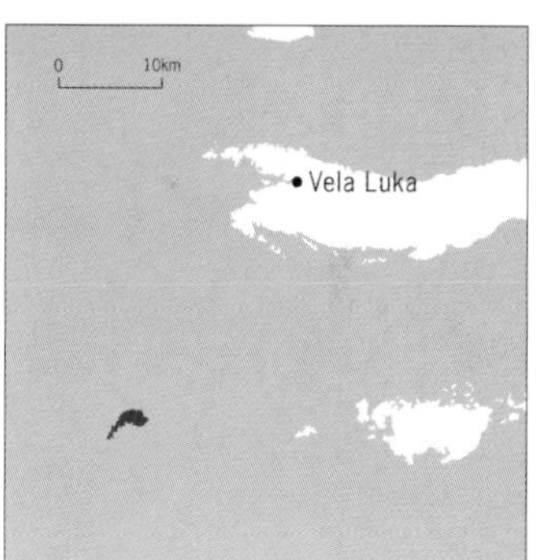
0
10km
Vela Luka

Ranking among all Mediterranean islands

	Rank
Area	223
Population	0
Visitor capacity	212
Crowdfactor	0

Susak

(PHOTO: MALI LOSINJ TOURIST BOARD)

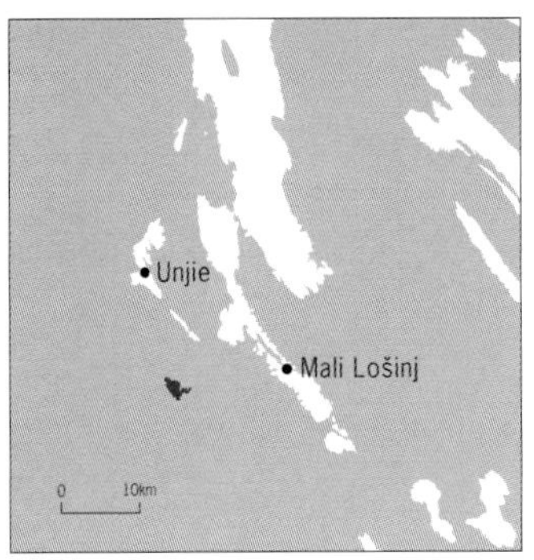

Unjie
Mali Lošinj
0
10km

44°30′ N 14°18′ E
Susak
Kvarner
Croatia

Susak is an unusual island, known for its unique national costume and its retention of the Old Croat dialect. It has no cars and is a very sandy island, with many lovely deserted beaches and very good wine.

★★☆☆☆ Tourism level
★★★★☆ Vegetation
★★★☆☆ Beaches
★★☆☆☆ History

Information
www.tz-malilosinj.hr
Telephone 051 231547

Map
Drzavna Geodetska Uprava (1:25000)

Area 3.77 sq km
Coastline 12 km
Highest point 96 m (Garba)

Permanent population 188

Visitor capacity 68
0 hotels
0 hotel beds
68 other beds
0 campsites

Crowdfactor
67 people per sq km

Access
Mali Losinj 1 hour

Connections
Mali Losinj 3 daily

Yacht facilities
no fuel

Ranking among all Mediterranean islands	Ra
Area	23
Population	15
Visitor capacity	16
Crowdfactor	11

4140 **Croatia** Kvarner

Sv Ivan na Pucini

45°02′ N 13°36′ E
Sv Ivan na Pucini
Istria
Croatia

The outermost of the islets lying off Rovinj, Sv Ivan na Pucini is a rock approximately 70 metres long by 50 wide with a 23m high lighthouse to stay in. There is shallow water on each side of the island and there are flat rocks to lie on. Fishing and diving complete the activities available for those who want to spend a holiday away from other people.

★☆☆☆☆ Tourism level
★☆☆☆☆ Vegetation
★☆☆☆☆ Beaches
★☆☆☆☆ History

Information
www.lighthouses-croatia.com
telephone 021 390609

Map
None

Area 0.0035 sq km
Coastline 0.2 km
Highest point 9 m

Permanent population 0

Visitor capacity 8
0 hotels
0 hotel beds
8 other beds
0 campsites

Crowdfactor

Access
Rovinj 30 minutes by private boat

Connections
None scheduled

Yacht facilities
no fuel

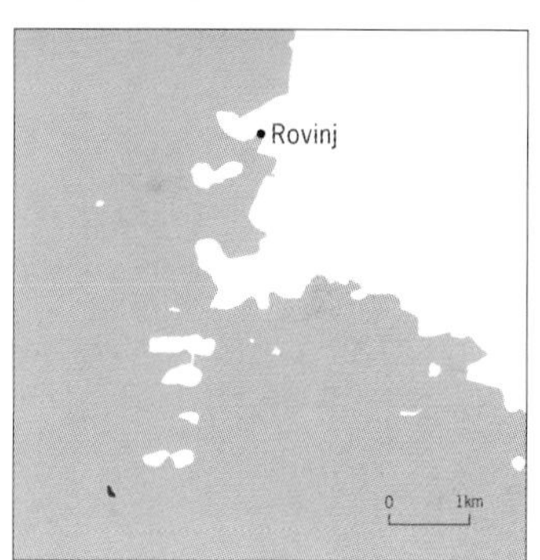
Rovinj
0 1km

Ranking among all Mediterranean islands

	Rank
Area	0
Population	0
Visitor capacity	212
Crowdfactor	0

Istria **Croatia** 4032

Sv Katarina

(PHOTO: GRANDHOTEL ZELL AM SEE)

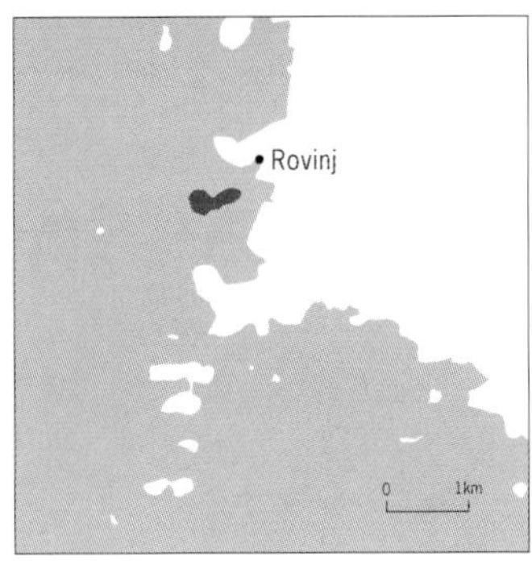
Rovinj
0 1km

45°04′ N 13°37′ E
Sv Katarina
Istria
Croatia

A lovely green little island covered mainly by a pine forest, with a vineyard, olive trees and an Austrian-run hotel.

★★★★☆ Tourism level
★★★★☆ Vegetation
★★☆☆☆ Beaches
★☆☆☆☆ History

Information
www.hotelinsel-katarina.com
Telephone 052 804100

Map
None

Area 0.12 sq km
Coastline 1.8 km
Highest point 25 m

Permanent population 0

Visitor capacity 240
1 hotel
240 hotel beds
0 other beds
0 campsites

Crowdfactor
2000 people per sq km

Access
Rovinj 5 minutes

Connections
Rovinj 15 daily

Yacht facilities
no fuel

Ranking among all Mediterranean islands	Ra
Area	86
Population	
Visitor capacity	13
Crowdfactor	

4020 **Croatia** Istria

43°09′ N 16°22′ E
Sveti Klement
Central Dalmatia
Croatia

The green island of Sveti Klement has a hotel with stone bungalows and a marina with 190 berths. It is a very relaxing place, especially for family holidays, with no cars but plenty of activities including fishing, diving, sailing and windsurfing. The food is delicious, especially shellfish and fresh vegetables grown on the island. There are magnificent botanical gardens and many beaches and coves.

★★★☆☆ Tourism level
★★★★☆ Vegetation
★★★☆☆ Beaches
★★☆☆☆ History

Information
www.palmizana.hr
Telephone 021 717270

Map
None

Area 5 sq km
Coastline 29 km
Highest point 94 m (Vela Glava)

Permanent population 0

Visitor capacity 63
1 hotel
47 hotel beds
16 other beds
0 campsites

Crowdfactor
11 people per sq km

Access
Hvar 20 minutes

Connections
Hvar 10 daily

Yacht facilities
no fuel

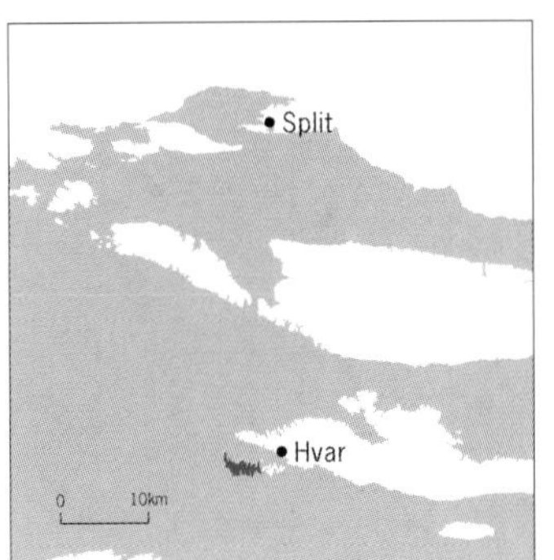
Split
Hvar
0
10km

Ranking among all Mediterranean islands

	Rank
Area	199
Population	0
Visitor capacity	168
Crowdfactor	197

Sv Nikola

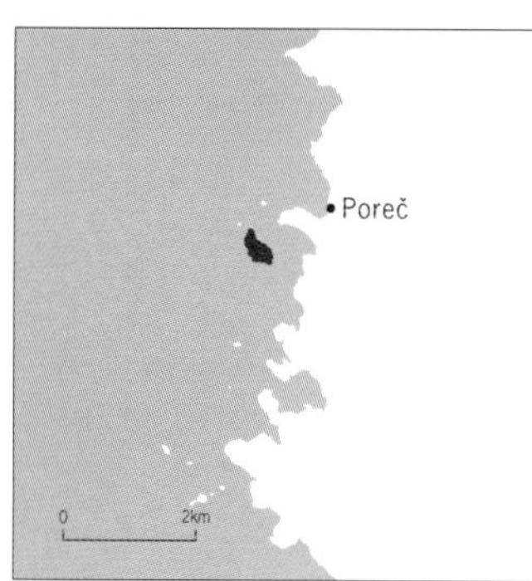
Poreč
0
2km

45°13′ N 13°35′ E
Sveti Nikola
Istria
Croatia

Sveti Nikola is a beautiful small island with a hotel, a small naturist beach and otherwise covered by a lovely mature park in which stands Isabella castle, now converted into holiday apartments.

★★★★☆ Tourism level
★★★★☆ Vegetation
★★☆☆☆ Beaches
★★☆☆☆ History

Information
www.valamar.com
Telephone 052 451293

Map
None

Area 0.12 sq km
Coastline 2.1 km
Highest point 25 m

Permanent population 0

Visitor capacity 354
1 hotel
354 hotel beds
0 other beds
0 campsites

Crowdfactor
2950 people per sq km

Access
⛴ Porec 5 minutes

Connections
⛴ Porec 36 daily

Yacht facilities
⛵ no fuel

Ranking among all Mediterranean islands

	Ran
Area	86
Population	(
Visitor capacity	12
Crowdfactor	

44°05' N 15°09' E
Ugljan
North Dalmatia
Croatia

Ugljan is a relaxed and rustic island known for its olives and popular with Croatian holidaymakers. It has a peaceful atmosphere and the food is good. Preko has a great medieval fortress and there are Franciscan monasteries at Ugljan (with a fine cloister) and on the islet of Galovac. Lukoran is a lovely place surrounded by pine forest and Kali is a picturesque village with a large fishing fleet.

★★★☆☆ Tourism level
★★★☆☆ Vegetation
★★★☆☆ Beaches
★★☆☆☆ History

Information
www.ugljan.hr
Telephone 023 288011

Map
Freytag & Berndt (1:100000)

Area 50 sq km
Coastline 68 km
Highest point 288 m (Scah)

Permanent population 6182

Visitor capacity 4707
2 hotels
1165 hotel beds
3542 other beds
8 campsites

Crowdfactor
216 people per sq km

Access
⛴ Zadar 15 minutes

Connections
⛴ Zadar 15 daily

Yacht facilities
⛵ Preko, Kali

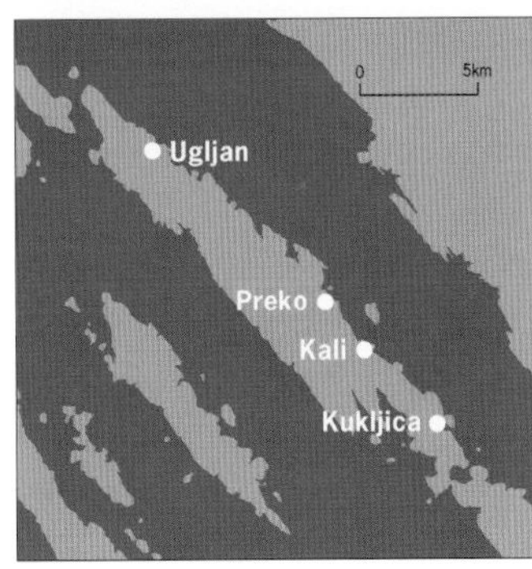
0
5km
Ugljan
Preko
Kali
Kukljica

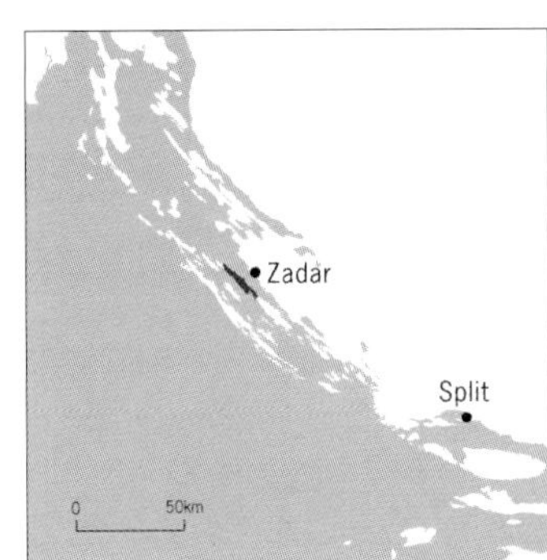
Zadar
Split
0
50km

Ranking among all Mediterranean islands	Rank
Area	76
Population	59
Visitor capacity	42
Crowdfactor	53

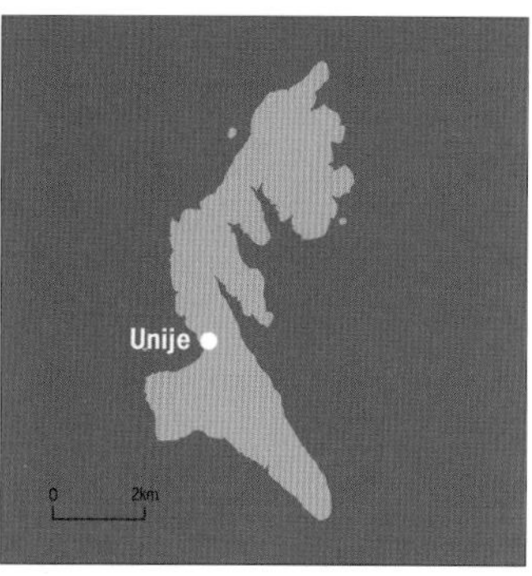
Unije
0 2km

Martinšćica
Mali Lošinj
0 10km

44°39' N 14°15' E
Unije
Kvarner
Croatia

Unije has olives and vines, many pebble beaches and Roman villa remains. It has no cars but it does have an airfield from which it is possible to fly to Mali Losinj every other day.

★★☆☆☆ Tourism level
★★☆☆☆ Vegetation
★★★☆☆ Beaches
★★★☆☆ History

Information
www.tz-malilosinj.hr
Telephone 051 231547

Map
Freytag & Berndt (1:100000)

Area 16 sq km
Coastline 36 km
Highest point 132 m (Kalk)

Permanent population 90

Visitor capacity 139
0 hotels
0 hotel beds
139 other beds
0 campsites

Crowdfactor
13 people per sq km

Access
✈ Unije
⛴ Mali Losinj 1½ hours

Connections
⛴ Mali Losinj, Martinscica 3 daily

Yacht facilities
⛵ no fuel

Ranking among all Mediterranean islands

	Rank
Area	12
Population	17
Visitor capacity	14
Crowdfactor	19

Veli Brijun

44°54' N 13°45' E
Veli Brijun
Istria
Croatia

Since the Brijuni archipelago (of about 15 islands) combines the functions of presidential residence, national park and tourist attraction, movement is not entirely free. Visitors are confined to the islands of Veli and Mali Brijun and tours are guided. Veli Brijun consists mainly of parkland which is toured in a 'train' (there are no cars). Activities include riding, golf and tennis and there is a small zoo.

★★★☆☆ Tourism level
★★★★★ Vegetation
★★☆☆☆ Beaches
★★★☆☆ History

Information
www.briuni.hr
Telephone 052 525883

Map
Reise-Know-How (1:75000)

Area 5 sq km
Coastline 23 km
Highest point 55 m (V Straza)

Permanent population 0

Visitor capacity 248
2 hotels
248 hotel beds
0 other beds
0 campsites

Crowdfactor
43 people per sq km

Access
⛴ Fazana 20 minutes

Connections
⛴ Fazana 4 daily

Yacht facilities
⛵ no fuel

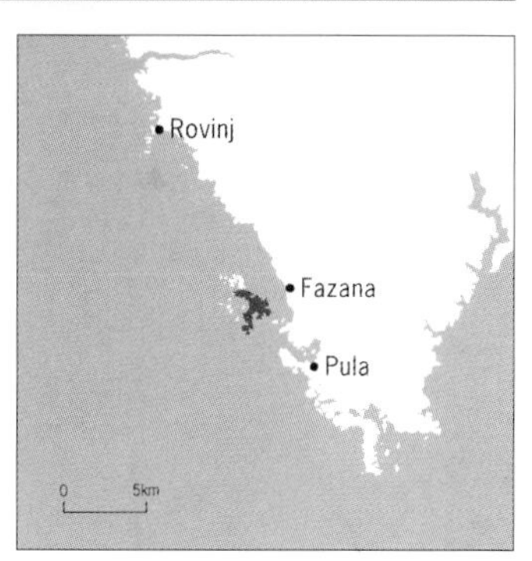
Rovinj
Fazana
Pula
0 5km

Ranking among all Mediterranean islands	Rank
Area	192
Population	0
Visitor capacity	130
Crowdfactor	136

Istria **Croatia** 4000

Veli Drvenik

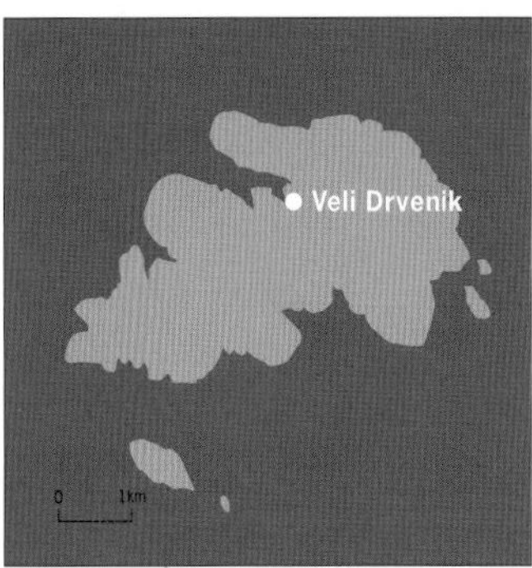
Veli Drvenik
0 1km

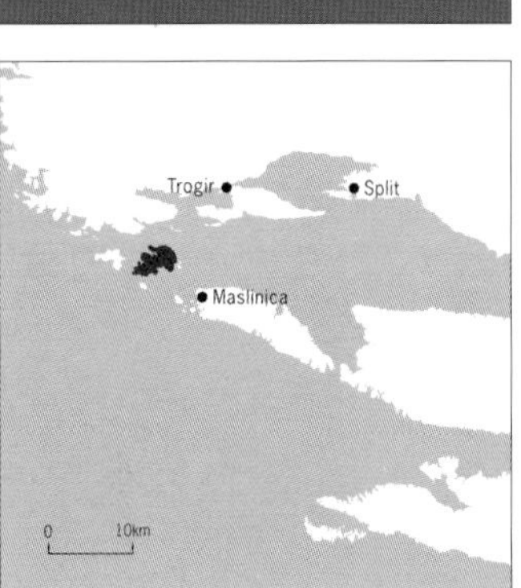
Trogir
Split
Maslinica
0 10km

43°27' N 16°08' E
Veli Drvenik
Central Dalmatia
Croatia

A quiet forest-covered island with good sandy and pebble beaches and coves, fishermen and farmers growing vines and olives, much visited by sailors.

★★☆☆☆ Tourism level
★★★☆☆ Vegetation
★★★☆☆ Beaches
★★☆☆☆ History

Information
Telephone 021 893038

Map
Freytag & Berndt (1:100000)

Area 12 sq km
Coastline 23 km
Highest point 178 m (Buhaj)

Permanent population 168

Visitor capacity 15
0 hotels
0 hotel beds
15 other beds
0 campsites

Crowdfactor
15 people per sq km

Access
Trogir 1 hour

Connections
Trogir 2 daily

Yacht facilities
no fuel

Ranking among all Mediterranean islands	Ra
Area	14
Population	15
Visitor capacity	20
Crowdfactor	18

4730 **Croatia** Central Dalmatia

44°18′ N 15°01′ E
Vir
North Dalmatia
Croatia

Linked to the mainland by a bridge, Vir is a mainly barren island, but has some vineyards and orchards. It is popular with Croatian holidaymakers but its sandy and pebble beaches are relatively quiet and its windy coast is good for surfers.

★★★☆☆ Tourism level
★★★☆☆ Vegetation
★★★☆☆ Beaches
★☆☆☆☆ History

Information
Telephone 023 362196

Map
Freytag & Berndt (1:100000)

Area 22 sq km
Coastline 27 km
Highest point 116 m (Barbenjak)

Permanent population 1608

Visitor capacity 8282
0 hotels
8282 other beds
4 campsites

Crowdfactor
441 people per sq km

Access
Bridge to mainland

Connections
None scheduled

Yacht facilities
⛵ no fuel

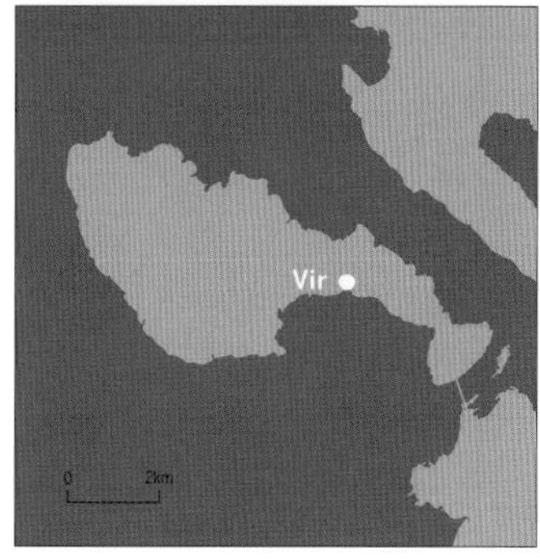
Vir
0
2km

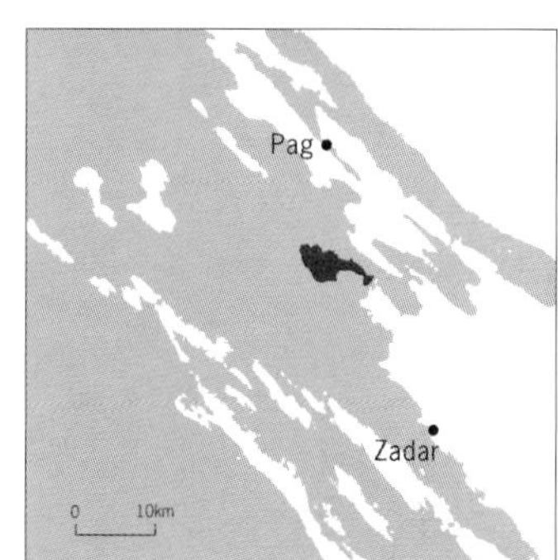
Pag
Zadar
0
10km

Ranking among all Mediterranean islands

	Rank
Area	106
Population	94
Visitor capacity	32
Crowdfactor	25

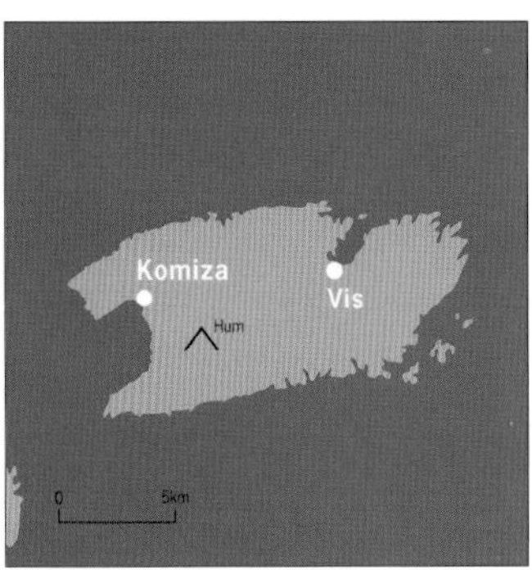
Komiza
Vis
Hum
0
5km

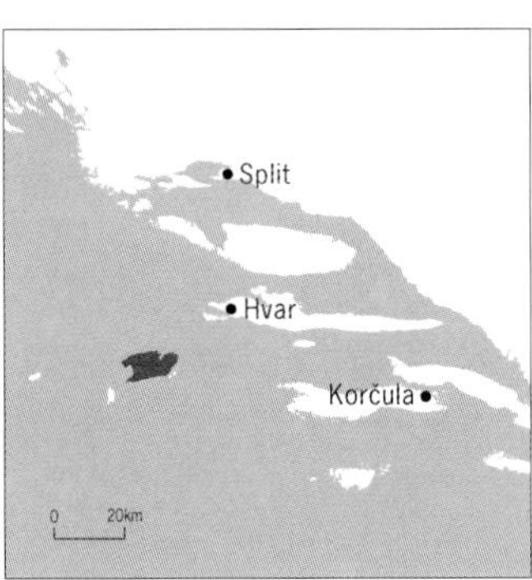
Split
Hvar
Korčula
0
20km

43°02' N 16°09' E
Vis
Central Dalmatia
Croatia

A wild mountainous island with fine views from the top of Hum, Vis is known for producing good wine both red and white. Vis town has lovely old houses and Komiza is an attractive town with a fine fortress and a Benedictine monastery. A popular excursion is to the beautiful blue cave on the island of Bisevo.

★★★☆☆ Tourism level
★★★★☆ Vegetation
★★☆☆☆ Beaches
★★★☆☆ History

Information
www.tz-vis.hr
Telephone 021 717017

Map
Freytag & Berndt (1:100000)

Area 90 sq km
Coastline 76 km
Highest point 587 m (Hum)

Permanent population 3617

Visitor capacity 3087
3 hotels
690 hotel beds
2397 other beds
0 campsites

Crowdfactor
74 people per sq km

Access
Split 1½ hours
Split 2½ hours

Connections
Split daily
Split 2 daily

Yacht facilities
Viska Luka

Ranking among all Mediterranean islands	Ra
Area	5
Population	6
Visitor capacity	5
Crowdfactor	1(

Vrgada

North Dalmatia **Croatia** 4620

43°51' N 15°30' E
Vrgada
North Dalmatia
Croatia

Vrgada is a quiet fertile island close to nature with pine forests and small sandy bays.

★★☆☆☆ Tourism level
★★★☆☆ Vegetation
★★★☆☆ Beaches
★★☆☆☆ History

Information
Telephone 023 212222

Map
None

Area 2.31 sq km
Coastline 9 km
Highest point 112 m (Strabinovac)

Permanent population 242

Visitor capacity 56
0 hotels
0 hotel beds
56 other beds
0 campsites

Crowdfactor
129 people per sq km

Access
Pakostane 35 minutes

Connections
None scheduled

Yacht facilities
no fuel

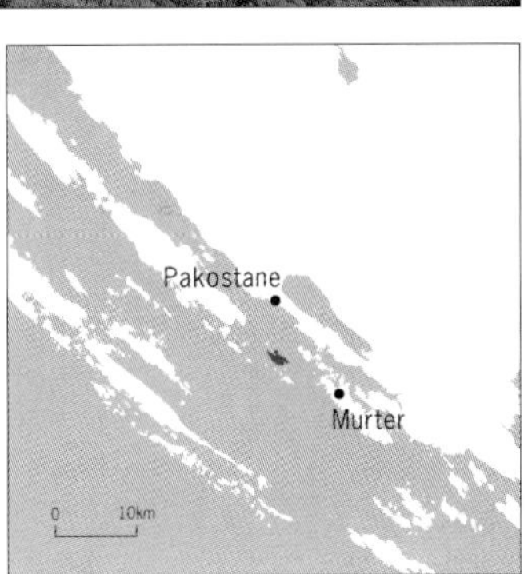
Pakostane
Murter
0
10km

Ranking among all Mediterranean islands

	Rank
Area	273
Population	143
Visitor capacity	172
Crowdfactor	76

Vrnik

4810 **Croatia** South Dalmatia

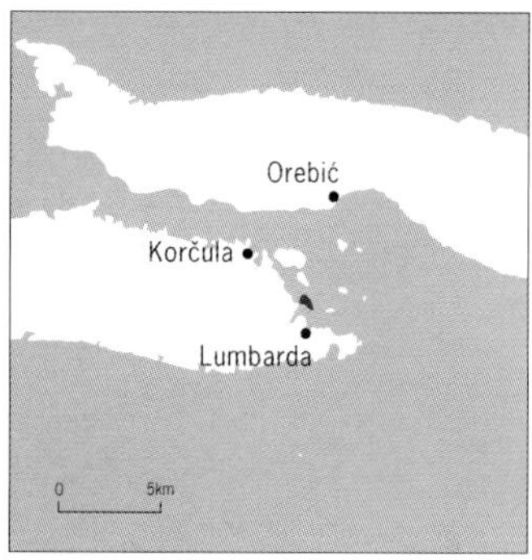

Orebić
Korčula
Lumbarda
0
5km

42°56′ N 17°10′ E
Vrnik
South Dalmatia
Croatia

Vrnik is a pretty little island with a number of rooms to let in private houses. Visits can be paid to the famous limestone quarries, which produced the stone for Agia Sofia in Istanbul.

★★☆☆☆ Tourism level
★★★☆☆ Vegetation
★★☆☆☆ Beaches
★★☆☆☆ History

Information
www.korculainfo.com
Telephone 020 715701

Map
None

Area 0.28 sq km
Coastline 2.3 km
Highest point 46 m

Permanent population 0

Visitor capacity 39
0 hotels
0 hotel beds
39 other beds
0 campsites

Crowdfactor
139 people per sq km

Access
Korčula 10 minutes

Connections
None scheduled

Yacht facilities
no fuel

Ranking among all Mediterranean islands

	Ra
Area	60
Population	
Visitor capacity	18
Crowdfactor	7

43°40′ N 15°39′ E
Žirje
North Dalmatia
Croatia

Žirje is a quiet green remote-feeling island with good basic food, growing fruit, vines and olives. It has a fishing community, many coves and is often visited by sailors.

★★☆☆☆ Tourism level
★★★☆☆ Vegetation
★★★☆☆ Beaches
★★☆☆☆ History

Information
www.otok-zirje.hr
Telephone 022 212075

Map
Freytag & Berndt (1:100000)

Area 15 sq km
Coastline 39 km
Highest point 134 m (Kapic)

Permanent population 124

Visitor capacity 84
0 hotels
0 hotel beds
84 other beds
0 campsites

Crowdfactor
13 people per sq km

Access
Sibenik 2 hours

Connections
Sibenik 2 daily

Yacht facilities
no fuel

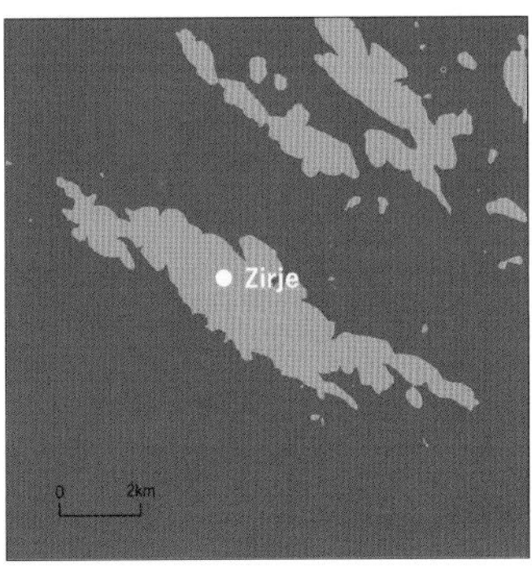
Zirje
0 2km

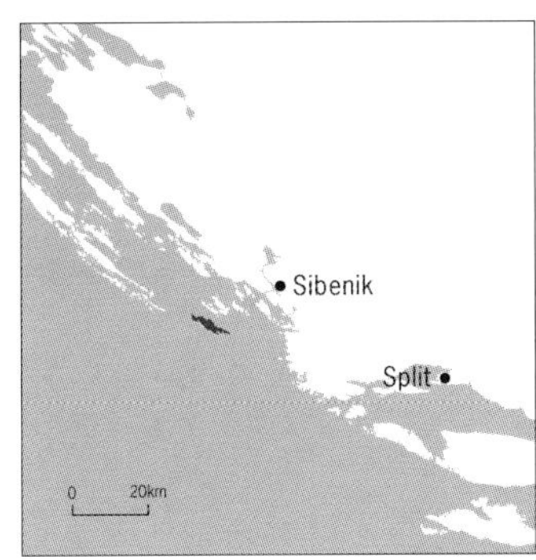
Sibenik
Split
0 20km

anking among all Mediterranean islands

	Rank
rea	131
opulation	167
sitor capacity	159
rowdfactor	192

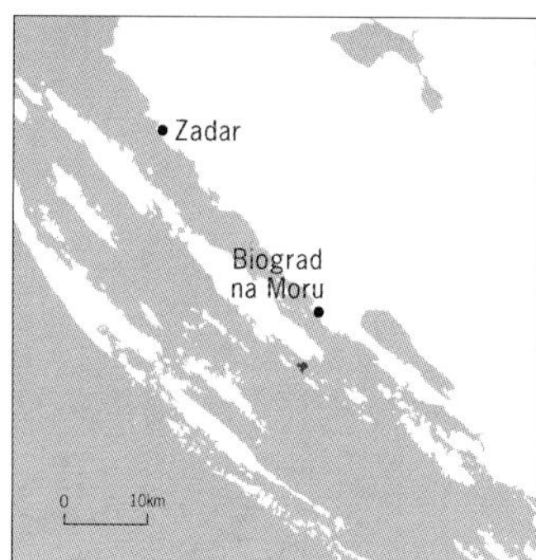
Zadar
Biograd
na Moru
0 10km

43°53' N 15°25' E
Žižanj
North Dalmatia
Croatia

Žižanj is a green island with a few fishermen's houses and holiday cottages, ideal for a quiet holiday fishing and bathing from rocks.

★☆☆☆☆ Tourism level
★★★☆☆ Vegetation
★★☆☆☆ Beaches
★☆☆☆☆ History

Information
www.pasman.hr
Telephone 023 285418

Map
None

Area 0.92 sq km
Coastline 4.5 km
Highest point 16 m

Permanent population 0

Visitor capacity 15
0 hotels
0 hotel beds
15 other beds
0 campsites

Crowdfactor
16 people per sq km

Access
Biograd 30 minutes

Connections
None sceduled

Yacht facilities
no fuel

Ranking among all Mediterranean islands

	Rar
Area	37
Population	
Visitor capacity	20
Crowdfactor	18

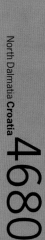

43°41' N 15°50' E
Zlarin
North Dalmatia
Croatia

Zlarin, known for its coral and sponges, is a quiet green island with no cars, is good for fishing and grows fruit, vines and olives.

★★★☆☆ Tourism level
★★★☆☆ Vegetation
★★★☆☆ Beaches
★★☆☆☆ History

Information
www.zlarin.tk
Telephone 022 553557

Map
Freytag & Berndt (1:100000)

Area 8 sq km
Coastline 18 km
Highest point 169 m (Klepac)

Permanent population 276

Visitor capacity 393
1 hotel
246 hotel beds
147 other beds
0 campsites

Crowdfactor
81 people per sq km

Access
Sibenik 30 minutes

Connections
Sibenik 4 daily

Yacht facilities
no fuel

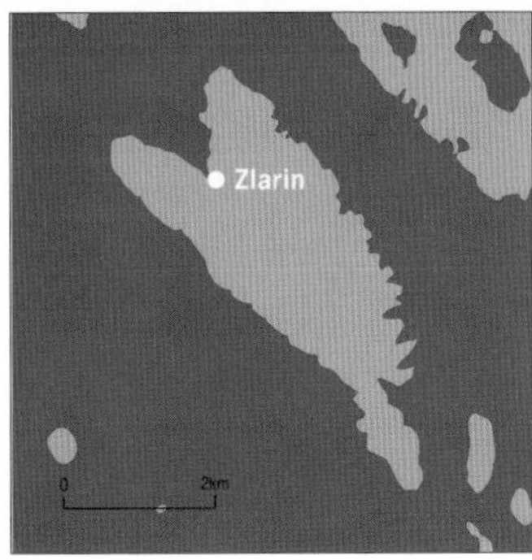
Zlarin
0
2km

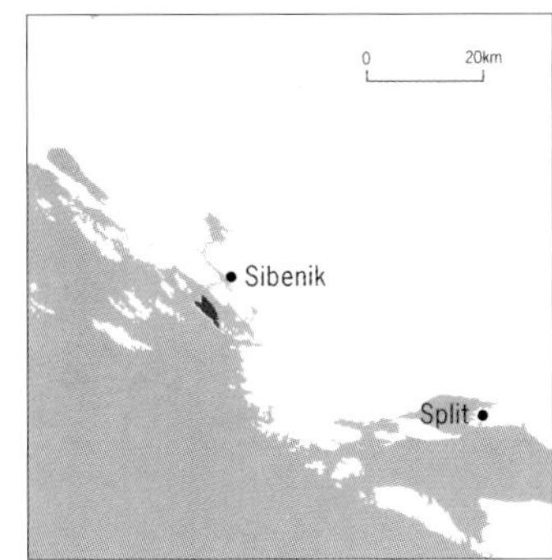
0
20km
Sibenik
Split

Ranking among all Mediterranean islands

	Rank
Area	173
Population	139
Visitor capacity	120
Crowdfactor	100

Žut

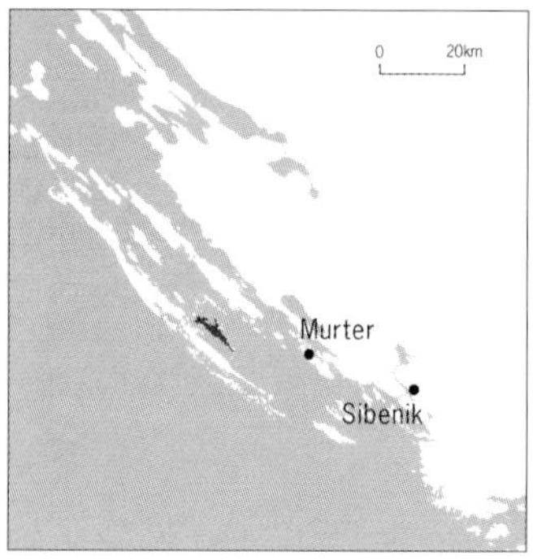
0 20km
Murter
Sibenik

43°53′ N 15°17′ E
Žut
North Dalmatia
Croatia

A green rocky island with cultivation of vines, figs and olives, Žut also has a marina with 120 berths. Day trips and private accommodation can be arranged in Murter.

★★☆☆☆ Tourism level
★★★☆☆ Vegetation
★★☆☆☆ Beaches
★★☆☆☆ History

Information
Telephone 022 436544

Map
Freytag & Berndt (1:100000)

Area 14 sq km
Coastline 45 km
Highest point 174 m (Gubavac)

Permanent population 0

Visitor capacity 200
0 hotels
0 hotel beds
200 other beds
0 campsites

Crowdfactor
13 people per sq km

Access
Private boat from Murter

Connections
None scheduled

Yacht facilities
⛵ no fuel

4570 **Croatia** North Dalmatia

Ranking among all Mediterranean islands

	Ran
Area	13
Population	
Visitor capacity	13
Crowdfactor	19

44°10′ N 14°55′ E
Zverinac
North Dalmatia
Croatia

Zverinac is thickly covered in vegetation and grows fruit, vines and olives. It also has a quiet fishing community and is much visited by sailors.

★★☆☆☆ Tourism level
★★★★☆ Vegetation
★★☆☆☆ Beaches
★★☆☆☆ History

Information
www.dugiotok.hr
Telephone 023 377094

Map
None

Area 4.17 sq km
Coastline 14 km
Highest point 117 m (Klis)

Permanent population 48

Visitor capacity 40
0 hotels
0 hotel beds
40 other beds
0 campsites

Crowdfactor
21 people per sq km

Access
Zadar 2½ hours

Connections
Zadar daily

Yacht facilities
no fuel

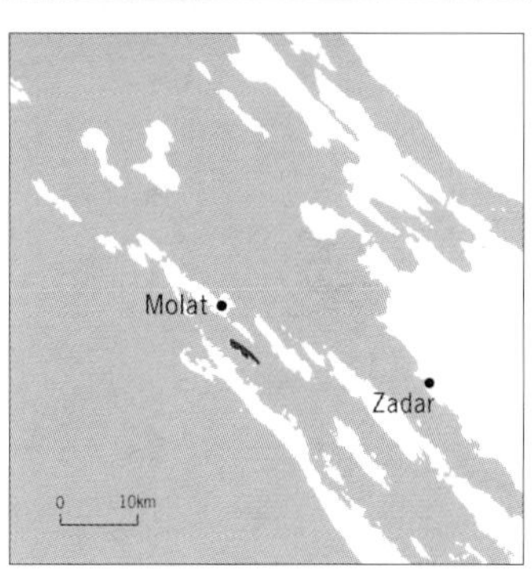
Molat
Zadar
0
10km

Ranking among all Mediterranean islands

	Rank
Area	220
Population	187
Visitor capacity	179
Crowdfactor	173

Zverinac

North Dalmatia **Croatia** 4410

Agathonísi

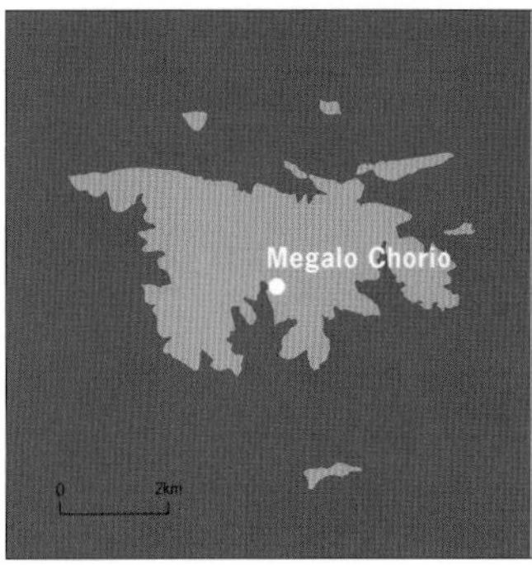

Megalo Chorio
0
2km

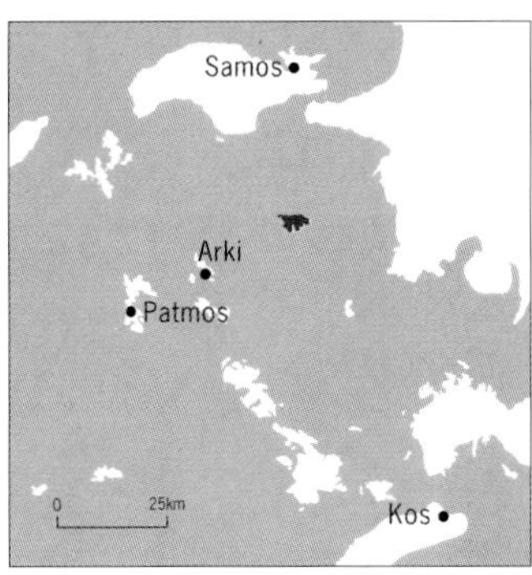

Samos
Arki
Patmos
Kos
0
25km

37°28' N 26°58' E
Agathonisi
Dodekanisa
Greece

Agathonisi is a very low-key peaceful island, surprisingly green and with pleasant walking and beaches.

★☆☆☆☆ Tourism level
★★☆☆☆ Vegetation
★★★☆☆ Beaches
★☆☆☆☆ History

Information
Telephone 22470 29062

Map
None

Area 13 sq km
Coastline 35 km
Highest point 208 m (Stifi)

Permanent population 152

Visitor capacity 38
0 hotels
0 hotel beds
38 other beds
0 campsites

Crowdfactor
14 people per sq km

Access
Samos, Arkí 1 hour

Connections
Samos, Arkí, Lipsoi 5 weekly
Leros, Kalymnos 4 weekly

Yacht facilities
Ag Georgiou

Ranking among all Mediterranean islands

	Ran
Area	14
Population	16
Visitor capacity	18
Crowdfactor	19

7480 **Greece** Dodekanisa

Agios Efstrátios

39°31' N 25°00' E
Agios Efstratios
Voreio Aigaio
Greece

Very little visited but surprisingly green, Agios Efstratios has good beaches and is a good island for exploring.

★☆☆☆☆ Tourism level
★★★☆☆ Vegetation
★★★☆☆ Beaches
★☆☆☆☆ History

Information
www.lemnos-island.com
Telephone 22540 93210

Map
Road Editions (1:50000)

Area 42 sq km
Coastline 37 km
Highest point 298 m (Lemoni Rachi)

Permanent population 307

Visitor capacity 120
1 hotel
30 hotel beds
90 other beds
0 campsites

Crowdfactor
10 people per sq km

Access
Limnos 1½ hours

Connections
Limnos 5 weekly
Lavrio 4 weekly

Yacht facilities
no fuel

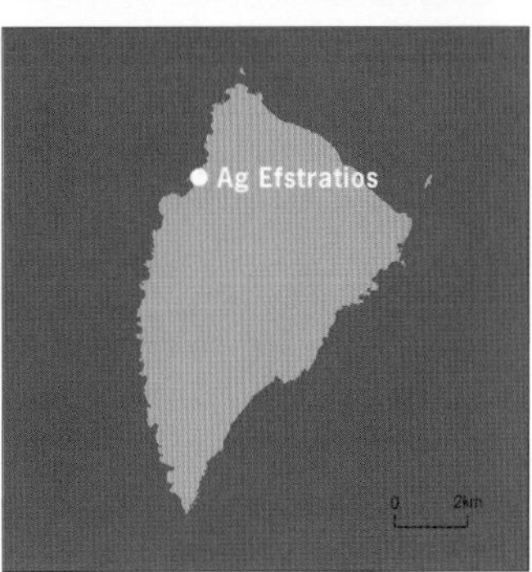
Ag Efstratios
0 2km

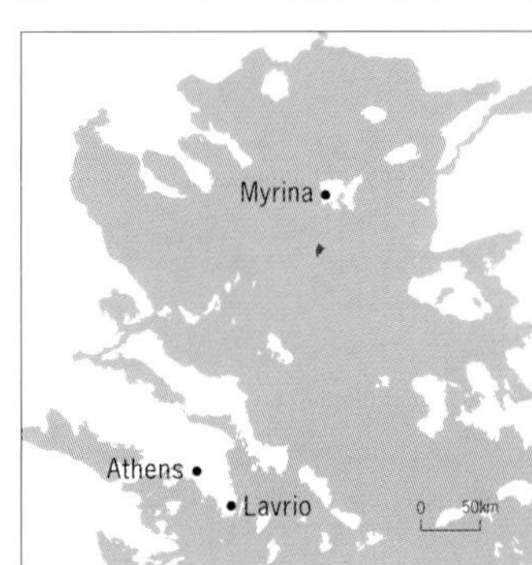
Myrina
Athens
Lavrio
0 50km

Voreio Aigaio **Greece** 7810

Ranking among all Mediterranean islands	Rank
Area	81
Population	133
Visitor capacity	153
Crowdfactor	200

Agkístri

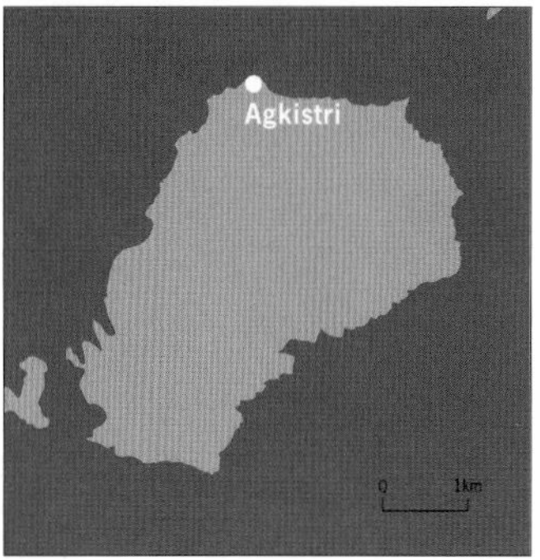

Agkistri
0
1km

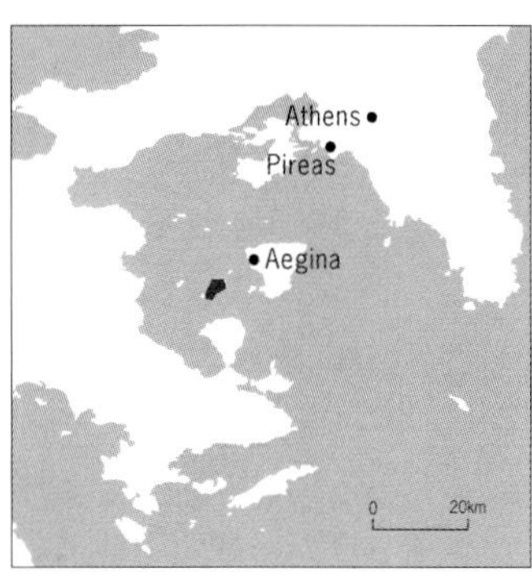

Athens
Pireas
Aegina
0
20km

37°42' N 23°21' E
Agkistri
Argosaronikos
Grrece

The area round the port is very ordinary, but the rest of this heavily wooded island is lovely with several good beaches and an attractive village at Limenaria. Daytrips are arranged to Poros, Ydra, Epidavros and Corinth.

★★☆☆☆ Tourism level
★★★★☆ Vegetation
★★★☆☆ Beaches
★☆☆☆☆ History

Information
www.agistri.gr
Telephone 22970 91356

Map
Road Editions (1:25000)

Area 11 sq km
Coastline 17 km
Highest point 275 m (Drimona)

Permanent population 886

Visitor capacity 1480
22 hotels
690 hotel beds
790 other beds
0 campsites

Crowdfactor
201 people per sq km

Access
Pireas 1 hour
Aigina 30 minutes
Pireas 2 hours

Connections
Pireas 3 daily
Aigina 8 daily

Yacht facilities
no fuel

Ranking among all Mediterranean islands	Ran
Area	15
Population	10
Visitor capacity	7
Crowdfactor	5

37°45' N 23°31' E
Aigina
Argosaronikos
Greece

For two years the capital of Greece, Aigina is now known for its fine pistachio nuts. The two major sights are the Doric temple of Aphaia in a magnificent setting on a wooded hill and the Venetian capital of Paleochora which has about 30 churches mostly dating from the 14th to 16th centuries. Other things to see are the lovely 13th century Omorfi Ekklisia with frescoes, the Panagia Chrysoleondissa convent, the view from the top of Oros and the fishing port of Perdika with a view over to the wooded island of Moni.

★★★★☆ Tourism level
★★★☆☆ Vegetation
★★★☆☆ Beaches
★★★★☆ History

Information
www.aroundaegina.com
Telephone 22970 26967

Map
Road Editions (1:25000)

Area 77 sq km
Coastline 56 km
Highest point 447 m (Oros)

Permanent population 12716

Visitor capacity 6997
80 hotels
3720 hotel beds
3277 other beds
0 campsites

Crowdfactor
255 people per sq km

Access
Pireas 40 minutes
Pireas 1 ½ hours

Connections
Pireas 5 daily
Methana, Poros 4 daily
Porto Cheli 2 daily
Pireas 20 daily
Agkistri 8 daily

Yacht facilities
Aigina, Perdika

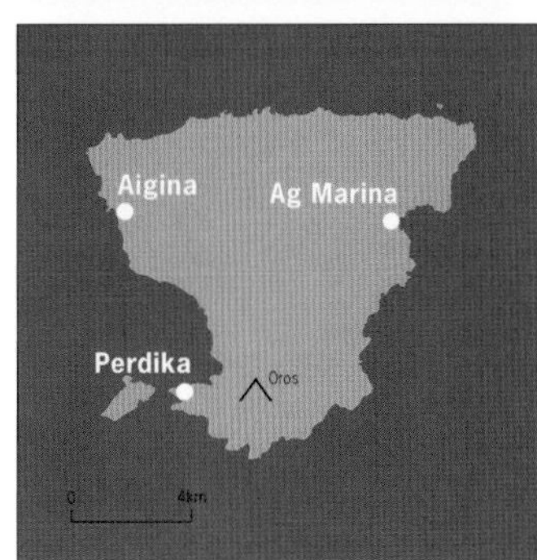
Aigina
Ag Marina
Perdika
Oros
0
4km

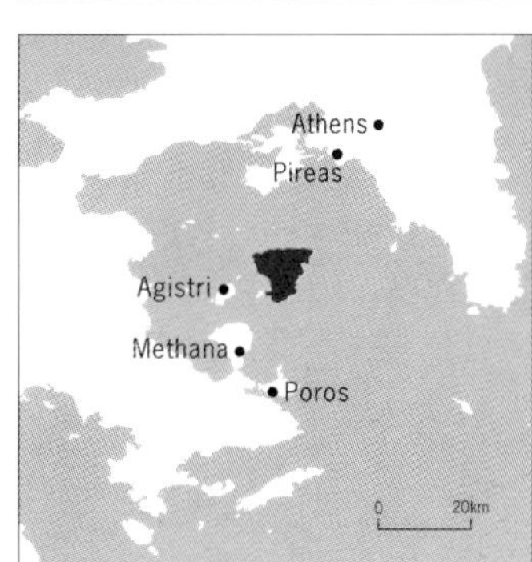
Athens
Pireas
Agistri
Methana
Poros
0
20km

Ranking among all Mediterranean islands	Rank
Area	62
Population	36
Visitor capacity	37
Crowdfactor	47

Alónnisos

6960 **Greece** Vories Sporades

(PHOTO: PREFECTURE OF MAGNESIA)

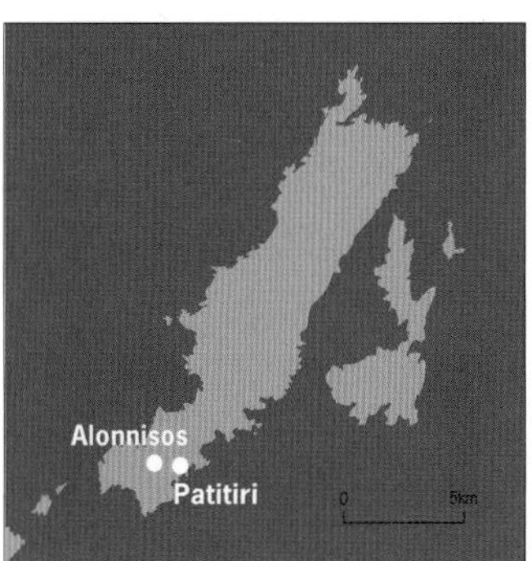
Alonnisos
Patitiri
0
5km

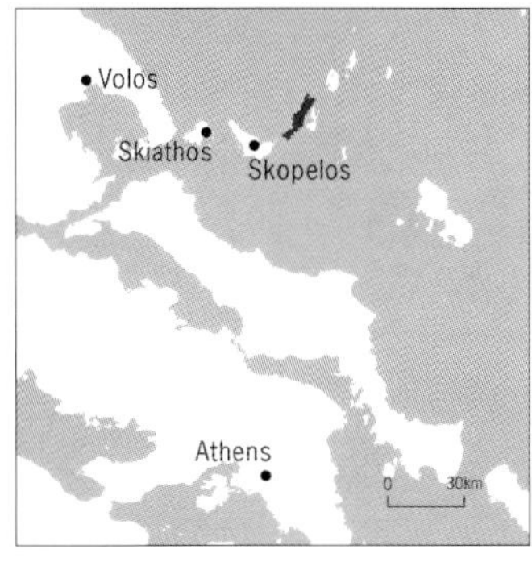
Volos
Skiathos
Skopelos
Athens
0
30km

39°12' N 23°55' E
Alonnisos
Vories Sporades
Greece

A very pretty wooded island with a relaxing port village and a recently restored capital above, from which there are fine views. The main delights of Alonnisos are the many lovely beaches reachable by caique and walking along the forest paths throughout the island. It is worth visiting the islands of Peristera opposite and the lovely Kyra Panagia with its monastery, but Gioura and Piperi are part of the Sporades Marine Park and visiting now requires special permission.

★★★☆☆ Tourism level
★★★★☆ Vegetation
★★★★☆ Beaches
★★☆☆☆ History

Information
www.alonissos.gr
Telephone 24240 65577

Map
Anavasi (1:25000)

Area 65 sq km
Coastline 81 km
Highest point 475 m (Kouvouli)

Permanent population 2399

Visitor capacity 1842
17 hotels
1012 hotel beds
830 other beds
0 campsites

Crowdfactor
64 people per sq km

Access
⛴ Skopelos 20 minutes

Connections
⛴ Skopelos 3 daily

Yacht facilities
⛵ Patitiri

Ranking among all Mediterranean islands	Ran
Area	6
Population	8
Visitor capacity	6
Crowdfactor	11

40°20′ N 23°54′ E
Ammouliani
Voreio Aigaio
Greece

An attractive little island with a pleasant village and a number of good beaches. It is well worth taking a boat to the lovely Drenia islets.

★★★☆☆ Tourism level
★★★☆☆ Vegetation
★★★★☆ Beaches
★☆☆☆☆ History

Information
www.ammouliani.com.gr
Telephone 23770 51273

Map
None

Area 7 sq km
Coastline 20 km
Highest point 100 m (Koukos)

Permanent population 547

Visitor capacity 893
9 hotels
397 hotel beds
496 other beds
1 campsite

Crowdfactor
201 people per sq km

Access
Trypiti 10 minutes

Connections
Trypiti 30 daily

Yacht facilities
Ammouliani

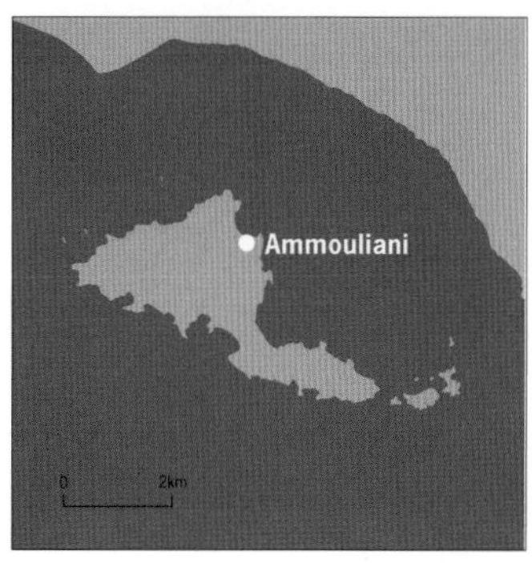
Ammouliani
0
2km

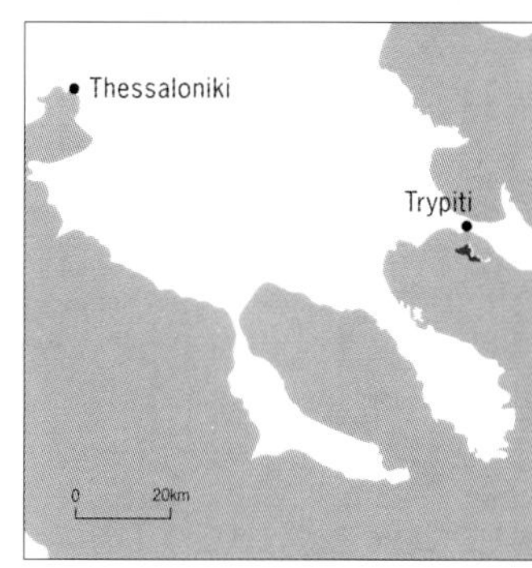
Thessaloniki
Trypiti
0
20km

Ranking among all Mediterranean islands

	Rank
Area	179
Population	121
Visitor capacity	90
Crowdfactor	56

Amorgós

(PHOTO: GREEK NATIONAL TOURISM ORGANISATION)

Aigiali
Katapola
Amorgos
0
10km

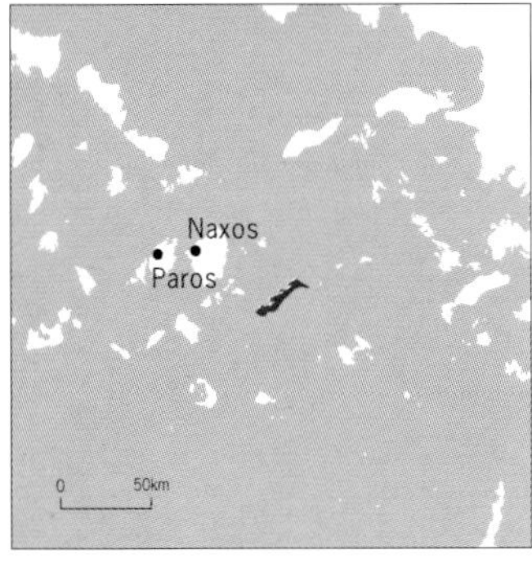
Naxos
Paros
0
50km

36°50′ N 25°53′ E
Amorgos
Kyklades
Greece

Amorgos is a long unspoilt mountainous island which joins two separate communities, with a spectacular walk between the two. At the western end is the charming Cycladic chora and the famous Chozoviotissa monastery clinging to the side of a cliff. At the eastern end is the charming small port of Aegiali with more fine walking and the lovely village of Langada beyond. Both the main offshore islands, Nikouria and Gramvousa, have good beaches.

★★☆☆☆ Tourism level
★★☆☆☆ Vegetation
★★★☆☆ Beaches
★★★☆☆ History

Information
www.amorgos.net
Telephone 22850 71246

Map
Anavasi (1:35000)

Area 121 sq km
Coastline 126 km
Highest point 827 m (Krikelo)

Permanent population 1851

Visitor capacity 984
8 hotels
298 hotel beds
686 other beds
3 campsites

Crowdfactor
23 people per sq km

Access
⛴ Naxos 2 hours

Connections
⛴ Naxos 2 daily
⛴ Pireas, Paros, Koufonisi, Donousa daily

Yacht facilities
⛵ Katapola

Ranking among all Mediterranean islands	Ran
Area	4
Population	9
Visitor capacity	8
Crowdfactor	16

6750 **Greece** Kyklades

36°22′ N 25°47′ E
Anafi
Kyklades
Greece

Anafi is an isolated barren island, but the people are friendly and the town is pretty. The only road is between the port and the chora and so journeys to the uncrowded sandy beaches or the 16th century Kalamiotissa monastery and nearby dragon's cave are made on foot or by boat.

★★☆☆☆ Tourism level
★☆☆☆☆ Vegetation
★★☆☆☆ Beaches
★★☆☆☆ History

Information
www.anafi.gr
Telephone 22860 61390

Map
None

Area 38 sq km
Coastline 38 km
Highest point 579 m (Vigla)

Permanent population 272

Visitor capacity 226
0 hotels
0 hotel beds
226 other beds
0 campsites

Crowdfactor
12 people per sq km

Access
Santorini 2 hours

Connections
Santorini daily

Yacht facilities
no fuel

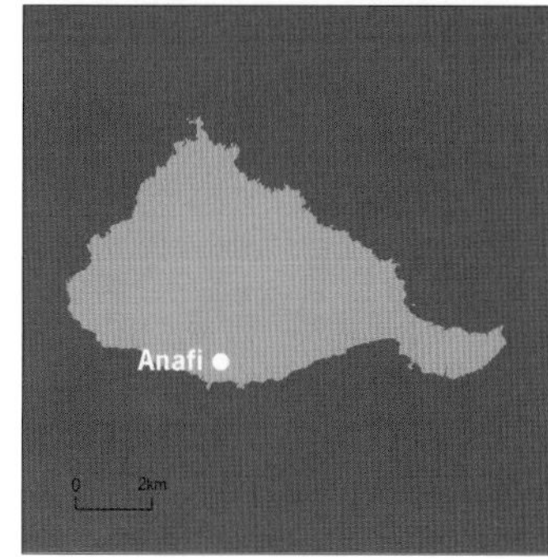
Anafi
0
2km

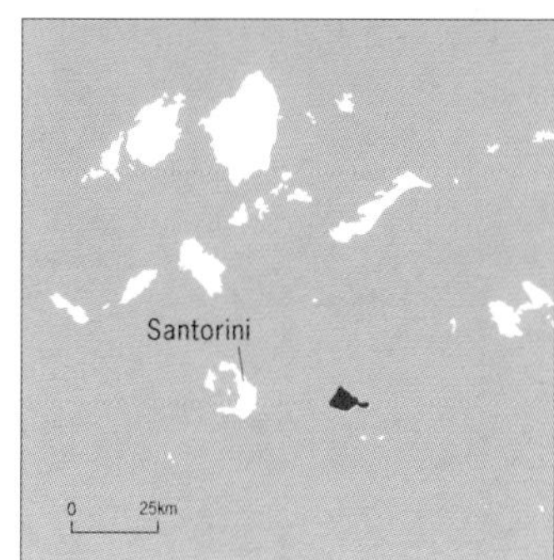
Santorini
0
25km

Ranking among all Mediterranean islands

	Rank
Area	85
Population	140
Visitor capacity	134
Crowdfactor	196

Ándros

6400 Greece Kyklades

(PHOTO: REGIONAL DEVELOPMENT AGENCY OF CYCLADES)

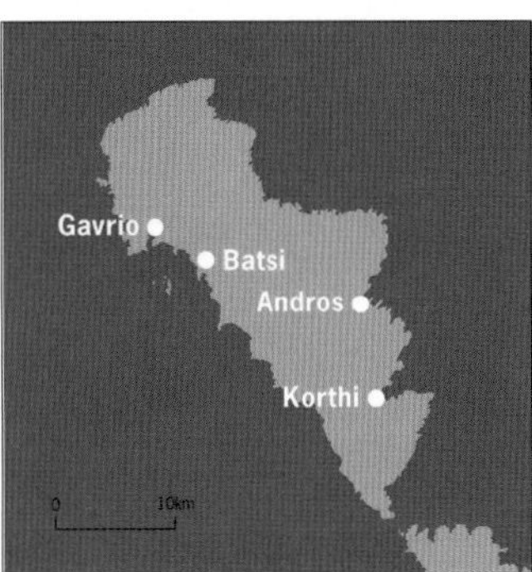
Gavrio
Batsi
Andros
Korthi
0
10km

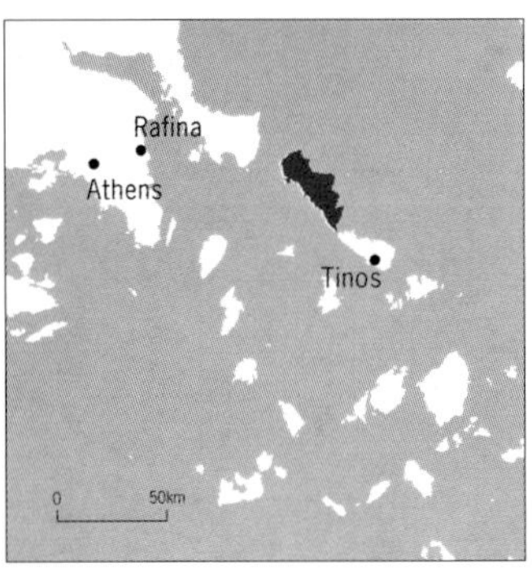
Rafina
Athens
Tinos
0
50km

37°51' N 24°51' E
Andros
Kyklades
Greece

Andros is a fertile island with an attractive capital and some lovely villages, notably Menites, Messaria, Katakilos and Stenies. The presence of many Athenians means that the food is good and wine lists are exceptional. There are lovely walks all over the island and the Panachrandou monastery is worth visiting. Batsi is the only place touched by tourism.

★★★☆☆ Tourism level
★★★☆☆ Vegetation
★★★★☆ Beaches
★★★☆☆ History

Information
www.andros.gr
Telephone 22820 22275

Map
Road Editions (1:50000)

Area 383 sq km
Coastline 176 km
Highest point 995 m (Profitis Ilias)

Permanent population 9285

Visitor capacity 2374
23 hotels
1228 hotel beds
1146 other beds
1 campsite

Crowdfactor
30 people per sq km

Access
Rafina 2 hours

Connections
Rafina, Tinos 5 daily

Yacht facilities
Gavrio, Batsi, Andros

Ranking among all Mediterranean islands	Ran
Area	2
Population	4
Visitor capacity	5
Crowdfactor	15

Antikýthira

35°52' N 23°18' E
Antikythira
Greece

Isolated and rugged but surprisingly fertile, producing fruit, vegetables, wine and honey, Antikythira is now making efforts to attract visitors interested in solitude, birds and flowers.

★☆☆☆☆ Tourism level
★★★☆☆ Vegetation
★☆☆☆☆ Beaches
★★☆☆☆ History

nformation
www.antikythira.gr
elephone 27360 33004

lap
ntikythira Community (1:10000)

Area 19 sq km
Coastline 32 km
Highest point 378 m (Plagaras)

Permanent population 39

Visitor capacity 35
0 hotels
0 hotel beds
35 other beds
0 campsites

Crowdfactor
3 people per sq km

Access
Kythira 2 hours

Connections
Kythira 4 weekly

Yacht facilities
no fuel

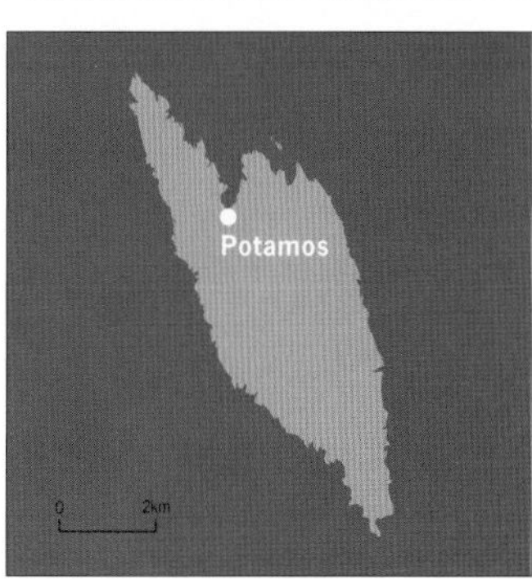
Potamos
0
2km

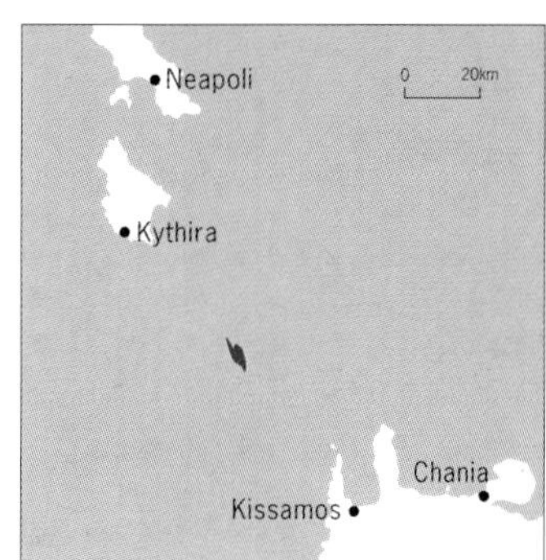
Neapoli
0
20km
Kythira
Chania
Kissamos

anking among all Mediterranean islands	Rank
rea	117
pulation	190
sitor capacity	188
rowdfactor	212

Greece
5510

Antíparos

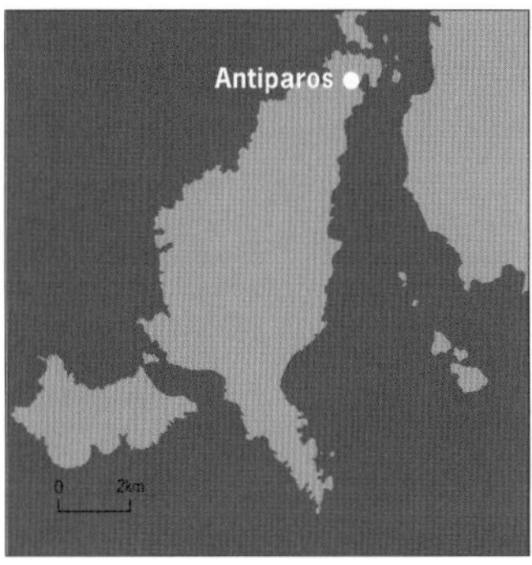

Antiparos
0 2km

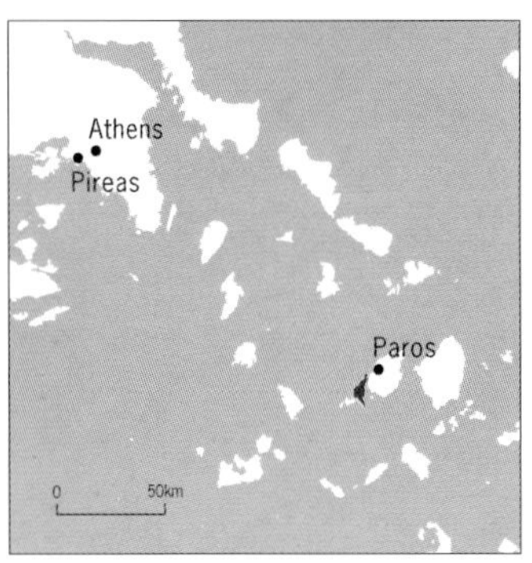

Athens
Pireas
Paros
0 50km

37°00' N 25°03' E
Antiparos
Kyklades
Greece

There has been a subtle shift in the character of Antiparos as those who spent an unforgettable summer on the nudist camping beach return 20 years later with their families. The village with its 15th century kastro is attractive and there are lovely beaches to be found down the east coast and in the south, but the famous cave has become rather over-visited.

★★★☆☆ Tourism level
★★☆☆☆ Vegetation
★★★★☆ Beaches
★★☆☆☆ History

Information
www.antiparos-isl.com
Telephone 22840 61570

Map
Road Editions (1:50000)

Area 35 sq km
Coastline 49 km
Highest point 301 m (Ag Ilias)

Permanent population 1010

Visitor capacity 527
9 hotels
343 hotel beds
184 other beds
1 campsite

Crowdfactor
43 people per sq km

Access
⛴ Pounda 10 minutes

Connections
⛴ Pounda 35 daily
⛴ Parikia 10 daily

Yacht facilities
⛵ no fuel

Ranking among all Mediterranean islands	Rar
Area	8
Population	10
Visitor capacity	11
Crowdfactor	13

6650 **Greece** Kyklades

Antípaxoi

39°09' N 20°14' E
Antipaxoi
Ionia Nisia
Greece

Frequent boats from Paxoi have made this small island less peaceful, but it is still possible to find a relatively deserted beach by walking away from the landing places and the interior covered with vines is lovely. There are two charming houses that can be rented.

★★☆☆☆ Tourism level
★★★☆☆ Vegetation
★★★☆☆ Beaches
★☆☆☆☆ History

Information
www.paxos-greece.com
telephone 26620 32401

Map
Heasdale (1:10000)

Area 4.59 sq km
Coastline 14 km
Highest point 116 m (Agrilida)

Permanent population 24

Visitor capacity 8
0 hotels
0 hotel beds
8 other beds
0 campsites

Crowdfactor
6 people per sq km

Access
Paxoi 30 minutes

Connections
Paxoi 6 daily

Yacht facilities
no fuel

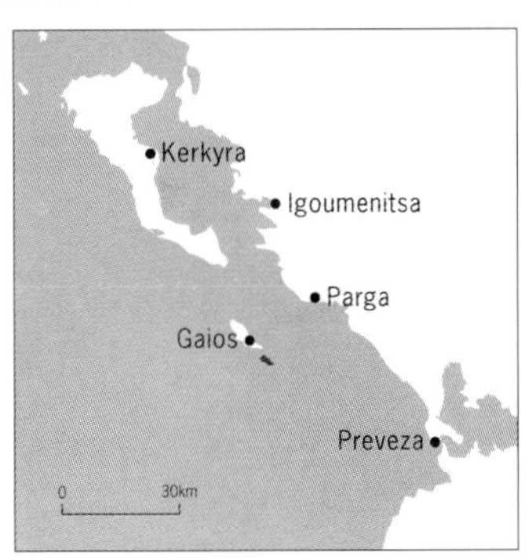
Kerkyra
Igoumenitsa
Parga
Gaios
Preveza
0
30km

Ranking among all Mediterranean islands

	Rank
Area	205
Population	193
Visitor capacity	212
Crowdfactor	209

Ionia Nisia **Greece** 5060

Arkoí

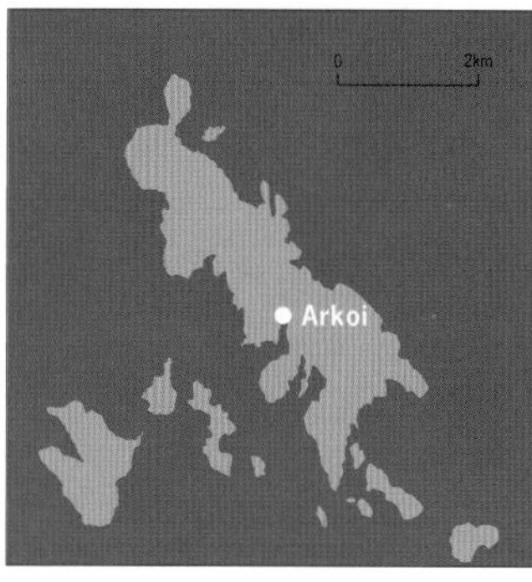
0 2km
Arkoi

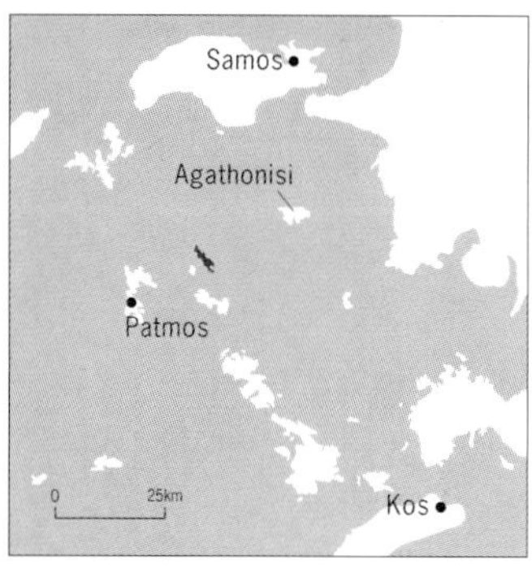
Samos
Agathonisi
Patmos
0 25km
Kos

37°23' N 26°45' E
Arkoi
Dodekanisa
Greece

Arkoi is a very quiet island, mostly barren and hilly and with only one beach at Tiganakia in the southeast.

★☆☆☆☆ Tourism level
★★☆☆☆ Vegetation
★★☆☆☆ Beaches
★☆☆☆☆ History

Information
Telephone 22470 32230

Map
Orama 329 (1:50000)

Area 6 sq km
Coastline 25 km
Highest point 111 m (Vardia)

Permanent population 50

Visitor capacity 64
0 hotels
0 hotel beds
64 other beds
0 campsites

Crowdfactor
17 people per sq km

Access
Patmos 30 minutes
Agathónisi 1 hour

Connections
Agathónisi 5 weekly
Patmos 4 weekly

Yacht facilities
no fuel

7460 **Greece** Dodekanisa

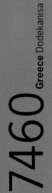

Ranking among all Mediterranean islands	Ra
Area	18
Population	18
Visitor capacity	16
Crowdfactor	18

36°33' N 26°19' E
Astypalaia
Dodekanisa
Greece

An attractive relaxed island whose Cycladic chora, dominated by a fine kastro dating from the 13th to 15th centuries, has a number of pretty churches and a photogenic line of windmills. Apart from the fertile Livadi valley, the island is mainly barren but attracts many species of birds and is pleasant to explore. Astypalaia is surrounded by numerous islets many of which can be visited by daily boats.

★★☆☆☆ Tourism level
★★☆☆☆ Vegetation
★★★☆☆ Beaches
★★☆☆☆ History

Information
www.astypalaia.gr
telephone 22430 61412

Map
Road Editions (1:40000)

Area 96 sq km
Coastline 128 km
Highest point 482 m (Vardia)

Permanent population 1385

Visitor capacity 821
8 hotels
271 hotel beds
550 other beds
1 campsite

Crowdfactor
22 people per sq km

Access
✈ Astypalaia
⛴ Kalymnos 2½ hours

Connections
⛴ Kalymnos 5 weekly
⛴ Amorgos 3 weekly

Yacht facilities
⛵ Skala

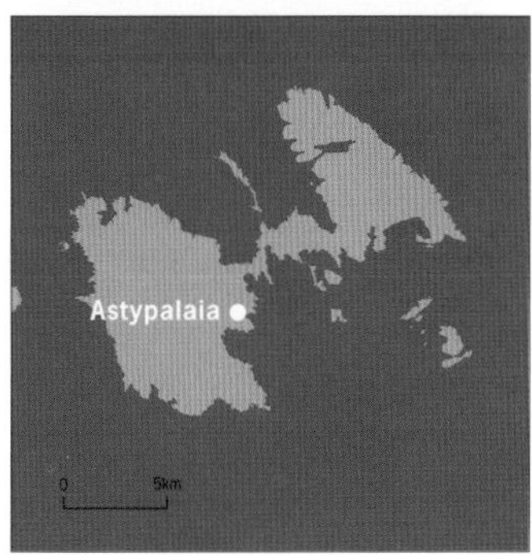
Astypalaia
0
5km

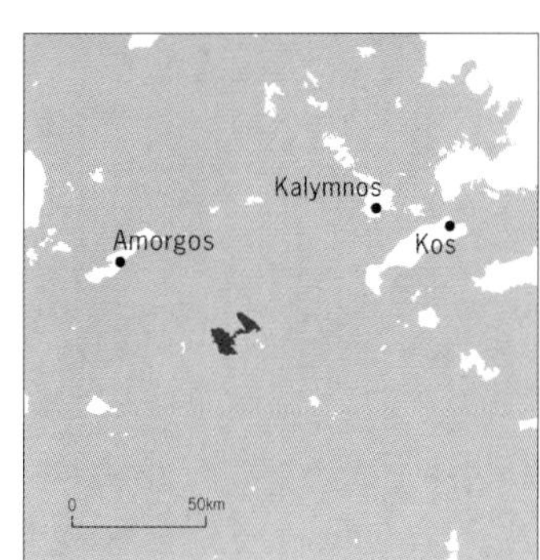
Kalymnos
Amorgos
Kos
0
50km

Ranking among all Mediterranean islands	Rank
Area	51
Population	98
Visitor capacity	91
Crowdfactor	169

Chálki

7020 **Greece** Dodekanisa

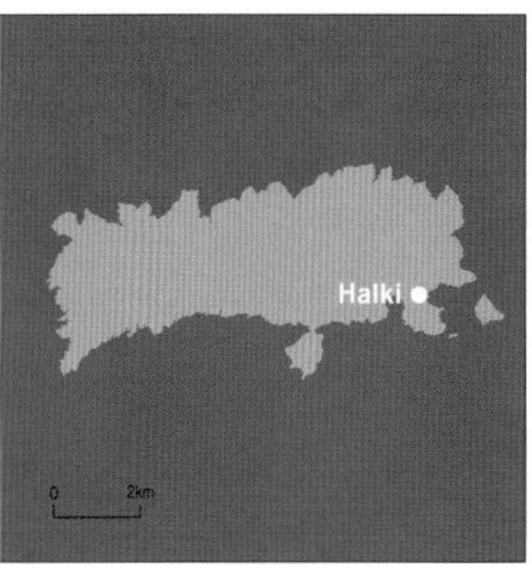
Halki
0
2km

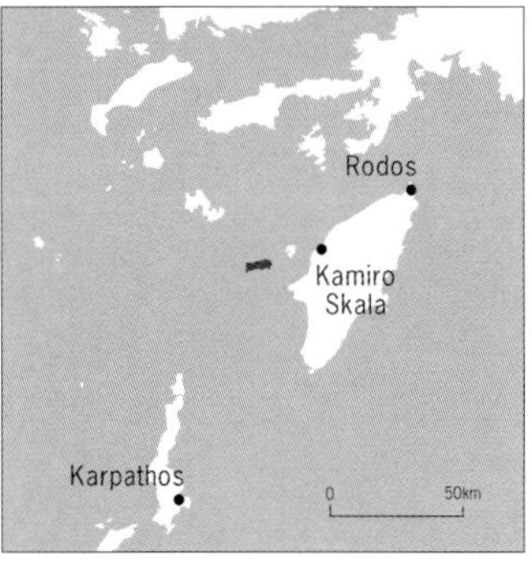
Rodos
Kamiro Skala
Karpathos
0
50km

36°14' N 27°36' E
Chalki
Dodekanisa
Greece

A barren island with no cars, Chalki can be explored either on foot or by boat. There are a number of coves around the island and a Knights' castle above Chora. Boats go to the uninhabited island of Alimia where there is also a castle.

★★☆☆☆ Tourism level
★☆☆☆☆ Vegetation
★★☆☆☆ Beaches
★★☆☆☆ History

Information
www.halkivisitor.com
Telephone 22460 45201

Map
Peace & Friendship (1:21000)

Area 26 sq km
Coastline 40 km
Highest point 593 m (Merovigli)

Permanent population 295

Visitor capacity 97
4 hotels
45 hotel beds
52 other beds
0 campsites

Crowdfactor
14 people per sq km

Access
Rodos 2 hours
Kamiro Skala 1½ hours

Connections
Rodos daily
Karpathos 4 weekly
Kamiro Skala daily

Yacht facilities
no fuel

Ranking among all Mediterranean islands	Ra
Area	9
Population	13
Visitor capacity	15
Crowdfactor	19

38°33′ N 26°03′ E
Chios
Voreio Aigaio
Greece

The north coast beyond Kardamyla, famous for its shipowners, is mountainous and green with lovely beaches. South of the capital are fine Genoese country houses with lovely citrus orchards, while further on is the area where mastic, used in chewing gum and raki, is grown and the fortified villages of Pyrgi and Mesta. The 11th century Nea Moni to the west of Chios town is a very fine Byzantine building in a lovely setting, while beyond it there is a wonderful view over the Aegean. Volissos is the reputed birthplace of Homer.

★★☆☆☆ Tourism level
★★★☆☆ Vegetation
★★★☆☆ Beaches
★★★★☆ History

Information
www.chiosnet.gr
Telephone 22710 44389

Map
Anavasi (1:60000)

Area 842 sq km
Coastline 229 km
Highest point 1297 m (Pelineo)

Permanent population 51773

Visitor capacity 3108
45 hotels
2422 hotel beds
686 other beds
1 campsite

Crowdfactor
65 people per sq km

Access
✈ Chios
⛴ Lesvos 3 hours

Connections
⛴ Pireas, Lesvos 2 daily
⛴ Inoússes, Cesme daily

Yacht facilities
⛵ 4 ports

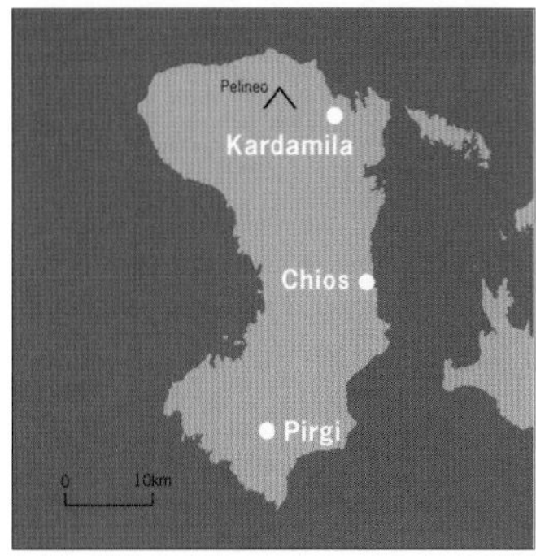
Pelineo
Kardamila
Chios
Pirgi
0
10km

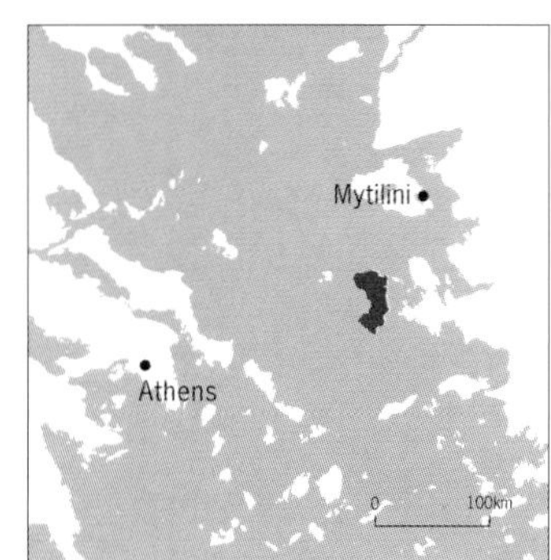
Mytilini
Athens
0
100km

Ranking among all Mediterranean islands	Rank
Area	10
Population	16
Visitor capacity	49
Crowdfactor	111

Voreio Aigaio **Greece** 7600

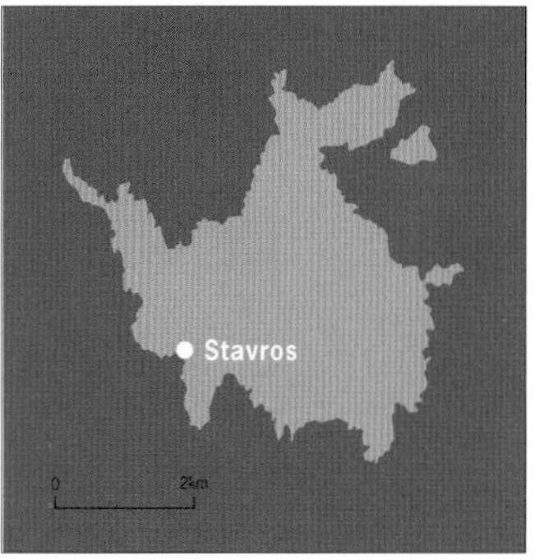
Stavros
0
2km

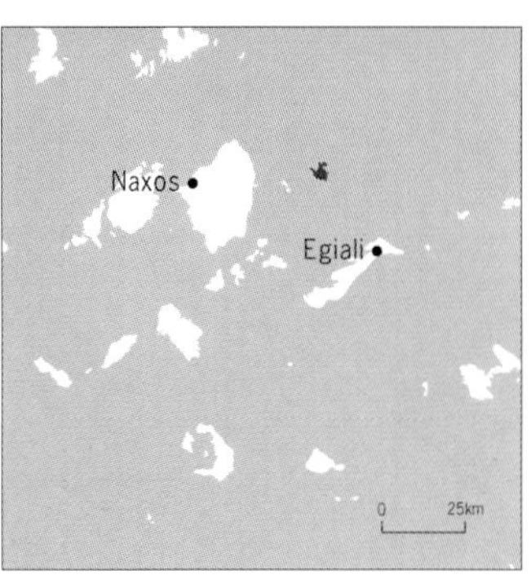
Naxos
Egiali
0
25km

37°06' N 25°49' E
Donousa
Kyklades
Greece

Donousa is a remote and wild but friendly island with good walking and fine beaches, particularly those at Kendros, Livadi and Kalotaritissa which can often be deserted.

★☆☆☆☆ Tourism level
★★☆☆☆ Vegetation
★★★☆☆ Beaches
★☆☆☆☆ History

Information
www.donoussa.info
Telephone 22850 51570

Map
Agoni Grammi (1:13500)

Area 13 sq km
Coastline 31 km
Highest point 383 m (Pappas)

Permanent population 166

Visitor capacity 50
0 hotels
0 hotel beds
50 other beds
0 campsites

Crowdfactor
15 people per sq km

Access
Amorgos 1½ hours
Naxos 2 hours

Connections
Amorgos daily
Koufonisi 4 weekly

Yacht facilities
no fuel

Ranking among all Mediterranean islands	Ra
Area	14
Population	15
Visitor capacity	17
Crowdfactor	18

Elafónisos

36°30' N 22°58' E
Elafonisos
Greece

Elafonisos has a pretty fishing village with a number of places to stay and a good choice of fish restaurants. It also has a huge and outstanding beach at Simos bay.

★★☆☆☆ Tourism level
★☆☆☆☆ Vegetation
★★★★☆ Beaches
★☆☆☆☆ History

nformation
www.elafonisos.net
elephone27340 61238

Map
Drama 352 (1:40000)

Area 17 sq km
Coastline 29 km
Highest point 276 m (Vardia)

Permanent population 746

Visitor capacity 414
4 hotels
94 hotel beds
320 other beds
0 campsites

Crowdfactor
64 people per sq km

Access
Viglafia 10 minutes

Connections
Viglafia 70 daily

Yacht facilities
no fuel

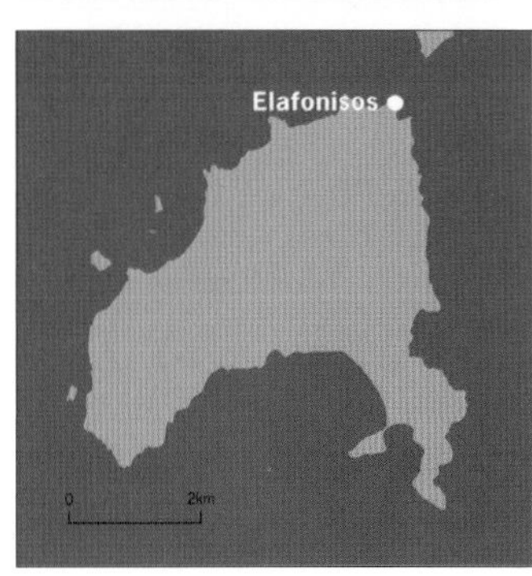
Elafonisos
0
2km

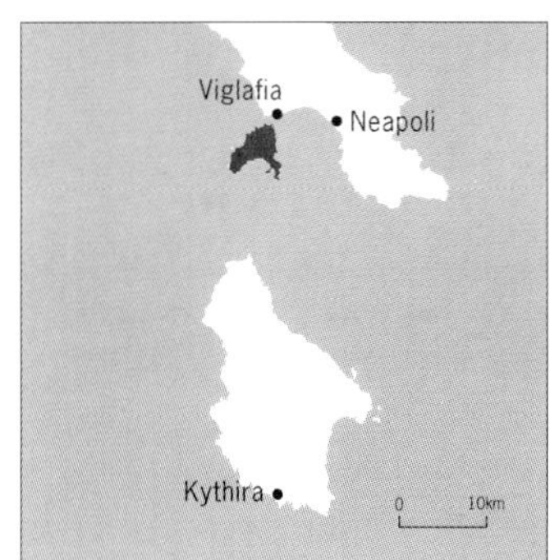
Viglafia
Neapoli
Kythira
0
10km

anking among all Mediterranean islands	Rank
rea	124
opulation	113
sitor capacity	117
rowdfactor	113

Greece 5520

Eríkousa

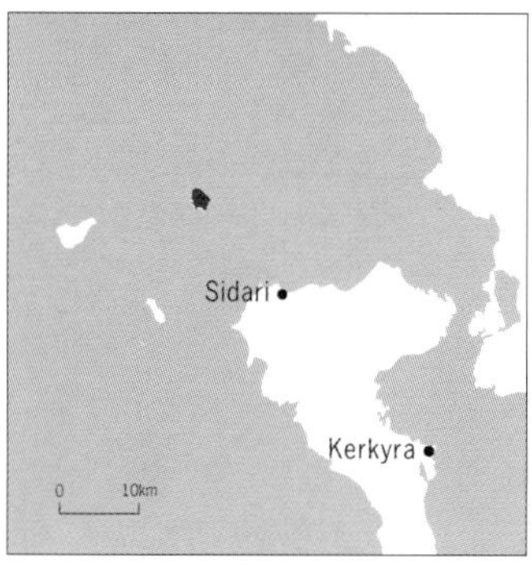

Sidari
Kerkyra
0
10km

39°53′ N 19°35′ E
Erikousa
Ionia Nisia
Greece

A wooded island, with cypresses and olives and a sandy beach usually covered with day visitors from Sidari.

★★☆☆☆ Tourism level
★★★☆☆ Vegetation
★★★☆☆ Beaches
★☆☆☆☆ History

Information
Telephone 26630 71555

Map
Road Editions (1:70000)

Area 4.38 sq km
Coastline 9 km
Highest point 121 m (Merovigla)

Permanent population 612

Visitor capacity 40
1 hotel
40 hotel beds
0 other beds
0 campsites

Crowdfactor
148 people per sq km

Access
Kerkyra 4 hours
Sidari 40 minutes

Connections
Kerkyra 2 weekly
Sidari daily

Yacht facilities
no fuel

Ranking among all Mediterranean islands

	Rar
Area	21
Population	11
Visitor capacity	17
Crowdfactor	6

5020 **Greece** Ionia Nisia

Évvoia

38°38' N 23°45' E
Evvoia
Greece

Evvoia is a beautiful island with dramatic scenery and forests, but is little visited. The villages of the north east surrounded by pine forests are as lovely as anywhere in Greece and the drive along the north coast is breathtaking if a little hazardous. The south of the island is lovely too with the chestnut forests round the west of Mount Ochi full of butterflies and stunning views from the Eagles Road over Marmari and the Petali islands. The newly excavated 10th to 8th century BC finds at Lefkanti are of serious interest.

★★★☆☆ Tourism level
★★★★★ Vegetation
★★★★☆ Beaches
★★★★☆ History

Information
www.aroundevvoia.com
Telephone 22210 82677

Map
Anavasi (1:100000)

Area 3661 sq km
Coastline 729 km
Highest point 1743 m (Delfi)

Permanent population 191009

Visitor capacity 16454
208 hotels
15046 hotel beds
1408 other beds
7 campsites

Crowdfactor
56 people per sq km

Access
2 bridges to mainland

Connections
Skiathos 2 daily
Skyros daily

Yacht facilities
8 ports

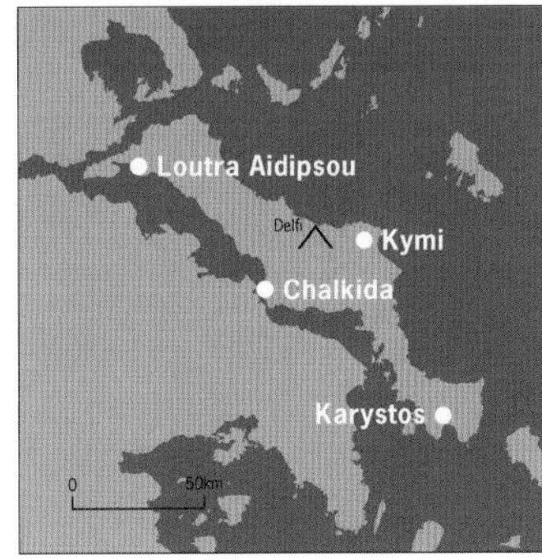
Loutra Aidipsou
Delfi
Kymi
Chalkida
Karystos
0
50km

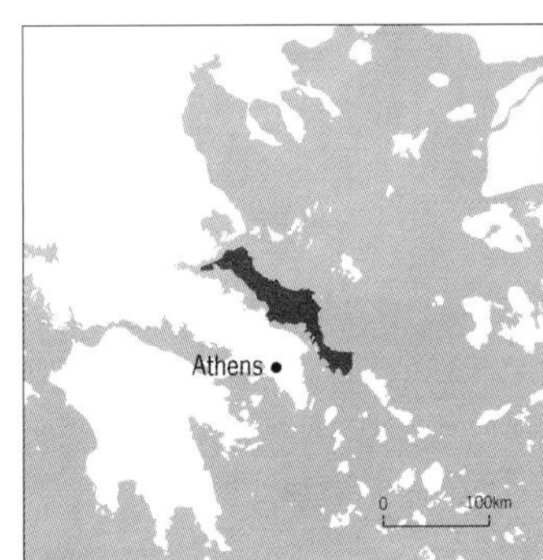
Athens
0
100km

Ranking among all Mediterranean islands

	Rank
Area	6
Population	8
Visitor capacity	22
Crowdfactor	123

Greece
6800

Folégandros

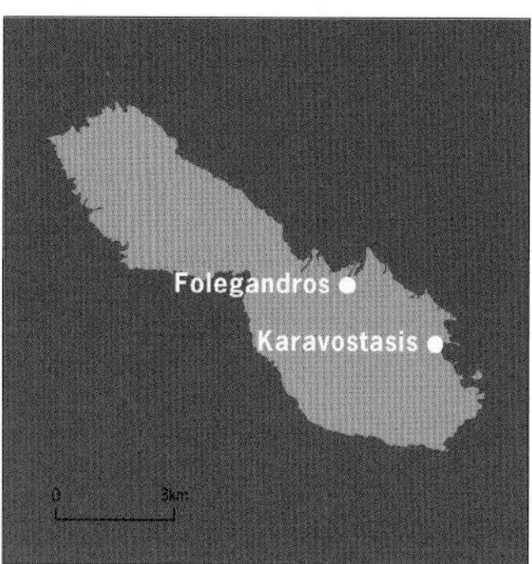
Folegandros
Karavostasis
0
3km

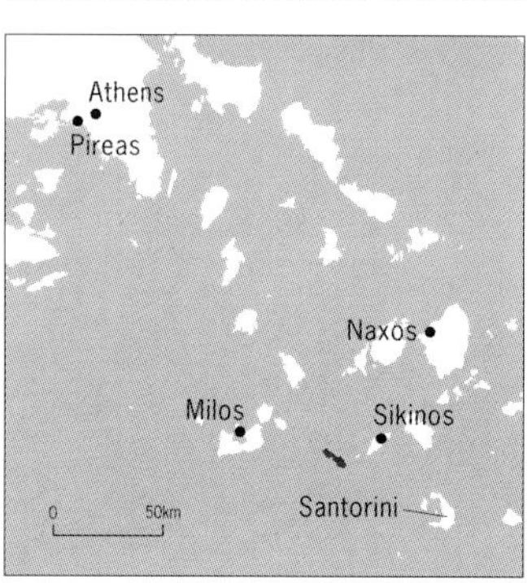
Athens
Pireas
Naxos
Milos
Sikinos
Santorini
0
50km

36°39' N 24°52' E
Folegandros
Kyklades
Greece

Folegandros is a small island with one road and a very pretty town, built along the edge of a cliff, which has a series of charming squares and a colourful 13th century fortified kastro. There are a few beaches but the main attraction of the island is walking along the bare ridges of the island which afford very fine views.

★★☆☆☆ Tourism level
★☆☆☆☆ Vegetation
★★☆☆☆ Beaches
★☆☆☆☆ History

Information
www.folegandros.com
Telephone 22860 41444

Map
Road Editions (1:40000)

Area 32 sq km
Coastline 42 km
Highest point 416 m (Agios Eleftherios)

Permanent population 676

Visitor capacity 747
19 hotels
637 hotel beds
110 other beds
1 campsite

Crowdfactor
43 people per sq km

Access
Sikinos 40 minutes
Ios 1½ hours

Connections
Sikinos daily

Yacht facilities
no fuel

6170 **Greece** Kyklades

Ranking among all Mediterranean islands	Ran
Area	92
Population	11(
Visitor capacity	9
Crowdfactor	13

Foúrnoi

37°35' N 26°30' E
Fournoi
Voreio Aigaio
Greece

ournoi is a very pleasant rugged low-key fishing island, with many good beaches and fish tavernas. The friendly town has a pretty square and there are boats to the northern village of Chrysomilia and the monastery of Ag oannis in the south.

★☆☆☆☆ Tourism level
★★☆☆☆ Vegetation
★★★☆☆ Beaches
★☆☆☆☆ History

nformation
ww.fourni.com
elephone 22750 51268

lap
oad Editions (1:50000)

Area 30 sq km
Coastline 74 km
Highest point 514 m (Korakas)

Permanent population 1333

Visitor capacity 256
0 hotels
0 hotel beds
256 other beds
0 campsites

Crowdfactor
52 people per sq km

Access
⛴ Ikaria 40 minutes
⛴ Samos 1½ hours

Connections
⛴ Ikaria 2 daily
⛴ Samos daily

Yacht facilities
⛵ Fournoi

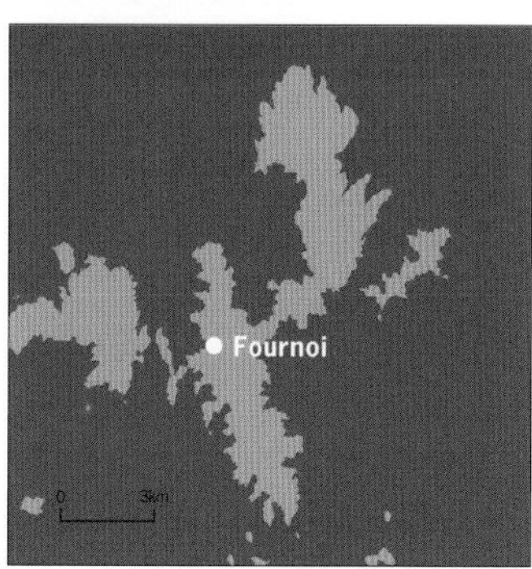
Fournoi
0
3km

Samos
Agios Kirikos
0
20km

Voreio Aigaio **Greece** 7520

anking among all Mediterranean islands	Rank
ea	94
pulation	100
sitor capacity	129
owdfactor	130

Gávdos

PHOTO: STIGMES MAGAZINE OF CRETE

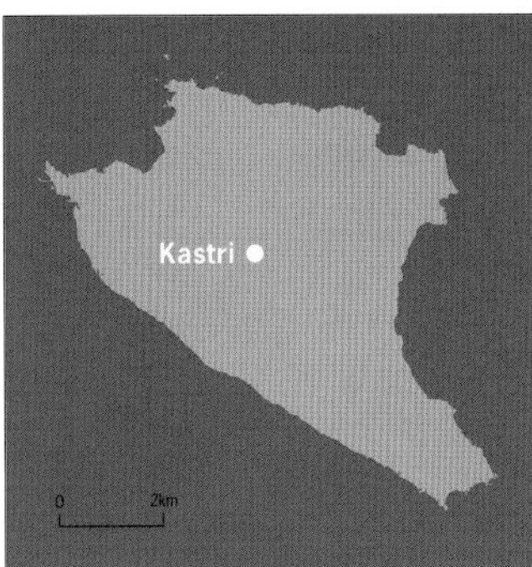
Kastri
0
2km

Chania
Rethymno
Paleochora
Chora Sfakion
0
50km

34°51' N 24°04' E
Gavdos
Greece

Gavdos, the southernmost part of Europe, is a good island for exploring, with five beaches, a large number of chapels and a surprising amount of vegetation, mostly pines and dwarf cypresses. Food is reasonable, with fish and goat being specialities, and it is possible to hire a car or a boat.

★☆☆☆☆ Tourism level
★★☆☆☆ Vegetation
★★☆☆☆ Beaches
★☆☆☆☆ History

Information
www.gavdos-online.com
Telephone 28230 83024

Map
Road Editions (1:100000)

Area 33 sq km
Coastline 38 km
Highest point 368 m (Fanari)

Permanent population 78

Visitor capacity 36
0 hotels
0 hotel beds
36 other beds
0 campsites

Crowdfactor
3 people per sq km

Access
Chora Sfakion 2 hours
Paleochora 4 hours

Connections
Chora Sfakion 5 weekly
Paleochora 2 weekly

Yacht facilities
no fuel

6050 Greece

Ranking among all Mediterranean islands	Ra
Area	9
Population	1
Visitor capacity	18
Crowdfactor	2

37°36' N 26°08' E
Ikaria
Voreio Aigaio
Greece

This mountainous island is one of the most rewarding to explore, particularly in the west where there is lovely walking and remote villages like Christos Rachon, Karkinagri and Manganitis. There is a spectacular road along the bare central ridge of the island with wooded slopes plunging down to the sea.

★★★☆☆ Tourism level
★★★☆☆ Vegetation
★★★☆☆ Beaches
★★☆☆☆ History

nformation
www.island-ikaria.com
Telephone 22750 22202

Map
Road Editions (1:50000)

Area 255 sq km
Coastline 107 km
Highest point 1037 m (Atheras)

Permanent population 8354

Visitor capacity 1160
24 hotels
934 hotel beds
226 other beds
0 campsites

Crowdfactor
37 people per sq km

Access
✈ Ikaria
⛴ Samos 1½ hours

Connections
⛴ Samos 3 daily
⛴ Pireas, Fournoi 2 daily
⛴ Naxos daily

Yacht facilities
⛵ Agios Kirykos

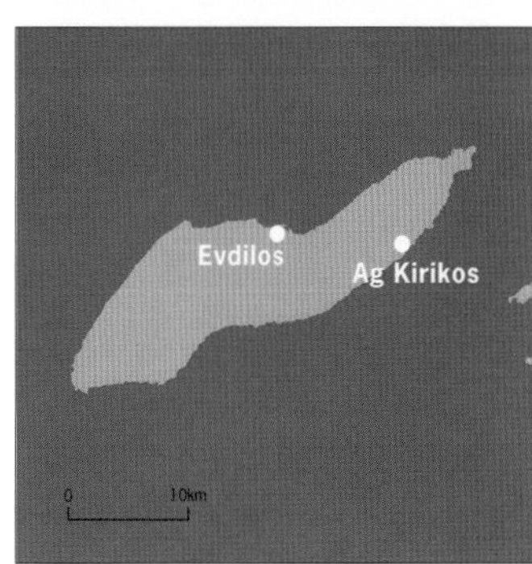
Evdilos
Ag Kirikos
0
10km

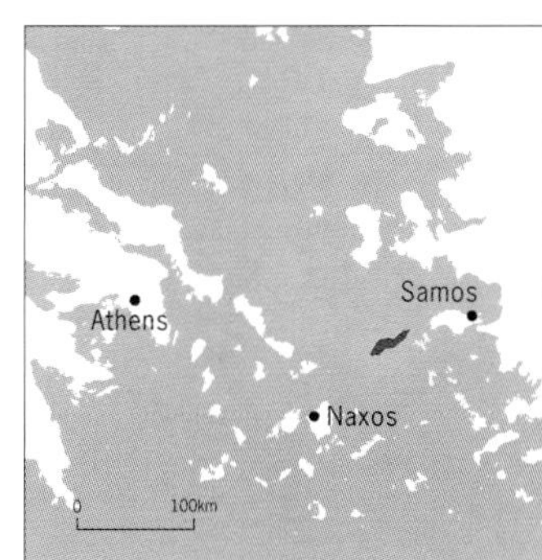
Athens
Samos
Naxos
0
100km

anking among all Mediterranean islands	Rank
rea	33
opulation	49
isitor capacity	78
rowdfactor	146

(PHOTO: GREEK NATIONAL TOURISM ORGANISATION)

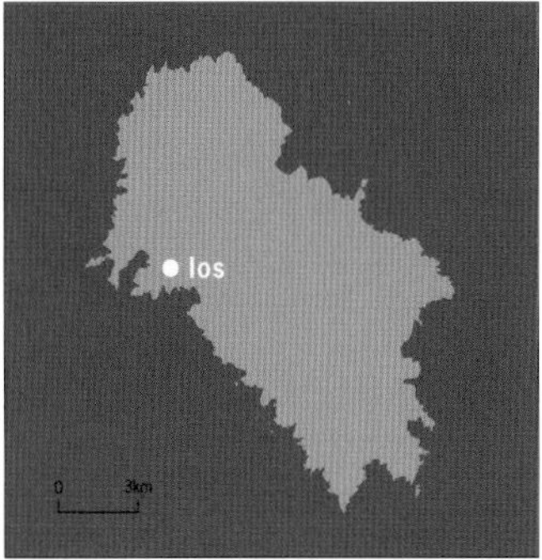
Ios
0 3km

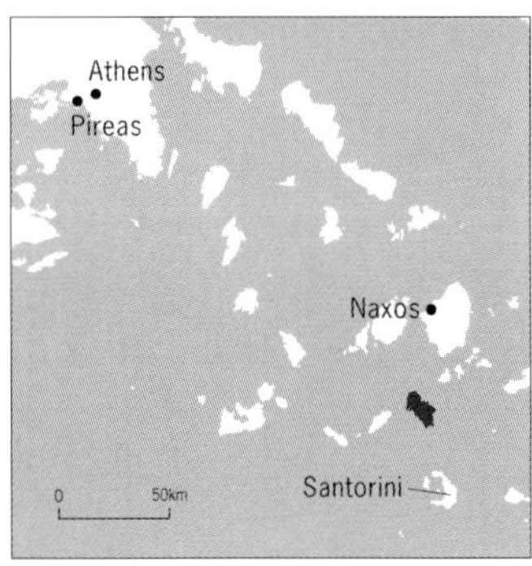
Athens
Pireas
Naxos
Santorini
0 50km

36°45′ N 25°18′ E
Ios
Kyklades
Greece

The island of young people is gradually trying to reposition itself in the market and is attracting more families. It has a lovely capital, with fine views from the top of the hill over to Santorini and Sikinos. There are still plenty of bars and discos and a large number of beaches some of which are not easy to get to and surprisingly uncrowded. The interior of the island is hilly and barren and there is little to see of the supposed tomb of Homer in the north of the island.

★★★★☆ Tourism level
★★☆☆☆ Vegetation
★★★★☆ Beaches
★★☆☆☆ History

Information
www.iosgreece.com
Telephone 22860 91505

Map
Road Editions (1:50000)

Area 108 sq km
Coastline 87 km
Highest point 713 m (Pyrgos)

Permanent population 1862

Visitor capacity 2731
43 hotels
2125 hotel beds
606 other beds
3 campsites

Crowdfactor
42 people per sq km

Access
Santorini 1 hour

Connections
Santorini 4 daily
Sikinos, Naxos, Paros daily

Yacht facilities
Ios

Ranking among all Mediterranean islands	Ran
Area	4
Population	9
Visitor capacity	5
Crowdfactor	13

36°50' N 25°27' E
Iraklia
Kyklades
Greece

The quietest of the Minor Cyclades, Iraklia has an attractive little port, a very small old chora, two good beaches at Ag Georgios and Livadi and a very fine cave at Ag Giannis.

★☆☆☆☆ Tourism level
★☆☆☆☆ Vegetation
★★★☆☆ Beaches
★☆☆☆☆ History

Information
www.iraklia.gr
Telephone 22850 71545

Map
None

Area 18 sq km
Coastline 29 km
Highest point 419 m (Papas)

Permanent population 133

Visitor capacity 36
0 hotels
0 hotel beds
36 other beds
0 campsites

Crowdfactor
9 people per sq km

Access
Ferry Naxos 1 hour
Ferry Amorgos 1 ½ hours

Connections
Ferry Schoinousa daily
Ferry Naxos 5 weekly

Yacht facilities
⛵ no fuel

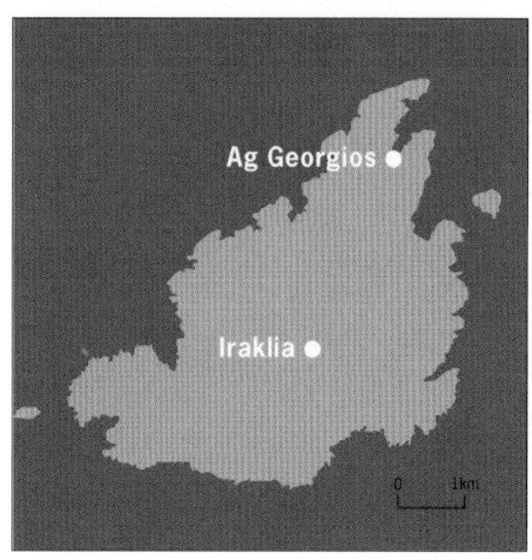
Ag Georgios
Iraklia
0
1km

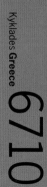

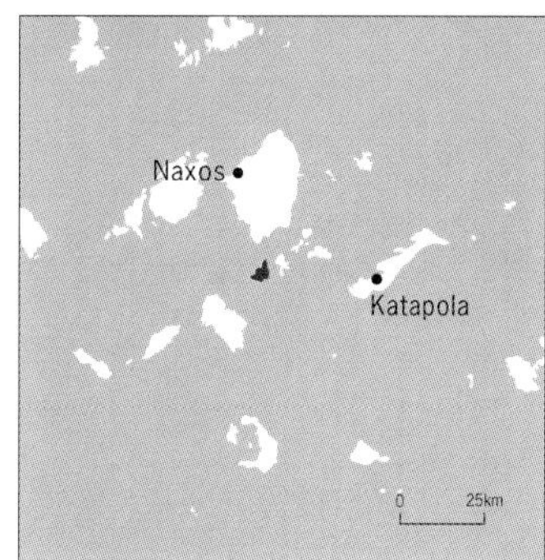
Naxos
Katapola
0
25km

Ranking among all Mediterranean islands

	Rank
Area	121
Population	165
Visitor capacity	186
Crowdfactor	202

6710

Itháki

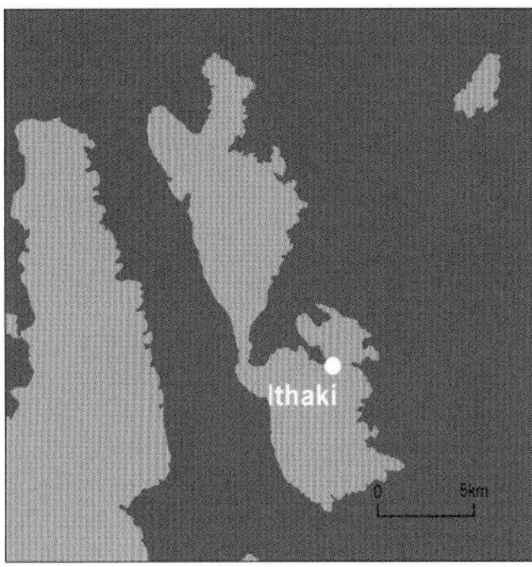
Ithaki
0
5km

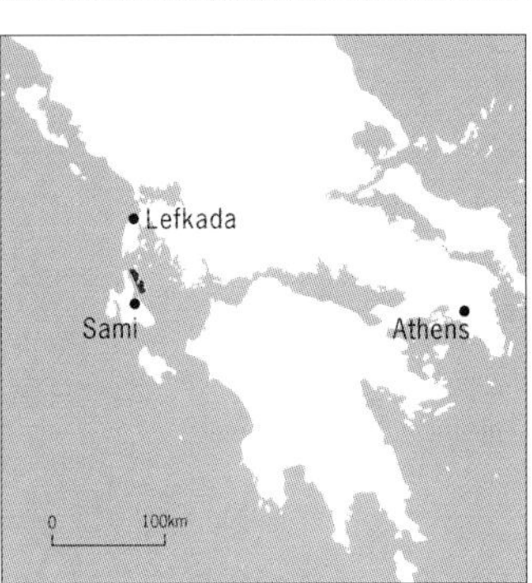
Lefkada
Sami
Athens
0
100km

38°23' N 20°40' E
Ithaki
Ionia Nisia
Greece

Ithaki is an island with little to see and poor beaches, but its hilly terrain offers a sense of freedom to the walker and fuels the imagination of those seeking Odysseus. The pleasant fishing villages of Kioni and Frikes are good places to stay.

★★★☆☆ Tourism level
★★☆☆☆ Vegetation
★★☆☆☆ Beaches
★★☆☆☆ History

Information
www.ithacagreece.com
Telephone 26740 33120

Map
Road Editions (1:70000)

Area 95 sq km
Coastline 105 km
Highest point 809 m (Nirito)

Permanent population 3210

Visitor capacity 373
5 hotels
195 hotel beds
178 other beds
0 campsites

Crowdfactor
37 people per sq km

Access
Kefalonia 1 hour

Connections
Kefalonia 4 daily

Yacht facilities
Vathy

Ranking among all Mediterranean islands	Rar
Area	5
Population	7
Visitor capacity	12
Crowdfactor	14

5300 **Greece** Ionia Nisia

Kálamos

38°38′ N 20°55′ E
Kalamos
Ionia Nisia
Greece

A hulk of an island, visited by daily boats from Mytikas, with a pleasant village and the possibility of some fine strenuous walking.

★☆☆☆☆ Tourism level
★★★☆☆ Vegetation
★★☆☆☆ Beaches
★☆☆☆☆ History

Information
www.kalamos.tk
Telephone 26460 91281

Map
Anavasi (1:100000)

Area 25 sq km
Coastline 32 km
Highest point 745 m (Vouni)

Permanent population 510

Visitor capacity 60
0 hotels
0 hotel beds
60 other beds
0 campsites

Crowdfactor
22 people per sq km

Access
Mytikas 30 minutes

Connections
Mytikas daily

Yacht facilities
no fuel

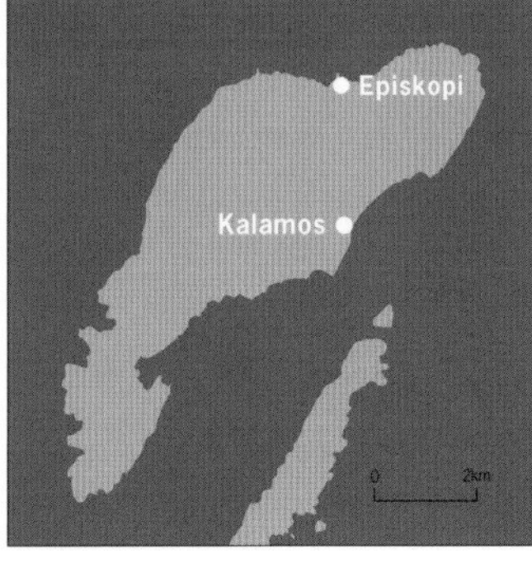
Episkopi
Kalamos
0
2km

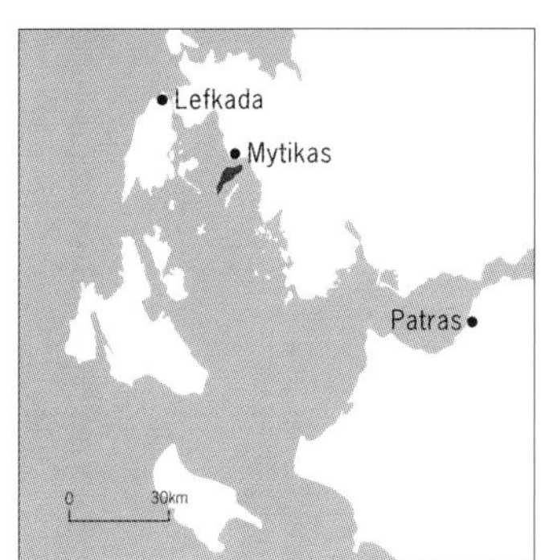
Lefkada
Mytikas
Patras
0
30km

Ranking among all Mediterranean islands	Rank
Area	100
Population	123
Visitor capacity	170
Crowdfactor	169

Ionia Nisia **Greece**

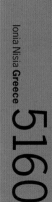

VIEW FROM ABOVE ARGOSTOLI, KEFALONIA (PHOTO: PEARCE MARCHBANK)

Kálymnos

7300 **Greece** Dodekanisa

(PHOTO: GREEK NATIONAL TOURISM ORGANISATION)

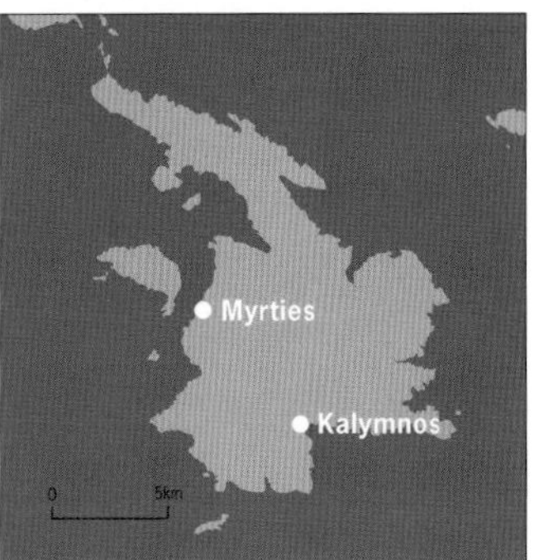

Myrties
Kalymnos
0
5km

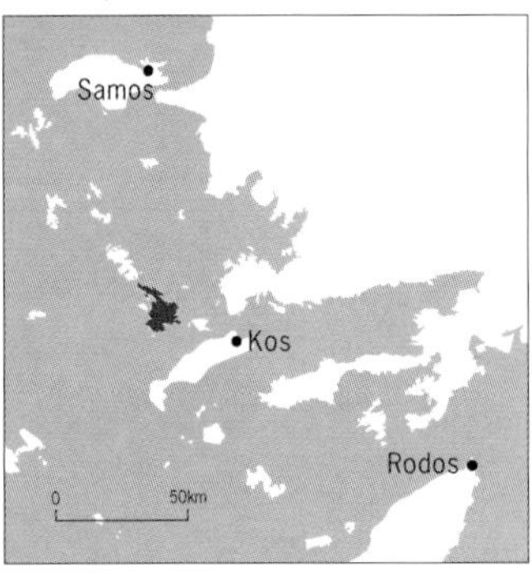

Samos
Kos
Rodos
0
50km

37°00' N 26°59' E
Kalymnos
Dodekanisa
Greece

Kalymnos is a mountainous island whose capital is more of a working town than a place for tourists. The Knights' castle and Taxiarchis Michailis monastery are worth seeing. The most attractive part of the island is the deep fertile valley of Vathi and there are boats to the cave of Kefalas and the islet of Nera with a monastery.

★★★☆☆ Tourism level
★★☆☆☆ Vegetation
★★★☆☆ Beaches
★★☆☆☆ History

Information
www.kalymnos-isl.gr
Telephone 22430 59056

Map
Anavasi (1:25000)

Area 110 sq km
Coastline 105 km
Highest point 678 m (Parasiva)

Permanent population 16368

Visitor capacity 2421
42 hotels
1769 hotel beds
652 other beds
0 campsites

Crowdfactor
169 people per sq km

Access
Kalymnos
Kos, Leros 45 minutes

Connections
Kos 6 daily
Leros 3 daily
Astypalaia 5 weekly

Yacht facilities
Pothia

Ranking among all Mediterranean islands	Ran
Area	4
Population	2
Visitor capacity	5
Crowdfactor	6

35°37' N 27°08' E
Karpathos
Dodekanisa
Greece

Karpathos is the wildest of all the Greek islands and offers a challenge to explorers. There are many attractive villages and good beaches all over the island but the roads are for the most part very poor. A worthwhile expedition is to take a boat from Diafani to the large uninhabited island of Saria where there is a large unexcavated city.

★★★☆☆ Tourism level
★★☆☆☆ Vegetation
★★★☆☆ Beaches
★★★☆☆ History

nformation
ww.karpathos.gr
elephone 22450 23926

lap
oad Editions (1:50000)

Area 300 sq km
Coastline 180 km
Highest point 1215 m (Kali Limni)

Permanent population 6543

Visitor capacity 5879
104 hotels
4719 hotel beds
1160 other beds
0 campsites

Crowdfactor
41 people per sq km

Access
Karpathos
Rodos, Kriti 4 hours

Connections
Rodos, Chalki 4 weekly
Kasos 3 weekly

Yacht facilities
Pigadia

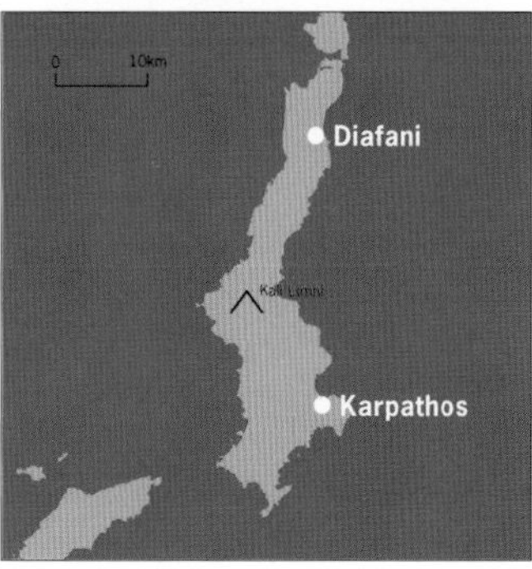
0
10km
Diafani
Kali Limni
Karpathos

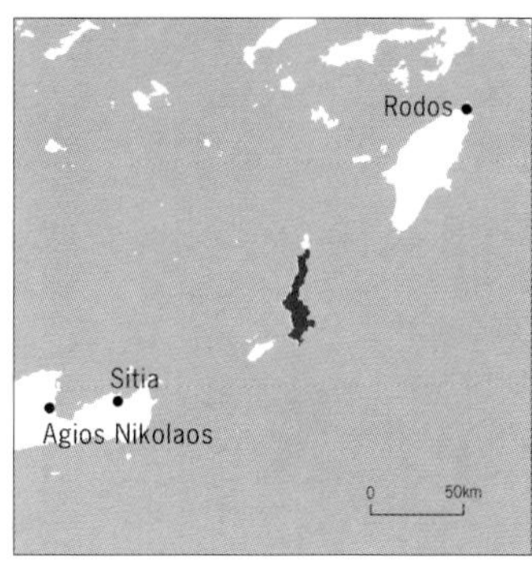
Rodos
Sitia
Agios Nikolaos
0
50km

anking among all Mediterranean islands	Rank
rea	26
opulation	56
isitor capacity	38
rowdfactor	140

Kásos

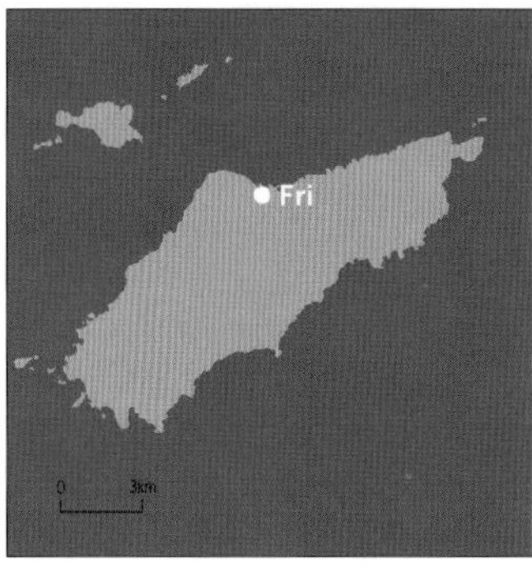
Fri
0 3km

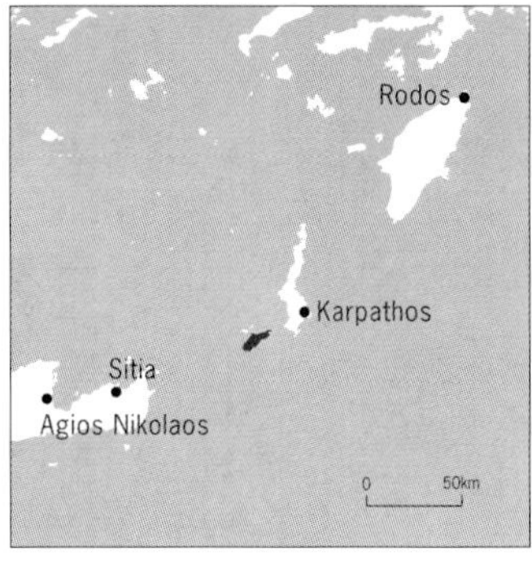
Rodos
Karpathos
Sitia
Agios Nikolaos
0 50km

35°24' N 26°56' E
Kasos
Dodekanisa
Greece

Kasos is a mountainous and mainly barren island little visited by tourists. Efforts are being made to encourage more visitors to one of the few traditional Greek islands left. The island is still principally a fishing community, but has good walking, cliffs, caves and a number of beaches, the best of which are on the islets of Armathia and Makra.

★☆☆☆☆ Tourism level
★★☆☆☆ Vegetation
★★★☆☆ Beaches
★★☆☆☆ History

Information
www.kasos.gr
Telephone 22450 41400

Map
Road Editions (1:50000)

Area 66 sq km
Coastline 59 km
Highest point 601 m (Prionas)

Permanent population 1013

Visitor capacity 49
3 hotels
41 hotel beds
8 other beds
0 campsites

Crowdfactor
15 people per sq km

Access
✈ Kasos
⛴ Karpathos 1½ hours

Connections
⛴ Karpathos, Kriti 3 weekly

Yacht facilities
⛵ Fri, Kasou

Ranking among all Mediterranean islands	Ran
Area	6
Population	10
Visitor capacity	17
Crowdfactor	18

7150 **Greece** Dodekanisa

Kastós

38°34' N 20°54' E
Kastos
Ionia Nisia
Greece

Kastos is a small quiet island with olive trees and a 17th century monastery Ag Ioannis.

★☆☆☆☆ Tourism level
★★★☆☆ Vegetation
★★☆☆☆ Beaches
★☆☆☆☆ History

Information
Telephone 26460 91484

Map
Anavasi (1:100000)

Area 5 sq km
Coastline 24 km
Highest point 155 m (Mavrachi)

Permanent population 89

Visitor capacity 10
0 hotels
0 hotel beds
10 other beds
0 campsites

Crowdfactor
16 people per sq km

Access
Mytikas 1 hour

Connections
Mytikas 5 weekly

Yacht facilities
no fuel

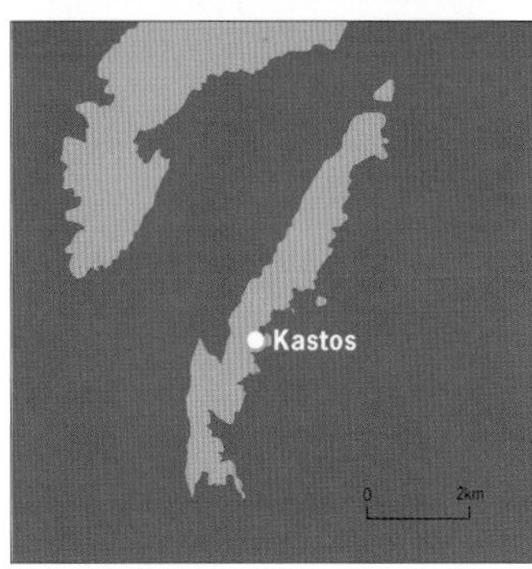
Kastos
0
2km

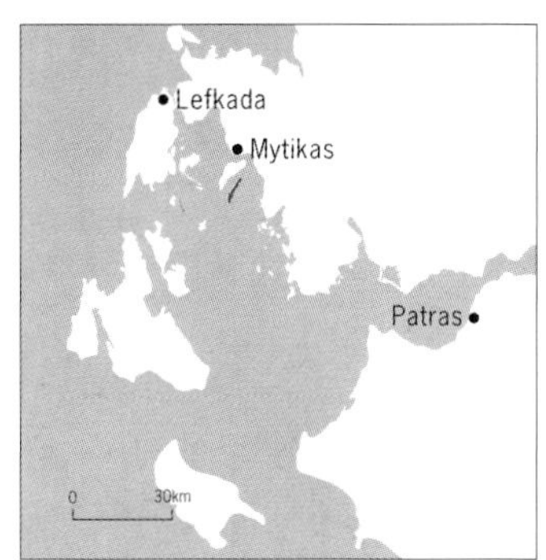
Lefkada
Mytikas
Patras
0
30km

Ranking among all Mediterranean islands

	Rank
Area	187
Population	173
Visitor capacity	206
Crowdfactor	182

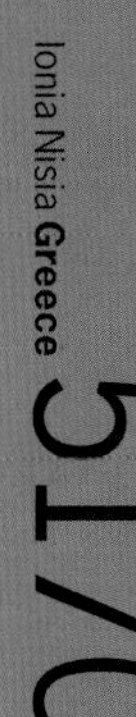
Ionia Nisia **Greece** 5170

Kéa

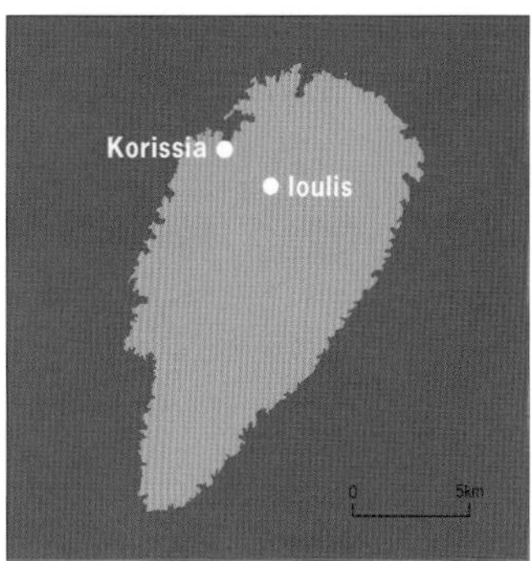
Korissia
Ioulis
0
5km

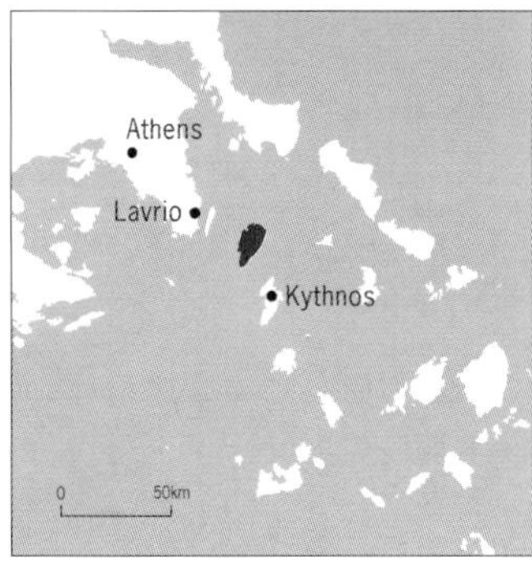
Athens
Lavrio
Kythnos
0
50km

37°38' N 24°20' E
Kea
Kyklades
Greece

Kea is a beautiful fertile island with a number of good beaches. Though slightly marred with holiday residences mostly owned by Athenians, it has fruit trees of all kinds and produces good red wine. It also has fine oak woods and is very pleasant for walking. The best known sights are the 6 metre long lion of Kea and the windmills above the chora.

★★★☆☆ Tourism level
★★★☆☆ Vegetation
★★★☆☆ Beaches
★★★☆☆ History

Information
www.kea.gr
Telephone 22880 22221

Map
Anavasi (1:25000)

Area 131 sq km
Coastline 88 km
Highest point 561 m (Profitis Ilias)

Permanent population 2158

Visitor capacity 740
6 hotels
282 hotel beds
458 other beds
1 campsite

Crowdfactor
22 people per sq km

Access
Lavrio 1 hour

Connections
Lavrio 4 daily
Kythnos 4 weekly

Yacht facilities
Ag Nikolaou

6280 **Greece** Kyklades

Ranking among all Mediterranean islands	Rar
Area	4
Population	8
Visitor capacity	9
Crowdfactor	16

Kefaloniá

38°15′N 20°31′E
Kefalonia
Ionia Nisia
Greece

One of the most impressive Greek islands, with terrific views from the top of Mount Aenos and along the west coast over Myrtos gulf. The position of Assos is lovely too set on the neck of a peninsular under a 16th century Venetian fortress and the road between the ports of Poros and Sami winds through an enchanting valley clad with cypress. Near Sami are the fine stalagmite cave of Drogarati and the Melissani cave with an underground lake which can be explored by boat. Exploration of the island needs a car.

★★★☆☆ Tourism level
★★★☆☆ Vegetation
★★★★☆ Beaches
★★☆☆☆ History

Information
www.kefaloniainfo.net
Telephone 26710 22248

Map
Road Editions (1:70000)

Area 734 sq km
Coastline 267 km
Highest point 1627 m (Ainos)

Permanent population 34544

Visitor capacity 10273
129 hotels
8565 hotel beds
1708 other beds
2 campsites

Crowdfactor
61 people per sq km

Access
✈ Kefalonia

Connections
⛴ Lefkada 4 daily
⛴ Kyllini 3 daily
⛴ Ithaki, Zakynthos 2 daily
⛴ Patras daily

Yacht facilities
⛵ 7 ports

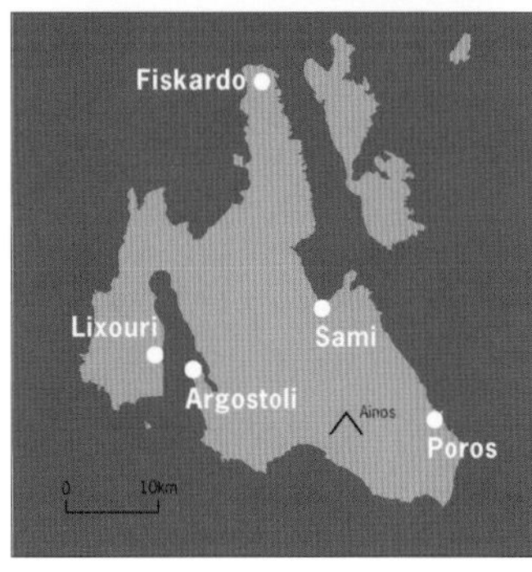
Fiskardo
Lixouri
Sami
Argostoli
Ainos
Poros
0
10km

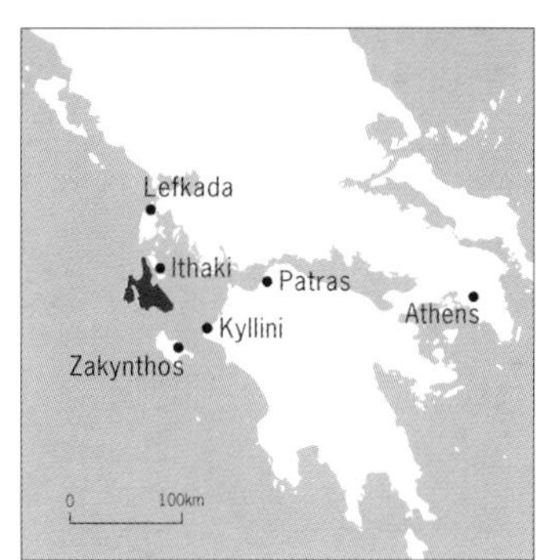
Lefkada
Ithaki
Patras
Athens
Kyllini
Zakynthos
0
100km

Ionia Nisia **Greece** 5200

Ranking among all Mediterranean islands	Rank
Area	11
Population	19
Visitor capacity	26
Crowdfactor	118

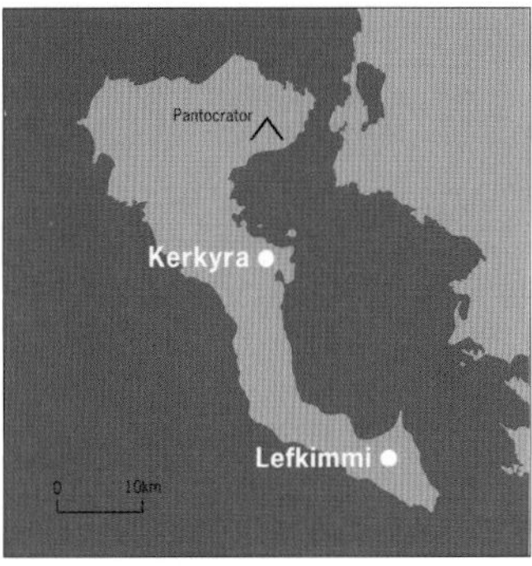
Pantocrator
Kerkyra
Lefkimmi
0 10km

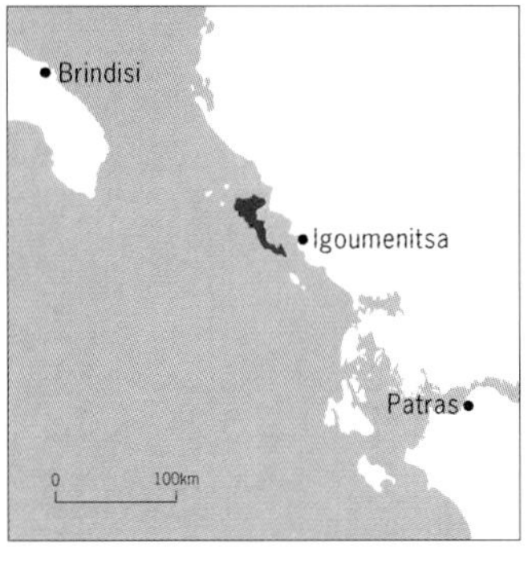
Brindisi
Igoumenitsa
Patras
0 100km

39°36′ N 19°51′ E
Kerkyra (Corfu)
Ionia Nisia
Greece

An enduringly lovely island, particularly in the north, where you can still wander endlessly through huge groves of olives and along country lanes teeming with luxuriant vegetation. Despite its popularity, the town is a fine place with its two fortresses, elegant Spianada, church of St Spiridon and Venetian theatre. Not to be missed are the view from Kanoni over the islets of Vlacherna and Pontikonisi and the views of Paleocastritsa from the Angelokastro road. Most of the best beaches are on the west coast.

★★★★☆ Tourism level
★★★★★ Vegetation
★★★★★ Beaches
★★★☆☆ History

Information
www.corfu-kerkyra.eu
Telephone 26610 37520

Map
Reise-Know-How (1:65000)

Area 585 sq km
Coastline 259 km
Highest point 911 m (Pantocrator)

Permanent population 107514

Visitor capacity 45995
404 hotels
43067 hotel beds
2928 other beds
10 campsites

Crowdfactor
262 people per sq km

Access
✈ Kerkyra
⛴ Igoumenitsa 1½ hours

Connections
Paxoi 2 daily
⛴ Igoumenitsa 30 daily
⛴ Brindisi 4 daily
⛴ Patras, Paxoi 2 daily
⛴ Bari daily

Yacht facilities
⛵ 5 ports

Ranking among all Mediterranean islands	Rar
Area	1
Population	1
Visitor capacity	1
Crowdfactor	4

Kímolos

36°48' N 24°33' E
Kimolos
‹yklades
Greece

Hardly a welcoming island with nowhere o stay at the port, no transport for hire, o bus, no taxi. If these problems can be vercome, it is worth visiting the chora vith its 16th century kastro and going long the pleasant south coast to Ag ndreas and the islet of Daskalio pposite where Mycenean remains have een found. Fuller's earth is still mined in he north east of the island where the ilvery white quarries are a memorable ight.

★★☆☆☆ Tourism level
★★☆☆☆ Vegetation
★★★☆☆ Beaches
★☆☆☆ History

formation
elephone 22870 51218

ap
oad Editions (1:50000)

Area 37 sq km
Coastline 45 km
Highest point 361 m (Paleokastro)

Permanent population 838

Visitor capacity 162
1 hotel
8 hotel beds
154 other beds
0 campsites

Crowdfactor
26 people per sq km

Access
Milos, Sifnos 1 hour

Connections
Milos 4 daily
Pireas, Sifnos daily

Yacht facilities
no fuel

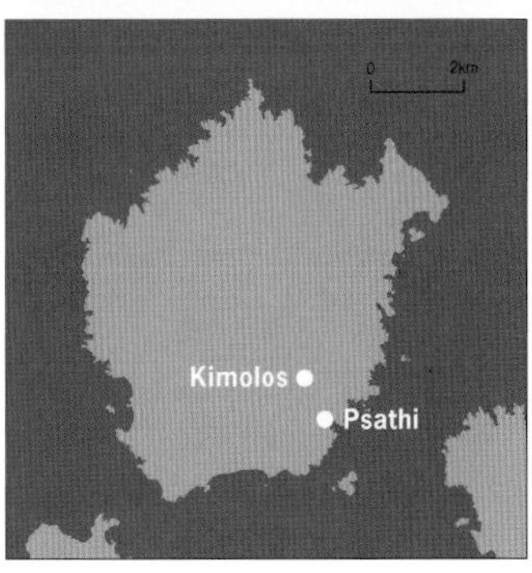

0 2km
Kimolos
Psathi

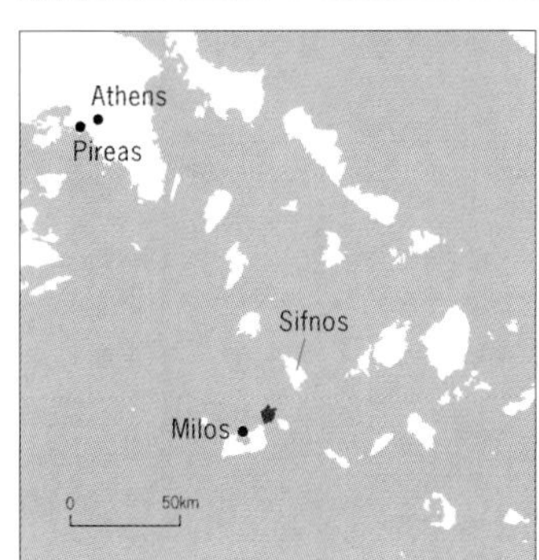

Athens
Pireas
Sifnos
Milos
0 50km

anking among all Mediterranean islands	Rank
ea	86
opulation	110
sitor capacity	144
owdfactor	162

Kos

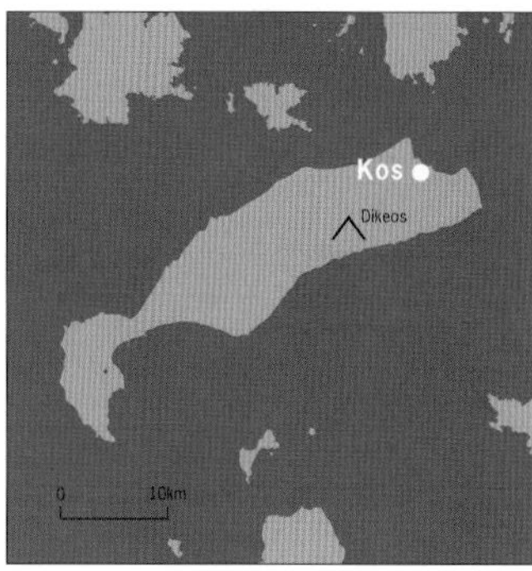

Kos
Dikeos
0
10km

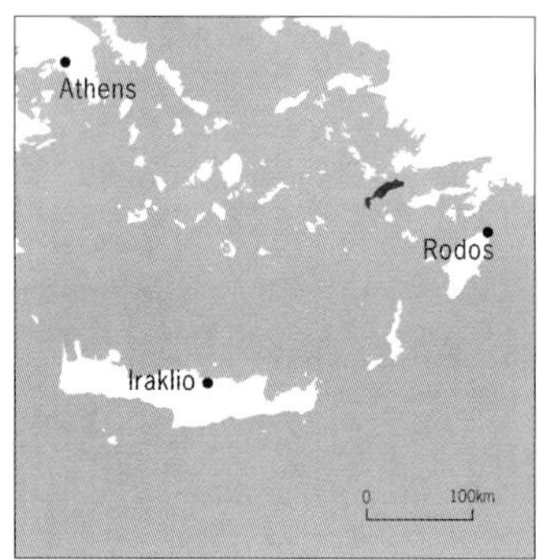

Athens
Rodos
Iraklio
0
100km

36°52' N 27°13' E
Kos
Dodekanisa
Greece

The island of Hippocrates has become a magnet for package tourism and much of it is crowded. The most famous sight is the Asklepion, consecrated to Asklepios the healing son of Apollo, and there are fine castles above Kos town, Antimachia and Kefalos. The view from the top of Dikteos is very fine and the monastery of Ag Ioannis at the west end of the island is worth seeing. There are daily boat trips to Nisyros, Pserimos and Bodrum.

★★★★★ Tourism level
★★☆☆☆ Vegetation
★★★☆☆ Beaches
★★★★☆ History

Information
www.kosinfo.gr
Telephone 22420 24460

Map
Road Editions (1:60000)

Area 287 sq km
Coastline 121 km
Highest point 843 m (Dikeos)

Permanent population 30828

Visitor capacity 39999
260 hotels
37809 hotel beds
2190 other beds
1 campsite

Crowdfactor
246 people per sq km

Access
✈ Kos

Connections
⛴ Kalymnos 10 daily
⛴ Rodos 5 daily
⛴ Nisyros, Leros, Symi 2 daily
⛴ Bodrum daily

Yacht facilities
⛵ Kos Marina

Ranking among all Mediterranean islands

Area
Population
Visitor capacity
Crowdfactor

Ra

7200 **Greece** Dodekanisa

Koufonísi

36°56′ N 25°37′ E
Koufonisi
Kyklades
Greece

The smallest and busiest of the Minor Cyclades, Koufonisi has a pretty fishing port, good fish tavernas and good beaches, particularly that at Finikas. It is possible to take boats to Kato Koufonisi, with a taverna and five beaches, and to the large uninhabited island of Keros which has a site over 4000 years old.

★★★☆☆ Tourism level
★★☆☆☆ Vegetation
★★★☆☆ Beaches
★☆☆☆☆ History

Information
www.koufonisia.gr
Telephone 22850 71379

Map
None

Area 5 sq km
Coastline 17 km
Highest point 114 m (Profitis Ilias)

Permanent population 376

Visitor capacity 381
6 hotels
179 hotel beds
202 other beds
1 campsite

Crowdfactor
131 people per sq km

Access
Amorgos 1 hour
Naxos 2 hours

Connections
Schoinousa, Amorgos, Naxos daily
Donousa 4 weekly

Yacht facilities
no fuel

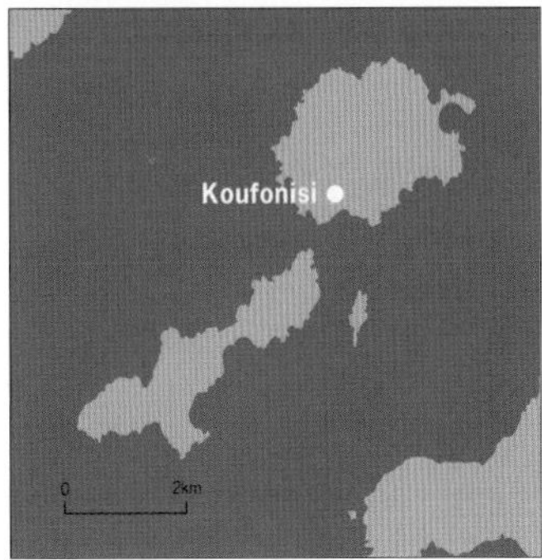
Koufonisi
0
2km

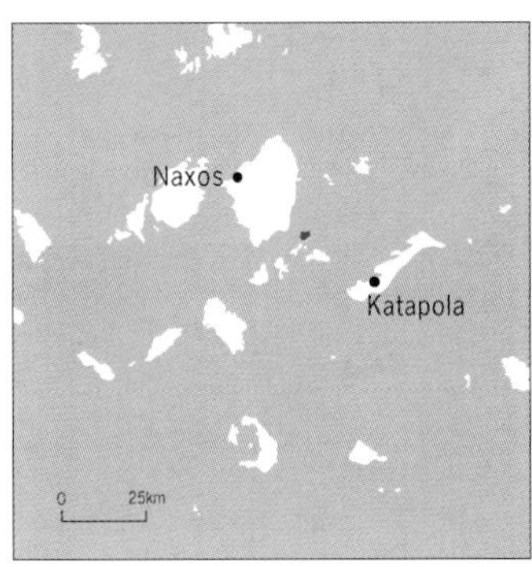
Naxos
Katapola
0
25km

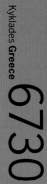

Kyklades **Greece** 6730

Ranking among all Mediterranean islands

	Rank
Area	190
Population	128
Visitor capacity	121
Crowdfactor	75

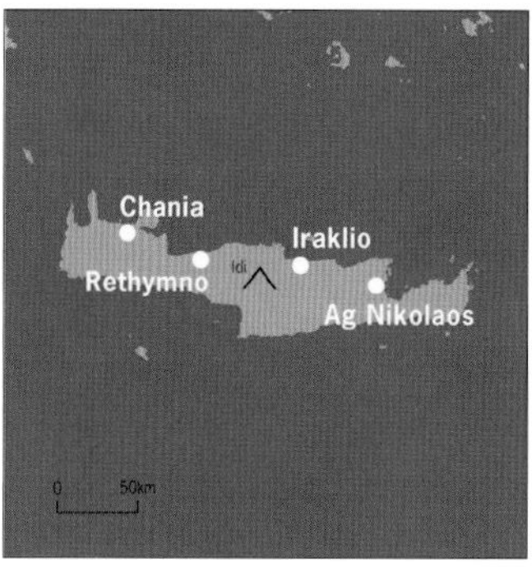
Chania
Iraklio
Rethymno
Idi
Ag Nikolaos
0 50km

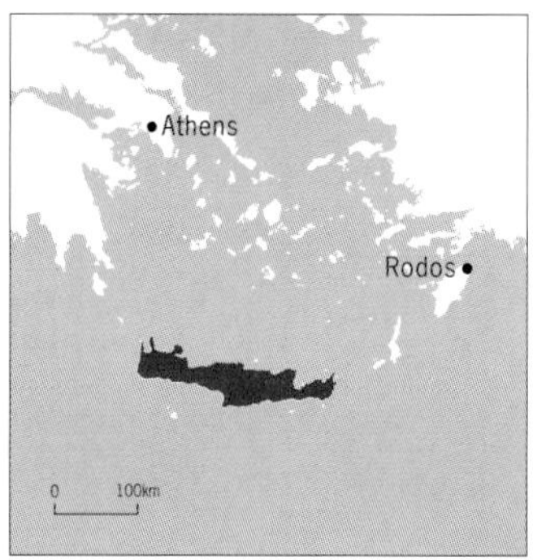
Athens
Rodos
0 100km

35°11' N 23°54' E
Kriti (Crete)
Greece

Crete is an island of great variety, with three great mountain ranges (Dikti, Psiloritis and Lefka Ori) and five major Minoan palaces at Knossos, Phaistos, Agia Triada, Malia and Zakros. Chania is lovely with a charming Venetian harbour and fine town houses, some of which are now hotels, and the archaeological museum at Iraklion is most impressive. Nearly all the tourism is concentrated on the north coast, while the south has the gorge of Samaria and many lovely beaches particularly in the SE and SW corners.

★★★☆☆ Tourism level
★★★☆☆ Vegetation
★★★★★ Beaches
★★★★★ History

Information
www.kriti.net
Telephone 2810 246298 (Iraklio)
28210 92943 (Chania)
28310 29148 (Rethymno)

Map
Anavasi (1:100000)

Area 8261 sq km
Coastline 1066 km
Highest point 2456 m (Idi)

Permanent population 594282

Visitor capacity 203592
1521 hotels
146073 hotel beds
57519 other beds
17 campsites

Crowdfactor
96 people per sq km

Access
✈ Iraklio, Chania

Connections
⛴ Pireas 4 daily
⛴ Santorini 2 daily
⛴ daily
⛴ Kasos 4 weekly

Yacht facilities
⛵ 20 ports

Ranking among all Mediterranean islands	Ran[illegible]
Area	[illegible]
Population	[illegible]
Visitor capacity	[illegible]
Crowdfactor	9[illegible]

36°13' N 22°58' E
Kythira
Greece

A most attractive but little visited island, Kythira has fine beaches, lovely villages and good food (but not good wine). The town of Kythira has a fine setting, with a Venetian castle and a lovely view over Kapsali. The hidden medieval capital of Paleochora is worth visiting and the village of Milopotamos is charming, offering delicious apple pies beside a stream with fine white ducks. The island also has a number of ravines which shelter figs and bananas. Australian is widely spoken and there is a Qantas office.

★★☆☆☆ Tourism level
★★★☆☆ Vegetation
★★★☆☆ Beaches
★★☆☆☆ History

Information
www.kythera.gr
Telephone 27360 31213

Map
Road Editions (1:50000)

Area 277 sq km
Coastline 118 km
Highest point 506 m (Mermingaris)

Permanent population 3532

Visitor capacity 2189
32 hotels
750 hotel beds
1439 other beds
1 campsite

Crowdfactor
20 people per sq km

Access
Kythira
Neapoli 1 hour

Connections
Neapoli 2 daily
Kriti 5 weekly

Yacht facilities
Agia Pelagia, Diakofti, Kapsali

Ag Pelagia
Potamos
Kythira
0
5km

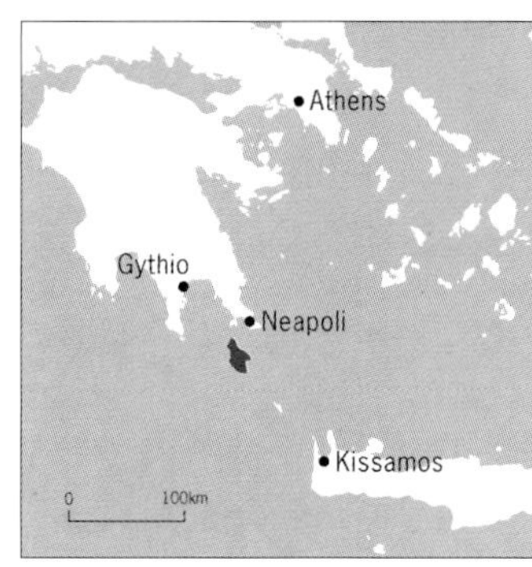
Athens
Gythio
Neapoli
Kissamos
0
100km

Ranking among all Mediterranean islands	Rank
Area	31
Population	70
Visitor capacity	59
Crowdfactor	174

Greece 5500

Kýthnos

(PHOTO: KLAZIEN MATTER-WALSTRA)

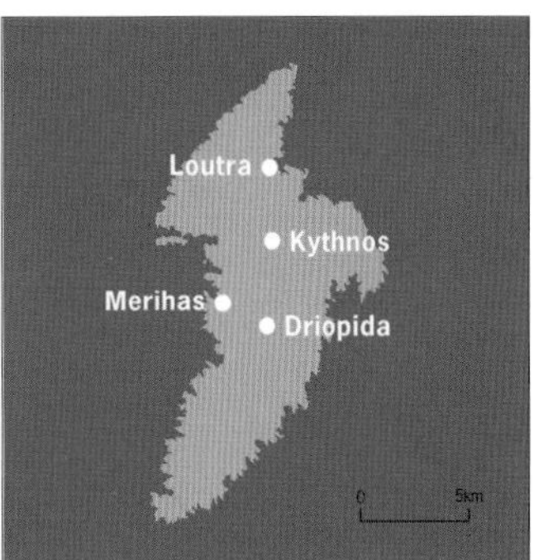
Loutra
Kythnos
Merihas
Driopida
0
5km

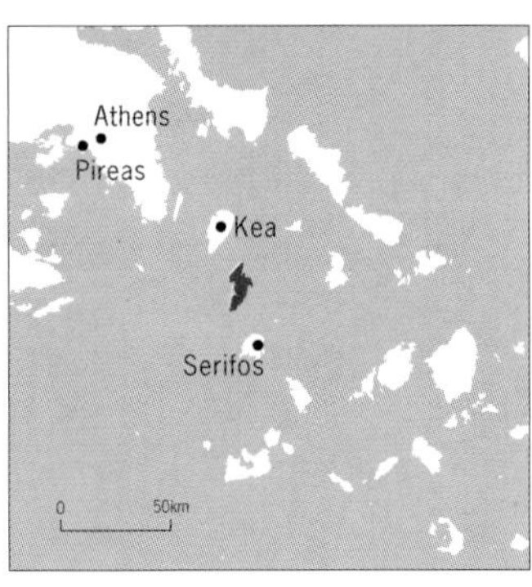
Athens
Pireas
Kea
Serifos
0
50km

37°23' N 24°25' E
Kythnos
Kyklades
Greece

A mostly barren island, usually overlooked by tourists, but still visited for its thermal waters. Rewarding for those seeking a quiet island not far from Athens, with two delightful old villages and 33 often deserted beaches. Difficult to explore without a car.

★★☆☆☆ Tourism level
★★☆☆☆ Vegetation
★★★☆☆ Beaches
★★☆☆☆ History

Information
www.kythnos-island.com
Telephone 22810 32250

Map
Road Editions (1:40000)

Area 99 sq km
Coastline 111 km
Highest point 356 m (Profitis Ilias)

Permanent population 1538

Visitor capacity 1105
5 hotels
305 hotel beds
800 other beds
0 campsites

Crowdfactor
26 people per sq km

Access
Pireas 3 hours
Serifos 1½ hours

Connections
Serifos 2 daily
Pireas daily
Kea 4 weekly

Yacht facilities
Loutra, Merichas

Ranking among all Mediterranean islands	Ran
Area	5
Population	9
Visitor capacity	8
Crowdfactor	16

Lefkáda

38°42' N 20°38' E
Lefkada
Ionia Nisia
Greece

Lefkada is a handsome island and yet rather lacking in character. The central mountain ridge is impressive and there are a number of very fine beaches all along the west coast. The south of the island is heavily wooded and is home to the windsurfing capital of Vasiliki. The main touristed part of the island is Nidri bay, which has a number of islands offshore, all of them privately owned, of which the prettiest is Madouri with the villa of the poet Valaoritis surrounded by a thick wood. The capital is low-key and pleasant.

★★★☆☆ Tourism level
★★★★☆ Vegetation
★★★★☆ Beaches
★★☆☆☆ History

Information
www.lefkada.gr
Telephone 26450 21713

Map
Anavasi (1:40000)

Area 301 sq km
Coastline 139 km
Highest point 1182 m (Elati)

Permanent population 20295

Visitor capacity 5568
87 hotels
4394 hotel beds
1174 other beds
7 campsites

Crowdfactor
85 people per sq km

Access
Bridge to mainland

Connections
Kefalonia 4 daily
Meganisi 3 daily
Ithaki 2 daily

Yacht facilities
5 ports

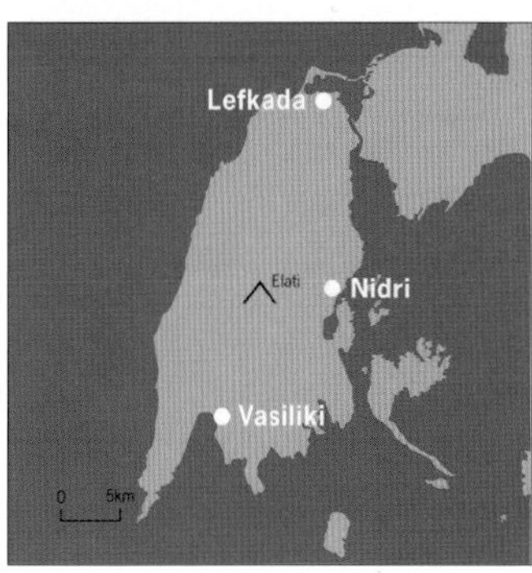
Lefkada
Elati
Nidri
Vasiliki
0
5km

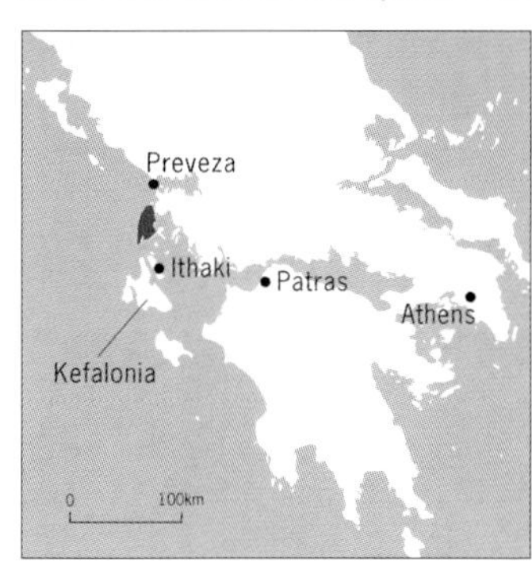
Preveza
Ithaki
Patras
Athens
Kefalonia
0
100km

Ranking among all Mediterranean islands	Rank
Area	25
Population	24
Visitor capacity	39
Crowdfactor	98

Ionia Nisia **Greece** 5100

Léros

AGIA MARINA (PHOTO: GREEK NATIONAL TOURISM ORGANISATION)

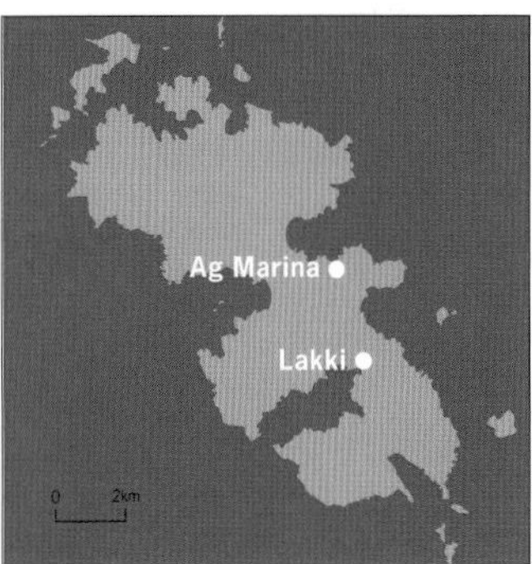
Ag Marina
Lakki
0 2km

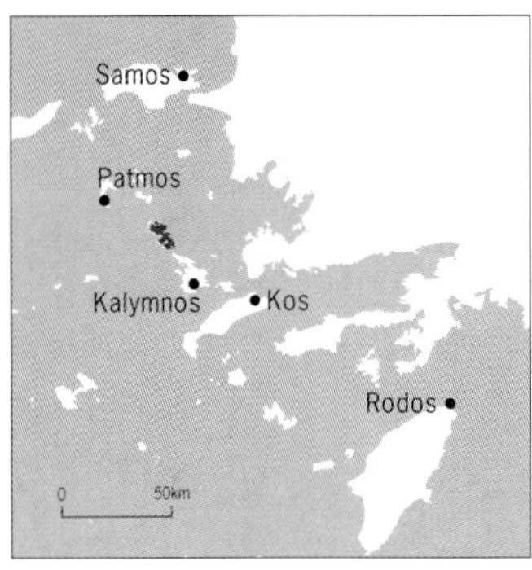
Samos
Patmos
Kalymnos
Kos
Rodos
0 50km

37°08' N 26°50' E
Leros
Dodekanisa
Greece

A pleasant mainly green hilly island with a number of good beaches, Leros suffers from its reputation as the main centre for mental hospitals in Greece. There is a fine 12th century Knights' castle at Platanos.

★★★☆☆ Tourism level
★★★☆☆ Vegetation
★★★☆☆ Beaches
★★☆☆☆ History

Information
www.lerosnet.com.gr
Telephone 22470 25520

Map
Orama 327 (1:30000)

Area 54 sq km
Coastline 82 km
Highest point 320 m (Klivi)

Permanent population 8087

Visitor capacity 2147
27 hotels
1197 hotel beds
950 other beds
1 campsite

Crowdfactor
189 people per sq km

Access
✈ Leros
⛴ Kalymnos 45 minutes
⛴ Patmos 1 hour

Connections
⛴ Kos, Kalymnos 4 daily
⛴ Lipsoi, Patmos 2 daily

Yacht facilities
⛵ 4 ports

7400

Greece Dodekanisa

Ranking among all Mediterranean islands	Ran
Area	7
Population	5
Visitor capacity	6
Crowdfactor	6

Lésvos

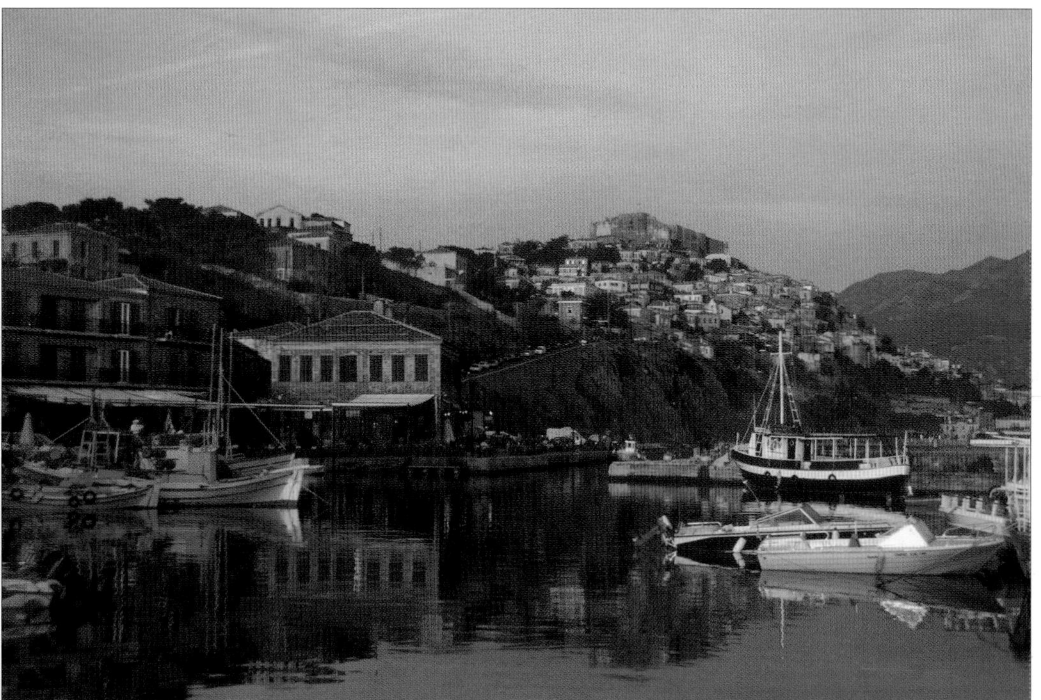

39°12′ N 26°16′ E
Lesvos
Voreio Aigaio
Greece

A fine island, noted for olives and birdlife, heavily wooded in the east, agricultural in the centre but rather bare in the west. The capital Mytilini has a fine Genoese castle, as does the pretty port of Mithymna, while Plomari is famous for its ouzo. Among many places worth visiting are the monastery of Ipsilou, the lovely hill village of Agiassos, the picturesque fishing port of Skala Sikaminias and Sigri with its Turkish castle. A car is essential for exploring this large island.

★★★☆☆ Tourism level
★★★☆☆ Vegetation
★★★★☆ Beaches
★★★☆☆ History

Information
www.lesvosonline.gr
Telephone 22510 42511

Map
Road Editions (1:70000)

Area 1635 sq km
Coastline 382 km
Highest point 968 m (Lepetymnos)

Permanent population 90436

Visitor capacity 7442
112 hotels
6606 hotel beds
836 other beds
1 campsite

Crowdfactor
59 people per sq km

Access
✈ Mytilini

Connections
⛴ Chios, Pireas 2 daily
⛴ Limnos, Ayvalik daily

Yacht facilities
⛵ 8 ports

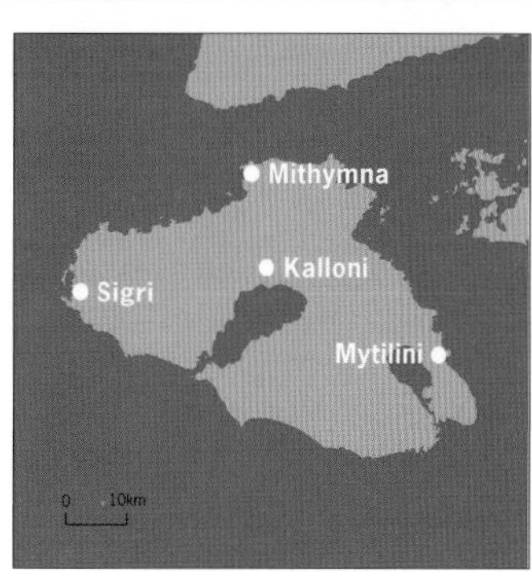
Mithymna
Kalloni
Sigri
Mytilini
0 10km

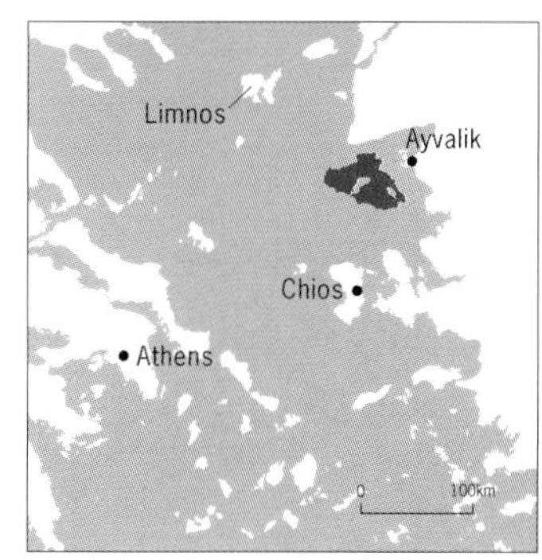
Limnos
Ayvalik
Chios
Athens
0 100km

Ranking among all Mediterranean islands	Rank
Area	8
Population	13
Visitor capacity	35
Crowdfactor	120

Límnos

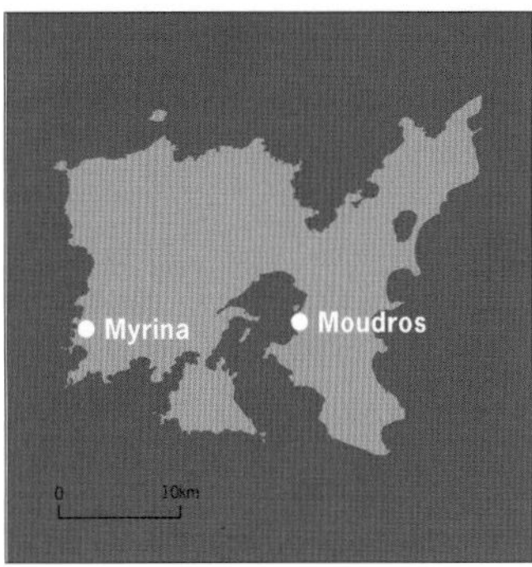
Myrina
Moudros
0 10km

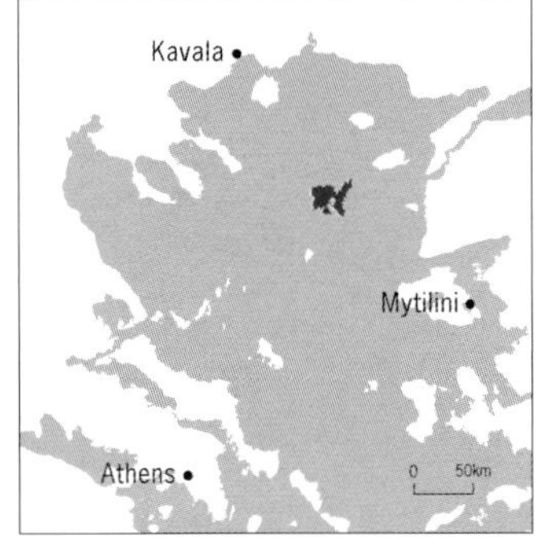
Kavala
Mytilini
Athens
0 50km

39°55' N 25°14' E
Limnos
Voreio Aigaio
Greece

This fertile volcanic island has many very good beaches and a long history going back to Polyochni, a town some 5000 years old thought to predate Troy. Myrina is dominated by a magnificent Venetian fortress, from which there are fine views over the town and island. There are also splendid views of Mount Athos in the evening, but it is not possible to go to the highest part of the island in the northwest, which is in the hands of the army. A car is needed to explore this large island. Many species of birds are to be seen.

★★★☆☆ Tourism level
★★☆☆☆ Vegetation
★★★★☆ Beaches
★★★☆☆ History

Information
www.lemnos-island.com
Telephone 22540 22208

Map
Road Editions (1:50000)

Area 476 sq km
Coastline 263 km
Highest point 430 m (Vigla)

Permanent population 17545

Visitor capacity 2392
24 hotels
1904 hotel beds
488 other beds
0 campsites

Crowdfactor
41 people per sq km

Access
✈ Limnos

Connections
⛴ Lesvos daily
⛴ Kavala 6 weekly
⛴ Agios Efstrátios 5 weekly
⛴ Samothraki 3 weekly

Yacht facilities
⛵ Myrina, Moudros

Ranking among all Mediterranean islands	Ran
Area	1
Population	2
Visitor capacity	5
Crowdfactor	14

7800 **Greece** Voreio Aigaio

37°19′ N 26°44′ E
Lipsoi
Dodekanisa
Greece

A charming peaceful relaxing island, with a number of good beaches, many chapels and pleasant walking.

★★☆☆☆ Tourism level
★★★☆☆ Vegetation
★★★★☆ Beaches
★☆☆☆☆ History

Information
www.lipsi-island.com
Telephone 22470 41250

Map
Drama 329 (1:50000)

Area 15 sq km
Coastline 39 km
Highest point 277 m (Skafi)

Permanent population 687

Visitor capacity 174
2 hotels
82 hotel beds
92 other beds
0 campsites

Crowdfactor
54 people per sq km

Access
Patmos 30 minutes

Connections
Patmos, Leros 4 daily

Yacht facilities
Lipsoi

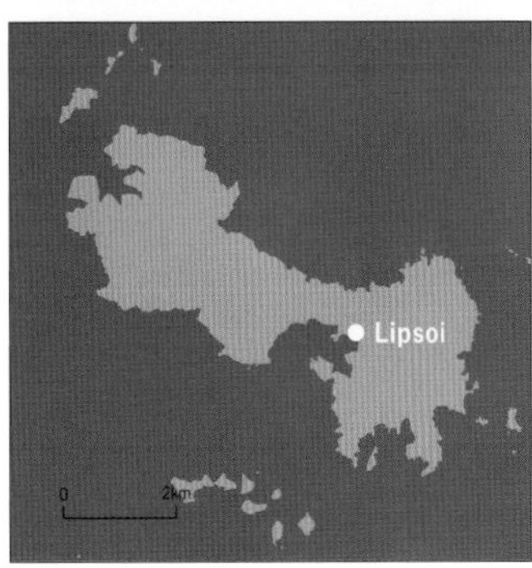
Lipsoi
0
2km

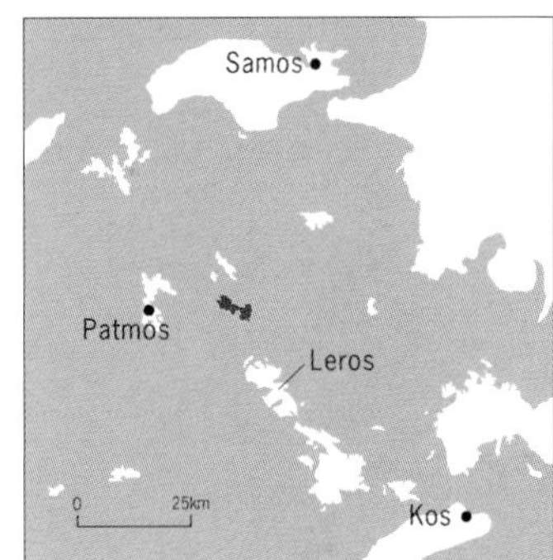
Samos
Patmos
Leros
Kos
0
25km

Lipsoí

Dodekanisa **Greece** 7450

Ranking among all Mediterranean islands

	Rank
Area	128
Population	115
Visitor capacity	143
Crowdfactor	127

Márathos

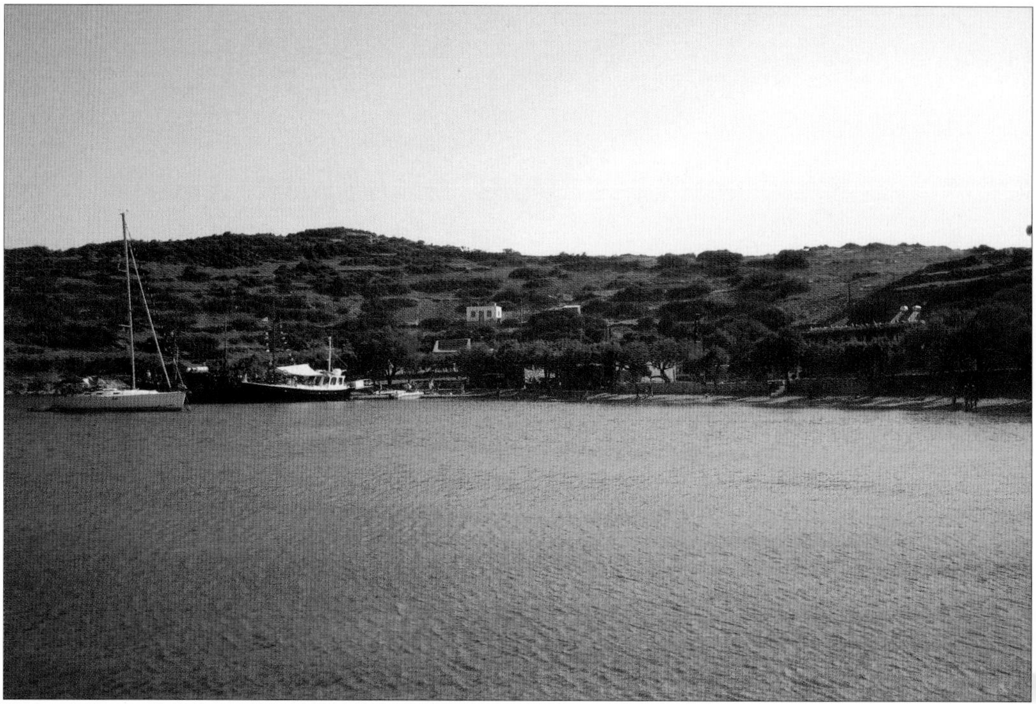

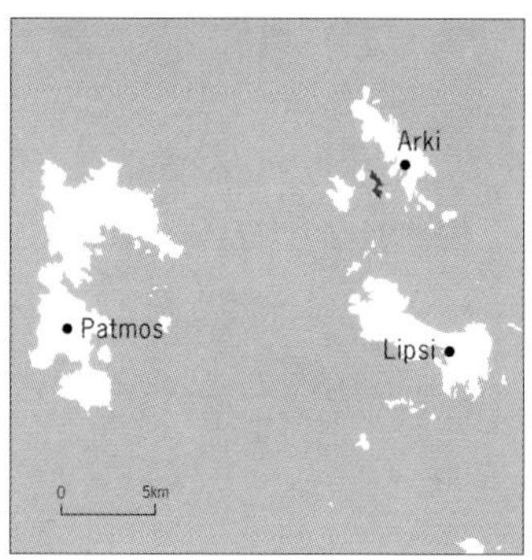
Arki
Patmos
Lipsi
0
5km

37°22' N 26°43' E
Marathos
Dodekanisa
Greece

Visited mainly by yachts or day trips from Patmos, Marathos is an attractive little island with a good beach and two friendly tavernas.

★★☆☆☆ Tourism level
★☆☆☆☆ Vegetation
★★★☆☆ Beaches
★☆☆☆☆ History

Information
Telephone 22470 32900
22470 32609

Map
None

Area 0.35 sq km
Coastline 3.8 km
Highest point 51 m (Vigla)

Permanent population 6

Visitor capacity 33
0 hotels
0 hotel beds
33 other beds
0 campsites

Crowdfactor
109 people per sq km

Access
Patmos 30 minutes

Connections
Patmos 2 daily

Yacht facilities
no fuel

Ranking among all Mediterranean islands	Ran
Area	53
Population	21
Visitor capacity	19
Crowdfactor	8

Mathráki

39°47′ N 19°31′ E
Mathraki
Ionia Nisia
Greece

A quiet thickly wooded island with a long expanse of beach where loggerhead turtles nest.

★☆☆☆☆ Tourism level
★★★★☆ Vegetation
★★★☆☆ Beaches
★☆☆☆☆ History

Information
Telephone 26630 72108

Map
Road Editions (1:70000)

Area 3 sq km
Coastline 9 km
Highest point 155 m (Vouno)

Permanent population 186

Visitor capacity 35
0 hotels
0 hotel beds
35 other beds
0 campsites

Crowdfactor
71 people per sq km

Access
Kerkyra 4 hours
Sidari 45 minutes

Connections
Kerkyra 3 weekly
Sidari daily

Yacht facilities
no fuel

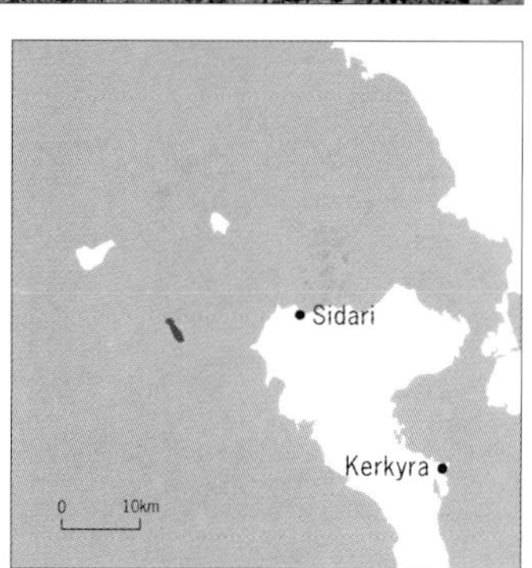
Sidari
Kerkyra
0
10km

Ranking among all Mediterranean islands	Rank
rea	244
opulation	155
isitor capacity	188
rowdfactor	107

Meganísi

PHOTO GIVEN BY MONTSE GENOVES

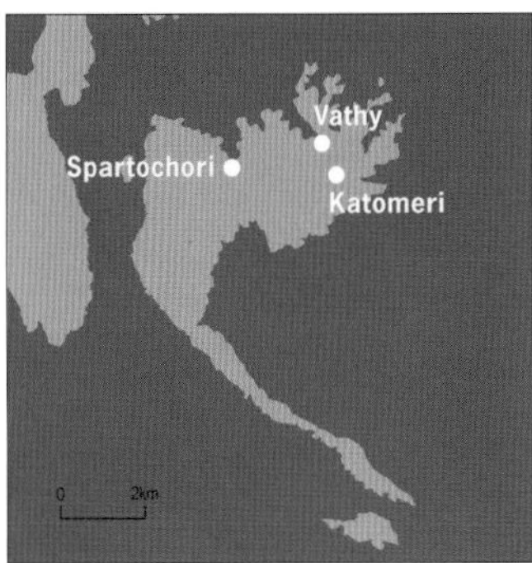
Vathy
Spartochori
Katomeri
0 2km

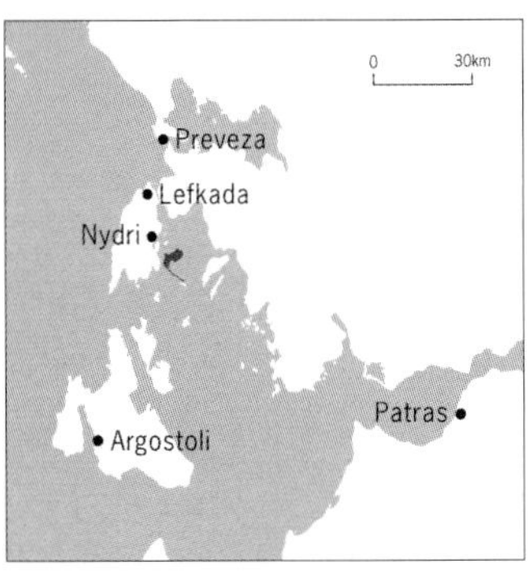
0 30km
Preveza
Lefkada
Nydri
Patras
Argostoli

38°39′ N 20°46′ E
Meganisi
Ionia Nisia
Greece

Meganisi is a pretty island with three flowery villages and a wild interior, ideal for a quiet relaxing holiday. It has a number of coves which can be reached on foot but others can only be accessed by boat. The only sight of note is the Papanikolis cave.

★★☆☆☆ Tourism level
★★★★☆ Vegetation
★★☆☆☆ Beaches
★☆☆☆☆ History

Information
www.meganisi.gr
Telephone 26450 51239

Map
Anavasi (1:40000)

Area 20 sq km
Coastline 53 km
Highest point 297 m (Megas Birnos)

Permanent population 992

Visitor capacity 142
1 hotel
28 hotel beds
114 other beds
0 campsites

Crowdfactor
56 people per sq km

Access
Nydri 25 minutes

Connections
Nydri 5 daily

Yacht facilities
Spartochori

5150 **Greece** Ionia Nisia

Ranking among all Mediterranean islands	Ran
Area	11
Population	10
Visitor capacity	14
Crowdfactor	12

Megísti (Kastellórizo)

36°08′ N 29°34′ E
Megisti (Kastellorizo)
Dodekanisa
Greece

The town, which is dominated by a 14th century castle, feels depopulated with a number of houses having been allowed to go to ruin. It is worth visiting the fine blue cave at Parasta and the Ag Triada and Ag Georgios monasteries. There are boat trips to Ro, Strongyli, Ag Georgios, with its chapel, and other islets and there are regular boats to the Turkish port of Kas.

★★☆☆☆ Tourism level
★★☆☆☆ Vegetation
★☆☆☆☆ Beaches
★★☆☆☆ History

Information
www.kastellorizo.org
Telephone 22460 49269

Map
Local Union (1:10000)

Area 9 sq km
Coastline 20 km
Highest point 277 m (Vigla)

Permanent population 369

Visitor capacity 117
3 hotels
73 hotel beds
44 other beds
0 campsites

Crowdfactor
53 people per sq km

Access
✈ Megisti

Connections
⛴ Rodos 4 weekly

Yacht facilities
⛵ Megisti

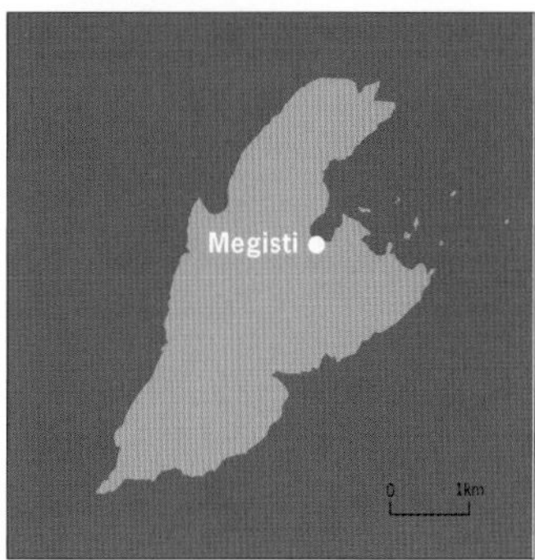
Megisti
0
1km

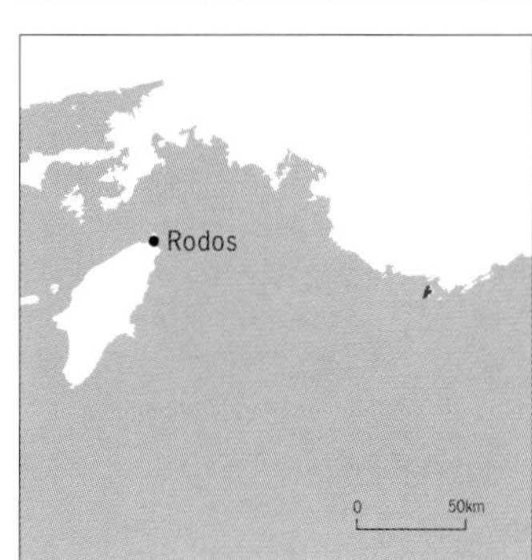
Rodos
0
50km

Ranking among all Mediterranean islands	Rank
Area	165
Population	129
Visitor capacity	154
Crowdfactor	129

Dodekanisa **Greece**

7010

Mílos

PHOTO: MARIN PASHOV

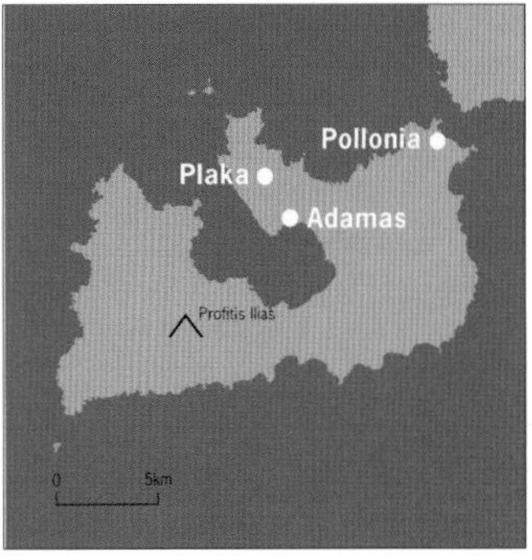
Pollonia
Plaka
Adamas
Profitis Ilias
0
5km

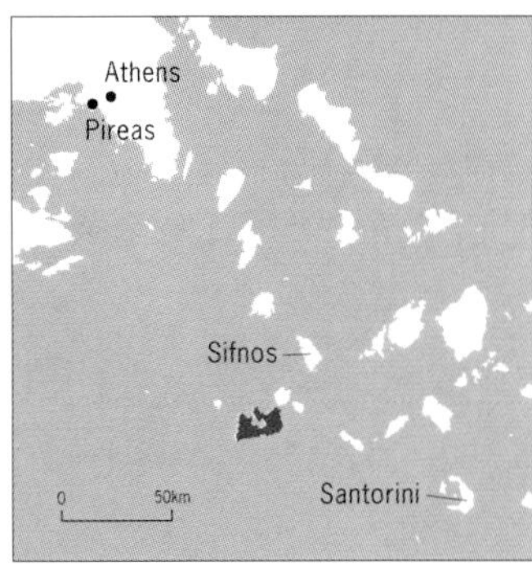
Athens
Pireas
Sifnos
Santorini
0
50km

36°40′ N 24°26′ E
Milos
Kyklades
Greece

This extinct volcano has some strange-looking scars where minerals have been and still are extracted. Apart from these Milos is quite an attractive island and has a pretty capital at Plaka, with first century catacombs and fine views from the top of the Venetian kastro. The south west of the island, which is best explored by car, is ruggedly grand and there are the two interesting monasteries of Ag Ioannis and Ag Marina. Milos also has fine beaches and there is good windsurfing at Pollonia.

★★★☆☆ Tourism level
★★☆☆☆ Vegetation
★★★☆☆ Beaches
★★☆☆☆ History

Information
www.milos-island.gr
Telephone 22870 21370

Map
Road Editions (1:50000)

Area 158 sq km
Coastline 139 km
Highest point 748 m (Profitis Ilias)

Permanent population 4736

Visitor capacity 1561
28 hotels
1057 hotel beds
504 other beds
1 campsite

Crowdfactor
39 people per sq km

Access
✈ Milos
⛴ Sifnos 1 hour

Connections
⛴ Pireas, Kimolos 4 daily
⛴ Sifnos 3 daily
⛴ Santorini 4 weekly

Yacht facilities
⛵ Adamas

Ranking among all Mediterranean islands	Ran
Area	4
Population	6
Visitor capacity	6
Crowdfactor	14

37°27′ N 25°23′ E
Mykonos
Kyklades
Greece

A fashionable cosmopolitan island with a lovely if crowded Cycladic town, whose narrow streets are full of boutiques. The Paraportiani church and the view over the harbour are famous. Ano Mera is worth visiting for the Tourliani monastery and is a good place to eat and also to stay if you do not want to be in the capital or by the sea. Mykonos is also the departure point for visits to the sacred island of Delos.

★★★★★ Tourism level
★☆☆☆☆ Vegetation
★★★★☆ Beaches
★★☆☆☆ History

Information
www.mykonos.gr
Telephone 22890 22201

Map
Road Editions (1:40000)

Area 86 sq km
Coastline 89 km
Highest point 373 m (Vardies)

Permanent population 9260

Visitor capacity 10032
160 hotels
9274 hotel beds
758 other beds
2 campsites

Crowdfactor
224 people per sq km

Access
✈ Mykonos
⛴ Tinos 20 minutes
⛴ Paros 1 hour

Connections
⛴ Tinos 10 daily
⛴ Paros 3 daily
⛴ Syros 2 daily
⛴ Naxos daily

Yacht facilities
⛵ Mykonos Marina

Mykonos
Ano Mera
0
4km

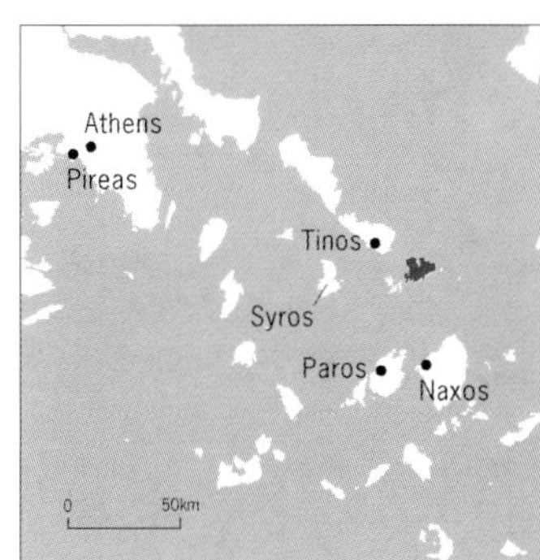
Athens
Pireas
Tinos
Syros
Paros
Naxos
0
50km

Ranking among all Mediterranean islands	Rank
Area	57
Population	45
Visitor capacity	27
Crowdfactor	52

Náxos

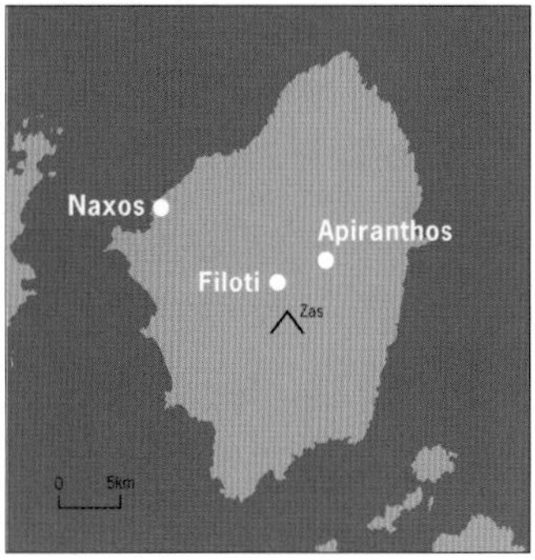
Naxos
Apiranthos
Filoti
Zas
0 5km

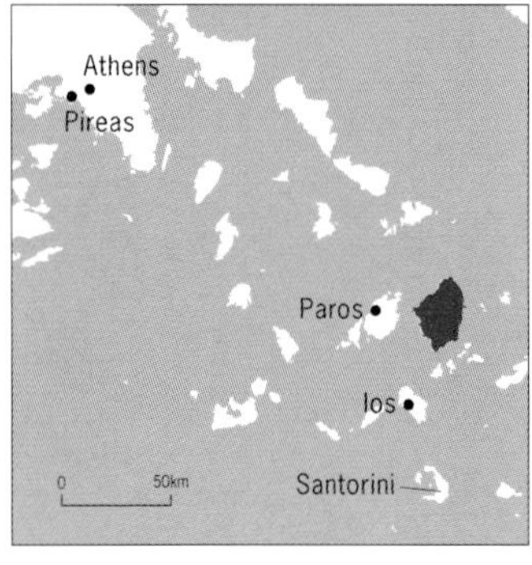
Athens
Pireas
Paros
Ios
Santorini
0 50km

37°04′ N 25°28′ E
Naxos
Kyklades
Greece

Naxos has the finest old town in the Cyclades, climbing through charming little winding streets up to the Venetian kastro, the seat of the dukes of Naxos. The interior of the island is very fertile. The marble quarries at the top of the island are impressive, especially if caught in the sunlight, and the emery mines on the east coast are interesting too. Fine frescoes are to be found in the churches of Ag Kyriaki in Apiranthos and Ag Artemios at Sangri. Naxos has some of the best beaches in the Cyclades.

★★★★☆ Tourism level
★★★★☆ Vegetation
★★★★☆ Beaches
★★★☆☆ History

Information
www.naxos-greece.net
Telephone 22850 22717

Map
Anavasi (1:40000)

Area 389 sq km
Coastline 133 km
Highest point 999 m (Zas)

Permanent population 17357

Visitor capacity 4925
108 hotels
4239 hotel beds
686 other beds
3 campsites

Crowdfactor
57 people per sq km

Access
✈ Naxos
⛴ Paros 1 hour

Connections
⛴ Paros 10 daily
⛴ Ios, Santorini 2 daily
⛴ Mykonos, Amorgos, Iraklia, Ikaria daily

Yacht facilities
⛵ Naxos

Ranking among all Mediterranean islands	Ran
Area	2
Population	2
Visitor capacity	4
Crowdfactor	12

36°36′ N 27°10′ E
Nisyros
Dodekanisa
Greece

Large numbers of day-trippers from Kos come to see the dormant volcano spanning most of the island, inside which are five smaller craters, fumaroles and evil-smelling sulphur deposits. The capital Mandraki is an attractive white town with pretty small streets and squares, dominated by a kastro enclosing the 15th century monastery of Panagia Spiliani. Also well worth seeing are the massive walls of Paleokastro and the monastery of Ag Ioannis. There are boats to beaches on the islets of Giali and Ag Antonios.

★★★☆☆ Tourism level
★★★☆☆ Vegetation
★★☆☆☆ Beaches
★★☆☆☆ History

Information
www.nisyrosinfo.com
Telephone 22420 31180

Map
Orama 328 (1:35000)

Area 41 sq km
Coastline 30 km
Highest point 698 m (Kratir)

Permanent population 915

Visitor capacity 241
5 hotels
233 hotel beds
8 other beds
0 campsites

Crowdfactor
28 people per sq km

Access
⛴ Kos, Tilos 1 hour

Connections
⛴ Kos 3 daily
⛴ Tilos 4 weekly

Yacht facilities
⛵ Mandraki

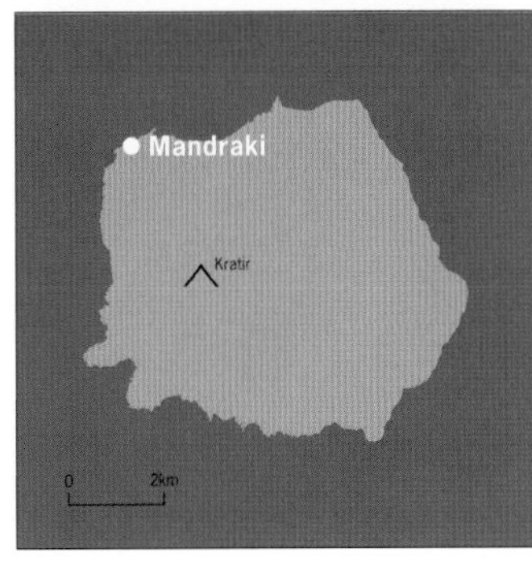
Mandraki
Kratir
0
2km

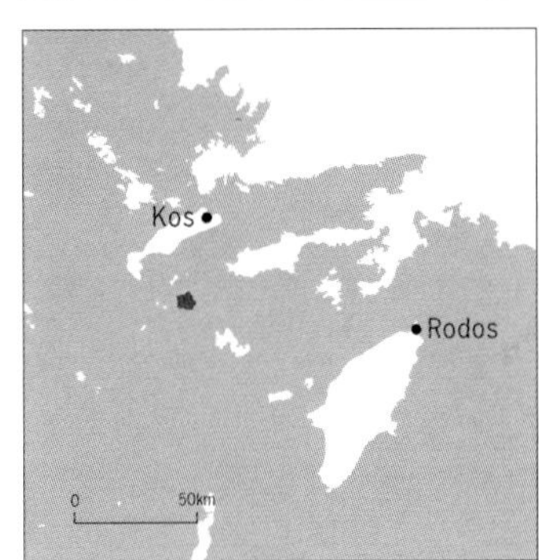
Kos
Rodos
0
50km

Ranking among all Mediterranean islands

	Rank
Area	83
Population	107
Visitor capacity	131
Crowdfactor	159

Oinoússes

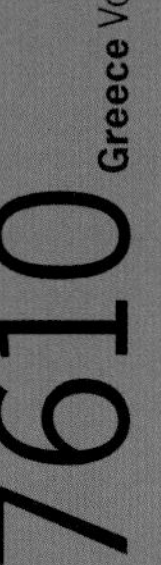

7610
Greece Voreio Aigaio

(PHOTO: NORTH AEGEAN REGION)

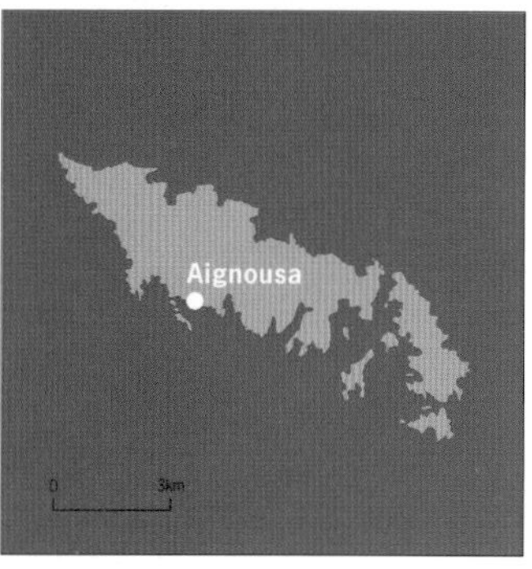

Aignousa
0
3km

38°32' N 26°13' E
Oinousses
Voreio Aigaio
Greece

A very quiet island with a private feel which is very much under the control of several well-known shipowning families. There is a nautical school and a few beaches.

★☆☆☆☆ Tourism level
★★☆☆☆ Vegetation
★★★☆☆ Beaches
★☆☆☆☆ History

Information
www.chiosnet.gr
Telephone 22720 51475

Map
Anavasi (1:60000)

Area 14 sq km
Coastline 35 km
Highest point 182 m (Voutiro)

Permanent population 855

Visitor capacity 23
1 hotel
23 hotel beds
0 other beds
0 campsites

Crowdfactor
61 people per sq km

Access
Chios 30 minutes

Connections
Chios daily

Yacht facilities
no fuel

Ranking among all Mediterranean islands

	Rank
Area	13[illegible]
Population	10[illegible]
Visitor capacity	19[illegible]
Crowdfactor	11[illegible]

Othonoí

39°51' N 19°23' E
Othonoi
Ionia Nisia
Greece

A friendly island much frequented by Italian sailors (it is the nearest Greek island to Italy), with a cheerful port, relatively good food, a dramatic tree-covered interior and a completely unspoilt traditional village near the top of the island.

★☆☆☆☆ Tourism level
★★★★☆ Vegetation
★★☆☆☆ Beaches
★☆☆☆☆ History

nformation
www.omogenia.com/othoni
elephone 26630 71545

Map
oad Editions (1:70000)

Area 10 sq km
Coastline 17 km
Highest point 393 m (Vitsetzakia)

Permanent population 340

Visitor capacity 79
1 hotel
35 hotel beds
44 other beds
0 campsites

Crowdfactor
40 people per sq km

Access
Kerkyra 4 hours
Agios Stefanos 1½ hours
Sidari 2 hours

Connections
Kerkyra 3 weekly
Agios Stefanos, Sidari 2 weekly

Yacht facilities
no fuel

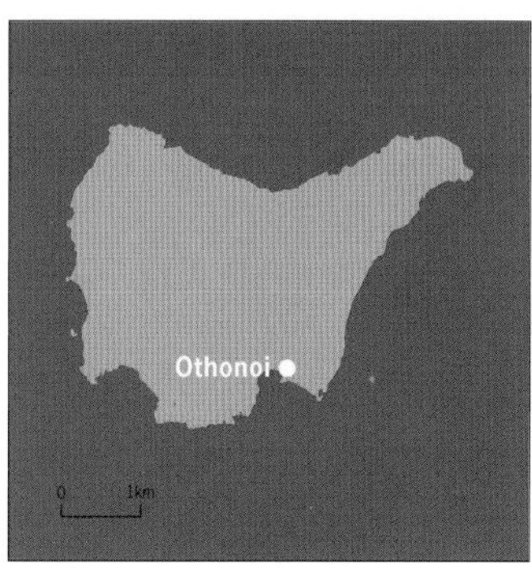
Othonoi
0
1km

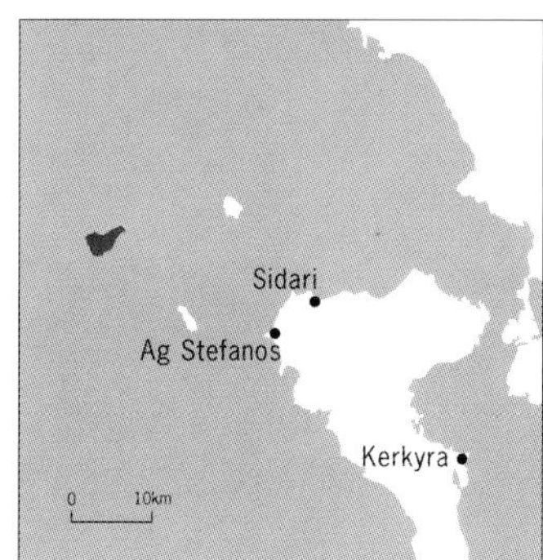
Sidari
Ag Stefanos
Kerkyra
0
10km

anking among all Mediterranean islands	Rank
rea	153
opulation	131
isitor capacity	162
rowdfactor	142

Ionia Nisia **Greece** 5010

Palaió Trikéri

6990 Greece

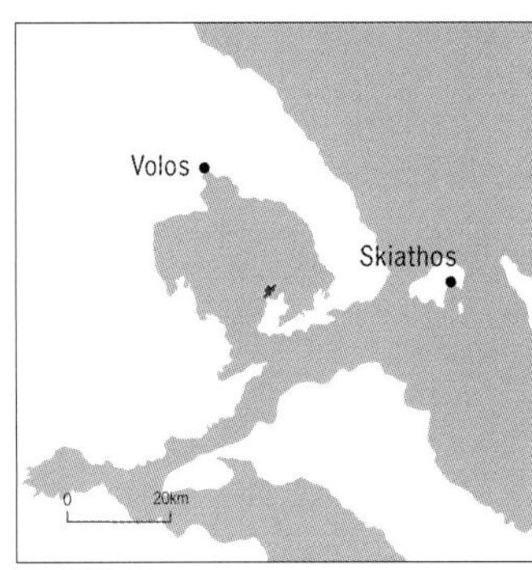

Volos
Skiathos
0
20km

39°09' N 23°04' E
Palaio Trikeri
Greece

A lovely little wooded island with quiet port and a large monastery.

★★☆☆☆ Tourism level
★★★★☆ Vegetation
★★☆☆☆ Beaches
★★☆☆☆ History

Information
Telephone 24230 91315

Map
Anavasi (1:10000)

Area 2.47 sq km
Coastline 11 km
Highest point 109 m (Schinorachi)

Permanent population 86

Visitor capacity 74
2 hotels
74 hotel beds
0 other beds
0 campsites

Crowdfactor
64 people per sq km

Access
Volos 45 minutes

Connections
Volos 2 daily

Yacht facilities
no fuel

Ranking among all Mediterranean islands	Ra
Area	26
Population	17
Visitor capacity	16
Crowdfactor	1

37°03' N 25°11' E
Paros
Kyklades
Greece

Paros seems to appeal to everyone. The capital Parikia is a charming Cycladic town built round a Venetian kastro and the 6th century Ekatontapiliani church is magnificent. Naoussa is also Cycladic and has a pretty port surrounded by restaurants. While the towns are crowded, the rest of the island is big enough to absorb its visitors. Good beaches and good restaurants are abundant and Lefkes, the old Turkish capital, is charming. It is worth visiting the monasteries of Ag Anargiri and Ag Minas, but the famous marble quarries are disappointing.

★★★★☆ Tourism level
★★★☆☆ Vegetation
★★★★★ Beaches
★★★☆☆ History

Information
www.paros.gr
Telephone 22840 51220

Map
Anavasi (1:40000)

Area 196 sq km
Coastline 111 km
Highest point 771 m (Agii Pantes)

Permanent population 12514

Visitor capacity 9154
145 hotels
6616 hotel beds
2538 other beds
8 campsites

Crowdfactor
110 people per sq km

Access
✈ Paros
⛴ Mykonos, Naxos 1 hour

Connections
⛴ Naxos 10 daily
⛴ Pireas 8 daily
⛴ Mykonos 2 daily
⛴ Syros daily

Yacht facilities
⛵ Parikia, Naousa

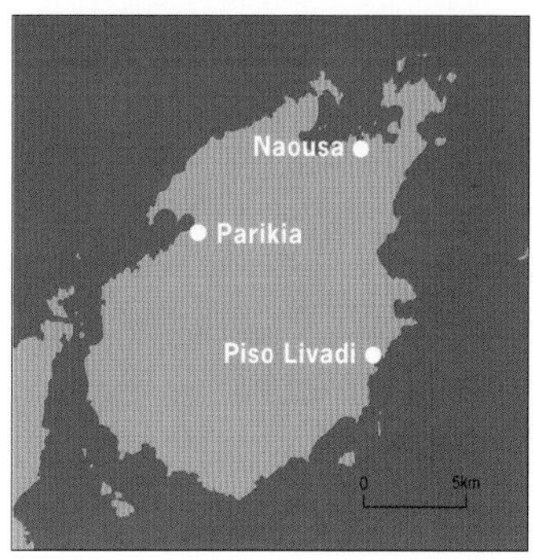
Naousa
Parikia
Piso Livadi
0
5km

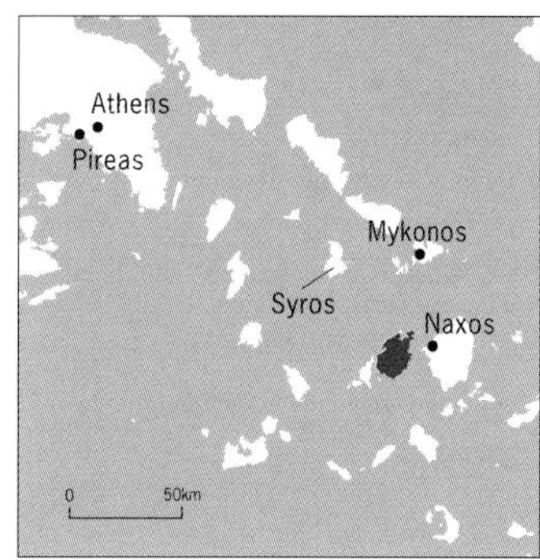
Athens
Pireas
Mykonos
Syros
Naxos
0
50km

Ranking among all Mediterranean islands

	Rank
Area	38
Population	37
Visitor capacity	30
Crowdfactor	80

Pátmos

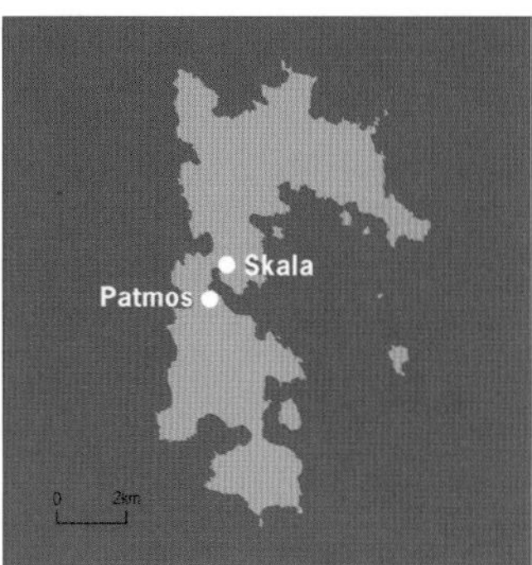
Skala
Patmos
0 2km

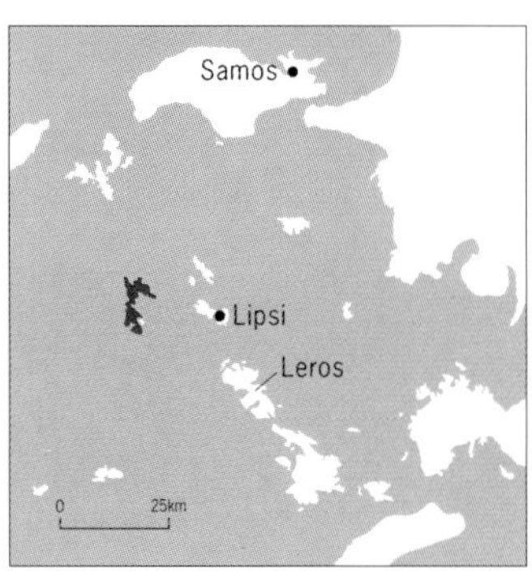
Samos
Lipsi
Leros
0 25km

37°19' N 26°32' E
Patmos
Dodekanisa
Greece

Patmos is famous for the huge monastery of St John, which dominates the capital and the island. It is a peaceful island with a large number of good beaches and some fine views.

★★★★☆ Tourism level
★☆☆☆☆ Vegetation
★★★☆☆ Beaches
★★★★☆ History

Information
www.patmos.gr
Telephone 22470 31666

Map
Orama 329 (1:50000)

Area 34 sq km
Coastline 72 km
Highest point 269 m (Profitis Ilias)

Permanent population 2997

Visitor capacity 1966
39 hotels
1698 hotel beds
268 other beds
1 campsite

Crowdfactor
145 people per sq km

Access
Leros 1 hour

Connections
Lipsoi, Samos 5 daily
Leros 4 daily
Fournoi, Arkoi 4 weekly
Ikaria 3 weekly

Yacht facilities
Skala

7430 **Greece** Dodekanisa

Ranking among all Mediterranean islands	Ran
Area	9
Population	7
Visitor capacity	6
Crowdfactor	7

39°12' N 20°10' E
Paxoi
Ionia Nisia
Greece

A relatively quiet and friendly island, Paxoi is almost entirely covered with trees particularly olives and offers very attractive walking. The west coast with its cliffs and caves is spectacular, but the rest of the island is gentle and relaxing with mostly pebble beaches. Shops and tavernas are quite sophisticated and the shortage of accommodation, combined with the daily visitors from Corfu, can give the impression that the island is more crowded than it is.

★★★☆☆ Tourism level
★★★★★ Vegetation
★★★☆☆ Beaches
★★☆☆☆ History

Information
www.paxos-greece.com
Telephone 26620 32100

Map
Bleasdale (1:10000)

Area 24 sq km
Coastline 37 km
Highest point 231 m (Arvanitakeika)

Permanent population 2405

Visitor capacity 296
6 hotels
282 hotel beds
14 other beds
0 campsites

Crowdfactor
109 people per sq km

Access
Kerkyra 1 hour
Kerkyra 2 hours

Connections
Kerkyra 2 daily
Kerkyra, Parga 2 daily
Igoumenitsa daily

Yacht facilities
Gaios, Lakka

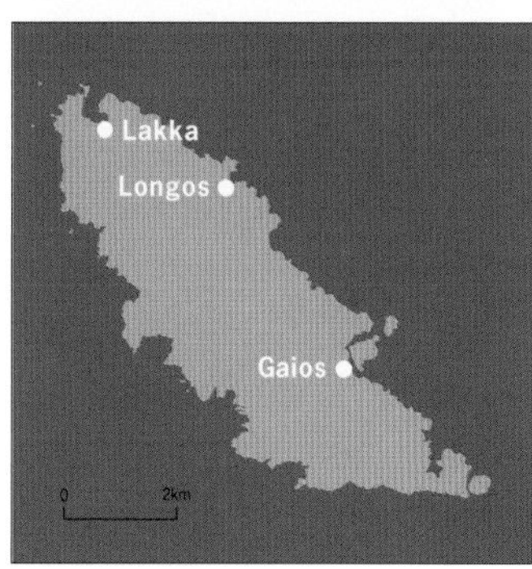
Lakka
Longos
Gaios
0
2km

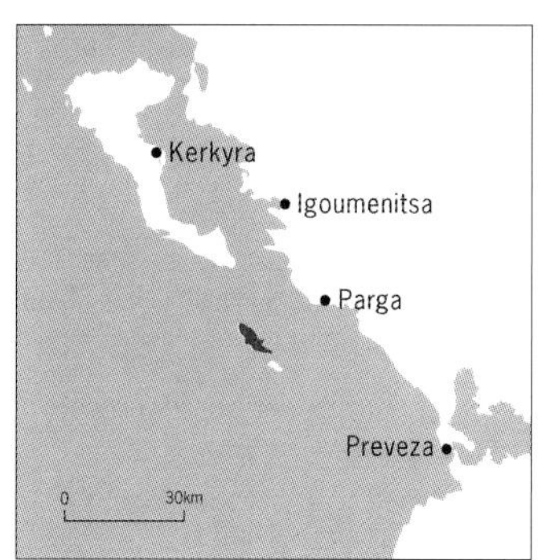
Kerkyra
Igoumenitsa
Parga
Preveza
0
30km

Ranking among all Mediterranean islands	Rank
Area	102
Population	85
Visitor capacity	127
Crowdfactor	82

Ionia Nisia **Greece** 5050

Póros

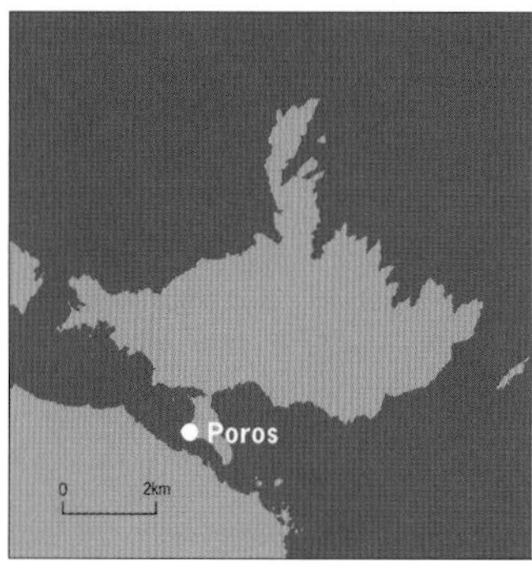
Poros
0 2km

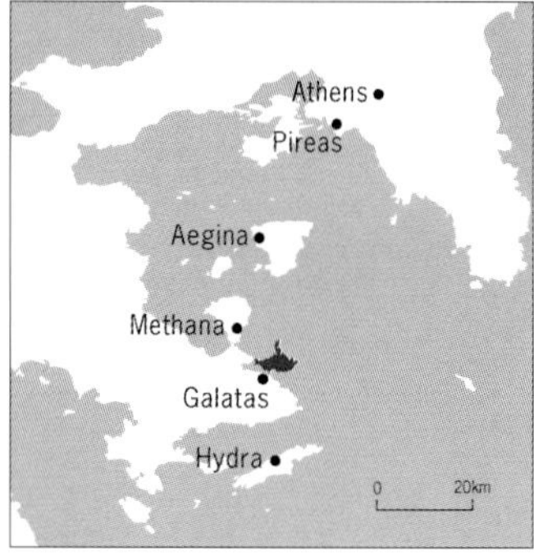
Athens
Pireas
Aegina
Methana
Galatas
Hydra
0 20km

37°31' N 23°29' E
Poros
Argosaronikos
Greece

The town has a fine setting on the islet of Sferia and there is a good view from the top of the campanile. There are lovely walks to the Panagia and Zoodochos Pigi monasteries and over the top of the island to the sanctuary of Poseidon and down through the pine forests to the lovely bays of the north coast. Most of the island is little visited and good to explore.

★★★★☆ Tourism level
★★★★☆ Vegetation
★★☆☆☆ Beaches
★★☆☆☆ History

Information
www.poros.com.gr
Telephone 22980 22311

Map
Orama 340 (1:20000)

Area 22 sq km
Coastline 42 km
Highest point 358 m (Vigla)

Permanent population 4182

Visitor capacity 4279
18 hotels
1229 hotel beds
3050 other beds
0 campsites

Crowdfactor
370 people per sq km

Access
Pireas 1 hour
Galatas 10 minutes

Connections
Pireas 12 daily
Aigina, Methana 8 daily
Ydra 5 daily
Galatas 50 daily

Yacht facilities
Poros

Ranking among all Mediterranean islands	Ran
Area	10
Population	6
Visitor capacity	4
Crowdfactor	2

5850 **Greece** Argosaronikos

38°35′ N 25°35′ E
Psara
Voreio Aigaio
Greece

Psara is a quiet barren island with no cars and little to see other than the Kimisis monastery in the north and good bird-watching.

★☆☆☆☆ Tourism level
★☆☆☆☆ Vegetation
★★☆☆☆ Beaches
★★☆☆☆ History

Information
www.chiosnet.gr
Telephone 22740 61293

Map
Anavasi (1:60000)

Area 40 sq km
Coastline 45 km
Highest point 531 m (Profitis Ilias)

Permanent population 478

Visitor capacity 84
3 hotels
26 hotel beds
58 other beds
0 campsites

Crowdfactor
13 people per sq km

Access
Chios 3½ hours

Connections
Chios 3 weekly

Yacht facilities
no fuel

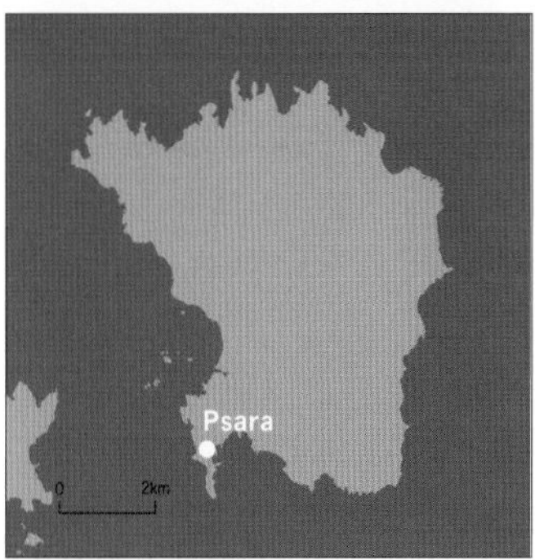
Psara
0
2km

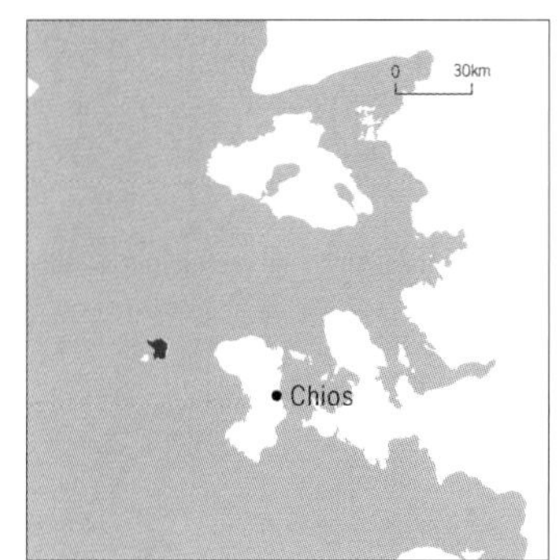
0
30km
Chios

Ranking among all Mediterranean islands	Rank
Area	84
Population	124
Visitor capacity	159
Crowdfactor	192

Psérimos

(PHOTO: CLAUDE HOSEMANN)

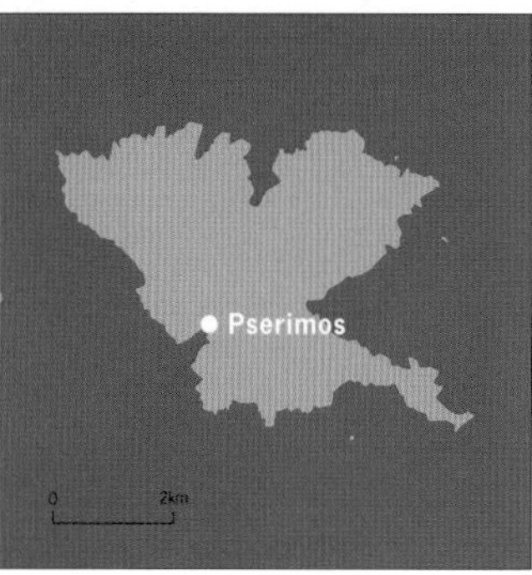

Pserimos
0
2km

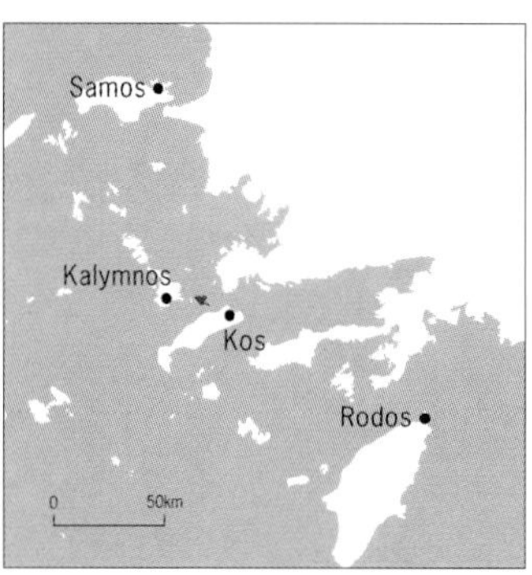

Samos
Kalymnos
Kos
Rodos
0
50km

36°56′ N 27°08′ E
Pserimos
Dodekanisa
Greece

An attractive little island usually overcrowded with day-trippers from Kos. It is possible to find more peace by walking away from the main beach or by visiting the Grafiotissa monastery.

★★★☆☆ Tourism level
★☆☆☆☆ Vegetation
★★☆☆☆ Beaches
★☆☆☆☆ History

Information
Telephone 22430 59056

Map
Orama 326 (1:75000)

Area 14 sq km
Coastline 28 km
Highest point 268 m (Vasiliki Vigla)

Permanent population 124

Visitor capacity 30
0 hotels
0 hotel beds
30 other beds
0 campsites

Crowdfactor
10 people per sq km

Access
Kos, Kalymnos 30 minutes

Connections
Kos daily
Kalymnos 3 weekly

Yacht facilities
no fuel

7320 **Greece** Dodekanisa

Ranking among all Mediterranean islands	Ran[k]
Area	13
Population	16
Visitor capacity	19
Crowdfactor	20

Ródos (Rhodes)

36°11' N 27°59' E
Rodos (Rhodes)
Dodekanisa
Greece

Rhodes was occupied for over two centuries by the Knights before they moved to Malta and they have left a wonderful medieval city. There are grand streets like the Odos Ippoton lined by Inns and many lesser streets which are also fascinating, the whole surrounded by magnificent walls. The rest of the island is also fine, with the spectacular sites of Lindos and Monolithos, and beyond Lindos the southern half of the island is very uncrowded.

★★★★☆ Tourism level
★★★☆☆ Vegetation
★★★★★ Beaches
★★★★★ History

Information
www.rhodes.gr
Telephone 22410 35226

Map
Road Editions (1:100000)

Area 1401 sq km
Coastline 253 km
Highest point 1216 m (Attaviros)

Permanent population 115334

Visitor capacity 76646
484 hotels
71526 hotel beds
4820 other beds
0 campsites

Crowdfactor
136 people per sq km

Access
✈ Rodos

Connections
⛴ Kos, Symi 4 daily
⛴ Chalki 2 daily
⛴ Tilos, Marmaris daily
⛴ Megisti 4 weekly

Yacht facilities
⛵ Mandraki, Langonia

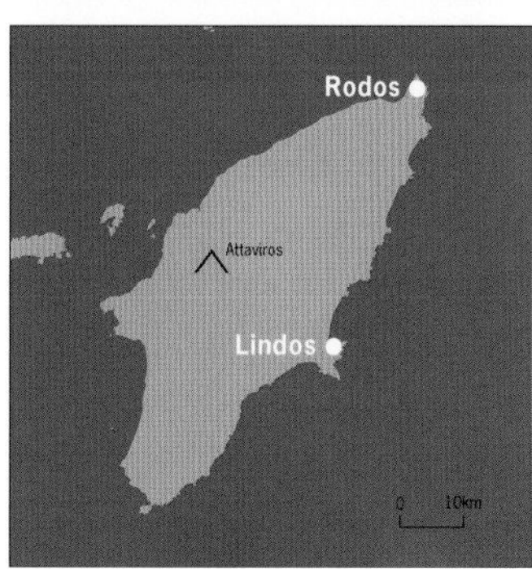
Rodos
Attaviros
Lindos
0 10km

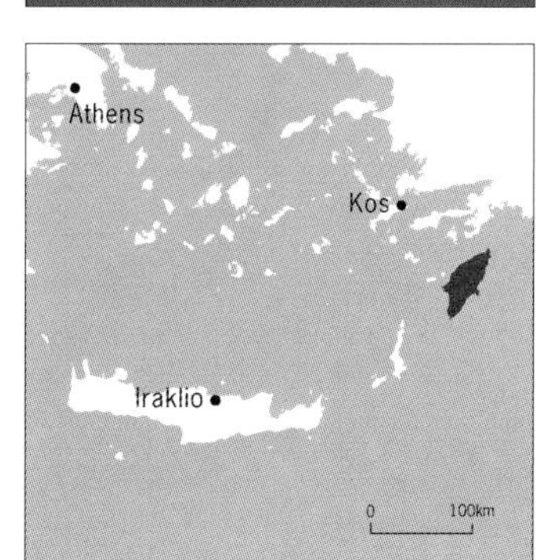
Athens
Kos
Iraklio
0 100km

Ranking among all Mediterranean islands	Rank
Area	9
Population	10
Visitor capacity	7
Crowdfactor	73

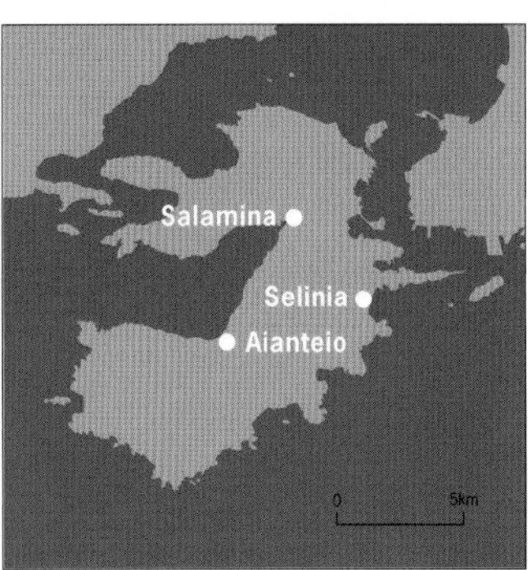
Salamina
Selinia
Aianteio
0
5km

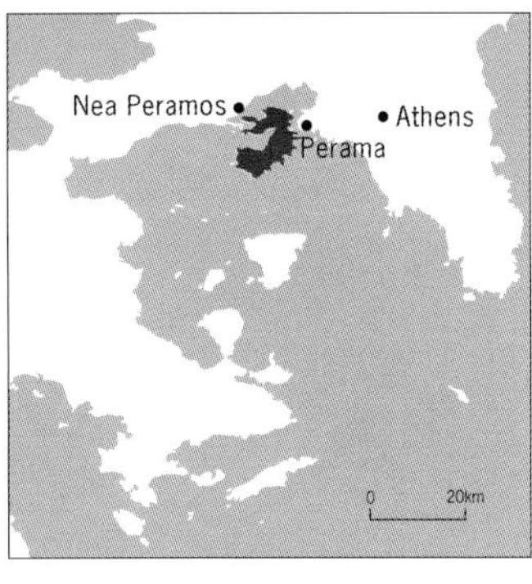
Nea Peramos
Athens
Perama
0
20km

37°55' N 23°28' E
Salamina
Argosaronikos
Greece

The largest island in the Argo-Saronic group is wrongly dismissed by many guidebooks. The pine forest of Kanakia ranks with the loveliest on any island and there have been recent discoveries thought to be the palace of Ajax and the cave of Euripides. Much of the island is covered by holiday homes with lemon trees and brightly coloured gardens. There is a fine view from Resti over to Eantio (and very good food), while the view from the little fishing village of Gyala over to Aegina seems a world away.

★★★☆☆ Tourism level
★★★★☆ Vegetation
★★☆☆☆ Beaches
★★★☆☆ History

Information
www.salamina.gr
Telephone 210 464 6000

Map
None

Area 91 sq km
Coastline 108 km
Highest point 365 m (Batsi)

Permanent population 34975

Visitor capacity 159
4 hotels
111 hotel beds
48 other beds
3 campsites

Crowdfactor
383 people per sq km

Access
Perama 20 minutes
Nea Peramos 10 minutes

Connections
Perama 70 daily
Nea Peramos 35 daily

Yacht facilities
Salamina, Ampelakia

Ranking among all Mediterranean islands	Ran
Area	5
Population	1
Visitor capacity	14
Crowdfactor	2

Sámos

37°43' N 26°49' E
Samos
Voreio Aigaio
Greece

A very wooded and fertile island with many fine views, Samos has lovely beaches and fine churches and monasteries. The best walking is in the west of the island, where the two wonderful Seitani beaches are also to be found. The area of the Heraion and Sacred Way is now disfigured by the airport, but the archaeological museum s one of the best in Greece. There are ɔoat excursions from Pythagorio to the ɔretty islet of Samiopoula.

★★★★☆ Tourism level
★★★★★ Vegetation
★★★★☆ Beaches
★★★★☆ History

nformation
ww.samos.gr
'elephone 22730 80005

lap
Road Editions (1:50000)

Area 477 sq km
Coastline 163 km
Highest point 1434 m (Kerkis)

Permanent population 33999

Visitor capacity 11057
184 hotels
9631 hotel beds
1426 other beds
0 campsites

Crowdfactor
94 people per sq km

Access
✈ Samos

Connections
⛴ Ikaria 3 daily
⛴ Fournoi, Patmos 2 daily
⛴ Agathónisi daily

Yacht facilities
⛵ 4 ports

Karlovasi
Kerkis
Samos
Pythagorio
0
10km

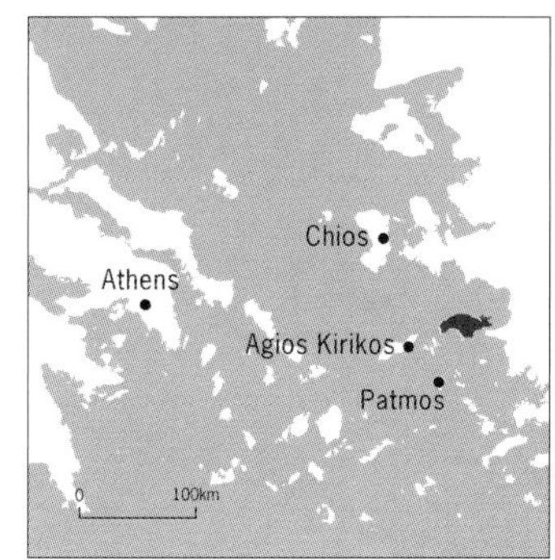
Chios
Athens
Agios Kirikos
Patmos
0
100km

Ranking among all Mediterranean islands	Rank
rea	16
opulation	20
isitor capacity	25
rowdfactor	92

Voreio Aigaio **Greece**

7500

FOREST OF KANAKIA, SALAMINA (PHOTO: ATHANASSIOS PAPACONSTANTINOU)

Samothráki

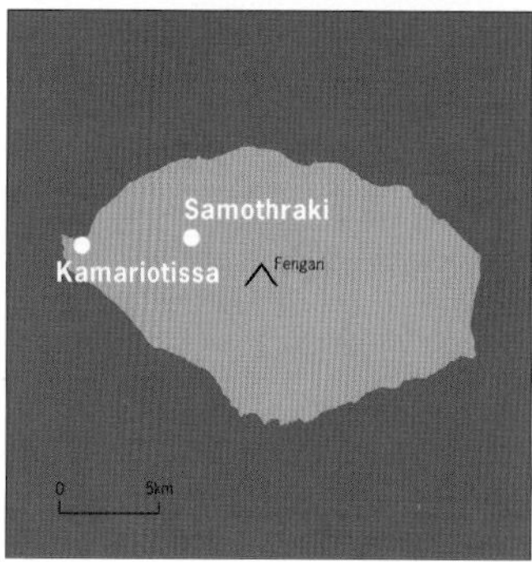
Samothraki
Kamariotissa
Fengari
0 5km

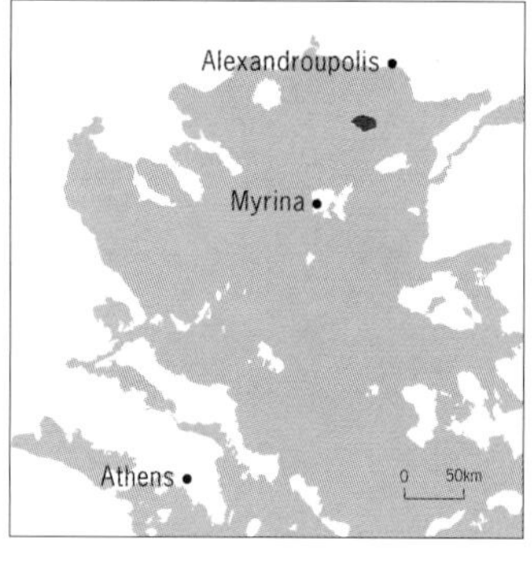
Alexandroupolis
Myrina
Athens
0 50km

40°26′ N 25°35′ E
Samothraki
Voreio Aigaio
Greece

A beautiful island with fine plane and chestnut forests in the north, while the south is mostly covered with olive trees. Goats are everywhere and are the island's main delicacy. Samothraki is famous for the Sanctuary of the Great Gods set in a forest in the north of the island. The island has the highest peak in the Aegean (not counting Evvoia), with some fine waterfalls and a very good beach in the south at Pachia Ammos. The chora is charming with a lovely ruined Byzantine castle.

★★☆☆☆ Tourism level
★★★☆☆ Vegetation
★★☆☆☆ Beaches
★★★★☆ History

Information
www.samothraki.com
Telephone 25510 41465

Map
Road Editions (1:30000)

Area 180 sq km
Coastline 59 km
Highest point 1611 m (Fengari)

Permanent population 2712

Visitor capacity 601
12 hotels
551 hotel beds
50 other beds
1 campsite

Crowdfactor
18 people per sq km

Access
Alexandroupolis 2 hours

Connections
Alexandroupolis 4 daily
Limnos 3 weekly

Yacht facilities
Kamariotissa, Therma

Ranking among all Mediterranean islands

	Ran
Area	3
Population	7
Visitor capacity	10
Crowdfactor	17

7850 **Greece** Voreio Aigaio

Santorini (Thíra)

36°23' N 25°27' E
Santorini (Thira)
Kyklades
Greece

Created by an eruption thought to have been 2½ times greater than Krakatoa, spectacular Santorini is best viewed from a boat or from Ia at the northern point if the island. The still smouldering volcano can be visited on the island of Nea Kameni. The recently discovered Mycenean settlement at Akrotiri is fascinating and the monastery at Profitis Ilias is worth a visit. The rich soil of Santorini produces good wines.

★★★★★ Tourism level
★★☆☆☆ Vegetation
★★☆☆☆ Beaches
★★★★★ History

Information
www.thira.gr
Telephone 22860 22231

Map
Reise-Know-How (1:25000)

Area 76 sq km
Coastline 67 km
Highest point 567 m (Profitis Ilias)

Permanent population 13447

Visitor capacity 13087
252 hotels
9789 hotel beds
3298 other beds
3 campsites

Crowdfactor
348 people per sq km

Access
✈ Santorini

Connections
⛴ Pireas, Ios 4 daily
⛴ Kriti, Naxos, Thirasia 2 daily
⛴ Anafi daily

Yacht facilities
⛵ Vlikada

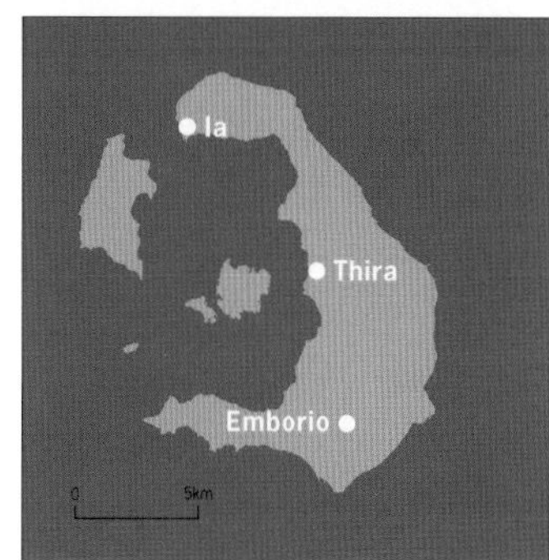
Ia
Thira
Emborio
0
5km

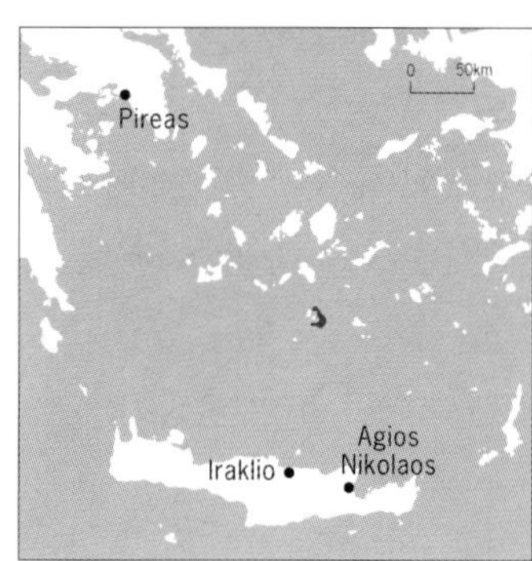
0
50km
Pireas
Iraklio
Agios Nikolaos

Kyklades **Greece** 6100

Ranking among all Mediterranean islands	Rank
Area	63
Population	33
Visitor capacity	24
Crowdfactor	33

Schoinoúsa

6720 **Greece** Kyklades

(PHOTO: CHARLES HAYNES)

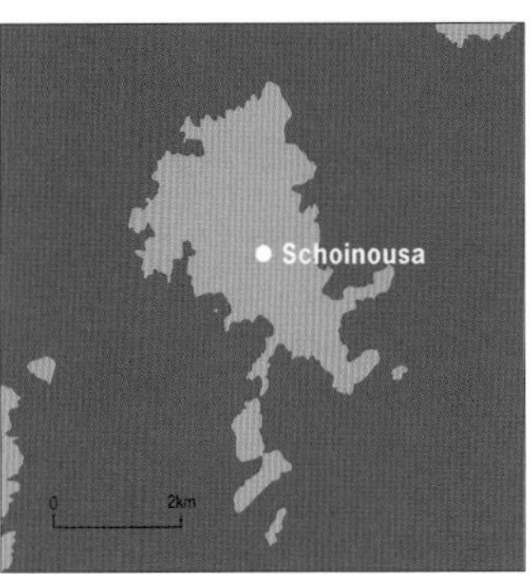

Schoinousa
0
2km

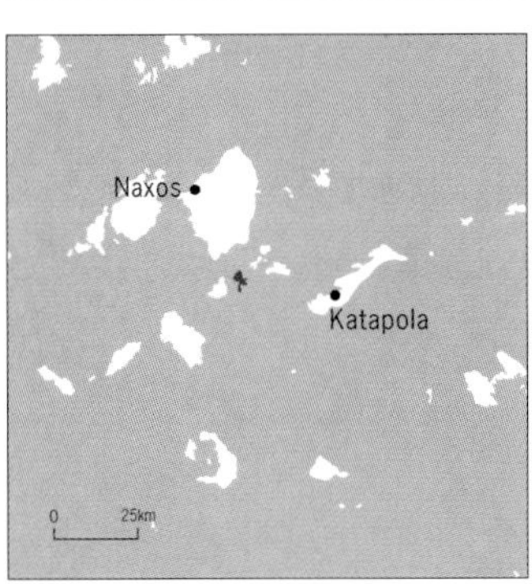

Naxos
Katapola
0
25km

36°53' N 25°31' E
Schoinousa
Kyklades
Greece

A rather attractive quiet island, with more than 15 beaches, some of them lovely, perfect for exploring on foot.

★☆☆☆☆ Tourism level
★☆☆☆☆ Vegetation
★★★☆☆ Beaches
★☆☆☆☆ History

Information
www.schinousa.gr
Telephone 22850 71170

Map
None

Area 8 sq km
Coastline 25 km
Highest point 134 m (Mylos)

Permanent population 197

Visitor capacity 83
1 hotel
58 hotel beds
25 other beds
0 campsites

Crowdfactor
34 people per sq km

Access
Naxos 1½ hours

Connections
Iraklia, Koufonisi, Naxos daily

Yacht facilities
no fuel

Ranking among all Mediterranean islands	Ran
Area	17
Population	15
Visitor capacity	16
Crowdfactor	15

37°09' N 24°29' E
Serifos
Kyklades
Greece

Serifos is mostly barren, but has an attractive chora with a marvellous view and some fine beaches. It is good walking country and the 16th century Taxiarchos monastery is worth visiting.

★★★☆☆ Tourism level
★★☆☆☆ Vegetation
★★★★☆ Beaches
★★☆☆☆ History

Information
www.serifos-island.com
Telephone 22810 51488

Map
Anavasi (1:20000)

Area 74 sq km
Coastline 83 km
Highest point 583 m (Troulos)

Permanent population 1262

Visitor capacity 592
10 hotels
306 hotel beds
286 other beds
1 campsite

Crowdfactor
24 people per sq km

Access
Pireas 2½ hours

Connections
Sifnos 4 daily
Pireas 3 daily
Kythnos 2 daily

Yacht facilities
Livadi

Serifos
Livadi
0
2km

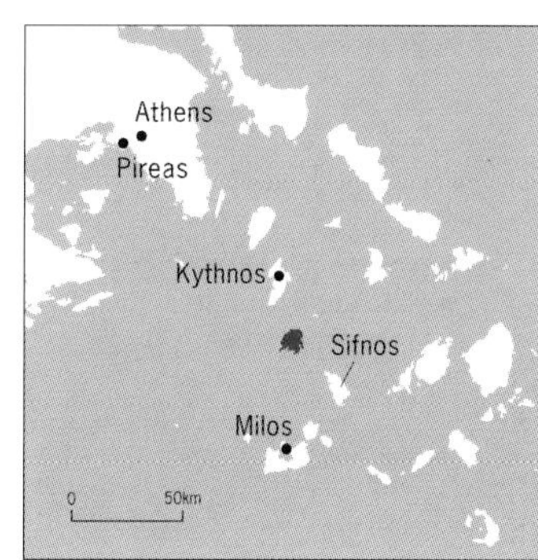
Athens
Pireas
Kythnos
Sifnos
Milos
0
50km

Ranking among all Mediterranean islands	Rank
Area	65
Population	101
Visitor capacity	107
Crowdfactor	164

Sífnos

Kamares
Apollonia
0
3km

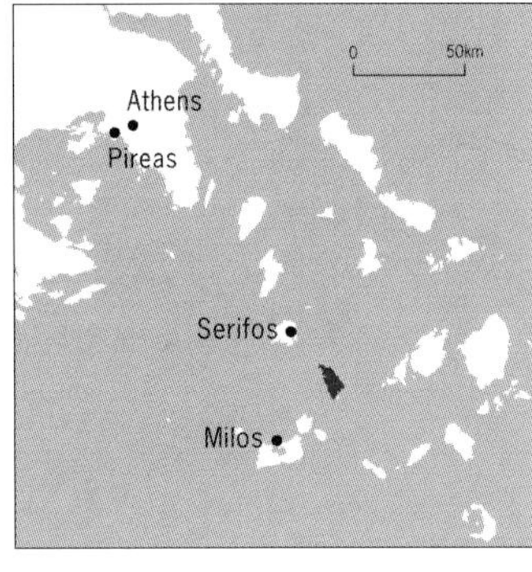

0
50km
Athens
Pireas
Serifos
Milos

37°00' N 24°42' E
Sifnos
Kyklades
Greece

The capital Apollonia and neighbouring Artemonas are attractive and the medieval kastro below is particularly so. There are fine views especially towards the archipelago of Paros and these, together with many chapels and towers, make Sifnos a good island for walking. It is not such a good island for driving, as the absence of road structure makes Apollonia a crossroads from all directions and often a bottleneck, but the bay of Vathi and the photogenic monastery of Chrysopigi are worth seeing. Sifnos is famous for food.

★★★☆☆ Tourism level
★★☆☆☆ Vegetation
★★★☆☆ Beaches
★★☆☆☆ History

Information
www.sifnos.e-sifnos.com
Telephone 22840 31977

Map
Anavasi (1:25000)

Area 77 sq km
Coastline 75 km
Highest point 682 m (Profitis Ilias)

Permanent population 2574

Visitor capacity 1180
26 hotels
832 hotel beds
348 other beds
2 campsites

Crowdfactor
48 people per sq km

Access
⛴ Serifos 30 minutes
⛴ Milos 1 hour

Connections
⛴ Serifos 4 daily
⛴ Milos 3 daily
⛴ Kimolos daily

Yacht facilities
⛵ Kamares

Ranking among all Mediterranean islands	Rar
Area	6
Population	8
Visitor capacity	7
Crowdfactor	13

6250 **Greece** Kyklades

36°41' N 25°08' E
Sikinos
Kyklades
Greece

The only road is from the port to the beautiful white unspoilt twin villages of Chora and Kastro. There are fine walks with splendid views in both directions from the capital, either past the ruined monastery of Zoodochos Pigi or through olive trees to the unusual monastery at Episkopi converted from a Byzantine church which had previously been a Roman mausoleum.

★★☆☆☆ Tourism level
★★☆☆☆ Vegetation
★★☆☆☆ Beaches
★★☆☆☆ History

Information
Telephone 22860 51238

Map
Anavasi (1:25000)

Area 41 sq km
Coastline 40 km
Highest point 553 m (Troulos)

Permanent population 238

Visitor capacity 95
1 hotel
37 hotel beds
58 other beds
0 campsites

Crowdfactor
7 people per sq km

Access
Ios 30 minutes

Connections
Ios, Folegandros daily

Yacht facilities
no fuel

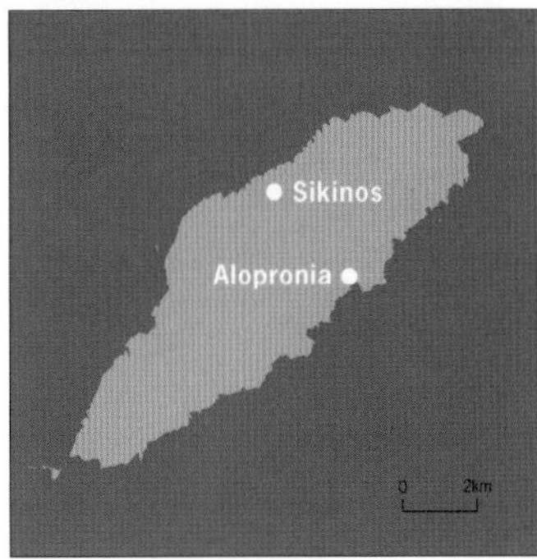
Sikinos
Alopronia
0
2km

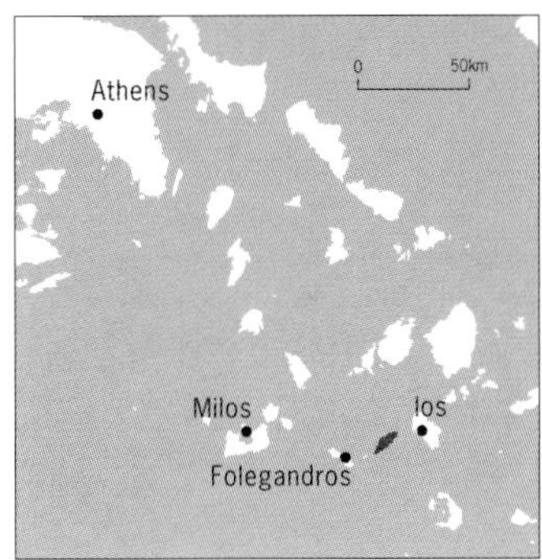
Athens
0
50km
Milos
Ios
Folegandros

Ranking among all Mediterranean islands

	Rank
Area	82
Population	144
Visitor capacity	158
Crowdfactor	205

Skiáthos

6900 **Greece** Vories Sporades

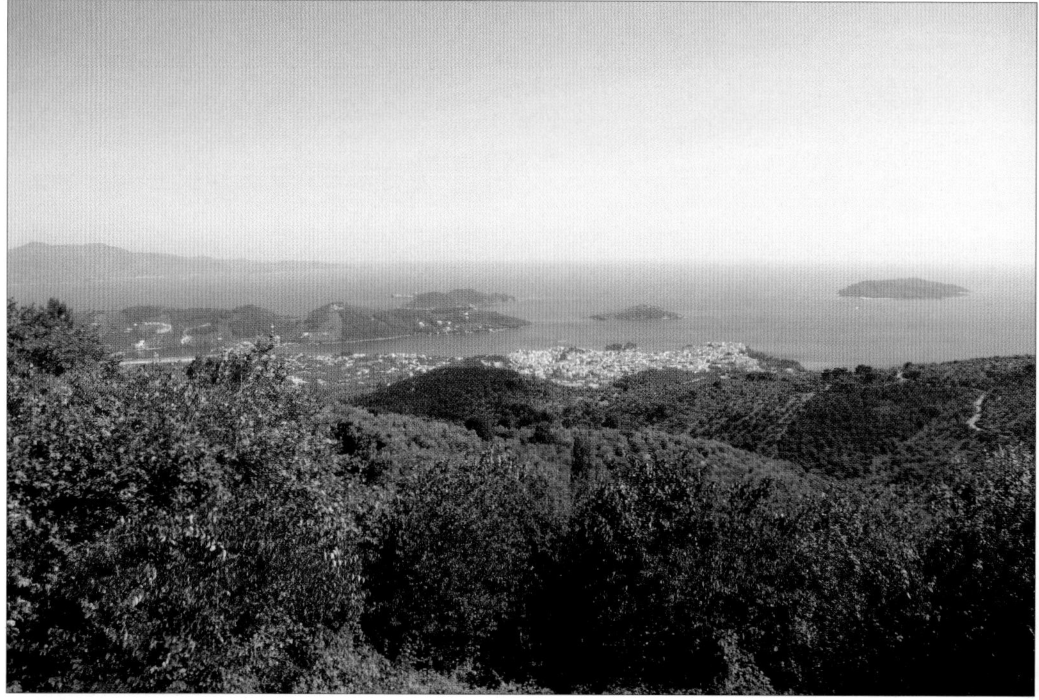

Skiathos
0 2km

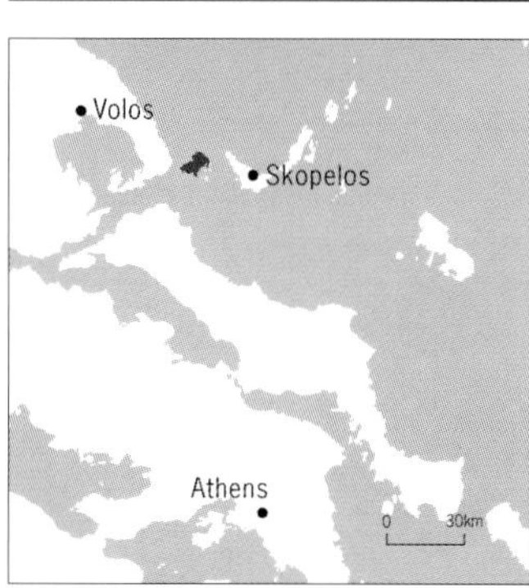

Volos
Skopelos
Athens
0 30km

39°10' N 23°28' E
Skiathos
Vories Sporades
Greece

Skiathos has a pretty town, rather crowded in summer, and the island is lovely, very wooded and with many fine beaches. The old kastro in the north of the island is worth visiting as are the monasteries of Evangelistria, Panagia Kechria and Kounistra. There are lovely views from the south coast over the offshore islets. Tsoungria in particular is a beautiful island and can be visited by boat.

★★★★☆ Tourism level
★★★★★ Vegetation
★★★★☆ Beaches
★★☆☆☆ History

Information
www.skiathos.gr
Telephone 24270 22990

Map
Anavasi (1:25000)

Area 47 sq km
Coastline 48 km
Highest point 433 m (Karafiltzanaka)

Permanent population 5788

Visitor capacity 7440
99 hotels
6514 hotel beds
926 other beds
1 campsite

Crowdfactor
280 people per sq km

Access
✈ Skiathos

Connections
⛴ Skopelos 4 daily
⛴ Volos 3 daily
⛴ Thessaloniki, Ag Konstantinos daily

Yacht facilities
⛵ Skiathos

Ranking among all Mediterranean islands	Ran
Area	7
Population	6
Visitor capacity	3
Crowdfactor	4

Skópelos

39°08' N 23°41' E
Skopelos
Vories Sporades
Greece

Heavily wooded Skopelos has a pretty town with many small churches and the road to the flowery village of Glossa at the other end of the island passes through magnificent scenery. It is also a fertile island, particularly known for its fine prunes, and has a number of monasteries and convents that are well worth visiting.

★★★☆☆ Tourism level
★★★★☆ Vegetation
★★★☆☆ Beaches
★★☆☆☆ History

Information
www.skopelos.gr
Telephone 24240 24567

Map
Anavasi (1:25000)

Area 95 sq km
Coastline 102 km
Highest point 681 m (Delfi)

Permanent population 4706

Visitor capacity 2849
47 hotels
2471 hotel beds
378 other beds
0 campsites

Crowdfactor
78 people per sq km

Access
Skiathos 20 minutes

Connections
Skiathos, Alonnisos 3 daily
Thessaloniki daily

Yacht facilities
Skopelos, Loutraki

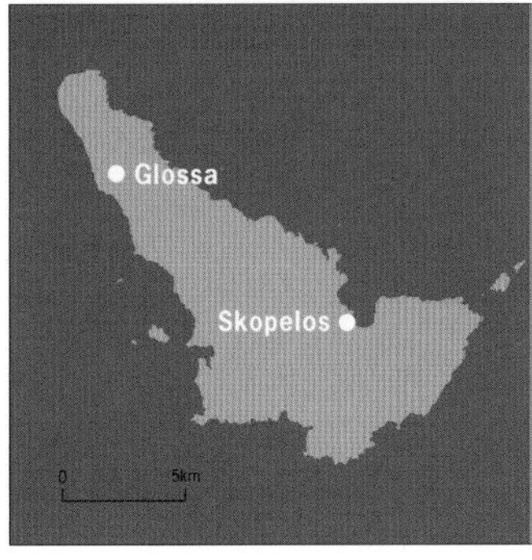
Glossa
Skopelos
0
5km

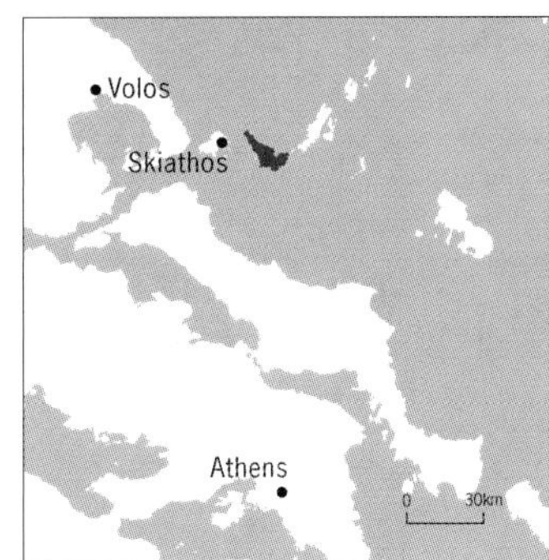
Volos
Skiathos
Athens
0
30km

Ranking among all Mediterranean islands

	Rank
Area	53
Population	64
Visitor capacity	52
Crowdfactor	101

Skýros

Atsitsa
Skyros
Linaria
0
5km

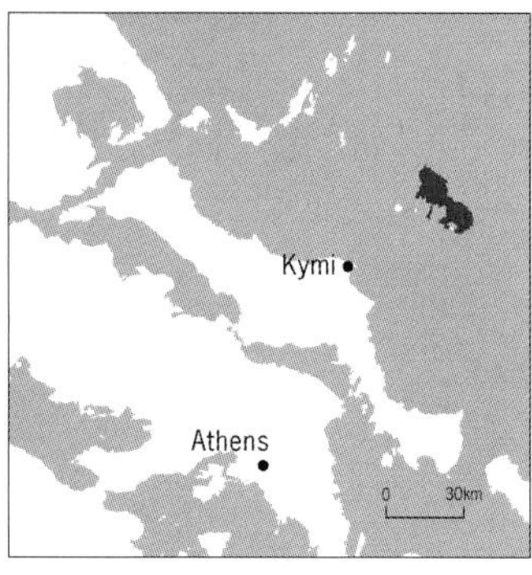
Kymi
Athens
0
30km

38°52' N 24°32' E
Skyros
Vories Sporades
Greece

Skyros is really two islands, the south barren and wild and the north wooded and lovely. It is a rewarding island to explore by foot or by car, but many of the roads are still rough. The town dominated by a Venetian castle looks as if it belongs in the Cyclades.

★★★☆☆ Tourism level
★★★☆☆ Vegetation
★★★☆☆ Beaches
★★☆☆☆ History

Information
www.inskyros.gr
Telephone 22290 91600

Map
Anavasi (1:40000)

Area 208 sq km
Coastline 134 km
Highest point 792 m (Kochilas)

Permanent population 2711

Visitor capacity 723
15 hotels
535 hotel beds
188 other beds
0 campsites

Crowdfactor
16 people per sq km

Access
Skyros
Kymi 2 hours

Connections
Kymi daily

Yacht facilities
Linaria

Ranking among all Mediterranean islands

	Ran
Area	3
Population	7
Visitor capacity	9
Crowdfactor	18

6850 **Greece** Vories Sporades

37°16' N 23°07' E
Spetses
Argosaronikos
Greece

A happy little island with horse-drawn carriages instead of cars where foreigners mix well with Athenians, many of whom own houses. The port is attractive and there are good beaches at Zogeria and Ag Anargiri, from where there is a lovely walk back over the top of the island through wonderfully scented pine forest. Boats run over to Kosta on the mainland opposite, where there are attractive secluded coves.

★★★★☆ Tourism level
★★★★★ Vegetation
★★★☆☆ Beaches
★★☆☆☆ History

Information
www.2spetses.gr
Telephone 22980 72215

Map
Road Editions (1:25000)

Area 20 sq km
Coastline 31 km
Highest point 245 m (Profitis Ilias)

Permanent population 3772

Visitor capacity 3149
19 hotels
961 hotel beds
2188 other beds
0 campsites

Crowdfactor
341 people per sq km

Access
Pireas 2 hours

Connections
Ydra 5 daily
Porto Cheli 3 daily
Kosta 6 daily

Yacht facilities
Baltiza, Dapia

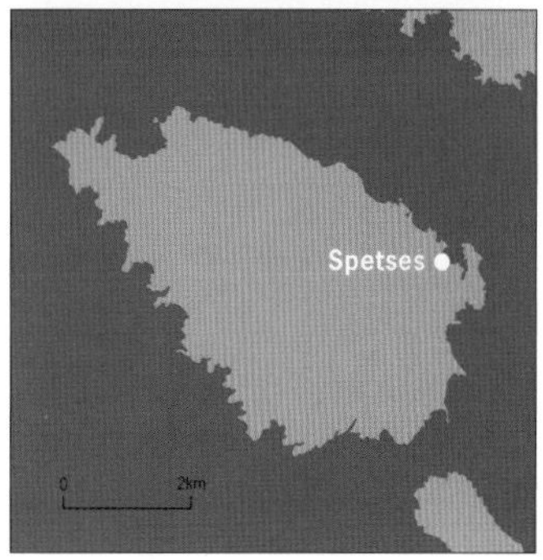
Spetses
0
2km

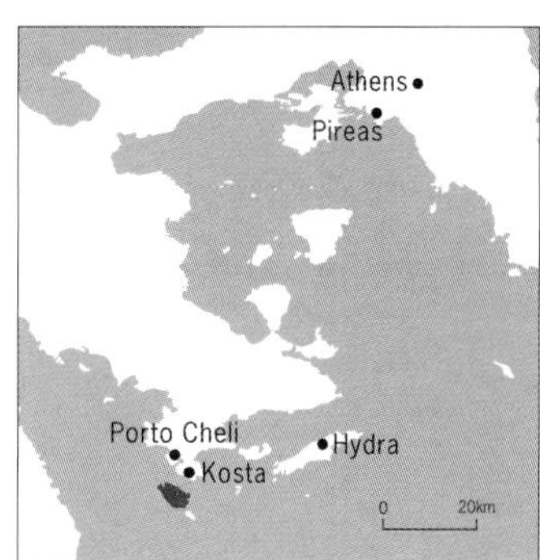
Athens
Pireas
Porto Cheli
Kosta
Hydra
0
20km

Ranking among all Mediterranean islands	Rank
Area	113
Population	68
Visitor capacity	48
Crowdfactor	34

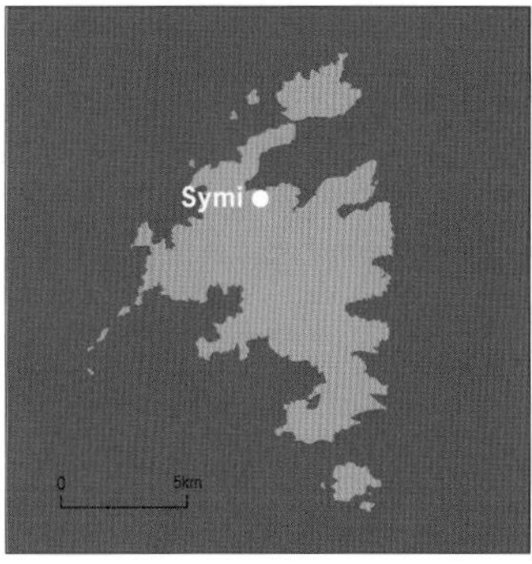
Symi
0
5km

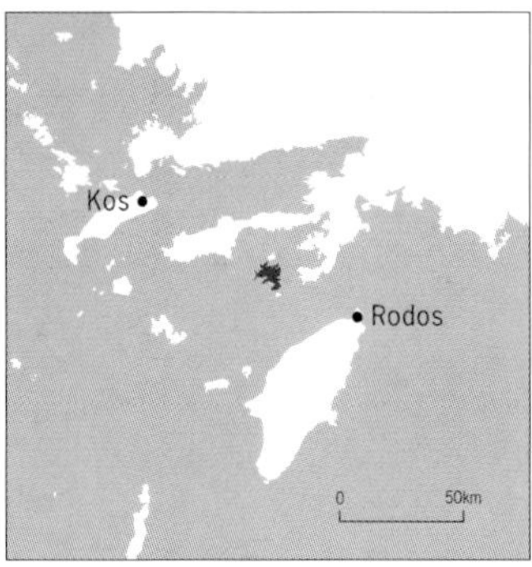
Kos
Rodos
0
50km

36°36' N 27°50' E
Symi
Dodekanisa
Greece

This otherwise quiet island is visited by large numbers of day-trippers from Rhodes. The town has elegant neo-classical houses and the upper town has a fine Knights' castle. In the south of the island is the huge Ag Panormitis monastery and there are walks to at least another dozen monasteries through rough arid terrain. Boats visit a number of beaches around the island and the neighbouring islands of Nimos and Seskli.

★★☆☆☆ Tourism level
★☆☆☆☆ Vegetation
★★☆☆☆ Beaches
★★☆☆☆ History

Information
www.symi.gr
Telephone 22460 71307

Map
Marengo (1:25000)

Area 57 sq km
Coastline 88 km
Highest point 617 m (Vigla)

Permanent population 2594

Visitor capacity 438
14 hotels
252 hotel beds
186 other beds
0 campsites

Crowdfactor
52 people per sq km

Access
⛴ Rodos 1 hour

Connections
⛴ Rodos 3 daily
⛴ Kos 2 daily

Yacht facilities
⛵ Symi

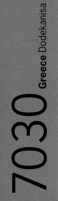

Ranking among all Mediterranean islands	Ran
Area	7
Population	8
Visitor capacity	11
Crowdfactor	13

37°28′ N 24°55′ E
Syros
Kyklades
Greece

An unusual island with a number of contrasts. Ermoupolis, the neo-classical capital of the Cyclades, is built round the impressive Plateia Miaoulis. Above is the medieval town Ano Syros and it is worth walking down from the Roman Catholic cathedral of St George to see one of the many fine views over Ermoupolis. The south of the island is built up and disappointing, while the north is wild and appealing. It can be seen either by driving up from Ano Syros or by staying in the little port of Kini and taking boats up to the beaches.

★★★☆☆ Tourism level
★☆☆☆☆ Vegetation
★★★☆☆ Beaches
★★☆☆☆ History

Information
www.welcome2syros.gr
Telephone 22810 83400

Map
Anavasi (1:25000)

Area 84 sq km
Coastline 84 km
Highest point 440 m (Pyrgos)

Permanent population 19793

Visitor capacity 3467
44 hotels
2127 hotel beds
1340 other beds
1 campsite

Crowdfactor
276 people per sq km

Access
✈ Syros
⛴ Pireas 3 hours

Connections
⛴ Pireas 7 daily
⛴ Tinos 4 daily
⛴ Paros, Rafina, Mykonos 2 daily

Yacht facilities
⛵ Ermoupolis, Finikas

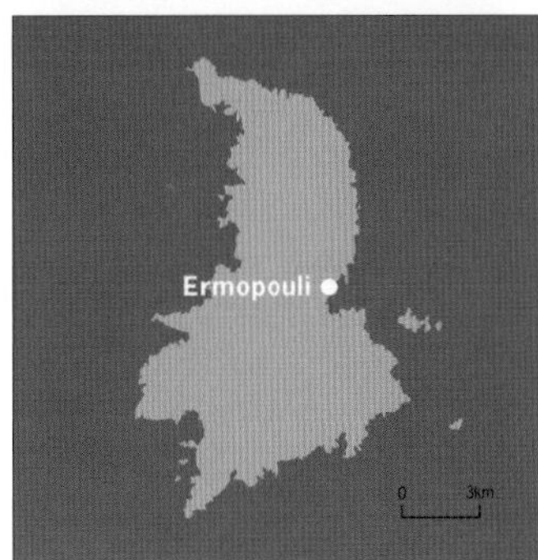
Ermopouli
0
3km

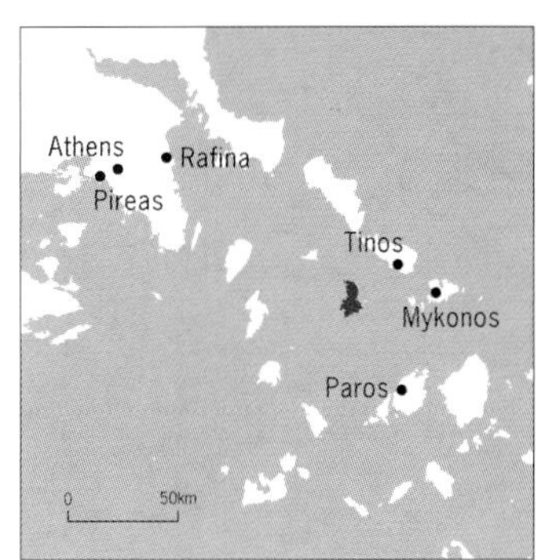
Athens
Rafina
Pireas
Tinos
Mykonos
Paros
0
50km

Ranking among all Mediterranean islands	Rank
Area	59
Population	25
Visitor capacity	47
Crowdfactor	44

Télendos

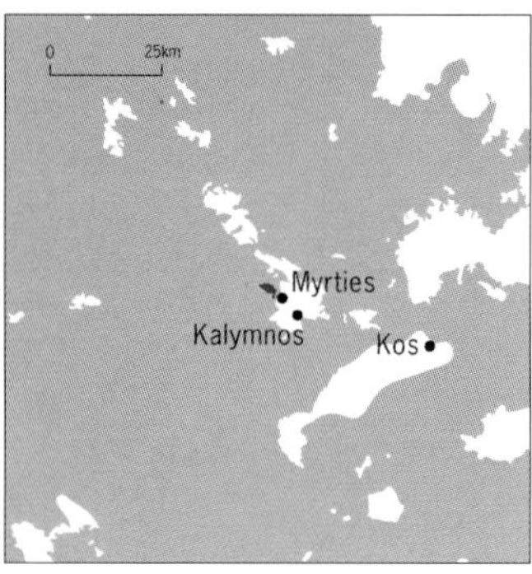
0
25km
Myrties
Kalymnos
Kos

37°01' N 26°54' E
Telendos
Dodekanisa
Greece

A relaxed little island with two monasteries, one ruined, good fish tavernas and strenuous walking.

★★☆☆☆ Tourism level
★★☆☆☆ Vegetation
★★☆☆☆ Beaches
★★☆☆☆ History

Information
www.telendos.com
Telephone 22430 47321

Map
Anavasi (1:25000)

Area 4.64 sq km
Coastline 12 km
Highest point 458 m (Rachi)

Permanent population 54

Visitor capacity 200
1 hotel
40 hotel beds
160 other beds
0 campsites

Crowdfactor
54 people per sq km

Access
Myrties 10 minutes

Connections
Myrties 30 daily

Yacht facilities
no fuel

Ranking among all Mediterranean islands

	Ran
Area	20
Population	18
Visitor capacity	13
Crowdfactor	12

7310 **Greece** Dodekanisa

Thásos

40°41' N 24°39' E
Thasos
Voreio Aigaio
Greece

Thasos is a beautiful mountainous green island with many fine beaches and wonderful walking. Although it has many visitors, the island is large enough to absorb them with ease. The town has one of the most interesting classical sites, with a fine theatre, several temple ruins, well-preserved 4th century walls and lovely views over the modern town.

★★★★☆ Tourism level
★★★★☆ Vegetation
★★★★☆ Beaches
★★★★☆ History

Information
www.gothassos.com
Telephone 25930 22546

Map
Drama 345 (1:70000)

Area 383 sq km
Coastline 116 km
Highest point 1205 m (Ipsario)

Permanent population 13447

Visitor capacity 8665
187 hotels
8037 hotel beds
628 other beds
6 campsites

Crowdfactor
57 people per sq km

Access
Kavala 45 minutes

Connections
Keramoti 12daily
Kavala 10 daily
Nea Peramos 3 daily

Yacht facilities
Thasos, Limenaria, Kalirachis

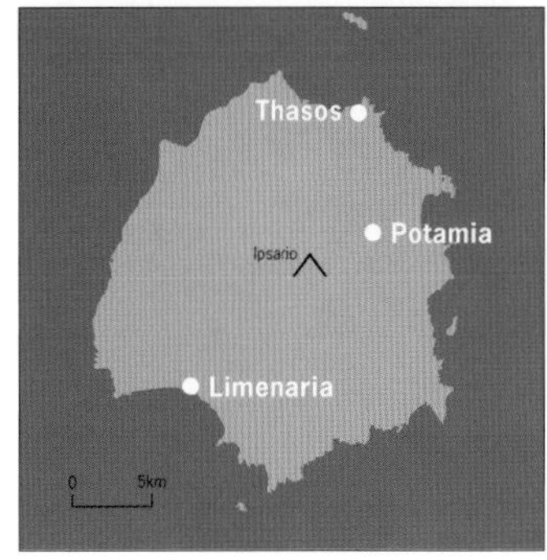
Thasos
Potamia
Ipsario
Limenaria
0
5km

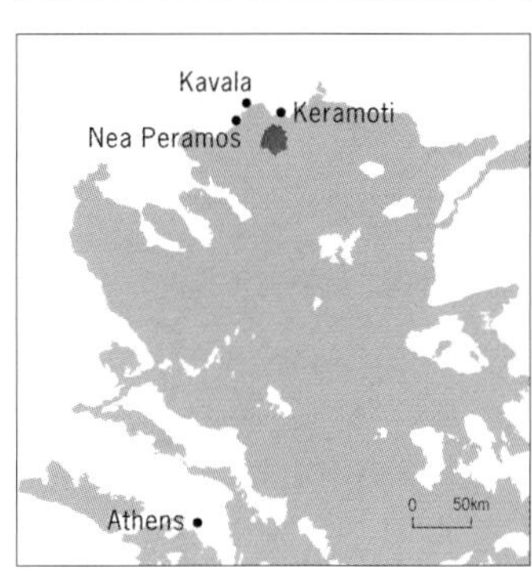
Kavala
Keramoti
Nea Peramos
Athens
0
50km

Ranking among all Mediterranean islands	Rank
Area	23
Population	33
Visitor capacity	31
Crowdfactor	121

Thirasía

6120 Greece Kyklades

(PHOTO: REGIONAL DEVELOPMENT AGENCY OF CYCLADES)

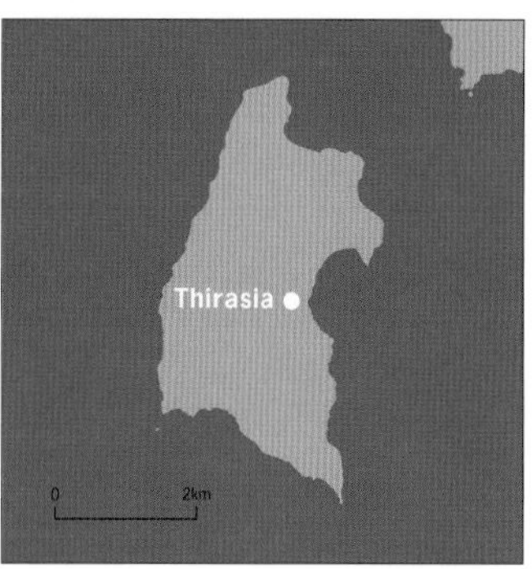

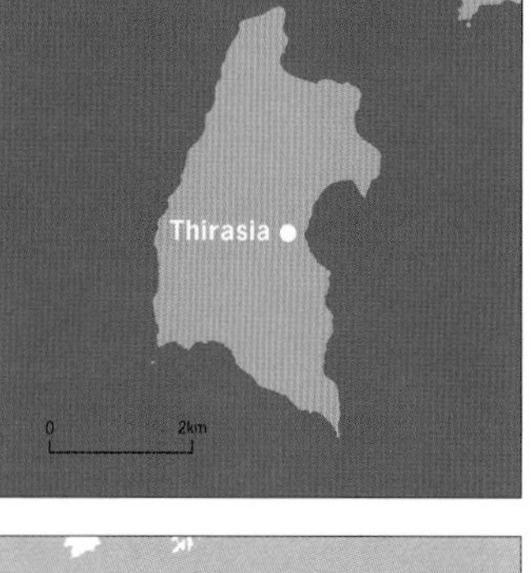
Thirasia
0
2km

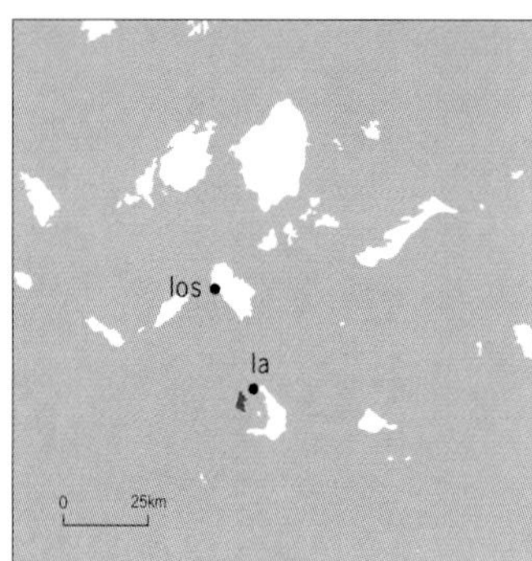
Ios
Ia
0
25km

36°26' N 25°20' E
Thirasia
Kyklades
Greece

The second largest piece of the rim of the Santorini volcano, Thirasia has a quiet pleasant village and spectacular views of Santorini itself.

★☆☆☆☆ Tourism level
★☆☆☆☆ Vegetation
★★☆☆☆ Beaches
★★☆☆☆ History

Information
www.thirasia.gr
Telephone 22860 29102

Map
Reise-Know-How (1:25000)

Area 9 sq km
Coastline 17 km
Highest point 294 m (Profitis Ilias)

Permanent population 278

Visitor capacity 18
0 hotels
0 hotel beds
18 other beds
0 campsites

Crowdfactor
32 people per sq km

Access
⛴ Ia 15 minutes

Connections
⛴ Ia 2 daily
⛴ Ios 3 weekly

Yacht facilities
⛵ no fuel

Ranking among all Mediterranean islands	Ran
Area	16
Population	13
Visitor capacity	19
Crowdfactor	15

37°35' N 26°25' E
Thymaina
Voreio Aigaio
Greece

Thymaina is a remote and traditional island, but has a friendly community. It has four beaches and is good for bird-watching.

★☆☆☆☆ Tourism level
★☆☆☆☆ Vegetation
★★☆☆☆ Beaches
★☆☆☆☆ History

Information
www.fourni.com
Telephone 22750 32797

Map
Road Editions (1:50000)

Area 10 sq km
Coastline 26 km
Highest point 470 m (Pasas)

Permanent population 151

Visitor capacity 9
0 hotels
0 hotel beds
9 other beds
0 campsites

Crowdfactor
15 people per sq km

Access
Fournoi 20 minutes

Connections
Fournoi, Samos 3 weekly

Yacht facilities
no fuel

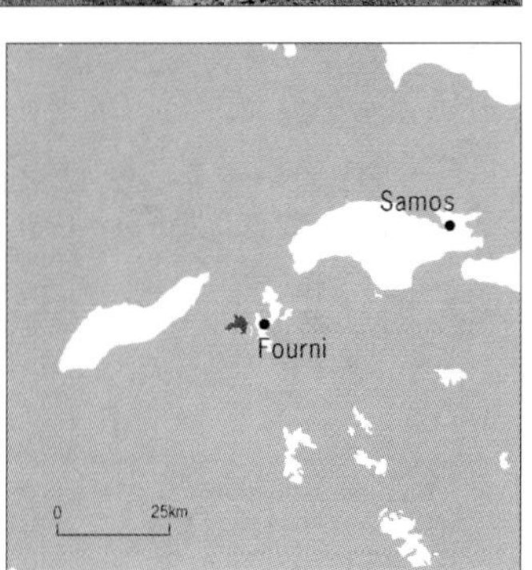
Samos
Fourni
0
25km

Ranking among all Mediterranean islands

	Rank
Area	157
Population	161
Visitor capacity	211
Crowdfactor	185

Tílos

7050 **Greece** Dodekanisa

(PHOTO: LAURA VIOLARDU)

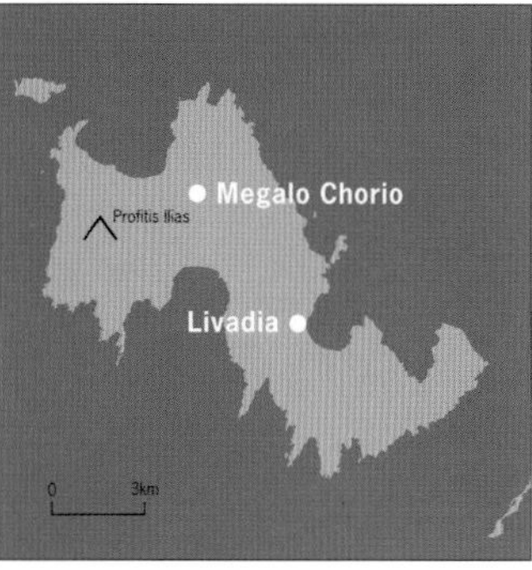
Megalo Chorio
Profitis Ilias
Livadia
0
3km

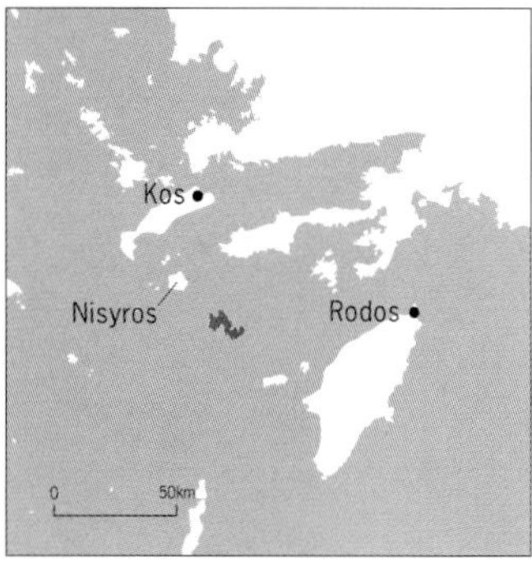
Kos
Nisyros
Rodos
0
50km

36°25' N 27°21' E
Tilos
Dodekanisa
Greece

A quiet and friendly island, Tilos has very good walking through attractive country often bare but sometimes fertile and always with very good views. The main sites are the 15th century Ag Pantelimon monastery on the west coast with a wonderful view and the fine setting of the castle above Megalo Chorio. There are several other castles on the island and a number of remote beaches, that at Eristos being the best.

★★☆☆☆ Tourism level
★★☆☆☆ Vegetation
★★★☆☆ Beaches
★★☆☆☆ History

Information
www.tilos.gr
Telephone 22460 44294

Map
Orama 332 (1:35000)

Area 61 sq km
Coastline 75 km
Highest point 651 m (Profitis Ilias)

Permanent population 521

Visitor capacity 442
4 hotels
204 hotel beds
238 other beds
0 campsites

Crowdfactor
15 people per sq km

Access
Rodos 2½ hours

Connections
Rodos 2 daily
Nisyros daily

Yacht facilities
Livadi

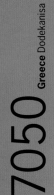

Ranking among all Mediterranean islands	Ran
Area	7
Population	12
Visitor capacity	11
Crowdfactor	18

37°37' N 25°10' E
Tinos
Kyklades
Greece

Tinos is a lovely island, best known for the miracle healing reputation of its Panagia Evangelistria shrine. The old village of Pyrgos in the north is delightful, with several marble sculptors' workshops and a charming little square in the middle. Sights worth seeing are the old Exombourgo fortress and the convent of Kechrovouni. The island is mostly bare but still a delight to explore with its many dovecotes and a large number of beaches.

★★★☆☆ Tourism level
★★★☆☆ Vegetation
★★★☆☆ Beaches
★★★☆☆ History

Information
www.tinos-tinos.com
Telephone 22830 23733

Map
Road Editions (1:40000)

Area 197 sq km
Coastline 114 km
Highest point 727 m (Tsiknias)

Permanent population 8115

Visitor capacity 3066
33 hotels
1872 hotel beds
1194 other beds
1 campsite

Crowdfactor
56 people per sq km

Access
Andros 1½ hours
Mykonos 30 minutes

Connections
Mykonos 10 daily
Rafina 7 daily
Syros, Andros 5 daily

Yacht facilities
Tinos

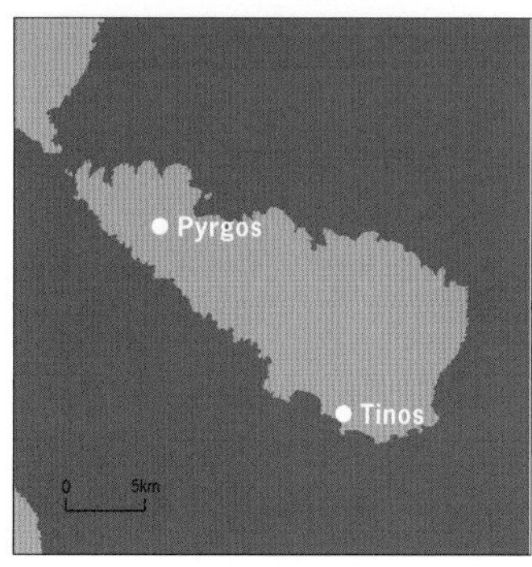
Pyrgos
Tinos
0
5km

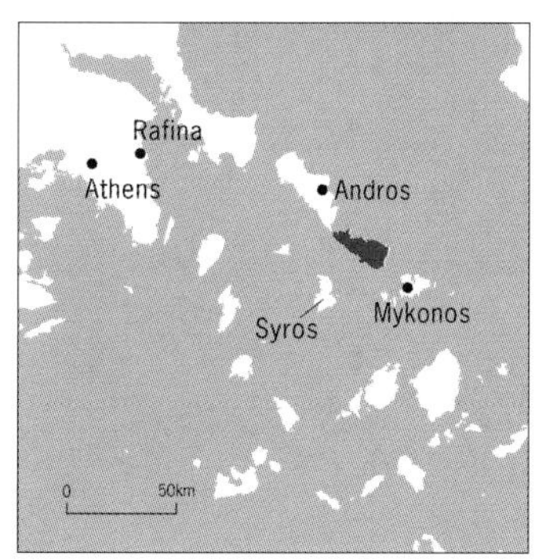
Rafina
Athens
Andros
Syros
Mykonos
0
50km

Ranking among all Mediterranean islands

	Rank
Area	37
Population	50
Visitor capacity	51
Crowdfactor	123

Trizónia

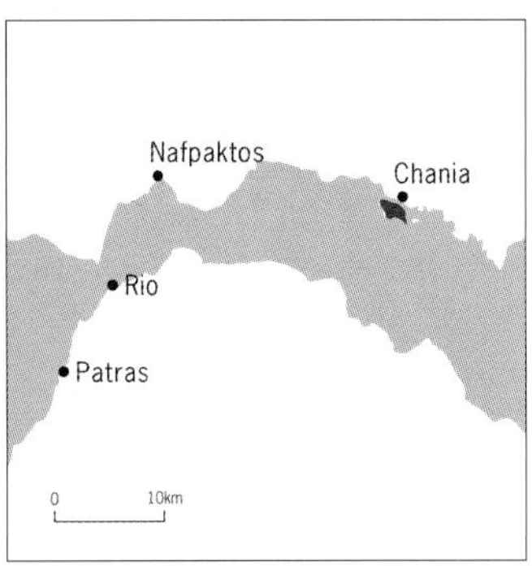
Nafpaktos
Chania
Rio
Patras
0
10km

38°22' N 22°04' E
Trizonia
Greece

Trizonia is a quiet and peaceful island with no cars, a fishing village and a harbour with 150 berths. It has a number of summer houses and a pleasant interior with olive groves.

★★★☆☆ Tourism level
★★★★☆ Vegetation
★★☆☆☆ Beaches
★☆☆☆☆ History

Information
Telephone 22660 71204

Map
None

Area 2.35 sq km
Coastline 9 km
Highest point 109 m (Aetorachi)

Permanent population 82

Visitor capacity 68
2 hotels
58 hotel beds
10 other beds
0 campsites

Crowdfactor
63 people per sq km

Access
Chania 5 minutes

Connections
Chania 15 daily

Yacht facilities
no fuel

5450 Greece

Ranking among all Mediterranean islands	Rar
Area	27
Population	17
Visitor capacity	16
Crowdfactor	11

37°21' N 23°30' E
Ydra
Argosaronikos
Greece

The town is attractive, with a number of fine old houses, but crowded mainly with day-trippers. There are no cars but lovely walks to the monasteries of Profitis Ilias and Zourvas and the convent of Ag Efpraxia.

★★★★☆ Tourism level
★☆☆☆☆ Vegetation
★★☆☆☆ Beaches
★★☆☆☆ History

Information
www.hydra-island.com
Telephone 22980 52184

Map
Anavasi (1:25000)

Area 49 sq km
Coastline 64 km
Highest point 588 m (Eros)

Permanent population 2629

Visitor capacity 1010
21 hotels
618 hotel beds
392 other beds
0 campsites

Crowdfactor
73 people per sq km

Access
⛴ Pireas 1 ½ hours

Connections
⛴ Spetses 3 daily
⛴ Pireas, Aigina 2 daily
⛴ Poros, Ermioni daily

Yacht facilities
⛵ no fuel

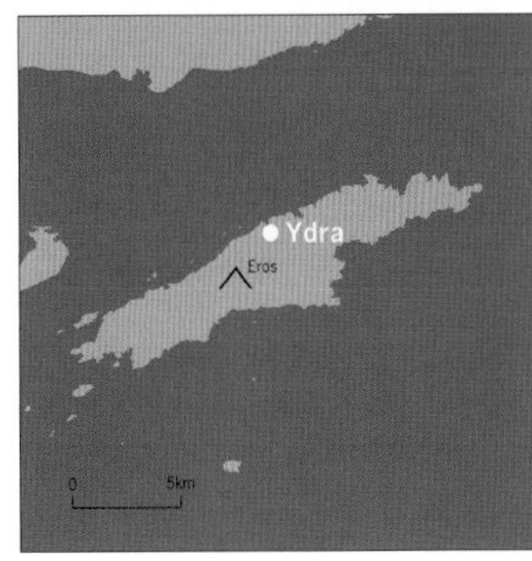
Ydra
Eros
0
5km

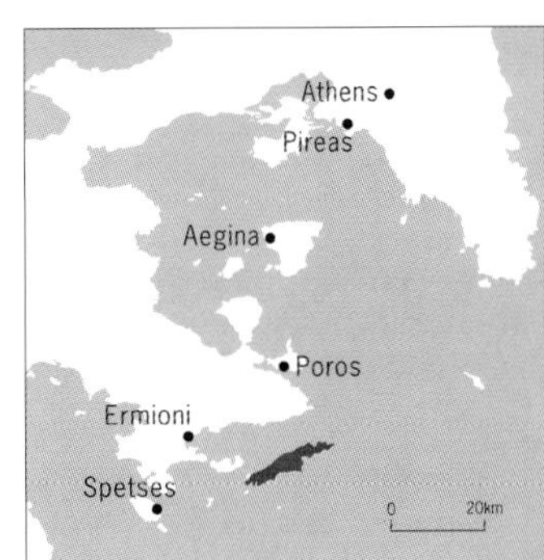
Athens
Pireas
Aegina
Poros
Ermioni
Spetses
0
20km

Ranking among all Mediterranean islands

	Rank
Area	77
Population	80
Visitor capacity	83
Crowdfactor	106

Zákynthos

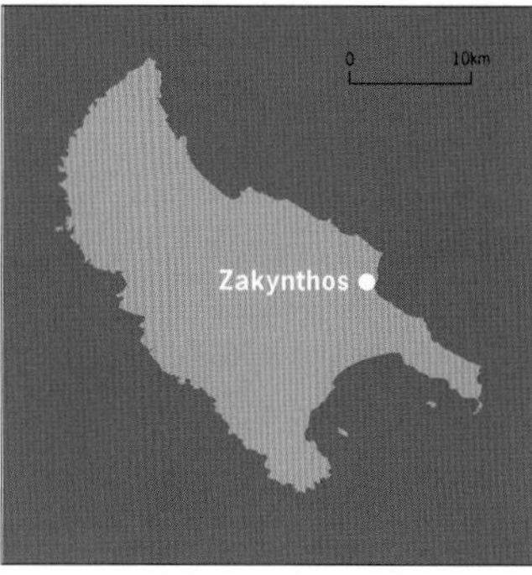
0 10km
Zakynthos

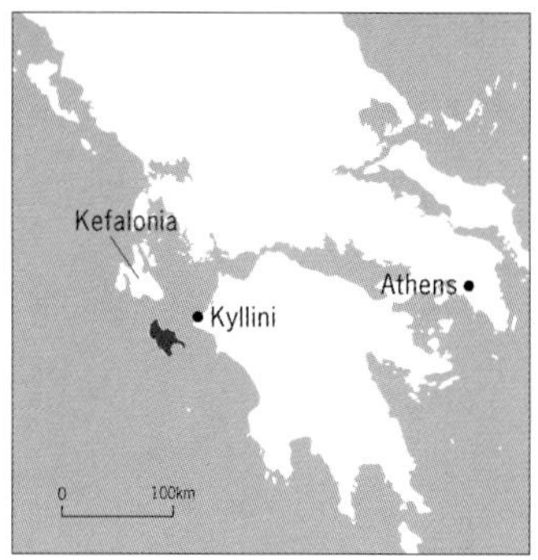
Kefalonia
Kyllini
Athens
0 100km

37°49' N 20°42' E
Zakynthos
Ionia Nisia
Greece

An island of great contrasts, with a bare and mountainous northwest and a very fertile centre famed for its currants and good wines. The fine town has suffered extensive earthquake damage, as have many though not all of the island's churches. The recent indiscriminate growth of mass market package tourism has spoilt much of the south and east of the island and created serious conflict with the largest turtle nesting grounds in the Mediterranean. The blue caves in the north and the views from flowery mount Skopos are worth seeing, but the natural tar springs at Keri have almost dried up.

★★★★☆ Tourism level
★★★★☆ Vegetation
★★★☆☆ Beaches
★★☆☆☆ History

Information
www.zakynthos.gr
Telephone 26950 22518

Map
Road Editions (1:60000)

Area 406 sq km
Coastline 156 km
Highest point 756 m (Vrachionas)

Permanent population 38825

Visitor capacity 27480
258 hotels
26426 hotel beds
1054 other beds
5 campsites

Crowdfactor
163 people per sq km

Access
✈ Zakynthos

Connections
⛴ Kyllini 8 daily
⛴ Kefalonia 2 daily

Yacht facilities
⛵ Zakynthos, Agios Nikolaos

Ranking among all Mediterranean islands	Ran
Area	1
Population	1
Visitor capacity	1
Crowdfactor	6

8300 Turkey

Alibey (Cunda)

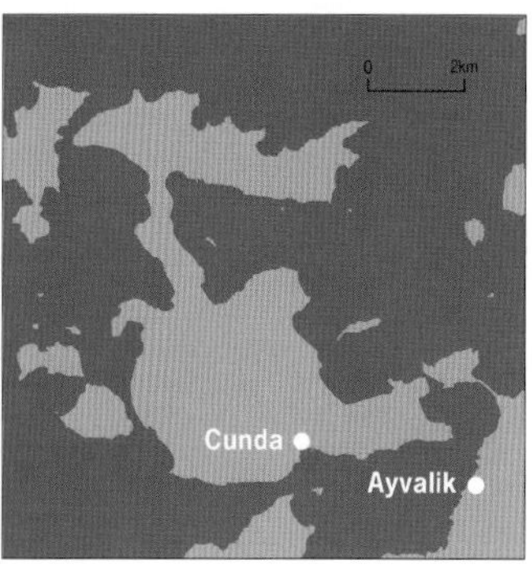
0
2km
Cunda
Ayvalik

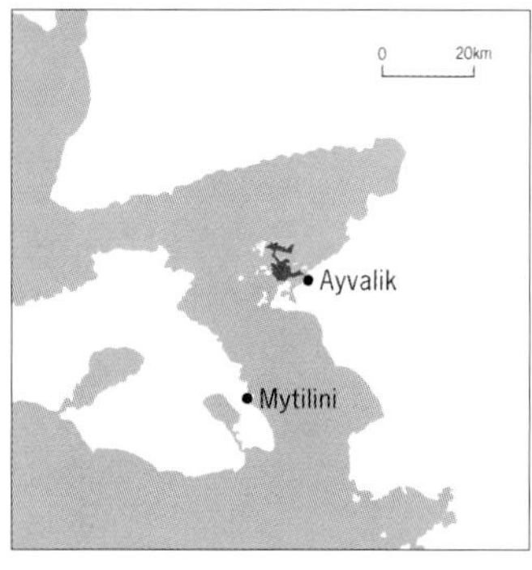
0
20km
Ayvalik
Mytilini

39°21' N 26°38' E
Alibey (Cunda)
Turkey

The largest of an archipelago of 20 islands not far from Lesvos. Alibey (sometimes called Cunda after its town) is a lovely island covered for the most part with fragrant pine trees and well endowed with beaches. All the churches dating from before the population exchange are now in ruins, but the town is otherwise attractive with winding cobbled streets and superb fish restaurants.

★★★☆☆ Tourism level
★★★★☆ Vegetation
★★★☆☆ Beaches
★★☆☆☆ History

Information

Map
None

Area 23 sq km
Coastline 28 km
Highest point 190 m (Alibey)

Permanent population 3500

Visitor capacity 1142
3 hotels
440 hotel beds
702 other beds
1 campsite

Crowdfactor
147 people per sq km

Access
Bridge to mainland

Yacht facilities
⛵ no fuel

Ranking among all Mediterranean islands

	Rank
Area	103
Population	87
Visitor capacity	79
Crowdfactor	69

Avşa (Turkeli)

40°30' N 27°31' E
Avşa (Turkeli)
Marmara Adalari
Turkey

This granite island is perhaps the most beautiful of the Marmara group, very green with lovely beaches and famous for its wine.

★★★☆☆ Tourism level
★★★☆☆ Vegetation
★★★★☆ Beaches
★★☆☆☆ History

Information
www.avsaadasi.org

Map
None

Area 20 sq km
Coastline 27 km
Highest point 191 m (Aliler)

Permanent population 2617

Visitor capacity 4737
10 hotels
2104 hotel beds
2633 other beds
0 campsites

Crowdfactor
356 people per sq km

Access
⛴ Istanbul 3 hours
⛴ Erdek 2 hours
⛴ Marmara 30 minutes

Connections
⛴ Istanbul 5 daily
⛴ Erdek 2 daily
⛴ Marmara daily

Yacht facilities
⛵ no fuel

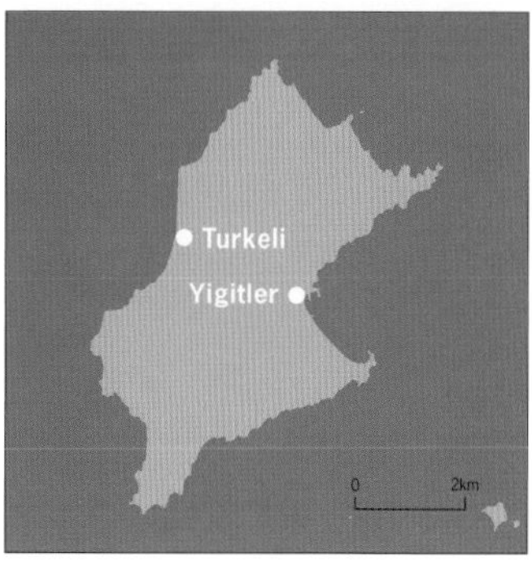
Turkeli
Yigitler
0
2km

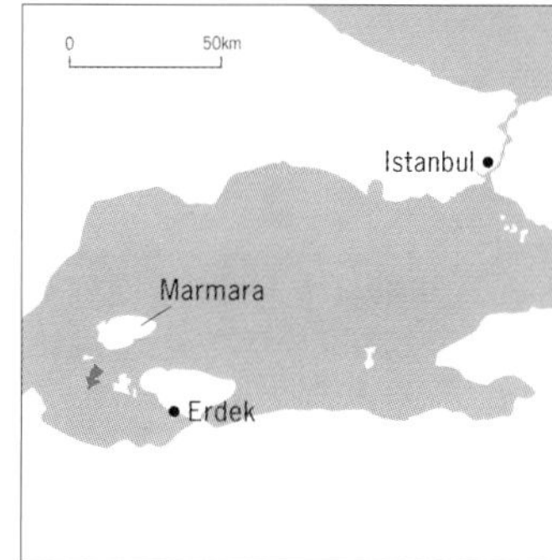
0
50km
Istanbul
Marmara
Erdek

Ranking among all Mediterranean islands	Rank
Area	110
Population	81
Visitor capacity	41
Crowdfactor	31

Marmara Adalari **Turkey** 8120

Bozcaada

Bozcaada
0 2km

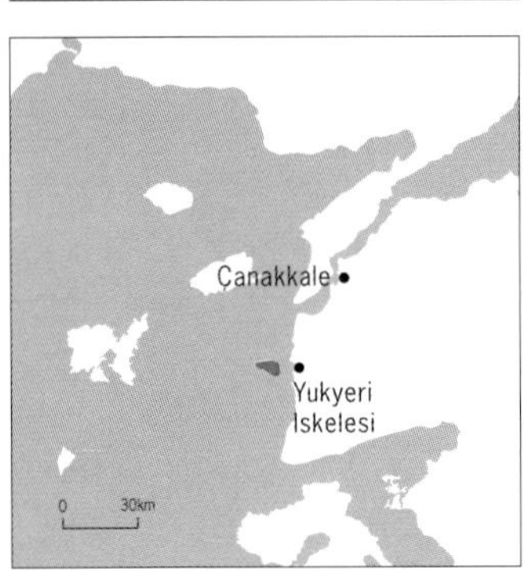
Çanakkale
Yukyeri
Iskelesi
0 30km

39°49′ N 26°02′ E
Bozcaada
Turkey

The ancient Tenedos, Bozcaada today is a quiet island, with an unspoilt little town of cobbled streets with overhanging houses, dominated by a magnificent fortress that dates back to before Venetian times. The south coast has fine sandy beaches, there are many vineyards producing an esteemed light white wine and there is almost no foreign tourism.

★★★☆☆ Tourism level
★★☆☆☆ Vegetation
★★★☆☆ Beaches
★★★☆☆ History

Information
www.bozcaadatenedos.com
Telephone

Map
None

Area 36 sq km
Coastline 34 km
Highest point 191 m (Goztepe)

Permanent population 2427

Visitor capacity 995
11 hotels
581 hotel beds
414 other beds
0 campsites

Crowdfactor
94 people per sq km

Access
Yukyeri Iskelesi 30 minutes

Connections
Yukyeri Iskelesi 4 daily

Yacht facilities
Bozcaada

8210 Turkey

Ranking among all Mediterranean islands

	Ra…
Area	8…
Population	8…
Visitor capacity	8…
Crowdfactor	9…

Burgazada

40°52' N 29°03' E
Burgazada
Prens Adalari
Turkey

A lovely pine-covered island still recovering from a devastating forest fire in 2003. The main sights are the church of St John the Baptist and the house of the famous Turkish writer Sait Faik.

★★★☆☆ Tourism level
★★★★☆ Vegetation
★★☆☆☆ Beaches
★★☆☆☆ History

nformation
'elephone 216 381 2660

Aap
None

Area 1.45 sq km
Coastline 5.7 km
Highest point 165 m (Christos Tepesi)

Permanent population 1578

Visitor capacity 45
1 hotels
45 hotel beds
0 other beds
0 campsites

Crowdfactor
1439 people per sq km

Access
Istanbul 40 minutes
Istanbul 1 hour

Connections
Istanbul 9 daily

Yacht facilities
no fuel

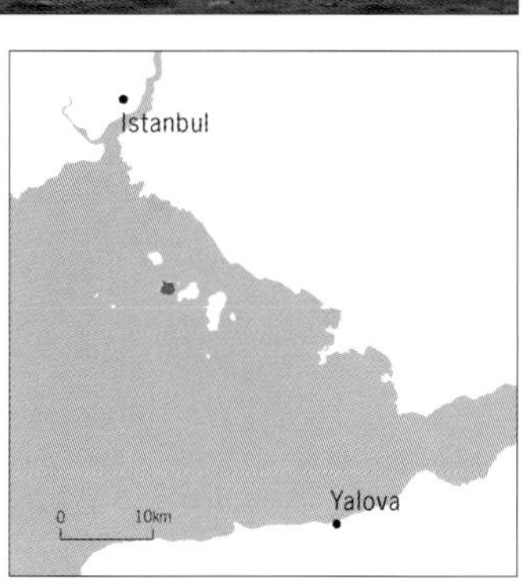
Istanbul
Yalova
0
10km

Prens Adalari **Turkey** 8020

anking among all Mediterranean islands	Rank
rea	315
opulation	90
isitor capacity	177
rowdfactor	15

Buyukada
0
1km

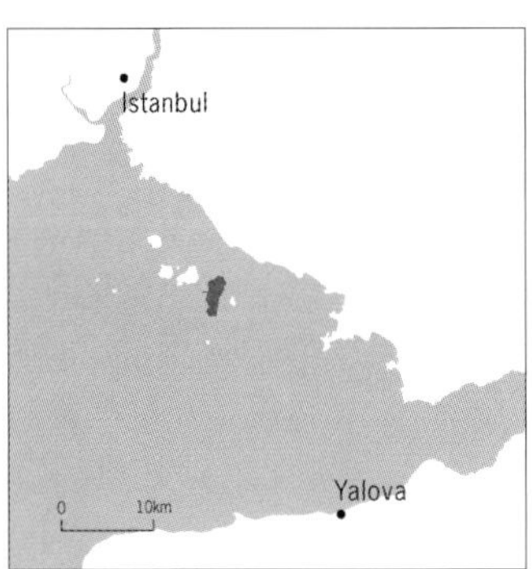
Istanbul
Yalova
0
10km

40°51' N 29°07' E
Büyükada
Prens Adalari
Turkey

The largest of the car-free Princes Islands, Büyükada is heavily populated in the north but quiet in the south which is covered in pine forest. Visitors choose between a short or long tour in a horse-drawn carriage, with the latter strongly recommended to take in the whole of this lovely island. The lanes lead past elegant villas through the scent of pine and jasmine to the top of the island with marvellous views, the monasteries of Christos and Ag Georgios, the church of Ag Dimitrios and the Hamidiye mosque.

★★★★☆ Tourism level
★★★★☆ Vegetation
★★☆☆☆ Beaches
★★★☆☆ History

Information
Telephone 216 282 7378

Map
Adalar Kultur Dernegi (1:15000)

Area 5 sq km
Coastline 14 km
Highest point 201 m (Yuce Tepesi)

Permanent population 7335

Visitor capacity 352
7 hotels
352 hotel beds
0 other beds
0 campsites

Crowdfactor
1366 people per sq km

Access
Istanbul 40 minutes

Connections
Istanbul, Yalova 15 daily

Yacht facilities
no fuel

Ranking among all Mediterranean islands	Ran
Area	19
Population	5
Visitor capacity	12
Crowdfactor	1

40°33' N 27°29' E
Ekinlik
Marmara Adalari
Turkey

Ekinlik is a peaceful small fishermen's island, quite green with olives and vines, on which a few rooms can be found.

★☆☆☆☆ Tourism level
★★★☆☆ Vegetation
★★☆☆☆ Beaches
★☆☆☆☆ History

Information
www.ekinlik.org

Map
None

Area 2.47 sq km
Coastline 10 km
Highest point 161 m

Permanent population 162

Visitor capacity 10
0 hotels
0 hotel beds
10 other beds
0 campsites

Crowdfactor
69 people per sq km

Access
Avşa 15 minutes
Marmara 45 minutes

Connections
Avşa, Marmara 4 weekly

Yacht facilities
no fuel

0
50km
İstanbul
Avsa
Erdek

Ranking among all Mediterranean islands	Rank
Area	264
Population	159
Visitor capacity	206
Crowdfactor	108

Imroz
0 5km

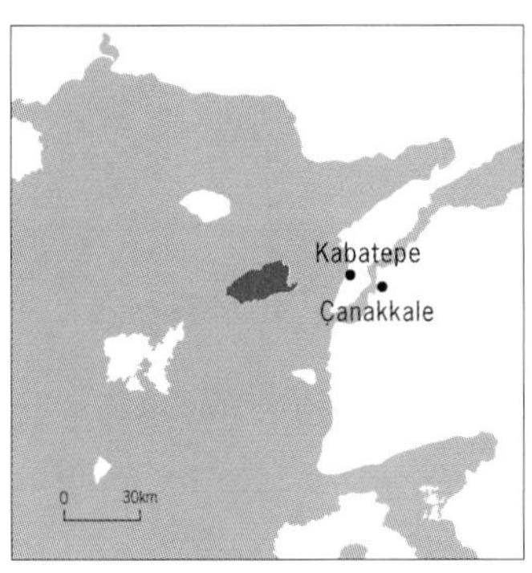
Kabatepe
Çanakkale
0 30km

40°10' N 25°50' E
Gökçeada (Imroz)
Turkey

The ancient Imbros, this mountainous island is mainly covered with sheep. For the most part it is relatively barren, but there is pine forest round Derekoy and cultivation of olives and vineyards making a reasonable wine. The capital has winding cobbled streets and a quiet charm.

★★★☆☆ Tourism level
★★★☆☆ Vegetation
★★★☆☆ Beaches
★★★☆☆ History

Information
www.gokceada.com

Map
None

Area 279 sq km
Coastline 92 km
Highest point 672 m (Aya Ilias Tepesi)

Permanent population 8875

Visitor capacity 585
7 hotels
537 hotel beds
48 other beds
0 campsites

Crowdfactor
24 people per sq km

Access
Kabatepe 1 ½ hours
Canakkale 3 hours

Connections
Kabatepe 6 daily
Canakkale daily

Yacht facilities
no fuel

Ranking among all Mediterranean islands	Ran
Area	3
Population	4
Visitor capacity	10
Crowdfactor	15

40°52′ N 29°05′ E
Heybeliada
Prens Adalari
Turkey

The visitor can choose between a long or short tour of this beautiful pine-covered island in a horse-drawn carriage. The main sights are the 11th century monastery of Ag Trias and the Byzantine Kamariotissa church and there are also the landmarks of the naval academy and sanatorium. The town has lovely old wooden houses but is relatively large and part of the island is occupied by the military.

★★★★☆ Tourism level
★★★★☆ Vegetation
★★☆☆☆ Beaches
★★☆☆☆ History

Information
Telephone 216 382 7378

Map
None

Area 2.46 sq km
Coastline 9 km
Highest point 136 m (Degirmen Tepesi)

Permanent population 5529

Visitor capacity 195
3 hotels
195 hotel beds
0 other beds
0 campsites

Crowdfactor
2735 people per sq km

Access
Istanbul 35 minutes
Istanbul 1½ hours

Connections
Istanbul 15 daily

Yacht facilities
no fuel

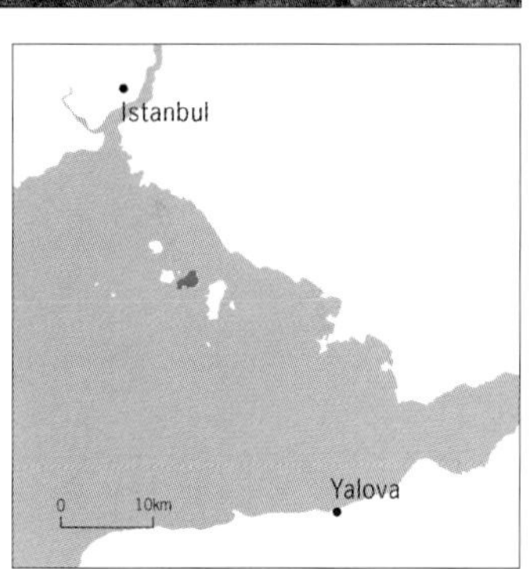
Istanbul
Yalova
0
10km

Ranking among all Mediterranean islands

	Rank
Area	265
Population	57
Visitor capacity	140
Crowdfactor	7

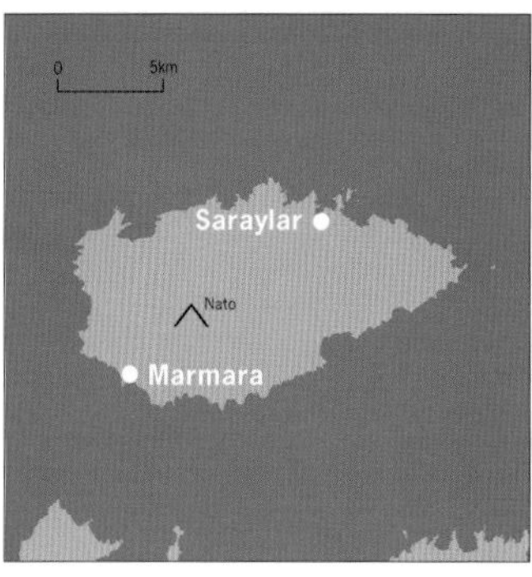
0
5km
Saraylar
Nato
Marmara

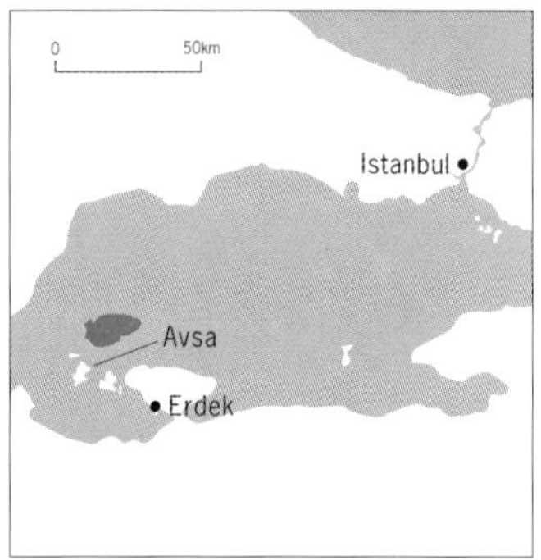
0
50km
Istanbul
Avsa
Erdek

40°37′ N 27°37′ E
Marmara
Marmara Adalari
Turkey

The largest of the Marmara group of islands and famous for the marble after which it is named. It is a well known holiday destination within Turkey but almost unknown outside the country.

★★★☆☆ Tourism level
★★★☆☆ Vegetation
★★★☆☆ Beaches
★★★☆☆ History

Information

Map
None

Area 117 sq km
Coastline 72 km
Highest point 699 m (Nato)

Permanent population 9446

Visitor capacity 10000
14 hotels
1200 hotel beds
8800 other beds
0 campsites

Crowdfactor
165 people per sq km

Access
Istanbul 3 hours
Erdek 2 hours
Avşa 30 minutes

Connections
Istanbul 5 daily
Erdek, Avşa daily

Yacht facilities
Marmara, Saraylar

Ranking among all Mediterranean islands	Ran
Area	4
Population	4
Visitor capacity	2
Crowdfactor	6

40°29' N 27°37' E
Paşalimanı
Marmara Adalari
Turkey

A simple unspoilt island, much less crowded than its two neighbours, which will appeal to those seeking a different and very quiet holiday. A knowledge of Turkish is essential.

★★☆☆☆ Tourism level
★★★☆☆ Vegetation
★★★☆☆ Beaches
★★☆☆☆ History

nformation

Map
None

Area 21 sq km
Coastline 40 km
Highest point 170 m

Permanent population 300

Visitor capacity 100
0 hotels
0 hotel beds
100 other beds
0 campsites

Crowdfactor
18 people per sq km

Access
Erdek, Avşa 1 hour

Connections
Erdek, Avşa 4 weekly

Yacht facilities
no fuel

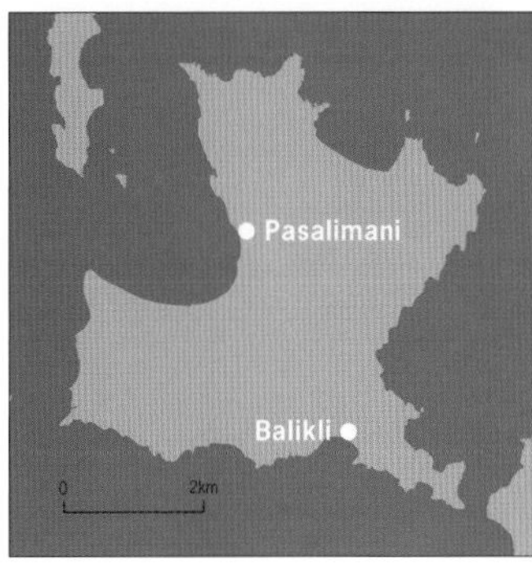
Pasalimani
Balikli
0
2km

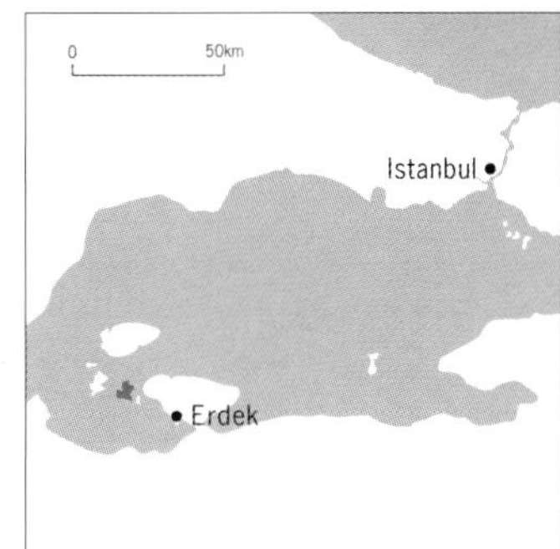
0
50km
Istanbul
Erdek

Ranking among all Mediterranean islands

	Rank
Area	108
Population	134
Visitor capacity	155
Crowdfactor	176

Nicosia
Olympus
Larnaca
Paphos
Limassol
0
50km

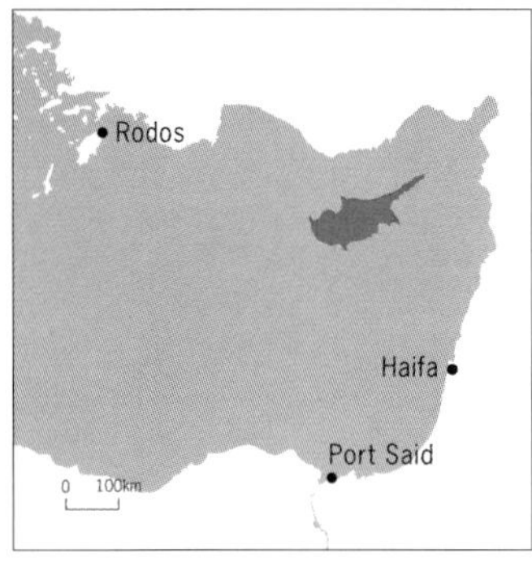
Rodos
Haifa
Port Said
0
100km

35°10' N 33°21' E
Cyprus

Cyprus has some of the finest beaches in the Mediterranean, particularly in the east, and the beach on the south side of the Karpas peninsular is unrivalled anywhere in Europe. Driving is on the left and more than half the visitors to the popular south coast are British. The centre of the island is dominated by the forest-covered Troodos mountains and the north by the steep narrow range of the mountains of Kyrenia, with the Mesaoria plain between. Communications between south and north are easing slowly.

★★★★☆ Tourism level
★★★☆☆ Vegetation
★★★★★ Beaches
★★★★☆ History

Information
www.visitcyprus.org
Telephone 22 691 100

Map
Insight (1:200000)

Area 9251 sq km
Coastline 782 km
Highest point 1953 m (Olympus)

Permanent population 953737

Visitor capacity 126380
700 hotels
89164 hotel beds
37216 other beds
10 campsites

Crowdfactor
116 people per sq km

Access
✈ Larnaca, Paphos, Ercan

Yacht facilities
⛵ 7 ports

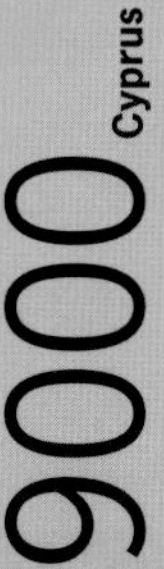

Ranking among all Mediterranean islands | Ran

Area
Population
Visitor capacity
Crowdfactor 7

36°01' N 14°20' E
Comino
Malta

Comino has many day-trippers who come to visit the famous Blue Lagoon opposite the islet of Cominotto with its very clear waters, but in the evening and early morning it is a peaceful place for those staying in the hotel, with pleasant walks and no cars.

★★★☆☆ Tourism level
★★☆☆☆ Vegetation
★★☆☆☆ Beaches
★★☆☆☆ History

Information
www.gozo.gov.mt
Telephone 22 915 000

Map
Malta Planning Authority (1:25000)

Area 2.7 sq km
Coastline 10 km
Highest point 75 m (Comino Hill)

Permanent population 4

Visitor capacity 282
1 hotel
282 hotel beds
0 other beds
0 campsites

Crowdfactor
102 people per sq km

Access
Cirkewwa 25 minutes
Mgarr 20 minutes

Connections
Cirkewwa, Mgarr 6 daily

Yacht facilities
no fuel

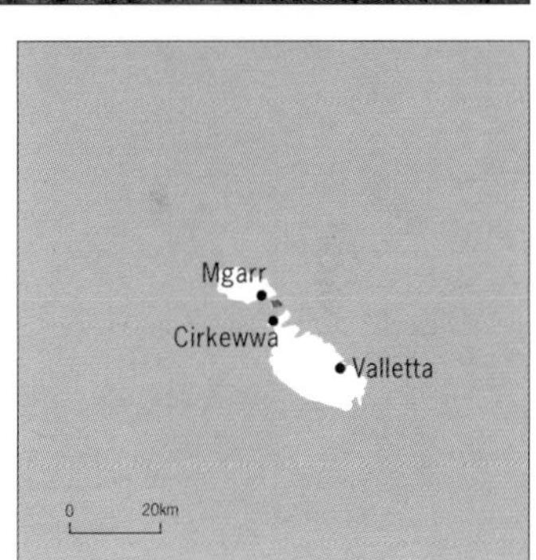
Mgarr
Cirkewwa
Valletta
0
20km

Ranking among all Mediterranean islands	Rank
Area	254
Population	218
Visitor capacity	128
Crowdfactor	86

Malta 9320

Gozo

(PHOTO: MALTA TOURISM AUTHORITY)

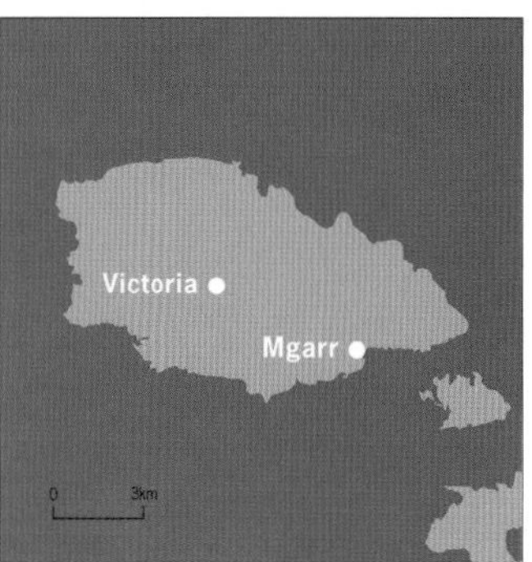
Victoria
Mgarr
0
3km

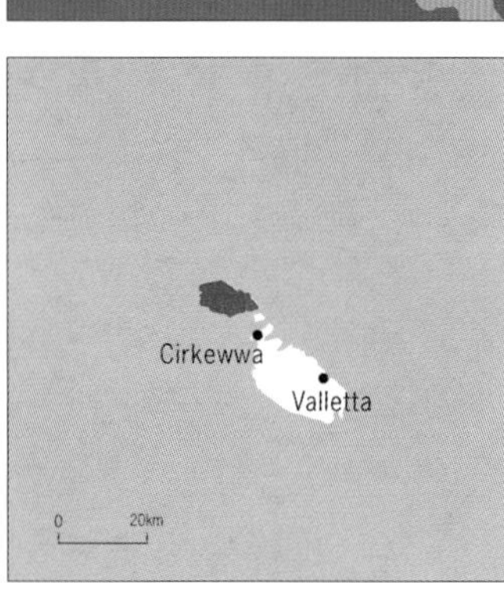
Cirkewwa
Valletta
0
20km

36°04′ N 14°13′ E
Gozo
Malta

Gozo has a different character from Malta, being quieter and greener with spectacular walks and views. There are several very nice hotels and well worth seeing are the fine old town of Victoria and the impressive megalithic temple at Ggantija.

★★★☆☆ Tourism level
★★★☆☆ Vegetation
★★☆☆☆ Beaches
★★★☆☆ History

Information
www.gozo.gov.mt
Telephone 22 915 000

Map
Malta Planning Authority (1:25000)

Area 67 sq km
Coastline 42 km
Highest point 191 m (Dbiegi)

Permanent population 31049

Visitor capacity 1504
9 hotels
1311 hotel beds
193 other beds
0 campsites

Crowdfactor
485 people per sq km

Access
⛴ Cirkewwa 25 minutes

Connections
⛴ Cirkewwa 25 daily

Yacht facilities
⛵ Mgarr

9310 Malta

Ranking among all Mediterranean islands	Rank
Area	66
Population	21
Visitor capacity	69
Crowdfactor	23

35°53′ N 14°30′ E
Malta

An immense sense of history pervades this densely populated island, starting with megalithic temples up to 6000 years old. The unique language has an Arabic base sprinkled with many words from Sicily, with which Malta shares a succession of cultures including Carthaginian, Saracen, Roman and Norman. Sights include the old capital Mdina, the catacombs of Rabat and the magnificent buildings left by the Knights.

★★★★★ Tourism level
★★☆☆☆ Vegetation
★★☆☆☆ Beaches
★★★★☆ History

Information
www.visitmalta.com
Telephone 22 915 000

Map
Malta Planning Authority (1:25000)

Area 245 sq km
Coastline 136 km
Highest point 253 m (Dingli Cliffs)

Permanent population 372986

Visitor capacity 37708
128 hotels
31094 hotel beds
6614 other beds
0 campsites

Crowdfactor
1671 people per sq km

Access
✈ Malta
⛴ Pozzallo 1½ hours

Connections
⛴ Pozzallo 4 weekly

Yacht facilities
⛵ Valletta, Msida, Taxbiex

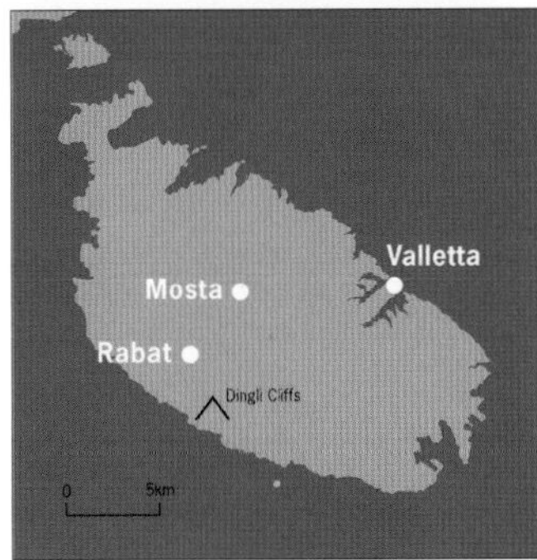
Valletta
Mosta
Rabat
Dingli Cliffs
0
5km

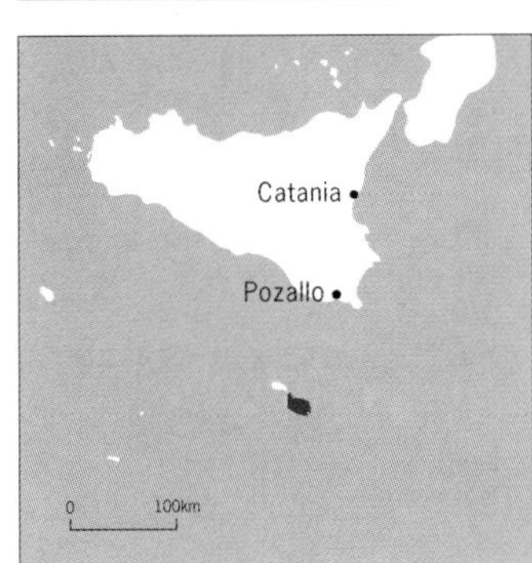
Catania
Pozallo
0
100km

Ranking among all Mediterranean islands	Rank
Area	34
Population	6
Visitor capacity	13
Crowdfactor	13

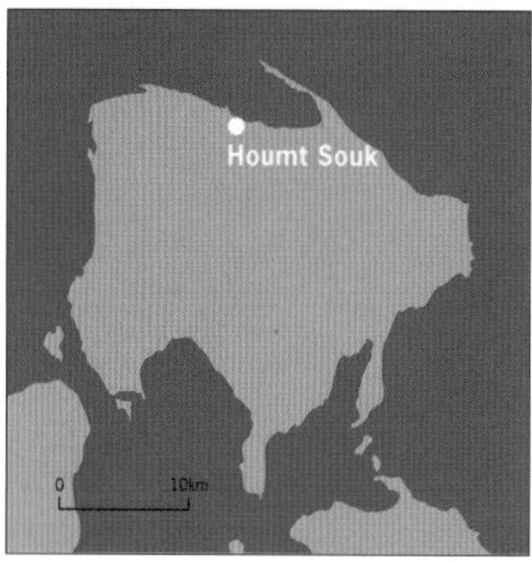
Houmt Souk
0
10km

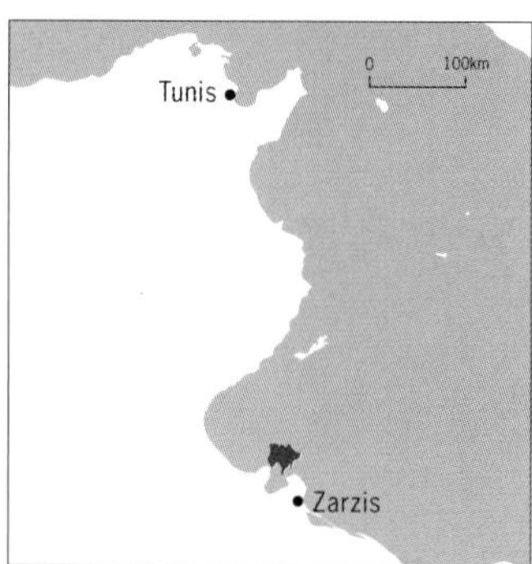
Tunis
0
100km
Zarzis

33°47' N 10°53' E
Djerba
Tunisia

Connected to the mainland by a 6 km long causeway, Djerba is a land of date oases and towards the centre of olives and fruit trees. The exception is the tourist strip of Sidi Mahrez in the north. Djerba is known for its crafts, particularly fine ceramics and weaving, and sights include the picturesque alleys of Houmt Souk, several fine mosques and the synagogue of La Ghriba.

★★★★☆ Tourism level
★★☆☆☆ Vegetation
★★★☆☆ Beaches
★★☆☆☆ History

Information
www.djerba.com
Telephone 075 650016

Map
Baedeker Mairs (1:75000)

Area 526 sq km
Coastline 137 km
Highest point 55 m (Musee ATP)

Permanent population 139544

Visitor capacity 54510
112 hotels
40610 hotel beds
13500 other beds
1 campsite

Crowdfactor
368 people per sq km

Access
✈ Djerba

Connections
Bridge to mainland

Yacht facilities
⛵ Houmt Souk

Ranking among all Mediterranean islands

	Ran
Area	1
Population	[illegible]
Visitor capacity	[illegible]
Crowdfactor	2

34°42′ N 11°11′ E
Kerkennah
Tunisia

The islands of Gharbi and Chergui are joined by a bridge to form Kerkennah. Flat and unspoilt, with very little tourist development, Kerkennah could be a perfect place for those seeking a quiet refuge. The arid landscape is broken by fig trees and palm trees, there are many wild flowers and species of birds and the shallow water is suitable for children.

★★★☆☆ Tourism level
★★☆☆☆ Vegetation
★★☆☆☆ Beaches
★★☆☆☆ History

Information
www.kerkennah.com
Telephone 074 497041

Map
None

Area 153 sq km
Coastline 138 km
Highest point 15 m

Permanent population 14400

Visitor capacity 687
3 hotels
383 hotel beds
304 other beds
0 campsites

Crowdfactor
98 people per sq km

Access
Sfax 1½ hours

Connections
Sfax 10 daily

Yacht facilities
no fuel

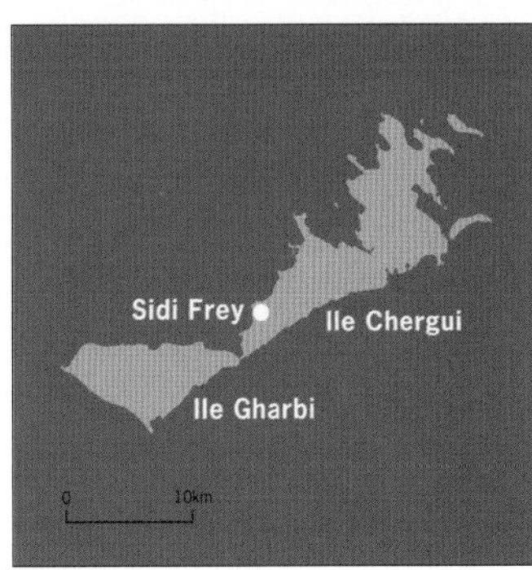
Sidi Frey
Ile Chergui
Ile Gharbi
0
10km

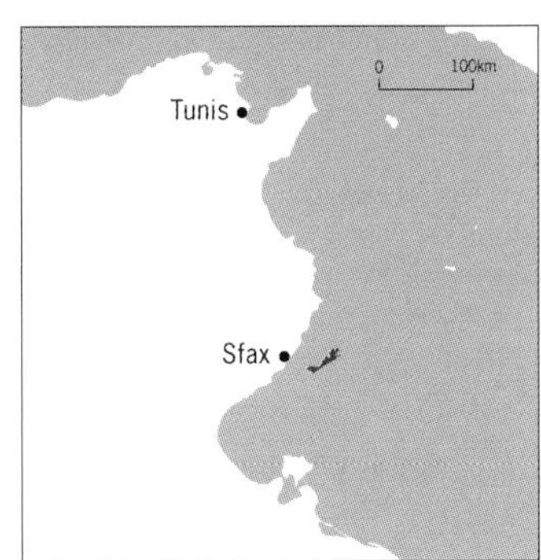
0
100km
Tunis
Sfax

Ranking among all Mediterranean islands

	Rank
Area	41
Population	31
Visitor capacity	100
Crowdfactor	89

The Islets

There are no generally accepted conventions about what defines an island and our first task has therefore been to make a definition of which islands to include in this book. We decided at the outset that we would include all islands with a surface area greater than one-tenth of a square kilometre, of which there are about 1,000 in the Mediterranean. All of these are listed and mapped in this section, apart from those which have already been covered in the Islands section, and we have also added some smaller islands which are of special interest. We have included only islands completely surrounded by the sea and so have excluded the islands of the Mar Menor, the Stagnone of Sicily and the lagoons of Mesologgi and Venice.

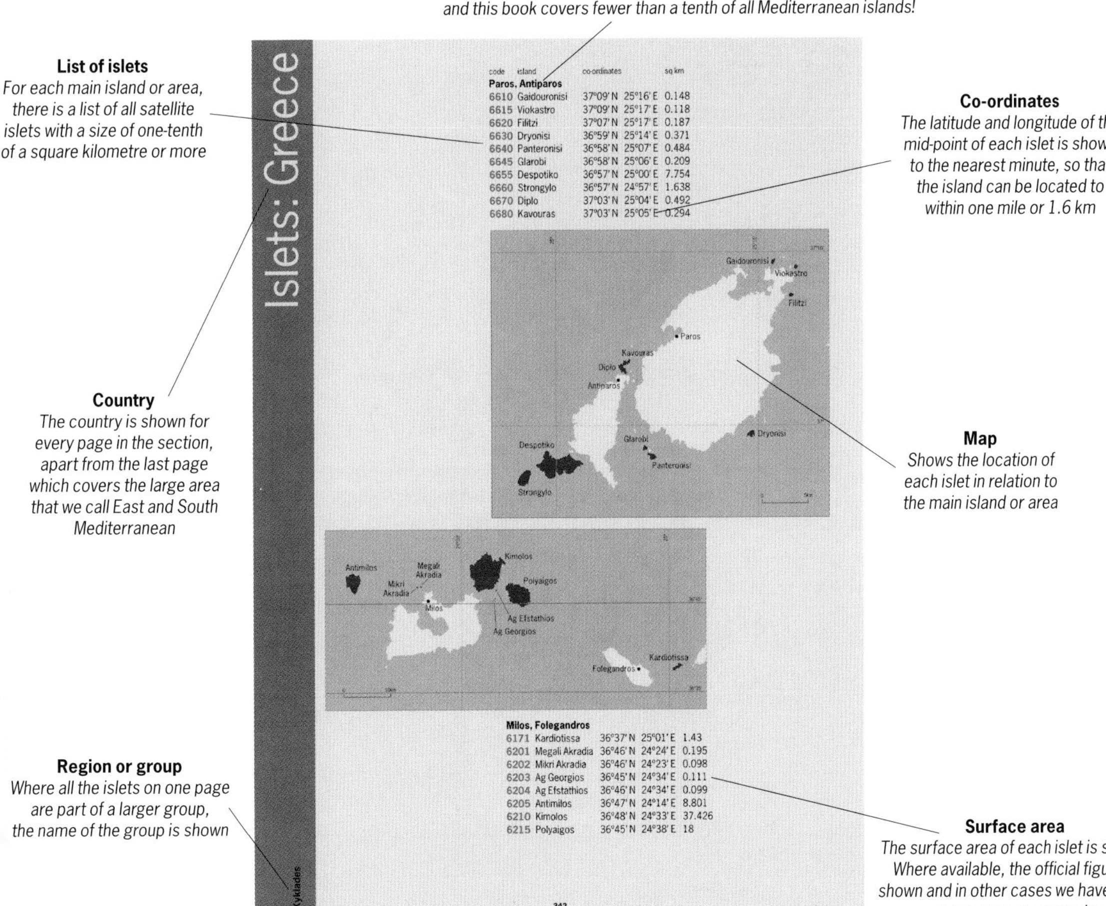

Names of islands
Names can change frequently in some countries, and there is scarcely an island which has not at some time had a different name. Where more than one name is in current use we show all and list each in the index. There is also the problem of shared names: a glance at the index will show how many islands have duplicate names (Agios Georgios, Piana or Tavsan for example) and this book covers fewer than a tenth of all Mediterranean islands!
List of islets
For each main island or area, there is a list of all satellite islets with a size of one-tenth of a square kilometre or more
Co-ordinates
The latitude and longitude of the mid-point of each islet is shown to the nearest minute, so that the island can be located to within one mile or 1.6 km
Country
The country is shown for every page in the section, apart from the last page which covers the large area that we call East and South Mediterranean
Map
Shows the location of each islet in relation to the main island or area
Region or group
Where all the islets on one page are part of a larger group, the name of the group is shown
Surface area
The surface area of each islet is shown. Where available, the official figure is shown and in other cases we have made our own measurements
Islets: Greece
code island co-ordinates sq km
Paros, Antiparos
6610 Gaidouronisi 37°09'N 25°16'E 0.148
6615 Viokastro 37°09'N 25°17'E 0.118
6620 Filitzi 37°07'N 25°17'E 0.187
6630 Dryonisi 36°59'N 25°14'E 0.371
6640 Panteronisi 36°58'N 25°07'E 0.484
6645 Glarobi 36°58'N 25°06'E 0.209
6655 Despotiko 36°57'N 25°00'E 7.754
6660 Strongylo 36°57'N 24°57'E 1.638
6670 Diplo 37°03'N 25°04'E 0.492
6680 Kavouras 37°03'N 25°05'E 0.294
Gaidouronisi
Viokastro
Filitzi
Paros
Kavouras
Diplo
Antiparos
Dryonisi
Despotiko
Glarobi
Panteronisi
Strongylo
Antimilos
Megali Akradia
Mikri Akradia
Kimolos
Polyaigos
Milos
Ag Efstathios
Ag Georgios
Kardiotissa
Folegandros
Milos, Folegandros
6171 Kardiotissa 36°37'N 25°01'E 1.43
6201 Megali Akradia 36°46'N 24°24'E 0.195
6202 Mikri Akradia 36°46'N 24°23'E 0.098
6203 Ag Georgios 36°45'N 24°34'E 0.111
6204 Ag Efstathios 36°46'N 24°34'E 0.099
6205 Antimilos 36°47'N 24°14'E 8.801
6210 Kimolos 36°48'N 24°33'E 37.426
6215 Polyaigos 36°45'N 24°38'E 18
Kyklades
342

code	island	co-ordinates		sq km
Mallorca, Cabrera				
1001	Dragonera	39°33′ N	02°18′ E	2.645
1002	Formentor	39°54′ N	03°08′ E	0.116
1050	Cabrera	39°08′ N	02°56′ E	11.479
1051	Conejera	39°10′ N	02°57′ E	1.375
1052	Redona	39°10′ N	02°58′ E	0.111

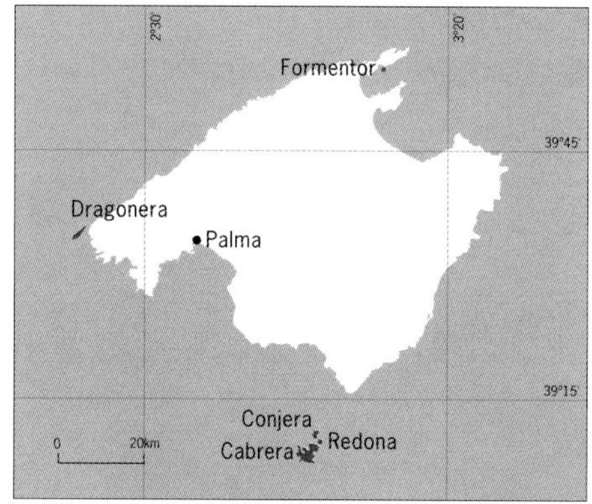
2°30′
3°20′
Formentor
39°45′
Dragonera
Palma
39°15′
Conjera
Cabrera
Redona
0
20km

Menorca

code	island	co-ordinates		sq km
1101	Colom	39°57′ N	04°16′ E	0.515
1102	Aire	39°48′ N	04°17′ E	0.328
1103	Lazareto	39°53′ N	04°17′ E	0.303

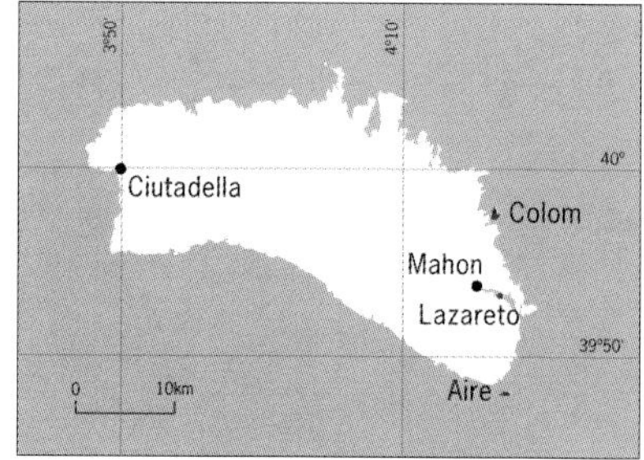
3°50′
4°10′
40°
Ciutadella
Colom
Mahon
Lazareto
39°50′
0
10km
Aire

1°20′
1°40′
Tagomago
Conejera
39°
Bosque
Espartar
Eivissa
Vedranell
Vedra
Espalmador
Espardell
La Savina
38°40′
0
10km

Eivissa, Formentera

code	island	co-ordinates		sq km
1201	Conejera	38°58′ N	01°12′ E	1.089
1202	Vedra	38°51′ N	01°11′ E	0.626
1203	Tagomago	39°02′ N	01°38′ E	0.617
1204	Espartar	38°57′ N	01°11′ E	0.203
1205	Bosque	38°58′ N	01°13′ E	0.181
1206	Vedranell	38°52′ N	01°12′ E	0.17
1301	Espalmador	38°47′ N	01°25′ E	1.435
1302	Espardell	38°47′ N	01°28′ E	0.513

Islets near mainland

code	island	co-ordinates		sq km
1400	Nueva Tabarca	38°09′ N	00°28′ W	0.43
1401	Meda Gran	42°02′ N	03°13′ E	0.182
1402	Columbretes	39°53′ N	00°40′ E	0.19
1403	Escombreras	37°31′ N	00°57′ W	0.04
1404	Alborán	35°55′ N	03°01′ W	0.0712
1405	Chafarinas	35°10′ N	02°25′ W	0.5
Algeria				
9500	Habibas	35°43′ N	01°07′ W	0.4
9501	Rachgoune	35°19′ N	01°28′ W	0.1

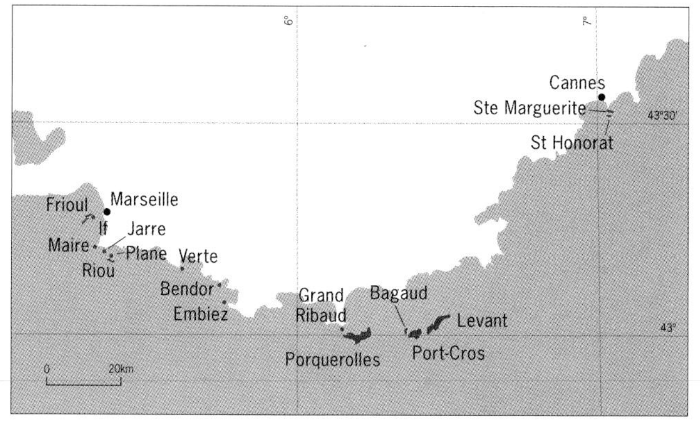

Cannes
Ste Marguerite
St Honorat
43°30'
Marseille
Frioul
If
Jarre
Maire
Plane
Verte
Riou
Bendor
Embiez
Grand
Ribaud
Bagaud
Levant
Porquerolles
Port-Cros
43°
0
20km
6°
7°

code	island	co-ordinates		sq km
Provence				
2100	Porquerolles	42°59' N	06°12' E	12.54
2101	Grand Ribaud	43°01' N	06°08' E	0.16
2200	Le Levant	43°01' N	06°27' E	9.96
2300	Port-Cros	43°00' N	06°23' E	6.75
2301	Bagaud	43°00' N	06°21' E	0.45
2400	Sainte Marguerite	43°31' N	07°02' E	2.1
2500	Saint Honorat	43°30' N	07°02' E	0.36
2600	Frioul	43°16' N	05°18' E	1.84
2601	If	43°16' N	05°19' E	0.035
2602	Riou	43°10' N	05°23' E	0.9
2603	Maire	43°12' N	05°20' E	0.28
2604	Jarre	43°11' N	05°21' E	0.18
2605	Plane	43°11' N	05°23' E	0.15
2606	Verte	43°09' N	05°37' E	0.15
2700	Embiez	43°04' N	05°45' E	0.9
2800	Bendor	43°07' N	05°44' E	0.08

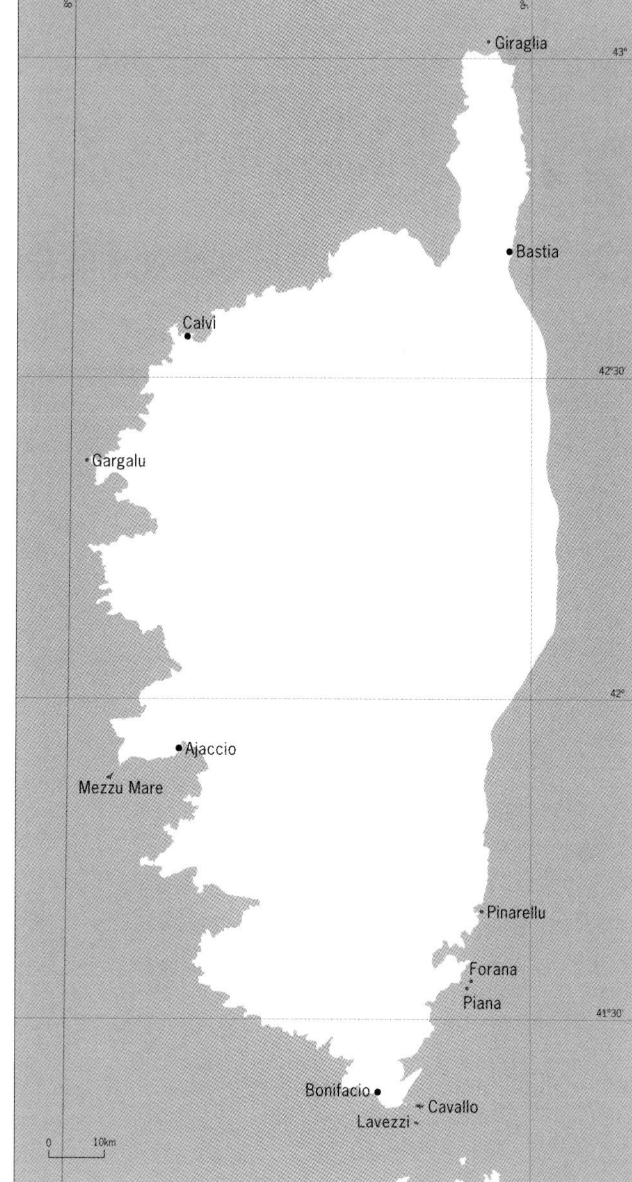

8°30'
9°30'
Giraglia
43°
Bastia
Calvi
42°30'
Gargalu
42°
Ajaccio
Mezzu Mare
Pinarellu
Forana
Piana
41°30'
Bonifacio
Cavallo
Lavezzi
0
10km

code	island	co-ordinates		sq km
Corsica				
010	Cavallo	41°22' N	09°15' E	1.204
020	Lavezzi	41°20' N	09°15' E	0.729
030	Mezzu Mare	41°52' N	08°35' E	0.372
040	Pinarellu	41°40' N	09°23' E	0.208
050	Piana (Cerbicale)	41°33' N	09°21' E	0.184
051	Forana	41°33' N	09°22' E	0.154
060	Gargalu	42°22' N	08°32' E	0.166
070	Giraglia	43°01' N	09°24' E	0.096

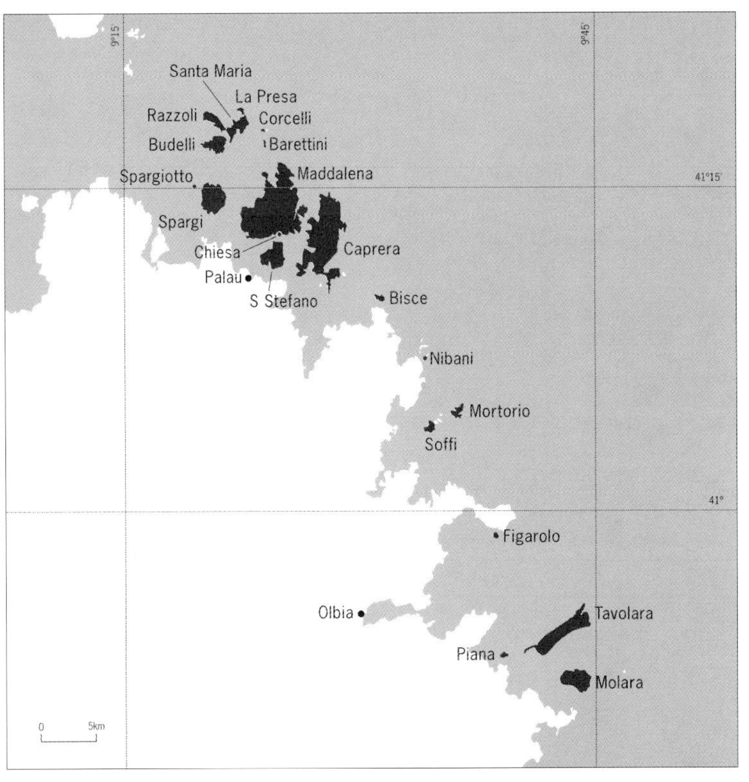
9°15'
9°45'
Santa Maria
La Presa
Razzoli
Corcelli
Budelli
Barettini
Spargiotto
Maddalena
41°15'
Spargi
Chiesa
Caprera
Palau
S Stefano
Bisce
Nibani
Mortorio
Soffi
41°
Figarolo
Olbia
Tavolara
Piana
Molara
0
5km

code	island	co-ordinates		sq km
Northeast Sardinia				
3550	Tavolara	40°54′ N	09°42′ E	4.7
3551	Piana (Tavolara)	40°53′ N	09°39′ E	0.13
3552	Molara	40°52′ N	09°43′ E	3.48
3553	Figarolo	40°58′ N	09°38′ E	0.22
3554	Soffi	41°03′ N	09°34′ E	0.43
3556	Mortorio	41°04′ N	09°36′ E	0.55
3558	Nibani	41°06′ N	09°34′ E	0.06
3559	Bisce	41°09′ N	09°31′ E	0.28
3600	Maddalena	41°13′ N	09°24′ E	20.17
3601	Chiesa	41°12′ N	09°25′ E	0.06
3610	Caprera	41°12′ N	09°27′ E	15.74
3620	Spargi	41°14′ N	09°20′ E	4.24
3525	Spargiotto	41°14′ N	09°19′ E	0.11
3630	Santo Stefano	41°11′ N	09°24′ E	3.01
3640	Santa Maria	41°17′ N	09°22′ E	1.86
3545	Corcelli	41°17′ N	09°24′ E	0.12
3648	Barettini	41°17′ N	09°24′ E	0.1
3650	Budelli	41°16′ N	09°20′ E	1.73
3660	Razzoli	41°18′ N	09°20′ E	1.64
3670	La Presa	41°18′ N	09°22′ E	0.29
Islets off Sardinia				
3510	Sant'Antioco	39°02′ N	08°24′ E	109.02
3515	Toro	38°56′ N	08°27′ E	0.13
3516	Rossa	38°54′ N	08°42′ E	0.11
3520	San Pietro	39°08′ N	08°16′ E	50.96
3525	Piana (San Pietro)	39°11′ N	08°19′ E	0.21
3530	Asinara	41°03′ N	08°15′ E	51.3
3535	Piana (Asinara)	40°58′ N	08°13′ E	118
3540	Mal di Ventre	39°59′ N	08°18′ E	0.88
3545	Piana (Capo Caccia)	40°36′ N	08°08′ E	0.13
3560	Cavoli	39°05′ N	09°31′ E	0.43
3570	Serpentera	39°08′ N	09°36′ E	0.32

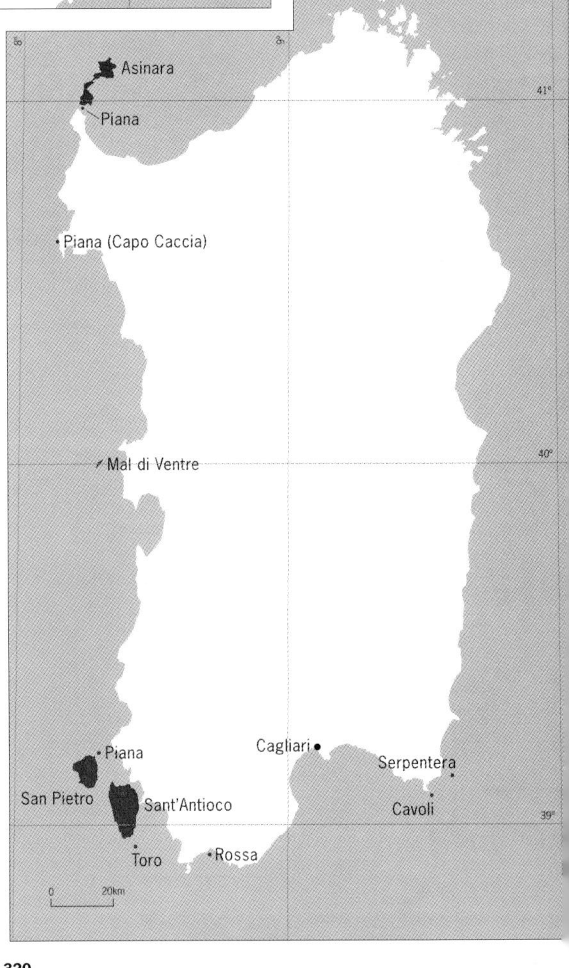
8°
9°
10°
Asinara
41°
Piana
Piana (Capo Caccia)
Mal di Ventre
40°
Piana
Cagliari
Serpentera
San Pietro
Sant'Antioco
Cavoli
39°
Toro
Rossa
0
20km

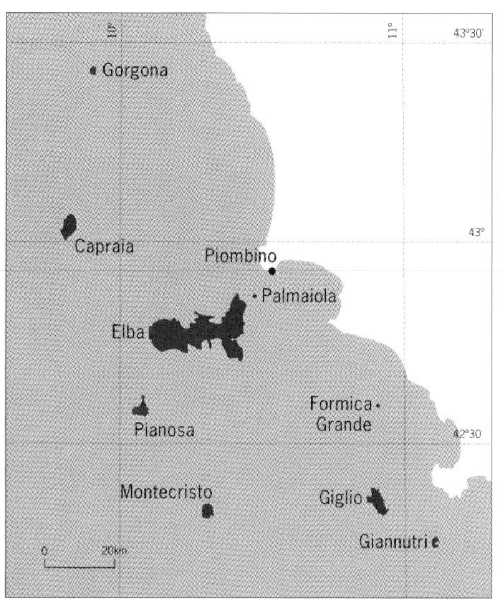

10°
11°
43°30'
Gorgona
43°
Capraia
Piombino
Palmaiola
Elba
Formica
Grande
Pianosa
42°30'
Montecristo
Giglio
Giannutri
0
20km

Arcipelago Toscano

code	island	co-ordinates		sq km
3400	Elba	42°46' N	10°17' E	223
3405	Palmaiola	42°51' N	10°28' E	0.09
3410	Capraia	43°02' N	09°49' E	19.24
3420	Gorgona	43°25' N	09°53' E	2.27
3430	Pianosa	42°34' N	10°04' E	10.41
3440	Montecristo	42°19' N	10°18' E	10.43
3450	Giglio	42°21' N	10°54' E	21.47
3451	Formica Grande	42°34' N	10°54' E	0.12
3460	Giannutri	42°14' N	11°05' E	2.39

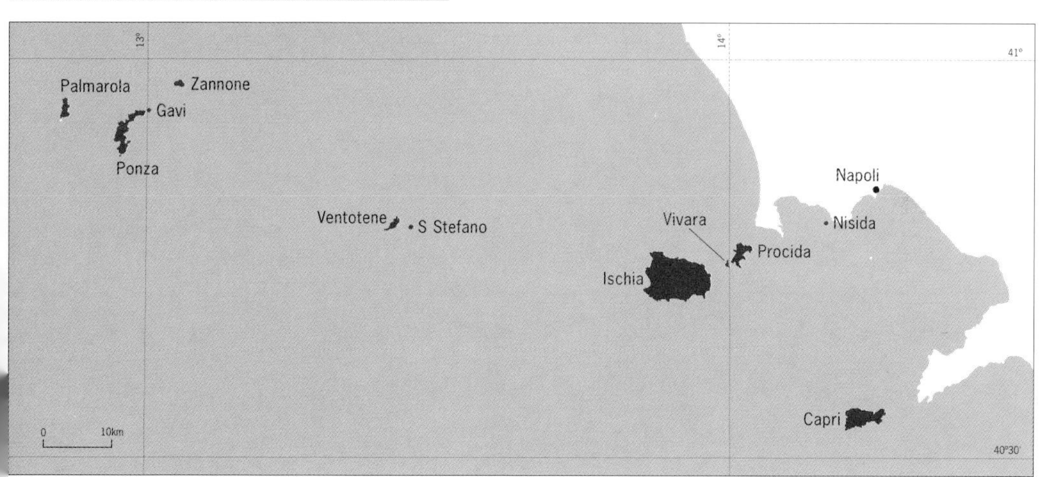

13°
14°
41°
Palmarola
Zannone
Gavi
Ponza
Napoli
Ventotene
S Stefano
Vivara
Nisida
Procida
Ischia
Capri
0
10km
40°30'

Isole Ponziane, Golfo di Napoli

code	island	co-ordinates		sq km
3700	Ponza	40°54' N	12°57' E	7.49
3705	Gavi	40°56' N	13°00' E	0.17
3710	Palmarola	40°56' N	12°51' E	1.24
3720	Zannone	40°58' N	13°03' E	1.04
3730	Ventotene	40°47' N	13°25' E	1.4
3735	Santo Stefano	40°47' N	13°27' E	0.29
3800	Capri	40°32' N	14°13' E	10.32
3810	Ischia	40°43' N	13°54' E	46.44
3820	Procida	40°45' N	14°00' E	3.89
3825	Vivara	40°44' N	13°59' E	0.36
3826	Nisida	40°47' N	14°09' E	0.3

Islets near mainland

code	island	co-ordinates		sq km
3480	Palmaria	44°02′ N	09°50′ E	1.61
3485	Tino	44°01′ N	09°51′ E	0.13
3490	Gallinara	44°01′ N	08°13′ E	0.1
3495	Bergeggi	44°14′ N	08°26′ E	0.04
3840	Dino	39°52′ N	15°46′ E	0.34
3850	San Pietro (Cheradi)	40°26′ N	17°09′ E	1.1
3855	Sant'Andrea (Gallipoli)	40°02′ N	17°57′ E	0.51
3856	Sant'Andrea (Brindisi)	40°39′ N	17°58′ E	0.12
3857	Grande	40°15′ N	17°53′ E	0.1

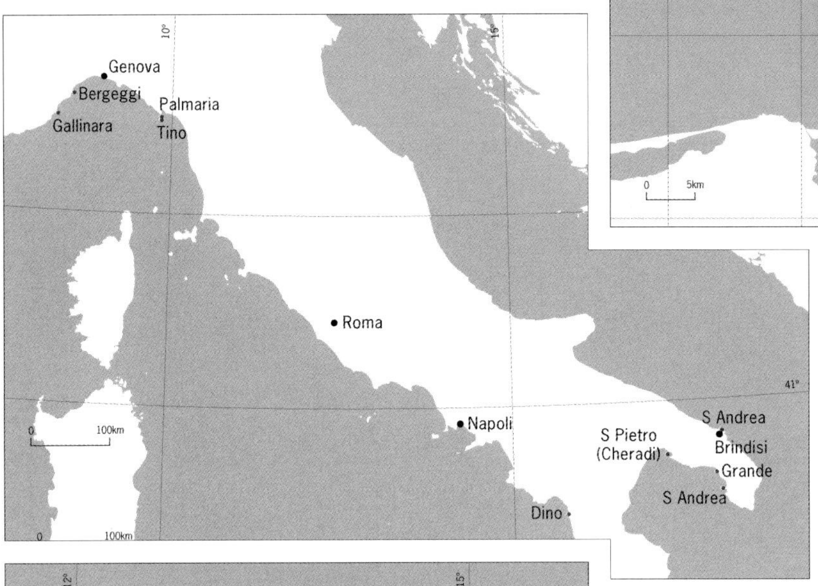
10°
15°
Genova
Bergeggi
Palmaria
Gallinara
Tino
Roma
41°
0
100km
Napoli
S Andrea
S Pietro
(Cheradi)
Brindisi
Grande
S Andrea
Dino

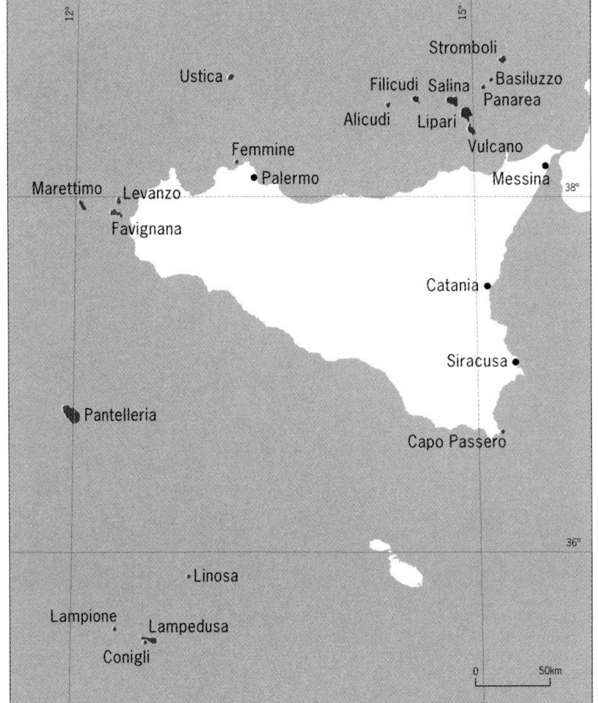
12°
15°
Stromboli
Ustica
Filicudi
Salina
Basiluzzo
Panarea
Alicudi
Lipari
Femmine
Vulcano
Palermo
Messina
Marettimo
Levanzo
38°
Favignana
Catania
Siracusa
Pantelleria
Capo Passero
36°
Linosa
Lampione
Lampedusa
Conigli
0
50km

Tremiti

code	island	co-ordinates		sq km
3900	San Domino	42°06′ N	15°29′ E	2.07
3910	Caprara	42°08′ N	15°30′ E	0.48
3920	San Nicola	42°07′ N	15°30′ E	0.44
3930	Pianosa	42°13′ N	15°44′ E	0.12

Sicily

code	island	co-ordinates		sq km
3020	Ustica	38°42′ N	13°10′ E	8.23
3030	Capo Passero	36°41′ N	15°08′ E	0.35
3040	Femmine	38°12′ N	13°14′ E	0.15
3050	Pantelleria	36°47′ N	11°59′ E	84.23
3100	Favignana	37°55′ N	12°18′ E	19.99
3110	Levanzo	37°59′ N	12°20′ E	5.87
3120	Marettimo	37°58′ N	12°03′ E	12.18
3200	Lampedusa	35°30′ N	12°36′ E	20.47
3205	Conigli	35°30′ N	12°33′ E	0.04
3210	Linosa	35°51′ N	12°51′ E	5.45
3220	Lampione	38°33′ N	12°19′ E	0.04
3300	Lipari	38°29′ N	14°56′ E	37.37
3310	Salina	38°33′ N	14°50′ E	26.14
3320	Vulcano	38°23′ N	14°58′ E	21.02
3330	Stromboli	38°47′ N	15°13′ E	12.51
3340	Filicudi	38°34′ N	14°33′ E	9.31
3350	Alicudi	38°32′ N	14°21′ E	5.05
3360	Panarea	38°38′ N	15°03′ E	3.38
3365	Basiluzzo	38°40′ N	15°06′ E	0.27

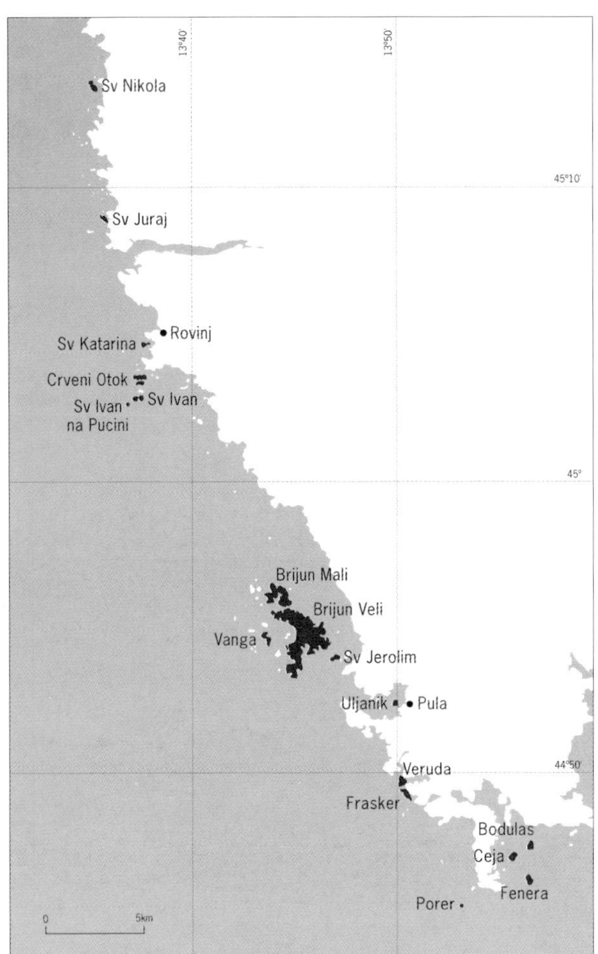
13°40'
13°50'
Sv Nikola
45°10'
Sv Juraj
Sv Katarina
Rovinj
Crveni Otok
Sv Ivan
Sv Ivan
na Pucini
45°
Brijun Mali
Brijun Veli
Vanga
Sv Jerolim
Uljanik
Pula
Veruda
44°50'
Frasker
Bodulas
Ceja
Fenera
Porer
0
5km

code	island	co-ordinates		sq km
Istria				
4000	Brijun Veli	44°54' N	13°45' E	5.72
4001	Brijun Mali	44°56' N	13°44' E	1.07
4002	Sv Jerolim	44°53' N	13°47' E	0.12
4003	Vanga	44°54' N	13°43' E	0.19
4010	Sv Nikola	45°13' N	13°35' E	0.12
4011	Sv Juraj	45°08' N	13°35' E	0.11
4020	Sv Katarina	45°04' N	1337' E	0.12
4030	Crveni Otok	45°03' N	13°37' E	0.23
4031	Sv Ivan	45°02' N	13°37' E	0.1
4032	Sv Ivan na Pucini	45°02' N	13°36' E	0.0035
4040	Uljanik	44°52' N	13°50' E	0.12
4041	Veruda	44°49' N	13°50' E	0.19
4042	Frasker	44°49' N	13°50' E	0.11
4050	Bodulas	44°47' N	13°56' E	0.12
4051	Ceja	44°47' N	13°56' E	0.18
4052	Fenera	44°46' N	13°56' E	0.16
4053	Porer	44°45' N	13°53' E	0.0012

Krk

code	island	co-ordinates		sq km
4101	Sv Marko	45°15' N	14°33' E	0.7
4102	Kosljun	45°01' N	14°37' E	0.072
4103	Prvic	44°54' N	14°48' E	13.45

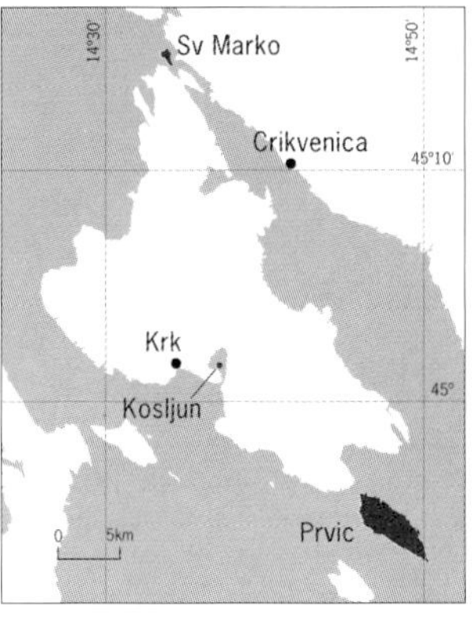
14°30'
14°50'
Sv Marko
Crikvenica
45°10'
Krk
Kosljun
45°
0
5km
Prvic

code	island	co-ordinates		sq km
Cres, Losinj				
4111	Zeca	44°46' N	14°18' E	2.54
4112	Plavnik	44°58' N	14°31' E	8.63
4113	Trstenik	44°40' N	14°34' E	0.33
4114	Oruda	44°33' N	14°35' E	0.4
4115	Palacol	44°32' N	14°35' E	0.05
4121	Koludarc	44°32' N	14°25' E	0.78
4122	Orjule Vele	44°29' N	14°33' E	1.05
4123	Orjule Male	44°29' N	14°33' E	0.33
4124	Kosjak	44°28' N	14°32' E	0.2
4130	Unije	44°39' N	14°15' E	16.92
4131	Srakane Vele	44°34' N	14°18' E	1.18
4132	Srakane Male	44°33' N	14°19' E	0.6
4140	Susak	44°30' N	14°18' E	3.77
4150	Ilovik	44°27' N	14°33' E	5.5
4151	Sv Petar	44°27' N	14°33' E	0.95

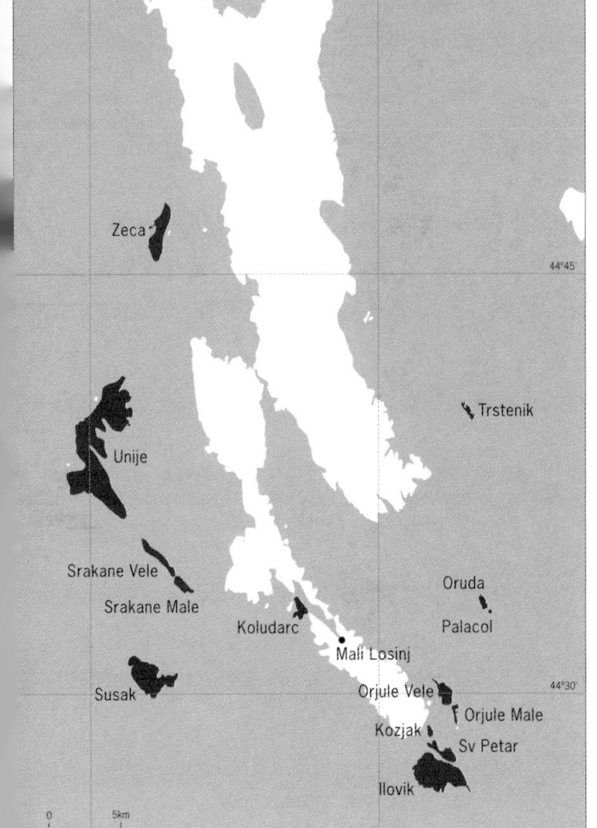

14°15'
14°30'
45°
Cres
Plavnik
Zeca
44°45'
Trstenik
Unije
Srakane Vele
Srakane Male
Koludarc
Oruda
Palacol
Mali Losinj
Susak
44°30'
Orjule Vele
Orjule Male
Kozjak
Sv Petar
Ilovik
0
5km

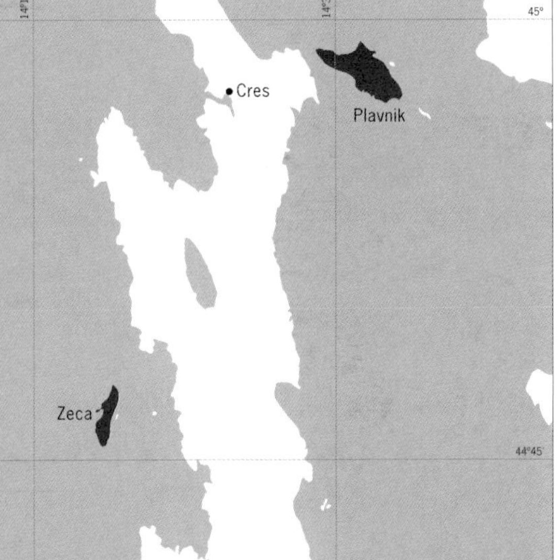

Rab

code	island	co-ordinates		sq km
4161	Dolin	44°42' N	14°48' E	4.61
4162	Goli	44°50' N	14°49' E	4.53
4163	Sv Grgur	44°51' N	14°45' E	6.37
4164	Maman	44°48' N	14°41' E	0.13

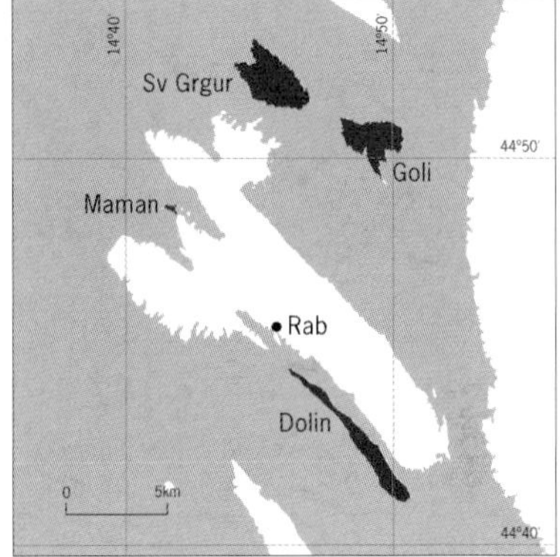

14°40'
14°50'
Sv Grgur
Goli
44°50'
Maman
Rab
Dolin
0
5km
44°40'

Pag

4201	Dolfin	44°41' N	14°41' E	0.25
4202	Skrda	44°28' N	14°51' E	2.05
4203	Maun	44°25' N	14°55' E	8.54
4204	Brusnjak Veli	44°23' N	14°59' E	0.18
4205	Zecevo	44°17' N	15°11' E	0.53
4206	Sikavac Veliki	44°18' N	15°13' E	0.14
4207	Sikavac Mali	44°17' N	15°14' E	0.13

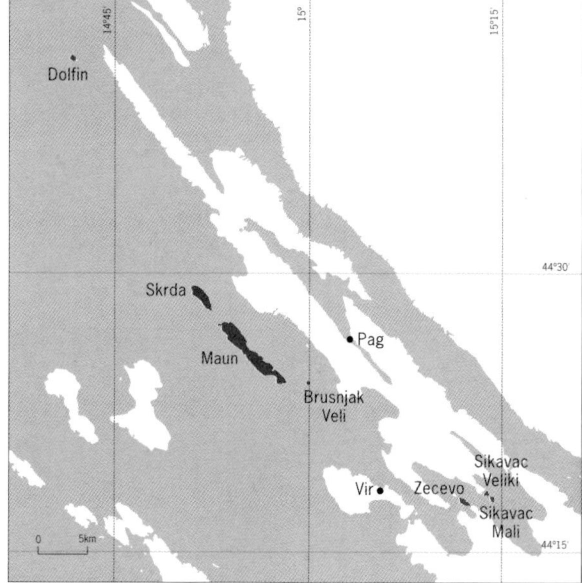
14°45'
15°
15°15'
Dolfin
44°30'
Skrda
Maun
Pag
Brusnjak Veli
Sikavac Veliki
Vir
Zecevo
Sikavac Mali
0 5km
44°15'

code	island	co-ordinates		sq km
Olib, Silba, Premuda, Ist, Molat				
4231	Planik	44°23' N	14°50' E	1.09
4232	Morovnik	44°25' N	14°44' E	0.2
4241	Greben Zapadni	44°19' N	14°41' E	0.13
4242	Greben Juzni	44°19' N	14°42' E	0.13
4251	Lutrosnjak	44°21' N	14°34' E	0.16
4255	Skarda	44°17' N	14°42' E	3.78
4261	Vodenjak	44°15' N	14°43' E	0.11
4271	Tun Veli	44°10' N	14°55' E	2.21
4272	Tun Mali	44°11' N	14°53' E	0.12
4273	Tramerka	44°13' N	14°46' E	0.74
4274	Tramercica	44°13' N	14°47' E	0.15
4275	Brguljski	44°13' N	14°50' E	0.096

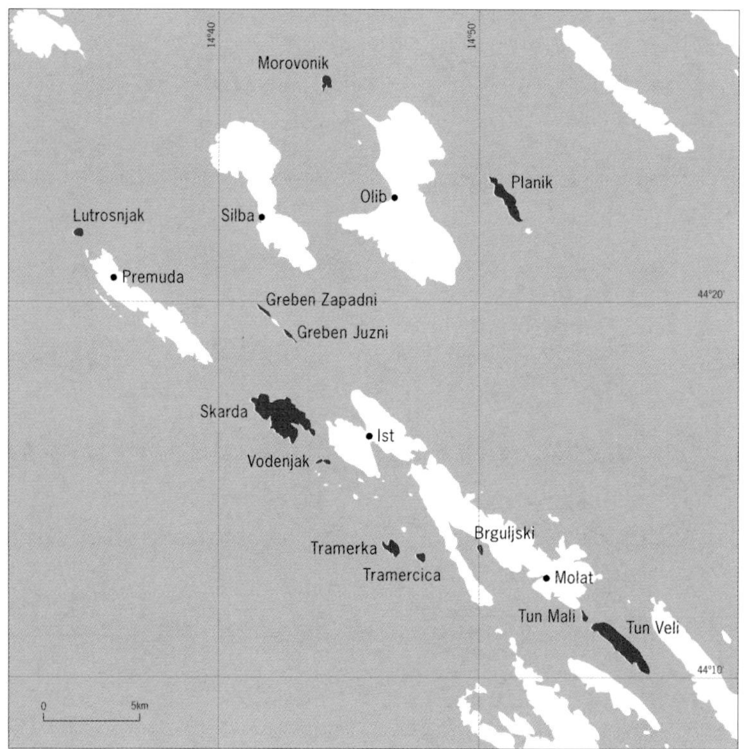
14°40'
14°50'
Morovonik
Planik
Olib
Lutrosnjak
Silba
Premuda
44°20'
Greben Zapadni
Greben Juzni
Skarda
Ist
Vodenjak
Brguljski
Tramerka
Tramercica
Molat
Tun Mali
Tun Veli
44°10'
0 5km

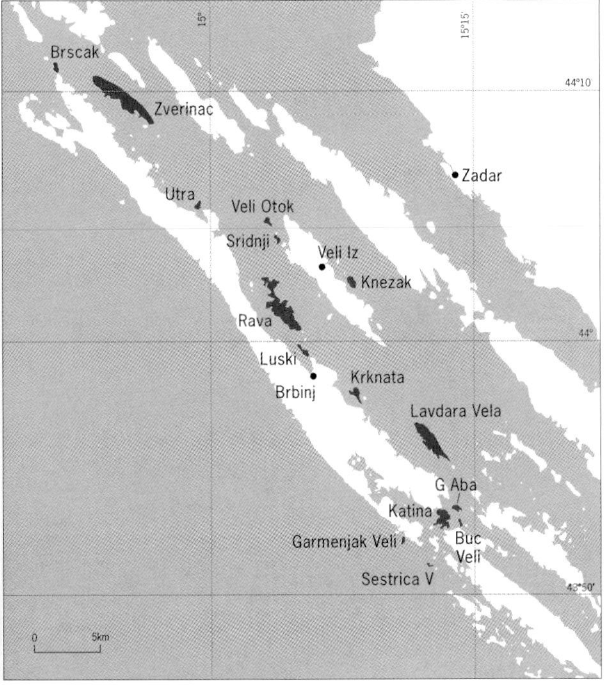
Brscak
15°
15°15'
44°10
Zverinac
Zadar
Utra
Veli Otok
Sridnji
Veli Iz
Knezak
Rava
44°
Luski
Brbinj
Krknata
Lavdara Vela
G Aba
Katina
Buc Veli
Garmenjak Veli
Sestrica V
43°50'
0 5km

code	island	co-ordinates		sq km
Dugi Otok, Iz				
4401	Brscak	44°10' N	14°51' E	0.18
4410	Zverinac	44°09' N	14°55' E	4.17
4411	Utra	44°05' N	14°59' E	0.2
4420	Rava	44°01' N	15°04' E	3.63
4421	Luski	43°59' N	15°05' E	0.29
4422	Krknata	43°57' N	15°08' E	0.39
4423	Lavdara Vela	43°56' N	15°12' E	2.27
4424	G Aba	43°53' N	15°13' E	0.22
4425	Buc Veli	43°52' N	15°14' E	0.1
4426	Katina	43°52' N	15°13' E	1.12
4427	Sestrica V	43°51' N	15°12' E	0.097
4428	Garmenjak Veli	43°52' N	15°10' E	0.13
4431	Knezak	44°02' N	15°08' E	0.35
4432	Sridnji	44°04' N	15°03' E	0.14
4433	Veli Otok	44°04' N	15°03' E	0.2

code	island	co-ordinates		sq km
Ugljan, Pasman				
4301	Osljak	44°04' N	15°12' E	0.33
4302	Idula	44°09' N	15°03' E	0.14
4303	V Skolj	44°01' N	15°12' E	0.17
4311	V Sestrica	44°11' N	14°59' E	0.18
4312	Sr Sestrica	44°10' N	15°00' E	0.1
4341	Galesnjak	43°58' N	15°23' E	0.13
4342	Komornik	43°57' N	15°23' E	0.15
4343	Babac	43°56' N	15°23' E	0.78
4344	Muntan	43°57' N	15°24' E	0.11
4346	Obun	43°51' N	15°27' E	0.17
4347	V Kotula	43°52' N	15°27' E	0.12
4348	Gangaro	43°51' N	15°26' E	0.79
4349	Kosara	43°53' N	15°24' E	0.57
4350	Zizanj	43°52' N	15°25' E	0.92

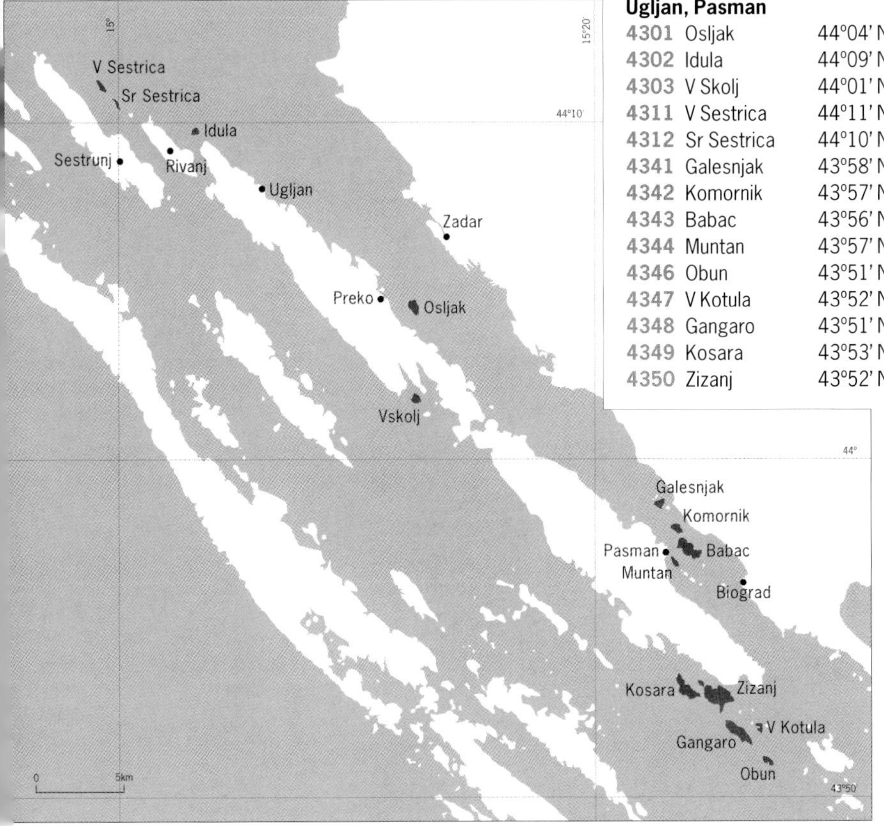
15°
15°20
V Sestrica
Sr Sestrica
44°10'
Idula
Sestrunj
Rivanj
Ugljan
Zadar
Preko
Osljak
Vskolj
44°
Galesnjak
Komornik
Pasman
Babac
Muntan
Biograd
Kosara
Zizanj
V Kotula
Gangaro
Obun
43°50'
0 5km

code	island	co-ordinates		sq km
Zut, Sit				
4570	Zut	43°52' N	15°18' E	14.82
4571	Gustac	43°52' N	15°20' E	0.19
4572	Zutska Aba	43°49' N	15°22' E	0.23
4573	Dajna Vela	43°48' N	15°21' E	0.17
4574	Glamoc	43°53' N	15°15' E	0.41
4575	Skala V	43°54' N	15°15' E	0.12
4590	Sit	43°55' N	15°18' E	1.77
4591	Scitna	43°54' N	15°19' E	0.31
4592	Gangarol	43°54' N	15°20' E	0.33
4593	Balabra Vela	43°56' N	15°16' E	0.16
4594	Brusnjak	43°55' N	15°16' E	0.16
4595	Kurba Mala	43°55' N	15°15' E	0.42

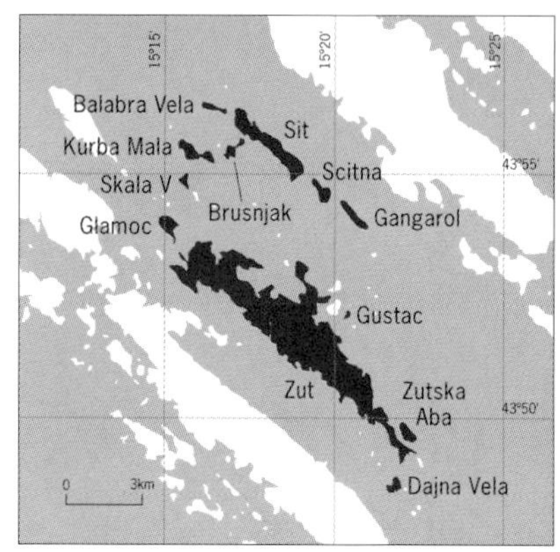

15°15'
15°20'
15°25'
Balabra Vela
Kurba Mala
Sit
Skala V
Scitna
43°55'
Brusnjak
Glamoc
Gangarol
Gustac
Zut
Zutska Aba
43°50'
0
3km
Dajna Vela

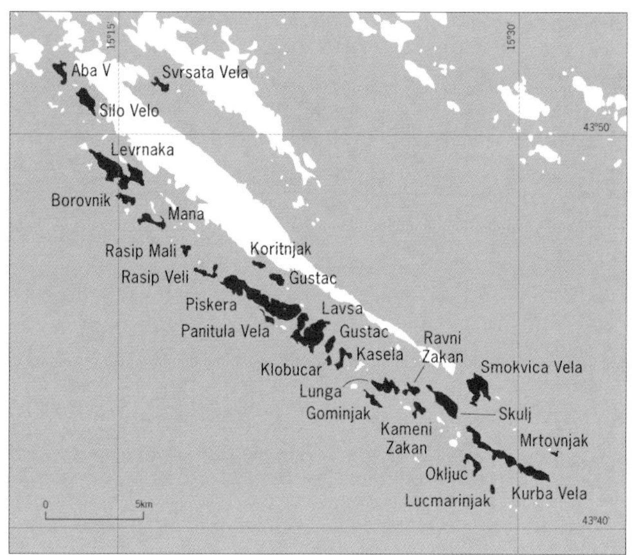

15°15'
15°30'
Aba V
Svrsata Vela
Silo Velo
43°50'
Levrnaka
Borovnik
Mana
Rasip Mali
Koritnjak
Rasip Veli
Gustac
Piskera
Lavsa
Panitula Vela
Gustac
Kasela
Ravni Zakan
Klobucar
Smokvica Vela
Lunga
Gominjak
Skulj
Kameni Zakan
Mrtovnjak
Okljuc
Lucmarinjak
Kurba Vela
0
5km
43°40'

code	island	co-ordinates		sq km
Kornat				
4501	Aba V	43°52' N	15°12' E	0.38
4502	Silo Velo	43°51' N	15°13' E	0.67
4503	Levrnaka	43°49' N	15°14' E	1.84
4504	Borovnik	43°48' N	15°15' E	0.27
4505	Mana	43°48' N	15°16' E	0.4
4506	Rasip Mali	43°47' N	15°17' E	0.15
4507	Rasip Veli	43°46' N	15°18' E	0.25
4510	Piskera	43°46' N	15°20' E	2.66
4511	Koritnjak	43°46' N	15°20' E	0.11
4512	Gustac	43°46' N	15°20' E	0.28
4513	Panitula Vela	43°45' N	15°20' E	0.15
4514	Lavsa	43°45' N	15°22' E	1.78
4515	Gustac	43°44' N	15°23' E	0.29
4516	Klobucar	43°44' N	15°22' E	0.11
4517	Kasela	43°44' N	15°23' E	0.34
4518	Lunga	43°43' N	15°25' E	0.6
4519	Gominjak	43°43' N	15°24' E	0.24
4520	Ravni Zakan	43°43' N	15°26' E	0.29
4521	Kameni Zakan	43°43' N	15°26' E	0.31
4522	Skulj	43°43' N	15°27' E	0.88
4523	Smokvica Vela	43°43' N	15°28' E	1.04
4524	Okljuc	43°41' N	15°28' E	0.35
4530	Kurba Vela	43°41' N	15°29' E	1.74
4531	Mrtovnjak	43°41' N	15°31' E	0.1
4532	Lucmarinjak	43°40' N	15°29' E	0.1
4540	Svrsata Vela	43°51' N	15°16' E	0.26

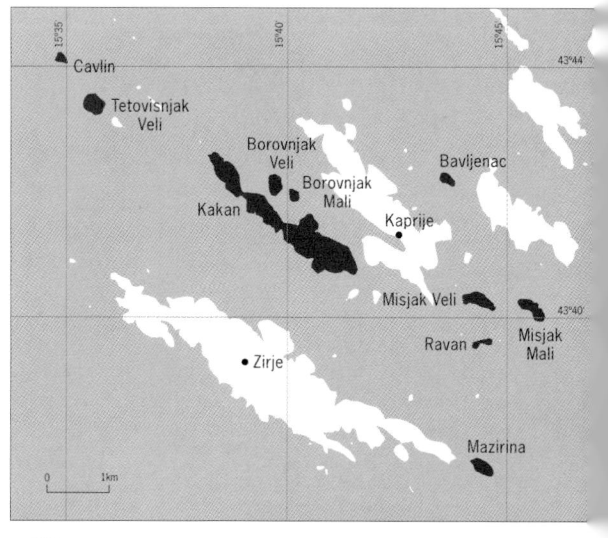

15°35'
15°40'
15°45'
Cavlin
43°44'
Tetovisnjak Veli
Borovnjak Veli
Bavljenac
Borovnjak Mali
Kakan
Kaprije
Misjak Veli
43°40'
Ravan
Misjak Mali
Zirje
Mazirina
0
1km

code	island	co-ordinates		sq km
Zirje, Kaprije				
4631	Mazirina	43°37' N	15°44' E	0.26
4640	Kakan	43°41' N	15°40' E	3.38
4641	Borovnjak Mali	43°41' N	15°40' E	0.1
4642	Borovnjak Veli	43°42' N	15°39' E	0.23
4643	Tetovisnjak Veli	43°43' N	15°35' E	0.34
4644	Cavlin	43°44' N	15°34' E	0.1
4651	Misjak Veli	43°40' N	15°44' E	0.34
4652	Misjak Mali	43°40' N	15°45' E	0.32
4653	Ravan	43°39' N	15°44' E	0.1
4654	Bavljenac	43°42' N	15°43' E	0.14

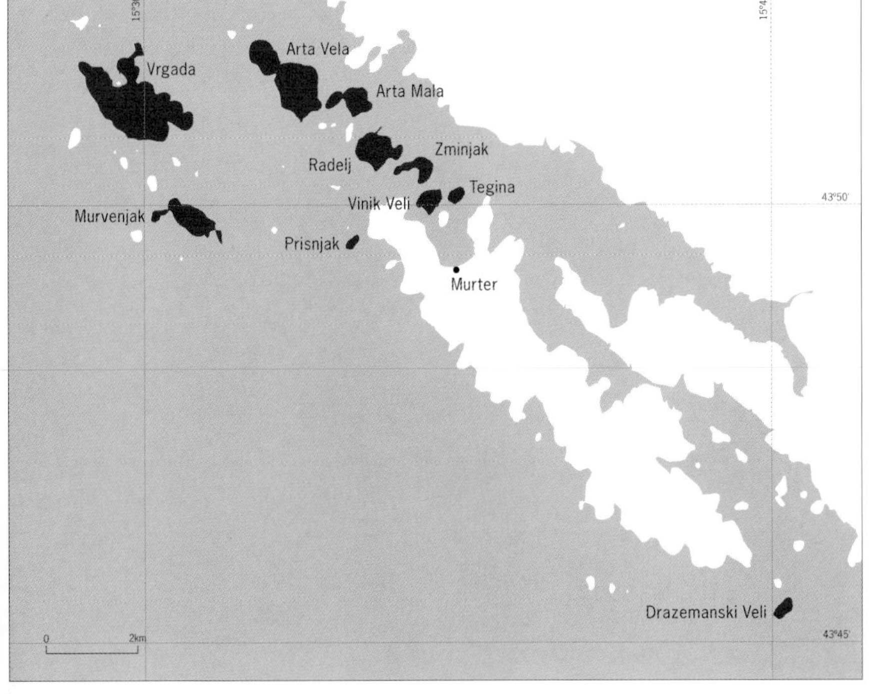
15°30'
15°40'
Vrgada
Arta Vela
Arta Mala
Zminjak
Radelj
Tegina
Vinik Veli
43°50'
Murvenjak
Prisnjak
Murter
Drazemanski Veli
0
2km
43°45'

code	island	co-ordinates		sq km
Murter				
4601	Drazemanski Veli	43°45' N	15°40' E	0.12
4602	Prisnjak	43°49' N	15°33' E	0.064
4603	Arta Vela	43°51' N	15°32' E	1.27
4604	Arta Mala	43°51' N	15°33' E	0.38
4605	Radelj	43°50' N	15°33' E	0.54
4606	Zminjak	43°50' N	15°34' E	0.22
4607	Vinik Veli	43°50' N	15°34' E	0.18
4608	Tegina	43°50' N	15°35' E	0.095
4620	Vrgada	43°51' N	15°30' E	2.31
4621	Murvenjak	43°49' N	15°31' E	0.6

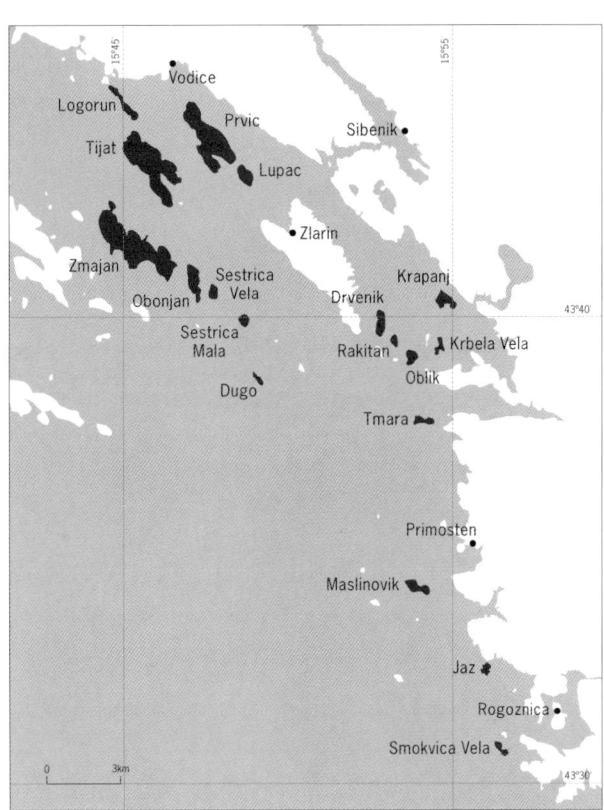
15°45'
15°55'
Vodice
Logorun
Prvic
Sibenik
Tijat
Lupac
Zlarin
Zmajan
Sestrica
Vela
Obonjan
Krapanj
Drvenik
43°40'
Sestrica
Mala
Rakitan
Krbela Vela
Oblik
Dugo
Tmara
Primosten
Maslinovik
Jaz
Rogoznica
Smokvica Vela
0
3km
43°30'

code	island	co-ordinates		sq km
Sibenik, Zlarin, Primosten				
4660	Prvic	43°43' N	15°47' E	2.4
4661	Lupac	43°43' N	15°48' E	0.33
4662	Tijat	43°43' N	15°45' E	2.77
4663	Logorun	43°44' N	15°45' E	0.38
4670	Zmajan	43°41' N	15°45' E	3.3
4671	Obonjan	43°40' N	15°47' E	0.55
4672	Sestrica Vela	43°40' N	15°47' E	0.21
4673	Sestrica Mala	43°39' N	15°48' E	0.16
4674	Dugo	43°38' N	15°49' E	0.11
4681	Drvenik	43°39' N	15°52' E	0.3
4682	Rakitan	43°39' N	15°53' E	0.11
4683	Oblik	43°39' N	15°53' E	0.24
4684	Krbela Vela	43°39' N	15°54' E	0.15
4690	Krapanj	43°40' N	15°54' E	0.35
4691	Tmara	43°37' N	15°54' E	0.21
4692	Maslinovik	43°34' N	15°53' E	0.35
4693	Jaz	43°32' N	15°56' E	0.13
4694	Smokvica Vela	43°30' N	15°56' E	0.17

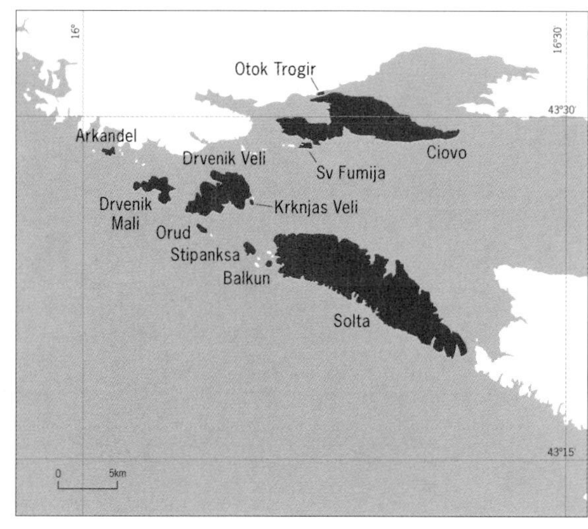

16°
16°30'
Otok Trogir
43°30'
Arkandel
Drvenik Veli
Ciovo
Sv Fumija
Drvenik Mali
Krknjas Veli
Orud
Stipanksa
Balkun
Solta
43°15'
0
5km

code	island	co-ordinates		sq km
Solta, Ciovo				
4710	Solta	43°22' N	16°17' E	58.98
4711	Balkun	43°23' N	16°11' E	0.23
4712	Stipanska	43°24' N	16°10' E	0.61
4720	Ciovo	43°29' N	16°17' E	28.8
4721	Sv Fumija	43°28' N	16°13' E	0.27
4722	Otok Trogir	43°30' N	16°15' E	0.11
4730	Drvenik Veli	43°26' N	16°08' E	12.07
4731	Orud	43°25' N	16°07' E	0.38
4732	Krknjas Veli	43°26' N	16°10' E	0.096
4740	Drvenik Mali	43°26' N	16°04' E	3.42
4741	Arkandel	43°28' N	16°01' E	0.47

Hvar

code	island	co-ordinates		sq km
4751	Zecevo	43°11' N	16°41' E	0.11
4760	Sv Klement	43°09' N	16°22' E	5.27
4761	Jerolim	43°09' N	16°25' E	0.2
4762	Marinkovac	43°09' N	16°25' E	0.68
4763	Planikovac	43°09' N	16°24' E	0.1
4764	Borovac	43°09' N	16°24' E	0.16
4765	Dobri	43°09' N	16°21' E	0.29
4766	Vodnjak Veli	43°10' N	16°18' E	0.25
4770	Scedro	43°05' N	16°42' E	8.36

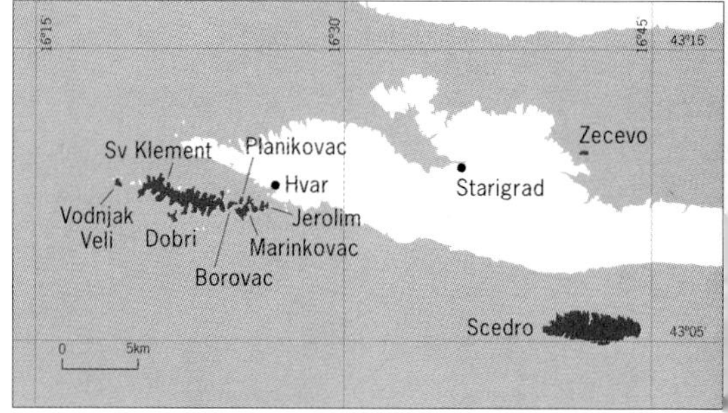

16°15'
16°30'
16°45'
43°15'
Zecevo
Sv Klement
Planikovac
Hvar
Starigrad
Vodnjak Veli
Dobri
Jerolim
Marinkovac
Borovac
Scedro
43°05'
0
5km

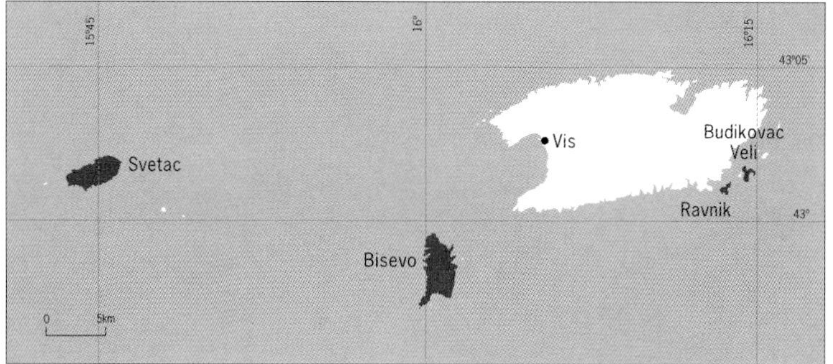

15°45'
16°
16°15'
43°05'
Vis
Budikovac Veli
Svetac
Ravnik
43°
Bisevo
0
5km

Vis

code	island	co-ordinates		sq km
4781	Bisevo	42°58' N	16°00' E	5.91
4782	Svetac	43°01' N	15°44' E	4.19
4783	Budikovac Veli	43°01' N	16°14' E	0.31
4784	Ravnik	43°01' N	16°13' E	0.26

code	island	co-ordinates		sq km
Korcula				
4801	Proizd	42°59' N	16°36' E	0.63
4802	Osjak	42°57' N	16°40' E	0.21
4803	Trstenik	42°54' N	16°40' E	0.27
4804	Prznjak Veli	42°54' N	16°41' E	0.2
4805	Prznjak Mali	42°54' N	16°41' E	0.096
4806	Zvirinovik	42°54' N	16°43' E	0.4
4807	Crklica	42°53' N	16°47' E	0.099
4808	Sridnjak	42°53' N	16°48' E	0.15
4809	Vrhovnjak	42°53' N	16°48' E	0.13
4810	Vrnik	42°56' N	17°10' E	0.28
4811	Sutvara	42°56' N	17°11' E	0.097
4812	Majsan	42°57' N	17°11' E	0.15
4813	Planjak	42°56' N	17°10' E	0.23
4815	Plocica	43°01' N	16°49' E	0.07
4820	Badija	42°57' N	17°09' E	0.97

16°45'
17°
17°15'
Plocica
43°
Proizd
Osjak
Badija
Majsan
Korcula
Planjak
Vrnik
Sutvara
42°55'
Trstenik
Zvirinovik
Vrhovnjak
Prznjak
Mali
Prznjak
Veli
Crklica
Sridnjak
0
5km

16°45'
17°
42°47'
Saplun
Mrcara
Prezba
Stomorina
Cesvinica
Lastovo
Krucica
Vlasnik
42°45'
Kopiste
Bratin
42°43'
0
2km

code	island	co-ordinates		sq km
Lastovo				
4901	Prezba	42°46' N	16°48' E	2.8
4902	Mrcara	42°46' N	16°47' E	1.45
4903	Kopiste	42°45' N	16°43' E	0.73
4904	Bratin	42°44' N	16°47' E	0.17
4905	Vlasnik	42°45' N	16°47' E	0.12
4906	Krucica	42°45' N	16°58' E	0.47
4907	Cesvinica	42°46' N	16°58' E	0.61
4908	Saplun	42°46' N	16°59' E	0.41
4909	Stomorina	42°46' N	16°57' E	0.29

code	island	co-ordinates		sq km
Mljet, Peljesac				
4941	Kobrava	42°47' N	17°24' E	0.52
4942	Moracnik	42°47' N	17°24' E	0.23
4943	Pomestak	42°47' N	17°20' E	0.23
4945	Tajan	42°55' N	17°30' E	0.25
4946	Dubovac	42°55' N	17°28' E	0.12

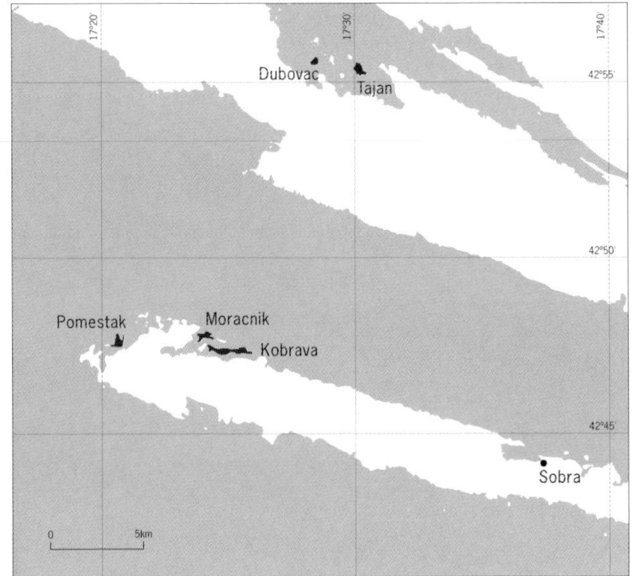
17°20'
17°30'
17°40'
Dubovac
Tajan
42°55'
42°50'
Pomestak
Moracnik
Kobrava
42°45'
Sobra
0
5km

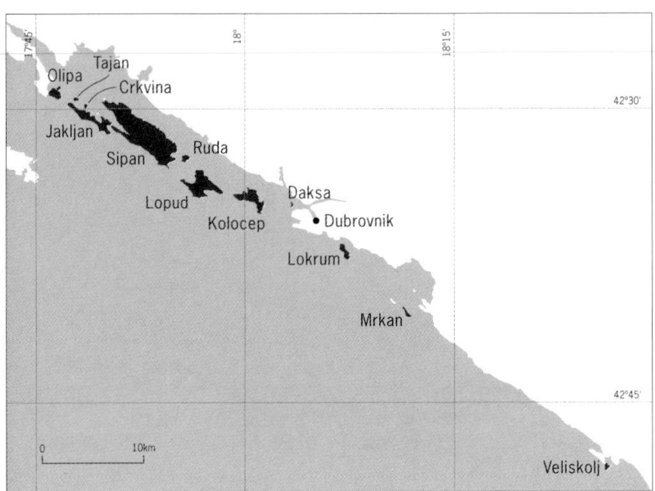
17°45'
18°
18°15'
Tajan
Olipa
Crkvina
42°30'
Jakljan
Ruda
Sipan
Lopud
Daksa
Kolocep
Dubrovnik
Lokrum
Mrkan
42°45'
0
10km
Veliskolj

code	island	co-ordinates		sq km
Elafiti, Dubrovnik				
4950	Jakljan	42°44' N	17°48' E	3.06
4951	Olipa	42°45' N	17°46' E	0.9
4952	Tajan	42°45' N	17°47' E	0.11
4953	Crkvina	42°45' N	17°48' E	0.099
4960	Sipan	42°43' N	17°52' E	15.81
4961	Ruda	42°42' N	17°55' E	0.29
4970	Lopud	42°41' N	17°56' E	4.37
4980	Kolocep	42°40' N	18°00' E	2.43
4981	Daksa	42°40' N	18°03' E	0.065
4982	Lokrum	42°37' N	18°07' E	0.69
4983	Mrkan	42°34' N	18°11' E	0.19
4984	Veli Skolj	42°26' N	18°25' E	0.16

code	island	co-ordinates		sq km
Albania, Corfu				
4990	Sazanit	40°29′ N	19°16′ E	5.7
5001	Vido/Ptychia	39°38′ N	19°55′ E	0.563
5005	Prasoudi	39°30′ N	20°09′ E	0.106
5006	Mourtos	39°24′ N	20°13′ E	0.742
5007	Ag Nikolaos	39°24′ N	20°13′ E	0.539
5008	Gourouni	39°23′ N	20°14′ E	0.181
5010	Othonoi	39°51′ N	19°23′ E	10.444
5020	Erikousa	39°53′ N	19°35′ E	4.381
5030	Mathraki	39°46′ N	19°31′ E	3.092
5031	Diaplon	39°46′ N	19°35′ E	0.31

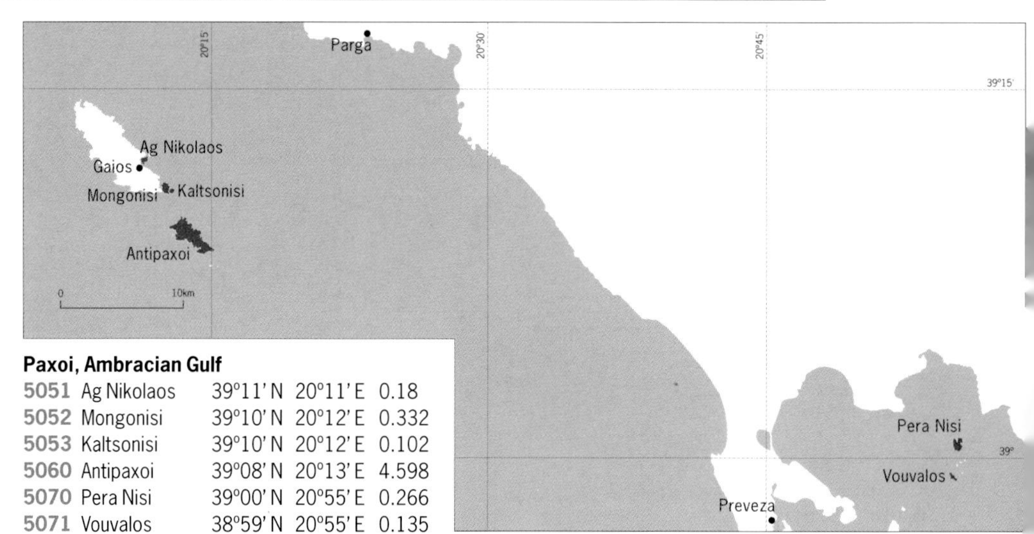
Parga
20°15′
20°30′
20°45′
39°15′
Ag Nikolaos
Gaios
Mongonisi
Kaltsonisi
Antipaxoi
0
10km
Pera Nisi
39°
Vouvalos
Preveza

Paxoi, Ambracian Gulf

code	island	co-ordinates		sq km
5051	Ag Nikolaos	39°11′ N	20°11′ E	0.18
5052	Mongonisi	39°10′ N	20°12′ E	0.332
5053	Kaltsonisi	39°10′ N	20°12′ E	0.102
5060	Antipaxoi	39°08′ N	20°13′ E	4.598
5070	Pera Nisi	39°00′ N	20°55′ E	0.266
5071	Vouvalos	38°59′ N	20°55′ E	0.135

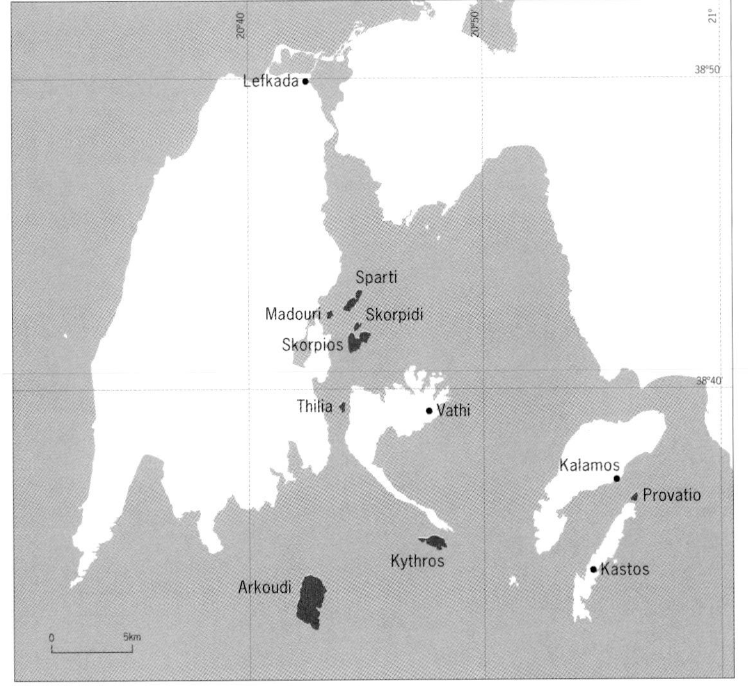

Lefkada
Sparti
Madouri
Skorpidi
Skorpios
Thilia
Vathi
Kalamos
Provatio
Kythros
Kastos
Arkoudi
0 5km
20°40'
20°50'
21°
38°50'
38°40'

Lefkada

code	island	co-ordinates		sq km
5101	Arkoudi	38°33' N	20°42' E	4.275
5102	Skorpios	38°41' N	20°44' E	0.878
5103	Skorpidi	38°42' N	20°44' E	0.118
5104	Sparti	38°42' N	20°44' E	0.538
5105	Madouri	38°42' N	20°43' E	0.127
5151	Kythros	38°35' N	20°44' E	0.814
5152	Thilia	38°39' N	20°44' E	0.155
5171	Provatio	38°36' N	20°56' E	0.107

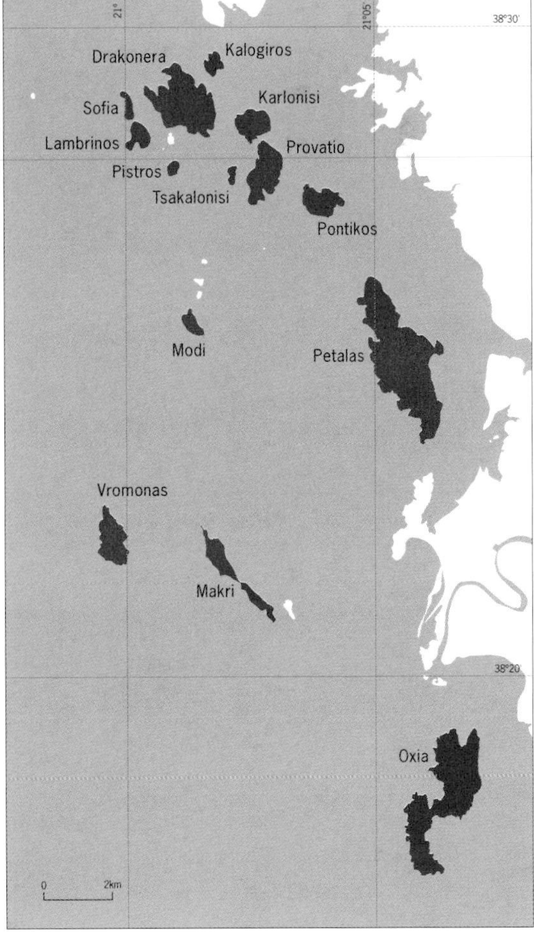

Drakonera
Kalogiros
Sofia
Karlonisi
Lambrinos
Provatio
Pistros
Tsakalonisi
Pontikos
Modi
Petalas
Vromonas
Makri
Oxia
0 2km
21°
21°05'
38°30'
38°20'

code	island	co-ordinates		sq km
Echinades				
5410	Oxia	38°18' N	21°06' E	4.223
5411	Petalas	38°24' N	21°05' E	5.497
5412	Makri	38°21' N	21°01' E	0.983
5414	Vromonas	38°22' N	20°59' E	1.047
5415	Modi	38°25' N	21°01' E	0.258
5419	Pontikos	38°27' N	21°03' E	0.736
5420	Provatio	38°27' N	21°02' E	1.21
5421	Tsalakonisi	38°27' N	21°02' E	0.1
5422	Karlonisi	38°28' N	21°02' E	0.719
5423	Kalogiros	38°29' N	21°01' E	0.249
5424	Drakonera	38°28' N	21°01' E	2.442
5425	Pistros	38°27' N	21°00' E	0.114
5427	Lambrinos	38°28' N	21°00' E	0.352
5428	Sofia	38°28' N	21°04' E	0.174

code	island	co-ordinates		sq km
Kefalonia, Ithaki				
5201	Vardiani	38°08' N	20°25' E	0.2
5301	Atokos	38°29' N	20°48' E	4.324
5302	Pera Pigadi/Lygia	38°20' N	20°44' E	0.115

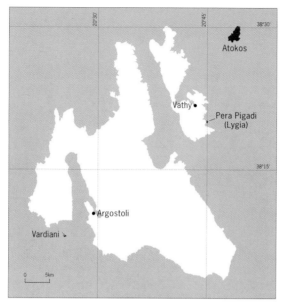

20°30'
20°45'
38°30'
Atokos
Vathy
Pera Pigadi (Lygia)
38°15'
Argostoli
Vardiani
0 5km

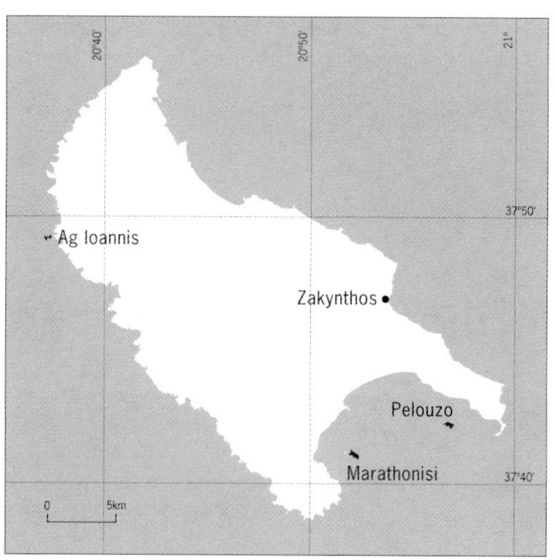
20°40'
20°50'
21°
37°50'
Ag Ioannis
Zakynthos
Pelouzo
Marathonisi
37°40'
0 5km

Zakynthos				
5401	Marathonisi	37°41' N	20°52' E	0.248
5402	Pelouzo	37°42' N	20°56' E	0.193
5403	Ag Ioannis	37°49' N	20°37' E	0.097

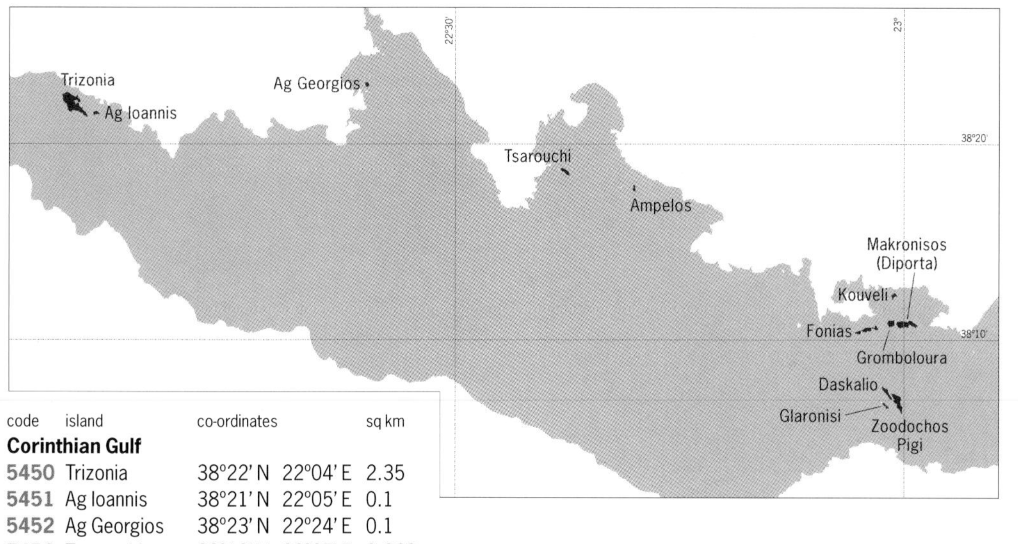
22°30'
23°
Trizonia
Ag Ioannis
Ag Georgios
38°20'
Tsarouchi
Ampelos
Makronisos
(Diporta)
Kouveli
Fonias
38°10'
Gromboloura
Daskalio
Glaronisi
Zoodochos
Pigi

code	island	co-ordinates		sq km
Corinthian Gulf				
5450	Trizonia	38°22' N	22°04' E	2.35
5451	Ag Ioannis	38°21' N	22°05' E	0.1
5452	Ag Georgios	38°23' N	22°24' E	0.1
5453	Tsarouchi	38°18' N	22°37' E	0.268
5454	Ampelos	38°17' N	22°42' E	0.106
5455	Fonias	38°10' N	22°57' E	0.579
5456	Gromboloura	38°10' N	22°59' E	0.33
5457	Kouveli	38°12' N	22°59' E	0.143
5458	Makronisos (Diporta)	38°10' N	23°00' E	0.927
5460	Zoodochos Pigi	38°06' N	22°59' E	0.702
5461	Daskalio	38°07' N	22°59' E	0.218
5462	Glaronisi	38°06' N	22°58' E	0.1

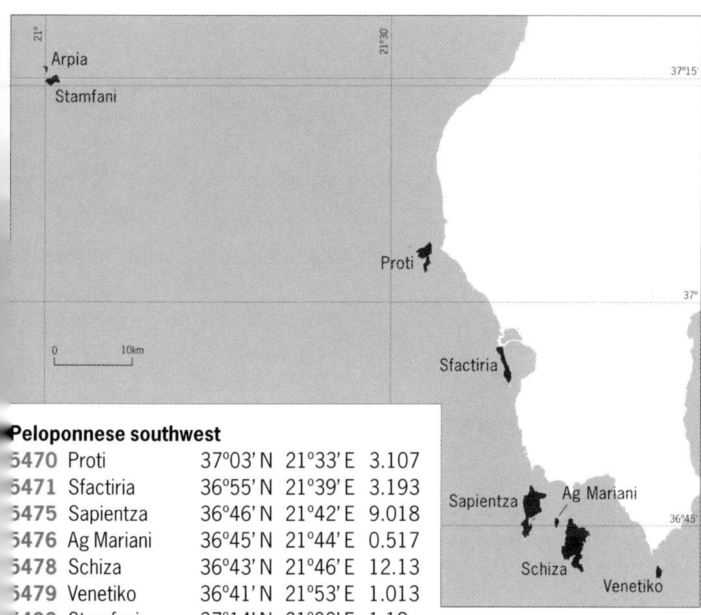
21°
21°30'
Arpia
Stamfani
37°15'
Proti
37°
0
10km
Sfactiria
Sapientza
Ag Mariani
36°45'
Schiza
Venetiko

code	island	co-ordinates		sq km
Peloponnese southwest				
5470	Proti	37°03' N	21°33' E	3.107
5471	Sfactiria	36°55' N	21°39' E	3.193
5475	Sapientza	36°46' N	21°42' E	9.018
5476	Ag Mariani	36°45' N	21°44' E	0.517
5478	Schiza	36°43' N	21°46' E	12.13
5479	Venetiko	36°41' N	21°53' E	1.013
5490	Stamfani	37°14' N	21°00' E	1.18
5491	Arpia	37°15' N	21°00' E	0.176

code	island	co-ordinates		sq km
Kythira				
5501	Avgo	36°06' N	23°00' E	0.318
5502	Dragonera	36°13' N	23°06' E	0.387
5503	Antidragonera	36°14' N	23°06' E	0.181
5504	Makronisi	36°16' N	23°04' E	0.38
5510	Antikythira	35°51' N	23°18' E	19.776
5511	Prasonisi	35°57' N	23°14' E	0.346
5520	Elafonisos	36°29' N	22°57' E	17.859

code	island	co-ordinates		sq km
Salamina				
5901	Kanakia	37°54' N	23°23' E	0.15
5902	Revithousa	37°57' N	23°24' E	0.144
5903	Makronisos	37°57' N	23°25' E	0.232
5904	Ag Georgios	37°57' N	23°32' E	0.203
5905	Leros	37°59' N	23°32' E	0.463
5906	Psyttalia	37°56' N	23°35' E	0.475

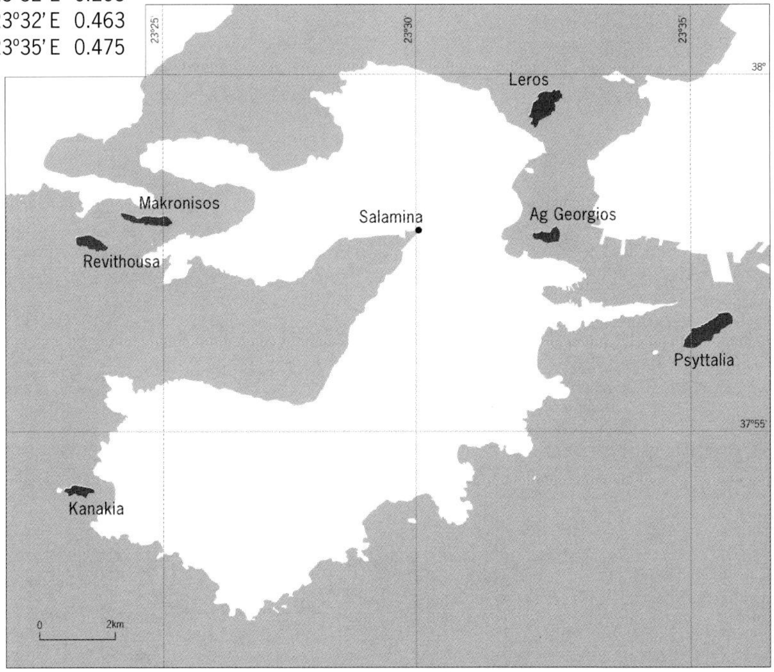

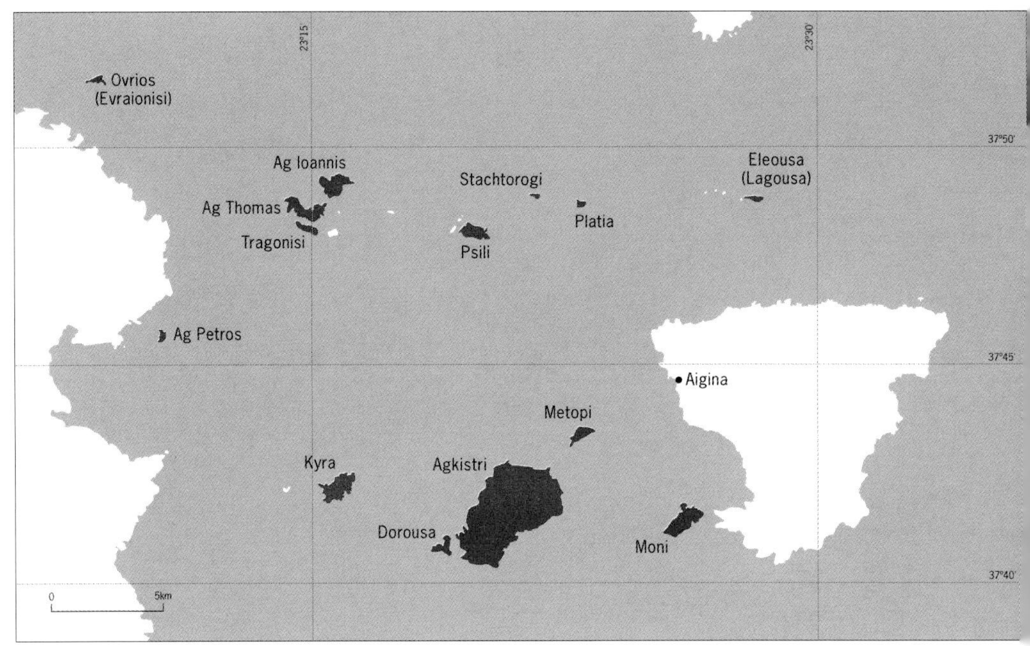
23°15'
23°30'
Ovrios
(Evraionisi)
37°50'
Ag Ioannis
Ag Thomas
Tragonisi
Stachtorogi
Psili
Platia
Eleousa
(Lagousa)
Ag Petros
37°45'
Aigina
Metopi
Kyra
Agkistri
Dorousa
Moni
37°40'
0
5km

Aigina

code	island	co-ordinates		sq km
5801	Moni	37°41' N	23°26' E	1.074
5802	Metopi	37°43' N	23°22' E	0.357
5803	Dorousa	37°40' N	23°18' E	0.317
5805	Psili	37°48' N	23°19' E	0.536
5806	Stachtorogi	37°48' N	23°21' E	0.097
5807	Platia	37°48' N	23°22' E	0.131
5808	Eleousa/Lagousa	37°48' N	23°28' E	0.176
5820	Agkistri	37°41' N	23°20' E	11.732
5821	Kyra	37°42' N	23°15' E	1.049
5830	Ag Ioannis	37°49' N	23°16' E	1.128
5831	Ag Thomas	37°49' N	23°15' E	1.048
5832	Tragonisi	37°49' N	23°15' E	0.226
5840	Ovrios/Evraionisi	37°51' N	23°08' E	0.157
5841	Ag Petros	37°45' N	23°10' E	0.109

code	island	co-ordinates		sq km
Spetses, Argos Gulf				
5601	Spetsopoula	37°13'N	23°10'E	1.956
5602	Velopoula/Parapola	36°54'N	23°27'E	1.83
5603	Falkonera	36°50'N	23°53'E	0.097
5610	Romvi/Tolo	37°30'N	22°51'E	1.195
5611	Platia	37°29'N	22°55'E	1.821
5612	Psili	37°26'N	22°58'E	2.14
5615	Koronida/Koilada	37°25'N	23°07'E	0.235
5616	Korakonisi	37°21'N	23°03'E	0.099

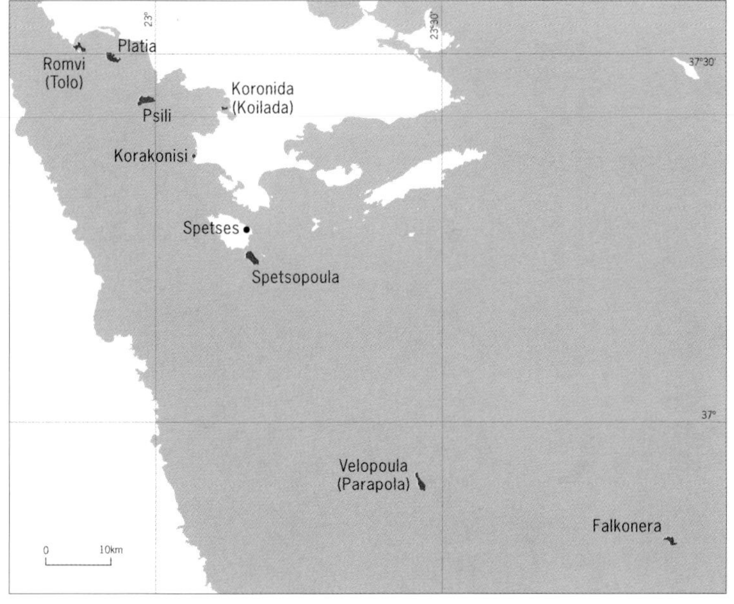

23°
23°30'
Platia
Romvi
(Tolo)
37°30'
Koronida
(Koilada)
Psili
Korakonisi
Spetses
Spetsopoula
37°
Velopoula
(Parapola)
Falkonera
0
10km

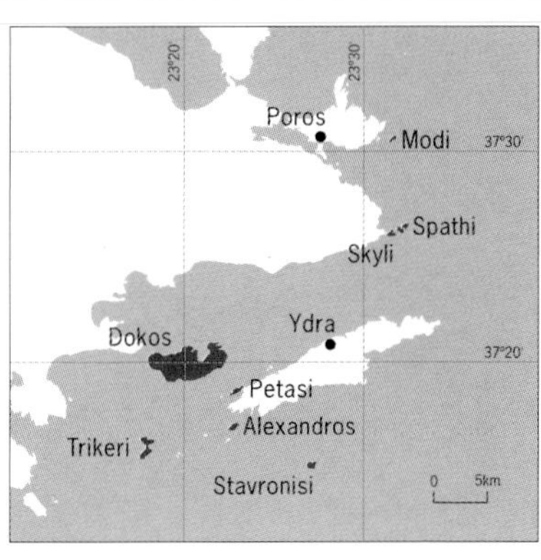

23°20'
23°30'
Poros
Modi
37°30'
Spathi
Skyli
Ydra
Dokos
37°20'
Petasi
Alexandros
Trikeri
Stavronisi
0
5km

code	island	co-ordinates		sq km
Ydra, Poros				
5701	Dokos	37°19'N	23°19'E	13.537
5702	Trikeri	37°15'N	23°16'E	0.923
5703	Alexandros	37°17'N	23°22'E	0.331
5704	Petasi	37°18'N	23°22'E	0.334
5705	Stavronisi	37°15'N	23°26'E	0.348
5851	Modi	37°30'N	23°31'E	0.148
5852	Skyli	37°26'N	23°31'E	0.387
5853	Spathi	37°26'N	23°32'E	0.34

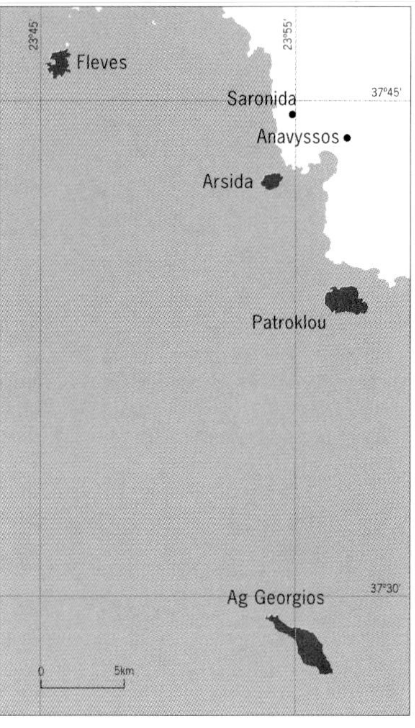

23°45'
23°55'
Fleves
Saronida
37°45'
Anavyssos
Arsida
Patroklou
37°30'
Ag Georgios
0
5km

code	island	co-ordinates		sq km
Attica southwest				
5910	Fleves	37°46'N	23°45'E	1.358
5920	Arsida	37°42'N	23°54'E	0.759
5930	Patroklou	37°39'N	23°56'E	2.787
5940	Ag Georgios	37°28'N	23°55'E	4.329

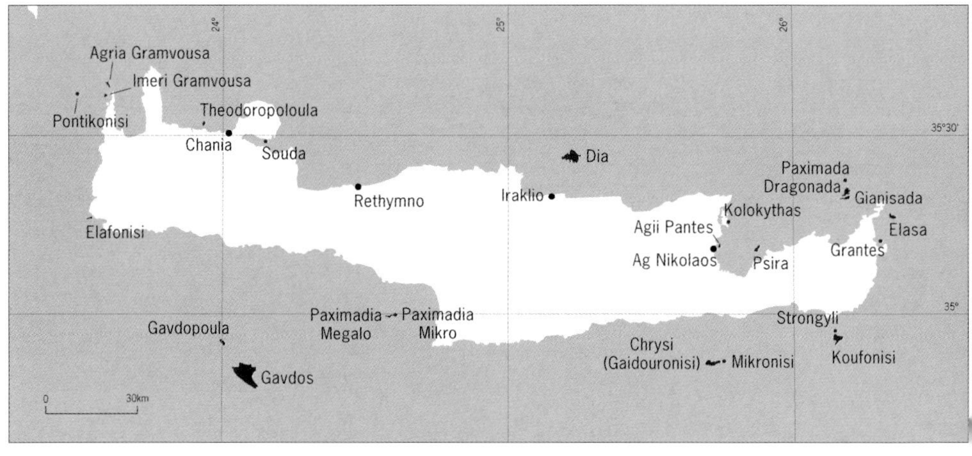
24°
25°
26°
35°30'
35°
Agria Gramvousa
Imeri Gramvousa
Pontikonisi
Theodoropoloula
Chania
Souda
Dia
Paximada
Dragonada
Gianisada
Rethymno
Iraklio
Kolokythas
Elasa
Elafonisi
Agii Pantes
Ag Nikolaos
Psira
Grantes
Paximadia
Megalo
Paximadia
Mikro
Strongyli
Gavdopoula
Chrysi
(Gaidouronisi)
Mikronisi
Koufonisi
Gavdos
0
30km

code	island	co-ordinates		sq km
Crete				
6001	Dia	35°27' N	25°13' E	11.909
6010	Souda	35°29' N	24°09' E	0.103
6015	Theodoropoula	35°32' N	23°55' E	0.905
6020	Imeri Gramvousa	35°36' N	23°34' E	0.722
6021	Agria Gramvousa	35°38' N	23°35' E	0.825
6022	Pontikonisi	35°35' N	23°28' E	0.266
6030	Elafonisi	35°16' N	23°31' E	0.435
6040	Paximadia Megalo	35°00' N	24°35' E	0.677
6041	Paximadia Mikro	35°00' N	24°36' E	0.566
6050	Gavdos	34°50' N	24°05' E	33.025
6051	Gavdopoula	34°55' N	24°00' E	1.775
6060	Chrysi (Gaidouronisi)	34°52' N	25°42' E	4.743
6061	Mikronisi	34°52' N	25°44' E	0.123
6070	Koufonisi	34°56' N	26°08' E	4.26
6071	Strongyli	34°57' N	26°08' E	0.151
6080	Elasa	35°16' N	26°20' E	1.746
6081	Grantes	35°12' N	26°17' E	0.302
6085	Gianisada	35°19' N	26°10' E	2.098
6086	Dragonada	35°20' N	26°10' E	2.892
6088	Paximada	35°22' N	26°10' E	0.311
6090	Psira	35°11' N	25°51' E	1.518
6091	Agii Pantes	35°11' N	25°43' E	0.346
6092	Kolokythas	35°15' N	25°45' E	0.144

Syros, Andros, Tinos

code	island	co-ordinates		sq km
6301	Didymi	37°25′ N	24°58′ E	0.47
6303	Aspro	37°23′ N	24°59′ E	0.116
6401	Megalo Gavronisi	37°50′ N	24°45′ E	0.25
6410	Gyaros	37°36′ N	24°43′ E	18
6411	Glaronisi	37°35′ N	24°45′ E	0.192
6451	Planitis/Panormos	37°39′ N	25°03′ E	0.126

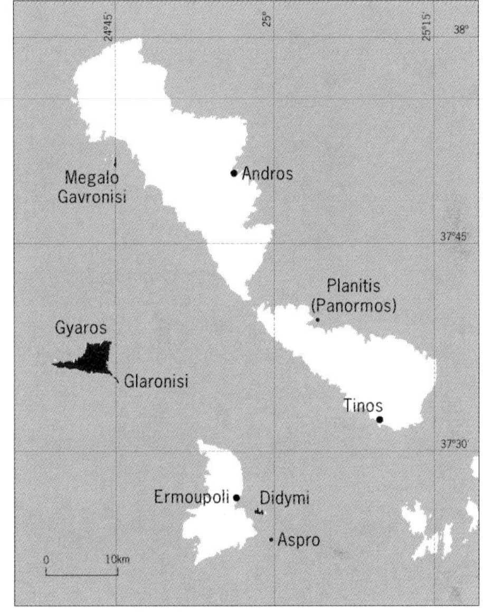
24°45'
25°
25°15'
38°
Megalo
Gavronisi
Andros
37°45'
Planitis
(Panormos)
Gyaros
Glaronisi
Tinos
37°30'
Ermoupoli
Didymi
Aspro
0
10km

Western Cyclades

code	island	co-ordinates		sq km
6251	Kitriani	36°54′ N	24°43′ E	0.937
6261	Serfopoula	37°15′ N	24°35′ E	1.859
6262	Vous	37°08′ N	24°33′ E	0.204
6271	Piperi	37°18′ N	24°31′ E	0.432
6285	Makronisos	37°42′ N	24°07′ E	18.427
6286	Raftis	37°52′ N	24°02′ E	0.096

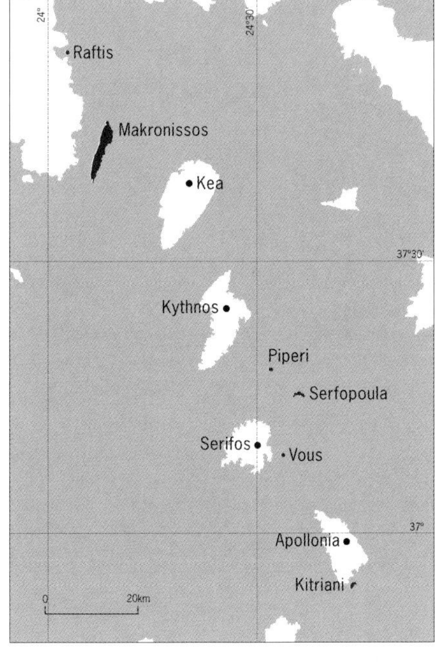
24°
24°30'
Raftis
Makronissos
Kea
37°30'
Kythnos
Piperi
Serfopoula
Serifos
Vous
37°
Apollonia
Kitriani
0
20km

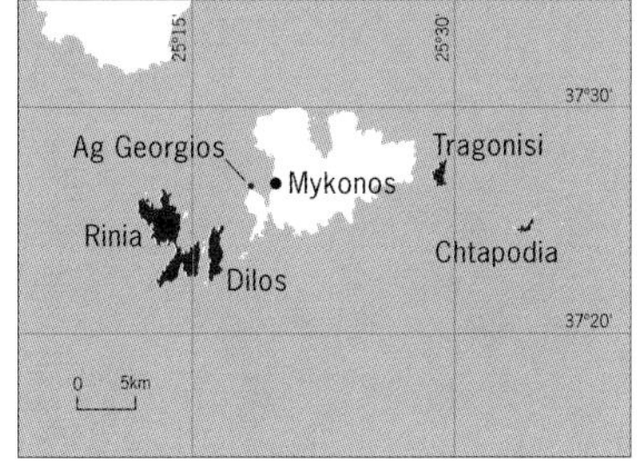
25°15'
25°30'
37°30'
Ag Georgios
Mykonos
Tragonisi
Rinia
Dilos
Chtapodia
37°20'
0
5km

Mykonos

code	island	co-ordinates		sq km
6501	Ag Georgios	37°26′ N	25°18′ E	0.132
6510	Tragonisi	37°26′ N	25°29′ E	1.402
6520	Chtapodia	37°24′ N	25°34′ E	0.452
6550	Dilos	37°23′ N	25°16′ E	3.536
6560	Rinia	37°24′ N	25°13′ E	14

code	island	co-ordinates		sq km
Paros, Antiparos				
6610	Gaidouronisi	37°09' N	25°16' E	0.148
6615	Viokastro	37°09' N	25°17' E	0.118
6620	Filitzi	37°07' N	25°17' E	0.187
6630	Dryonisi	36°59' N	25°14' E	0.371
6640	Panteronisi	36°58' N	25°07' E	0.484
6645	Glarobi	36°58' N	25°06' E	0.209
6655	Despotiko	36°57' N	25°00' E	7.754
6660	Strongylo	36°57' N	24°57' E	1.638
6670	Diplo	37°03' N	25°04' E	0.492
6680	Kavouras	37°03' N	25°05' E	0.294

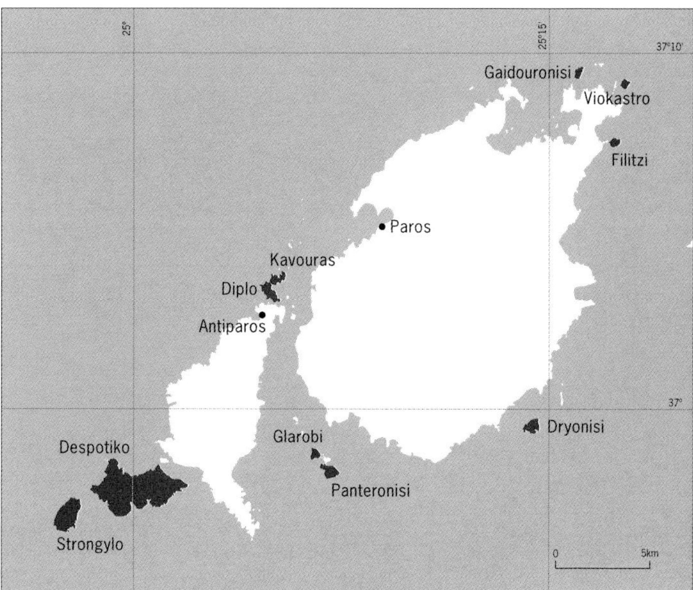
25°
25°15'
37°10'
Gaidouronisi
Viokastro
Filitzi
Paros
Kavouras
Diplo
Antiparos
37°
Dryonisi
Glarobi
Despotiko
Panteronisi
Strongylo
0
5km

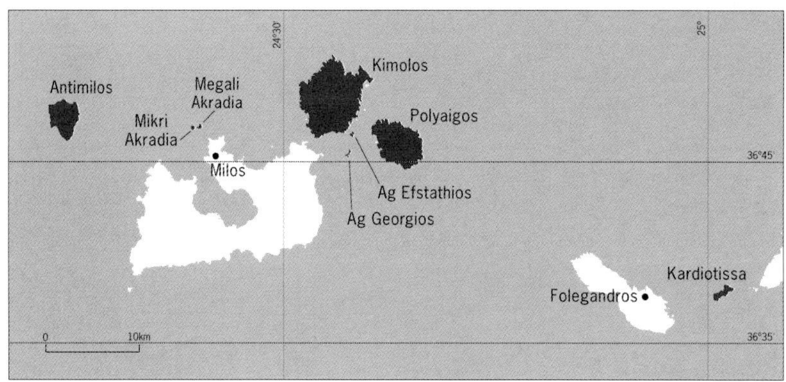
24°30'
25°
Kimolos
Antimilos
Megali
Akradia
Polyaigos
Mikri
Akradia
Milos
36°45'
Ag Efstathios
Ag Georgios
Kardiotissa
Folegandros
0
10km
36°35'

code	island	co-ordinates		sq km
Milos, Folegandros				
6171	Kardiotissa	36°37' N	25°01' E	1.43
6201	Megali Akradia	36°46' N	24°24' E	0.195
6202	Mikri Akradia	36°46' N	24°23' E	0.098
6203	Ag Georgios	36°45' N	24°34' E	0.111
6204	Ag Efstathios	36°46' N	24°34' E	0.099
6205	Antimilos	36°47' N	24°14' E	8.801
6210	Kimolos	36°48' N	24°33' E	37.426
6215	Polyaigos	36°45' N	24°38' E	18

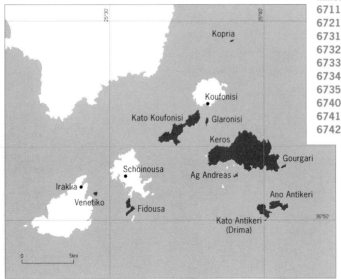

code	island	co-ordinates		sq km
Minor Cyclades				
6711	Venetiko	36°51′ N	25°29′ E	0.121
6721	Fidousa	36°50′ N	25°31′ E	0.63
6731	Glaronisi	36°54′ N	25°36′ E	0.156
6732	Ag Andreas	36°52′ N	25°38′ E	0.103
6733	Gourgari	36°52′ N	25°41′ E	0.119
6734	Kopria	36°58′ N	25°38′ E	0.145
6735	Kato Koufonisi	36°54′ N	25°34′ E	3.879
6740	Keros	36°53′ N	25°38′ E	15
6741	Ano Antikeri	36°50′ N	25°40′ E	1.077
6742	Kato Antikeri/Drima	36°50′ N	25°39′ E	1.079

Amorgos

code	island	co-ordinates		sq km
6751	Anydros	36°37′ N	25°41′ E	0.907
6752	Gramvousa	36°48′ N	25°44′ E	0.825
6753	Grabonisi	36°52′ N	25°53′ E	0.164
6754	Nikouria	36°53′ N	25°54′ E	2.744
6780	Donousa	37°06′ N	25°48′ E	13.652
6781	Skylonisi	37°07′ N	25°50′ E	0.243
6790	Makares/Ag Nikolaos	37°05′ N	25°41′ E	0.912
6791	Strongylo	37°04′ N	25°42′ E	0.354
6792	Ag Paraskevi	37°04′ N	25°42′ E	0.275

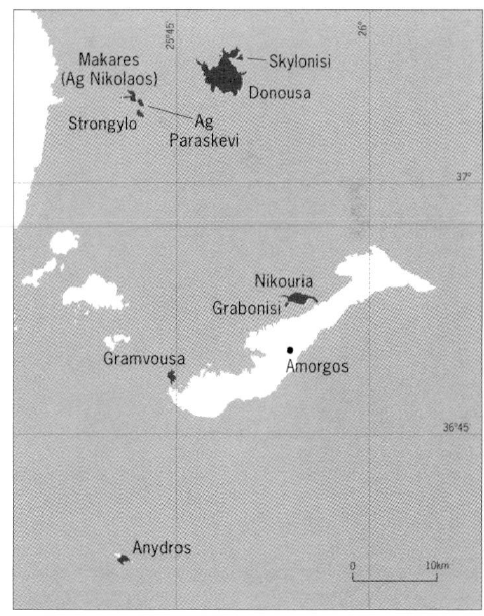
25°45′
26°
Makares
(Ag Nikolaos)
Skylonisi
Donousa
Strongylo
Ag
Paraskevi
37°
Nikouria
Grabonisi
Amorgos
Gramvousa
36°45′
Anydros
0
10km

Santorini, Anafi

code	island	co-ordinates		sq km
6101	Nea Kammeni	36°24′ N	25°23′ E	3.338
6102	Palaia Kammeni	36°23′ N	25°22′ E	0.525
6104	Aspronisi	36°22′ N	25°20′ E	0.142
6110	Christiani	36°14′ N	25°12′ E	1.188
6111	Askania	36°14′ N	25°12′ E	0.257
6120	Thirasia	36°26′ N	25°20′ E	9.246
6141	Pachia	36°16′ N	25°49′ E	1.425
6142	Makra	36°16′ N	25°53′ E	0.569

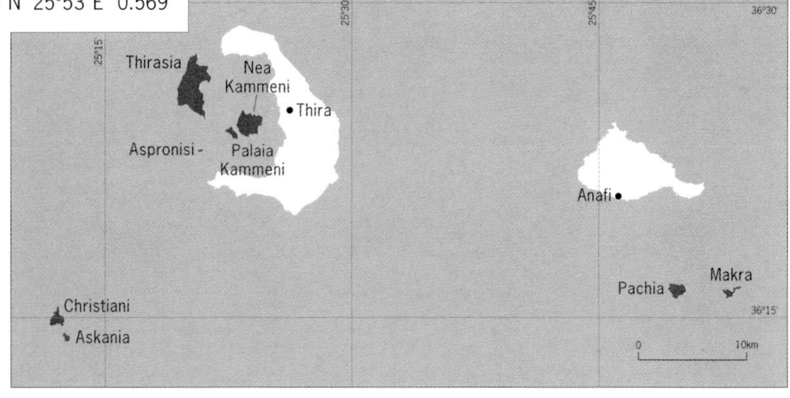
25°15′
25°30′
25°45′
36°30′
Thirasia
Nea
Kammeni
Thira
Aspronisi
Palaia
Kammeni
Anafi
Pachia
Makra
36°15′
Christiani
Askania
0
10km

code	island	co-ordinates		sq km
Skyros				
6851	Valaxa	38°49′ N	24°29′ E	4.336
6852	Skyropoula	38°50′ N	24°21′ E	3.797
6853	Sarakino (Despoti)	38°45′ N	24°36′ E	3.383
6854	Platia	38°45′ N	24°35′ E	0.619
6855	Rinia	38°49′ N	24°25′ E	0.541
6856	Koulouri	38°52′ N	24°26′ E	0.292
6857	Mesa Podia	39°01′ N	24°28′ E	0.131
6858	Exo Podies	38°59′ N	24°29′ E	0.12

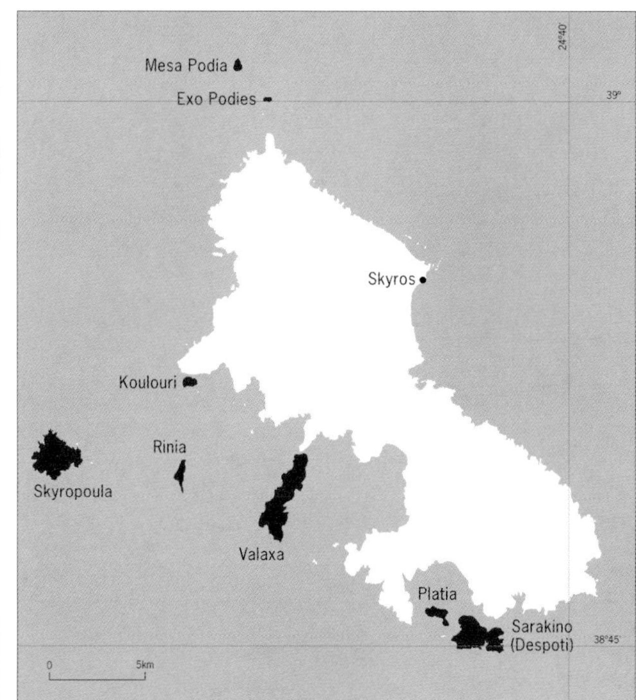
Mesa Podia
Exo Podies
Skyros
Koulouri
Rinia
Skyropoula
Valaxa
Platia
Sarakino
(Despoti)
24°40′
39°
38°45′
0
5km

23°
Pontikonisi
Argyronisi
Monolia
Atalanti
Gaidaros
Koili
Kymi
Kyponisi
(Gaidaros)
Chalkida
Oniron
(Pezonisos)
Kavalliani
Parthenopi
Styra
Petousi
Akio
Elafi
Lamperousa
Tragonisi
Chersonisi
Founti
Megalonisos
Mandilou
38°
0
20km

code	island	co-ordinates		sq km
Evvoia				
6801	Mandilou	37°56′ N	23°49′ E	0.47
6810	Megalonisos	37°59′ N	24°15′ E	17
6811	Chersonisi	38°01′ N	24°17′ E	3.833
6812	Tragonisi	38°01′ N	24°16′ E	0.268
6813	Founti	38°01′ N	24°14′ E	0.128
6814	Lamperousa	38°02′ N	24°16′ E	0.332
6815	Elafi	38°04′ N	24°12′ E	0.132
6820	Styra	38°10′ N	24°09′ E	3.048
6821	Petousi	38°09′ N	24°09′ E	0.152
6822	Akio	38°05′ N	24°09′ E	0.207
6823	Parthenopi	38°11′ N	24°05′ E	0.1
6825	Kavalliani	38°13′ N	24°6′ E	1.971
6826	Oniron/Pezonisos	38°23′ N	23°48′ E	0.069
6830	Gaidaros	38°38′ N	23°06′ E	1.675
6831	Monolia	38°49′ N	22°49′ E	0.345
6832	Atalanti	38°40′ N	23°05′ E	1.674
6840	Argyronisi	39°00′ N	23°04′ E	0.357
6845	Pontikonisi	39°02′ N	23°20′ E	0.359
6846	Ktyponisi/Gaidaros	38°29′ N	23°30′ E	0.249
6847	Koili	38°40′ N	24°07′ E	0.182

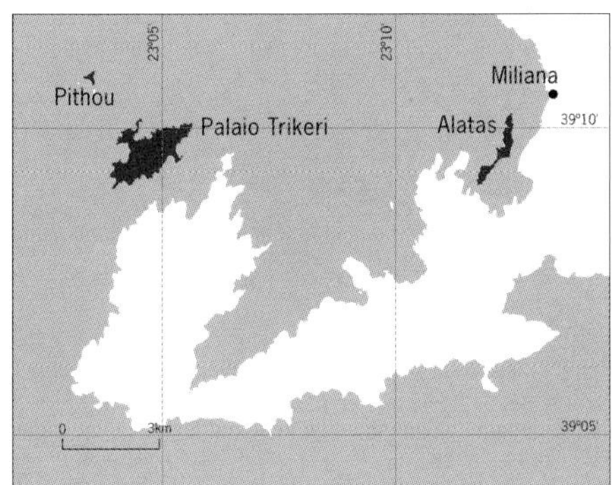
23°05'
23°10'
Pithou
Palaio Trikeri
Miliana
Alatas
39°10'
0
3km
39°05'

Pagasitic Gulf

code	island	co-ordinates		sq km
6990	Palaio Trikeri	39°09' N	23°04' E	2.476
6991	Pithou	39°10' N	23°03' E	0.176
6992	Alatas	39°09' N	23°12' E	0.566

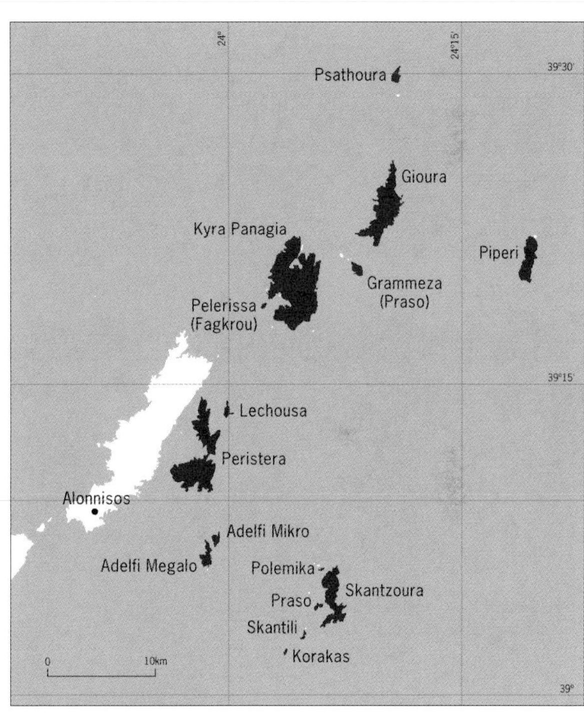
24°
24°15'
39°30'
Psathoura
Gioura
Kyra Panagia
Piperi
Grammeza
(Praso)
Pelerissa
(Fagkrou)
39°15'
Lechousa
Peristera
Alonnisos
Adelfi Mikro
Adelfi Megalo
Polemika
Skantzoura
Praso
Skantili
Korakas
0
10km
39°

code	island	co-ordinates		sq km
Alonnisos				
6961	Adelfi Megalo	39°06' N	23°58' E	1.032
6962	Adelfi Mikro	39°07' N	23°59' E	0.392
6965	Peristera	39°11' N	23°58' E	14.513
6966	Lechousa	39°13' N	23°59' E	0.527
6970	Skantzoura	39°04' N	24°06' E	6.333
6971	Polemika	39°06' N	24°06' E	0.114
6972	Praso	39°04' N	24°05' E	0.262
6973	Skantili	39°02' N	24°04' E	0.214
6974	Korakas	39°02' N	24°03' E	0.122
6980	Kyra Panagia	39°19' N	24°04' E	24.973
6981	Pelerissa/Fagkrou	39°18' N	24°02' E	0.174
6982	Grammeza/Praso	39°20' N	24°8' E	0.843
6985	Gioura	39°23' N	24°10' E	11
6986	Piperi	39°20' N	24°19' E	4.166
6987	Psathoura	39°29' N	24°10' E	0.762

23°30'
23°45'
Aspronisо
Skiathos
39°10'
Arkos
Ag Georgios
Dasia
Skopelos
Tsougkria
39°05'
0
5km

Skiathos, Skopelos

code	island	co-ordinates		sq km
6901	Tsougkria	39°07' N	23°29' E	1.173
6902	Arkos	39°09' N	23°31' E	0.414
6903	Aspronisо	39°10' N	23°31' E	0.173
6951	Dasia	39°06' N	23°38' E	0.34
6952	Ag Georgios	39°08' N	23°48' E	0.417

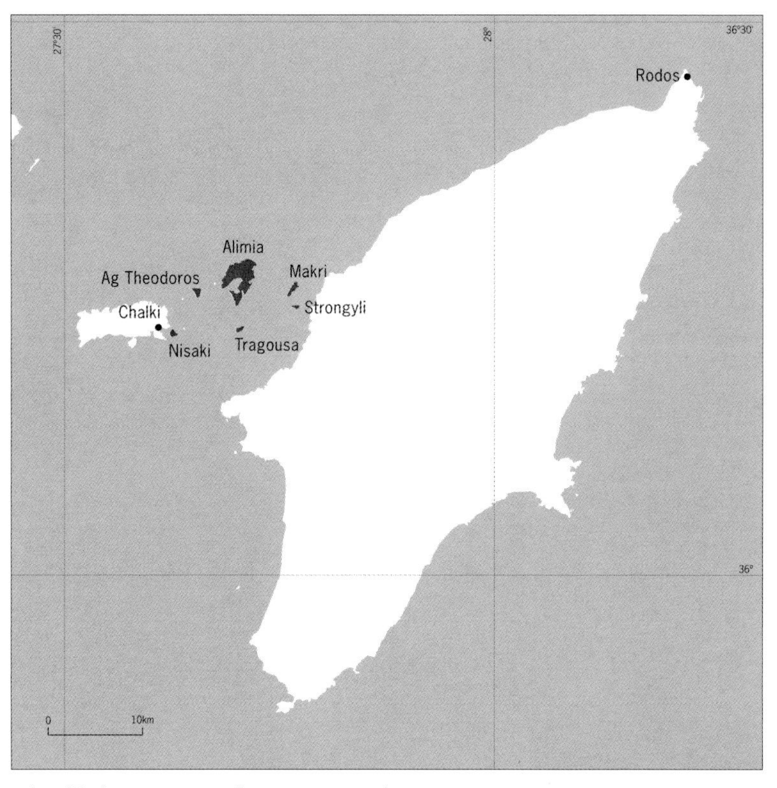

27°30'
28°
36°30'
Rodos
Alimia
Ag Theodoros
Makri
Strongyli
Chalki
Nisaki
Tragousa
36°
0
10km

code	island	co-ordinates		sq km
Rhodes, Chalki				
7001	Makri	36°15' N	27°46' E	0.581
7006	Strongyli	36°14' N	27°46' E	0.22
7021	Nisaki	36°13' N	27°37' E	0.313
7022	Ag Theodoros	36°15' N	27°39' E	0.651
7023	Tragousa	36°16' N	27°42' E	0.279
7025	Alimia	36°16' N	27°42' E	7

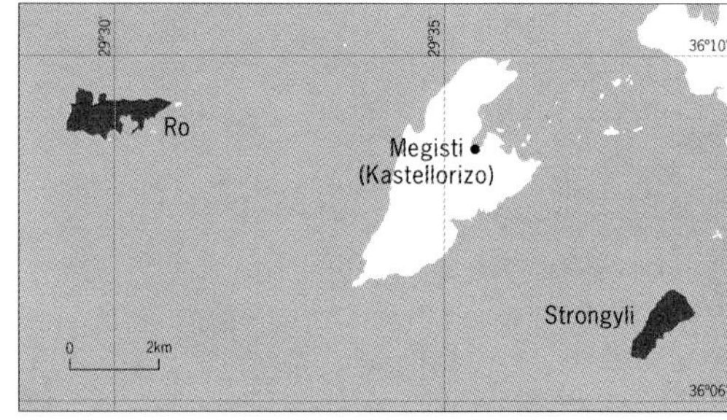

29°30'
29°35'
36°10'
Ro
Megisti
(Kastellorizo)
Strongyli
0
2km
36°06'

code	island	co-ordinates		sq km
Megisti (Kastellorizo)				
7011	Ro	36°09' N	29°30' E	1.476
7012	Strongyli	36°06' N	29°38' E	0.22

Symi

7031	Seskli	36°31′N	27°51′E	1.835
7032	Gialesina	36°34′N	27°45′E	0.117
7033	Megalonisi	36°34′N	27°45′E	0.109
7034	Kouloundros	36°30′N	27°52′E	0.152
7035	Nimos	36°39′N	27°50′E	4.657
7036	Chondros	36°39′N	27°49′E	0.19

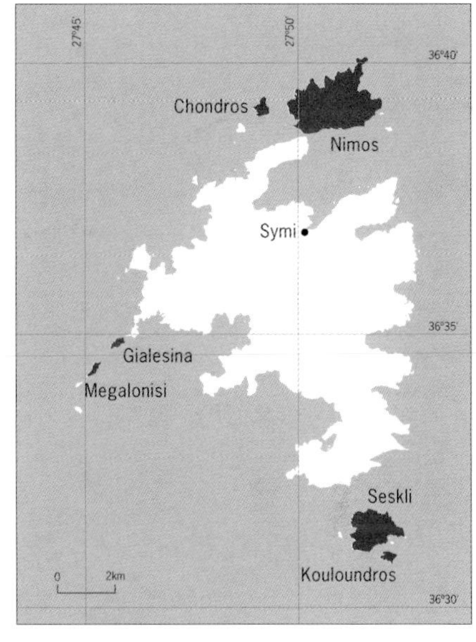
27°45'
27°50'
36°40'
Chondros
Nimos
Symi
36°35'
Gialesina
Megalonisi
Seskli
0
2km
Kouloundros
36°30'

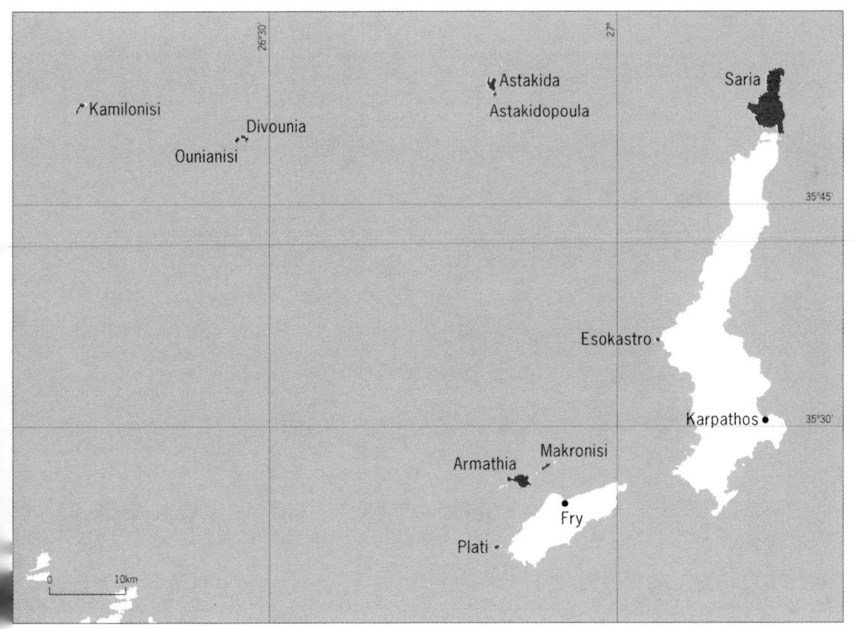
26°30'
27°
Astakida
Astakidopoula
Saria
Kamilonisi
Divounia
Ounianisi
35°45'
Esokastro
Karpathos
35°30'
Makronisi
Armathia
Fry
Plati
0
10km

code	island	co-ordinates		sq km
Karpathos, Kasos				
7110	Saria	35°51′N	27°13′E	20.429
7145	Esokastro	35°35′N	27°03′E	0.119
7152	Makronisi	35°27′N	26°53′E	0.296
7153	Plati	35°21′N	26°49′E	0.205
7155	Armathia	35°26′N	26°51′E	2.532
7160	Astakida	35°53′N	26°49′E	0.984
7161	Astakidopoula	35°52′N	26°49′E	0.136
7170	Divounia	35°49′N	26°27′E	0.275
7171	Ounianisi	35°49′N	26°27′E	0.211
7180	Kamilonisi	35°51′N	26°13′E	0.429

code	island	co-ordinates		sq km
Tilos, Nisyros				
7051	Gaidouronisi	36°28' N	27°17' E	0.794
7055	Antitilos	36°22' N	27°27' E	0.509
7056	Gaidaros	36°26' N	27°23' E	0.176
7221	Kandeliousa	36°30' N	26°58' E	1.363
7222	Pergousa	36°35' N	27°02' E	1.169
7223	Pachia	36°34' N	27°04' E	1.184
7224	Strongyli	36°40' N	27°10' E	0.217
7225	Gyali	36°39' N	27°07' E	4.558

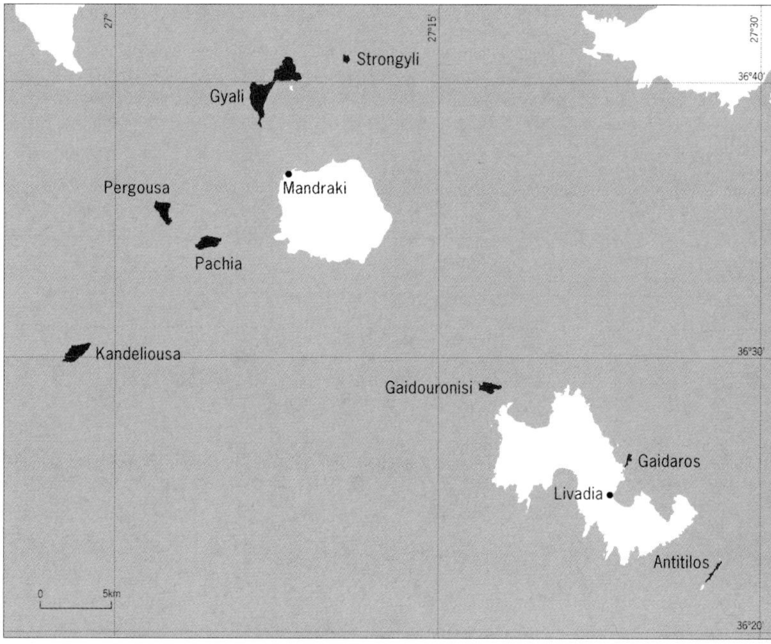
27°
27°15'
27°30'
36°40'
Strongyli
Gyali
Mandraki
Pergousa
Pachia
Kandeliousa
36°30'
Gaidouronisi
Gaidaros
Livadia
Antitilos
0
5km
36°20'

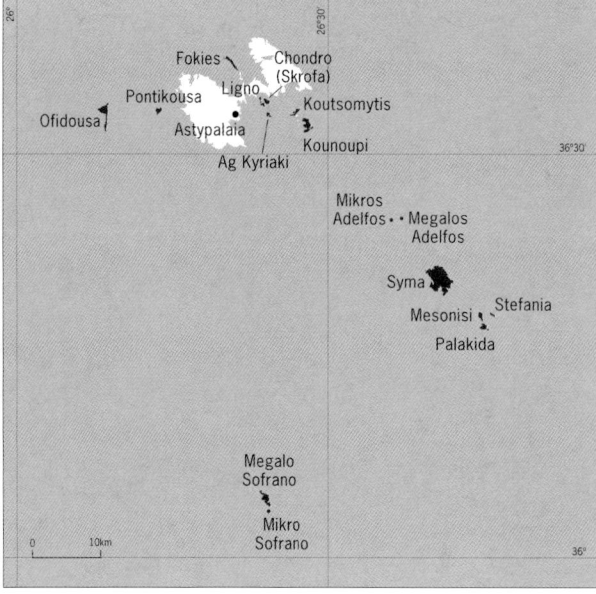
26°
26°30'
Fokies
Chondro
(Skrofa)
Pontikousa
Ligno
Koutsomytis
Ofidousa
Astypalaia
Kounoupi
36°30'
Ag Kyriaki
Mikros
Adelfos
Megalos
Adelfos
Syrna
Stefania
Mesonisi
Palakida
Megalo
Sofrano
Mikro
Sofrano
0
10km
36°

code	island	co-ordinates		sq km
Astypalaia				
7351	Ofidousa	36°33' N	26°08' E	1.94
7352	Pontikousa	36°33' N	26°13' E	0.982
7353	Fokies	36°36' N	26°21' E	0.569
7360	Ligno	36°33' N	26°23' E	0.238
7361	Chondro (Skrofa)	36°33' N	26°24' E	0. 387
7362	Ag Kyriaki	36°32' N	26°24' E	0.254
7363	Koutsomytis	36°33' N	26°26' E	0.459
7364	Kounoupi	36°32' N	26°28' E	1.457
7370	Megalos Adelfos	36°25' N	26°36' E	0.226
7371	Mikros Adelfos	36°25' N	26°36' E	0.133
7380	Syrna	36°20' N	26°40' E	7.885
7385	Palakida	36°17' N	26°44' E	0.514
7386	Mesonisi	36°17' N	26°44' E	0.416
7387	Stefania	36°18' N	26°45' E	0.144
7390	Megalo Sofrano	36°04' N	26°24' E	1.281
7391	Mikro Sofrano	36°03' N	26°24' E	0.104

26°30'
27°
37°30'
Psathonisi (Plato)
Neronisi
Megalo Horio
Kouneli
Anydros
Strongyli
Arkoi
Agrelousa
Makronisi
Kalovolos
Arefousa
Marathos
Patmos
Chiliomodi
Lipsoi
Tragonisi
Farmakonisi
Makronisi
Fragkos
Archangelos
Strongyli
Faradonisia
Ag Kyriaki
Lakki
Piganousa
Mavro Megalo
Mavro Mikro
Levitha
37°
Kinaros
Laros
Liadi
0
10km

code	island	co-ordinates		sq km
Leros, Patmos, Lipsoi, Arkoi, Agathonisi				
7401	Piganousa	37°06' N	26°54' E	0.371
7402	Ag Kyriaki	37°08' N	26°53' E	0.125
7403	Faradonisia	37°11' N	26°45' E	0.229
7404	Strongyli	37°12' N	26°49' E	0.174
7405	Archangelos	37°12' N	26°46' E	1.621
7410	Farmakonisi	37°17' N	27°05' E	3.866
7420	Levitha	37°00' N	26°27' E	9.121
7421	Mavro Megalo	36°59' N	26°22' E	0.152
7422	Mavro Mikro	36°59' N	26°22' E	0.133
7430	Kinaros	36°58' N	26°17' E	4.577
7431	Laros	36°59' N	26°19' E	0.177
7435	Liadi	36°54' N	26°09' E	0.333
7441	Fragkos	37°15' N	26°43' E	0.223
7442	Arefousa	37°19' N	26°42' E	0.18
7443	Makronisi	37°16' N	26°44' E	0.195
7451	Chiliomodi	37°18' N	26°36' E	0.28
7452	Tragonisi	37°17' N	26°34' E	0.379
7453	Anydros	37°24' N	26°29' E	0.307
7461	Strongyli	37°22' N	26°42' E	0.21
7462	Makronisi	37°21' N	26°45' E	0.258
7463	Kalovolos	37°21' N	26°45' E	0.306
7465	Agrelousa	37°21' N	26°42' E	1.328
7470	Marathos	37°22' N	26°43' E	0.355
7481	Kouneli	37°25' N	26°58' E	0.213
7482	Psathonisi/Plato	37°29' N	26°57' E	0.124
7483	Neronisi	37°28' N	26°59' E	0.433

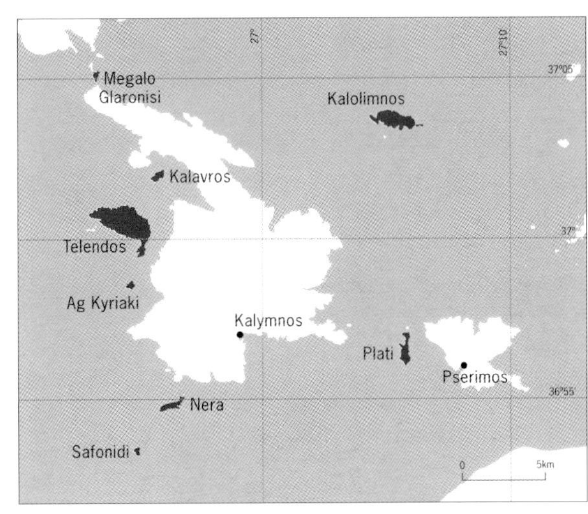
27°
27°10'
37°05'
Megalo Glaronisi
Kalolimnos
Kalavros
37°
Telendos
Ag Kyriaki
Kalymnos
Plati
Pserimos
36°55'
Nera
Safonidi
0
5km

code	island	co-ordinates		sq km
Kalymnos				
7301	Kalavros	37°01' N	26°55' E	0.296
7302	Megalo Glaronisi	37°05' N	26°53' E	0.127
7305	Kalolimnos	37°03' N	27°05' E	1.912
7306	Nera	36°54' N	26°56' E	0.456
7307	Safonidi	36°53' N	26°55' E	0.155
7308	Ag Kyriaki	36°58' N	26°54' E	0.147
7310	Telendos	37°00' N	26°54' E	4.648
7321	Plati	36°56' N	27°05' E	0.726

code	island	co-ordinates		sq km
Samos				
7501	Ag Nikolaos	37°47' N	26°58' E	0.119
7502	Kasonisi	37°44' N	27°02' E	0.107
7505	Samiopoula	37°37' N	26°47' E	1.018

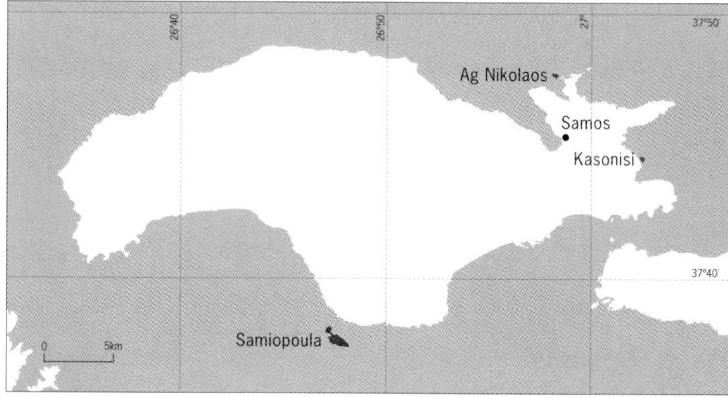
26°40'
26°50'
27°
37°50'
Ag Nikolaos
Samos
Kasonisi
37°40'
0
5km
Samiopoula

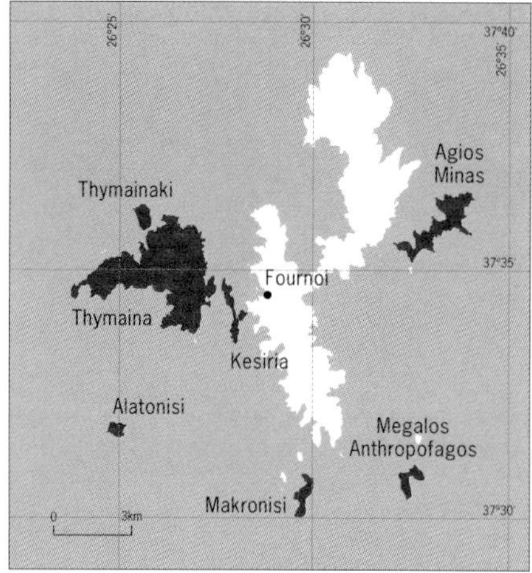
26°25'
26°30'
37°40'
26°35'
Agios
Minas
Thymainaki
37°35'
Fournoi
Thymaina
Kesiria
Alatonisi
Megalos
Anthropofagos
0
3km
Makronisi
37°30'

code	island	co-ordinates		sq km
Fournoi				
7521	Makronisi	37°30' N	26°29' E	0.655
7522	Alatonisi	37°31' N	26°24' E	0.299
7523	Agios Minas	37°35' N	26°33' E	2.343
7525	Kesiria	37°34' N	26°28' E	0.667
7526	Megalos Anthropofagos	37°31' N	26°32' E	0.557
7530	Thymaina	37°35' N	26°25' E	10.071
7531	Thymainaki	37°36' N	26°25' E	0.416

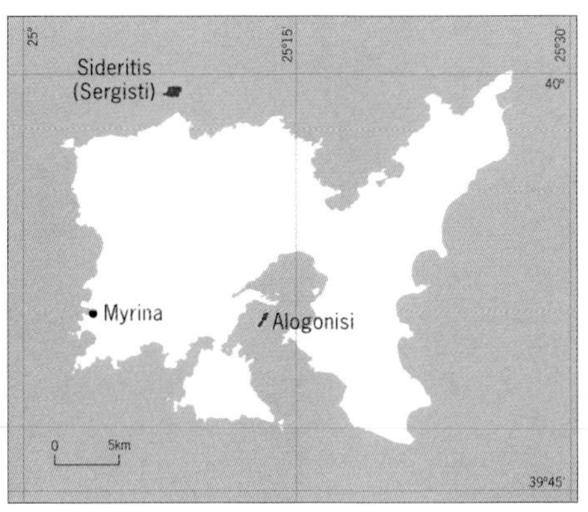
25°
25°15'
25°30'
40°
Sideritis
(Sergisti)
Myrina
Alogonisi
0
5km
39°45'

code	island	co-ordinates		sq km
Limnos				
7801	Alogonisi	39°51' N	25°13' E	0.281
7805	Sideritis/Sergitsi	40°01' N	25°08' E	0.946

code	island	co-ordinates		sq km
Lesvos				
7701	Tomaronisi/Barbalias	39°18' N	26°26' E	0.531
7702	Aspronisos	39°17' N	26°26' E	0.133
7703	Panagia	39°18' N	26°26' E	0.122
7705	Megalonisi	39°12' N	25°50' E	0.818
7706	Ag Georgios	39°20' N	26°08' E	0.155

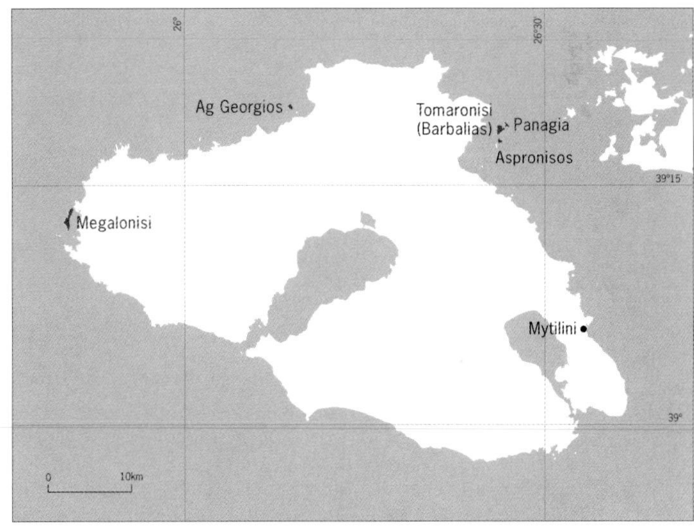
26°
26°30'
Ag Georgios
Tomaronisi
(Barbalias)
Panagia
Aspronisos
39°15'
Megalonisi
Mytilini
39°
0
10km

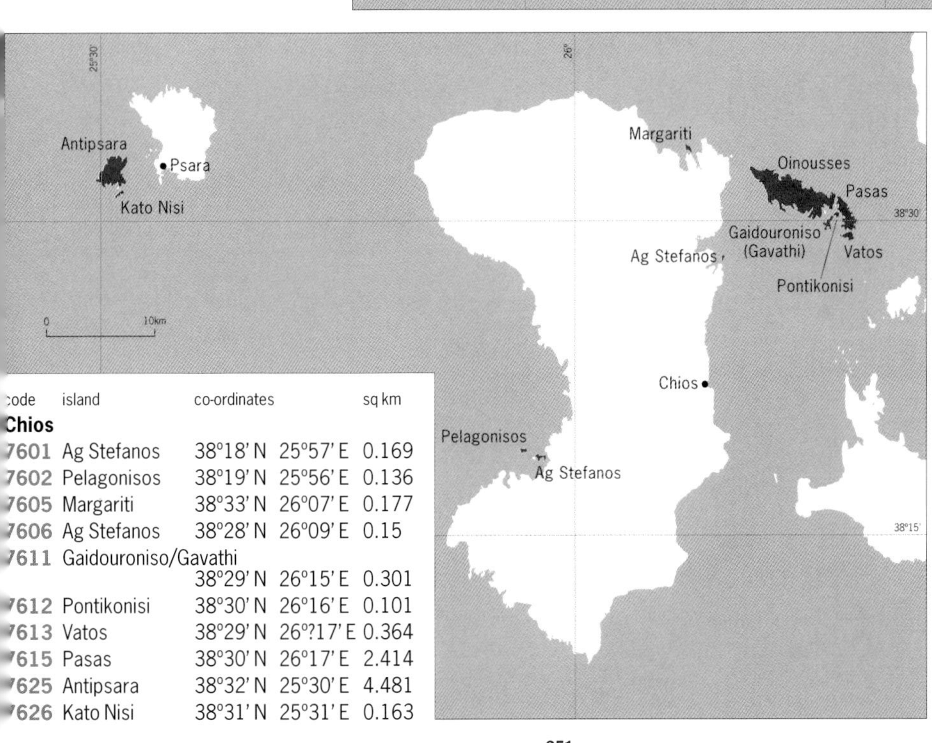
25°30'
26°
Antipsara
Psara
Kato Nisi
Margariti
Oinousses
Pasas
38°30'
Gaidouroniso
(Gavathi)
Vatos
Ag Stefanos
Pontikonisi
0
10km
Chios
Pelagonisos
Ag Stefanos
38°15'

code	island	co-ordinates		sq km
Chios				
7601	Ag Stefanos	38°18' N	25°57' E	0.169
7602	Pelagonisos	38°19' N	25°56' E	0.136
7605	Margariti	38°33' N	26°07' E	0.177
7606	Ag Stefanos	38°28' N	26°09' E	0.15
7611	Gaidouroniso/Gavathi	38°29' N	26°15' E	0.301
7612	Pontikonisi	38°30' N	26°16' E	0.101
7613	Vatos	38°29' N	26°?17' E	0.364
7615	Pasas	38°30' N	26°17' E	2.414
7625	Antipsara	38°32' N	25°30' E	4.481
7626	Kato Nisi	38°31' N	25°31' E	0.163

code	island	co-ordinates		sq km
Thasos				
7901	Koinyra	40°39′ N	24°46′ E	0.356
7902	Panagia	40°33′ N	24°37′ E	0.187
7903	Xeronisi	40°52′ N	24°20′ E	0.144
7905	Thasopoula	40°49′ N	24°42′ E	0.716

24°30′
24°45′
Xeronisi
Thasopoula
40°50′
Thasos
40°40′
Koinyra
0 5km
Panagia

Thraki, Samothraki

code	island	co-ordinates		sq km
7851	Zourafa	40°27′ N	25°50′ E	0.125
7980	Asanis	40°47′ N	26°01′ E	0.393
7981	Karaviou Xirafi	40°46′ N	26°01′ E	0.225

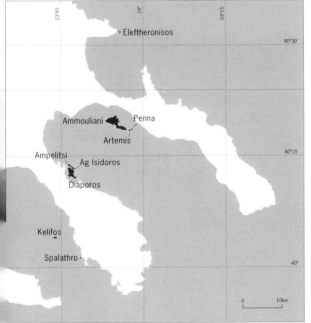

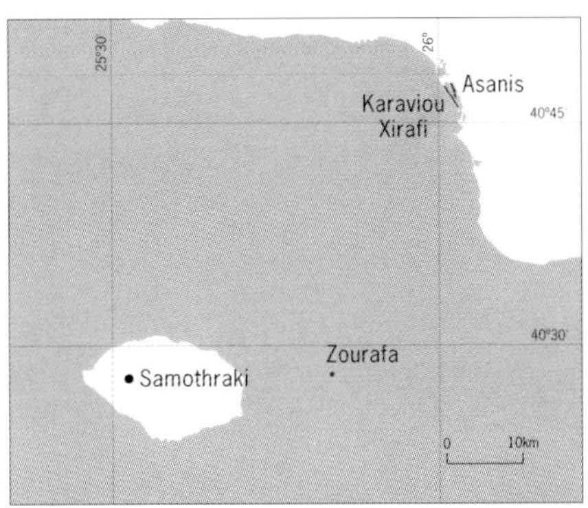
25°30′
26°
Asanis
Karaviou
Xirafi
40°45′
40°30′
Zourafa
Samothraki
0 10km

Chalkidiki

code	island	co-ordinates		sq km
7950	Ammouliani	40°19′ N	23°54′ E	7.136
7951	Artemis	40°18′ N	23°57′ E	0.168
7952	Penna	40°18′ N	23°57′ E	0.12
7960	Diaporos	40°12′ N	23°46′ E	3.162
7961	Ampelitsi	40°13′ N	23°46′ E	0.102
7962	Ag Isidoros	40°13′ N	23°47′ E	0.9
7970	Kelifos	40°03′ N	23°43′ E	0.78
7971	Spalathro	40°01′ N	23°48′ E	0.11
7973	Eleftheronisos	40°31′ N	23°55′ E	0.121

code	island	co-ordinates		sq km
Princes Islands				
8015	Kasikada	40°53' N	29°04' E	0.06
8030	Kinaliada	40°54' N	29°02' E	1.32
8040	Sedef	40°50' N	29°08' E	0.34
8050	Yassiada	40°51' N	28°59' E	0.12
8060	Sivriada	40°52' N	28°58' E	0.1
8070	Tavsanadasi	40°49' N	29°06' E	0.11

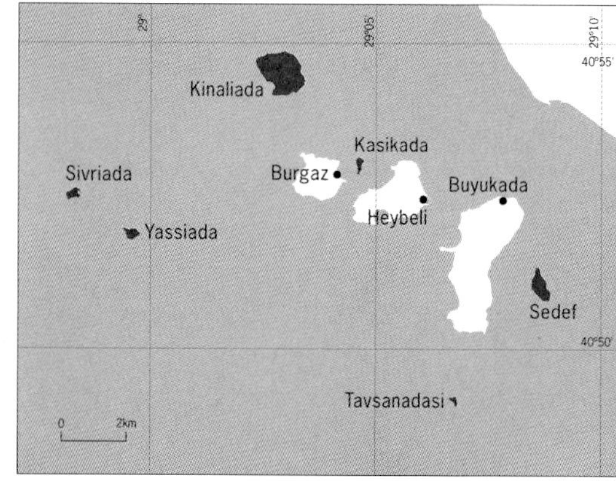
29°
29°05'
29°10'
40°55'
Kinaliada
Kasikada
Sivriada
Burgaz
Buyukada
Heybeli
Yassiada
Sedef
40°50'
Tavsanadasi
0
2km

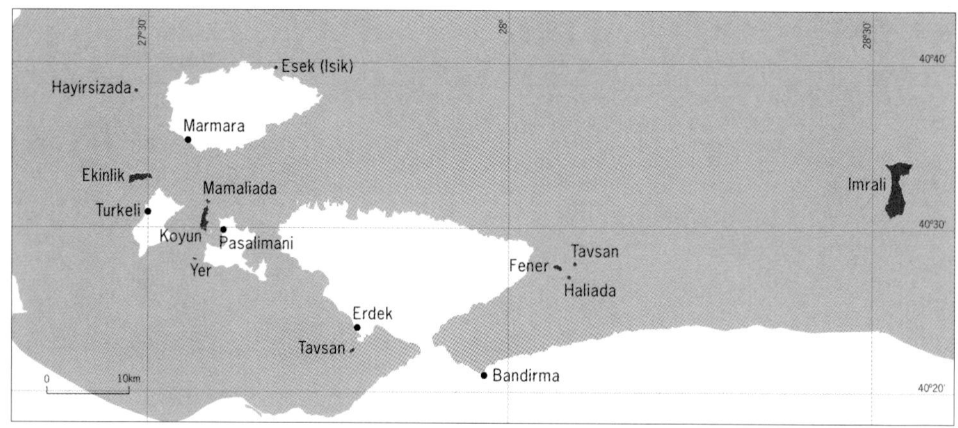
27°30'
28°
28°30'
40°40'
Esek (Isik)
Hayirsizada
Marmara
Ekinlik
Mamaliada
Imrali
Turkeli
Koyun
Pasalimani
40°30'
Yer
Tavsan
Fener
Haliada
Erdek
Tavsan
Bandirma
0
10km
40°20'

Balikesir, Sea of Marmara

code	island	co-ordinates		sq km
8101	Hayirsizada	40°38' N	27°29' E	0.39
8102	Esek/Isik	40°39' N	27°40' E	0.11
8111	Koyun	40°30' N	27°34' E	1.71
8112	Mamaliada	40°31' N	27°35' E	0.19
8113	Yer	40°28' N	27°33' E	0.14
8114	Tavsan	40°22' N	27°47' E	0.25
8130	Ekinlik	40°32' N	27°29' E	2.47
8141	Fener	40°27' N	28°04' E	0.57
8142	Tavsan	40°27' N	28°05' E	0.14
8143	Haliada	40°27' N	28°05' E	0.14
8150	Imrali	40°32' N	28°31' E	9.98

Gokceada
(Imroz)
Tavsan
Bozcaada
Kuthu
(Karaada)
Hasirada
Balik
Madenada
Kiz (Ulva)
Kucukmaden
Cicek
Gunes
Dolap
Cunda
Karaada (Balkan)
Moskoada
(Pinar)
Yellice
(Poyrazada)
Ciplakada
Mytilini
0 10km

Balikesir, Aegean Coast, Canakkale

code	island	co-ordinates		sq km
8201	Tavsan	39°56′ N	26°03′ E	0.93
8301	Madenada	39°23′ N	26°35′ E	2.99
8302	Moskoada/Pinar	39°20′ N	26°36′ E	1.06
8303	Gunes	39°19′ N	26°32′ E	0.65
8304	Yellice/Poyrazada	39°20′ N	26°35′ E	0.64
8305	Karaada	39°20′ N	26°34′ E	0.27
8306	Kucukmaden	39°22′ N	26°34′ E	0.21
8311	Balik	39°22′ N	26°42′ E	0.49
8312	Dolap	39°20′ N	26°41′ E	0.48
8313	Cicek	39°22′ N	26°45′ E	0.27
8314	Kiz/Ulva	39°24′ N	26°42′ E	0.14
8315	Kuthu/Karaada	39°22′ N	26°41′ E	0.14
8316	Hasirada	39°21′ N	26°40′ E	0.11
8320	Ciplakada	39°17′ N	26°35′ E	2.31

Izmir

code	island	co-ordinates		sq km
8401	Kalem	39°00′ N	26°47′ E	0.48
8402	Garip	39°00′ N	26°47′ E	0.4
8403	Mardalic/Kizkulesi	38°55′ N	26°49′ E	1.46
8404	Karaada	38°54′ N	26°50′ E	0.21
8405	Tavsan	38°51′ N	26°52′ E	0.74
8406	Hayirsizada	38°42′ N	26°42′ E	0.5
8407	Orak	38°41′ N	26°42′ E	0.93
8408	Incir	38°40′ N	26°43′ E	0.18
8409	Fener/Oglak	38°40′ N	26°42′ E	0.14
8410	Uzunada	38°30′ N	26°42′ E	25.39
8411	Hekim	38°26′ N	26°45′ E	2.31
8412	Yassicaada	38°24′ N	26°47′ E	0.31
8413	Pirnalliada	38°23′ N	26°47′ E	0.28
8414	Incirliada/Esek	38°24′ N	26°46′ E	0.58
8415	Karantina	38°22′ N	26°47′ E	0.35
8417	Yilan	38°19′ N	26°40′ E	0. 13
8419	Kucukada/Balta	38°25′ N	26°22′ E	0.33
8420	Uzunadalar	38°24′ N	26°18′ E	0.18
8421	Karada/Goni	38°26′ N	26°20′ E	6.9
8422	Karabag	38°23′ N	26°27′ E	0.49
8423	Cifteadalar	38°23′ N	26°26′ E	0.11
8424	Mustafa Celebi	38°21′ N	26°27′ E	0.6
8425	Yassiada	38°22′ N	26°27′ E	0.17
8426	Bogaz	38°17′ N	26°12′ E	0.14
8427	Bogurtlen	38°11′ N	26°26′ E	0.24
8428	Carufa	38°11′ N	26°25′ E	0.17
8429	Cirakan	38°11′ N	26°26′ E	0.13
8430	Kanliada/Esek	38°11′ N	26°46′ E	0.11

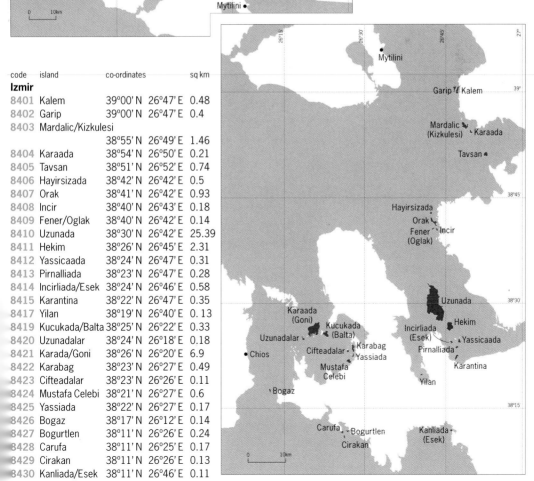

code	island	co-ordinates		sq km
Aydin, Mugla north				
8501	Tavsan/Cil	37°39' N	27°00' E	0.13
8502	Neo/Su	37°39' N	27°00' E	0.11
8503	Panayiada	37°19' N	27°19' E	0.44
8504	Toprak	37°16' N	27°22' E	0.24
8601	Salih	37°09' N	27°31' E	5.67
8602	Ikizadalar	37°07' N	27°28' E	0.37
8603	Buyuk/Tokatbasi	37°08' N	27°23' E	0.34
8604	Apostol/Konel	37°10' N	27°22' E	1.01
8605	Kiremit Buyuk	37°05' N	27°12' E	0.51
8606	Kiremit Kucuk	37°05' N	27°14' E	0.18
8607	Eskifener/Cavus	37°02' N	27°12' E	0.16
8608	Catalada	37°00' N	27°12' E	0.74
8609	Celebi	37°00' N	27°21' E	0.13
8610	Icada/Gorecik	36°59' N	27°23' E	0.44
8611	Karaada	36°58' N	27°27' E	9.08
8612	Orak	36°58' N	27°35' E	0.83
8613	Kistak	36°58' N	27°34' E	0.05
8615	Gelibolu/Camli	37°00' N	28°14' E	0.19
8616	Sehirola/Sideyri	36°59' N	28°12' E	0.22
8617	Karacaada	36°57' N	28°11' E	0.44
8618	Yediadalar	36°52' N	28°02' E	0.35
8619	Murdala/Akcali	36°46' N	27°27' E	0.14

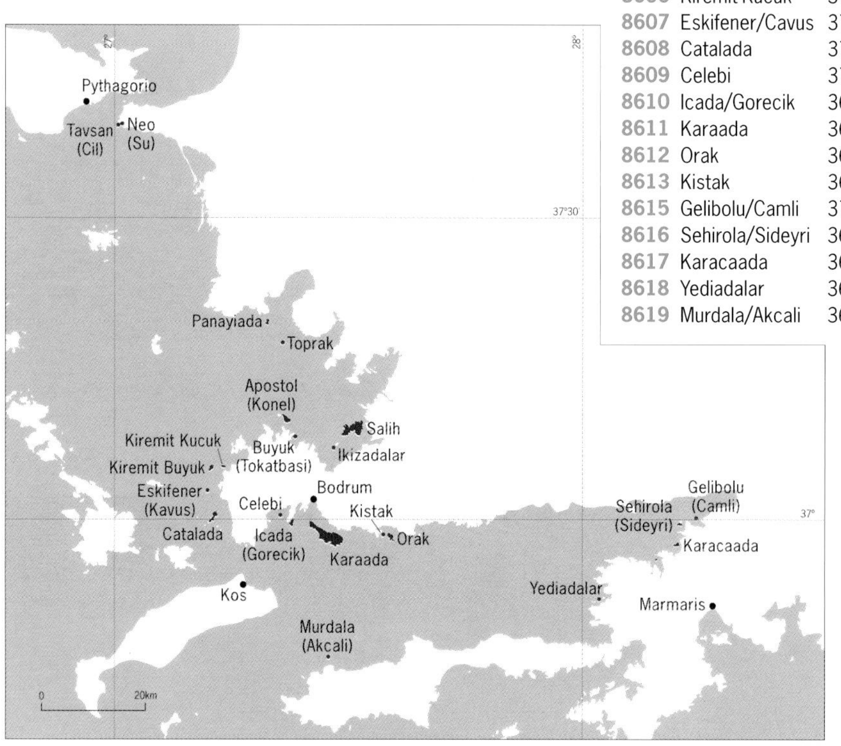

27°
28°
Pythagorio
Tavsan (Cil)
Neo (Su)
37°30'
Panayiada
Toprak
Apostol (Konel)
Salih
Kiremit Kucuk
Kiremit Buyuk
Buyuk (Tokatbasi)
Ikizadalar
Eskifener (Kavus)
Bodrum
Celebi
Kistak
Catalada
Icada (Gorecik)
Karaada
Orak
Sehirola (Sideyri)
Gelibolu (Camli)
Karacaada
37°
Kos
Yediadalar
Marmaris
Murdala (Akçali)
0
20km

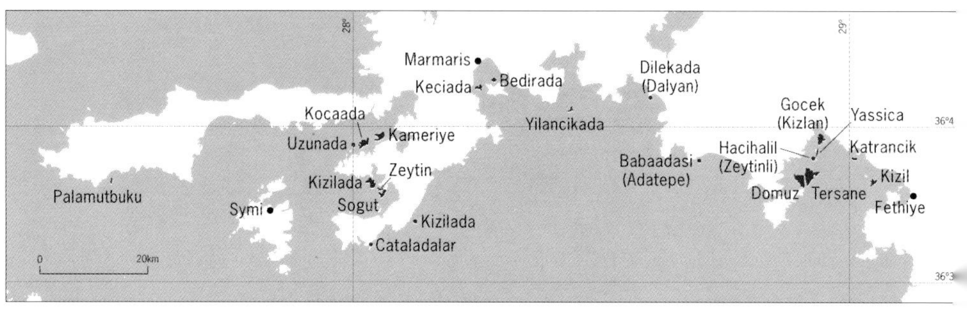

28°
29°
Marmaris
Keciada
Bedirada
Dilekada (Dalyan)
Kocaada
Uzunada
Kameriye
Yilancikada
Gocek (Kizlan)
Yassica
Hacihalil (Zeytinli)
Katrancik
Babaadasi (Adatepe)
Zeytin
Kizilada
Sogut
Palamutbuku
Symi
Kizilada
Cataladalar
Domuz
Tersane
Kizil
Fethiye
0
20km

code	island	co-ordinates		sq km
Mugla south				
8701	Palamutbuku	36°39' N	27°30' E	0.16
8702	Kameriye	36°43' N	28°03' E	1.17
8703	Kocaada	36°43' N	28°01' E	1.67
8704	Uzunada	36°43' N	28°00' E	0.16
8705	Kizilada	36°39' N	28°02' E	1.72
8706	Zeytin	36°38' N	28°03' E	0.16
8707	Sogut	36°38' N	28°03' E	0.76
8708	Cataladalar	36°33' N	28°02' E	0.13
8709	Kizilada	36°35' N	28°07' E	0.24
8710	Keciada	36°48' N	28°15' E	0.76
8711	Bedirada	36°49' N	28°17' E	0.14
8712	Yilancikada	36°46' N	28°26' E	0.49
8713	Dilekada/Dalyan	36°47' N	28°35' E	0.38
8714	Babaadasi/Adatepe	36°41' N	28°41' E	0.13
8715	Domuz	36°39' N	28°54' E	1.93
8716	Tersane	36°40' N	28°55' E	3.68
8717	Hacihalil/Zeytinli	36°41' N	28°55' E	0.32
8718	Yassica	36°42' N	28°56' E	0.26
8719	Gocek/Kizlan	36°43' N	28°56' E	1.48
8720	Katrancik	36°41' N	29°00' E	0.28
8721	Kizil	36°39' N	29°02' E	0.68

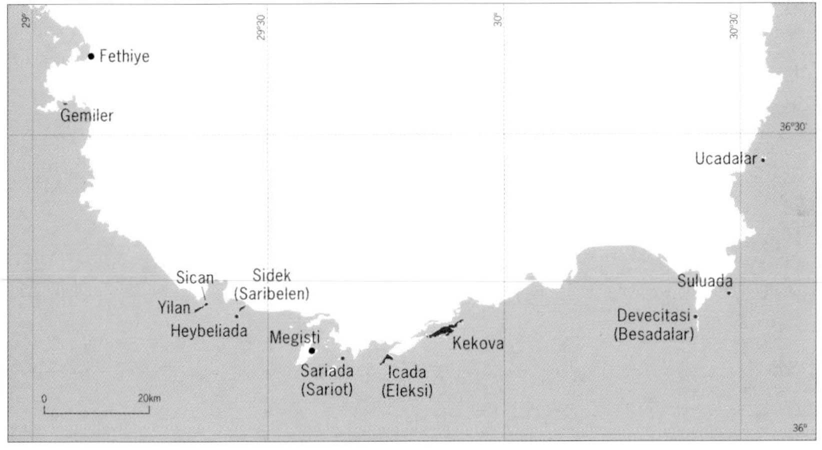
Fethiye
Gemiler
Ucadalar
Sican
Sidek
(Saribelen)
Yilan
Heybeliada
Megisti
Sariada
(Sariot)
Icada
(Eleksi)
Kekova
Suluada
Devecitasi
(Besadalar)
0
20km
29°
29°30'
30°
30°30'
36°30'
36°

code	island	co-ordinates		sq km
Antalya				
8801	Gemiler	36°33' N	29°04' E	0.2
8802	Yilan	36°12' N	29°21' E	0.53
8803	Sican	36°13' N	29°22' E	0.23
8804	Heybeliada	36°12' N	29°26' E	0.1
8805	Sidek/Saribelen	36°13' N	29°26' E	0.33
8806	Sariada/Sariot	36°07' N	29°39' E	0.25
8807	Icada/Eleksi	36°07' N	29°44' E	1.35
8808	Kekova	36°10' N	29°50' E	5.74
8809	Devecitasi/Besadalar	36°11' N	30°24' E	0.19
8810	Suluada	36°14' N	30°28' E	0.28
8811	Ucadalar	36°27' N	30°32' E	0.11

code	island	co-ordinates		sq km
Icel, Cyprus, Syria, Lebanon				
8812	Babadil/Besparmak	36°07' N	33°31' E	0.18
8813	Dana/Kargincik	36°11' N	33°46' E	2.69
9001	Klides	35°42' N	34°36' E	0.15
9100	Arwad	34°51' N	35°51' E	0.2
9200	Palm/An Nakhl	34°29' N	35°46' E	0.2

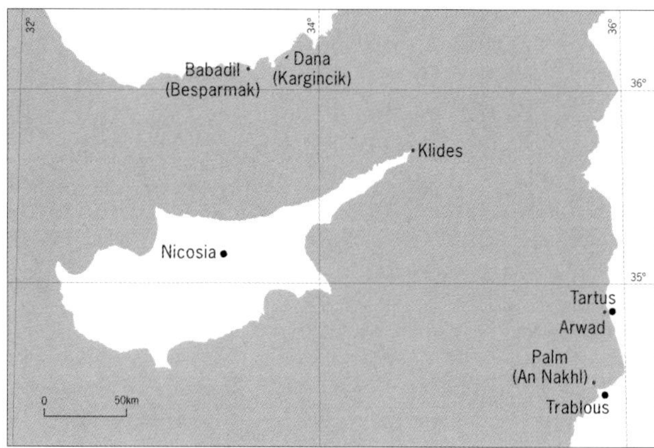
32°
34°
36°
36°
35°
Babadil
(Besparmak)
Dana
(Kargincik)
Klides
Nicosia
Tartus
Arwad
Palm
(An Nakhl)
Trablous
0
50km

Malta

code	island	co-ordinates		sq km
9301	St Paul's	35°57' N	14°24' E	0.101
9320	Comino	36°00' N	14°20' E	2.784
9321	Cominotto	36°00' N	14°19' E	0.098

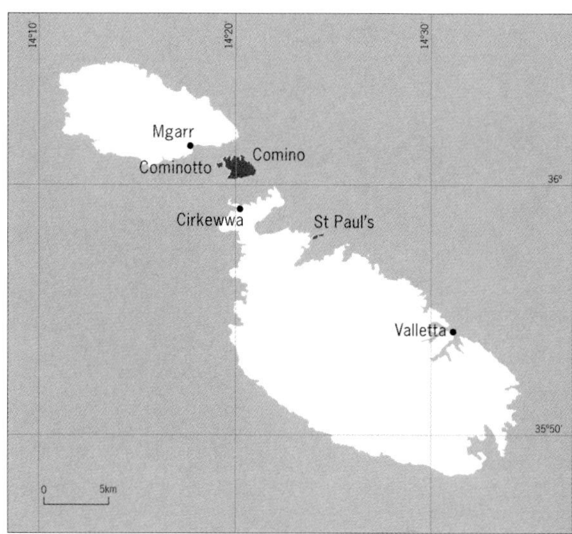
14°10'
14°20'
14°30'
36°
35°50'
Mgarr
Comino
Cominotto
Cirkewwa
St Paul's
Valletta
0
5km

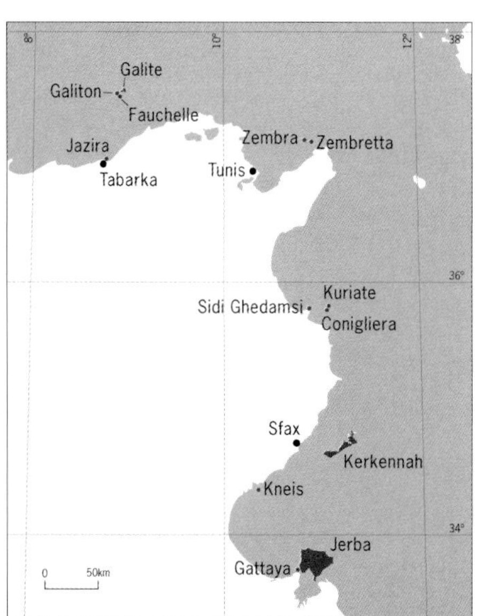
8°
10°
12°
38°
36°
34°
Galite
Galiton
Fauchelle
Jazira
Tabarka
Zembra
Zembretta
Tunis
Sidi Ghedamsi
Kuriate
Conigliera
Sfax
Kerkennah
Kneis
Jerba
Gattaya
0
50km

Tunisia

code	island	co-ordinates		sq km
9400	Djerba	33°47' N	10°53' E	526.46
9401	Gattaya el Baharia	33°43'N	10°43' E	0. 86
9410	Kerkennah	34°42' N	11°11' E	153.51
9420	Galite	37°31' N	08°55' E	7.48
9421	Galiton	37°30' N	08°52' E	0.28
9422	Fauchelle	37°29' N	08°53' E	0.14
9425	Jazira	36°56' N	08°44' E	0.6
9430	Kneis	34°22' N	10°19' E	4.13
9440	Zembra	37°08' N	10°48' E	3.59
9441	Zembretta	37°07' N	10°52' E	0.05
9450	Kuriate	35°47' N	11°02' E	2.71
9451	Conigliera	35°46' N	11°00' E	0.55
9452	Sidi Ghedamsi	35°47' N	10°50' E	0.13

Statistics

Much of the statistical information in this section has been compiled especially for this book and is not available anywhere else.

This is the first time that a comparative study of the islands of the Mediterranean has been published. Never before have they been ranked and listed by size or by population.

The length of the coastline of each country, both mainland and islands, is also set out for the first time. The accuracy of coastline and area measurement is now improving greatly as a result of satellite mapping and computer measurement techniques.

While we have tried to ensure that the best data available have been selected in every case, there is room for improvement. For example, the Hellenic Navy Hydrographic Service (HNHS) is currently engaged in a major reassessment of the islands in Greek waters.

This is also the first time that a comparative study has been made of the number of visitors to the Mediterranean islands.

Some of the visitor statistics that we have received appear to be incomplete and the figures for the turnover of visitor accommodation, the key measure of efficiency for the tourism industry, show huge differences between one country and another. These will no doubt be studied closely by national tourism organisations.

The compilation of these statistics has also given rise to our unique 'Crowdfactor' measurement, the number of visitors plus residents per square kilometre, which differs greatly from one island to another but is a reliable indicator of the crowdedness of an island.

It should be noted that Cyprus has been treated as a single entity throughout the book, but readers may be interested to know that the occupied part of the island comprises 36% of its land area, 27% of its population following large migrations from Turkey, 24% of its tourist capacity, 22% of its visitors and 52% of its coastline, a further 9% of which is taken by military bases.

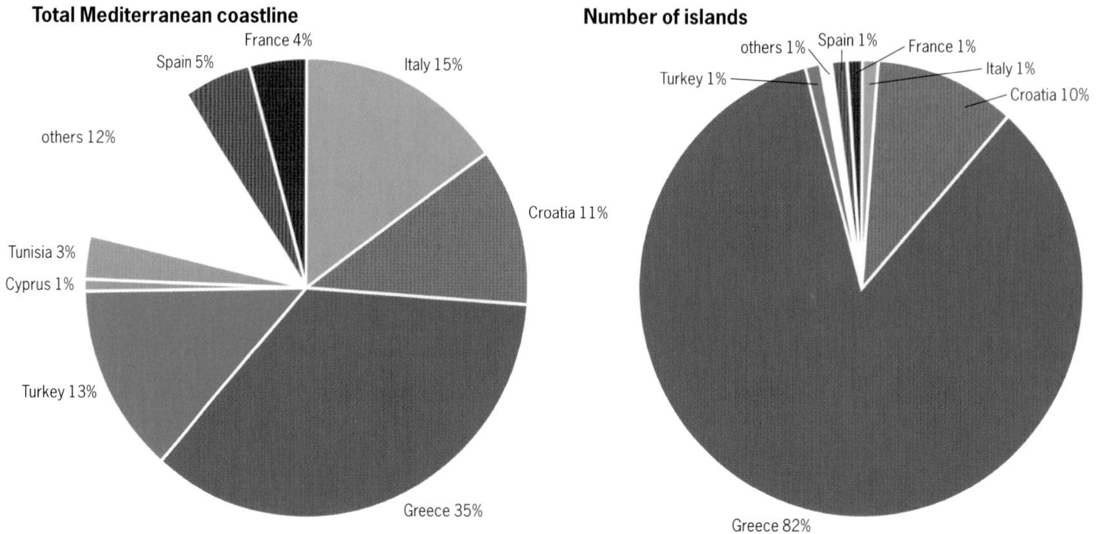
Total Mediterranean coastline
France 4%
Spain 5%
Italy 15%
others 12%
Croatia 11%
Tunisia 3%
Cyprus 1%
Turkey 13%
Greece 35%
Number of islands
others 1%
Spain 1%
France 1%
Turkey 1%
Italy 1%
Croatia 10%
Greece 82%

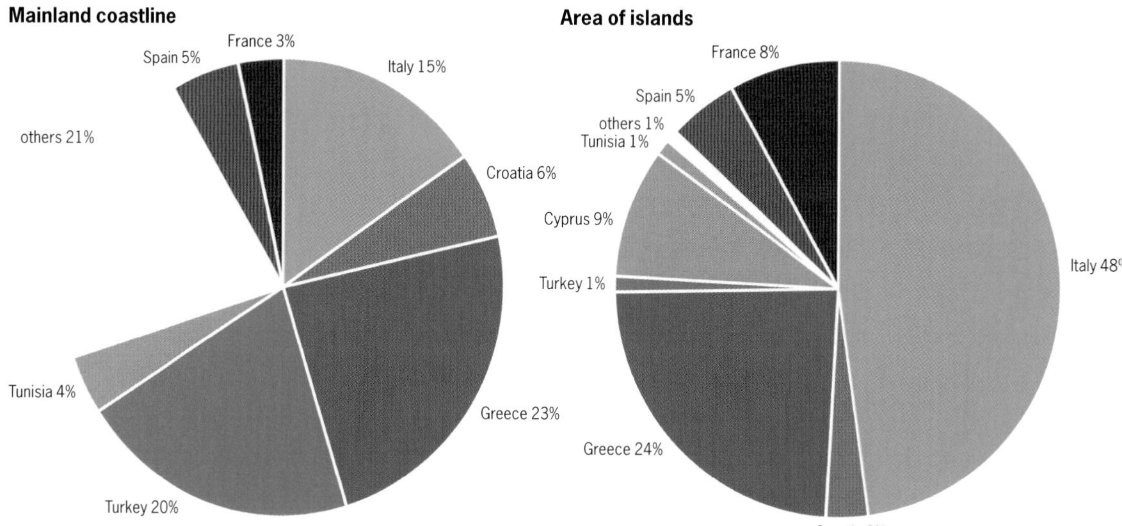
Mainland coastline
France 3%
Spain 5%
Italy 15%
others 21%
Croatia 6%
Tunisia 4%
Greece 23%
Turkey 20%
Area of islands
France 8%
Spain 5%
others 1%
Tunisia 1%
Cyprus 9%
Turkey 1%
Italy 48
Greece 24%
Croatia 3%

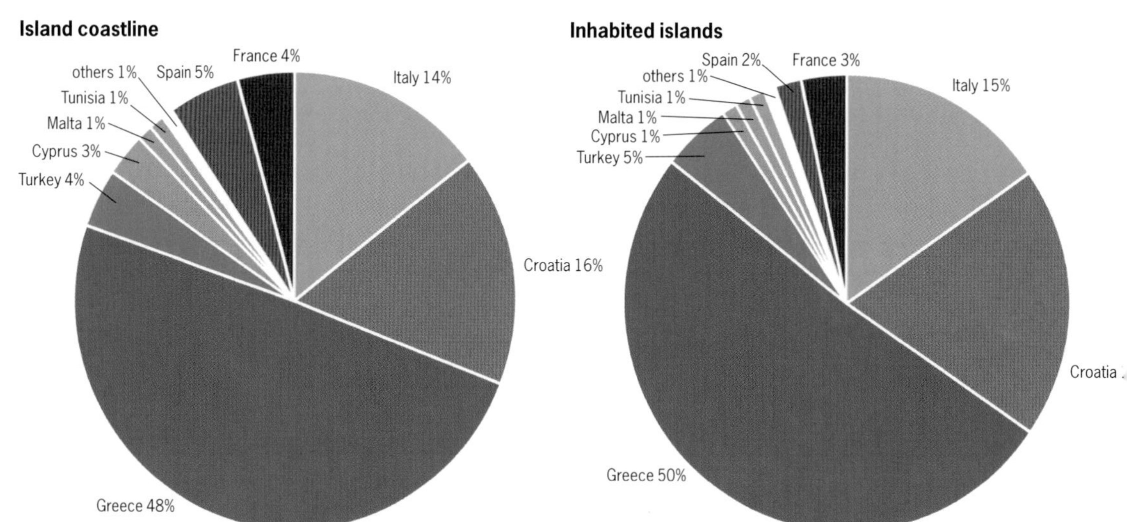
Island coastline
France 4%
others 1%
Spain 5%
Italy 14%
Tunisia 1%
Malta 1%
Cyprus 3%
Turkey 4%
Croatia 16%
Greece 48%
Inhabited islands
Spain 2%
France 3%
others 1%
Italy 15%
Tunisia 1%
Malta 1%
Cyprus 1%
Turkey 5%
Croatia
Greece 50%

Percentages by country

Percentage shares by country differ hugely with different measurements. It is difficult to say which is the most important island country in the Mediterranean. Many people would say Greece, which ranks first by number of islands, both inhabited and uninhabited, by coastline length, by number of islands providing accommodation and by number of hotels and visitor beds. Italy however ranks first by island area and population, while Spain has by far the greatest number of visitors to its islands.

	total coastline (km)	mainland coastline (km)	island coastline (km)	number of islands	area of islands ('000 sq km)	inhabited islands
Total	52374	27752	24622	11879	102.8	243
	100%	100%	100%	100%	100%	100%
Italy	7911	4320	3591	215	50.0	38
	15%	15%	14%	1%	48%	15%
Croatia	5835	1777	4058	1246	3.3	47
	11%	6%	16%	10%	3%	19%
Greece	18400	6400	12000	9835	25.0	123
	35%	23%	48%	82%	24%	50%
Turkey	6677	5610	1067	158	0.6	13
	13%	20%	4%	1%	1%	5%
Cyprus	782	0	782	4	9.2	1
	1%	0%	3%	0%	9%	1%
Malta	190	0	190	6	0.3	3
	0%	0%	1%	0%	0%	1%
Tunisia	1641	1297	344	19	0.6	2
	3%	4%	1%	0%	1%	1%
Spain	3037	1609	1428	188	5.0	6
	5%	5%	5%	1%	5%	2%
France	2056	994	1062	202	8.7	8
	4%	3%	4%	1%	8%	3%
9 countries total	46529	22007	24522	11873	102.7	241
	88%	79%	99%	99%	99%	99%

	population of islands ('000s)	islands with accomm	number of hotels	number of visitor beds ('000s)	number of visitors (millions est)
Total	11231	218	10769	1710	38.0
	100%	100%	100%	100%	100%
Italy	6711	35	2723	261	8.4
	59%	16%	25%	15%	22%
Croatia	121	66	111	162	2.5
	1%	30%	1%	9%	6%
Greece	1594	87	5530	568	5.3
	14%	40%	51%	33%	14%
Turkey	42	10	56	18	0.5
	1%	4%	0%	1%	1%
Cyprus	953	1	700	126	3.1
	8%	0%	6%	7%	8%
Malta	404	3	138	39	1.1
	3%	1%	1%	2%	3%
Tunisia	153	2	115	55	1.1
	1%	1%	1%	3%	3%
Spain	983	5	978	423	12.8
	8%	2%	9%	24%	33%
France	261	9	418	56	3.2
	2%	4%	4%	3%	8%
9 countries total	11227	218	10769	1710	38.0
	99%	100%	100%	100%	100%

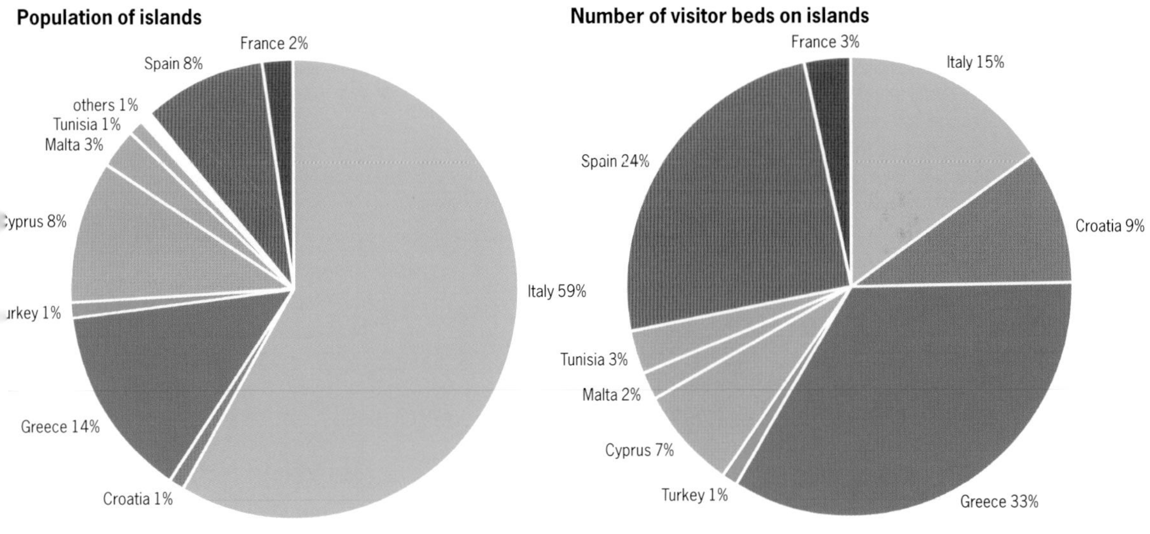
Population of islands
France 2%
Spain 8%
others 1%
Tunisia 1%
Malta 3%
yprus 8%
rkey 1%
Greece 14%
Croatia 1%
Italy 59%
Number of visitor beds on islands
France 3%
Italy 15%
Spain 24%
Croatia 9%
Tunisia 3%
Malta 2%
Cyprus 7%
Turkey 1%
Greece 33%

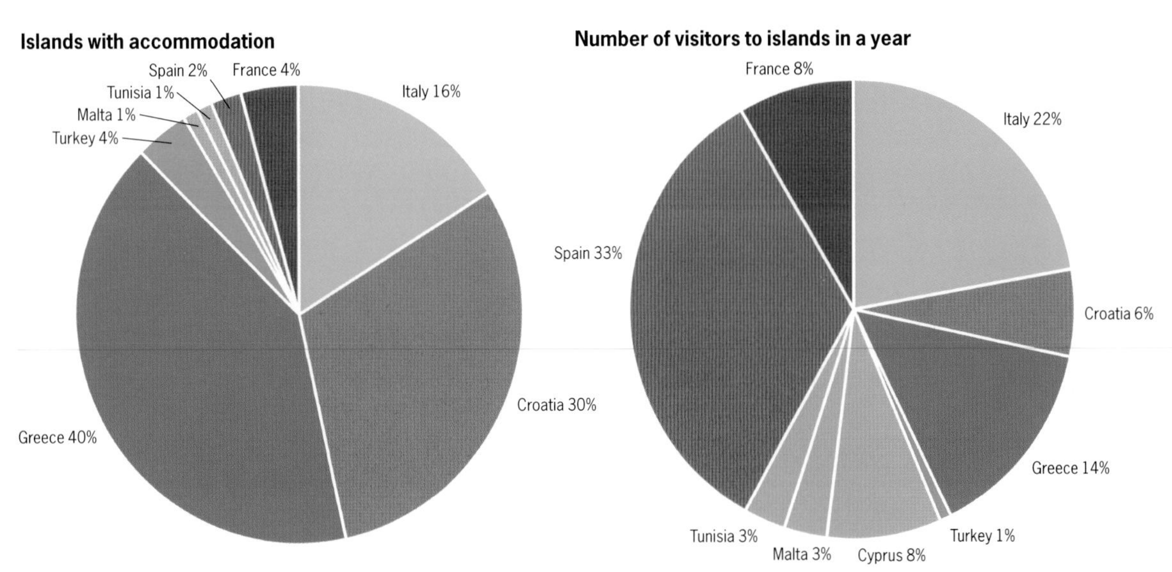
Islands with accommodation
Spain 2%
France 4%
Tunisia 1%
Malta 1%
Turkey 4%
Italy 16%
Croatia 30%
Greece 40%
Number of visitors to islands in a year
France 8%
Italy 22%
Spain 33%
Croatia 6%
Greece 14%
Tunisia 3%
Malta 3%
Cyprus 8%
Turkey 1%

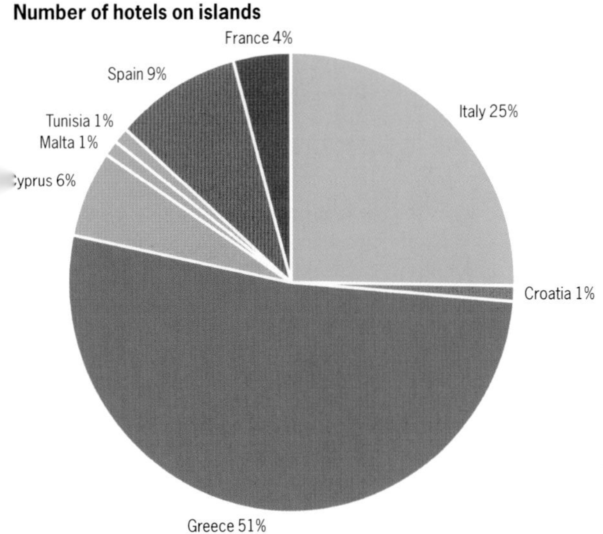
Number of hotels on islands
France 4%
Spain 9%
Italy 25%
Tunisia 1%
Malta 1%
yprus 6%
Croatia 1%
Greece 51%

Ranking by size: the top 200 islands

There are exactly 200 islands in the Mediterranean with a surface area greater than five square kilometres.

Only Greece and Croatia publish island measurement statistics for their islands on a regular basis and figures for the islands of other countries are derived from our own research.

rank	code	island	square kilometres
1	3000	**Sicilia**	25426.200
2	3500	**Sardegna**	23812.600
3	9000	**Kypros (Cyprus)**	9251.000
4	2000	**Corse (Corsica)**	8679.800
5	6000	**Kriti (Crete)**	8261.183
6	6800	**Evvoia**	3661.637
7	1000	**Mallorca**	3620.858
8	7700	**Lesvos**	1635.998
9	7000	**Rodos (Rhodes)**	1401.459
10	7600	**Chios**	842.796
11	5200	**Kefalonia**	734.014
12	1100	**Menorca**	693.587
13	5000	**Kerkyra (Corfu)**	585.312
14	1200	**Eivissa (Ibiza)**	568.935
15	9400	**Djerba**	526.460
16	7500	**Samos**	477.942
17	7800	**Limnos**	476.288
18	5400	**Zakynthos**	406.619
19	4100	**Krk**	405.780
19	4110	**Cres**	405.780
21	4700	**Brac**	394.570
22	6700	**Naxos**	389.434
23	7900	**Thasos**	383.672
24	6400	**Andros**	383.022
25	5100	**Lefkada**	301.106
26	7100	**Karpathos**	300.152
27	4750	**Hvar**	299.660
28	7200	**Kos**	287.611
29	4200	**Pag**	284.560
30	8200	**Gokceada**	279.240
31	5500	**Kythira**	277.746
32	4800	**Korcula**	276.030
33	7550	**Ikaria**	255.320
34	9300	**Malta**	245.728
35	3400	**Elba**	223.000
36	6850	**Skyros**	208.594
37	6450	**Tinos**	197.044
38	6600	**Paros**	196.755
39	7850	**Samothraki**	180.364
40	6200	**Milos**	158.403
41	9410	**Kerkennah**	153.510
42	6280	**Kea**	131.693
43	6750	**Amorgos**	121.464
44	8100	**Marmara**	117.180
45	4400	**Dugi Otok**	114.440
46	7300	**Kalymnos**	110.581
47	3510	**Sant'Antioco**	109.020
48	6150	**Ios**	108.713
49	4940	**Mljet**	100.410
50	6270	**Kythnos**	99.432
51	7350	**Astypalaia**	96.420
52	5300	**Ithaki**	95.821
53	6950	**Skopelos**	95.684
54	5900	**Salamina**	91.503
55	4160	**Rab**	90.840
56	4780	**Vis**	90.260
57	6500	**Mykonos**	86.125
58	3050	**Pantelleria**	84.230
59	6300	**Syros**	84.069
60	1300	**Formentera**	81.079
61	6250	**Sifnos**	77.371
62	5800	**Aigina**	77.014
63	6100	**Santorini (Thira)**	76.194
64	4120	**Losinj**	74.680
65	6260	**Serifos**	74.331
66	9310	**Gozo**	67.078
67	7150	**Kasos**	66.419
68	6960	**Alonnisos**	65.390
69	4340	**Pasman**	63.340
70	7050	**Tilos**	61.487
71	4710	**Solta**	58.980
72	7030	**Symi**	57.865
73	7400	**Leros**	54.052
74	3530	**Asinara**	51.300
75	3520	**San Pietro**	50.960
76	4300	**Ugljan**	50.210
77	5700	**Ydra**	49.586
78	6900	**Skiathos**	47.212
79	4900	**Lastovo**	46.870
80	3810	**Ischia**	46.440
81	7810	**Agios Efstratios**	42.030
82	6160	**Sikinos**	41.676
83	7220	**Nisyros**	41.263
84	7620	**Psara**	40.667
85	6140	**Anafi**	38.636
86	6210	**Kimolos**	37.426
87	3300	**Lipari**	37.370
88	8210	**Bozcaada**	36.030
89	6650	**Antiparos**	35.090
90	7430	**Patmos**	34.142
91	6050	**Gavdos**	33.025
92	6170	**Folegandros**	32.384
93	4500	**Kornat**	32.300
94	7520	**Fournoi**	30.500
95	4720	**Ciovo**	28.800
96	7020	**Chalki**	26.988
97	3310	**Salina**	26.140
98	4230	**Olib**	26.090
99	8410	**Uzunada**	25.390
100	5160	**Kalamos**	25.122
101	6980	**Kyra Panagia**	24.973
102	5050	**Paxoi**	24.648
103	8300	**Alibey**	23.360
104	5850	**Poros**	22.841
105	4270	**Molat**	22.820
106	4220	**Vir**	22.380
107	3450	**Giglio**	21.470
108	8110	**Pasalimani**	21.370
109	3320	**Vulcano**	21.020
110	8120	**Avsa**	20.620
111	3200	**Lampedusa**	20.470
112	7110	**Saria**	20.429
113	5600	**Spetses**	20.263
114	3600	**Maddalena**	20.170
115	5150	**Meganisi**	20.100
116	3100	**Favignana**	19.990
117	5510	**Antikythira**	19.776
118	3410	**Capraia**	19.240
119	4600	**Murter**	18.600
120	6285	**Makronisos**	18.427
121	6710	**Iraklia**	18.078
122	6215	**Polyaigos**	18.000
122	6410	**Gyaros**	18.000
124	5520	**Elafonisos**	17.859

rank	code	island	square kilometres
125	4430	**Iz**	17.590
126	6810	**Megalonisos (Petali)**	17.000
127	4130	**Unije**	16.920
128	7450	**Lipsoi**	15.842
129	4960	**Sipan**	15.810
130	3610	**Caprera**	15.740
131	4630	**Zirje**	15.060
132	4330	**Sestrunj**	15.030
133	6740	**Keros**	15.000
134	4240	**Silba**	14.980
135	4570	**Zut**	14.820
136	7320	**Pserimos**	14.615
137	6965	**Peristera**	14.513
138	7610	**Oinousses**	14.382
139	6560	**Rinia**	14.000
140	6780	**Donousa**	13.652
141	5701	**Dokos**	13.537
142	4103	**Prvic (Krk)**	13.450
143	7480	**Agathonisi**	13.417
144	2100	**Porquerolles**	12.540
145	3330	**Stromboli**	12.510
146	3120	**Marettimo**	12.180
147	5478	**Schiza**	12.130
148	4730	**Drvenik Veli**	12.070
149	6001	**Dia**	11.909
150	5820	**Agkistri**	11.732
151	1050	**Cabrera**	11.479
152	6985	**Gioura**	11.000
153	5010	**Othonoi**	10.444
154	3440	**Montecristo**	10.430
155	3430	**Pianosa**	10.410
156	3800	**Capri**	10.320
157	7530	**Thymaina**	10.071
158	8150	**Imrali**	9.980
159	2200	**Le Levant**	9.960
160	4260	**Ist**	9.730
161	3340	**Filicudi**	9.310
162	4250	**Premuda**	9.250
163	6120	**Thirasia**	9.246
164	6770	**Levitha**	9.121
165	7010	**Megisti (Kastellorizo)**	9.113
166	8611	**Karaada (Mugla)**	9.080
167	5475	**Sapientza**	9.018
168	6205	**Antimilos**	8.801
169	4112	**Plavnik**	8.630
170	4203	**Maun**	8.540
171	4770	**Scedro**	8.360
172	3020	**Ustica**	8.230
173	4680	**Zlarin**	8.190
174	6720	**Schoinousa**	8.144
175	7280	**Syrna**	7.885
176	6655	**Despotiko**	7.754
177	3700	**Ponza**	7.490
178	9420	**Galite**	7.480
179	7950	**Ammouliani**	7.136
180	7005	**Alimia**	7.000
181	4650	**Kaprije**	6.970
182	8421	**Karaada (Goni)**	6.900
183	2300	**Port-Cros**	6.750
184	7460	**Arkoi**	6.697
185	4163	**Sveti Grgur**	6.370
186	6970	**Skantzoura**	6.333

rank	code	island	square kilometres
187	5170	**Kastos**	5.915
188	4781	**Bisevo**	5.910
189	3110	**Levanzo**	5.870
190	6730	**Koufonisi**	5.770
191	8808	**Kekova**	5.740
192	4000	**Veli Brijun**	5.720
193	4990	**Sazanit**	5.700
194	8601	**Salih**	5.670
195	4150	**Ilovik**	5.500
196	5411	**Petalas**	5.497
197	3210	**Linosa**	5.450
198	8000	**Buyukada**	5.360
199	4760	**Sveti Klement**	5.270
200	3350	**Alicudi**	5.050

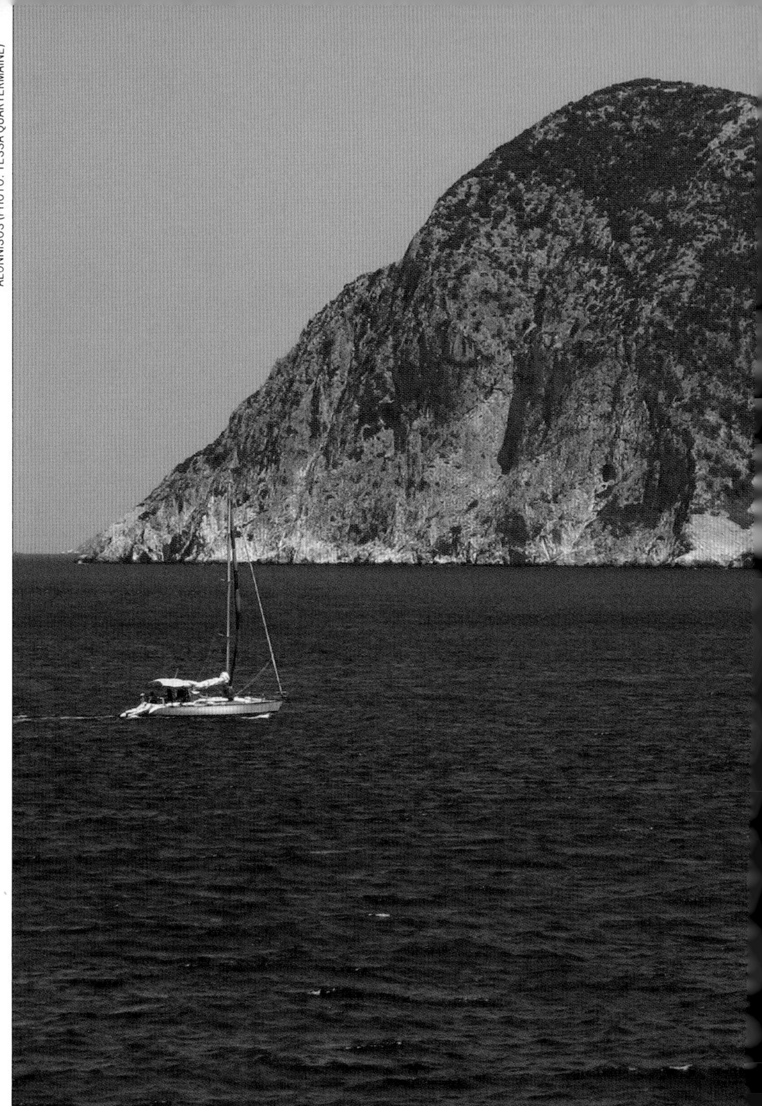

ALONNISOS (PHOTO: TESSA QUARTERMAINE)

Coastlines
This table shows the national totals that make up the length of the Mediterranean coastline. The length of its coastline has been defined publicly by Croatia, but elsewhere the figures are vague. Greece has a current estimate of 18,400 kilometres of coastline (mainland 6,400 and islands 12,000) and the precise figure will be clearer when the Hellenic Navy Hydrographic Service (HNHS) reassessment has been completed. In all other countries there are conflicting figures, from which we have selected those that appear to be the most reliable.

	total (km)	mainland (km)	islands (km)
Greece	18400	6400	
			12000
Croatia	5835	1777	
			4058
Italy	7911	4320	
			3591
Spain	3037	1609	
			1428
Turkey	6677	5610	
			1067
France	2056	994	
			1062
Cyprus	782		
			782
Tunisia	1641	1297	
			344
Malta	190		
			190
Others	5845	5745	
			100
Total	52374	27752	**24622**

Ranking by Population

This table shows all islands which returned a figure for permanent population at the last national census.

Only Greece and Croatia publish island population statistics on a regular basis.

rank	code	island	population
1	3000	**Sicilia**	4937301
2	3500	**Sardegna**	1602406
3	9000	**Kypros (Cyprus)**	953737
4	1000	**Mallorca**	777821
5	6000	**Kriti (Crete)**	594282
6	9300	**Malta**	372986
7	2000	**Corse (Corsica)**	260196
8	6800	**Evvoia**	191009
9	9400	**Djerba**	139544
10	7000	**Rodos (Rhodes)**	115334
11	1200	**Eivissa (Ibiza)**	111107
12	5000	**Kerkyra (Corfu)**	107514
13	7700	**Lesvos**	90436
14	1100	**Menorca**	86697
15	3810	**Ischia**	56105
16	7600	**Chios**	51773
17	5400	**Zakynthos**	38825
18	5900	**Salamina**	34975
19	5200	**Kefalonia**	34544
20	7500	**Samos**	33999
21	9310	**Gozo**	31049
22	7200	**Kos**	30828
23	3400	**Elba**	24988
24	5100	**Lefkada**	20295
25	6300	**Syros**	19793
26	4100	**Krk**	17860
27	7800	**Limnos**	17545
28	6700	**Naxos**	17357
29	7300	**Kalymnos**	16368
30	4800	**Korcula**	16182
31	9410	**Kerkennah**	14400
32	4700	**Brac**	14031
33	6100	**Santorini (Thira)**	13447
33	7900	**Thasos**	13447
35	3800	**Capri**	12919
36	5800	**Aigina**	12716
37	6600	**Paros**	12514
38	3510	**Sant'Antioco**	11670
39	3600	**Maddalena**	11275
40	4750	**Hvar**	11103
41	3820	**Procida**	10575
42	4160	**Rab**	9480
43	8100	**Marmara**	9446
44	6400	**Andros**	9285
45	6500	**Mykonos**	9260
46	8200	**Gokceada**	8875
47	3300	**Lipari**	8677
48	4200	**Pag**	8398
49	7550	**Ikaria**	8354
50	6450	**Tinos**	8115
51	7400	**Leros**	8087
52	4120	**Losinj**	7771
53	1300	**Formentera**	7506
54	3050	**Pantelleria**	7224
55	8000	**Buyukada**	6975
56	7100	**Karpathos**	6543
57	8010	**Heybeliada**	6534
58	3520	**San Pietro**	6444
59	4300	**Ugljan**	6182
60	6900	**Skiathos**	5788
61	3200	**Lampedusa**	5703
62	4600	**Murter**	5060
63	6200	**Milos**	4736
64	6950	**Skopelos**	4706
65	4720	**Ciovo**	4455
66	5850	**Poros**	4182
67	8030	**Kinaliada**	3862
68	5600	**Spetses**	3772
69	4780	**Vis**	3617
70	5500	**Kythira**	3532
71	5300	**Ithaki**	3210
72	4110	**Cres**	3184
73	3100	**Favignana**	3176
74	3700	**Ponza**	3107
75	9100	**Arwad**	3000
76	7430	**Patmos**	2997
77	7850	**Samothraki**	2712
78	4340	**Pasman**	2711
78	6850	**Skyros**	2711
80	5700	**Ydra**	2629
81	8120	**Avsa**	2617
82	7030	**Symi**	2594
83	6250	**Sifnos**	2574
84	8210	**Bozcaada**	2427
85	5050	**Paxoi**	2405
86	6960	**Alonnisos**	2399
87	8300	**Alibey**	2300
87	3310	**Salina**	2300
89	6280	**Kea**	2158
90	8020	**Burgazada**	2042
91	6150	**Ios**	1862
92	6750	**Amorgos**	1851
93	4400	**Dugi Otok**	1772
94	4220	**Vir**	1608
95	6270	**Kythnos**	1538
96	4710	**Solta**	1479
97	3450	**Giglio**	1406
98	7350	**Astypalaia**	1385
99	3020	**Ustica**	1335
100	7520	**Fournoi**	1333
101	6260	**Serifos**	1262
102	4940	**Mljet**	1111
103	7150	**Kasos**	1013
104	6650	**Antiparos**	1010
105	4990	**Sazanit**	1000
106	5150	**Meganisi**	992
107	7220	**Nisyros**	915
108	5820	**Agkistri**	886
109	7610	**Oinousses**	855
110	6210	**Kimolos**	838
111	4900	**Lastovo**	835
112	3320	**Vulcano**	749
113	5520	**Elafonisos**	746
114	3120	**Marettimo**	725
115	7450	**Lipsoi**	687
116	6170	**Folegandros**	676
117	3730	**Ventotene**	633
118	5020	**Erikousa**	612
119	3330	**Stromboli**	568
120	4430	**Iz**	557
121	7950	**Ammouliani**	547
122	7050	**Tilos**	521
123	5160	**Kalamos**	510
124	7620	**Psara**	478

rank	code	island	population
125	4660	**Prvic (Sibenik)**	453
126	3210	**Linosa**	438
127	4960	**Sipan**	436
128	6730	**Koufonisi**	376
129	7010	**Megisti (Kastellorizo)**	369
130	2100	**Porquerolles**	342
131	5010	**Othonoi**	340
132	3410	**Capraia**	333
133	7810	**Agios Efstratios**	307
134	8110	**Pasalimani**	300
134	3420	**Gorgona**	300
136	7020	**Chalki**	295
137	4980	**Kolocep**	294
138	6120	**Thirasia**	278
139	4680	**Zlarin**	276
140	6140	**Anafi**	272
141	4970	**Lopud**	269
142	4240	**Silba**	265
143	4620	**Vrgada**	242
144	6160	**Sikinos**	238
145	4690	**Krapanj**	237
146	3900	**San Domino**	236
147	3110	**Levanzo**	235
148	3360	**Panarea**	230
149	3340	**Filicudi**	225
150	4270	**Molat**	207
151	4260	**Ist**	202
152	6720	**Schoinousa**	197
153	1405	**Chafarinas**	190
154	4140	**Susak**	188
155	2200	**Le Levant**	186
155	5030	**Mathraki**	186
157	4730	**Drvenik Veli**	168
158	6780	**Donousa**	166
159	8130	**Ekinlik**	162
160	7480	**Agathonisi**	152
161	7530	**Thymaina**	151
162	2600	**Frioul**	150
163	4230	**Olib**	147
164	4650	**Kaprije**	143
165	6710	**Iraklia**	133
166	3920	**San Nicola**	131
167	4630	**Zirje**	124
167	7320	**Pserimos**	124
169	3350	**Alicudi**	105
170	4150	**Ilovik**	104
171	4420	**Rava**	98
172	4130	**Unije**	90
173	5170	**Kastos**	89
174	6990	**Palaio Trikeri**	86
175	5450	**Trizonia**	82
176	6050	**Gavdos**	78
177	3610	**Caprera**	77
178	7485	**Farmakonisi**	74
179	1400	**Nueva Tabarca**	66
180	4250	**Premuda**	58
180	5490	**Stamfanion**	58
182	2500	**Saint Honorat**	57
183	7310	**Telendos**	54
183	4740	**Drvenik Mali**	54
185	2700	**Embiez**	50
185	7460	**Arkoi**	50

rank	code	island	population
187	2300	**Port-Cros**	48
187	4410	**Zverinac**	48
187	4330	**Sestrunj**	48
190	5510	**Antikythira**	39
191	2400	**Sainte Marguerite**	28
191	7305	**Kalolimnos**	28
193	5060	**Antipaxoi**	24
194	3460	**Giannutri**	23
195	4310	**Rivanj**	22
195	7110	**Saria**	22
197	7011	**Ro**	21
198	3430	**Pianosa**	20
199	4781	**Bisevo**	19
200	5478	**Schiza**	17
201	8716	**Tersane**	16
202	6550	**Dilos**	14
203	7012	**Strongyli**	13
203	7225	**Gyali**	13
203	5701	**Dokos**	13
206	6980	**Kyra Panagia**	10
207	3601	**Chiesa**	9
207	6961	**Adelfi**	9
207	6770	**Levitha**	9
210	4131	**Srakane Vele**	8
210	5601	**Spetsopoula**	8
212	4500	**Kornat**	7
212	5611	**Platia**	7
212	5475	**Sapientza**	7
215	7470	**Marathos**	6
216	6992	**Alatas**	5
216	6965	**Peristera**	5
218	9320	**Comino**	4
218	3640	**Santa Maria**	4
218	5615	**Koronida/Koilada**	4
218	7901	**Koinyra**	4
218	5460	**Zoodochos Pigi**	4
218	5702	**Trikeri**	4
218	6285	**Makronisos**	4
225	7971	**Spalathronisia**	3
225	6051	**Gavdopoula**	3
225	7523	**Agios Minas**	3
225	6060	**Chrysi**	3
229	7153	**Plati**	2
229	4132	**Srakane Male**	2
229	8721	**Kizil (Fethiye)**	2
229	5102	**Skorpios**	2
229	6986	**Piperi**	2
229	3620	**Spargi**	2
229	5301	**Atokos**	2
229	6760	**Kinaros**	2
229	6001	**Dia**	2
238	3630	**Santo Stefano**	1
238	7505	**Samiopoula**	1
238	6742	**Kato Antikeri**	1
238	3650	**Budelli**	1
238	4782	**Svetac**	1
238	6655	**Despotiko**	1

Hotel and summer islands

Some islands have no permanent population but come alive in summer because they have hotels or holiday houses.

2800 **Bendor**
4030 **Crveni Otok**
4348 **Gangaro**
4423 **Lavdara**
4514 **Lavsa**
4902 **Mrcara**
4671 **Obonjan**
4301 **Osljak**
3710 **Palmarola**
3630 **Santo Stefano (Maddalena)**
4770 **Scedro**
4590 **Sit**
4523 **Smokvica**
4020 **Sveta Katarina**
4760 **Sveti Klement**
4010 **Sveti Nikola**
4000 **Veli Brijun**
4810 **Vrnik**
4350 **Zizanj**
4570 **Zut**

Islands with restricted access

Some islands are inaccessible or have restricted access because they house prisons or are used for military purposes or are strict nature reserves. Examples are...

1404 **Alboran**
3420 **Gorgona**
8411 **Hekim**
8150 **Imrali**
2200 **Le Levant (94%)**
3440 **Montecristo**
3430 **Pianosa**
6986 **Piperi**
5805 **Psili (Saronic Gulf)**
3440 **San Pietro (Cheradi)**
4990 **Sazanit**
5478 **Schiza**
3550 **Tavolara**
8410 **Uzunada**
8050 **Yassiada**

Visitor-heavy islands

This table shows those islands whose visitor beds outnumber the permanent population.

code	island	visitor beds	population	ratio
4500	**Kornat**	200	7	28.57
3610	**Caprera**	1384	77	17.97
4690	**Krapanj**	2268	237	9.56
3900	**San Domino**	1366	236	5.78
7470	**Marathos**	33	6	5.50
4220	**Vir**	8282	1608	5.15
3460	**Giannutri**	100	23	4.34
7310	**Telendos**	200	54	3.70
4200	**Pag**	24788	8398	2.95
4970	**Lopud**	779	269	2.89
2300	**Port-Cros**	135	48	2.81
2100	**Porquerolles**	949	342	2.77
4240	**Silba**	700	265	2.64
2200	**Le Levant**	470	186	2.52
4160	**Rab**	22847	9480	2.41
3360	**Panarea**	534	230	2.32
4100	**Krk**	36860	17860	2.06
8120	**Avsa**	4737	2617	1.81
4120	**Losinj**	13465	7771	1.73
5820	**Agkistri**	1480	886	1.67
7950	**Ammouliani**	893	547	1.63
4750	**Hvar**	17714	11103	1.59
3320	**Vulcano**	1187	749	1.58
4130	**Unije**	139	90	1.54
4600	**Murter**	7449	5060	1.47
6150	**Ios**	2731	1862	1.46
4400	**Dugi Otok**	2563	1772	1.44
4980	**Kolocep**	407	294	1.38
4110	**Cres**	4365	3184	1.37
4660	**Prvic**	618	453	1.36
4700	**Brac**	19009	14031	1.35
7200	**Kos**	39999	30828	1.29
6900	**Skiathos**	7440	5788	1.28
7460	**Arkoi**	64	50	1.28
4940	**Mljet**	1349	1111	1.21
4710	**Solta**	1766	1479	1.19
4430	**Iz**	640	557	1.14
3210	**Linosa**	485	438	1.10
6170	**Folegandros**	747	676	1.10
6500	**Mykonos**	10032	9260	1.06
8100	**Marmara**	10000	9446	1.05
3330	**Stromboli**	596	568	1.04
3410	**Capraia**	343	333	1.03
5850	**Poros**	4279	4182	1.02
1300	**Formentera**	7668	7506	1.02
4270	**Molat**	210	207	1.01
6730	**Koufonisi**	381	376	1.01

Ranking by visitor beds

Of the 218 islands which offer some form of accommodation, just five islands account for more than half the total of visitor beds. 14 islands account for 80% of all visitor beds and 21 islands for 90%. The remaining 10% of beds is therefore spread among 90% of the islands.

rank	code	island	visitor beds
1	1000	**Mallorca**	286408
2	6000	**Kriti (Crete)**	203592
3	3500	**Sardegna**	175869
4	3000	**Sicilia**	128750
5	9000	**Kypros (Cyprus)**	126380
6	1200	**Eivissa (Ibiza)**	79864
7	7000	**Rodos (Rhodes)**	76646
8	9400	**Djerba**	54510
9	2000	**Corse (Corsica)**	54000
10	1100	**Menorca**	49172
11	5000	**Kerkyra (Corfu)**	45995
12	7200	**Kos**	39999
13	9300	**Malta**	37708
14	4100	**Krk**	36860
15	5400	**Zakynthos**	27480
16	4200	**Pag**	24788
17	3810	**Ischia**	22936
18	4160	**Rab**	22847
19	3400	**Elba**	22181
20	4700	**Brac**	19009
21	4750	**Hvar**	17714
22	6800	**Evvoia**	16454
23	4120	**Losinj**	13465
24	6100	**Santorini (Thira)**	13087
25	7500	**Samos**	11057
26	5200	**Kefalonia**	10273
27	6500	**Mykonos**	10032
28	8100	**Marmara**	10000
29	4800	**Korcula**	9616
30	6600	**Paros**	9154
31	7900	**Thasos**	8665
32	4220	**Vir**	8282
33	1300	**Formentera**	7668
34	4600	**Murter**	7449
35	7700	**Lesvos**	7442
36	6900	**Skiathos**	7440
37	5800	**Aigina**	6997
38	7100	**Karpathos**	5879
39	5100	**Lefkada**	5568
40	6700	**Naxos**	4925
41	8120	**Avsa**	4737
42	4300	**Ugljan**	4707
43	4110	**Cres**	4365
44	5850	**Poros**	4279
45	4720	**Ciovo**	4182
46	3800	**Capri**	3824
47	6300	**Syros**	3467
48	5600	**Spetses**	3149
49	7600	**Chios**	3108
50	4780	**Vis**	3087
51	6450	**Tinos**	3066
52	6950	**Skopelos**	2849
53	6150	**Ios**	2731
54	4400	**Dugi Otok**	2563
55	7300	**Kalymnos**	2421
56	7800	**Limnos**	2392
57	6400	**Andros**	2374
58	4690	**Krapanj**	2268
59	5500	**Kythira**	2189
60	7400	**Leros**	2147
61	4340	**Pasman**	2146
62	3510	**Sant'Antioco**	2139

rank	code	island	visitor beds
63	3300	**Lipari**	2100
64	7430	**Patmos**	1966
65	6960	**Alonnisos**	1842
66	4710	**Solta**	1766
67	3200	**Lampedusa**	1616
68	6200	**Milos**	1561
69	9310	**Gozo**	1504
70	3100	**Favignana**	1484
71	3050	**Pantelleria**	1481
72	5820	**Agkistri**	1480
73	3610	**Caprera**	1384
74	3900	**San Domino**	1366
75	4940	**Mljet**	1349
76	3320	**Vulcano**	1187
77	6250	**Sifnos**	1180
78	7550	**Ikaria**	1160
79	8300	**Alibey**	1142
80	6270	**Kythnos**	1105
81	3020	**Ustica**	1067
82	3600	**Maddalena**	1059
83	5700	**Ydra**	1010
84	4671	**Obonjan**	1000
85	8210	**Bozcaada**	995
86	6750	**Amorgos**	984
87	3520	**San Pietro**	973
88	3700	**Ponza**	958
89	2100	**Porquerolles**	949
90	7950	**Ammouliani**	893
91	7350	**Astypalaia**	821
92	3820	**Procida**	810
93	4970	**Lopud**	779
94	3450	**Giglio**	768
95	6170	**Folegandros**	747
96	6280	**Kea**	740
97	6850	**Skyros**	723
98	4030	**Crveni Otok**	721
99	4240	**Silba**	700
100	9410	**Kerkennah**	687
101	4430	**Iz**	640
102	3630	**Santo Stefano**	639
103	4900	**Lastovo**	633
104	4660	**Prvic (Sibenik)**	618
105	7850	**Samothraki**	601
106	3330	**Stromboli**	596
107	6260	**Serifos**	592
108	8200	**Gokceada**	585
109	2700	**Embiez**	580
110	3310	**Salina**	577
111	3360	**Panarea**	534
112	6650	**Antiparos**	527
113	3210	**Linosa**	485
114	2200	**Le Levant**	470
115	7050	**Tilos**	442
116	7030	**Symi**	438
117	5520	**Elafonisos**	414
118	4980	**Kolocep**	407
119	3525	**Piana**	400
120	4680	**Zlarin**	393
121	6730	**Koufonisi**	381
122	5300	**Ithaki**	373
123	4010	**Sveti Nikola**	354
124	8000	**Buyukada**	352

rank	code	island	visitor beds
125	3410	**Capraia**	343
126	4960	**Sipan**	301
127	5050	**Paxoi**	296
128	9320	**Comino**	282
129	7520	**Fournoi**	256
130	4000	**Veli Brijun**	248
131	7220	**Nisyros**	241
132	4020	**Sveta Katarina**	240
133	3730	**Ventotene**	239
134	6140	**Anafi**	226
135	4270	**Molat**	210
136	7310	**Telendos**	200
136	2400	**Sainte Marguerite**	200
136	4500	**Kornat**	200
136	4570	**Zut**	200
140	8010	**Heybeliada**	195
141	4260	**Ist**	192
142	3120	**Marettimo**	181
143	7450	**Lipsoi**	174
144	6210	**Kimolos**	162
145	5900	**Salamina**	159
146	2600	**Frioul**	154
147	5150	**Meganisi**	142
148	2800	**Bendor**	140
149	4130	**Unije**	139
150	2300	**Port-Cros**	135
151	4650	**Kaprije**	125
152	3340	**Filicudi**	123
153	7810	**Agios Efstratios**	120
154	7010	**Megisti (Kastellorizo)**	117
155	8110	**Pasalimani**	100
155	3460	**Giannutri**	100
157	7020	**Chalki**	97
158	6160	**Sikinos**	95
159	7620	**Psara**	84
159	4630	**Zirje**	84
161	6720	**Schoinousa**	83
162	5010	**Othonoi**	79
163	6990	**Palaio Trikeri**	74
164	3110	**Levanzo**	69
165	4140	**Susak**	68
165	5450	**Trizonia**	68
167	7460	**Arkoi**	64
168	1400	**Nueva Tabarca**	63
168	4760	**Sveti Klement**	63
170	5160	**Kalamos**	60
171	4301	**Osljak**	57
172	4620	**Vrgada**	56
173	6780	**Donousa**	50
173	4230	**Olib**	50
173	3920	**San Nicola**	50
176	7150	**Kasos**	49
177	8020	**Burgazada**	45
177	4250	**Premuda**	45
179	5020	**Erikousa**	40
179	3350	**Alicudi**	40
179	2500	**Saint Honorat**	40
179	4410	**Zverinac**	40
179	4590	**Sit**	40
184	4810	**Vrnik**	39
185	7480	**Agathonisi**	38
186	6710	**Iraklia**	36

rank	code	island	visitor beds
186	6050	**Gavdos**	36
188	5030	**Mathraki**	35
188	5510	**Antikythira**	35
190	7470	**Marathos**	33
191	7320	**Pserimos**	30
191	4330	**Sestrunj**	30
191	4348	**Gangaro**	30
194	4902	**Mrcara**	26
195	4150	**Ilovik**	25
195	4523	**Smokvica**	25
197	7610	**Oinousses**	23
198	4514	**Lavsa**	20
199	6120	**Thirasia**	18
199	4423	**Lavdara**	18
201	4420	**Rava**	17
202	4730	**Drvenik Veli**	15
202	4740	**Drvenik Mali**	15
202	4350	**Zizanj**	15
205	4801	**Plocica**	14
206	8130	**Ekinlik**	10
206	5170	**Kastos**	10
206	3640	**Santa Maria**	10
206	3710	**Palmarola**	10
206	4770	**Scedro**	10
211	7530	**Thymaina**	9
212	5060	**Antipaxoi**	8
212	4310	**Rivanj**	8
212	4053	**Porer**	8
212	4032	**Sveti Ivan na Pucini**	8
212	4840	**Palagruza**	8
212	4830	**Susac**	8
218	4602	**Prisnjak**	4

Visitor numbers: top 50 islands by visitor beds

With regard to tourism statistics, only the Balearics, Cyprus and Malta publish figures for either the number of beds available or the number of visitors. For other countries, we have assembled figures with the help of the national tourism authorities, particularly in Croatia, Greece and Tunisia. Not surprisingly, some statistics are more reliable than others. In particular, some islands appear not to have recorded the full number of their visitors, with the result that visitor turnover is understated.

It should be noted that this section does not include islands which receive large numbers of day-trippers, such as the Tremiti (estimated at 800,000 a year), Sainte Marguerite (400,000), Porquerolles (300,000) or Nueva Tabarca (150,000).

code	island	capacity total beds	turnover	visitors ('000s)
1000	**Mallorca**	286408	33	9614
6000	**Kriti**	203592	8	1732
3500	**Sardegna**	175869	11	1962
3000	**Sicilia**	128750	33	4300
9000	**Kypros**	126380	24	3116
1200	**Eivissa**	79864	23	1870
7000	**Rodos**	76646	13	1063
9400	**Djerba**	54510	20	1115
2000	**Corse**	54000	43	2357
1100	**Menorca**	49172	22	1093
5000	**Kerkyra**	45995	12	570
7200	**Kos**	39999	9	387
9300	**Malta**	39494	28	1124
4100	**Krk**	36860	14	542
5400	**Zakynthos**	27480	10	275
4200	**Pag**	24788	8	201
3810	**Ischia**	22936	22	506
4160	**Rab**	22847	10	233
3400	**Elba**	22181	21	474
4700	**Brac**	19009	9	178
4750	**Hvar**	17714	12	230
6800	**Evia**	16454	10	167
4120	**Losinj**	13465	17	232
6100	**Santorini**	13087	3	40
7500	**Samos**	11057	8	94
5200	**Kefalonia**	10273	8	89
6500	**Mykonos**	10032	17	175
8100	**Marmara**	10000	15	150
4800	**Korcula**	9616	15	148
6600	**Paros**	9154	5	50
7900	**Thasos**	8665	9	80
4220	**Vir**	8282	4	35
1300	**Formentera**	7668	14	110
4600	**Murter**	7449	22	165
7700	**Lesbos**	7442	15	114
6900	**Skiathos**	7440	11	83
5800	**Aegina**	6997	2	20
7100	**Karpathos**	5879	3	23
5100	**Lefkada**	5568	10	59
6700	**Naxos**	4925	1	3
8120	**Avsa**	4737	15	75
4300	**Ugljan**	4707	5	28
4110	**Cres**	4365	60	262
5850	**Poros**	4279	2	11
4720	**Ciovo**	4182	7	31
3800	**Capri**	3824	43	167
6300	**Syros**	3467	4	14
5600	**Spetses**	3149	2	8
7600	**Chios**	3108	16	52
4780	**Vis**	3087	8	26

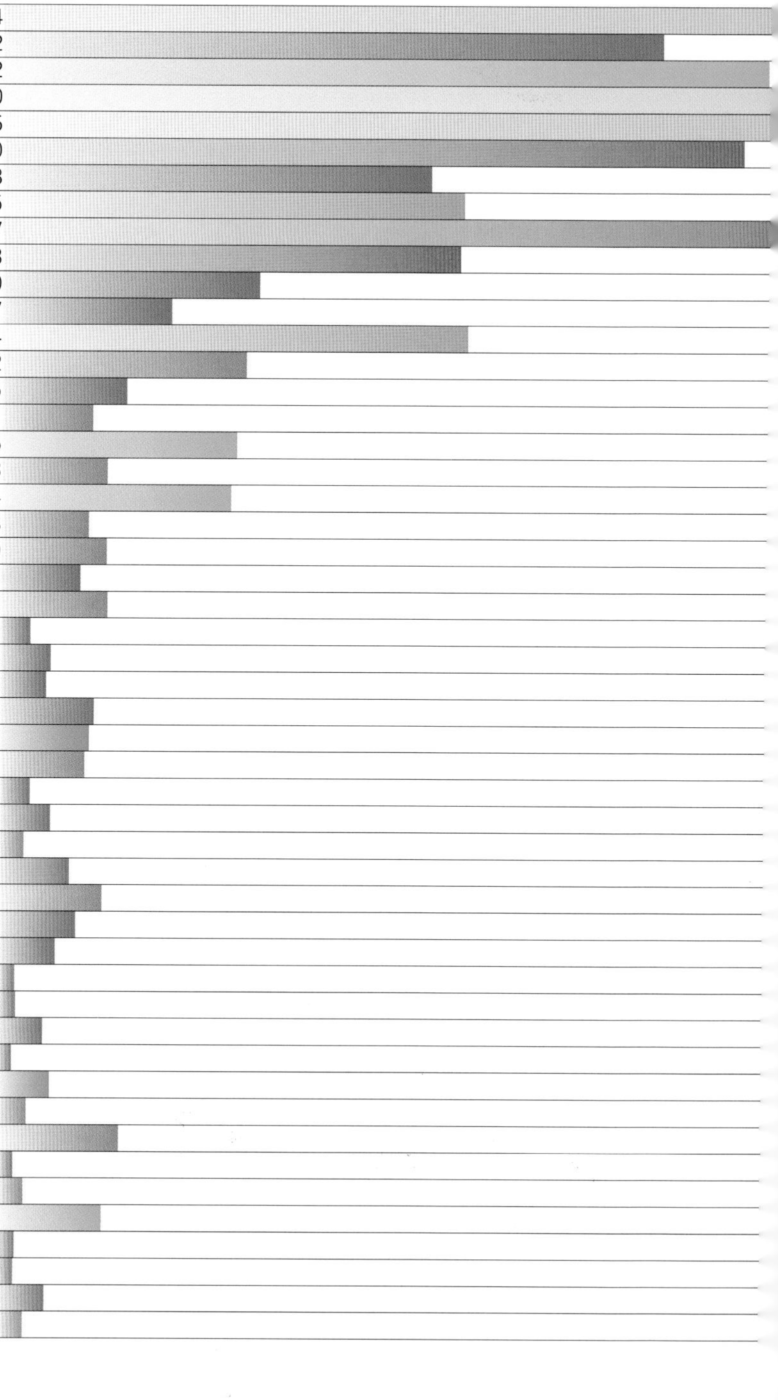

Mallorca continues off page
to twice this length

Ranking by Crowdfactor

Crowdfactor is the theoretical number of people that would be encountered on average per square kilometre, if all the permanent inhabitants were present on the island and all the visitor capacity were full. Although it is only a theoretical figure, and subject to a number of possible distortions, there seem to us to be very few instances where the Crowdfactor figure is not a good indicator of the crowdedness of an island. The only instances where it could be unreliable are in the cases of islands which receive large numbers of day visitors or which have large numbers of campers, neither of which is taken into account in the calculation of Crowdfactor.

rank	code	island	crowdfactor
1	9100	**Arwad**	15000
2	4690	**Krapanj**	7157
3	4030	**Crveni Otok**	3134
4	4010	**Sveti Nikola**	2950
5	3820	**Procida**	2926
6	8030	**Kinaliada**	2925
7	8010	**Heybeliada**	2735
8	4020	**Sveta Katarina**	2000
9	3525	**Piana**	1904
10	4671	**Obonjan**	1818
11	2800	**Bendor**	1750
12	3810	**Ischia**	1702
13	9300	**Malta**	1671
14	3800	**Capri**	1622
15	8020	**Burgazada**	1439
16	8000	**Buyukada**	1366
17	3900	**San Domino**	773
18	2700	**Embiez**	700
19	4600	**Murter**	672
20	3730	**Ventotene**	622
21	3600	**Maddalena**	611
22	3700	**Ponza**	542
23	9310	**Gozo**	485
24	4660	**Prvic (Sibenik)**	446
25	4220	**Vir**	441
26	3920	**San Nicola**	411
27	5900	**Salamina**	383
28	5850	**Poros**	370
29	9400	**Djerba**	368
30	3200	**Lampedusa**	357
31	8120	**Avsa**	356
32	4160	**Rab**	355
33	6100	**Santorini (Thira)**	348
34	5600	**Spetses**	341
35	1200	**Eivissa (Ibiza)**	335
36	1400	**Nueva Tabarca**	300
37	4720	**Ciovo**	299
38	1000	**Mallorca**	293
39	3020	**Ustica**	291
40	3300	**Lipari**	288
40	4980	**Kolocep**	288
42	4120	**Losinj**	284
43	6900	**Skiathos**	280
44	6300	**Syros**	276
45	2500	**Saint Honorat**	269
46	5000	**Kerkyra (Corfu)**	262
47	5800	**Aigina**	255
48	7200	**Kos**	246
49	4970	**Lopud**	239
50	3100	**Favignana**	233
51	3360	**Panarea**	226
52	6500	**Mykonos**	224
53	4300	**Ugljan**	216
54	3630	**Santo Stefano**	212
55	3400	**Elba**	211
56	5820	**Agkistri**	201
56	7950	**Ammouliani**	201
58	3000	**Sicilia**	199
59	1100	**Menorca**	195
60	7400	**Leros**	189
61	1300	**Formentera**	187
62	4301	**Osljak**	172
63	7300	**Kalymnos**	169
63	3210	**Linosa**	169
65	8100	**Marmara**	165
65	2600	**Frioul**	165
67	5400	**Zakynthos**	163
68	5020	**Erikousa**	148
69	8300	**Alibey**	147
70	3520	**San Pietro**	145
70	7430	**Patmos**	145
72	4810	**Vrnik**	139
73	7000	**Rodos (Rhodes)**	136
74	4100	**Krk**	134
75	6730	**Koufonisi**	131
76	4620	**Vrgada**	129
77	3510	**Sant'Antioco**	126
78	9000	**Kypros (Cyprus)**	116
78	4200	**Pag**	116
80	6600	**Paros**	110
80	3310	**Salina**	110
82	5050	**Paxoi**	109
82	7470	**Marathos**	109
84	2400	**Sainte Marguerite**	108
85	3050	**Pantelleria**	103
86	2100	**Porquerolles**	102
86	9320	**Comino**	102
88	3450	**Giglio**	101
89	9410	**Kerkennah**	98
90	6000	**Kriti (Crete)**	96
90	4750	**Hvar**	96
92	7500	**Samos**	94
92	8210	**Bozcaada**	94
94	4800	**Korcula**	93
94	3330	**Stromboli**	93
96	3320	**Vulcano**	92
96	3610	**Caprera**	92
98	5100	**Lefkada**	85
99	4700	**Brac**	83
100	4680	**Zlarin**	81
101	6950	**Skopelos**	78
102	4340	**Pasman**	76
103	3500	**Sardegna**	74
103	4780	**Vis**	74
103	3120	**Marettimo**	74
106	5700	**Ydra**	73
107	5030	**Mathraki**	71
108	8130	**Ekinlik**	69
109	4430	**Iz**	68
110	4140	**Susak**	67
111	7600	**Chios**	65
111	2200	**Le Levant**	65
113	6960	**Alonnisos**	64
113	5520	**Elafonisos**	64
113	4240	**Silba**	64
113	6990	**Palaio Trikeri**	64
117	5450	**Trizonia**	63
118	5200	**Kefalonia**	61
118	7610	**Oinousses**	61
120	7700	**Lesvos**	59
121	6700	**Naxos**	57
121	7900	**Thasos**	57
123	6800	**Evvoia**	56
123	6450	**Tinos**	56

rank	code	island	crowdfactor
123	5150	**Meganisi**	56
126	4710	**Solta**	55
127	7450	**Lipsoi**	54
127	7310	**Telendos**	54
129	7010	**Megisti (Kastellorizo)**	53
130	7030	**Symi**	52
130	7520	**Fournoi**	52
132	3110	**Levanzo**	51
132	3460	**Giannutri**	51
134	6250	**Sifnos**	48
135	4960	**Sipan**	46
136	6650	**Antiparos**	43
136	6170	**Folegandros**	43
136	4000	**Veli Brijun**	43
139	6150	**Ios**	42
140	7800	**Limnos**	41
140	7100	**Karpathos**	41
142	5010	**Othonoi**	40
142	4260	**Ist**	40
144	6200	**Milos**	39
145	4650	**Kaprije**	38
146	7550	**Ikaria**	37
146	4400	**Dugi Otok**	37
146	5300	**Ithaki**	37
146	3340	**Filicudi**	37
146	4348	**Gangaro**	37
151	2000	**Corse (Corsica)**	36
152	3410	**Capraia**	35
153	6720	**Schoinousa**	34
154	6120	**Thirasia**	32
155	4900	**Lastovo**	31
155	4420	**Rava**	31
157	6400	**Andros**	30
158	7220	**Nisyros**	28
158	3350	**Alicudi**	28
160	2300	**Port-Cros**	27
161	6270	**Kythnos**	26
161	6210	**Kimolos**	26
163	8200	**Gokceada**	24
163	4940	**Mljet**	24
163	6260	**Serifos**	24
163	4523	**Smokvica**	24
167	6750	**Amorgos**	23
167	4150	**Ilovik**	23
169	6280	**Kea**	22
169	7350	**Astypalaia**	22
169	5160	**Kalamos**	22
169	4590	**Sit**	22
173	4410	**Zverinac**	21
174	5500	**Kythira**	20
174	4740	**Drvenik Mali**	20
176	4110	**Cres**	18
176	7850	**Samothraki**	18
176	4270	**Molat**	18
176	8110	**Pasalimani**	18
180	7460	**Arkoi**	17
180	4902	**Mrcara**	17
182	6850	**Skyros**	16
182	5170	**Kastos**	16
182	4350	**Zizanj**	16
185	7150	**Kasos**	15
185	7050	**Tilos**	15
185	6780	**Donousa**	15
185	4730	**Drvenik Veli**	15
185	7530	**Thymaina**	15
190	7020	**Chalki**	14
190	7480	**Agathonisi**	14
192	7620	**Psara**	13
192	4130	**Unije**	13
192	4630	**Zirje**	13
192	4570	**Zut**	13
196	6140	**Anafi**	12
197	4250	**Premuda**	11
197	4760	**Sveti Klement**	11
197	4514	**Lavsa**	11
200	7810	**Agios Efstratios**	10
200	7320	**Pserimos**	10
202	6710	**Iraklia**	9
203	4310	**Rivanj**	8
203	3710	**Palmarola**	8
205	6160	**Sikinos**	7
205	4230	**Olib**	7
205	4423	**Lavdara**	7
205	3640	**Santa Maria**	7
209	4500	**Kornat**	6
209	5060	**Antipaxoi**	6
211	4330	**Sestrunj**	5
212	6050	**Gavdos**	3
212	5510	**Antikythira**	3
214	4770	**Scedro**	1

Satellite Atlas

Every island offering accommodation is shown in the atlas pages, which are at a scale of 2,500,000:1. It will be seen that these islands are concentrated in certain areas, particularly in the Croatian Adriatic and in the Aegean Sea, and also that there are very large tracts of the Mediterranean Sea which have virtually no islands at all.

Every island named
Every island in the Islands section is named, as are all the island groups, together with longitude and latitude

NASA Landsat data
The mapping used in this atlas, and our wall map, is licensed from PlanetObserver. It is based on data supplied by the NASA Landsat 5 and 7 satellites, which orbit the earth at a height of approximately 705 km at a speed of 27,000 kph

Mediterranean Islands

Accuracy and true colour
The sophisticated image processing technology ensures the translation of the satellite data into exceptionally accurate information and guarantees that the maps have true colours

Large wall poster map
To order a copy of the large 154 x70 cm Mediterranean Islands *poster version of this map, visit our website* www.mediterraneanislands.org *or see the mail order details inside the back cover*

West of Greenwich
0° East of Greenwich
40° N
Mallorca
Eivissa
Illes Balears
Formentera
Nueva Tabarca
38° N
0
100 Kms
0°

6° E
8° E
44° N
Ste Marguerite
St Honorat
Lerins
Frioul
Bendor
Embiez
Levant
Porquerolles
Port-Cros
Iles d'Hyeres
Corse
42° N
Arcipelago
Maddalenino
Santa Maria
Maddalena
Caprera
Santo Stefano
Sardegna
40° N
Piana
San Pietro
Sant'Antioco
Arcipelago
Sulcitano
6° E
8° E

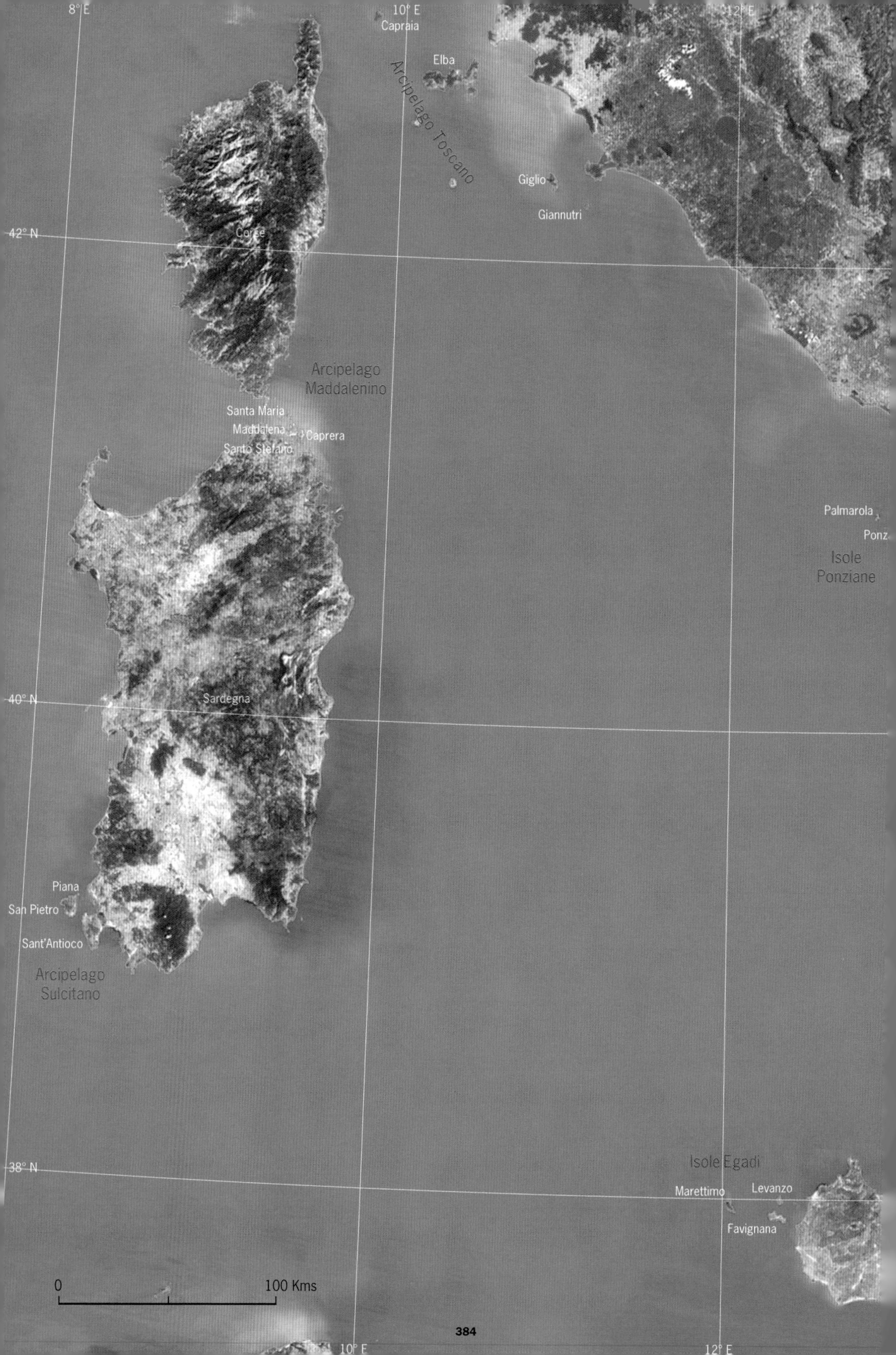
8° E
10° E
12° E
Capraia
Elba
Arcipelago Toscano
Giglio
Giannutri
42° N
Corse
Arcipelago
Maddalenino
Santa Maria
Maddalena
Caprera
Santo Stefano
Palmarola
Ponz
Isole
Ponziane
40° N
Sardegna
Piana
San Pietro
Sant'Antioco
Arcipelago
Sulcitano
38° N
Isole Egadi
Marettimo
Levanzo
Favignana
0
100 Kms
10° E
12° E

14° E
16° E
18° E
Vis
Pločica
Korčula
Vrnik
Šipan
Lopud
Koločep
Mrcara
Sušac
Lastovo
Mljet
South Dalmatia
Palagruža
Isole Tremiti
San Domino
San Nicola
42° N
Procida
Ischia
Capri
40° N
Isole Eolie
Stromboli
Filicudi
Salina
Panarea
Alicudi
Lipari
Vulcano
38° N
Sicilia
14° E
16° E
18° E

8° E
10° E
12° E
Sant'Antioco
Arcipelago
Sulcitano
38° N
Isole Egadi
Marettimo
Le
Favigna
Pantel
Kerkennah
Djerba
10° E
12° E

14° E
16° E
Isole Eolie
Stromboli
Ustica
Filicudi
Salina
Panarea
Alicudi
Lipari
Vulcano
38° N
Sicilia
Gozo
Comino
36° N
Linosa
Malta
Lampedusa
34° N
0
100 Kms
14° E
16° E

12° E
14° E
Istria
Sv Nikola
Sv Katarina
Crveni Otok
Sv Ivan na Pučini
Veli Brijun
Porer
Krk
Cres
Kvarner
Rab
Unije
Lošinj
Pag
Susak
Ilovik
Silba
Olib
Premuda
Ist
Vir
Molat
Sestrunj
Rivanj
Zverinac
Ugljan
Dugi Otok
Iž
Rava
Lavdara
Kornat
Žižanj
Gangaro
Lavsa
North Dalmatia
44° N
Elba
Arcipelago Toscano
Giglio
Giannutri
42° N
Palmarola
Ponza
Isole Ponziane
Ventotene
Procida
Ischia
Capri
0
100 Kms
40° N
12° E
14° E

16° E
18° E
20° E
44° N
42° N
40° N
Prisnjak
Prvić
Zlarin
Krapanj
Čiovo
Veli Drvenik
Mali Drvenik
Šolta
Brač
Sv Klement
Hvar
Šćedro
Vis
Pločica
Korčula
Vrnik
Šipan
Lopud
Koločep
Mrcara
Sušac
Lastovo
Mljet
South Dalmatia
Palagruža
Tremiti
Nicola
Erikousa
Othonoi
Mathraki
Kerkyra
16° E
18° E
20° E

20° E
22° E
24° E
42° N
40° N
38° N
Erikousa
Othonoi
Mathraki
Kerkyra
Ionia Nisia
Paxoi
Antipaxoi
Lefkada
Kalamos
Meganisi
Kastos
Ithaki
Kefalonia
Zakynthos
Trizonia
Ammouliani
Skiathos
Palaio Trikeri
Skopelos
Salamina
Agkistri
Aigina
Poros
Ydra
Spetses
Elafonisos
Kythira
0
100 Kms
20° E
22° E

26° E
28° E
30° E
Burgazada
Heybeliada
Büyükada
Prens Adalari
Marmara
Adalari
Marmara
Ekinlik
Avşa
Paşalimani
40° N
Thasos
Samothraki
oreio Aigaio
Gökçeada
Limnos
Bozcaada
Alibey
Ag Efstratios
Lesvos
ories
rades
Skyros
Oinousses
Psara
38° N
Chios
Voreio Aigaio
Samos
Andros
Ikaria
Fournoi
Thymaina
Agathonisi
Tinos
Marathos
Arkoi
Mykonos
Lipsoi
Kea
Patmos
Leros
Syros
Kythnos
Kyklades
Telendos
Donousa
Kalymnos
Pserimos
Paros
Naxos
Serifos
Antiparos
Koufonisi
Kos
Sifnos
Schoinousa
Amorgos
Iraklia
Nisyros
Symi
Dodekanis
Kimolos
Ios
Tilos
Astypalaia
Sikinos
Milos
Folegandros
Chalki
Rodos
36° N
Anafi
Thirasia
Santorini
24° E
26° E
28° E
Karpathos

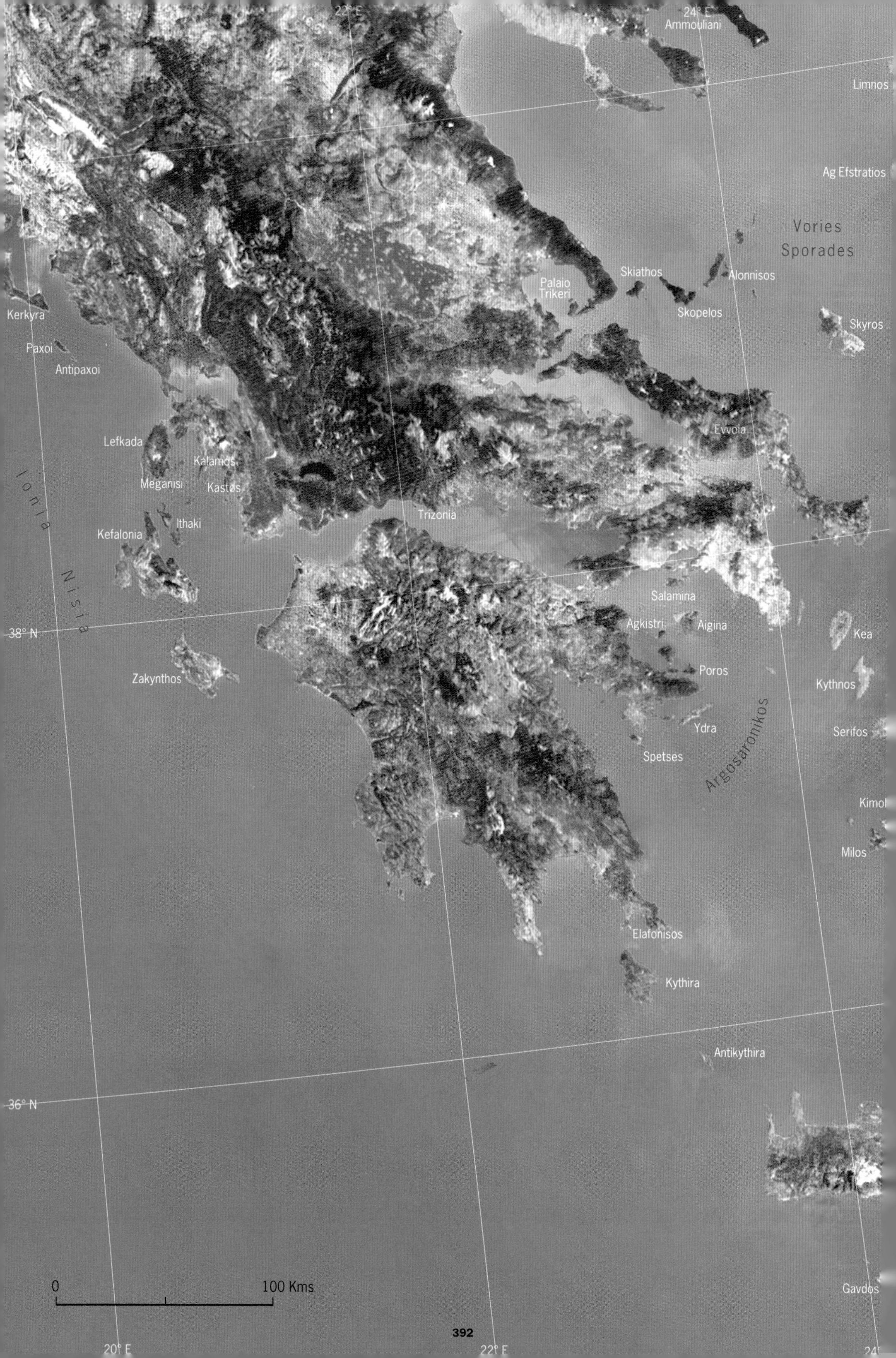
22° E
24° E
Ammouliani
Limnos
Ag Efstratios
Vories Sporades
Skiathos
Alonnisos
Palaio Trikeri
Skopelos
Skyros
Kerkyra
Paxoi
Antipaxoi
Evvoia
Lefkada
Kalamos
Meganisi
Kastos
Ionia Nisia
Ithaki
Kefalonia
Trizonia
Salamina
Agkistri
Aigina
Kea
38° N
Zakynthos
Poros
Kythnos
Argosaronikos
Ydra
Serifos
Spetses
Kimol
Milos
Elafonisos
Kythira
Antikythira
36° N
0
100 Kms
Gavdos
20° E
22° E

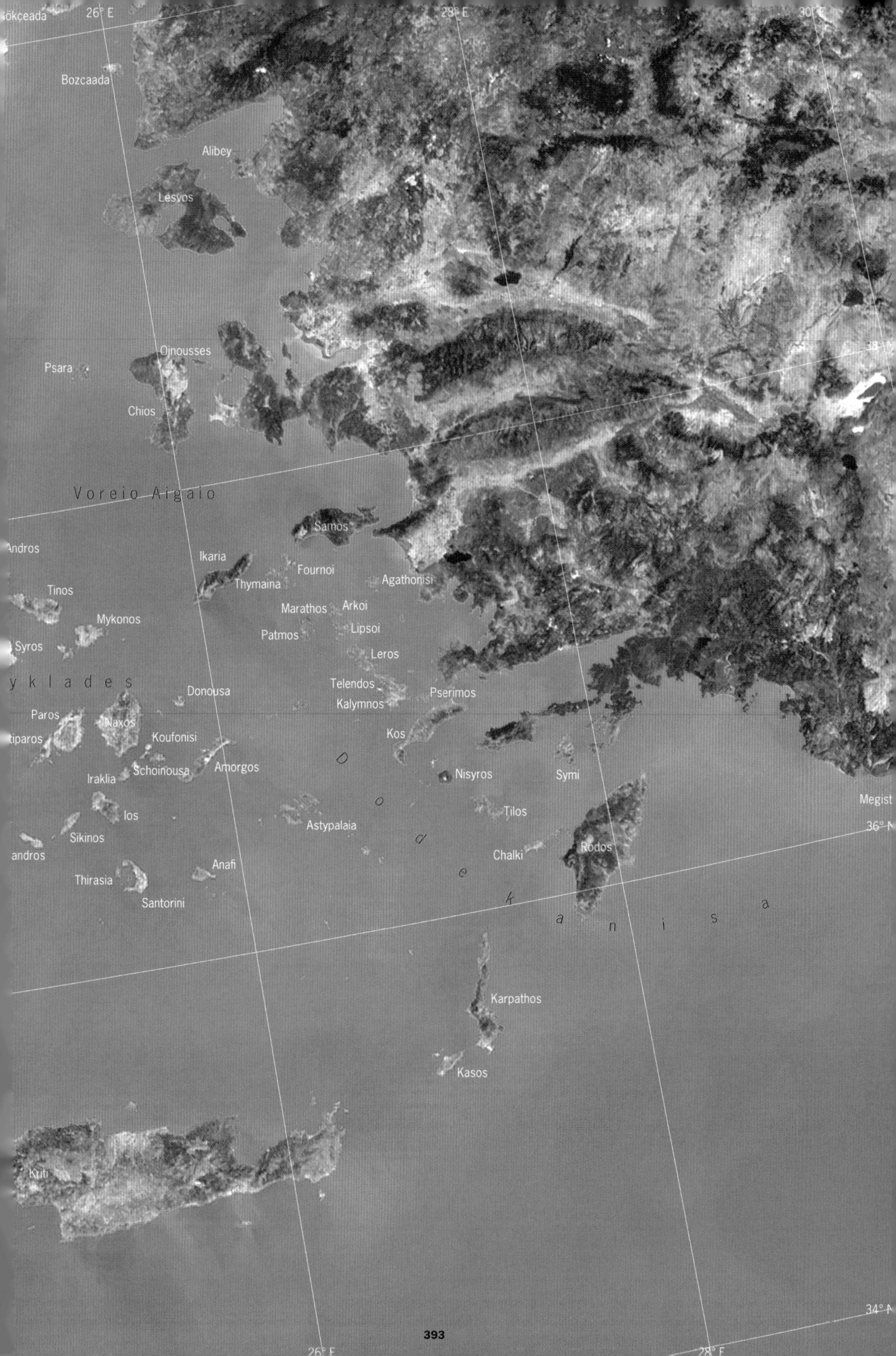

ökceada
26° E
28° E
30° E
Bozcaada
Alibey
Lesvos
Oinousses
Psara
Chios
38° N
Voreio Aigaio
Samos
Andros
Ikaria
Fournoi
Thymaina
Agathonisi
Tinos
Marathos
Arkoi
Mykonos
Patmos
Lipsoi
Syros
Leros
Kyklades
Telendos
Donousa
Kalymnos
Pserimos
Paros
Naxos
Koufonisi
Kos
Antiparos
Schoinousa
Amorgos
Iraklia
Nisyros
Symi
Dodekanisa
Megist
Tilos
Ios
Astypalaia
Sikinos
36° N
Rodos
Folegandros
Chalki
Anafi
Thirasia
Santorini
Karpathos
Kasos
Kriti
34° N

Marmara
Ekinlik
Avsa
Marmara
Pasalimani
28° E
30° E
40° N
38° N
36° N
Samos
Fournoi
Agathonisi
Arkoi
Marathos
Lipsoi
Patmos
Leros
Telendos
Kalymnos
Pserimos
Kos
Nisyros
Symi
Tilos
Astypalaia
Chalki
Rodos
Megisti
D o d e k a n i s a
Karpathos
Kasos
0
100 Kms
28° E
30° E

34° E
36° E
38° N
36° N
Kypros
34° N
32° E
34° E

Island Locator

An alphabetical index of all the islands featured in the Islands and Islets sections, together with the privately owned islands listed on page 83. The region or group of each island is shown and in some cases a more specific locality is added. Each island has a coloured code number, which indicates its country as shown on the inside front cover flap.

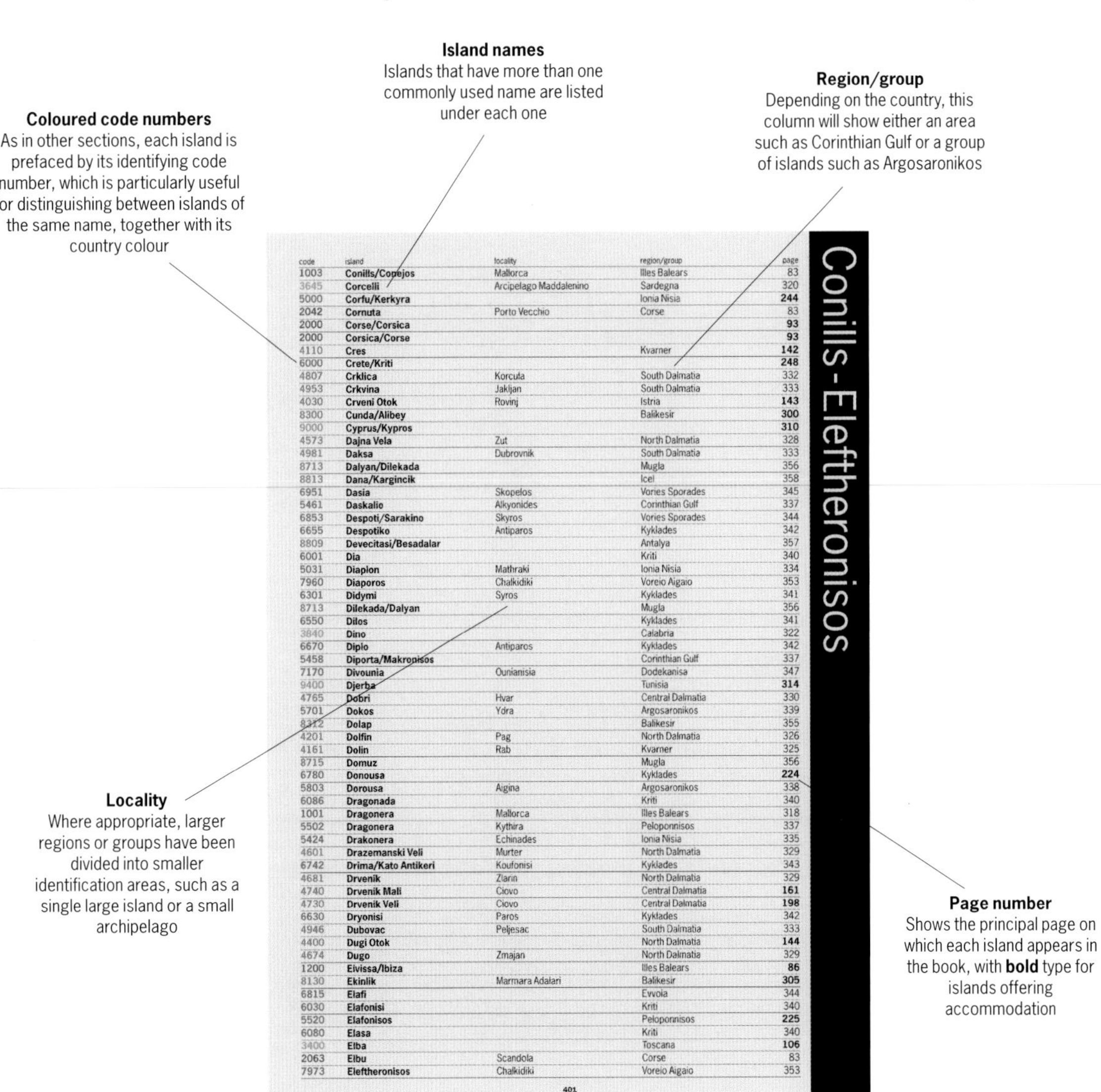
Island names
Islands that have more than one commonly used name are listed under each one
Region/group
Depending on the country, this column will show either an area such as Corinthian Gulf or a group of islands such as Argosaronikos
Coloured code numbers
As in other sections, each island is prefaced by its identifying code number, which is particularly useful for distinguishing between islands of the same name, together with its country colour
Locality
Where appropriate, larger regions or groups have been divided into smaller identification areas, such as a single large island or a small archipelago
Page number
Shows the principal page on which each island appears in the book, with **bold** type for islands offering accommodation
Conills - Eleftheronisos

code	island	locality	region/group	page
1003	**Conills/Conejos**	Mallorca	Illes Balears	83
3645	**Corcelli**	Arcipelago Maddalenino	Sardegna	320
5000	**Corfu/Kerkyra**		Ionia Nisia	**244**
2042	**Cornuta**	Porto Vecchio	Corse	83
2000	**Corse/Corsica**			**93**
2000	**Corsica/Corse**			**93**
4110	**Cres**		Kvarner	**142**
6000	**Crete/Kriti**			**248**
4807	**Crklica**	Korcula	South Dalmatia	332
4953	**Crkvina**	Jakljan	South Dalmatia	333
4030	**Crveni Otok**	Rovinj	Istria	**143**
8300	**Cunda/Alibey**		Balikesir	**300**
9000	**Cyprus/Kypros**			**310**
4573	**Dajna Vela**	Zut	North Dalmatia	328
4981	**Daksa**	Dubrovnik	South Dalmatia	333
8713	**Dalyan/Dilekada**		Mugla	356
8813	**Dana/Kargincik**		Icel	358
6951	**Dasia**	Skopelos	Vories Sporades	345
5461	**Daskalio**	Alkyonides	Corinthian Gulf	337
6853	**Despoti/Sarakino**	Skyros	Vories Sporades	344
6655	**Despotiko**	Antiparos	Kyklades	342
8809	**Devecitasi/Besadalar**		Antalya	357
6001	**Dia**		Kriti	340
5031	**Diaplon**	Mathraki	Ionia Nisia	334
7960	**Diaporos**	Chalkidiki	Voreio Aigaio	353
6301	**Didymi**	Syros	Kyklades	341
8713	**Dilekada/Dalyan**		Mugla	356
6550	**Dilos**		Kyklades	341
3840	**Dino**		Calabria	322
6670	**Diplo**	Antiparos	Kyklades	342
5458	**Diporta/Makronisos**		Corinthian Gulf	337
7170	**Divounia**	Ounianisia	Dodekanisa	347
9400	**Djerba**		Tunisia	**314**
4765	**Dobri**	Hvar	Central Dalmatia	330
5701	**Dokos**	Ydra	Argosaronikos	339
8312	**Dolap**		Balikesir	355
4201	**Dolfin**	Pag	North Dalmatia	326
4161	**Dolin**	Rab	Kvarner	325
8715	**Domuz**		Mugla	356
6780	**Donousa**		Kyklades	**224**
5803	**Dorousa**	Aigina	Argosaronikos	338
6086	**Dragonada**		Kriti	340
1001	**Dragonera**	Mallorca	Illes Balears	318
5502	**Dragonera**	Kythira	Peloponnisos	337
5424	**Drakonera**	Echinades	Ionia Nisia	335
4601	**Drazemanski Veli**	Murter	North Dalmatia	329
6742	**Drima/Kato Antikeri**	Koufonisi	Kyklades	343
4681	**Drvenik**	Zlarin	North Dalmatia	329
4740	**Drvenik Mali**	Ciovo	Central Dalmatia	**161**
4730	**Drvenik Veli**	Ciovo	Central Dalmatia	**198**
6630	**Dryonisi**	Paros	Kyklades	342
4946	**Dubovac**	Peljesac	South Dalmatia	333
4400	**Dugi Otok**		North Dalmatia	**144**
4674	**Dugo**	Zmajan	North Dalmatia	329
1200	**Eivissa/Ibiza**		Illes Balears	**86**
8130	**Ekinlik**	Marmara Adalari	Balikesir	**305**
6815	**Elafi**		Evvoia	344
6030	**Elafonisi**		Kriti	340
5520	**Elafonisos**		Peloponnisos	**225**
6080	**Elasa**		Kriti	340
3400	**Elba**		Toscana	**106**
2063	**Elbu**	Scandola	Corse	83
7973	**Eleftheronisos**	Chalkidiki	Voreio Aigaio	353

401

code	island	locality	region/group	page
6205	**Antimilos**	Milos	Kyklades	342
6650	**Antiparos**		Kyklades	**218**
5060	**Antipaxoi**		Ionia Nisia	**219**
7625	**Antipsara**	Psara	Voreio Aigaio	351
7055	**Antitilos**	Tilos	Dodekanisa	348
6751	**Anydros**	Amorgos	Kyklades	343
7453	**Anydros**	Patmos	Dodekanisa	349
5416	**Apaso**	Echinades	Ionia Nisia	83
8604	**Apostol/Konel**		Mugla	356
7405	**Archangelos**	Leros	Dodekanisa	349
7442	**Arefousa**	Lipsoi	Dodekanisa	349
6840	**Argyronisi**		Evvoia	344
4741	**Arkandel**	Mali drvenik	Central Dalmatia	330
7460	**Arkoi**		Dodekanisa	**220**
6902	**Arkos**	Skiathos	Vories Sporades	345
5101	**Arkoudi**	Lefkada	Ionia Nisia	335
7155	**Armathia**	Kasos	Dodekanisa	347
5491	**Arpia**	Strofades	Ionia Nisia	337
5920	**Arsida**	Saronic Gulf	Argosaronikos	339
4604	**Arta Mala**	Murter	North Dalmatia	329
4603	**Arta Vela**	Murter	North Dalmatia	329
7951	**Artemis**	Ammouliani	Voreio Aigaio	353
9100	**Arwad**	Tartus	Syria	358
7980	**Asanis**	Evros	Voreio Aigaio	353
3530	**Asinara**	Sardegna	Sardegna	320
6111	**Askania**	Santorini	Kyklades	343
6303	**Aspro**	Syros	Kyklades	341
6104	**Aspronisi**	Santorini	Kyklades	343
6903	**Aspronisо**	Skiathos	Vories Sporades	345
7702	**Aspronisos**	Lesvos	Voreio Aigaio	351
7160	**Astakida**	Kasos	Dodekanisa	347
7161	**Astakidopoula**	Kasos	Dodekanisa	347
7350	**Astypalaia**		Dodekanisa	**221**
6832	**Atalanti**		Fthiotida	344
5301	**Atokos**	Ithaki	Ionia Nisia	336
1006	**Aucanada**	Mallorca	Illes Balears	83
5501	**Avgo**	Kythira	Peloponnisos	337
8120	**Avsa**	Marmara Adalari	Balikesir	**301**
8714	**Babaadasi/Adatepe**		Mugla	356
4343	**Babac**	Pasman	North Dalmatia	327
8812	**Babadil/Besparmak**		Icel	358
4820	**Badija**	Korcula	South Dalmatia	332
2301	**Bagaud**	Port-Cros	Provence	319
4593	**Balabra Vela**	Sit	North Dalmatia	328
8311	**Balik**		Balikesir	355
4711	**Balkun**	Solta	Central Dalmatia	330
8419	**Balta/Kucukada**		Izmir	355
7701	**Barbalias/Tomaronisi**	Lesvos	Voreio Aigaio	351
3648	**Barettini**	Arcipelago Maddalenino	Sardegna	320
3365	**Basiluzzo**	Isole Eolie	Sicilia	322
4654	**Bavljenac**	Kaprije	North Dalmatia	328
8711	**Bedirada**		Mugla	356
2800	**Bendor**	Bandol	Provence	**92**
3495	**Bergeggi**		Liguria	322
8809	**Besadalar/Devecitasi**		Antalya	357
8812	**Besparmak/Babadil**		Antalya	358
3559	**Bisce**		Sardegna	320
4781	**Bisevo**	Vis	Central Dalmatia	330
1209	**Bleda Plana**	Eivissa	Illes Balears	83
4050	**Bodulas**	Medulin	Istria	324
8426	**Bogaz**		Izmir	355
8427	**Bogurtlen**		Izmir	355
4764	**Borovac**	Hvar	Central Dalmatia	330

code	island	locality	region/group	page
4504	**Borovnik**	Kornat	North Dalmatia	328
4641	**Borovnjak Mali**	Kakan	North Dalmatia	328
4642	**Borovnjak Veli**	Kakan	North Dalmatia	328
1205	**Bosque**	Eivissa	Illes Balears	318
8210	**Bozcaada**		Canakkale	**302**
4700	**Brac**		Central Dalmatia	**140**
4904	**Bratin**	Lastovo	South Dalmatia	332
4275	**Brguljski**	Molat	North Dalmatia	326
4001	**Brijun Mali**		Istria	324
4000	**Brijun Veli**		Istria	**197**
4401	**Brscak**	Dugi Otok	North Dalmatia	327
4594	**Brusnjak**	Sit	North Dalmatia	328
4204	**Brusnjak Veli**	Pag	North Dalmatia	326
4425	**Buc Veli**	Dugi Otok	North Dalmatia	327
3650	**Budelli**	Arcipelago Maddalenino	Sardegna	320
4783	**Budikovac Veli**	Vis	Central Dalmatia	330
8020	**Burgazada**	Prens Adalari	Istanbul	**303**
8603	**Buyuk/Tokatbasi**		Mugla	356
8000	**Buyukada**	Prens Adalari	Istanbul	**304**
1050	**Cabrera**		Illes Balears	318
2021	**Camaro Canto**	Lavezzi	Corse	83
8615	**Camli/Gelibolu**		Mugla	356
3030	**Capo Passero**		Sicilia	322
3410	**Capraia**		Toscana	**103**
3910	**Caprara**	Tremiti	Puglia	322
3610	**Caprera**	Arcipelago Maddalenino	Sardegna	**104**
3800	**Capri**		Campania	**105**
8428	**Carufa**		Izmir	355
8608	**Catalada**		Mugla	356
8708	**Cataladalar**		Mugla	356
2010	**Cavallo**	Bonifacio	Corse	319
4644	**Cavlin**	Kakan	North Dalmatia	328
3560	**Cavoli**		Sardegna	320
8607	**Cavus/Eskifener**		Mugla	356
4051	**Ceja**	Medulin	Istria	324
8609	**Celebi**		Mugla	356
4907	**Cesvinica**	Lastovo	South Dalmatia	332
1405	**Chafarinas**		Moroccan coast	318
7020	**Chalki**		Dodekanisa	**222**
6811	**Chersonisi**	Petalioi	Evvoia	344
3601	**Chiesa**	Arcipelago Maddalenino	Sardegna	320
7451	**Chiliomodi**	Patmos	Dodekanisa	349
7600	**Chios**		Voreio Aigaio	**223**
7361	**Chondro/Skrofa**	Astypalaia	Dodekanisa	348
7036	**Chondros**	Symi	Dodekanisa	347
6110	**Christiani**	Santorini	Kyklades	343
6060	**Chrysi/Gaidouronisi**		Kriti	340
6520	**Chtapodia**	Mykonos	Kyklades	341
8313	**Cicek**		Balikesir	355
8423	**Cifteadalar**		Izmir	355
8501	**Cil/Tavsan**		Aydin	356
4720	**Ciovo**		Central Dalmatia	**141**
8320	**Ciplakada**		Balikesir	355
8429	**Cirakan**		Izmir	355
1101	**Colom**	Menorca	Illes Balears	318
1402	**Columbretes**		Castellon	318
9320	**Comino**		Malta	**311**
9321	**Cominotto**		Malta	358
1051	**Conejera**	Cabrera	Illes Balears	318
1201	**Conejera**	Eivissa	Illes Balears	318
1003	**Conejos/Conills**	Mallorca	Illes Balears	83
3205	**Conigli**	Lampedusa	Sicilia	322
9451	**Conigliera**	Monastir	Tunisia	358

code	island	locality	region/group	page
8807	**Eleksi/Icada**		Antalya	357
5808	**Eleousa/Lagousa**	Aigina	Argosaronikos	338
2700	**Embiez**	Sanary	Provence	**94**
5020	**Erikousa**	Diapontia	Ionia Nisia	**226**
1403	**Escombreras**	Cartagena	Murcia	318
8430	**Esek/Kanliada**		Izmir	355
8414	**Esek/Incirliada**		Izmir	355
8102	**Esek/Isik**	Marmara Adalari	Balikesir	354
8607	**Eskifener/Cavus**		Mugla	356
7145	**Esokastro**	Karpathos	Dodekanisa	347
1301	**Espalmador**	Formentera	Illes Balears	318
1302	**Espardell**	Formentera	Illes Balears	318
1204	**Espartar**	Eivissa	Illes Balears	318
6800	**Evia/Evvoia**			**227**
5840	**Evraionisi/Ovrios**		Argosaronikos	338
6800	**Evvoia/Evia**			**227**
6858	**Exo Podies**	Skyros	Vories Sporades	344
6981	**Fagkrou/Pelerissa**	Kyra Panagia	Vories Sporades	345
5603	**Falkonera**		Argosaronikos	339
7403	**Faradonisia**	Leros	Dodekanisa	349
2044	**Farina**	Porto Vecchio	Corse	83
7410	**Farmakonisi**	Leros	Dodekanisa	349
9422	**Fauchelle**	Galite	Tunisia	358
2041	**Fautea**	Porto Vecchio	Corse	83
3100	**Favignana**	Egadi	Sicilia	**107**
3040	**Femmine**		Sicilia	322
8141	**Fener**	Bandirma	Balikesir	354
8409	**Fener/Oglak**		Izmir	355
4052	**Fenera**	Medulin	Istria	324
6721	**Fidousa**	Schoinousa	Kyklades	343
3553	**Figarolo**		Sardegna	320
3340	**Filicudi**	Isole Eolie	Sicilia	**108**
6620	**Filitzi**	Paros	Kyklades	342
2071	**Finocchiarola**	Cap Corse	Corse	83
5910	**Fleves**	Saronic Gulf	Argosaronikos	339
7353	**Fokies**	Astypalaia	Dodekanisa	348
6170	**Folegandros**		Kyklades	**228**
5455	**Fonias**		Corinthian Gulf	337
2051	**Forana**	Cerbicale	Corse	319
1300	**Formentera**		Illes Balears	**87**
1002	**Formentor**	Mallorca	Illes Balears	318
3451	**Formica Grande**	Grosseto	Toscana	321
6813	**Founti**	Petalioi	Evvoia	344
7520	**Fournoi**		North Aegean	**229**
7441	**Fragkos**	Lipsoi	Dodekanisa	349
4042	**Frasker**	Pula	Istria	324
2600	**Frioul**	Marseille	Provence	**95**
6830	**Gaidaros**		Fthiotida	344
7056	**Gaidaros**	Tilos	Dodekanisa	348
6846	**Gaidaros/Ktyponisi**		Evvoia	344
7051	**Gaidouronisi**	Tilos	Dodekanisa	348
6610	**Gaidouronisi**	Paros	Kyklades	342
6060	**Gaidouronisi/Chrysi**		Kriti	340
7611	**Gaidouroniso/Gavathi**	Oinousses	Voreio Aigaio	351
4341	**Galesnjak**	Pasman	North Dalmatia	327
9420	**Galite**	Tabarka	Tunisia	358
9421	**Galiton**	Galite	Tunisia	358
3830	**Galli**	Positano	Campania	83
3490	**Gallinara**		Liguria	322
4348	**Gangaro**	Pasman	North Dalmatia	**145**
4592	**Gangarol**	Sit	North Dalmatia	328
2060	**Gargalu**	Scandola	Corse	319
8402	**Garip**		Izmir	355

code	island	locality	region/group	page
5200	**Kefalonia**		Ionia Nisia	**243**
8808	**Kekova**		Antalya	357
7970	**Kelifos**	Chalkidiki	Voreio Aigaio	353
9410	**Kerkennah**	Sfax	Tunisia	**315**
5000	**Kerkyra/Corfu**		Ionia Nisia	**244**
6740	**Keros**	Koufonisi	Kyklades	343
7525	**Kesiria**	Fournoi	Voreio Aigaio	350
6210	**Kimolos**		Kyklades	**245**
8030	**Kinaliada**	Prens Adalari	Istanbul	354
7430	**Kinaros**	Leros	Dodekanisa	349
8605	**Kiremit Buyuk**		Mugla	356
8606	**Kiremit Kucuk**		Mugla	356
8613	**Kistak**		Mugla	356
6251	**Kitriani**	Sifnos	Kyklades	341
8314	**Kiz/Ulva**		Balikesir	355
8721	**Kizil**	Fethiye	Mugla	356
8705	**Kizilada**		Mugla	356
8709	**Kizilada**		Mugla	356
8403	**Kizkulesi/Mardalic**		Izmir	355
8719	**Kizlan/Gocek**		Mugla	356
9001	**Klides**		Kypros	358
4516	**Klobucar**	Kornat	North Dalmatia	328
9430	**Kneis**	Sfax	Tunisia	358
4431	**Knezak**	Iz	North Dalmatia	327
4941	**Kobrava**	Mljet	South Dalmatia	333
8703	**Kocaada**		Mugla	356
5615	**Koilada/Koronida**	Argos Gulf	Argosaronikos	339
6847	**Koili**		Evvoia	344
7901	**Koinyra**	Thasos	Voreio Aigaio	353
4980	**Kolocep**	Elafiti	South Dalmatia	**151**
6092	**Kolokythas**		Kriti	340
4121	**Koludarc**	Losinj	Kvarner	325
4342	**Komornik**	Pasman	North Dalmatia	327
8604	**Konel/Apostol**		Mugla	356
4903	**Kopiste**	Lastovo	South Dalmatia	332
6734	**Kopria**	Koufonisi	Kyklades	343
6974	**Korakas**	Skantzoura	Vories Sporades	345
5616	**Korakonisi**	Argos Gulf	Argosaronikos	339
4800	**Korcula**		South Dalmatia	**152**
4511	**Koritnjak**	Kornat	North Dalmatia	328
4500	**Kornat**		North Dalmatia	**153**
5615	**Koronida/Koilada**	Argos Gulf	Argosaronikos	339
7200	**Kos**		Dodekanisa	**246**
4349	**Kosara**	Pasman	North Dalmatia	327
4124	**Kosjak**	Losinj	Kvarner	325
4102	**Kosljun**	Krk	Kvarner	324
6730	**Koufonisi**		Kyklades	**247**
6070	**Koufonisi**		Kriti	340
7034	**Kouloundros**	Symi	Dodekanisa	347
6856	**Koulouri**	Skyros	Vories Sporades	344
7481	**Kouneli**	Agathonisi	Dodekanisa	349
7364	**Kounoupi**	Astypalaia	Dodekanisa	348
7363	**Koutsomytis**	Astypalaia	Dodekanisa	348
5457	**Kouveli**		Corinthian Gulf	337
8111	**Koyun**		Balikesir	354
4124	**Kozjak**	Losinj	Kvarner	325
4690	**Krapanj**	Sibenik	North Dalmatia	**154**
4684	**Krbela Vela**	Zlarin	North Dalmatia	329
6000	**Kriti/Crete**			**248**
4100	**Krk**		Kvarner	**155**
4422	**Krknata**	Dugi Otok	North Dalmatia	327
4732	**Krknjas Veli**	Veli Drvenik	Central Dalmatia	330
4906	**Krucica**	Lastovo	South Dalmatia	332

code	island	locality	region/group	page
6846	**Ktyponisi/Gaidaros**		Evvoia	344
8419	**Kucukada/Balta**		Izmir	355
8306	**Kucukmaden**	Alibey	Balikesir	355
4595	**Kurba Mala**	Sit	North Dalmatia	328
4530	**Kurba Vela**	Kornat	North Dalmatia	328
9450	**Kuriate**	Monastir	Tunisia	358
8315	**Kuthu/Karaada**		Balikesir	355
9000	**Kypros/Cyprus**			**310**
5821	**Kyra**	Agkistri	Argosaronikos	338
6980	**Kyra Panagia**	Alonnisos	Vories Sporades	345
5500	**Kythira**		Peloponnisos	**249**
6270	**Kythnos**		Kyklades	**250**
5151	**Kythros**	Meganisi	Ionia Nisia	335
3670	**La Presa**	Arcipelago Maddalenino	Sardegna	320
5808	**Lagousa/Eleousa**	Aigina	Argosaronikos	338
5427	**Lambrinos**	Echinades	Ionia Nisia	335
3200	**Lampedusa**	Isole Pelagie	Sicilia	**112**
6814	**Lamperousa**	Petalioi	Evvoia	344
3220	**Lampione**	Isole Pelagie	Sicilia	322
7431	**Laros**	Kinaros	Dodekanisa	349
4900	**Lastovo**		South Dalmatia	**156**
4423	**Lavdara Vela**	Dugi Otok	North Dalmatia	**157**
2020	**Lavezzi**	Bonifacio	Corse	319
4514	**Lavsa**	Kornat	North Dalmatia	**158**
1103	**Lazareto**	Menorca	Illes Balears	318
2200	**Le Levant**	Iles d'Hyeres	Provence	**96**
6966	**Lechousa**	Alonnisos	Vories Sporades	345
5100	**Lefkada**		Ionia Nisia	**251**
7400	**Leros**		Dodekanisa	**252**
5905	**Leros**	Salamina	Argosaronikos	338
7700	**Lesvos**		Voreio Aigaio	**253**
3110	**Levanzo**	Egadi	Sicilia	**113**
7420	**Levitha**	Leros	Dodekanisa	349
4503	**Levrnaka**	Kornat	North Dalmatia	328
7435	**Liadi**	Kinaros	Dodekanisa	349
7360	**Ligno**	Astypalaia	Dodekanisa	348
7800	**Limnos**		Voreio Aigaio	**254**
3210	**Linosa**	Isole Pelagie	Sicilia	**114**
3300	**Lipari**	Isole Eolie	Sicilia	**115**
7440	**Lipsoi**		Dodekanisa	**255**
1208	**Llarga**	Eivissa	Illes Balears	83
4663	**Logorun**	Tijat	North Dalmatia	329
4982	**Lokrum**	Dubrovnik	South Dalmatia	333
4970	**Lopud**	Elafiti	South Dalmatia	**159**
4120	**Losinj**		Kvarner	**160**
4532	**Lucmarinjak**	Kurba Vela	North Dalmatia	328
4518	**Lunga**	Kornat	North Dalmatia	328
4661	**Lupac**	Prvic	North Dalmatia	329
4421	**Luski**	Dugi Otok	North Dalmatia	327
4251	**Lutrosnjak**	Premuda	North Dalmatia	326
5302	**Lygia/Pera Pigadi**	Ithaki	Ionia Nisia	336
3600	**Maddalena**	Arcipelago Maddalenino	Sardegna	**116**
8301	**Madenada**		Balikesir	355
5105	**Madouri**	Lefkada	Ionia Nisia	335
2052	**Maestro Maria**	Cerbicales	Corse	83
2603	**Maire**	Marseille	Provence	319
4812	**Majsan**	Korcula	South Dalmatia	332
6142	**Makra**	Anafi	Kyklades	343
5412	**Makri**	Echinades	Ionia Nisia	335
7001	**Makri**	Rodos	Dodekanisa	346
7521	**Makronisi**	Fournoi	Voreio Aigaio	350
5504	**Makronisi**	Kythira	Peloponnisos	337
7152	**Makronisi**	Kasos	Dodekanisa	347

code	island	locality	region/group	page
4942	**Moracnik**	Mljet	South Dalmatia	333
4232	**Morovnik**	Olib	North Dalmatia	326
3556	**Mortorio**		Sardegna	320
8302	**Moskoada/Pinar**		Balikesir	355
5006	**Mourtos**	Sivota	Ionia Nisia	334
4902	**Mrcara**	Lastovo	South Dalmatia	**164**
4983	**Mrkan**	Dubrovnik	South Dalmatia	333
4531	**Mrtovnjak**	Kurba Vela	North Dalmatia	328
4344	**Muntan**	Pasman	North Dalmatia	327
8619	**Murdala/Akcali**		Mugla	356
4600	**Murter**		North Dalmatia	**165**
4621	**Murvenjak**	Vrgada	North Dalmatia	329
8424	**Mustafa Celebi**		Izmir	355
6500	**Mykonos**		Kyklades	**261**
6700	**Naxos**		Kyklades	**262**
6101	**Nea Kammeni**	Santorini	Kyklades	343
8502	**Neo/Su**		Aydin	356
7306	**Nera**	Kalymnos	Dodekanisa	349
7483	**Neronisi**	Agathonisi	Dodekanisa	349
3558	**Nibani**		Sardegna	320
6754	**Nikouria**	Amorgos	Kyklades	343
7035	**Nimos**	Symi	Dodekanisa	347
7021	**Nisaki**	Chalki	Dodekanisa	346
3826	**Nisida**	Pozzuoli	Campania	321
7220	**Nisyros**		Dodekanisa	**263**
1400	**Nueva Tabarca**	Santa Pola	Alicante	**90**
4683	**Oblik**	Zlarin	North Dalmatia	329
4671	**Obonjan**	Zmajan	North Dalmatia	**166**
4346	**Obun**	Pasman	North Dalmatia	327
7351	**Ofidousa**	Astypalaia	Dodekanisa	348
8409	**Oglak/Fener**		Izmir	355
7610	**Oinousses**		Voreio Aigaio	**264**
4524	**Okljuc**	Kornat	North Dalmatia	328
4230	**Olib**		North Dalmatia	**167**
4951	**Olipa**	Jakljan	South Dalmatia	333
6826	**Oniron/Pezonisos**		Evvoia	344
8407	**Orak**		Izmir	355
8612	**Orak**		Mugla	356
4123	**Orjule Male**	Losinj	Kvarner	325
4122	**Orjule Vele**	Losinj	Kvarner	325
4731	**Orud**	Veli Drvenik	Central Dalmatia	330
4114	**Oruda**	Losinj	Kvarner	325
4802	**Osjak**	Korcula	South Dalmatia	332
4301	**Osljak**	Ugljan	North Dalmatia	**168**
5010	**Othonoi**	Diapontia	Ionia Nisia	**265**
4722	**Otok Trogir**	Trogir	Central Dalmatia	330
7171	**Ounianisi**	Kasos	Dodekanisa	347
5840	**Ovrios/Evraionisi**	Saronic Gulf	Argosaronikos	338
5410	**Oxia**	Echinades	Ionia Nisia	335
4115	**Palacol**	Oruda	Kvarner	325
6141	**Pachia**	Anafi	Kyklades	343
7223	**Pachia**	Nisyros	Dodekanisa	348
4200	**Pag**		North Dalmatia	**169**
4840	**Palagruza**		South Dalmatia	**170**
6102	**Palaia Kammeni**	Santorini	Kyklades	343
6990	**Palaio Trikeri**	Pagasitic Gulf	Pagasitic Gulf	**266**
7385	**Palakida**	Tria Nisia	Dodekanisa	348
8701	**Palamutbuku**		Mugla	356
2062	**Palazzu**	Scandola	Corse	83
9200	**Palm/An Nakhl**	Trablous	Lebanon	358
3405	**Palmaiola**	Elba	Toscana	321
3480	**Palmaria**		Liguria	322
3710	**Palmarola**	Isole Ponziane	Lazio	**118**

code	island	locality	region/group	page
7902	**Panagia**	Thasos	Voreio Aigaio	353
7703	**Panagia**	Lesvos	Voreio Aigaio	351
3360	**Panarea**	Isole Eolie	Sicilia	**119**
8503	**Panayiada**		Aydin	356
4513	**Panitula Vela**	Kornat	North Dalmatia	328
6451	**Panormos/Planitis**		Kyklades	341
3050	**Pantelleria**		Sicilia	**122**
6640	**Panteronisi**	Paros	Kyklades	342
5602	**Parapola/Velopoula**	Spetses	Argosaronikos	339
6600	**Paros**		Kyklades	**267**
6823	**Parthenopi**		Evvoia	344
8110	**Pasalimani**	Marmara Adalari	Balikesir	**309**
7615	**Pasas**	Oinousses	Voreio Aigaio	351
4340	**Pasman**		North Dalmatia	**171**
7450	**Patmos**		Dodekanisa	**268**
5930	**Patroklou**	Saronic Gulf	Argosaronikos	339
6088	**Paximada**		Kriti	340
6040	**Paximadia Megalo**		Kriti	340
6041	**Paximadia Mikro**		Kriti	340
5050	**Paxoi**		Ionia Nisia	**269**
7602	**Pelagonisos**	Chios	Voreio Aigaio	351
6981	**Pelerissa/Fagkrou**	Kyra Panagia	Vories Sporades	345
5402	**Pelouzo**	Zakynthos	Ionia Nisia	336
7952	**Penna**	Ammouliani	Voreio Aigaio	353
5070	**Pera Nisi**	Ambracian Gulf	Ambracian Gulf	334
5302	**Pera Pigadi/Lygia**	Ithaki	Ionia Nisia	336
7222	**Pergousa**	Nisyros	Dodekanisa	348
6965	**Peristera**	Alonnisos	Vories Sporades	345
5411	**Petalas**	Echinades	Ionia Nisia	335
5704	**Petasi**	Ydra	Argosaronikos	339
1105	**Petita d'Addaia**	Menorca	Illes Balears	83
6821	**Petousi**		Evvoia	344
6826	**Pezonisos/Oniron**		Evvoia	344
2007	**Piana**	Ajaccio	Corse	83
2023	**Piana**	Lavezzi	Corse	83
2050	**Piana**	Cerbicale	Corse	319
3525	**Piana**	Sulcis	Sardegna	**123**
3535	**Piana**	Asinara	Sardegna	320
3545	**Piana**	Capo Caccia	Sardegna	320
3551	**Piana**	Tavolara	Sardegna	320
3930	**Pianosa**	Tremiti	Puglia	322
3430	**Pianosa**		Toscana	321
2053	**Pietricaggiosa**	Cerbicale	Corse	83
7401	**Piganousa**	Leros	Dodekanisa	349
8302	**Pinar/Moskoada**		Balikesir	355
2040	**Pinarellu**	Porto Vecchio	Corse	319
6986	**Piperi**	Alonnisos	Vories Sporades	345
6271	**Piperi**	Kythnos	Kyklades	341
8413	**Pirnalliada**		Izmir	355
4510	**Piskera**	Kornat	North Dalmatia	328
5425	**Pistros**	Echinades	Ionia Nisia	335
6991	**Pithou**	Pagasitic Gulf	Pagasitic Gulf	345
2605	**Plane**	Marseille	Provence	319
4231	**Planik**	Olib	North Dalmatia	326
4763	**Planikovac**	Hvar	Central Dalmatia	330
6451	**Planitis/Panormos**	Tinos	Kyklades	341
4813	**Planjak**	Korcula	South Dalmatia	332
7321	**Plati**	Pserimos	Dodekanisa	349
7153	**Plati**	Kasos	Dodekanisa	347
6854	**Platia**	Skyros	Vories Sporades	344
5807	**Platia**	Aigina	Argosaronikos	338
5611	**Platia**	Argos Gulf	Argosaronikos	339
7482	**Plato/Psathonisi**	Agathonisi	Dodekanisa	349

code	island	locality	region/group	page
4112	**Plavnik**	Cres	Kvarner	325
4815	**Plocica**	Korcula	South Dalmatia	**174**
6971	**Polemika**	Skantzoura	Vories Sporades	345
6215	**Polyaigos**	Milos	Kyklades	342
4943	**Pomestak**	Mljet	South Dalmatia	333
6845	**Pontikonisi**		Evvoia	344
6022	**Pontikonisi**		Kriti	340
7612	**Pontikonisi**	Oinousses	Voreio Aigaio	351
5419	**Pontikos**	Echinades	Ionia Nisia	335
7352	**Pontikousa**	Astypalaia	Dodekanisa	348
3700	**Ponza**	Isole Ponziane	Lazio	**124**
4053	**Porer**	Premantura	Istria	**175**
5850	**Poros**		Argosaronikos	**270**
2100	**Porquerolles**	Iles d'Hyeres	Provence	**97**
1109	**Porros**	Menorca	Illes Balears	83
2080	**Port**	Figari	Corse	83
2300	**Port-Cros**	Iles d'Hyeres	Provence	**98**
8304	**Poyrazada/Yellice**	Alibey	Balikesir	355
6972	**Praso**	Skantzoura	Vories Sporades	345
5429	**Praso**	Echinades	Ionia Nisia	83
6982	**Praso/Grammeza**	Alonnisos	Vories Sporades	345
5511	**Prasonisi**	Antikythira	Peloponnisos	337
5005	**Prasoudi**	Igoumenitsa	Ionia Nisia	334
4250	**Premuda**		North Dalmatia	**176**
4901	**Prezba**	Lastovo	South Dalmatia	332
4602	**Prisnjak**	Murter	North Dalmatia	**177**
3820	**Procida**		Campania	**125**
4801	**Proizd**	Korcula	South Dalmatia	332
5470	**Proti**		Peloponnisos	337
5420	**Provatio**	Echinades	Ionia Nisia	335
5171	**Provatio**	Kastos	Ionia Nisia	335
4103	**Prvic**	Krk	Kvarner	324
4660	**Prvic**		North Dalmatia	**178**
4805	**Prznjak Mali**	Korcula	South Dalmatia	332
4804	**Prznjak Veli**	Korcula	South Dalmatia	332
7620	**Psara**		Voreio Aigaio	**271**
7482	**Psathonisi/Plato**	Agathonisi	Dodekanisa	349
6987	**Psathoura**	Alonnisos	Vories Sporades	345
7320	**Pserimos**		Dodekanisa	**272**
5612	**Psili**	Argos Gulf	Argosaronikos	339
5805	**Psili**	Aigina	Argosaronikos	338
6090	**Psira**		Kriti	340
5906	**Psyttalia**	Salamina	Argosaronikos	338
5001	**Ptychia/Vido**	Kerkyra	Ionia Nisia	334
4160	**Rab**		Kvarner	**179**
9501	**Rachgoune**	Beni Saf	Algeria	318
4605	**Radelj**	Murter	North Dalmatia	329
6286	**Raftis**	Porto Rafti	Attiki	341
4682	**Rakitan**	Zlarin	North Dalmatia	329
4506	**Rasip Mali**	Kornat	North Dalmatia	328
4507	**Rasip Veli**	Kornat	North Dalmatia	328
4420	**Rava**	Dugi Otok	North Dalmatia	**180**
4653	**Ravan**	Kaprije	North Dalmatia	328
1108	**Ravells**	Menorca	Illes Balears	83
4520	**Ravni Zakan**	Kornat	North Dalmatia	328
4784	**Ravnik**	Vis	Central Dalmatia	330
3660	**Razzoli**	Arcipelago Maddalenino	Sardegna	320
1052	**Redona**	Cabrera	Illes Balears	318
1207	**Redona**	Eivissa	Illes Balears	83
5902	**Revithousa**	Salamina	Argosaronikos	338
6675	**Revmatonisi**	Antiparos	Kyklades	83
7000	**Rhodes/Rodos**		Dodekanisa	**273**
6560	**Rinia**	Mykonos	Kyklades	341

code	island	locality	region/group	page
6250	**Sifnos**		Kyklades	**282**
4207	**Sikavac Mali**	Pag	North Dalmatia	326
4206	**Sikavac Veliki**	Pag	North Dalmatia	326
6160	**Sikinos**		Kyklades	**283**
4240	**Silba**		North Dalmatia	**184**
4502	**Silo Velo**	Kornat	North Dalmatia	328
4960	**Sipan**	Elafiti	South Dalmatia	**185**
4590	**Sit**		North Dalmatia	**186**
8060	**Sivriada**	Prens Adalari	Istanbul	354
4575	**Skala Vela**	Zut	North Dalmatia	328
6973	**Skantili**	Skantzoura	Vories Sporades	345
6970	**Skantzoura**	Alonnisos	Vories Sporades	345
4255	**Skarda**	Premuda	North Dalmatia	326
6900	**Skiathos**		Vories Sporades	**284**
6950	**Skopelos**		Vories Sporades	**285**
5103	**Skorpidi**	Lefkada	Ionia Nisia	335
5102	**Skorpios**	Lefkada	Ionia Nisia	335
4202	**Skrda**	Pag	North Dalmatia	326
7361	**Skrofa/Chondro**	Astypalaia	Dodekanisa	348
4522	**Skulj**	Kornat	North Dalmatia	328
5852	**Skyli**	Poros	Argosaronikos	339
6781	**Skylonisi**	Donousa	Kyklades	343
6852	**Skyropoula**	Skyros	Vories Sporades	344
6850	**Skyros**		Vories Sporades	**286**
4523	**Smokvica Vela**	Kornat	North Dalmatia	**187**
4694	**Smokvica Vela**	Primosten	North Dalmatia	329
3554	**Soffi**		Sardegna	320
5428	**Sofia**	Echinades	Ionia Nisia	335
8707	**Sogut**		Mugla	356
4710	**Solta**		Central Dalmatia	**188**
5417	**Soros**	Echinades	Ionia Nisia	83
6010	**Souda**		Kriti	340
7971	**Spalathro**	Chalkidiki	Voreio Aigaio	353
3620	**Spargi**	Arcipelago Maddalenino	Sardegna	320
3625	**Spargiotto**	Arcipelago Maddalenino	Sardegna	320
5104	**Sparti**	Lefkada	Ionia Nisia	335
5853	**Spathi**	Poros	Argosaronikos	339
5600	**Spetses**		Argosaronikos	**287**
5601	**Spetsopoula**	Spetses	Argosaronikos	339
4132	**Srakane Male**	Losinj	Kvarner	325
4131	**Srakane Vele**	Losinj	Kvarner	325
4312	**Srednji Sestrica**	Rivanj	North Dalmatia	327
4808	**Sridnjak**	Korcula	South Dalmatia	332
4432	**Sridnji**	Iz	North Dalmatia	327
9301	**St Paul's**		Malta	358
5806	**Stachtorogi**	Aigina	Argosaronikos	338
5490	**Stamfani**	Strofades	Ionia Nisia	337
5705	**Stavronisi**	Ydra	Argosaronikos	339
7387	**Stefania**	Tria Nisia	Dodekanisa	348
4712	**Stipanska**	Solta	Central Dalmatia	330
4909	**Stomorina**	Lastovo	South Dalmatia	332
3330	**Stromboli**	Isole Eolie	Sicilia	**135**
7012	**Strongyli**	Megisti	Dodekanisa	346
7006	**Strongyli**	Rodos	Dodekanisa	346
7224	**Strongyli**	Nisyros	Dodekanisa	348
7461	**Strongyli**	Arkoi	Dodekanisa	349
7404	**Strongyli**	Leros	Dodekanisa	349
6071	**Strongyli**		Kriti	340
6660	**Strongylo**	Antiparos	Kyklades	342
6791	**Strongylo**	Makares	Kyklades	343
6820	**Styra**		Evvoia	344
8502	**Su/Neo**		Aydin	356
2061	**Sulana**	Scandola	Corse	83

code	island	locality	region/group	page
4803	**Trstenik**	Korcula	South Dalmatia	332
5421	**Tsakalonisi**	Echinades	Ionia Nisia	335
5453	**Tsarouchi**		Corinthian Gulf	337
6901	**Tsougkria**	Skiathos	Vories Sporades	345
4272	**Tun Mali**	Molat	North Dalmatia	326
4271	**Tun Veli**	Molat	North Dalmatia	326
8120	**Turkeli/Avsa**	Marmara Adalari	Balikesir	**301**
8811	**Ucadalar**		Antalya	357
4300	**Ugljan**		North Dalmatia	**195**
4040	**Uljanik**	Pula	Istria	324
8314	**Ulva/Kiz**		Balikesir	355
4130	**Unije**	Losinj	Kvarner	**196**
3020	**Ustica**		Sicilia	**136**
4411	**Utra**	Dugi Otok	North Dalmatia	327
8410	**Uzunada**		Izmir	355
8704	**Uzunada**		Mugla	356
8420	**Uzunadalar**		Izmir	355
6851	**Valaxa**	Skyros	Vories Sporades	344
4003	**Vanga**	Brijuni	Istria	324
5201	**Vardiani**	Kefalonia	Ionia Nisia	336
7613	**Vatos**	Oinousses	Voreio Aigaio	351
1202	**Vedra**	Eivissa	Illes Balears	318
1206	**Vedranell**	Eivissa	Illes Balears	318
4347	**Vela Kotula**	Pasman	North Dalmatia	327
4311	**Vela Sestrica**	Rivanj	North Dalmatia	327
4000	**Veli Brijun**		Istria	**197**
4730	**Veli Drvenik**	Ciovo	Central Dalmatia	**198**
4433	**Veli Otok**	Iz	North Dalmatia	327
4303	**Veli Skolj**	Ugljan	North Dalmatia	327
4984	**Veli Skolj**	Molunat	South Dalmatia	333
5602	**Velopoula/Parapola**	Spetses	Argosaronikos	339
5479	**Venetiko**		Peloponnisos	337
6711	**Venetiko**	Iraklia	Kyklades	343
3730	**Ventotene**	Isole Ponziane	Lazio	**137**
2606	**Verte**	La Ciotat	Provence	319
4041	**Veruda**	Pula	Istria	324
5001	**Vido/Ptychia**	Kerkyra	Ionia Nisia	334
4607	**Vinik Veli**	Murter	North Dalmatia	329
6615	**Viokastro**	Paros	Kyklades	342
4220	**Vir**	Pag	North Dalmatia	**199**
4780	**Vis**	Vis	Central Dalmatia	**200**
3825	**Vivara**	Procida	Campania	321
4905	**Vlasnik**	Lastovo	South Dalmatia	332
4261	**Vodenjak**	Ist	North Dalmatia	326
4766	**Vodnjak Veli**	Hvar	Central Dalmatia	330
6262	**Vous**	Serifos	Kyklades	341
5071	**Vouvalos**	Ambracian Gulf	Ambracian Gulf	334
4620	**Vrgada**		North Dalmatia	**201**
4809	**Vrhovnjak**	Korcula	South Dalmatia	332
4810	**Vrnik**	Korcula	South Dalmatia	**202**
5414	**Vromonas**	Echinades	Ionia Nisia	335
3320	**Vulcano**	Isole Eolie	Sicilia	**138**
7903	**Xeronisi**	Thasos	Voreio Aigaio	353
8425	**Yassiada**		Izmir	355
8050	**Yassiada**	Prens Adalari	Istanbul	354
8718	**Yassica**		Mugla	356
8412	**Yassicaada**		Izmir	355
5700	**Ydra**		Argosaronikos	**297**
8618	**Yediadalar**		Mugla	356
8304	**Yellice/Poyrazada**		Balikesir	355
8113	**Yer**		Balikesir	354
8802	**Yilan**		Antalya	357
8417	**Yilan**		Izmir	355

www.mediterraneanislands.org